T0322081

SPATIAL MULTIDIMENSIONAL COOPERATIVE TRANSMISSION
Theories and Key Technologies

SPATIAL MULTIDIMENSIONAL
COOPERATIVE TRANSMISSION
Theories and Key Technologies

Lin Bai
Beihang University, China

Xianling Liang
Shanghai Jiao Tong University, China

Zhenyu Xiao
Beihang University, China

Ronghong Jin
Shanghai Jiao Tong University, China

Quan Yu
Chinese Academy of Engineering, China

World Scientific

NEW JERSEY · LONDON · SINGAPORE · BEIJING · SHANGHAI · HONG KONG · TAIPEI · CHENNAI · TOKYO

Published by

World Scientific Publishing Co. Pte. Ltd.

5 Toh Tuck Link, Singapore 596224

USA office: 27 Warren Street, Suite 401-402, Hackensack, NJ 07601

UK office: 57 Shelton Street, Covent Garden, London WC2H 9HE

Library of Congress Cataloging-in-Publication Data

Names: Bai, Lin (Associate professor), author. | Liang, Xianling, author. | Xiao, Zhenyu, author. |
    Jin, Ronghong, author. | Yu, Quan (Engineer), author.
Title: Spatial multidimensional cooperative transmission : theories and key technologies /
    Lin Bai, Beihang University, China, Xianling Liang, Shanghai Jiao Tong University, China,
    Zhenyu Xiao, Beihang University, China, Ronghong Jin, Shanghai Jiao Tong University, China,
    Quan Yu, Chinese Academy of Engineering, China.
Description: Singapore ; Hackensack, NJ : World Scientific, [2020] | Includes index.
Identifiers: LCCN 2020013219 | ISBN 9789811202452 (hardcover) | ISBN 9789811202469 (ebook) |
    ISBN 9789811202476 (ebook other)
Subjects: LCSH: Radio--Transmitters and transmission. | Antenna arrays. |
    MIMO systems. | Cell phone systems.
Classification: LCC TK6561 .B27 2020 | DDC 621.382/4--dc23
LC record available at https://lccn.loc.gov/2020013219

British Library Cataloguing-in-Publication Data

A catalogue record for this book is available from the British Library.

空间多维协同传输理论与关键技术
Originally published in China by Posts & Telecom Press
Copyright © Posts & Telecom Press 2016

For any available supplementary material, please visit
https://www.worldscientific.com/worldscibooks/10.1142/11336#t=suppl

Desk Editors: Ramya Gangadharan/Yu Shan Tay

Typeset by Stallion Press
Email: enquiries@stallionpress.com

Printed in Singapore

Preface

The development of mobile communication technology has witnessed mainly four generations so far. The first generation of mobile terminals that appeared in 1995 could only be used for voice communication. And the second generation of mobile terminals that were in use between 1996 and 1997 appeared with the addition of data transmitting and receiving functions, such as sending and receiving e-mails or web browsing. With the rapid development of communication and computer technology, Internet access service was introduced from the third generation of mobile communication, and then the mobile communication service entered a rapid development period of mobile Internet dominated by data services. Furthermore, the fourth generation of mobile communication reflected the demand for Internet-like communication services based on high-speed data streams. CCID data showed that by June 2012, the number of mobile Internet users had exceeded the number of computer users for the first time. Mobile Internet is changing the social interaction lifestyle of people as never before, and it has become one of the necessary means for modern human information interaction.

Faced with the growing demand for broadband communication and the rapid development of mobile Internet industry, how to realize large-capacity data transmission at anytime and anywhere has become an important issue in wireless communication. According to Shannon's theory, the demand for wireless spectrum resources has also increased correspondingly, thus leading to the shortage of spectrum resources suitable for wireless communication. It has become the main bottleneck restricting the development of wireless communication. From the first generation to the third generation, the core technologies of mobile communication are FDMA, TDMA, and CDMA, respectively, which use resources such as frequency, time, and code element to improve the spectrum efficiency of the system. When people try to take full use of time, frequency, and code resources to improve spectrum utilization, the rational use of space resources and the development of the corresponding multi-antenna technology will become the core issues and key technologies of mobile communication in the future.

At the same time, with the continuous improvement of aerospace technology and the rapid growth of the types and quantities of space-based and air-based platforms, the space–air–ground-integrated information network consisting of satellites, stratospheric balloons and various aerospace vehicles is developing rapidly. The resulting space–air–ground-integrated mobile Internet will become an information bridge for human beings to understand space, enter space, use space, and develop space in the future. The rational use of the multi-antenna technology to realize efficient spatial multidimensional signal cooperative transmission is the premise of healthy development of the future space–air–ground-integrated mobile Internet and also provides theoretical basis and technical support for its development. Based on the principle of spatial multidimensional signal transmission and multi-antenna system, this book, respectively, introduces how to maximize the use of spatial dimension resources to improve system performance and spectral efficiency in ground-based, air-based, and space-based cooperative transmission systems.

In the first chapter, the book outlines the history of mobile communication and the characteristics of ground-based, air-based, and space-based cooperative communication systems. And then in the first part, the multi-antenna system and the key technologies of signal transmission and reception are discussed. Focusing on these issues, the vector space and multi-antenna system, adaptive system, MIMO multi-antenna system, and spatial multidimensional signal reception and iterative processing technologies are introduced in Chapters 2–5. Based on the above theories and technologies, the application and the corresponding key technologies of spatial multidimensional cooperative transmission in ground-based, air-based, and space-based communication systems are introduced in Chapters 6–8 of the second part.

Our team has worked on the research of space–air–ground-integrated transmission for many years and has undertaken many national-level scientific research projects. We have relevant foundations both in theory and engineering practice. The content of this book is taken from the results of many years of our research, and the principles and methods are expounded by combining theory with engineering practice. This book provides a step-by-step elaboration of the theories, which is very suitable for college graduates with a certain level of professional foundation as well as for researchers and engineers in research institutions.

Based on the principle of multidimensional signal transmission and multi-antenna system, this book provides suggestions on how to maximize the use of spatial dimension resources to improve system performance and spectrum efficiency in ground-based, air-based, and space-based cooperative transmission systems. The main contents of this book include basic theories and key technologies such as adaptive antenna system, spatial multidimensional signal transmission and reception, multi-antenna design, and iterative signal processing in a MIMO multi-antenna system. Based on the above theories and technologies, this book also presents the characteristics and applications of spatial multidimensional cooperative transmission in ground-based, air-based, and space-based communication systems from the perspective of practical application.

The book is rich in content and clear in structure. It is a technical book with emphasis on both theory and practice. It can be used as a postgraduate textbook for the major of mobile Internet communication and serve as a handbook also suitable for researchers engaged in related fields.

About the Authors

Lin Bai received the B.Sc. degree in electronic and information engineering from the Huazhong University of Science and Technology, Wuhan, China, in 2004, the M.Sc. degree (Hons.) in communication systems from the University of Wales, Swansea, U.K., in 2007, and the Ph.D. degree in advanced telecommunications from the School of Engineering, Swansea University, U.K., in 2010. Since 2011, he has been with Beihang University (Beijing University of Aeronautics and Astronautics, BUAA), Beijing, China, where he is currently a Professor at the School of Cyber Science and Technology. His research interests include multiple-input multiple-output (MIMO), Internet-of-Things (IoT), and unmanned aerial vehicle (UAV) communications. He authored two books published by Springer in 2012 and 2014. He was invited to serve as a Symposium Co-Chair of IEEE GLOBECOM 2019 and a Tutorial Co-Chair of IEEE/CIC ICCC 2019. He has served as a Lead Guest Editor for *IEEE Wireless Communications* and a Guest Editor for *IEEE Internet of Things Journal*. Currently, he is on the Editorial Board of several journals, including *IEEE Transactions on Signal Processing* and *IEEE Transactions on Wireless Communications*, and serves as the Managing Editor of *Journal of Communications and Information Networks*. Prof. Bai is a Distinguished Lecturer of the IEEE Vehicular Technology Society and a senior member of the IEEE.

 **Xianling Liang** received a B.S. degree in electronic engineering from Xidian University, Xi'an, China, in 2002, and a Ph.D. degree in electronic engineering from Shanghai University, Shanghai, China, in 2007. From 2007 to 2008, he was a Post-Doctoral Research Fellow of EMT-INRS, University of Quebec. In 2009, he joined the Department of Electronic Engineering, Shanghai Jiao Tong University (SJTU), Shanghai, as a Lecturer, where he became an Associate Professor in 2012. He has authored or co-authored about 260 papers including over 150 journal papers, and co-authored one book and three chapters on antenna fields. He holds over 20 patents in antenna technologies. His current research interests are on modern antenna technology and applications, including OAM-EM wave propagation theory and antennas, time-modulated/4-D arrays, anti-interference antennas, integrated active arrays, and UWB wide-angle scanning phased arrays. Dr. Liang is a senior member of IEEE, and member of communication appraisal expert of the National Natural Science Foundation of China and the Degree Center of the Ministry of Education. He was a recipient of the Award of Shanghai Municipal Excellent Doctoral Dissertation in 2008, the Nomination of the National Excellent Doctoral Dissertation in 2009, the Best Paper Award presented at the International Workshop on Antenna Technology: Small Antennas, Innovative Structures, and Materials in 2010, the SMC Excellent Young Faculty and the Excellent Teacher Award of SJTU in 2012, the Shanghai Natural Science Award in 2013, the Best Paper Award presented at the IEEE International Symposium on Microwave, Antenna, Propagation, and EMC Technologies in 2015, the 4th China Publishing Government Book Award, and the Okawa Foundation Research Grant in 2017.

Zhenyu Xiao received a B.E. degree from the Department of Electronics and Information Engineering, Huazhong University of Science and Technology, Wuhan, China, in 2006, and a Ph.D. degree from the Department of Electronic Engineering, Tsinghua University, Beijing, China, in 2011. From 2011 to 2013, he held a post-doctoral position with the Department of Electronic Engineering, Tsinghua University. From 2013 to 2016 he was a Lecturer with the School of Electronic and Information Engineering, Beihang University, Beijing, China, where he is currently an Associate Professor. He had visited the University of Delaware and Imperial College London from 2012 to 2013 and 2015 to 2016, respectively. Dr. Xiao has published over 70 papers in journals including IEEE JSAC, IEEE TWC, IEEE TSP, IEEE TVT, IEEE COMML, IEEE WCL, and IET COMM, and is serving as a reviewer for these journals. He has been a TPC member of IEEE GLOBECOM, IEEE WCSP, IEEE ICC, IEEE ICCC, etc. He is currently an Associate Editor for IEEE Transactions on Cognitive Communications and Networking, China Communications, IET Communications, IEEE Access, and KSII transactions on Internet and Information Systems. He has also been a leading Guest Editor for IEEE Access, Special Issue on Millimeter Wave Communications. Dr. Xiao received the 2017 Best Reviewer Award of IEEE TWC, 2019 Exemplary Reviewer Award of IEEE WCL, and the 4th China Publishing Government Award. He has won the Second Prize from the Natural Science of China Electronics Society and the First Prize from Technical Invention of China Society of Aeronautics and Astronautics. Dr. Xiao is an active researcher with broad interests in millimeter wave communications, UAV and Near-Space communications and networking, NOMA, etc. He is a senior member of the IEEE.

 **Ronghong Jin** received a B.S. degree in electronic engineering, an M.S. degree in electromagnetic and microwave technology, and a Ph.D. degree in communication and electronic systems from Shanghai Jiao Tong University (SJTU), Shanghai, China, in 1983, 1986, and 1993, respectively. In 1986, he joined the Faculty of the Department of Electronic Engineering, SJTU, where he was an Assistant Professor, a Lecturer, and an Associate Professor. From 1997 to 1999, he was a Visiting Scholar with the Department of Electrical and Electronic Engineering, Tokyo Institute of Technology, Tokyo, Japan. From 2001 to 2002, he was a Special Invited Research Fellow with the Communication Research Laboratory, Tokyo. From 2006 to 2009, he was a Guest Professor with the University of Wollongong, Wollongong, NSW, Australia. He is currently a Professor with SJTU. He is a Distinguish Guest Scientist with the Commonwealth Scientific and Industrial Research Organization, Sydney, NSW, Australia. He has authored or co-authored more than 400 papers in refereed journals and conference proceedings and co-authored four books. He holds about 70 patents in antenna and wireless technologies. His current research interests include antennas, electromagnetic theory, numerical techniques of solving field problems, and wireless communication. Dr. Jin is a Fellow of IEEE, and a committee member of the Radiowave Propagation Branch and the Antenna Branch of the Chinese Institute of Electronics (CIE), Beijing, China. He was a recipient of the National Technology Innovation Award, the National Nature Science Award, the 2012 Nomination of National Excellent Doctoral Dissertation (Supervisor), the Shanghai Nature Science Award, and the Shanghai Science and Technology Progress Award.

Quan Yu received his Ph.D. degree in fiber optics from the University of Limoges in 1992. Since 1992, he joined the faculty of the Institute of China Electronic System Engineering Corporation. He is currently a principal research scientist at Peng Cheng Laboratory. His main areas of research interest are the architecture of wireless networks, optimization of protocols, and cognitive radios. He is an Academician of the Chinese Academy of Engineering (CAE) and the founding Editor-in-Chief of the *Journal of Communications and Information Networks*.

Acknowledgments

We would like to thank many colleagues who worked together, including Professor Jun Zhang, Professor Feng Liu, and Associate Professor Chen Chen. They gave many suggestions and helped in the completion of this book. In addition, we especially thank the students who worked hard for the preparation and proofreading of this book, including Chao Han, Shengyue Dou, Min Zhang, Yao Li, Xin Zhang, Shengsen Pan, Wenjie Bai, Yuewen Zhao, Shang Dang, Yezhen Li, and He Zhu.

In addition, I would like to thank the National Key Research and Development Program of China (Grant No. 2017YFB0503002) and the National Natural Science Foundation of China (Grant No. 61922010).

Finally, I am very grateful to my family for their strong support and understanding of my work.

Lin Bai, Xianling Liang, Zhenyu Xiao,
Ronghong Jin and Quan Yu
Beijing and Shanghai

Common Symbol Table

1. $\mathbf{A}$ and $\mathbf{a}$ represent complex-value vectors and matrices, respectively.
2. For matrix $\mathbf{A}$, $\mathbf{A}^{\mathrm{T}}$, $\mathbf{A}^{\mathrm{H}}$, $\mathbf{A}^{-1}$, and $\mathbf{A}^*$ represent its transpose, conjugate transpose, inverse of the matrix, and conjugate matrix, respectively.
3. $[\mathbf{A}]_{i,j}$ denotes the element of the ith row and the jth column of matrix $\mathbf{A}$.
4. $\mathbf{A}(a{:}b, c{:}d)$ represents a sub-array of matrix $\mathbf{A}$ whose elements are the $a, \ldots, b$ rows and $c, \ldots, d$ columns of matrix $\mathbf{A}$.
5. $\mathbf{A}(n,:)$ and $\mathbf{A}(:,n)$ represent the nth row and the nth column of the matrix $\mathbf{A}$, respectively.
6. $\Re(z)$ and $\Im(z)$ represent the real and the imaginary parts of complex z, respectively.
7. $\| \cdot \|$ represents the 2 norm of the vector or matrix and $\| \cdot \|_{\mathrm{F}}$ represents the Frobenius norm of the vector or matrix.
8. $\lfloor \alpha \rfloor$ represents the largest integer less than α and $\lceil \alpha \rfloor$ represents the nearest integer to α.
9. $|\alpha|$ represents the absolute value of α.
10. \ represents set subtraction.
11. $\mathbf{I}_n$ represents the $n \times n$ identity matrix.
12. $\mathcal{K} = \{k_{(1)}, k_{(2)}, \ldots\}$ represents the set containing elements $k_{(1)}, k_{(2)}, \ldots$.
13. $\mathrm{tr}(\mathbf{A})$ represents the trace of matrix $\mathbf{A}$.
14. $\det(\mathbf{A})$ represents the determinant of matrix $\mathbf{A}$.
15. $\mathcal{D}(\mathbf{A})$ represents the length of the shortest non-zero vector in the lattice generated by matrix $\mathbf{A}$.
16. $\mathcal{OD}_M(\mathbf{A})$ represents the orthogonal separating degree of matrix $\mathbf{A}$ with M column vectors.

17. $\lambda(\mathbf{A})$ and $\lambda_{\min}(\mathbf{A})$ represent the eigenvalues of matrix $\mathbf{A}$ and the minimum eigenvalue of matrix $\mathbf{A}$, respectively.

18. $\mathcal{L}(\mathbf{A})$ represents the lattice generated by the matrix $\mathbf{A}$.

19. $\mathrm{E}[\cdot]$ represents statistical expectation.

20. $\langle \mathbf{a}, \mathbf{b} \rangle$ represents the inner product of the vectors $\mathbf{a}$ and $\mathbf{b}$.

21. $\mathcal{CN}(m, C)$ represents a complex Gaussian vector with a mean of m and a variance of C.

22. $\log(\cdot)$ represents the natural logarithm.

23. $\mathbf{0}$ represents a matrix with all zero elements.

24. $\mathbb{Z}$ represents a set of all integers.

25. $\mathbf{A} \otimes \mathbf{B}$ represents the Kronecker product of the matrices $\mathbf{A}$ and $\mathbf{B}$.

Contents

Chapter 1

Introduction

With the rapid development of wireless broadband communication and the swift progress in the Internet industry, mobile Internet is showing a booming trend with its unprecedented way to change people's social lives and lifestyles, and it has become one of the necessary means for modern human information interaction. Traditional wireless communication is mostly based on ground-based cellular communication. However, with the continuous improvement of aerospace technology and the rapid growth of the types and quantities of space-based and air-based platforms, the space–air–ground integrated information network consisting of satellites, stratospheric balloons, and various aerospace vehicles is developing rapidly. The resulting space–air–ground integrated mobile Internet will become an information bridge for human beings to understand, enter, use, and develop space in the future.

Since the birth of wireless communication, the shortage of spectrum resources has been the biggest bottleneck restricting its development. The efficient use of spectrum resources and the development of the corresponding spatial multidimensional cooperative transmission technology have brought new growth points for future wireless communication and also provided theoretical and technical guarantee for the healthy development of the space–air–ground integrated mobile Internet in the future. This chapter will outline the characteristics and development history of ground-based, air-based, and space-based wireless communication.

1.1 Overview of Ground-based Wireless Communication System

Since the concept of mobile communication was proposed by Bell Labs in the United States in 1947,[1] mobile communication technology has made rapid progress in the past 30 years and has become one of the indispensable communication means in modern ground-based communication networks. In this section, we will first expound the development of the four generations of ground-based mobile communications and the corresponding key technologies.[2]

1.1.1 *The first generation of mobile communication system*

The first generation of mobile communication systems (1G) was born in the 1970s and 1980s when the integrated circuits, microcomputers, and microprocessor technologies were rapidly developed. In 1978, Bell Labs of the United States introduced an analog cellular mobile communication system, extending mobile communication into personal field. In 1983, the US advanced mobile phone service (AMPS)[1] was put into commercial use. The AMPS system employed a 7-cell multiplexing mode and could use "sectorization" and "cell splitting" to increase capacity when needed. At the same time, Europe and Japan had also established their own mobile communication networks, including the UK's extended total access communication system (ETACS) and Japan's narrowband total access communication system (NTACS). The wireless communication system of this period mainly used analog modulation and frequency division multiple access (FDMA) technology. There is no doubt that the first generation of mobile communication system has many shortcomings, such as limited user capacity, difficulty in system expansion, mixed modulation methods, inability to achieve international roaming, poor confidentiality, low call quality, and inability to provide data services.

1.1.2 *The second generation of mobile communication system*

In 1992, with the birth of the first digital cellular mobile communication network, namely the global system for mobile (GSM) communications, mobile communication entered the second generation (2G). Due to its superior performance, GSM made rapid progress worldwide. In 1993, the first all-digital mobile phone GSM system was completed in China, and then both China Telecom and China Unicom adopted GSM. The GSM system has the following main characteristics: microcell structure, digitalization of voice signals, new modulation methods (GMSK, QPSK, etc.), the use of FDMA or time division multiple access (TDMA) technology, high spectrum utilization, high confidentiality, etc.

In 1995, Qualcomm proposed another digital cellular system technology solution using code division multiple access (CDMA), which is IS-95 CDMA. It is currently used in Hong Kong, South Korea, and North America with good reviews from users. The CDMA system mainly has the following characteristics: the user access mode adopting CDMA, soft capacity, soft cut-in, large system capacity, anti-multipath fading, voice activation, and diversity reception, etc.

Compared with the 1G system, 2G system has higher spectrum utilization, stronger security, and better voice quality. Up to now, the 2G system standards have become more and more perfect, and the technology is relatively mature. However, as people's demand for data services continues to increase, the rate provided by the 2G system is no longer sufficient, and a stronger system is needed to support high-speed mobile communications.

1.1.3 *The third generation of mobile communication system*

The concept of the third-generation mobile communication system was proposed by the ITU in 1985 and it was named the future public land mobile telecommunications system (FPLMTS). In 1996, it was renamed the international mobile telecommunications 2000 (IMT-2000) system, which worked in the 2000-MHz band and could provide a data transmission rate of up to 2000 kbit/s. The purpose of 3G is to achieve a unified standard for cellular mobile communication and establish a globally popular seamless roaming system. Meanwhile, it can support high-quality multimedia services and enhance network capacity and multiple-user management capabilities. Therefore, IMT-2000s requirements for 3G technology are as follows: (1) high data transmission rate including the minimum rate of satellite link 9.6 kbit/s, indoor environment at least 2 Mbit/s, outdoor walking and vehicle environment at least 384 kbit/s and 144 kbit/s, respectively, (2) transmission rate allocation on demand, (3) uplink and downlink adapting to the needs of asymmetric services, (4) simple cell structure and easy-to-manage channel structure, (5) flexible frequency and radio resource management, system configuration, and service facilities, and (6) the combination of wireless network and wired network, trying to achieve the same transmission quality as that of the wired network.

On October 19, 2007, the ITU officially approved the IEEE 802.16-based worldwide interoperability for microwave access (WiMax) to become the 3G standard. WCDMA and cdma2000 have been commercialized on a global scale, and China also began commercialization based on TD-SCDMA 3G system in 2008. However, 3G has its limitations which are as follows: (1) Using CDMA it is difficult to achieve high communication rate due to multi-user interference, (2) due to the limitation of the air interface to the core network, the dynamic range of service rates provided by 3G is not large enough to meet various service types, (3) the frequency resources allocated to 3G have become saturated, (4) the voice switching architecture adopted by 3G still inherits 2G circuit switching rather than pure IP, and (5) the applications of streaming media are not satisfactory. Therefore, more advanced technologies are needed to further improve the quality of mobile services.

1.1.4 *The fourth generation of mobile communication system*

Along with the rapid development of the first three generations of mobile communication systems and intelligent mobile terminals, the users' demand for services has changed from voice-based to Internet-based communication modes based on high-speed data streams. As users' demand for transmission rate continues to increase, people are beginning to develop the next-generation system based on the first three generations of mobile communication systems to better support high-speed broadband mobile communication services. The World Radio Conference in 2007 allocated spectrum for IMT-Advanced, and IMT-Advanced standards began to be collected in March 2008. By October 2009, a total of six candidate proposals were collected, which can be classified into 3GPP LTE-Advanced[3] and IEEE802.16m.[4] At present, international standards for 4G mobile communication technologies mainly include FDD-LTE, FDD-LTE-Advance, TD-LTE, and TD-LTE-Advanced. Among them, TD-LTE and TD-LTE-Advanced are 4G international standards led by China.

LTE is an evolution of 3G. It improves 3G air access technology, using orthogonal frequency division multiplexing (OFDM) and multiple-input multiple-output (MIMO) technologies as its wireless evolution technology.

The LTE mobile communication system can provide a downlink rate of 100 Mbit/s (TD-LTE) or 150 Mbit/s (FDD-LTE), an uplink rate of 50 Mbit/s (TD-LTE) or 40 Mbit/s (FDD-LTE), and peak rates in a 20-MHz spectrum bandwidth. TD-LTE is the 4G international standard led by China, and it is adopted by China Mobile.

LTE-Advanced can be divided into FDD-LTE-Advanced and TD-LTE-Advanced. It is optimized for indoor environments and uses technologies such as carrier aggregation. It flexibly allocates spectrum for a wider spectrum bandwidth and effectively supports new frequency band and large-bandwidth applications. It can provide a downlink rate of 1 Gbit/s and an uplink rate of 500 Mbit/s in a 100-MHz spectrum bandwidth.

WiMax is an IEEE 802.16 standard that provides a maximum access rate of 70 Mbit/s and a working frequency range of 2–66 GHz without authorization. The main advantages of WiMax are as follows: (1) it is beneficial to avoid known interference, (2) it is beneficial to save spectrum resources, (3) flexible bandwidth adjustment capability is beneficial for operators to coordinate spectrum resources, and (4) wireless signal transmission distance can be up to 50 km. However, it cannot meet the seamless connection of wireless networks under high speed in terms of mobile performance. Therefore, WiMax is not a wireless mobile communication technology, but only a wireless broadband LAN technology.

Wireless MAN-Advanced is an upgraded version of WiMax, namely the IEEE 802.16m standard, which has the ability to seamlessly switch under high speed. It can effectively solve mobile performance problems of WiMax. IEEE 802.16m is compatible with 4G networks. Its advantages are as follows: (1) expand network coverage to achieve seamless network connectivity, (2) improve spectrum efficiency, (3) provide 1 Gib/s wireless transmission rate in roaming mode or high-efficiency/strong signal mode.

1.1.5 *The fifth generation of mobile communication system*

The fifth-generation mobile communication system (5G) is a next-generation wireless mobile communication system that is being developed in order to meet the rapid spread of intelligent terminals and the rapid development of mobile Internet after 4G. It is a wireless mobile communication system for the needs of the human information society after 2020.

5G has become an active research in the field of mobile communication systems at home and abroad. In 2013, the 7th Framework Program, which was jointly undertaken by 29 participants including China's Huawei

Corporation, launched the mobile and wireless communications enablers for the 2020 information society (METIS) project[5] for 5G research. China's 863 Program also launched the first and second phase of 5G major projects in June 2013 and March 2014, respectively. At present, countries around the world are conducting extensive discussions on the development, application requirements, candidate frequency bands, and key technical indicators of 5G, and striving to reach a consensus at the 2015 World Radio Conference. And standardization process started in 2016.[6]

For the future vision and application of 5G, there have been relevant descriptions in academia and industry, from which we can summarize the technical needs of the future 5G. Compared with the traditional mobile communication network, 5G should have the following basic characteristics such as: (1) the data traffic is increased by 1000 times, (2) the number of networked devices is increased by 100 times, (3) the peak rate is at least 10 Gbit/s, (4) the rate users can obtain is 10 Mbit/s, and it can be up to 100 Mbit/s for special needs, (5) short delay and high reliability, and (6) high spectrum utilization and low network energy consumption.

At present, the key technologies of 5G are still in research. Technologies such as large-scale MIMO technology, beamforming technology, and cooperative wireless communication technology all have the possibility to become the key technologies of 5G.

MIMO technology can effectively improve the spectral efficiency of wireless communication and obtain receive diversity gain (RDG), which is recognized as the core technology of the next-generation mobile communication system. A typical $M \times N$ MIMO system is shown in Fig. 1.1.

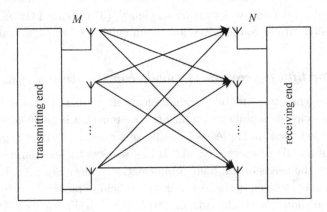

Fig. 1.1.   An $M \times N$ MIMO system.

Since each receiving antenna will receive a superimposed signal from all transmitting antennas, the received signal can be expressed as

$$
\boldsymbol{y} = \begin{bmatrix} y_1 \\ y_2 \\ \vdots \\ y_n \end{bmatrix} = \begin{bmatrix} h_{11} & h_{12} & \cdots & h_{1m} \\ h_{21} & h_{22} & \cdots & h_{2m} \\ \vdots & \vdots & \ddots & \vdots \\ h_{n1} & h_{n2} & \cdots & h_{nm} \end{bmatrix} \begin{bmatrix} s_1 \\ s_2 \\ \vdots \\ s_m \end{bmatrix} + \begin{bmatrix} n_1 \\ n_2 \\ \vdots \\ n_n \end{bmatrix}
$$

$$
= \mathbf{Hs} + \mathbf{n} \tag{1.1}
$$

where y_n, h_{nm}, s_m, and n_n, respectively represent the received signal of the nth receiving antenna, the channel gain from the mth transmitting antenna to the nth receiving antenna, the transmitted signal of the mth transmitting antenna, and the noise of the nth receiving antenna. It can be seen from Eq. (1.1) that each transmitted signal will have N backups at the receiving end, which is called reception diversity. However, signals from different transmitting antennas form interference at the receiving end. In order to detect the transmitted signal at the receiving end, signals from different transmitting antennas must be extracted. Therefore, the detection algorithm of the MIMO receiver is an indispensable component of the MIMO system.

Besides, beamforming is also a key technology to achieve space diversity gain. Beamforming technology is widely used in directional antenna array radar, sonar hydroacoustic positioning and classification, ultrasonic optical imaging, geophysical exploration, petroleum exploration, biomedical imaging, and wireless communication. At the transmitting end, beamforming technology is used to appropriately weight the signals transmitted by the corresponding antennas in the antenna array to generate a directional virtual beam. Thereby the purpose of enhancing the desired signal and suppressing interference and improving the communication capacity and quality can be achieved. At the receiving end, signals from different receiving antennas are combined in the receiver to achieve coherent superposition and improve the reception quality of the signals. Beamforming technology can be divided into two categories, namely array beamforming based on antenna array and multi-antenna beamforming based on signal pre-processing, which utilize the spatial correlation and independence of different antenna channels, respectively. Array beamforming technology utilizes the strong correlation of spatial channels and the principle of interference of electromagnetic waves. By weighting the correlation of the output signals of multiple antennas in terms of amplitude and phase, the signals will be superimposed in a certain direction and phase cancellation in other directions will be done to enhance the target signal and suppress interference. And for the multi-antenna beamforming technology, it utilizes the independence between different antenna channels to improve the space diversity gain of the system.

For a cellular communication system, when a user is at the cell edge, a signal from a neighboring cell base station will be received. The conventional method is to simply consider the signal from the neighboring cell base station as an interference signal. Because this competition-causing strategy will significantly reduce communication performance, coordinated multipoint (CoMP) technology has attracted widespread attention in 5G communication systems. By utilizing the interaction of mobile channel information and data information between adjacent base stations, the CoMP technology performs an interference avoidance strategy for the interfered users or joint transmission for mobile users by multiple base stations. Increasing the throughput of edge users and the coverage area of the high data transmission rate, reducing the interference of edge users, and improving the throughput of the cell can thus be realized. Downlink CoMP can be divided into two categories, joint processing (JP) and joint transmission (JT). For JP, the cooperative clusters not only share channel information but also share data information and perform joint pre-processing on user data to eliminate interference between base stations. For JT, a user terminal simultaneously receives data information transmitted by several transmission nodes and combines the information to improve the quality of the received signal.

In summary, the core technologies of 1G–5G are FDMA, TDMA, CDMA, OFDMA, and MIMO technologies, respectively, which utilize frequency, time, code element, space, and other resources to improve the spectrum efficiency of the system. Faced with the increasing communication demand in the future, the growing need for multimedia services and the rapid development of Internet technology, how to realize large-capacity data transmission at anytime and anywhere has become an important issue in wireless communication. Considering that there is still a broad prospect for the utilization of air-based and space-based wireless communication systems in the future, how to construct the space–air–ground integrated mobile Internet from the perspective of space–air–ground integration has become the main trend of the development of mobile communication networks. In the following, we will outline the space-based and air-based communication systems.

1.2 The Overview of Air-Based Cooperative Transmission System

With the rapid development of wireless communication systems, higher spectrum utilization, larger system capacity, more flexible network coverage, and lower construction cost are increasingly required. However, the current wireless communication platforms are mainly ground platforms and satellite platforms, and each has its own drawbacks. For example, the ground platform requires large investment in large-scale coverage and high construction cost, and its configuration is inflexible. Serious channel fading happens in urban construction-intensive areas. The satellite platform has problems such as high terminal cost, difficulty in updating and repairing on-board equipment, and limited system capacity. Under this circumstance, the research of the new high-altitude communication platform has received increasing attention and become a research hotspot in the field of wireless communication.[7]

The air-based wireless communication system based on the high-altitude platform is a new type of communication system currently under research in the world. The carriers of the high-altitude platform are mainly tethered balloons and airships. The former's height is generally below 10 km, and the latter is generally located in the stratosphere with its height of 20–50 km. The stratosphere is located above the troposphere in the atmosphere, where the air is thin, the density is a few percent of that at the sea level, the buoyancy is small, but the airflow is relatively stable, and the wind is weak. It is an ideal airspace for deploying high-altitude hovering airships.[8]

The concept of stratospheric communication was proposed during the Second World War, and it began to attract the attention of scientists and technicians in the 1970s. With the breakthrough of several key technologies and the overall progress of technology level, research hotspots have been formed in recent years. Organizations such as NASA and companies such as SKYTOWER in the United States plan to deploy a stratospheric platform for security purpose with the support of the government. Japan uses the stratospheric platform for digital high-definition television broadcasting and IMT-2000 network construction, which is led by the Stratospheric Communication Platform Development Association. The European stratospheric communication projects are funded by the European Space Agency and governments to conduct research on stratospheric broadband communications. In 2004, the German Aerospace Center successfully implemented large data transmission from balloons floating in the stratosphere to the ground. South Korea and the United States also conducted similar studies. They divided the study of stratospheric communication into three phases and made rapid progress. In China, Tsinghua University used a helium airship to fly for 2 hours at a height of 300 meters to demonstrate the video conferencing system,[9] and Peking University has established a professional organization studying the solar stratospheric suspension platform system. Although there have been many achievements in this field, no unified international standards have yet been put forward.

Compared with the communication satellite, the distance between the stratospheric platform and the ground is 1/1800 of the distance between the synchronous satellite and the ground. The free space attenuation and delay time are greatly reduced, which is conducive to miniaturization and broadbandization of the communication terminal. Besides, it is low in cost, fast in construction, can be recyclable, and is easy to maintain. Compared to ground-based cellular systems, the coverage of stratospheric platforms is much greater than that of groundcellular systems, and channel conditions (by Rice attenuation) are superior to ground systems (by Rayleigh attenuation). The stratospheric platform is not only suitable for urban use being an effective complement to ground mobile communication systems but also suitable for use in areas where ground mobile communication systems are inconvenient to deploy such as oceans and mountains. Stratospheric platforms can also be quickly transferred for use in battlefield areas or in the monitoring and communication in areas natural disaster occurred (such as floods). In the long run, the high-altitude platform communication system may also become the third wireless communication system in addition to the ground mobile communication system and the satellite communication system.

The current research of high-altitude platform mobile communication is generally based on the third-generation mobile communication (3G) technology,[10] mainly using CDMA technology. The third generation of mobile communication still has many shortcomings in many issues such as air interface, system architecture, and openness. With the continuous increase of communication users and business volume and the increasing requirements for communication quality, it is of utmost importance to develop a new generation of mobile communication system with higher

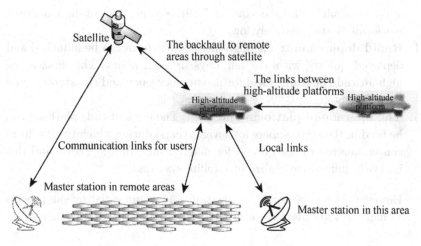

Fig. 1.2. High-altitude platform communication scenario.

speed, larger capacity, a more complete and open system. The new generation of mobile communication systems is generally called beyond3G (B3G) or the fourth generation (4G).

Figure 1.2 depicts a typical high-altitude platform communication scenario. The advantages of the high-altitude platform are detailed in the following points.[11]

(1) **Larger coverage compared to ground mobile systems:** Generally, the radius of the coverage of the high-altitude platform covers several tens of kilometers, but the radius of the range covered by the ground mobile system spans several kilometers.

(2) **Flexibility to high-volume needs:** Within its coverage, the high-altitude platform can centrally support the cellular system architecture and can flexibly perform frequency reuse and set the size of the cell. Therefore, in the high-altitude platform system, the process of reasonably allocating resources can be adopted to deal with the demand for large capacity of the system network.

(3) **Lower cost compared to satellite systems:** Compared with the constellation network composed of geostationary orbit satellites and low-orbit satellites, the cost of high-altitude platforms in network construction and platform launching will be greatly reduced. Meanwhile, for some ground mobile communication networks that need to build

a large number of base station facilities, the cost of high-altitude platforms is also relatively low.

(4) **Rapid deployment:** The high-altitude platform can be launched and deployed quickly within a few days or even hours. This makes the high-altitude platform ideal for use in emergency and disaster-affected environments.

(5) **The upgrade of platform and load:** The high-altitude platform can be used in the stratosphere for several years, during which the platform can be lowered to the ground for maintenance and upgrades, and this is clearly difficult to realize in satellite systems.

However, the engineering realization and commercialization process of the high-altitude platform also face some difficulties and challenges as follows:

(1) **Mass and volume of the load:** Compared to the ground mobile systems, the payload mass and volume of the high-altitude platform system are very limited. The limitation of the payload will limit the system capacity provided by the high-altitude platform, even if it covers a large geographical area.

(2) **Power supply:** Power supply is a common constraint for any aeronautical system. High-altitude platforms of the unmanned aerial vehicle (UAV) type mainly rely on fuel power. Then how the power system meets the needs of communication load is a big challenge for the high-altitude platform. Long-running airship-type high-altitude platform systems mainly rely on solar energy. During the day, the solar panels convert solar energy into electrical energy to maintain the stability and communication load of the high-altitude platform, and the excess power is stored for use at night. However, the currently available fuel cell technology is not mature enough, and the efficiency of photovoltaic panels needs to be improved.

In order to support the deployment and implementation of high-altitude platforms, the international telecommunication union (ITU) has adopted the high-altitude platform communication system as an alternative to the International Mobile Telecom System-2000 (IMT-2000) wireless communication service. The spectrum allocation of high-altitude platforms is listed in Table 1.1. It can be seen that the ITU has allocated the 48-GHz frequency band (worldwide) and the 31/28-GHz frequency band (selected countries) to the high-altitude platform communication system.[12,13] At the same time, the ITU also allocates the frequency bands used by the 3G system to

Table 1.1. High-altitude platform spectrum allocation table.

Distribution frequency	Description	Scope of application
48/47 GHz	The bandwidth of uplink and downlink is 300 MHz.	Worldwide
31/28 GHz	It was revised to 31/28 GHz at the World Radio communication Conference with a bandwidth of 300 MHz.	More than 40 countries, including all countries in North and South America, excluding Europe.
2 GHz	High-altitude platform system is selected as the alternative for IMT-2000 wireless communication service.	Worldwide
6 GHz	WRC is considering the use of this band for high-altitude platforms as a gateway link for IMT-2000.	No explanation

the high-altitude platform system.[14] Therefore, integrating high-altitude platforms into the network of the 3G communication deployment is an emerging and forward-looking task.

The high-altitude platform can provide a wide variety of services and applications for fixed or mobile, personal or group users, and therefore must comply with the existing wireless standard protocols or develop protocols that are consistent with them. Only in this way, more user terminals can use the high-altitude platform. At present, there is no established standard protocol for high-altitude platforms. The international telecommunication union radio communication group (ITU-R) stipulates that the high-altitude platform uses 2 GHz when it provides communication services as a 3G base station. However, the actual broadband fixed access and mobile radio access bands have been increased to the millimeter band. More specifically, the frequencies are 31/28 GHz and 48/47 GHz. There are a number of candidate standards that can be adopted,[15] in particular the IEEE 802 series of standards (IEEE 802.11, IEEE 802.16, and IEEE 802.20), the data over cable service interface specification (DOCSIS) which includes multichannel microware distribution system (MMDS) and Local multipoint distribution service (LMDS), and the digital video broadcasting (DVB) standards, such as DVB-S/S2 and DVB-RCS.

At present, many countries have actively carried out research projects on high-altitude platforms, including the recently completed HeliNet project[16] and the ongoing CAPANINA project.[17] The HeliNet project began in January 2000 and ended in May 2003, and its outcomes had been presented to the fifth European Commission Framework Plan. Meanwhile, a large-scale project called Heliplat has also been carried out to implement three experimental applications: broadband communication, environmental monitoring, and remote sensing. This is also the first time in the history of the European Union funding has been provided for projects on high-altitude platforms. The CAPANINA project is funded by the European Commission to further develop wireless and optical broadband technologies for high-altitude platform systems. Its goal is to provide effective network coverage and low-cost broadband communication services for users in remote locations, users very long distance from ground communications facilities, and users on high-speed trains. At the same time, the project requires a transmission rate of 120 Mbit/s within the coverage of 60 km. Millimeter wave technology and free space optical communication technology have become the research focus of the project.

The high-altitude platform is to serve as a candidate technology for supporting and complementing the world's two best communications systems, ground mobile communications system and satellite system. And thus, it requires that high-altitude platform systems have efficient spectrum multiplexing technology in order to ensure high spectral efficiency of the system. Therefore, the integration of high-altitude platforms into mobile cellular networks for frequency reuse is an actively studied area in high-altitude platforms research. In addition, the frequency bands used by the above-mentioned high-altitude platforms are also used by other systems. Therefore, some scholars have studied the sharing of spectrums between high-altitude platforms and other systems.[18] It is worth emphasizing that array antennas are almost the best choice for high-altitude platforms. The stable coverage of multiple cells in the presence of random fluttering at high-altitude platforms can only be achieved by multi-beam pointing through the antenna array. Therefore, in order to provide communication services from high-altitude platforms for the ground, it is more important to rationally design multi-beam antenna arrays for high-altitude platforms and multi-cell planning based on antenna arrays. A little different from other systems, the high-altitude platform will suffer worse stability and aerial positioning, which requires a more precise design of the high-altitude platform and the ground receiving end to ensure that the beam of the antenna can maintain the correct orientation, thus maintaining a stable communication link.

Compared with the ground mobile network, the most significant advantage of the high-altitude platform is that the cellular network it generates can periodically move within a certain area, and thus, its coverage is not subject to geographical conditions. Since the coverage area of the high-altitude platform is large, multiple cells can be sourced from the same high-altitude platform at the same time, which can effectively improve the utilization of communication resources. In addition, the coexistence systems of high-altitude platforms and ground wireless network will bring new issues such as radio network planning and avoiding inter-system interference. The network coverage of groundcellular systems is mainly affected by objects such as buildings, trees, and hills. However, the network coverage of high-altitude platforms is determined only by the direction of the antenna. Therefore, although the high-altitude platform can be used as an auxiliary communication system, it will also cause stronger interference to the ground cellular network. These problems have recently been extensively studied and discussed. The main solution is to use cognitive radio technology and dynamic spectrum sensing technology. Both technologies are highly promising solutions to avoid interference problems. Therefore, the research and development in this field will also promote the commercialization of high-altitude platform systems.

1.3 The Overview of Space-Based Cooperative Transmission System

The traditional space-based cooperative transmission system is a communication system taking satellite as the forwarding center. Since satellites are usually located at high altitudes away from the ground, space-based systems have incomparable advantages in terms of coverage. Satellite communication systems play an important role in data transmission and global information interaction, especially in maritime, earth observation, and all-weather surveillance. With the increasing demand for bandwidth, service providers and related agencies have to increase the number, bandwidth, and power of satellites. However, the lack of orbital positions for GEO satellites and the lack of available spectrum resources, as well as the increased complexity and increased operating costs caused by power improvements, make these improvements for satellite difficult to achieve. Considering these factors, the space-based cooperative transmission system is proposed to collaborate the multi-coorbital satellites and adopt the technical advantage of multi-antenna systems. Multi-coorbital satellites technology keeps multiple satellites with the same or similar functions in the same orbital position Synchronization and data exchange are achieved through satellite links to form a satellite group with cooperative transmission and forwarding capabilities. Therefore, the utilization rate of satellite orbit resources can be effectively improved, and the deficiencies of single-satellite platform load and power limitation can be compensated. For the multi-antenna technology, by configuring the active antenna array, the coorbital multi-satellites can realize the efficient transmission mechanism of the multi-beam system and obtain the channel capacity gain and also adaptively optimize the transmission mode and improve the energy efficiency according to the continuous change of its structure.

1.3.1   *The current situation and development trend of space-based cooperative transmission system*

With the development of aerospace technology, the types and functions of space platforms using satellites as backbone networks are becoming more and more perfect. Different satellite systems separately used for information acquisition, transmission, and processing in space are connected organically by space-based transmission technology, and thus, a satellite-based space information network has been established. The characteristics of flexible networking, wide coverage, fast network construction, and no geographical restrictions make satellite networks have significant advantages in long-distance wireless communications. Many countries have carried out related research projects. For example, NASA and the US Air Force's Advanced Extremely High Frequency (AEHF) military communications satellite and Transformational Satellite Communications System (TSAT) projects[19] can achieve rapid information acquisition on a global scale. In addition, the German Aerospace Center proposed the TanDEM-X program,[20] the French Space Agency proposed the CartWheel program,[21] Italy proposed the BISSAT program,[22] and Canada proposed the RadarSat-2/3 program.[23]

The AEHF satellite system[24, 25] is a project of the US Department of Defense. It aims to provide a new generation of strategic and tactical communications satellites and ground-matching systems that can be used for military conflicts at all levels with global precision, high confidentiality, high communication capacity, and high survivability for the United States and its allies. In addition to the existing techniques of spread spectrum, frequency modulation, inter-satellite link, and on-board processing on the "military satellite", the AEHF space segment satellite also uses phased-array antenna technology and beamforming technology.[26] Phased-array antenna technology can change the direction of the RF beam by electronic means to make the beam between users jump instantaneously, thereby improving the transmission efficiency and flexibility. The beamforming network can use the automatic zeroing method to suppress the interference signal while providing services for legitimate users.

On June 21, 2010, the successful launch of the German radar satellite TanDEM-X symbolized the beginning of a new era in the global digital elevation model (WorldDEM). TanDEM-X and TerraSAR-X together form a high-precision radar interferometer that can acquire basic data for homologous WorldDEM. The two satellites form a unique satellite formation, flying in a tightly controlled spiral formation. They are very close with a minimum relative distance of only a few hundred meters. The main task is to produce a WorldDEM with good quality, high precision, and wide coverage. The accuracy of the WorldDEM will be higher than any existing satellite-based WorldDEM and has the following unique advantages: (1) relative vertical accuracy of 2 m and absolute vertical accuracy of 10 m, (2) 12 m × 12 m scanning raster, (3) global homology, (4) no ground control information is required. The TerraSAR-X and TanDEM-X binary star systems developed by the German Aerospace Center also form flexible beam pointing through active phased-array antenna technology to provide array gain. Although it can improve the signal power and transmission efficiency to a certain extent, it does not significantly increase the channel capacity and is largely subject to the load and power of the satellite.[27]

The TSAT program[28] was proposed by the US Air Force. Its core mission is using the virtual radar array established by cooperative communication of formation satellites to perform tasks such as passive radio radiation measurement, navigation, and communication (mobile tactical communication), thereby verifying that the formation satellites have the ability to achieve effective multitasking through cooperative communication.[29] The satellite can achieve high-capacity global communications and can deliver highly mobile, over-the-horizon, and protected communications to thousands of users by the use of new technologies such as laser links and Internet Protocol (IP). It provides tactical users with medium-rate communication capacity and also provides greater capacity of connectivity to the onboard intelligence, surveillance, and reconnaissance platforms. Due to funding and other reasons, TSAT program was on hold in 2009, but its concept of global networking and building spatial information network has not disappeared. The technology of space routers accumulated in the early stage of research continues to develop.

In the same period with TSAT program, the Applied Physics Laboratory at Johns Hopkins University and the US National Security Space Office proposed the idea of performing military missions in the geostationary orbit (GEO) with separation modules, namely the space-based group, to overcome the shortcomings of large mass, complicated technology, high cost, long developing cycle, and difficult maintenance of the complex large satellites loaded with multiple payloads.[30] The space-based group uses a main satellite to provide core services such as the space–ground link for the group and uses other low-cost, low-tech, task-specific sub-satellites and a main satellite to form a satellite group to perform tasks such as communication and remote sensing. And the group also includes on-orbit service satellites to provide support for satellite life extension and system reconstruction. Its key technologies include a high-speed low-power wireless network technology. Due to the working distance of only a few kilometers, the size, quality, and power consumption of wireless network equipment are exponentially lower than traditional satellite–ground links. It also combines IP routing technology with wireless networking and is equipped with a plug-and-play interface, which will be verified on-orbit. In terms of on-orbit service technology, the US Department of Defense Advanced Research Projects Agency (DARPA) has used the "Orbital Express" project to conduct tests such as fuel filling and equipment replacement. Recently, DARPA launched a research project codenamed "Phoenix", also known as the "Zombie Satellite" program. The project aims to recycle the scrapped satellites that become space debris and integrate the components especially antennas of space debris to form an antenna array, which will eventually become a low-cost "communication center". It can provide information services for the ground US military, realize the reuse of space resources, and reduce the cost of space development. The program will first launch a geosynchronous satellite (GEO) and then launch a series of small satellites that will work as controllers for the specified moving position. A robotic manipulator carried by the GEO will mount the recovered antennas on the launched small satellites. Finally, recyclable parts removed from space debris can form a "zombie antenna array".

In order to build a future-oriented, flexible, and efficient spacecraft architecture, the DARPA proposed the F6 program.[31–33] It is based on the idea of decomposing the traditional spacecraft into multiple combinable separation modules of different tasks and functions. These separate spacecraft modules can be mass-produced and independently launched on the ground. When operating normally in satellite orbit, they work together by the means of formation flight, wireless data transmission, and wireless energy transmission to combine the discrete modules into one complete unit. This "space-based group" transmission technology based on separation modules provides a new idea for the development of satellite communication systems.

Through the analysis above, the characteristics of the development trend of foreign space-based transmission systems can be summarized as follows:

(1) from single satellite to spatial information network;
(2) from completing the complex function by a single satellite to completing the complex function by a cooperative satellite group consisting of satellites with multiple functions;
(3) from adopting phased-array antennas to improve the received signal-to-noise ratio to adopting active antenna arrays to improve the channel capacity and transmission efficiency and achieve spatial multiplexing gain.

1.3.2 *The basic principle of space-based cooperative transmission system*

We will introduce the basic principles of spatial multiplexing gain obtained by the space-based cooperative transmission system. Based on the active antenna array, we take the downlink between a ground receiver consisting of M_E receiving antennas and a cooperative satellite group consisting of M_S satellites, as shown in Fig. 1.3. Among them, each satellite is equipped with M_L transmitting antenna arrays.

The frequency-selective MIMO satellite communication channel can be described by its channel matrix $\mathbf{H}(f)$. Due to the characteristics of the satellite communication system, the link is actually a non-fading and shadowless LOS channel. In groundwireless communication systems, we have demonstrated that orthogonal channels in the LOS channel can provide optimal channel capacity,[34] which requires that the channel response between the transmitting and receiving antennas meets special requirements and is quasi-static. Since groundwireless system terminals are almost mobile, the assumption of quasi-static channels is not true in groundcellular mobile systems.

Fortunately, in the satellite communication system, the ground station has a very low movement speed relative to the satellite in most cases. The geometric arrangement of the receiving and transmitting antenna arrays is

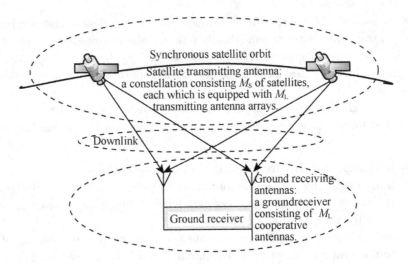

Fig. 1.3.   Downlink of space-based cooperative transmission system.

almost constant in a short time, and thus, the LOS channel can be approximated as static. Therefore, the satellite channel has unique advantages in realizing channel capacity optimization. Through the cooperative multi-beam transmission technology of constellation, we can achieve theoretically optimal antenna configuration, thereby increasing the capacity gain of the satellite communication system.

Regardless of the noise generated during signal propagation, the propagation process of a frequency stationary signal from constellation in MIMO channel can be expressed as

$$y = Hx \tag{1.2}$$

where the groundreceiving signal vector is $\mathbf{y} = [y_1, \ldots, y_{m_E}]^T$, the transmitting signal vector of constellation is $\mathbf{x} = [x_1, \ldots, x_{m_S}]^T$, and the channel matrix is $\mathbf{H} \in \mathbb{C}^{M_R \times M_T}$. The number of transmitting antennas is $M_T = M_S M_L$ and the number of receiving antennas is $M_R = M_E$.

For a MIMO system, the highest spectral efficiency of the channel can be calculated by Telatar's famous formula.[35]

$$C = \mathrm{lb}[\det(\mathbf{I}_{M_R} + \rho \cdot \mathbf{H}\mathbf{H}^H)] \tag{1.3}$$

where $(\cdot)^H$ is the transpose of matrix and ρ is the linear signal-to-noise ratio of the channel. The signal-to-noise ratio of the channel is defined as $\mathrm{SNR} = 10 \lg(\rho) = \mathrm{EIRP} + (G-T) - \kappa - \beta[\mathrm{dB}]$, where EIRP, $(G-T)$, κ, and β

are the effective isotropic radiated power, the quality factor, the Boltzmann constant, and the logarithm of downlink bandwidth, respectively. Since the distance between the satellite and the ground is much larger than the distance between array antennas, each element in the transfer matrix **H** can be considered to be of the same magnitude. Therefore, the transfer matrix **H** of the MIMO channel satisfying the maximum multiplexing gain is an orthogonal matrix. The theoretically optimal channel capacity can be achieved by adjusting the distance between the antennas and the distance between the constellations. The accessibility and conditions of the optimal channel capacity will be discussed in detail in Chapter 8.

1.4 Summary

Traditional wireless communication mainly uses ground-based wireless communication systems. However, with the rapid development of wireless communication systems, it is increasingly requiring higher spectrum utilization, greater system capacity, more flexible network coverage, and lower construction costs. With the continuous improvement of aerospace technology and the rapid growth of the types and quantities of space-based and air-based platforms, the space–air–ground integrated information network consisting of satellites, stratospheric balloons, and various aerospace vehicles is developed. This chapter mainly summarizes the characteristics and development process of the ground-based, air-based, and space-based wireless communication systems. In the following chapters, we will elaborate on the space–air–ground integrated cooperative transmission theories and key technologies.

References

1. Macdonald VH. The cellular concept. *Bell System Technical Journal*, 1979, 58: 15–41.
2. Bai L, Li Y, Huang Q, Dong X and Yu Q. Spatial Signal Combining Theories and Key Technologies. Posts&Telecom Press, Beijing, 2013.
3. Young WR. Advanced mobile phone service: Introduction, background, and objectives. *Bell System Technical Journal*, 1979, 58: 1–14.
4. TIA/EIA/IS-95 Interim Standard. Mobile Station-Base Station Compatibility Standard for Dual-Mode Wideband Spread Spectrum Cellular System, 1993.
5. 3GPP TR 36.913 v.8.0.1 Requirements for Further Advancements for E-UTRA. Tech. Report, 3rd Generation Partnership Project, 2009.

6. IEEE P802.16m/D3. Part 16: Air Interface for Broadband Wireless Access Systems, Advanced Air Interface, 2009.

7. METIS. Mobile And Wireless Communications Enablers For The 2020 Information society[EB/OL]. http://www.metis2020.com.

8. Wen T and Zhu PY. 5G: A technology vision 2013. 2014 National Wireless And Mobile Communication Academic Conference (WMC'14), Liaoning, China, 2014, 5–9.

9. Eguchi K. Overview of stratospheric platform airship R&D program in Japan. *The Proceeding of the First Stratospheric Platform Systems Workshop*, Yokosuka, Japan, 1999.

10. Wu YS. High altitude platform stations information system—new generation-wireless communications system. *ChinaRadio*, 2003, 6.

11. Sun ZQ. The rapid development of high-altitude platform communication system. *People's Posts and Telecommunications News*, 2004, 06–17.

12. Taha-Ahmcd B, Calm-Ramon M, Haro-Arict DE. High altitude platforms (HAPs) W-CDMA system over cities. *IEEE Vehicular Technology Conference*, 2005, 2673–2677.

13. Tozer TC, and Grace D. High-altitude platforms for wireless communications. *IEEE Electronics and Communications Engineering Journal*, 2001, 13(3): 127–137.

14. ITU Recommendation ITU-R F.1500, Preferred Characteristics of Systems in the Fixed Service Using High Altitude Platforms Operating in the Bands 47.2–47.5 GHz and 47.9–48.2 GHz. International Telecommunications Union, Geneva, Switzerland, 2000.

15. ITU Recommendation ITU-RF.1569, Technical and Operational Characteristics for the Fixed Service Using High Altitude Platform Stations in the Bands 7.5–28.35 GHz and 31–31.3 GHz. International Telecommunications Union, Geneva, Switzerland, 2002.

16. ITU Recommendation M.1456, Minimum Performance Characteristics and Operational Conditions for HAPS Providing IMT-2000 in the Bands 1885–1980 MHz, 2010–2025 MHz and 2110–2170 MHz in Regions 1 and 3 and 1885–1980 MHz and 2110–2160 MHz in Region 2. International Telecommunications Union, Geneva, Switzerland, 2000.

17. Mohorcic M, Javorinik T, Lavric A, *et al.* Selection of Broadband Communication Standard for High-Speed Mobile Scenario, FP6 CAPANINA Project. https://www.capanina.com/documents/CAP-D09-WP21-JSI-PUB-01.pdf, 2005.

18. Grace D, Thornton J, Konefal T, *et al.* Broadband communications from high altitude platforms the HeliNet solution. *Personalized Multimedia Communication Conference*, Aalborg, Denmark, 2001, 75–80.

19. Grace D, Capstick MH, Mohorcic M, *et al.* Integrating users into the wider broadband network via high altitude platforms. *IEEE Wireless Communications*, 2005, 12: 98–105.

20. Oodo M, Miura R, Hori T, *et al.* Sharing and compatibility study between fixed service using high altitude platform stations (HAPs) and other services in 31/28 GHz bands. *Wireless Personal Communications*, 2002, 23: 3–14.

21. Burns R, Mclaughlin CA, Leitner J, *et al.* TechSat 21: Formation design, control, and simulation. *IEEE Aerospace Conference*, 2000, 7: 19–25.
22. Krieger G, Moreira A, Fiedler H, *et al.* TanDEM-X: A satellite formation for high-resolution SAR interferometry. *IEEE Transactions on Geoscience and Remote Sensing*, 2007, 45(11): 3317–3341.
23. Amiot T, Douchin F, Thouvenot E, *et al.* The interferometric cartwheel: A multi-purpose formation of passive radar microsatellites. *IEEE International Geoscience and Remote Sensing Symposium*, 2002, 1: 435–437.
24. D'errico M, Moccia A. The BISSAT mission: A bistatic SAR operating information with COSMO/SkyMed X-band radar. *IEEE Aerospace Conference*, 2002, 2: 809–818.
25. Girard R, Lee PF, James K. The RADARSAT-2&3 topographic mission: An overview. *IEEE International Geoscience and Remote Sensing Symposium*, 2002, 3: 1477–1479.
26. Yang HP, Hu XH and Li Y. Advanced Extreme High Frequency (AEHF). *Digital Communication World*, 2008, (6): 84–87.
27. Hang GR and Kang XL. Propulsion system of USA AEHF military communication satellite and its application on AEHF-1 Satellite. *Journal of Rocket Propulsion*, 2011, 37(6): 1–8.
28. Wu XZ, Wu B and He RL. Foreign military's next-generation satellite communication system key technologies. *Communication Technology*, 2012, 45(9): 7–12.
29. Arapolou PD, Liolis K, Bertinelli M, *et al.* MIMO over satellite: A review. *IEEE Communications Surveys & Tutorials*, 2011, 13(1): 27–51.
30. Steyskal H, Schindler JK, Franchi P, *et al.* Pattern synthesis for TechSat21- A distributed Space-based radar system. *IEEE Antennas and Propagation Magazine*, 2003, 45(4): 19–25.
31. Feng SD, Zhang WF and Zhang JX. Design of the US army's next-generation transformational satellite operation system. *Digital Communication World*, 2009, (9): 59–63.
32. Gou L, Wei YJ, Shen Z, *et al.* Research on fractionated spacecraft. *Journal of Spacecraft TT&C Technology*, 2012, 31(2): 7–12.
33. Liu H and Liang W. Development of DARPA's F6 Program. *Spacecraft Engineering*, 2010, 19(2): 92–98.
34. Telatar E. Capacity of multi-antenna Gaussian channels. *AT&TBell Technical Memorandum*, 1995.
35. Maral G and Bousquet M. *Satellite Communications Systems: Systems, Techniques and Technology*. New Jersey, Wiley, 2002.

Chapter 2

The Overview of Multi-Antenna Signal and System

Wireless communication faces many challenges such as limited available wireless spectrum resources and complex space–time variation in the wireless communication environment. How to effectively utilize the optimal spatial signal combination method to improve the performance and spectrum efficiency of wireless communication systems is a very important and difficult technology for the next generation of wireless communication. This chapter will first introduce the basic theories of multi-antenna spatial signal combination and detection and then introduce the basic knowledge of array antenna from the perspective of signal space propagation. The pattern synthesis technology in the array antenna will be the focus of discussion. Finally, another wide application of multi-antenna technology will be introduced, namely the basic principle and signal detection method of multi-input and multi-output (MIMO) systems.

2.1 Spatial Signal Combination and Detection Basis

The received signal combination is a technology for combining multiple received signal values, and it is particularly significant in attenuating signal fading in the processing of wireless communication matrix signals. By providing multiple receiving antennas at the receiving end of the wireless communication system, better signal receiving performance can be obtained. This section assumes that multiple antennas at the receiving end can be equivalently replaced, and each receiving antenna can be regarded as a receiving device corresponding to a specific wireless channel. Since multiple receiving antennas can obtain multiple received signals, in order to obtain a larger signal gain, we need to properly combine the multiple received signals. In this section, we will consider the statistical characteristics of background noise on the basis of the statistics and certainty of the signals, and then combine the received signals.

Among the various signal combination technologies currently in existence, the technology that is easiest to implement is the linear signal combination technology, which is also the focus of our research.

2.1.1 *Spatial signal combination*

In a wireless communication system, it is assumed that there are N receiving antennas at the receiving end. In general, the source signal received by the receiving end must contain signal attenuation or distortion due to channel noise interference when transmitting in a specific channel. Since multiple receiving antennas can obtain observations of multiple received signals, the received signal can be represented by a signal vector in the signal vector space. As N increases, the number of dimensions in the signal vector space increases accordingly. Therefore, a subvector space of a signal vector with a high signal gain must be produced.

If s is used to denote the transmitted signal, then the signal received by the n pairs of receiving antennas at the receiving end can be expressed as

$$y_1 = h_1 s + n_1$$
$$y_2 = h_2 s + n_2$$
$$\vdots$$
$$y_N = h_N s + n_N \tag{2.1}$$

where h_k represents the channel gain corresponding to the kth received signal and n_k represents the noise of the kth received signal. It can be represented by a vector as follows:

$$\mathbf{y} = [y_1 \ y_2 \cdots y_N]^{\mathrm{T}}$$
$$= [h_1 \ h_2 \cdots h_N]^{\mathrm{T}} s + [n_1 \ n_2 \cdots n_N]^{\mathrm{T}}$$
$$= \mathbf{h}s + \mathbf{n} \tag{2.2}$$

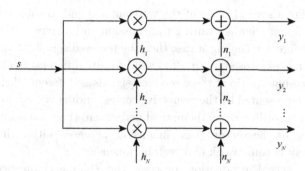

Fig. 2.1. Schematic diagram of the system model for receiving signals from multiple antennas.

where $\mathbf{h} = [h_1 \; h_2 \; \cdots \; h_N]^T \in \mathbb{C}^{N \times 1}$ is the channel gain vector and $\mathbf{n} = [n_1 \; n_2 \; \cdots \; n_N]^T \in \mathbb{C}^{N \times 1}$ is the noise vector. The channel gain $\mathbf{h}$ which describes the channel transmission characteristics is one of the key parameters in the combination of received signals.

Figure 2.1 is the schematic diagram of a system model for receiving signals from the N pairs of antennas at the receiving end. Since multiple receiving antennas can receive multiple observations for the same signal at the same time, a more accurate signal estimation can be obtained by properly combining these different observations.

Using a linear combination of a vector $\mathbf{y}$, the estimated value of s can be obtained as follows:

$$
\begin{aligned}
\hat{s} &= \sum_{k=1}^{N} w_k^* y_k \\
&= [w_1 \; w_2 \; \cdots \; w_N][y_1 \; y_2 \; \cdots \; y_N]^T \\
&= \mathbf{w}^H \mathbf{y}
\end{aligned}
\tag{2.3}
$$

where $\mathbf{w} = [w_1 \; w_2 \; \cdots \; w_N]^T$ represents a linear combination vector.

Of the various signal combination technologies currently available, the technology that can be easily implemented is through the linear signal combination technology, and the mathematical analysis is also relatively simple. Therefore, we will focus on the linear signal combination technology.

In a wireless communication system, utilizing a certain technology to obtain multiple copies of the same source signal at the receiving end can effectively improve the reliability of signal transmission, such as the multi-antenna receiving technology mentioned above, or repeatedly transmitting the same signal several times at the transmitting end. If each signal passes through different channels during transmission and arrives at the receiving end with different receiving states, then the received signal strength of each signal which is expressed in Eq. (2.1) will be quite different. In other words, the signal-to-noise ratio of these received signals is different. If the received signals are represented by the respective corresponding vectors in the vector space, then according to mathematical derivation, the total signal strength will increase as the vector space dimension increases, although the signal strength may become weak in a certain dimension.

In the actual production process, the channel gain between the transmitter and the receiver is affected by many factors such as transmission distance and multipath propagation. The transmission distance determines the average gain of the channel, while multipath propagation and the motion of the transmitter and receiver affect the instantaneous channel gain. In addition, moving the obstacles between the transmitter and the receiver can also result in time-varying channel gains. Due to the influence of various factors, the channel in wireless communication system is often a fading channel. In the fading channel environment, the signal-to-noise ratio (SNR) can be regarded as a time-varying random variable. However, when the SNR is below a certain threshold, the receiver cannot detect the signal. Therefore, we should try to reduce the probability that the SNR is lower than the threshold, namely reducing the probability of interruption. To solve this problem, we can use multi-receiving antenna diversity technology to reduce the probability of interruption, so as to obtain better signal detection performance. The gain obtained from this diversity is called the spatial diversity gain.

We call the vector space of the received signal as Space Domain, and the channel gain generated by the multidimensional signal (or multiple copies of the same signal) is known as the spatial diversity gain. In what follows, we will focus on several ways of combining signals in a wireless communication system.

2.1.1.1 *The combining method of known channels*

Based on the models expressed in Eqs. (2.2) and (2.3), when the channel state information **h** is known, the signal combination method can be designed separately according to the optimal discriminant criteria of different linear combination vectors **w**. In the following, the combination methods of received signals such as the minimum mean square error, the maximum SNR, the maximum likelihood estimation, the maximum ratio, and the general selection diversity will be introduced.

(1) Minimum mean square error combining

The minimum mean square error algorithm determines the combining signal vector $\mathbf{w}$ by minimizing the mean square error between the transmitted signal s and a linear combiner output.

If the signal and noise both obey Gaussian distribution, then the ideal MMSE combination is also a linear MMSE combination. In order to implement the linear MMSE combination algorithm, the statistical properties of $\mathbf{h}$, s, and $\mathbf{n}$ need to be known first. It is generally assumed that $E(\mathbf{n}) = \mathbf{0}$, $E(s) = 0$, $E(|s|^2) = \sigma_s^2$, and $E(\mathbf{n}\mathbf{n}^H) = \mathbf{R}_n$, where, $E(\cdot)$ represents the mathematical expectation of a random variable. In this section, we assume that the covariance matrix $\mathbf{R}_n$ is full rank.

The output of the linear combiner, namely the MSE of signal s and its estimated value $\hat{s}$, is

$$E(|s - \hat{s}|^2) = E(|s - \mathbf{w}^H y|^2) \tag{2.4}$$

It is easy to know that the MSE is a function of vector $\mathbf{w}$. According to the orthogonality principle, the optimal combining vector is

$$\mathbf{w}_{\text{MMSE}} = \arg \min_{w} E(|s - \mathbf{w}^H \mathbf{y}|^2)$$

$$= (E(\mathbf{y}\mathbf{y}^H))^{-1} E(\mathbf{y}s^*)$$

$$= \mathbf{R}_r^{-1} \mathbf{c} \tag{2.5}$$

where $\mathbf{R}_r = E(\mathbf{y}\mathbf{y}^H)$ is the covariance matrix of the received signal vector $\mathbf{y}$ and $\mathbf{c} = E(\mathbf{y}s^*)$ is the correlation vector of vectors $\mathbf{y}$ and s^*. If s and $\mathbf{n}$ are not related, then $\mathbf{R}_r = \mathbf{h}\mathbf{h}^H\sigma_s^2 + \mathbf{R}_n$, $\mathbf{c} = \mathbf{h}\sigma_s^2$. By substituting it in Eq. (2.5), the optimal MMSE combination vector can be obtained.

$$\mathbf{w}_{\text{MMSE}} = (\mathbf{h}\mathbf{h}^H\sigma_s^2 + \mathbf{R}_n)^{-1}\mathbf{h}\sigma_s^2$$

$$= \frac{\sigma_s^2}{1 + \sigma_s^2 \mathbf{h}^H \mathbf{R}_n^{-1} \mathbf{h}} \mathbf{R}_n^{-1} \mathbf{h}$$

$$= \alpha \mathbf{R}_n^{-1} \mathbf{h} \tag{2.6}$$

where $\alpha = \frac{\sigma_s^2}{1 + \sigma_s^2 \mathbf{h}^H \mathbf{R}_n^{-1} \mathbf{h}}$.

Therefore, MMSE is

$$\varepsilon_{\min}^2 = \mathrm{E}(|s - \mathbf{w}_{\mathrm{MMSE}}^{\mathrm{H}} \mathbf{y}|^2)$$
$$= \sigma_s^2(1 - \mathbf{h}^{\mathrm{H}}(\mathbf{h}\mathbf{h}^{\mathrm{H}}\sigma_s^2 + \mathbf{R}_n)^{-1}\mathbf{h}\sigma_s^2)$$
$$= \frac{\sigma_s^2}{1 + \sigma_s^2\mathbf{h}^{\mathrm{H}}\mathbf{R}_n^{-1}\mathbf{h}}$$
$$= \alpha \qquad (2.7)$$

It can be seen from Eq. (2.7) that the value of MMSE depends on the transmitted signal s, the channel transmission vector $\mathbf{h}$, and the noise covariance matrix $\mathbf{R}_n$. Taking the extreme value as an example, when $\sigma_s^2 \to \infty$, Eq. (2.7) can be simplified as $\lim_{\sigma_s^2 \to \infty} \varepsilon_{\min}^2 = \frac{1}{\mathbf{h}^{\mathrm{H}}\mathbf{R}_n^{-1}\mathbf{h}}$. In this case, although $\sigma_s^2 \to \infty$, MMSE will never reach zero because $\mathbf{h}^{\mathrm{H}}\mathbf{R}_n^{-1}\mathbf{h}$ is limited.

Substituting Eq. (2.7) into Eq. (2.6) we get

$$\mathbf{w}_{\mathrm{MMSE}} = \varepsilon_{\min}^2 \mathbf{R}_n^{-1}\mathbf{h} \qquad (2.8)$$

substituting Eq. (2.8) into Eq. (2.3), we can obtain the estimated signal based on MMSE.

$$\hat{s}_{\mathrm{MMSE}} = \varepsilon_{\min}^2 \mathbf{h}^{\mathrm{H}}\mathbf{R}_n^{-1}\mathbf{r}$$
$$= \varepsilon_{\min}^2 \mathbf{h}^{\mathrm{H}}\mathbf{R}_n^{-1}\mathbf{h}s + w \qquad (2.9)$$

where, $w = \varepsilon_{\min}^2 \mathbf{h}^{\mathrm{H}}\mathbf{R}_n^{-1}\mathbf{h}$, $\mathrm{E}(|w|^2) = \varepsilon_{\min}^4 \mathbf{h}^{\mathrm{H}}\mathbf{R}_n^{-1}\mathbf{h}$. And then the SNR of the received signal can be defined as

$$\mathrm{SNR} = \frac{\mathrm{E}(|ws|^2)}{\mathrm{E}(|w|^2)}$$
$$= \sigma_s^2\mathbf{h}^{\mathrm{H}}\mathbf{R}_n^{-1}\mathbf{h}$$
$$= \frac{\sigma_s^2}{\lim_{\sigma_s^2 \to \infty} \varepsilon_{\min}^2} \qquad (2.10)$$

(2) Maximum SNR combining

If the criterion for maximizing SNR is used in the linear combination, then for the combined vector $\mathbf{w}$, the combined signal can be written as

$$\hat{s} = \mathbf{w}^{\mathrm{H}}\mathbf{y}$$
$$= \mathbf{w}^{\mathrm{H}}\mathbf{h}s + \mathbf{w}^{\mathrm{H}}\mathbf{n} \qquad (2.11)$$

where the first item and the second item on the right-hand side are the signal and noise, respectively. Thus, the SNR is given as follows:

$$
\begin{aligned}
\text{SNR} &= \frac{E(|\mathbf{w}^H \mathbf{h} s|^2)}{E(|\mathbf{w}^H \mathbf{n}|^2)} \\
&= \frac{|\mathbf{w}^H \mathbf{h}|^2 \sigma_s^2}{\mathbf{w}^H \mathbf{R}_n \mathbf{w}} \\
&= \frac{\left| \left(\mathbf{R}_n^{\frac{1}{2}} \mathbf{w} \right)^H \left(\left(\mathbf{R}_n^{-\frac{1}{2}} \right)^H \mathbf{h} \right) \right|^2 \sigma_s^2}{\left(\mathbf{R}_n^{\frac{1}{2}} \mathbf{w} \right)^H \left(\mathbf{R}_n^{\frac{1}{2}} \mathbf{w} \right)} \\
&\leq \frac{\left\| \mathbf{R}_n^{\frac{1}{2}} \mathbf{w} \right\|^2 \left\| \left(\mathbf{R}_n^{-\frac{1}{2}} \right)^H \mathbf{h} \right\|^2 \sigma_s^2}{\left(\mathbf{R}_n^{-\frac{1}{2}} \mathbf{w} \right)^H \left(\mathbf{R}_n^{\frac{1}{2}} \mathbf{w} \right)} \\
&= \left\| \left(\mathbf{R}_n^{-\frac{1}{2}} \right)^H \mathbf{h} \right\|^2 \sigma_s^2 \\
&= \mathbf{h}^H \mathbf{R}_n^{-1} \mathbf{h} \sigma_s^2
\end{aligned}
\tag{2.12}
$$

where the full rank covariance matrix $\mathbf{R}_n$ must be a positive definite matrix (matrix decomposition $\mathbf{R}_n = (\mathbf{R}_n^{\frac{1}{2}})^H \mathbf{R}_n^{\frac{1}{2}}$ is used in the derivation from row 2 to row 3 of Eq. (2.12)). In addition, if and only if $\mathbf{R}_n^{\frac{1}{2}} \mathbf{w} = \alpha (\mathbf{R}_n^{-\frac{1}{2}})^H \mathbf{h}$ (α is a non-zero constant), the equal sign can be used from row 3 to row 4 of Eq. (2.12). In order to make the inequality take the maximum value, it should set

$$
\begin{aligned}
\mathbf{w} &= \alpha \mathbf{R}_n^{-\frac{1}{2}} \left(\mathbf{R}_n^{-\frac{1}{2}} \right)^H \mathbf{h} \\
&= \alpha \left(\left(\mathbf{R}_n^{\frac{1}{2}} \right)^H \mathbf{R}_n^{\frac{1}{2}} \right)^{-1} \mathbf{h} \\
&= \alpha \mathbf{R}_n^{-1} \mathbf{h}
\end{aligned}
\tag{2.13}
$$

and then the combined vector with the maximum signal-to-noise ratio (MSNR) can be expressed as

$$
\mathbf{w}_{\text{MSNR}} = \alpha \mathbf{R}_n^{-1} \mathbf{h}
\tag{2.14}
$$

Comparing Eq. (2.14) with Eq. (2.6), we see that the MMSE combination is essentially an MSNR combination.

(3) Maximum likelihood combining

If the transmitted signal s is considered as an estimated parameter, the signal s can be estimated by the maximum likelihood (ML) estimation algorithm. Assuming that vector $\mathbf{n}$ in Eq. (2.2) is a zero-mean CSCG random variable, namely $\mathbf{n} \sim \mathcal{CN}(\mathbf{0}, \mathbf{R}_n)$, then for vector $\mathbf{r}$ given in Eq. (2.2), the probability density of the signal s is

$$f(\mathbf{y}|s) = \frac{1}{\det(\pi\mathbf{R}_n)}e^{-(\mathbf{y}-\mathbf{h}s)^{\mathrm{H}}\mathbf{R}_n^{-1}(\mathbf{y}-\mathbf{h}s)} \tag{2.15}$$

Therefore, the maximum likelihood estimate for signal s is

$$\begin{aligned}
\hat{s}_{\mathrm{ML}} &= \arg\max_s f(\mathbf{y}|s) \\
&= \arg\min_s (\mathbf{y} - \mathbf{h}s)^{\mathrm{H}}\mathbf{R}_n^{-1}(\mathbf{y} - \mathbf{h}s) \\
&= \frac{(\mathbf{R}_n^{-1}\mathbf{h})^{\mathrm{H}}\mathbf{y}}{\mathbf{h}^{\mathrm{H}}\mathbf{R}_n^{-1}\mathbf{h}} \\
&= \left(\frac{1}{\mathbf{h}^{\mathrm{H}}\mathbf{R}_n^{-1}\mathbf{h}}\mathbf{R}_n^{-1}\mathbf{h}\right)^{\mathrm{H}}\mathbf{y} \\
&= \mathbf{w}_{\mathrm{ML}}^{\mathrm{H}}\mathbf{y}
\end{aligned} \tag{2.16}$$

where the maximum likelihood combining vector is

$$\mathbf{w}_{\mathrm{ML}} = \frac{1}{\mathbf{h}^{\mathrm{H}}\mathbf{R}_n^{-1}\mathbf{h}}\mathbf{R}_n^{-1}\mathbf{h} \tag{2.17}$$

It is easy to know that the maximum likelihood estimation is actually achieved by adjusting the weight vector $\mathbf{w}_{\mathrm{ML}}$ through a linear combination operation, which we call the maximum likelihood combining.

Comparing Eq. (2.17) with Eq. (2.14), the maximum likelihood combining is essentially an MSNR combination.

(4) Maximum ratio combining

Maximum ratio combining (MRC) is a linear combination technology often used in the fading channel environment, which can effectively improve the system performance of the fading channel. In fact, MRC can be seen as a special case of MSNR combination.

In order to derive the MRC algorithm, we assume that the noise terms in Eq. (2.1) are uncorrelated and their variances are equal, namely

$E(\mathbf{n}\mathbf{n}^H) = N_0\mathbf{I}$. In this case, the SNR can be obtained according to Eq. (2.12).

$$\text{SNR} = \frac{|\mathbf{w}^H\mathbf{h}|^2\sigma_s^2}{N_0\|\mathbf{w}\|^2} \tag{2.18}$$

According to the Cauchy–Schwartz inequality, it is easy to prove that the combined vector that maximizes SNR is $\mathbf{w} = \alpha\mathbf{h}$. This is also a special case of the MSNR combination vector in Eq. (2.14). The linear combination of linear combination vectors $\mathbf{w} = \alpha\mathbf{h}$ is called MRC.

When the MRC algorithm is applied, the SNR can be obtained.

$$\text{SNR}_{\text{MRC}} = \frac{\|\mathbf{h}\|^2\sigma_s^2}{N_0}$$
$$= \sum_{k=1}^{N} \frac{|h_k|^2\sigma_s^2}{N_0} \tag{2.19}$$

(5) Generalized selection diversity combining

In wireless communication systems, selection diversity (SD) is also a common spatial diversity technology. Different from the principle that the MRC algorithm combines all the received signals to maximize SNR, the SD algorithm picks out only the strongest signal of the N received signals for processing, which makes it easy to implement.

The SNR of the SD algorithm is

$$\text{SNR}_{\text{SD}} = \max\{\text{SNR}_1, \text{SNR}_2, \ldots, \text{SNR}_N\} \tag{2.20}$$

where $\text{SNR}_k = \frac{|h_k|^2\sigma_s^2}{N_0}$, $k = 1, 2, \ldots, N$.

In order to improve the performance of SD, a generalized SD combining (GSDC) algorithm is proposed in related literatures. The generalized SD combining selects M signals from the N received signals. When $M = N$, GSDC is equivalent to the optimal MRC combining. When $M = 1$, GSDC is a common SD algorithm. It is easy to see that GSDC algorithm has a good balance between performance and computational complexity.

If M signals are obtained under the MSNR standard, the final SNR is

$$\text{SNR}_{\text{GSDC}} = \sum_{k=1}^{M} \text{SNR}_{(k)} \tag{2.21}$$

where $\text{SNR}_{(k)}$ is the kth maximum SNR of SNR_k, $k = 1, 2, \ldots, N$.

2.1.1.2 *The combining method of unknown channels*

The signal combining technologies we discussed above are all based on the assumption that the channel transmission vector $\mathbf{h}$ is known. However, in some cases, the channel transmission vector $\mathbf{h}$ is difficult to accurately measure, or $\mathbf{h}$ is a random variable and there is no accurate value. In this case, when it is necessary to perform a mathematical estimate of the channel transmission vector, the channel transmission vector is regarded as a random variable by considering of the inevitable estimation error.

In the following, the MMSE combining method where the channel transmission vector is a random variable is further analyzed.

Assuming that the expectation and variance of the channel transmission vector $\mathbf{h}$ are known, they are given as

$$
\begin{aligned}
\mathrm{E}(\mathbf{h}) &= \overline{\mathbf{h}} \\
\mathrm{E}((\mathbf{h} - \overline{\mathbf{h}})(\mathbf{h} - \overline{\mathbf{h}})^{\mathrm{H}}) &= \mathbf{C}
\end{aligned}
\tag{2.22}
$$

When estimating the channel transmission vector $\mathbf{h}$, we can replace its mean vector with the estimated value of $\mathbf{h}$ and replace its covariance matrix $\mathbf{C}$ with the estimated error covariance of h. In this case, the MMSE combining vector is

$$
\begin{aligned}
\mathbf{W}_{\mathrm{MMSE}} &= \mathrm{E}(|s - \mathbf{w}^{\mathrm{H}}\mathbf{y}|^2) \\
&= (\mathrm{E}(\mathbf{h}\mathbf{h}^{\mathrm{H}})\sigma_s^2 + \mathbf{R_n})^{-1}\overline{\mathbf{h}}\sigma_s^2 \\
&= ((\mathbf{C} + \overline{\mathbf{h}}\overline{\mathbf{h}}^{\mathrm{H}})\sigma_s^2 + \mathbf{R_n})^{-1}\overline{\mathbf{h}}\sigma_s^2
\end{aligned}
\tag{2.23}
$$

If $\overline{\mathbf{h}} = \mathbf{0}$, the MMSE combining vector is also $\mathbf{0}$, and this indicates the failure of the MMSE combining method. In order to avoid such problems, we need to correct the MMSE combining method, and the correction methods are different based on different applications.

In the following, we will illustrate the correction of the MMSE combining method.

Assume that the channel transmission vector $\mathbf{h} = \mathrm{e}^{\mathrm{j}\phi}\mathbf{h_0}$, where ϕ is a random phase vector and $\mathbf{h_0}$ is a non-zero constant vector. If ϕ is uniformly distributed, $\overline{\mathbf{h}} = \mathbf{0}$, then the amplitude of the channel transmission vector gain is also constant, but its phase is time-varying. If the time-varying phase changes slowly, some conventional signal modulation technologies can be used to detect the received signal with an unknown phase estimation.

If the received signal is expressed as

$$\mathbf{y} = e^{j\phi}\mathbf{h}_0 s + \mathbf{n}$$
$$= \mathbf{h}_0 e^{j\phi} s + \mathbf{n} \tag{2.24}$$

and $c = e^{j\phi}s$ is regarded as a new detection signal, then the MMSE combining vector is

$$\mathbf{w}_{\text{MMSE}} = \mathbf{w}_{\text{MMSE},0}$$
$$= \arg\min_{\mathbf{w}} E(|e^{j\phi}s - \mathbf{w}^H\mathbf{y}|^2)$$
$$= (\mathbf{h}_0\mathbf{h}_0^H\sigma_s^2 + \mathbf{R}_n)^{-1}\mathbf{h}_0\sigma_s^2 \tag{2.25}$$

However, it should be noted that the MMSE combining vector here is not time-varying. The output of the MMSE combiner is

$$\hat{c} = \mathbf{w}_{\text{MMSE}}^H\mathbf{y}$$
$$= \mathbf{w}_{\text{MMSE}}^H\mathbf{h}_0 c + \mathbf{w}_{\text{MMSE}}^H\mathbf{n} \tag{2.26}$$

According to $\hat{c}$, the receiver can detect the signal.

In general, if the time-varying random channel transmission vector can be decomposed into the known constant and the random variable, then we can realize the application of MMSE in the actual production process by modifying the known signals.

2.1.2 *Received signal detection*

In Section 2.1.1, we briefly introduced how to use the different criteria to obtain the optimal linear combination vector to design different signal combinations. Under ideal conditions, we can assume that the receiver can only receive the target signals. However, the receiver actually often receives interference signals from other devices while receiving the target signals. For these interference signals, traditional signal combining methods generally classify them into noise for processing, but such solutions have obvious drawbacks and sometimes lead to large performance losses.

As a result, the method of extracting the target signal in the mixed signal, namely the signal detection method, is beginning to be studied. Multi-signal detection method has always been an important problem to be solved in wireless communication. As shown in Fig. 2.2, in a cellular system, if users in two cells use the same transmission channel to transmit signals, the base station can receive the user signal in the cell of the base station and

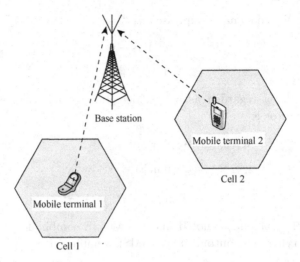

Fig. 2.2.   Multi-user monitoring model of the cellular system.

can also receive the signal in another cell. And in this case, the base station needs to detect different signals. In addition, when a transmitter transmits signals through multiple transmitting antennas, the receiving end also needs to detect multiple received signals. And when multiple antennas are used by both the transmitter and the receiver, point-to-point signal detection can also be regarded as a virtual multi-signal detection technique due to interference between the antennas. In addition, when multiple antennas are used by both the transmitter and the receiver, point-to-point signal detection can also be regarded as a virtual multi-signal detection technology due to the interference between the antennas.

The above examples illustrate several common application scenarios for multi-signal detection, and multi-signal detection technology will play a significant role for a long time.

2.1.2.1 *Binary waveform signal detection*[a]

In a wireless communication system, the channel transmits an analog signal rather than a discrete signal. For binary waveform signals, the received

---

[a]Reprinted/adapted by permission from Springer Nature Customer Service Centre GmbH: Springer "Low Complexity MIMO Receivers" by Bai L, Choi J and Yu Q, 2014.

signal can be written as

$$R(t) = X(t) + N(t), \quad 0 \le t < T \qquad (2.27)$$

where T represents the duration of the signal, $N(t)$ is Gaussian white noise and $E(N(t)) = 0$, $E(N(t)N(\rho)) = \frac{N_0}{2}\delta(t - \rho)$ with $\delta(t)$ representing a Dirac function, otherwise called a unit pulse function. The wireless channel of Eq. (2.27) is called an Additive White Gaussian Noise (AWGN) channel. Meanwhile, $X(t)$ is a binary waveform signal, i.e.

$$X(t) = \begin{cases} s_0(t), & S_0 \text{ holds} \\ s_0(t), & S_1 \text{ holds} \end{cases} \qquad (2.28)$$

whose transmission rate is $1/T$ bit/s.

(1) Waveform signal detection

First, we will discuss a heuristic algorithm for waveform signal detection and then extend the waveform to generalize a general waveform detection method.

If the signal is judged according to $R(t)(0 \le t < T)$ at the receiving end, the observation values of $R(t)$ and $N(t)$ are represented by $r(t)$ and $n(t)$, respectively, L times sampling on $r(t)$ has been performed, and define $r_l = \int_{(l-1)T/L}^{lT/L} y(t)\,\mathrm{d}t$, $s_{m,l} = \int_{(l-1)T/L}^{lT/L} s_m(t)\,\mathrm{d}t$, $n_l = \int_{(l-1)T/L}^{lT/L} n(t)\,\mathrm{d}t$, we can obtain

$$\begin{aligned} S_0 \text{ holds}: \ r_l &= s_{0,l} + n_l \\ S_1 \text{ holds}: \ r_l &= s_{1,l} + n_l \end{aligned} \qquad (2.29)$$

Since $N(t)$ is white noise and n_l is independent of each other, the mean of n_l is zero and the variance is

$$\sigma^2 = E(n_l^2)$$

$$= E\left(\left(\int_{(l-1)T/L}^{lT/L} n(t)\,\mathrm{d}t\right)^2\right)$$

$$= \int_{(l-1)T/L}^{lT/L} \int_{(l-1)T/L}^{lT/L} E(N(t)N(\rho))\,\mathrm{d}t\,\mathrm{d}\rho$$

$$= \int_{(l-1)T/L}^{lT/L} \int_{(l-1)T/L}^{lT/L} \frac{N_0}{2}\delta(t-\rho)\,\mathrm{d}t\,\mathrm{d}\rho$$

$$= \frac{N_0 T}{2L} \tag{2.30}$$

Defining $\mathbf{r} = [r_1\ r_2\ \cdots\ r_L]^{\mathrm{T}}$, the likelihood ratio of L is obtained as

$$
\begin{aligned}
\mathrm{LLR}(r) &= \log \frac{\prod_{l=1}^{L} f(r_l|S_0)}{\prod_{l=1}^{L} f(r_l|S_1)} \\[2mm]
&= \log \frac{f_0(\mathbf{r})}{f_1(\mathbf{r})} \\[2mm]
&= \sum_{l=1}^{L} \log \frac{f_0(r_l)}{f_1(r_l)} \\[2mm]
&= \sum_{l=1}^{L} \log \left(e^{-\frac{1}{N_0}((r_l - s_{0,l})^2 - (r_l - s_{1,l})^2)} \right) \\[2mm]
&= \frac{1}{N_0} \sum_{l=1}^{L} ((r_l - s_{1,l})^2 - (r_l - s_{0,l})^2) \\[2mm]
&= \frac{1}{N_0} (2\mathbf{r}^{\mathrm{T}}(\mathbf{s}_0 - \mathbf{s}_1) - (\mathbf{s}_0^{\mathrm{T}}\mathbf{s}_0 - \mathbf{s}_1^{\mathrm{T}}\mathbf{s}_1)) \tag{2.31}
\end{aligned}
$$

where $\mathbf{s}_m = [s_{m,1}\ s_{m,2}\ \cdots\ s_{m,L}]^{\mathrm{T}}$.

According to the likelihood ratio of L, the MAP criterion can be obtained.

$$
\begin{cases}
S_0 : \mathbf{r}^{\mathrm{T}}(\mathbf{s}_0 - \mathbf{s}_1) > \sigma^2 \log \left(\frac{P(S_0)}{P(S_1)} \right) + \frac{1}{2}(\mathbf{s}_0^{\mathrm{T}}\mathbf{s}_0 - \mathbf{s}_1^{\mathrm{T}}\mathbf{s}_1) \\[3mm]
S_1 : \mathbf{r}^{\mathrm{T}}(\mathbf{s}_0 - \mathbf{s}_1) < \sigma^2 \log \left(\frac{P(S_0)}{P(S_1)} \right) + \frac{1}{2}(\mathbf{s}_0^{\mathrm{T}}\mathbf{s}_0 - \mathbf{s}_1^{\mathrm{T}}\mathbf{s}_1)
\end{cases} \tag{2.32}
$$

If we consider the criterion based on the likelihood ratio and use the threshold ρ instead of $\frac{P(S_0)}{P(S_1)}$, then we have

$$
\begin{cases}
S_0 : \mathbf{r}^{\mathrm{T}}(\mathbf{s}_0 - \mathbf{s}_1) > \sigma^2 \log \rho + \frac{1}{2}(\mathbf{s}_0^{\mathrm{T}}\mathbf{s}_0 - \mathbf{s}_1^{\mathrm{T}}\mathbf{s}_1) \\[3mm]
S_1 : \mathbf{r}^{\mathrm{T}}(\mathbf{s}_0 - \mathbf{s}_1) < \sigma^2 \log \rho + \frac{1}{2}(\mathbf{s}_0^{\mathrm{T}}\mathbf{s}_0 - \mathbf{s}_1^{\mathrm{T}}\mathbf{s}_1)
\end{cases} \tag{2.33}
$$

(2) Correlation detector and its performance

In the sampling process of $r(t)$, if it has a low sampling frequency within the duration Ts of the signal, the information may be missing due to the sampling process. To avoid this distortion, the value of L is assumed to be large enough to be close to $\mathbf{r}^T\mathbf{s}_i \approx \frac{1}{T}\int_0^T r(t)s_m(t)\,dt$. On this basis, the judging criteria based on the likelihood ratio can be rewritten as

$$\begin{cases} S_0 : \int_0^T r(t)(s_0(t) - s_1(t))\,dt > \sigma^2 \log\rho + \frac{1}{2}\int_0^T (s_0^2(t) - s_1^2(t))\,dt \\ S_1 : \int_0^T r(t)(s_0(t) - s_1(t))\,dt < \sigma^2 \log\rho + \frac{1}{2}\int_0^T (s_0^2(t) - s_1^2(t))\,dt \end{cases}$$

$$(2.34)$$

Define $V_T = \sigma^2 \log\rho + \frac{1}{2}\int_0^T (s_0^2(t) - s_1^2(t))\,dt$, then the judging criteria in Eq. (2.34) become

$$\begin{cases} S_0 : \int_0^T r(t)(s_0(t) - s_1(t))\,dt > V_T \\ S_1 : \int_0^T r(t)(s_0(t) - s_1(t))\,dt < V_T \end{cases} \qquad (2.35)$$

The judging criteria can be implemented by the model shown in Fig. 2.3, which is called a correlation detector.

In order to make an analysis of the detector's performance, the maximum likelihood judging criteria are first considered, namely setting $\rho = 1$ in the judging criteria based on the likelihood ratio. In this case, $V_T = \frac{1}{2}\int_0^T (s_0^2(t) - s_1^2(t))\,dt$. Define $X = \int_0^T r(t)(s_0(t) - s_1(t))\,dt - V_T$, and it is easy to know

$$\begin{cases} P(D_0|S_1) = P(X > 0|S_1) \\ P(D_1|S_0) = P(X < 0|S_0) \end{cases} \qquad (2.36)$$

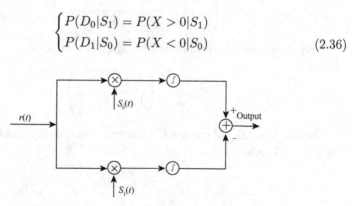

Fig. 2.3. Correlation detector for binary waveform signals.

Second, the bit error rate is calculated based on the statistical properties of the random variable X. Since the noise $N(t)$ is assumed to follow the Gaussian random process, it can be seen that X is also a Gaussian random variable. Note that when S_m is true, $R(t) = s_m(t) + N(t)$, and thus, the statistical properties of X depend on S_m. In order to obtain the statistical properties of X, the mean and variance of the Gaussian random variable X need to be determined, respectively.

$$E(X|S_m) = \int_0^T E(R(t)|S_m)(s_0(t) - s_1(t)) \, dt - V_T$$

$$= \int_0^T s_m(t)(s_0(t) - s_1(t)) \, dt - V_T \tag{2.37}$$

$$\sigma_m^2 = E((X - E(X|S_m))^2|S_m) \tag{2.38}$$

The average energy of the signal is defined as $E_s = \frac{1}{2} \int_0^T (s_0^2(t) + s_1^2(t)) \, dt$. Assume $s_m(t)$ is transmitted by equal probability with $m = 0, 1$. Define $\tau = \frac{1}{E_s} \int_0^T s_0(t)s_1(t) \, dt$ and $\sigma^2 = \sigma_0^2 = \sigma_1^2 = N_0 E_s(1 - \tau)$, then

$$\begin{cases} E(X|S_0) = E_s(1 - \tau) \\ E(X|S_1) = -E_s(1 - \tau) \end{cases} \tag{2.39}$$

Therefore, in the case where S_0 and S_1 are, respectively, established, the probability density of X is

$$\begin{cases} f_0(g) = \dfrac{e^{-\frac{(g - E_s(1-\tau))^2}{2N_0 E_s(1-\tau)}}}{\sqrt{2\pi N_0 E_s(1 - \tau)}} \\[4mm] f_1(g) = \dfrac{e^{-\frac{(g + E_s(1-\tau))^2}{2N_0 E_s(1-\tau)}}}{\sqrt{2\pi N_0 E_s(1 - \tau)}} \end{cases} \tag{2.40}$$

And then the error probability in signal detection is

$$P_{\text{ER}} = Q\left(\sqrt{\frac{E_s(1 - \tau)}{N_0}}\right) \tag{2.41}$$

For the fixed signal energy E_s, the error probability can be minimized when $\tau = -1$, namely

$$P_{\text{ER}} = Q\left(\sqrt{\frac{2E_s}{N_0}}\right) \tag{2.42}$$

It is easy to prove that the signal that minimizes the error probability has the opposite polarity, namely $s_0(t) = -s_1(t)$. For the orthogonal signal set, $\tau = 0$ and the error probability is

$$P_{\text{ER}} = \mathcal{Q}\left(\sqrt{\frac{E_s}{N_0}}\right) \tag{2.43}$$

It can be seen from Eqs. (2.42) and (2.43) that the SNR between the orthogonal signal set and the signal set with the opposite polarity is 3 dB.

2.1.2.2 *M-ary signal detection*

The detection problem of the binary waveform signal when $M = 2$ has been introduced above, and then we will analyze the detection problem of the M-ary signal.

It is assumed that in the M-ary communication, there is a set $\{s_1(t), s_2(t), \ldots, s_M(t)\}$, $0 \leq t < T$ consisting of M signal waveforms. At this time, the data transmission rate is $\frac{\text{lb}M}{T}$ bit/s. It can be seen that the data transmission rate increases as M increases, which means that the larger the M value is, the better. However, in general, the detection performance of the signal will be worse as the value of M increases.

In the case of M hypotheses, assuming that the received signal is $R(t) = s_m(t) + N(t)$, $0 \leq t < T$. The likelihood function and log-likelihood function of the L samples are expressed as

$$f_m(\mathbf{r}) = \prod_{l=1}^{L} f_m(r_l) = \frac{1}{(\pi N_0)^{\frac{L}{2}}} \prod_{l=1}^{L} e^{-\frac{(r_l - s_{m,l})^2}{N_0}}$$

$$\log f_m(\mathbf{r}) = \log \frac{1}{(\pi N_0)^{\frac{L}{2}}} + \sum_{l=1}^{L} \log\left(e^{-\frac{(r_l - s_{m,l})^2}{N_0}}\right)$$

$$= \log \frac{1}{(\pi N_0)^{\frac{L}{2}}} - \frac{(r_l - s_{m,l})^2}{N_0} \tag{2.44}$$

If the common terms in all hypotheses are ignored, the log-likelihood function becomes

$$\log f_m(\mathbf{r}) = \frac{1}{N_0}\left(\sum_{l=1}^{L} r_l s_{m,l} - \frac{1}{2}|s_{m,l}|^2\right) \tag{2.45}$$

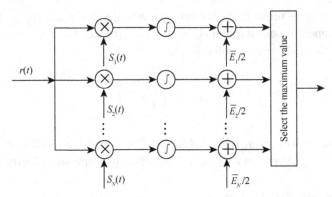

Fig. 2.4. Maximum likelihood detector for M-ary signal detection based on a set of correlation detectors.

Using $r(t)$ to represent the observed value of $R(t)$, when L tends to infinity, the following equation can be obtained:

$$\log f_m(r(t)) = \frac{1}{N_0}\left(\int_0^T r(t)s_m(t)\,\mathrm{d}t - \frac{1}{2}\int_0^T s_m^2(t)\,\mathrm{d}t\right) \qquad (2.46)$$

where $E_m = \int_0^T s_m^2(t)\,\mathrm{d}t$ is the energy of the mth signal $s_m(t)$ and $\int_0^T r(t)s_m(t)\,\mathrm{d}t$ is the correlation function of $r(t)$ and $s_m(t)$.

According to the expression of the log-likelihood function, the maximum likelihood judging criteria for accepting S_m should be $\log f_m(r(t)) \geq \log f_{m'}(r(t))$ or $\log \frac{f_m(r(t))}{f_{m'}(r(t))} \geq 0$, $m' \in \{1, 2, \ldots, M\}\backslash\{m\}$. The symbol "$\backslash$" is defined as $A\backslash B = \{x | x \in A, x \notin B\}$.

Based on the preceding conclusions, the process of connecting a series of correlation detectors to achieve the maximum likelihood judging criteria is shown in Fig. 2.4.

2.1.2.3 *Signal detection in vector space*

In the process of wireless communication, in addition to receiving multiple target signals, the receiving end is also affected by the noise generated by the wireless channel and other devices. For these interferences, all of them are regarded as noise in the traditional signal combining method, which usually leads to a large performance loss. Considering this problem, the technology of signal detection in vector space is extensively studied to distinguish and detect target signals in mixed signals. Before introducing the signal detection in vector space, the expansion of space vector signal, namely Karhunen–Loeve Expansion, is first introduced.

The Karhunen–Loeve expansion can represent a function with the sum of multiple basis functions with different weights. Assume that there is a set $\{\phi_l(t)\}$ $(l = 1, 2, \ldots, L, \ 0 \le t < T)$ consisting of L orthogonal basis functions, and if the received signal can be decomposed into

$$s_m(t) = \sum_{l=1}^{L} s_{m,l}\phi_l(t), \quad 0 \le t \le T, \tag{2.47}$$

then the coefficient $s_{m,l}$ in Eq. (2.47) is called the Karhunen–Loeve expansion coefficient. According to the characteristics of the orthogonal basis function,

$$\begin{cases} \displaystyle\int_0^T \phi_l(t)\phi_m^*(t)\,\mathrm{d}t = 1, & \text{if } m = l \\ \displaystyle\int_0^T \phi_l(t)\phi_m^*(t)\,\mathrm{d}t = 0, & \text{else} \end{cases} \tag{2.48}$$

Therefore, we can obtain

$$s_{m,l} = \int_0^T s_m(t)\phi_l^*(t)\,\mathrm{d}t \tag{2.49}$$

As shown in Eq. (2.47), if $s_{m,l}$ is known, then we can re-solve $s_m(t)$.

Define a vector $\mathbf{s}_m = [s_{1,m} \ s_{2,m} \ \cdots \ s_{L,m}]^{\mathrm{T}}$. Obviously, $\mathbf{s}_m$ and $s_m(t)$ are equivalent, where $s_m(t)$ represents the mth signal in the function space (or waveform space) and $\mathbf{s}_m$ represents the mth signal in the vector space. Therefore, the energy of the two signals and the distance between the signals are both equal.

$$E_m = \int_0^T |s_m(t)|^2\,\mathrm{d}t = \|\mathbf{s}_m\|^2$$

$$d_{m,k} = \sqrt{\int_0^T |s_m(t) - s_k(t)|^2\,\mathrm{d}t} = \|\mathbf{s}_m - \mathbf{s}_k\| \tag{2.50}$$

where $d_{m,k}$ represents the distance between the mth signal and the kth signal.

Using the Karhunen–Loeve expansion, we obtain

$$y_l = \int_0^T r(t)\phi_l^*(t)\,\mathrm{d}t$$

$$= s_{m,l} + \int_0^T N(t)\phi_l^*(t)\,\mathrm{d}t$$

$$= s_{m,l} + n_l, \quad l = 1, 2, \ldots, L \tag{2.51}$$

Define

$$\mathbf{y} = [y_1 \; y_2 \; \cdots \; y_L]^{\mathrm{T}}$$
$$= \mathbf{s}_m + \mathbf{n} \tag{2.52}$$

where $\mathbf{n} = [n_1 n_2 \ldots n_L]^{\mathrm{T}}$. The noise signal can be expressed as

$$N(t) = \left(\sum_{l=1}^{L} n_l \phi_l(t) \right) + \left(N(t) - \sum_{l=1}^{L} n_l \phi_l(t) \right)$$
$$= \overline{N}(t) + \tilde{N}(t), \quad 0 \le t < T \tag{2.53}$$

where $\overline{N}(t) = \sum_{l=1}^{L} n_l \phi_l(t)$ and $\tilde{N}(t)$ represents the noise that cannot be expanded by the Karhunen–Loeve expansion, $\tilde{N}(t) = N(t) - \sum_{l=1}^{L} n_l \phi_l(t)$. It is worth noting that the noise $\tilde{N}(t)$ does not appear in vector $\mathbf{y}$ as shown in Eq. (2.52).

Since $N(t)$ is additive white Gaussian noise, n_l is a white Gaussian random vector whose mean and variance are given as

$$\mathrm{E}(n_l) = \int_0^T \mathrm{E}(N(t)\phi_l^*(t)) \, \mathrm{d}t = 0$$

$$\mathrm{E}(|n_l|^2) = \mathrm{E}\left(\left(\int_0^T N(t)\phi_l^*(t) \, \mathrm{d}t \right) \left(\int_0^T N(\tau)\phi_l^*(\tau) \mathrm{d}\tau \right)^* \right)$$
$$= \int_0^T \int_0^T \mathrm{E}(N(t)N(\tau))\phi_l^*(t)\phi_l(\tau) \, \mathrm{d}t \, \mathrm{d}\tau \tag{2.54}$$
$$= \frac{N_0}{2}$$

where $\int_0^T |\phi_l(t)|^2 \, \mathrm{d}t = 1$, as the base function is assumed to be orthogonal.

According to the Karhunen–Loeve expansion, it can be assumed that the received signal can be represented by a space vector, i.e.

$$\mathbf{y} = \mathbf{s}_m + \mathbf{n}, \quad m = 0, 1, \ldots, M - 1 \tag{2.55}$$

Generally, it can be assumed that $\mathbf{s}_m$ and $\mathbf{n}$ are both complex vectors. In addition, $\mathbf{n}$ is assumed to be a circularly symmetric complex Gaussian (CSCG) random vector with $\mathrm{E}(\mathbf{n}) = 0$ and $\mathrm{E}(\mathbf{n}\mathbf{n}^{\mathrm{H}}) = \mathbf{R}_n$. For convenience, $\mathcal{CN}(\mathbf{m}, \mathbf{R}_x)$ is used to represent the probability density of a CSCG random variable whose mean vector is $\mathbf{m}$ and covariance matrix is $\mathbf{R}_x$.

For a given vector $\mathbf{y}$, the maximum likelihood judging criteria for receiving $s_m(t)$ are $f_m(\mathbf{y}) \geq f_{m'}(\mathbf{y})$, where $m' \neq m$, $f_m(\mathbf{y})$ is the mth hypothesis or the likelihood function of $\mathbf{s}_m$. Since the noise is assumed to be a CSCG random vector, the likelihood function of $\mathbf{s}_m$ can be written as

$$f(\mathbf{y}|\mathbf{s}_m) = \frac{1}{\pi^L \det(\mathbf{R}_n)} \exp(-(\mathbf{y} - \mathbf{s}_m)^H \mathbf{R}_n^{-1}(\mathbf{y} - \mathbf{s}_m)) \qquad (2.56)$$

Then the log-likelihood function is

$$\log f_m(\mathbf{y}) = -(\mathbf{y} - \mathbf{s}_m)^H \mathbf{R}_n^{-1}(\mathbf{y} - \mathbf{s}_m) + \text{constant}$$
$$\log f_m(\mathbf{y}) = 2\mathcal{R}(\mathbf{s}_m^H \mathbf{R}_n^{-1} \mathbf{y}) - \mathbf{s}_m^H \mathbf{R}_n^{-1} \mathbf{s}_m + \text{constant} \qquad (2.57)$$

Therefore, the maximum likelihood judging criteria for receiving $s_m(t)$ can be simplified as $\mathcal{R}(\mathbf{s}_m^H \mathbf{R}_n^{-1} \mathbf{y}) - \frac{\mathbf{s}_m^H \mathbf{R}_n^{-1} \mathbf{s}_m}{2} \geq \mathcal{R}(\mathbf{s}_m^H \mathbf{R}_n^{-1} \mathbf{y}) - \frac{\mathbf{s}_{m'}^H \mathbf{R}_n^{-1} \mathbf{s}_{m'}}{2}$, where $m' \neq m$.

When $M = 2$ which is a binary signal, the L-likelihood ratio is

$$\text{LLR}(\mathbf{y}) = \log\left(\frac{f_0(\mathbf{y})}{f_1(\mathbf{y})}\right)$$
$$= ((\mathbf{y} - \mathbf{s}_1)^H \mathbf{R}_n^{-1}(\mathbf{y} - \mathbf{s}_1) - (\mathbf{y} - \mathbf{s}_0)^H \mathbf{R}_n^{-1}(\mathbf{y} - \mathbf{s}_0)) \qquad (2.58)$$

As a special case, if it is assumed that n_l are independent of each other, then the variances between n_l are the same, which means $\mathbf{R}_n = N_0 \mathbf{I}$ ($N_0 > 0$). In this case, the L-likelihood ratio is

$$\text{LLR}(\mathbf{y}) = \frac{1}{N_0}((\mathbf{s}_0^H \mathbf{y} + \mathbf{y}^H \mathbf{s}_0) - (\mathbf{s}_1^H \mathbf{y} + \mathbf{y}^H \mathbf{s}_1) + (\mathbf{s}_1^H \mathbf{s}_1 - \mathbf{s}_0^H \mathbf{s}_0))$$
$$= \frac{1}{N_0}(2\mathcal{R}((\mathbf{s}_0 - \mathbf{s}_1)^H \mathbf{y}) + \mathbf{s}_1^H \mathbf{s}_1 - \mathbf{s}_0^H \mathbf{s}_0) \qquad (2.59)$$

2.2 Array Antenna Pattern Synthesis Technology

An antenna is a device used to transmit and receive electromagnetic energy. In many cases, the task of transmitting and receiving electromagnetic energy can be performed well by a single radiator. Various commonly used antennas, such as the vibrator antenna, microstrip antenna, horn antenna, and reflector antenna, can work independently. However, once these antenna forms are selected, their radiation characteristics are relatively fixed, such as beam pointing, beam width, gain, and so on. And this leads to the fact that a single antenna cannot work and multiple antennas need to work together to form an array antenna in some special applications, such as shaped beams, multiple beams, and scanning beams.

2.2.1 *Array antenna arrangement*

Array antennas are generally classified according to the arrangement of the units. The array antennas with the center of each unit arranged along a line are called line arrays and the unit spacing can be equal or unequal. The array antennas with the center of each unit arranged in a plane are called planar arrays, and if all the units of the planar array are arranged according to the matrix grid, they are then called rectangular arrays. And the array antennas with the center of all units arranged on a concentric ring or an elliptical ring are called circular or elliptical arrays.

Figure 2.5 shows the arrangement of the four common array antennas. The independent units that make up the antenna array in a linear array, a planar array, and a tri-dimensional array are called antenna units or array elements. The array elements can be various types of antennas.

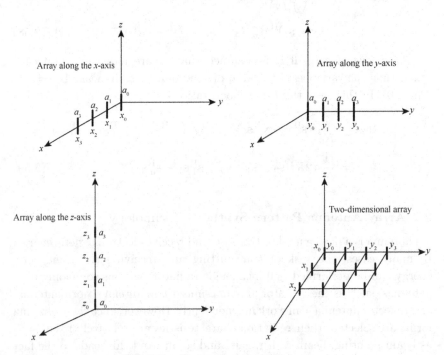

Fig. 2.5.   Common array antennas.

The analysis and synthesis of discrete array antennas mainly depend on the following four factors: the number of array elements, the position of array elements in space, the current amplitude distribution of array elements, and the current phase distribution of array elements.

Array analysis is based on the above four factors and is used to determine the radiation characteristics of the array, including the pattern, gain, impedance, and so on. And the synthesis problem is to design the optimal array parameters (the above four factors) according to their radiation characteristics. As for the selection of the array element type, it is mainly determined by the working bandwidth, the pattern characteristics, and the polarization characteristics. In phased-array antennas, it is also related to the scan range.

In the general array antenna theory, if the mutual coupling effect between the array elements is a fixed factor with less variation, the field pattern function of the array antenna can be expressed by the product of the array factor and the array element pattern function. Let's take a simple example to illustrate this problem, as shown in Fig 2.6.

The phase factors are (as shown in Fig. 2.6(a))

$$e^{jkd_0} = 1 \tag{2.60}$$

$$e^{jkd_0} = e^{jk_x d} = e^{jkd\sin\theta\cos\phi} \tag{2.61}$$

or (as shown in Fig. 2.6(b))

$$e^{jkd_0} = e^{-jk_x d/2} = e^{-jk(d/2)\sin\theta\cos\phi} \tag{2.62}$$

$$e^{jkd_1} = e^{jk_x d/2} = e^{jk(d/2)\sin\theta\cos\phi} \tag{2.63}$$

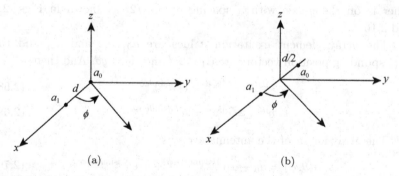

Fig. 2.6. Linear array antenna. (a) The origin of the coordinate system is at a unit. (b) The origin of the coordinate system is at the center of two units.

Let $a = (a_0, a_1)$ be the array element coefficient, then the array factors are given as follows:

The array in Fig. 2.6(a) : $A_1(\theta, \phi) = a_0 + a_1 e^{jkd\sin\theta\cos\phi}$ (2.64)

The array in Fig. 2.6(b) : $A_2(\theta, \phi) = a_0 e^{-jk(d/2)\sin\theta\cos\phi}$

$$+ a_1 e^{jk(d/2)\sin\theta\cos\phi} \quad (2.65)$$

Only one phase constant difference exists between the above two expressions, which will not affect the pattern. When $\theta = 90°$, namely in the xoy plane, the above array factor can be written as

$$A(\theta) = |a_0 + a_1 e^{jkd\cos\phi}| \quad (2.66)$$

The power pattern can be expressed as

$$g(\phi) = |A(\phi)|^2 = |a_0 + a_1 e^{jkd\cos\phi}|^2 \quad (2.67)$$

Figure 2.7 shows the antenna pattern when $a = (a_0, a_1) = (1, 1)$, $a = (a_0, a_1) = (1, -1)$, $a = (a_0, a_1) = (1, -j)$ with excitation values of $d = 0.25\lambda$, $d = 0.5\lambda$, and $d = \lambda$, respectively.

The main beam-pointing direction of the pattern changes with the relative phases of the excitation values a_0 and a_1. When the main beam points to $\phi = 0°$ or $\phi = 180°$, the antenna array is called an end-fire array.

As shown in Fig. 2.7, the main lobe width gradually increases with the main lobe of the pattern moving from $\phi = 90°$ to $\phi = 0°$.

In addition, when $d \geq \lambda$, there will be multiple main lobes in the pattern, which is called the grating lobe as shown in Fig. 2.8.

Consider a two-dimensional array and three half-wave oscillators placed along the z-axis, among which one is at the origin on the x-axis and the other is on the y-axis with a spacing $d = \lambda/2$, as shown in Figs. 2.9 and 2.10.

The array element excitation values are a_0, a_1, and a_2, and the corresponding position vectors are $\mathbf{d}_1 = \hat{x}d$ and $\mathbf{d}_2 = \hat{y}d$. And then

$$e^{jkd_1} = e^{jk_x d} = e^{jkd\sin\theta\cos\phi} \quad (2.68)$$

$$e^{jkd_2} = e^{jk_y d} = e^{jkd\sin\theta\cos\phi} \quad (2.69)$$

The array factor of the antenna array is

$$A(\theta, \phi) = a_0 + a_1 e^{jkd\sin\theta\cos\phi} + a_2 e^{jkd\sin\theta\cos\phi} \quad (2.70)$$

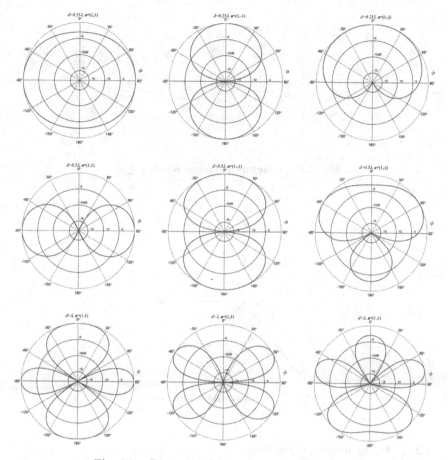

Fig. 2.7. Patterns of array antenna (Fig. 2.6).

Therefore, the normalized gain of the array is

$$g_{\text{tot}}(\theta, \phi) = |A(\theta, \phi)|^2 g(\theta, \phi) = |A(\theta, \phi)|^2 \left| \frac{\cos(0.5\pi \cos\theta)}{\sin\theta} \right|^2 \qquad (2.71)$$

where $g(\theta, \phi)$ is the pattern function of the half-wave oscillator.

In the xoy plane ($\theta = 90°$), the gain pattern is given as

$$g_{\text{tot}}(\theta, \phi) = |A(\theta, \phi)|^2 g(\theta, \phi) = |A(\theta, \phi)|^2 \left| \frac{\cos(0.5\pi \cos\theta)}{\sin\theta} \right|^2 \qquad (2.72)$$

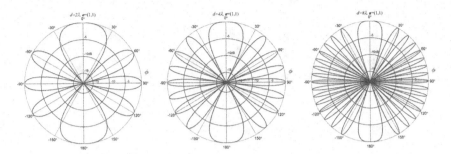

Fig. 2.8.   Antenna patterns when $d \geq \lambda$.

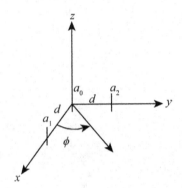

Fig. 2.9.   Two-dimensional array.

2.2.2 *Array antenna freedom*

A binary array with two weighting coefficients can maximize the response of the antenna in a desired signal direction or produce a zero in an interference direction by adjusting the weighting coefficients, which is defined as a degree of freedom. When M array elements are used, the degree of freedom of the antenna array is $M - 1$. This property has important applications in the pattern synthesis of array antennas.

Assume that the radiation pattern of the array is

$$f(\theta) = \mathbf{W}^{\mathrm{H}} \mathbf{a}(\theta) \tag{2.73}$$

where $\mathbf{a}(\theta) = (1, \mathrm{e}^{\mathrm{j}\varphi_2(\theta)}, \ldots, \mathrm{e}^{\mathrm{j}\varphi_M(\theta)})^{\mathrm{T}}$ is the array steering vector and $\mathbf{W}$ is the array element weight vector. By expanding the above equation, we

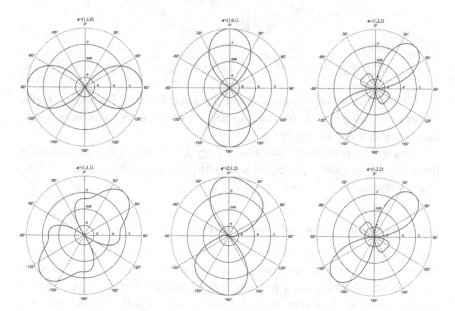

Fig. 2.10.   Patterns of the two-dimensional antenna array (Fig. 2.9).

can obtain

$$f(\theta) = w_1^* + w_2^* e^{j\varphi_2(\theta)} + \cdots + w_M^* e^{j\varphi_M(\theta)}$$
$$= w_1^* \left(1 + \frac{w_2^*}{w_1^*} e^{j\varphi_2(\theta)} + \cdots + \frac{w_M^*}{w_1^*} e^{j\varphi_M(\theta)} \right) \qquad (2.74)$$

which refers to

$$\begin{cases} f^*(\theta_1) = w_1 + w_2^{e-j\varphi_2(\theta_1)} + \cdots + w_M e^{-j\varphi_M(\theta_1)} = 0 \\ \qquad\qquad \vdots \\ f^*(\theta_L) = w_1 + w_2^{e-j\varphi_2(\theta_L)} + \cdots + w_M^{e-j\varphi_M(\theta_L)} = 0 \end{cases} \qquad (2.75)$$

In Eq. (2.74), when $L \leq M - 1$, the equations have a non-zero solution.

And it also needs to establish a constraint equation when it is required by the pattern to produce a maximum in a certain direction.

$$f(\theta)|_{\theta=\theta_{\max}} = f_{\max} \qquad (2.76)$$

$$\frac{\mathrm{d}f(\theta)}{\mathrm{d}\theta}\bigg|_{\theta=\theta_{\max}} = 0 \tag{2.77}$$

$$w_2^* \varphi_2'(\theta_{\max}) \mathrm{e}^{\mathrm{j}\varphi_2(\theta_{\max})} + \cdots + w_M^* \varphi_M'(\theta_{\max}) \mathrm{e}^{\mathrm{j}\varphi_M(\theta_{\max})} = 0 \tag{2.78}$$

This is also a homogeneous linear equation for w_m. Therefore, it also requires the degrees of freedom of an array when generating a beam maximum in a certain direction.

In a word, there are M weighted M-ary arrays with $(M-1)$ degrees of freedom, and at most L_1 independent beam maxima and $L_2 = M - 1 - L_1$ beam zeros can be achieved.

2.2.3 *Array antenna pattern synthesis*

The analytical methods of array antenna pattern synthesis are mainly for uniform linear arrays and uniform planar arrays, while numerical methods are generally used for non-uniform arrays. For more than half a century, many analytical methods for array antenna pattern synthesis have been studied. The two most basic methods, namely the Dolph–Chebyshev pattern synthesis method and the Taylor single parameter pattern synthesis method, are introduced here.

2.2.3.1 *Dolph–Chebyshev pattern synthesis method*

For a uniform linear array, the first sidelobe is approximately 13.5 dB lower than the main lobe when the same excitation is used for each array element. For many practical applications, lower sidelobe levels are often required. In 1946, C.L. Dolphy proposed a method for obtaining lower sidelobe patterns in a classic paper. This method considers the properties of the Chebyshev polynomial and establishes the relationship from polynomial to array sidelobe level.

The Chebyshev polynomial $T_{2N}(u)$ has the characteristics of an undamped oscillation function when $-1 \leq u \leq 1$, and the monotonic increase is characteristic of the absolute value outside this oscillation interval. The undamped oscillation characteristics correspond to equal sidelobe levels, while the monotonic characteristics correspond to the main lobe. The Chebyshev polynomial whose order is $2N$ and number of elements is $2N + 1$ can be expressed as

$$T_{2N}(u) = \begin{cases} \cos(2N \arccos u), & -1 \leq u \leq 1 \\ \cosh(2N \operatorname{arccosh} u), & |u| \geq 1 \end{cases} \tag{2.79}$$

The relationship between the Chebyshev polynomial and the array antenna parameters is

$$\varphi = kd(\cos\theta - \cos\theta_0) \qquad (2.80)$$

$$u = \cos(\varphi/2) \qquad (2.81)$$

where θ denotes the angle between the spatial orientation and the array.

The sidelobe level of the array antenna is expressed as $20\lg\eta$ in dB, where $\eta = T_{2N}(u_0)$.

The above polynomial can also be expressed in the product form of the polynomial root.

$$T_{2N}(u) = cf(u) = \prod_{p=1}^{N}(u - u_p) \qquad (2.82)$$

where c is a constant and the root is given by

$$\cos\left(\frac{\varphi_p}{2}\right) = \left(\frac{1}{u_0}\right)\left[\frac{\cos(2p-1)\pi}{4N}\right], \quad p = 1, 2, \ldots, 2N \qquad (2.83)$$

When the excitation current is symmetrically distributed, the root of the polynomial is a pair of complex conjugates. And through a series of mathematical derivations, the pattern can be expressed as

$$f(u) = u^N 4^N \prod_{p=1}^{N} \sin\left(\frac{\varphi - \varphi_p}{2}\right)\sin\left(\frac{\varphi + \varphi_p}{2}\right) \qquad (2.84)$$

This is the Chebyshev pattern with $2N + 1$ array elements.

The above Chebyshev pattern gives an array antenna pattern synthesis method which can control the sidelobe level to minimize the maximum sidelobe level. However, the method has the following problems as well. The excitation current between the antenna intermediate unit and the external unit varies greatly, which is difficult to implement. The far-sidelobe level is too high. These problems make the Chebyshev pattern encounter some difficulties in practical applications, which means that its physical achievability is poor.

2.2.3.2 *Taylor single-parameter pattern synthesis method*

In 1953, T.T. Taylor presented a pattern synthesis method derived from the uniform excitation array pattern $\sin(\pi u)/\pi u$. The zero interval of the pattern is an integer, and the descent velocity of sidelobe envelope is $1/u$. Therefore, it is necessary to control the height of the first sidelobe level, which is realized by adjusting the zero point of the pattern function. The zero point of the array pattern is given by $u = \sqrt{n^2 + B^2}$.

B is an undetermined parameter and then the description of the antenna pattern becomes

$$F(u) = \begin{cases} \dfrac{\sinh \pi \sqrt{B^2 - u^2}}{\pi \sqrt{B^2 - u^2}}, & u \geq B \\[3mm] \dfrac{\sinh \pi \sqrt{u^2 - B^2}}{\pi \sqrt{u^2 - B^2}}, & u \leq B \end{cases} \tag{2.85}$$

when $u = B$, the pattern changes from a hyperbolic function to a sinc function.

SLR is the ratio of peak to sinc, and it is expressed in dB by

$$\text{SLR} = 20 \lg \frac{\sinh \pi B}{\pi B} + 13.26\,\text{dB} \tag{2.86}$$

The method determines all parameters of the pattern by a single parameter B, including sidelobe level, beamwidth, and beam efficiency. The aperture distribution of the array is the inverse of the pattern, i.e.

$$g(p) = I_0(\pi B \sqrt{1 - p^2}) \tag{2.87}$$

where p is the distance from the center of the aperture to one end and I_0 is the modified Bessel function. The excitation efficiency is

$$\eta = 2 \sinh^2(\pi B) / \pi B \overline{I}_0(2\pi B) \tag{2.88}$$

where $\overline{I}_0$ is the list integration.

When using this method, B is calculated from Eq. (2.86) according to the SLR of the designed pattern, and the excitation value of the array is obtained from the aperture distribution equation. The characteristic parameters of the Taylor single-parameter pattern synthesis are shown in Table 2.1.

In addition to the two methods described above, the analytical methods for antenna pattern synthesis also include Taylor n, Villenenve n, and so on. The analytical methods for planar array pattern synthesis include Hansen single-parameter circle distribution, Taylor n circle distribution, and so on.

2.3 Overview of the MIMO System

In a conventional wireless communication system, the transmitting end and the receiving end usually use one antenna each. This single-antenna

Table 2.1. Characteristic parameters of Taylor single-parameter pattern synthesis.

SLR/dB	B	u_3/rad	η	ηb
13.26	0	0.442 9	1	0.902 8
20	0.738 6	0.511 9	0.933	0.982
25	1.022 9	0.558	0.862 6	0.995
30	1.276 2	0.600 2	0.801 4	0.998 6
35	1.531 6	0.639 1	0.750 9	0.999 6
40	1.741 5	0.675 2	0.709	0.999 9
45	1.962 8	0.709 1	0.674	1
50	2.179 3	0.741 1	0.645 1	1

Note: u_3 denotes half-power beamwidth and ηb denotes beam efficiency.

system is also called a single-input single-output (SISO) system. For such a system, Shannon[1] proposed the channel capacity formula in 1948 as follows: $C = B \operatorname{lb}(1 + S/N)$, where B represents the channel bandwidth and S/N represents the signal-to-noise ratio at the receiving end. It determines the upper limit rate for reliable communication in noisy channels. No matter what channel coding method and modulation method is used, it can only be accessed little by little but cannot be surpassed. This seems to be a recognized and insurmountable boundary and becomes a bottleneck in the development of wireless communications. According to Shannon's channel capacity formula, increasing the SNR can improve the efficiency of the spectrum. For every 3-dB increase in SNR, the channel capacity increases by 1 bit/Hz/s. However, in the actual communication system, it is not recommended to increase the transmission power of the transmitting end in consideration of the actual conditions such as electromagnetic pollution, performance of radio frequency circuit, and the interferences among users. Diversity technique is another way to increase the spectrum usage efficiency. If a single antenna is used at the transmitting end and multiple antennas are used at the receiving end, this diversity is often called diversity reception which is also known as the single-input multiple-output (SIMO) system. The use of optimal combined diversity reception techniques generally improves the SNR at the receiving end, thereby increasing the channel capacity and the spectrum usage efficiency. If multiple antennas are used at the transmitting end and a single antenna is used at the receiving end, this diversity is often called the transmit diversity, which is also known as the multiple-input single-output (MISO) system. However, if the state information of the channel is not known at the transmitting end, beamforming technology and adaptive allocation cannot be used in the multi-transmitting antenna for transmitting power, and thus, the channel capacity cannot be improved much. The development and integration of SIMO and MISO technologies have evolved into MIMO technology, which is an effective method to break through the SISO channel capacity bottleneck. The core idea of the system is to synthesize the signals at both ends of the spatial sampling by way of generating effective multi-parallel spatial data channels (increasing the data traffic), so as to greatly improve the channel capacity, or by way of increasing the diversity to improve communication (reduce bit error rate).

2.3.1 *Diversity technique*

The particularity of a wireless link is that it is affected by random fluctuations in signal levels across time, space, and frequency. This characteristic is fading and affects the system performance (symbol or bit error rate). Take the SISO Rayleigh fading channel transmitted by binary phase shift keying (BPSK) as an example.

When there is no fading ($h = 1$), in the additive white Gaussian noise (AWGN) channel, the bit error rate (SER) is

$$\overline{P} = Q\left(\sqrt{\frac{2E_S}{\sigma_n^2}}\right) = Q(\sqrt{2\rho}) \tag{2.89}$$

When considering the fading, the level of the received signal fluctuates with $S\sqrt{E_S}$ and the bit error rate is given as

$$\overline{P} = \int_0^\infty Q(\sqrt{2\rho s})p_s(s)\mathrm{d}s \tag{2.90}$$

where $p_s(s)$ is the distribution function of the fading. For Rayleigh fading, the integration of the above equation yields

$$\overline{P} = \frac{1}{2}\left(1 - \sqrt{\frac{\rho}{1+\rho}}\right) \tag{2.91}$$

When the SNR is large, the bit error rate in Eq. (2.91) becomes

$$\overline{P} \cong \frac{1}{4\rho} \tag{2.92}$$

In order to overcome the negative impact of fading on the bit error rate, diversity techniques are often employed. The principle of diversity is to provide the receiver with multiple copies of the same transmitted signal, and each replica acts as a diversity branch. If this replication is affected by independent fading conditions, the probability that all branches will be in a fading state at the same time can be greatly reduced. Therefore, diversity stabilizes the link by channel enhancement, which improves the bit error rate performance of the system.

As fading can occur in time, frequency, and space domains, diversity techniques can be used in these domains. For example, time diversity can be obtained by coding and interleaving, and frequency diversity can exploit the time spread of the channel (in the τ domain) by equalization techniques or multi-carrier modulation. Obviously, time and frequency diversity techniques can result in a loss of time or bandwidth due to the introduction of redundancy. Conversely, because multiple antennas are used at one or both ends of the link, space or polarization diversity does not sacrifice time and bandwidth.

2.3.2 *SIMO system*

The SIMO system relies on the number of antennas at the receiving end $M_R \geq 2$ to realize diversity. If these antennas are sufficiently spaced (such as a wavelength), then when the physical channel exhibits good characteristics, the system will fade independent of the diversity of each branch. Reception diversity can be achieved in two different ways: selective combining and gain combining.

2.3.2.1 *Reception diversity through selective combining*

Among M_R received signals, the combiner selects a branch having the largest SNR (or the highest absolute power, bit error rate, etc.) for signal detection. Suppose that M_R channels are subject to unit Rayleigh energy independent and identical distribution and the noise level is equal on each antenna. At this time, the selection algorithm compares the instantaneous amplitude of each channel $s_n (n = 1, \ldots, M_R)$ and selects the branch having the largest amplitude $s_{max} = \max\{s_1, \ldots, s_{M_n}\}$. The probability that s_{max} is below a certain threshold S^2 is given by

$$P[s_{max} < S] = P[s_1, \ldots, s_{M_R} \leq S] = [1 - e^{-s^2}]^{M_R} \qquad (2.93)$$

The distribution corresponding to s_{max} can be obtained by the differentiation of Eq. (2.93).

$$p_{s_{max}}(s) = M_R 2s e^{-s^2} [1 - e^{-s^2}]^{M_R - 1} \qquad (2.94)$$

The average SNR of the combiner output is[3]

$$\rho_{\text{out}} = \int_0^\infty \rho s^2 p_{s_{\max}}(s) \mathrm{d}s = \rho \sum_{n=1}^{M_{\mathrm{R}}} \frac{1}{n} \tag{2.95}$$

when M_{R} is large, the array gain is approximately

$$g_a = \frac{\rho_{\text{out}}}{\rho} = \sum_{n=1}^{M_{\mathrm{R}}} \frac{1}{n} \cong \gamma + \log(M_{\mathrm{R}}) + \frac{1}{2M_{\mathrm{R}}} \tag{2.96}$$

where $\gamma \approx 0.577\,215\,66$ is the Euler constant.

The diversity obtained by the selective combining can be estimated by calculating the bit error rate using the fading distribution given by Eq. (2.94). For the system using BPSK modulation and owning a two-branch diversity, the bit error rate as a function of the average SNR can be expressed corresponding to each channel ρ[4] as follows:

$$\overline{P} = \int_0^\infty Q(\sqrt{2\rho s}) p_{s_{\max}}(s) \mathrm{d}s$$

$$= \frac{1}{2} - \sqrt{\frac{\rho}{1+\rho}} + \frac{1}{2}\sqrt{\frac{\rho}{2+\rho}} \tag{2.97}$$

when the SNR is high,

$$\overline{P} \cong \frac{3}{8\rho^3} \tag{2.98}$$

The slope of the bit error rate curve is 2. In general, the diversity gain of the M_{R}-branch selection diversity scheme is equal to M_{R}, which indicates that the selection diversity collects all possible diversity from the channel.

2.3.2.2 *Reception diversity based on gain combining*

In gain combining, the signal z used for detection is a linear combination of all branches.

$$z = \mathbf{W}^{\mathrm{T}} \mathbf{y} = \sum_{n=1}^{M_{\mathrm{R}}} W_n y_n \tag{2.99}$$

where W_n denotes the combined weight and $\mathbf{W} = [W_1, \ldots, W_{M_{\mathrm{R}}}]^{\mathrm{T}}$. According to the selection of these weights, there are different gain combining methods. It is assumed that the data symbol c is transmitted by the channel and received by M_{R} antennas. Each antenna is described by the channel $h_n = |h_n| e^{\mathrm{j}\phi_n} (n = 1, \ldots, M_{\mathrm{R}})$. Suppose they obey the unit variance Rayleigh distribution and all channels are independent. Combining signals from all antennas, the detected variable can be expressed as

$$z = \sqrt{E_S}\mathbf{W}^{\mathrm{T}}\mathbf{h}c + \mathbf{W}^{\mathrm{T}}\mathbf{n} \tag{2.100}$$

where $\mathbf{h} = [h_1, \ldots, h_{M_{\mathrm{R}}}]^{\mathrm{T}}$.

(1) Equal gain combining

The weight of equal gain combining is $W_n = \mathrm{e}^{-\mathrm{j}\phi_n}$, indicating that the signals from different antennas are in phase and can be added together. This approach requires the combiner to have a complete knowledge of the known signal phase. And the post-combiner signal of Eq. (2.100) becomes

$$z = \sqrt{E_S}\sum_{n=1}^{M_{\mathrm{R}}} |h_n|c + n' \tag{2.101}$$

where $n' = \sum_{m=1}^{M_{\mathrm{R}}} n_m \mathrm{e}^{-\mathrm{j}\phi_m}$ is the Gaussian white noise.

When the channel is a Rayleigh distribution, the mean value of the output SNR can be obtained.

$$\rho_{\mathrm{out}} = \frac{\mathrm{E}\left\{\left[\sum_{n=1}^{M_{\mathrm{R}}} \sqrt{E_S}|h_n|\right]^2\right\}}{\mathrm{E}\{|n|^2\}} = \frac{E_S}{M_{\mathrm{R}}\sigma_n^2}\mathrm{E}\left\{\left[\sum_{n=1}^{M_{\mathrm{R}}} |h_n|\right]^2\right\}$$

$$= \frac{\rho}{M_{\mathrm{R}}}\left[\mathrm{E}\left\{\sum_{n=1}^{M_{\mathrm{R}}} |h_n|^2\right\} + \sum_{n=1}^{M_{\mathrm{R}}}\sum_{\substack{m=1 \\ m \neq n}}^{M_{\mathrm{R}}} \mathrm{E}\{|h_n|\}\mathrm{E}\{|h_m|\}\right]$$

$$= \frac{\rho}{M_{\mathrm{R}}}\left[M_{\mathrm{R}} + M_{\mathrm{R}}(M_{\mathrm{R}} - 1)\frac{\pi}{4}\right] = \rho\left[1 + (M_{\mathrm{R}} - 1)\frac{\pi}{4}\right] \tag{2.102}$$

It can be seen that the array gain increases linearly with M_{R}, and it is greater than the array gain of selective combining. In addition, the diversity gain of equal gain combining is M_{R}, which is similar to that of the selective combining.

(2) Maximum ratio combining

The selection weight of maximum ratio combining is $W_n = h_n^*$, and its post-combiner signal

$$z = \sqrt{E_S}\|\mathbf{h}\|^2 c + n' \tag{2.103}$$

where $n' = \mathbf{h}^H\mathbf{n}$. Because it maximizes the output SNR ρ_{out}, this strategy is called maximum ratio combining. And

$$\rho_{\text{out}} = \frac{1}{\sigma_n^2}\mathrm{E}\left\{\frac{E_S\|\mathbf{h}\|^4}{\|\mathbf{h}\|^2}\right\} = \rho\mathrm{E}\{\|\mathbf{h}\|^2\} = \rho M_{\text{R}} \qquad (2.104)$$

In the maximum ratio combining diversity scheme, the array gain g_a is always equal to M_{R}.

Consider the case of transmitting with BPSK modulation. It is well known that when $u = \|\mathbf{h}\|^2$ and different channels are independently distributed Rayleigh channels, u obeys $2M_{\text{R}}$ degrees of freedom χ^2 distribution.

$$p_u(u) = \frac{1}{(M_{\text{R}} - 1)!}u^{M_{\text{R}}-1}e^{-u} \qquad (2.105)$$

The bit error rate can be given by

$$\begin{aligned}
\overline{P} &= \int_0^\infty Q(\sqrt{2\rho u})p_u(u)\mathrm{d}u \\
&= \left[\frac{1 - \sqrt{\rho/1+\rho}}{2}\right]^{M_{\text{R}}}\sum_{n=1}^{M_{\text{R}}}\binom{M_{\text{R}} + n - 2}{n - 1}\left[\frac{1 + \sqrt{\rho/1+\rho}}{2}\right]^{n-1}
\end{aligned}$$

$$(2.106)$$

when the SNR is large, the above equation becomes

$$\overline{P} = (4\rho)^{-M_{\text{R}}}\binom{2M_{\text{R}} - 1}{M_{\text{R}}} \qquad (2.107)$$

It can be seen that the diversity gain is still M_{R}.

For other constellations, using maximum likelihood detection,[5] the error probability is

$$\overline{P} \approx \int_0^\infty \overline{N}_e Q\left(d_{\min}\sqrt{\frac{\rho u}{2}}\right)p_u(u)\mathrm{d}u \qquad (2.108)$$

where $\overline{N}_e$ and $d_{\min}$ are the nearest neighbor and the minimum separation distance of the constellation, respectively. The analytical solution of the above expression can be obtained by following Eq. (2.106). The upper bound of the bit error rate is usually obtained using the Chernoff bound.

Equation (2.108) can also be written as

$$\overline{P} \approx \overline{N}_e \mathrm{E}\left\{Q\left(d_{\min}\sqrt{\frac{\rho u}{2}}\right)\right\} \le \overline{N}_e \mathrm{E}\left\{e^{-\frac{d_{\min}^2 \rho u}{4}}\right\} \tag{2.109}$$

Since u is a χ^2 variable, the average upper bound above is

$$\overline{P} \le \overline{N}_e \prod_{n=1}^{M_R} \frac{1}{1 + \rho d_{\min}^2/4} \tag{2.110}$$

when the SNR is large, Eq. (2.110) is simplified to

$$\overline{P} \le \overline{N}_e \left(\frac{\rho d_{\min}^2}{4}\right)^{-M_R} \tag{2.111}$$

Similar to the case of BPSK, the diversity gain is equal to the number of receiving branches in an independent and identically distributed Rayleigh channel.

(3) Minimum mean square error combining

When the noise is spatially correlated or non-Gaussian interference occurs, the maximum ratio combining is no longer optimal. In this case, the minimum mean-squared error combining is an optimal gain combining, from which the weight is obtained by minimizing the mean square error between the transmitted symbol c and the combiner output z, namely

$$\mathbf{W}^* = \arg\min_{W} \mathrm{E}\{|\mathbf{W}^T\mathbf{y} - c|^2\} \tag{2.112}$$

And it is easy to get the optimal weight vector

$$\mathbf{W}^* = \mathbf{R}_{ni}^{-1}\mathbf{h}^* \tag{2.113}$$

where $\mathbf{R}_{ni}$ is the correlation matrix of noise and interference. When there is no interference, $\mathbf{R}_{ni} = E\{\mathbf{n}\mathbf{n}^H\}$. If the noise across the antenna is white noise, then $\mathbf{R}_{ni} = \sigma_n^2 \mathbf{I}_{M_R}$, and the minimum mean square error combining diversity is simplified to a maximum ratio combining diversity with only one coefficient difference.

2.3.2.3 Reception diversity through hybrid selection combining or gain combining

A hybrid approach combines the selection algorithm with the maximum ratio combining. At each moment, the receiver first selects M_R' branches with the largest SNR among M_R branches and then combines them by the maximum ratio combining algorithm. This strategy is called augmentation selection.

Obviously, it can be concluded that the average SNR of the combiner output is the sum of the two items. The first item corresponds to the maximum ratio combining M_R' branches and the second item is generated from the M_R' branches of the M_R branches, which is the extension of Eq. (2.95). Therefore, the overall array gain is

$$g_a = M_R' + M_R' \sum_{n=M_R'+1}^{M_R} \frac{1}{n} \tag{2.114}$$

Similarly, for selective combining ($M_R' = 1$), the diversity gain of the hybrid selection combining and maximum ratio combining is equal to M_R instead of M_R'.

2.3.3 *MISO system*

The MISO system utilizes M_T transmitting antennas with pre-processing or precoding to perform diversity at the transmitting end. And the obvious difference from reception diversity is that the transmitter may not have knowledge of the MISO system channel. Since the channel characteristics can be estimated at the receiving end, while the channel information needs to be fed back from the receiver to the transmitter at the transmitting end, there are basically two ways to obtain direct transmit diversity.

- When the transmitter has complete channel knowledge, beamforming can be achieved by various optimization metrics such as SNR and SINR to obtain diversity and array gain.
- When the transmitter has no channel information, the so-called space–time coding pre-processing can be used to obtain the diversity gain, but the array gain cannot be obtained.

In the following, different beamformers will be evaluated and several indirect transmit diversity techniques will be discussed, which can convert space diversity into time or frequency diversity.

2.3.3.1 *Transmit diversity formed by matched beamforming*

This beamforming technique is also known as transmitting maximum ratio combining and it assumes that the transmitter knows all the information about the channel. In order to use diversity, signal c is appropriately weighted before being transmitted to each antenna. At the receiving end, the signal can be expressed as

$$y = \sqrt{E_S}\mathbf{h}\mathbf{W}c + n \tag{2.115}$$

where $\mathbf{h} = [h_1, \ldots, h_{M_R}]$ denotes the MISO channel vector and $\mathbf{W}$ is the weight vector. And the weight vector that maximizes the received SNR is

$$\mathbf{W} = \frac{\mathbf{h}^H}{\|\mathbf{h}\|} \tag{2.116}$$

where the denominator guarantees that the average total transmitting power remains unchanged and is equal to E_S. This vector makes the transmission in the direction of the matched channel and is therefore also called the matched beamforming or conventional beamforming. Similarly, for reception maximum ratio combining, the average output SNR is $\rho_{\text{out}} = M_T\rho$, and therefore, the array gain is equal to the number of transmitting antennas M_T. If the bit error rate has the following upper bound at a high SNR, the diversity gain is also equal to M_R.

$$\overline{P} \leq \overline{N}_e \left(\frac{\rho d_{\min}^2}{4}\right)^{-M_T} \tag{2.117}$$

Therefore, the matched beamformer exhibits the same performance as the reception maximum ratio combining. It requires knowledge of the complete information of the transmitting channel, which means there is feedback from the receiver in the time duplex system. If frequency duplexing is adopted, the interchangeability of the upper and lower channels is no longer guaranteed, and the understanding of the channel information at the transmitting end is greatly reduced. In addition, the matched beamformer is optimal in the absence of interfering signals but cannot cancel the interference.

Similar to the aforementioned augmented selection algorithm for SIMO systems, the matched beamformer can be combined with the selective combining algorithm. In the beamformer, the transmitter selects M_T' antennas out of M_T antennas. Obviously, this technique yields a full-diversity gain M_T, but reduces the transmit array gain.

2.3.3.2 *Space–time coded transmit diversity*

The beamforming technique described previously requires channel information for the transmitter to obtain optimal weights. Conversely, Alamouti proposes a particularly simple but original diversity approach for the two transmit antenna systems, called the Alamouti algorithm, which does not require information on the transmit channel. Considering that in the first symbol period, two symbols c_1 and c_2 are simultaneously transmitted from antenna 1 and antenna 2, and then two symbols $-c_2^*$ and c_1^* are transmitted from antenna 1 and antenna 2 in the second symbol period, it is assumed that the flat fading channel remains unchanged during these two symbol periods, which is expressed as $\mathbf{h} = [h_1, h_2]$ (the subscript indicates the antenna number rather than the symbol period). The symbol received in the first symbol period is

$$y_1 = \sqrt{E_S} h_1 \frac{c_1}{\sqrt{2}} + \sqrt{E_S} h_2 \frac{c_2}{\sqrt{2}} + n_1 \tag{2.118}$$

The symbol received in the second symbol period is

$$y_2 = \sqrt{E_S} h_1 \frac{c_2^*}{\sqrt{2}} + \sqrt{E_S} h_2 \frac{c_1^*}{\sqrt{2}} + n_2 \tag{2.119}$$

where each symbol is divided by $\sqrt{2}$, and then the vector $\mathbf{c} = [c_1/\sqrt{2} \ \ c_2/\sqrt{2}]$ has a unit average energy (assuming that c_1 and c_2 are obtained from the unit average energy constellation). n_1 and n_2 are the corresponding terms of additive noise in each symbol period (in this case, the subscript represents the symbol period rather than the antenna number). Combining Eq. (2.118) with Eq. (2.119), we get

$$\mathbf{y} = \begin{bmatrix} y_1 \\ y_2^* \end{bmatrix} = \sqrt{E_S} \underbrace{\begin{bmatrix} h_1 & h_2 \\ h_2^* & -h_1^* \end{bmatrix}}_{\mathbf{H}_{\text{eff}}} \underbrace{\begin{bmatrix} c_1/\sqrt{2} \\ c_2/\sqrt{2} \end{bmatrix}}_{c} + \begin{bmatrix} n_1 \\ n_2^* \end{bmatrix} \tag{2.120}$$

It can be seen that the two symbols are extended on two antennas over two symbol periods. Therefore, $\mathbf{H}_{\text{eff}}$ represents a space–time channel. Adding the matched filter $\mathbf{H}_{\text{eff}}^{\text{H}}$ to the received vector $\mathbf{y}$ can effectively decouple the transmitted symbols, such as

$$\mathbf{z} = \begin{bmatrix} z_1 \\ z_2 \end{bmatrix} = \mathbf{H}_{\text{eff}}^{\text{H}} \begin{bmatrix} y_1 \\ y_2^* \end{bmatrix} = \sqrt{E_S} [|h_1|^2 + |h_2|^2] \mathbf{I}_2 \begin{bmatrix} c_1/\sqrt{2} \\ c_2/\sqrt{2} \end{bmatrix} + \mathbf{H}_{\text{eff}}^{\text{H}} \begin{bmatrix} n_1 \\ n_2^* \end{bmatrix}$$

$$= \sqrt{E_S} \|\mathbf{h}\|^2 \mathbf{I}_2 \mathbf{c} + \mathbf{n}' \tag{2.121}$$

where $\mathbf{n}'$ satisfies $E\{\mathbf{n}'\} = \mathbf{0}_{\times 1}$, $E\{\mathbf{n}'\mathbf{n}'^{H}\} = \|\mathbf{h}\|^2\sigma_n^2\mathbf{I}_2$. The average output SNR is

$$\rho_{\text{out}} = \frac{1}{\sigma_n^2}E\left\{\frac{E_S[\|\mathbf{h}\|^2]^2}{2\|\mathbf{h}\|^2}\right\} = \rho \qquad (2.122)$$

It shows that the Alamouti algorithm cannot provide array gain due to a lack of information about the transmitting channel (note $E\{\|\mathbf{h}\|^2\} = M_T = 2$).

However, for independent and identically distributed Rayleigh channels, the average bit error rate of the above problem has the following upper bound at high SNR.

$$\overline{P} \leq \overline{N}_e\left(\frac{\rho d_{\min}^2}{8}\right)^{-2} \qquad (2.123)$$

It means that despite the lack of transmit channel information, the diversity gain is equal to $M_T = 2$, which is the same as the transmit maximum ratio combining. From a global perspective, the Alamouti algorithm has a lower performance than the transmit or receive maximum ratio combining due to its zero array gain.

2.3.3.3 *Indirect transmit diversity*

The technique of obtaining space diversity by combining or space–time coding described above belongs to the direct transmit diversity technique. By using well-known SISO techniques, converting space diversity to time or frequency diversity can also be realized.

Assuming $M_T = 2$, the phase shift is achieved by delaying the signal on the second transmit branch by one symbol period or by selecting the appropriate frequency shift. If the channels h_1 and h_2 are independent and identically distributed Rayleigh channels, the space diversity (using two antennas) is converted to frequency and time diversity, respectively. Indeed, the receiver has a frequency or time fading problem for an effective two-branch summed SISO channel, which can be overcome by conventional diversity techniques, such as forward error correction or interleaving for frequency diversity.

2.3.4 *MIMO system*

As mentioned above, in order to obtain a sufficiently high transmission rate, we can install multiple antennas on both the transmitter and the receiver to improve the spectral efficiency. The corresponding multi-antenna system is also called the MIMO system. When multiple antennas are used at both ends of the link, in addition to improving diversity gain and array gain, the system's throughput can also be increased by the spatial multiplexing capability of the MIMO channel. However, it must be pointed out that it is impossible to maximize spatial multiplexing capability and diversity gain simultaneously. Besides, the array gain in the Rayleigh channel is also limited, which is smaller than $M_R M_T$. In the following, the MIMO technologies will be classified according to the understanding of the channel information by the transmitter.

2.3.4.1 *MIMO system with complete transmit channel information*

(1) The dominant eigenmode transmission

First, the diversity gain of the $M_R \times M_T$ MIMO system is maximized, which can be realized by selecting $M_T \times 1$ weight vector $\mathbf{W}_T$ and transmitting the same signal from all transmit antennas. In the receiving array, the antenna outputs are combined into a scalar signal z according to the $M_R \times 1$ weight vector $\mathbf{W}_R$. Thereafter, the transmission can be expressed as

$$\mathbf{y} = \sqrt{E_S}\mathbf{H}\mathbf{W}_T c + \mathbf{n} \tag{2.124}$$

$$z = \mathbf{W}_R^H \mathbf{y} = \sqrt{E_S}\mathbf{W}_R^H \mathbf{H}\mathbf{W}_T c + \mathbf{W}_R^H \mathbf{n} \tag{2.125}$$

By maximizing $\|\mathbf{W}_R^H \mathbf{H}\mathbf{W}_T\|_F^2 / \|\mathbf{W}_R\|_F^2$, the maximized received SNR can be achieved. In order to solve this optimization problem, it is necessary to perform singular value decomposition for $\mathbf{H}$.

$$\mathbf{H} = \mathbf{U}_\mathbf{H} \sum_\mathbf{H} \mathbf{V}_\mathbf{H}^H \tag{2.126}$$

where $\mathbf{U}_\mathbf{H}$ and $\mathbf{V}_\mathbf{H}$ are $M_R \times r(\mathbf{H})$ and $M_T \times r(\mathbf{H})$ dimensional unitary matrices, respectively. $r(\mathbf{H})$ is the rank of matrix $\mathbf{H}$ and $\sum_\mathbf{H} = \text{diag}\{\sigma_1, \sigma_2, \dots, \sigma_{r(\mathbf{H})}\}$ is a singular value diagonal matrix containing matrix $\mathbf{H}$. By the decomposition of the channel matrix, it can be clearly seen that when $\mathbf{W}_T$ and $\mathbf{W}_R$ are the transmitting and receiving singular vectors corresponding to the maximum singular value $\sigma_{max} = \max\{\sigma_1, \sigma_2, \dots, \sigma_{r(\mathbf{H})}\}$ of $\mathbf{H}$, the received SNR is maximized.[6] This technique is known as the dominant eigenmode transmission, and Eq. (2.125) can be rewritten as

$$z = \sqrt{E_S}\sigma_{max}c + \tilde{n} \tag{2.127}$$

where the variance of $\tilde{n} = \mathbf{W}_R^H \mathbf{n}$ is σ_n^2.

As can be seen from Eq. (2.127), the array gain is equal to $\mathrm{E}\{\sigma_{max}^2\} = \mathrm{E}\{\lambda_{max}\}$ with λ_{max} representing the maximum eigenvalue of $\mathbf{HH}^H$. For an independent and identically distributed Rayleigh channel, the upper bound of the array gain is

$$\max\{M_T, M_R\} \leq g_a \leq M_T M_R \tag{2.128}$$

The asymptotic array gain of the dominant eigenmode transmission (when M_T and M_R are large) is given by

$$g_a = (\sqrt{M_T} + \sqrt{M_R})^2 \tag{2.129}$$

Finally, the diversity gain has upper and lower bounds at high SNR[7] (Chernoff bound is a good approximation of SER at high SNR)

$$\overline{N}_e \left(\frac{\rho d_{min}^2}{4\min\{M_T, M_R\}} \right)^{-M_T M_R} \geq \overline{P} \geq \overline{N}_e \left(\frac{\rho d_{min}^2}{4} \right)^{-M_T M_R} \tag{2.130}$$

It means that the error rate is a function of the SNR and the slope of the curve is $M_T M_R$. The full diversity gain $M_T M_R$ is obtained by the dominant eigenmode transmission.

(2) The dominant eigenmode transmission with antenna selection

The principle of the dominant eigenmode transmission with antenna selection is as follows. First, the matrix set $\mathbf{H}'$ consisting of $(M_T - M_T')$ columns of matrix $\mathbf{H}$ is removed according to the definition. The set of all possible $\mathbf{H}'$ is $\mathbf{S}\{\mathbf{H}'\}$, and its potential is $\binom{M_T}{M_T'}$. At each instantaneous time, the selection algorithm uses the matrix to provide the largest singular value $\sigma_{max}' = \max\{\sigma_1', \sigma_2', \ldots, \sigma_{r(\mathbf{H})}'\}$ for a dominant eigenmode transmission. Therefore, the output SNR becomes

$$\rho_{\text{out}} = \rho \max_{S\{H'\}} \{\sigma'_{\max}\} \qquad (2.131)$$

The average SNR can be calculated according to the method provided in Ref. 7, and the corresponding array gain is

$$g_a = \sum_{k=M'_T}^{M_T - M'_T + 1} X_k \qquad (2.132)$$

where

$$X_k = \frac{M_T!}{(k-1)!(M_T - k)!(M_R - 1)!} \sum_{l=0}^{k-1} \left[(-1)^l \binom{k-1}{l} \times \sum_{m=0}^{(M_R-1)(M_T-k+l)} \right.$$

$$\left. a_{M_T-k+l} \frac{\Gamma(1 + M_R + m)}{(M_T - k + l + 1)^{1+M_R+m}} \right] \qquad (2.133)$$

where a_S is the coefficient of u^m of $\sum_{i=0}^{M_R-1} (u^i/u!)^S$.

Similar to the traditional dominant eigenmode transmission, if all transmit antennas are used, the antenna selection algorithm can obtain the same diversity gain, which means the diversity gain is $M_T M_R$.

(3) Multi-eigenmode transmission

The eigenmode transmission will not achieve multiplexing gain when the same symbol is sent to all transmit antennas. As an alternative, the system throughput can be increased by maximizing spatial multiplexing gain. For this purpose, the symbols are spread over the non-zero eigenmode of all channels. Assuming $M_R \geq M_T$, the channel matrix is an independent and identically distributed Rayleigh channel, and singular value decomposition is made for the channel matrix by Eq. (2.125). If the transmitter uses the precoding matrix $\mathbf{V_H}$ to multiply the input vector $\mathbf{c}(M_T \times 1)$ and the receiver uses matrix $\mathbf{U_H^H}$ to multiply the received vector, the input–output relationship can be written as

$$\mathbf{y} = \sqrt{E_S} \mathbf{U_H^H H V_H c} + \mathbf{U_H^H n} = \sqrt{E_S} \sum_{\mathbf{H}} \mathbf{c} + \tilde{\mathbf{n}} \qquad (2.134)$$

It can be seen that the channel has been decomposed into M_T parallel SISO channels given by $\{\sigma_1, \ldots, \sigma_{n_t}\}$. It should be noted that if M_T virtual data channels are established, all of these channels will be fully decoupled. Therefore, the mutual information of the MIMO channel is the sum of the SISO channel capacities.

$$I = \sum_{k=1}^{M_T} \text{lb}(1 + \rho p_k \sigma_k^2) \tag{2.135}$$

where $\{p_1, \ldots, p_{M_T}\}$ is the eigenmode power allocation for each channel, satisfying the normalization condition $\sum_{k=1}^{M_T} p_k = 1$. The capacity is linear with M_T, so the spatial multiplexing gain is equal to M_T. This transmission mode might not achieve full diversity gain $M_T M_R$, but at least provides a M_R-times array and diversity gain. Multi-eigenmode transmission can also be combined with antenna selection at the receiving end. As long as $M_R' \geq M_T$, the multiplexing gain is still M_T, but the array gain and diversity gain are reduced.

2.3.4.2 *MIMO system without transmit channel information*

When the transmitter has no channel information, multiple antennas can be used at the transmitter and receiver ends to achieve diversity and increase the system capacity. This can be realized by spreading the symbols over the antenna (space) and time using the so-called space–time coding. In the following, the space–time block code will be briefly introduced.

Similar to MISO system, two symbols c_1 and c_2 are simultaneously transmitted from antenna 1 and antenna 2 in the first symbol period, and the symbols $-c_2^*$ and c_1^* are transmitted from antenna 1 and antenna 2 in the next symbol period.

Assuming that the flat fading channel remains unchanged in the two consecutive symbol periods, the 2×2 channel matrix can be expressed as

$$\mathbf{H} = \begin{bmatrix} h_{11} & h_{12} \\ h_{21} & h_{22} \end{bmatrix} \tag{2.136}$$

It is worth noting that the subscripts here represent the receive and transmit antenna labels instead of the symbol periods. The signal vector received by the receiving array in the first symbol period is

$$\mathbf{y}_1 = \sqrt{E_S}\mathbf{H} \begin{bmatrix} c_1/\sqrt{2} \\ c_2/\sqrt{2} \end{bmatrix} + \mathbf{n}_1 \tag{2.137}$$

The signal vector received in the second symbol period is

$$\mathbf{y}_2 = \sqrt{E_S}\mathbf{H} \begin{bmatrix} -c_2^*/\sqrt{2} \\ c_1^*/\sqrt{2} \end{bmatrix} + \mathbf{n}_2 \tag{2.138}$$

where $\mathbf{n}_1$ and $\mathbf{n}_2$ are additive noise components per symbol period of the receive antenna array (the subscripts represent symbol periods instead of antenna labels). Therefore, the receiver produces a mixed signal vector

$$\mathbf{y} = \begin{bmatrix} \mathbf{y}_1 \\ \mathbf{y}_2^* \end{bmatrix} = \underbrace{\begin{bmatrix} h_{11} & h_{12} \\ h_{21} & h_{22} \\ h_{12}^* & -h_{11}^* \\ h_{22}^* & -h_{21}^* \end{bmatrix}}_{\mathbf{H}_{\text{eff}}} \underbrace{\begin{bmatrix} c_1/\sqrt{2} \\ c_2/\sqrt{2} \end{bmatrix}}_{c} + \begin{bmatrix} \mathbf{n}_1 \\ \mathbf{n}_2^* \end{bmatrix} \tag{2.139}$$

Similar to the MISO system, two symbols c_1 and c_2 are transmitted during two symbol periods of two transmit antennas. Therefore, matrix $\mathbf{H}_{\text{eff}}$ is orthogonal to all channel information, namely $\mathbf{H}_{\text{eff}}^{\text{H}}\mathbf{H}_{\text{eff}} = \|\mathbf{H}\|_F^2 \mathbf{I}_2$. If $\mathbf{z} = \mathbf{H}_{\text{eff}}^{\text{H}}\mathbf{y}$, then

$$\mathbf{z} = \begin{bmatrix} z_1 \\ z_2 \end{bmatrix} \mathbf{H}_{\text{eff}}^{\text{H}}\mathbf{y} = \|\mathbf{H}\|_F^2 \mathbf{I}_2 c + \mathbf{n}' \tag{2.140}$$

where $\mathbf{n}'$ satisfies $E\{\mathbf{n}'\} = \mathbf{0}_{2\times 1}$ and $E\{\mathbf{n}'\mathbf{n}'^{\text{H}}\} = \|\mathbf{H}\|_F^2 \sigma_n^2 \mathbf{I}_2$. The above equation shows that the transmission of the symbols c_1 and c_2 is completely decoupled, which means

$$z_k = \sqrt{E_S/2}\|\mathbf{H}\|_F^2 c_k + \tilde{n}_k, \quad k = 1, 2 \tag{2.141}$$

The average output SNR is

$$\rho_{\text{out}} = \frac{1}{\sigma_n^2} E\left\{ \frac{E_S[\|\mathbf{H}\|_F^2]^2}{2\|\mathbf{H}\|_F^2} \right\} = 2\rho \tag{2.142}$$

The Alamouti algorithm of the 2×2 structure obtains the receive array gain ($g_a = M_R = 2$) but does not get the transmit array gain (because there is no channel information). The above method can get the full diversity ($g_d^0 = M_T M_R = 4$)

$$\overline{P} \leq \overline{N}_e \left(\frac{\rho d_{\min}^2}{8} \right)^{-4} \tag{2.143}$$

The diversity gain of both the Alamouti algorithm and the dominant eigenmode transmission is 4, but the array gain of the dominant eigenmode transmission is 3 dB larger than the Alamouti algorithm. Alamouti algorithm can also be used for any number of receive antennas ($g_a = M_R, g_d^0 = 2M_R$), but the number of transmit antennas of the system should be less than or equal to 2.

2.3.4.3 *MIMO system with partial transmit channel information*

If the transmitter has only partial channel information, it is also possible to exploit the gain of the array. The complete channel information at the transmitter requires high-speed feedback links at both ends of the receiver and transmitter to ensure that the latter can continuously obtain channel state information. On the converse, exploiting the statistical property of the channel at the transmitter or the quantitative description of the channel requires only a lower rate feedback link.

Precoding techniques usually combine a multi-mode beamformer that can spread codewords in orthogonal directions of the channel distribution-related direction with a constellation shaper, or more simply, with a power allocation algorithm. There are many similarities with various eigenmode transmissions, while the difference is that the eigenbeam is based on the statistical property of matrix **H** rather than its instantaneous value.

Similarly, the antenna selection technique may also only depend on partial channel information, namely the first- and second-order statistics of the matrix **H** to select the transmitting or receiving antenna. Intuitively, they are selected from the antenna pair with the lowest selective correlation ratio. Such techniques do not minimize transient error performance metrics, but minimize the average error probability.

By quantization precoding, the generalization of antenna selection is to derive limited feedback from the transmitter. This technique depends on the selection of codebooks in the precoding matrix, which is a finite set of precoders. It can be designed offline and is known to both the transmitter and the receiver. The receiver estimates the best precoder as a function of the current channel and then feeds the index of the best precoder back into the codebook.

2.4 MIMO Traditional Detection Technology

In Section 2.3.4, we introduced the basic concepts and principles of the MIMO systems. In the following, we will discuss the signal detection problem at the receiving end of the MIMO system from the perspective of the MIMO receiver.

2.4.1 *System model*

The MIMO system model is shown in Fig. 2.11. Consider the system with two transmitting antennas and two receiving antennas as an example. Since each receiving antenna can receive signals from different transmitting antennas, the received signals from the two receiving antennas can be expressed as

$$y_1 = h_{11}s_1 + h_{12}s_2 + n_1$$
$$y_2 = h_{21}s_1 + h_{22}s_2 + n_2 \tag{2.144}$$

where h_{ij}, s_j, and n_i represent the channel gain from the jth transmitting antenna to the ith receiving antenna, the transmitted signal of the jth transmitting antenna, and the additive noise of the ith receiving antenna, respectively. Defining $\mathbf{y} = [y_1 \ y_2]^\mathrm{T}$, the received signal vector can be expressed by the matrix multiplication.

$$\mathbf{y} = \mathbf{Hs} + \mathbf{n} \tag{2.145}$$

where channel matrix $\mathbf{H} = \begin{bmatrix} h_{11} & h_{12} \\ h_{21} & h_{22} \end{bmatrix}$, transmitted signal vector $\mathbf{s} = \begin{bmatrix} s_1 \\ s_2 \end{bmatrix}$, and noise vector $\mathbf{n} = \begin{bmatrix} n_1 \\ n_2 \end{bmatrix}$. The corresponding system model can be extended to any MIMO system with M transmitting antennas and N receiving antennas. The system model expression can still be expressed by Eq. (2.145), and the channel can be assumed to be an additive white Gaussian noise channel. In the AWGN channel, the received noise vector

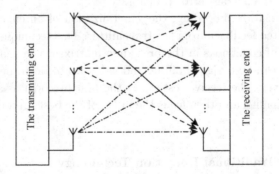

Fig. 2.11. The MIMO system model.

$\mathbf{n}$ is assumed to be a zero-average CSCG random vector,[8,9] whose mean value is $\mathrm{E}(\mathbf{n}\mathbf{n}^H) = N_0\mathbf{I}$, covariance matrix is $\mathbf{R}$, namely $\mathbf{n} \sim \mathcal{CN}(0, \mathbf{R})$.

2.4.2 Uncoded MIMO signal detection[b]

2.4.2.1 Maximum likelihood MIMO signal detection

It can be seen from Eq. (2.145) that the purpose of detecting the MIMO signal is to estimate the unknown transmitted signal vector $\mathbf{s}$ when the received signal vector $\mathbf{y}$ and the channel matrix $\mathbf{H}$ are known. Although we are unable to obtain accurate information of the noise vector $\mathbf{n}$, all possible cases of transmitting the signal vector $\mathbf{s}$ can be obtained in advance according to the modulation method. For an MIMO system with M transmitting antennas, if the transmitted symbols are taken from a constellation symbol set, then the number of all possible transmitted signal vectors is $|\mathcal{S}|^M$, where $|\mathcal{S}|$ denotes the number of symbol elements in the set. For example, when the modulation method adopts 4-quadrature amplitude modulation (QAM) and the number of transmit antennas M is 2, the number of all possible transmitted signal vectors $\mathbf{s}$ is $4^2 = 16$. It can be easily found that the number of possible transmitted signal vectors increases exponentially with M.

In summary, maximum likelihood MIMO signal detection can be accomplished by retrieving all possible transmitted signals and calculating the corresponding likelihood function values. Defining $f(\mathbf{y}|\mathbf{s})$ as a likelihood function that transmits signal vector $\mathbf{s}$ when signal $\mathbf{y}$ is received, the transmitted signal vector of maximum likelihood can be expressed as

$$\mathbf{s}_{\mathrm{ml}} = \arg \max_{\mathbf{s} \in \mathcal{S}^M} f(\mathbf{y}|\mathbf{s})$$

$$= \arg \min_{\mathbf{s} \in \mathcal{S}^M} \|\mathbf{y} - \mathbf{H}\mathbf{s}\|^2 \qquad (2.146)$$

Since the maximum likelihood detection requires exhaustive retrieval and the number of all possible transmitted signal vectors is $|\mathcal{S}|^M$, the computational complexity of the ML detection algorithm increases exponentially with the number of transmit antennas M.

---

[b]Reprinted/adapted by permission from Springer Nature Customer Service Centre GmbH: Springer "Low Complexity MIMO Detection" by Bai L and Choi J, 2012.

2.4.2.2 *Linear MIMO signal detection*

In order to reduce the complexity of detection, we can also consider using the linear filtering method to complete the detection process. In the linear MIMO signal detection, each transmitted signal can be detected separately after the received signal $\mathbf{y}$ is filtered by a linear filter. Therefore, the function of a linear filter is to separate the interference signals.

First, we consider zero forcing (ZF) detection. The ZF detection linear filter is defined as

$$\mathbf{W}_{zf} = \mathbf{H}(\mathbf{H}^H\mathbf{H})^{-1} \tag{2.147}$$

And the corresponding ZF signal is estimated as

$$\begin{aligned}
\tilde{\mathbf{s}}_{zf} &= \mathbf{W}_{zf}^H\mathbf{y} \\
&= (\mathbf{H}^H\mathbf{H})^{-1}\mathbf{H}^H\mathbf{y} \\
&= \mathbf{s} + (\mathbf{H}^H\mathbf{H})^{-1}\mathbf{H}^H\mathbf{n}
\end{aligned} \tag{2.148}$$

With $\tilde{\mathbf{s}}_{zf}$ and $\mathcal{S}$, the hard decision of the transmitted signal vector $\mathbf{s}$ can be made by the symbol-level estimation.

It should be noted that since the noise term, namely the effect of $(\mathbf{H}^H\mathbf{H})^{-1}\mathbf{H}^H\mathbf{n}$ in Eq. (2.148), will be amplified, the equivalent noise will be amplified when the channel matrix $\mathbf{H}$ is nearly singular. Therefore, the performance of the ZF detection cannot be well guaranteed. In order to reduce the influence caused by the equivalent noise being amplified in the ZF detection, the MMSE detection utilizes the statistical property of the noise to improve the ZF detection method. The calculation of the MMSE filter matrix is based on the minimum mean square error criterion.

$$\begin{aligned}
\mathbf{W}_{\text{MMSE}} &= \arg\min_{\mathbf{w}} \mathrm{E}[\|\mathbf{s} - \mathbf{W}^H\mathbf{y}\|^2] \\
&= (\mathrm{E}(\mathbf{y}\mathbf{y}^H))^{-1}\mathrm{E}(\mathbf{y}\mathbf{s}^H) \\
&= \mathbf{H}\left(\mathbf{H}^H\mathbf{H} + \frac{N_0}{E_s}\mathbf{I}\right)^{-1}
\end{aligned} \tag{2.149}$$

where E_s represents the signal energy. The corresponding estimate of the transmitted signal vector can be expressed as

$$\begin{aligned}
\tilde{\mathbf{s}}_{\text{MMSE}} &= \mathbf{W}_{\text{MMSE}}^H\mathbf{y} \\
&= \left(\mathbf{H}^H\mathbf{H} + \frac{N_0}{E_s}\mathbf{I}\right)^{-1}\mathbf{H}^H\mathbf{y}
\end{aligned} \tag{2.150}$$

Therefore, the MMSE hard decision $\widetilde{s}_{MMSE}$ of the signal vector s can be obtained.

2.4.2.3 *Successive interference cancellation (SIC) detection*

With the consideration of the existence of interference signals, how to realize high-performance signal detection has become a key issue that modern wireless communication needs to solve. For example, assume that the signal received by the receiver is

$$y = \mathbf{h}_1 s_1 + \mathbf{h}_2 s_2 + \mathbf{n} \tag{2.151}$$

where s_i and $\mathbf{h}_i$ represent the ith signal and the channel gain experienced by the signal, respectively, and $\mathbf{n}$ represents the background noise. When detecting the signal s_1, the signal-to-interference plus noise ratio can be expressed as

$$\text{SINR}_1 = \frac{|\mathbf{h}_1|^2 E_1}{|\mathbf{h}_2|^2 E_2 + N_0} \tag{2.152}$$

where $\text{E}[|s_i|^2] = E_i$ and $\text{E}[|n|^2] = N_0$. If the received power of the two signals is assumed to be the same, namely $E_1 = E_2$, and the channel gain is also assumed to be the same, namely $|\mathbf{h}_1|^2 = |\mathbf{h}_2|^2$, then the SINR of signal s_1 will be less than $0\,\text{dB}$, which brings great difficulty to the signal detection.

Successive interference cancellation is an alternative method to improve the performance of signal detection. Assuming $E_1 > E_2$, the SINR of s_1 is relatively high at this time, and it is possible to detect s_1 first. Let $\hat{s}_1$ be the detection value of s_1, and if the detection of $\hat{s}_1$ is correct, then it is possible to eliminate the interference of s_1 during the detection process of s_2. Therefore, the interference-free detection of s_2 can be realized, which is expressed as

$$u_2 = \mathbf{y} - \mathbf{h}_1\widehat{s}_1$$

$$= \mathbf{h}_2 s_2 + \mathbf{n} \tag{2.153}$$

This detection method is called Successive Interference Cancellation (SIC) and can be applied to MIMO joint signal detection.

In order to realize SIC, QR decomposition plays an important role in the SIC-based detection process.[10, 11] QR decomposition is a common method of matrix decomposition, which can be decomposed into the product of an orthogonal matrix and an upper triangular matrix. And how the 2×2 MIMO system performs QR decomposition will be introduced first in this section.

Assume that there is a 2×2 channel matrix $\mathbf{H} = [\mathbf{h}_1 \ \mathbf{h}_2]$, where $\mathbf{h}_i$ represents the ith column vector of $\mathbf{H}$. Define the inner product of the two vectors to be $\langle \mathbf{a}, \mathbf{b} \rangle = \mathbf{a}^H \mathbf{b}$. In order to find an orthogonal vector with the same lattice as $\mathbf{H}$, we define

$$\mathbf{r}_1 = \mathbf{h}_1$$
$$\mathbf{r}_2 = \mathbf{h}_2 - \omega \mathbf{h}_1 \tag{2.154}$$

where

$$\omega = \frac{\langle \mathbf{h}_2, \mathbf{r}_1 \rangle}{\|\mathbf{r}_1\|^2} = \frac{\langle \mathbf{h}_2, \mathbf{h}_1 \rangle}{\|\mathbf{h}_1\|^2} \tag{2.155}$$

According to the linear relationship described by Eq. (2.154), it can be judged that $[\mathbf{h}_1 \ \mathbf{h}_2]$ and $[\mathbf{r}_1 \ \mathbf{r}_2]$ can span the same subspace. And if $\mathbf{r}_i$ is a non-zero vector $(i = 1, 2)$, it can be found that

$$
\begin{aligned}
[\mathbf{h}_1 \ \mathbf{h}_2] &= [\mathbf{r}_1 \ \mathbf{r}_2] \begin{bmatrix} 1 & \omega \\ 0 & 1 \end{bmatrix} \\
&= [\mathbf{q}_1 \ \mathbf{q}_2] \begin{bmatrix} \|\mathbf{r}_1\| & 0 \\ 0 & \|\mathbf{r}_2\| \end{bmatrix} \begin{bmatrix} 1 & \omega \\ 0 & 1 \end{bmatrix} \\
&= [\mathbf{q}_1 \ \mathbf{q}_2] \begin{bmatrix} \|\mathbf{r}_1\| & \omega\|\mathbf{r}_1\| \\ 0 & \|\mathbf{r}_2\| \end{bmatrix}
\end{aligned} \tag{2.156}
$$

where $\mathbf{q}_i = \mathbf{r}_i / \|\mathbf{r}_i\|$. Based on Eq. (2.156), an orthogonal matrix $\mathbf{Q} = [\mathbf{q}_1 \ \mathbf{q}_2]$ and an upper triangular matrix $\mathbf{R} = \begin{bmatrix} \|\mathbf{r}_1\| & \omega\|\mathbf{r}_1\| \\ 0 & \|\mathbf{r}_2\| \end{bmatrix}$ can be obtained, and thus, the QR decomposition of $\mathbf{H}$ is achieved. It is worth noting that if $\mathbf{r}_2 = \mathbf{h}_2$ and $\mathbf{r}_1 = \mathbf{h}_1 - \omega \mathbf{h}_2$, another QR decomposition result of $\mathbf{H}$ can be obtained.

The successive interference cancellation of the received signal can be performed according to the QR decomposition of the channel matrix. This section only discusses the case where the channel matrix $\mathbf{H}$ is a square matrix or a thin matrix $(M \leq N)$ whose number of rows is larger than the number of columns.

1. H is a square matrix

$\mathbf{H}$ can be decomposed into an $M \times M$ unitary matrix $\mathbf{Q}$ and an $M \times M$ upper triangular matrix $\mathbf{R}$.

$$\mathbf{H} = \mathbf{QR}$$

$$= \mathbf{Q} \left. \begin{bmatrix} r_{1,1} & r_{1,2} & \cdots & r_{1,M} \\ 0 & r_{2,2} & \cdots & r_{2,M} \\ \vdots & \vdots & \ddots & \vdots \\ 0 & 0 & \cdots & r_{M,M} \end{bmatrix} \right\} M \qquad (2.157)$$

$$\underbrace{\qquad\qquad\qquad\qquad}_{M}$$

where $r_{p,q}$ is defined as the (p,q)th element of $\mathbf{R}$. By the premultiplication of $\mathbf{Q}^{\mathrm{H}}$, the received signal can be expressed as

$$\mathbf{x} = \mathbf{Q}^{\mathrm{H}} \mathbf{y}$$

$$= \mathbf{Rs} + \mathbf{Q}^{\mathrm{H}} \mathbf{n} \qquad (2.158)$$

where $\mathbf{Q}^{\mathrm{H}} \mathbf{n}$ is a zero-mean CSCG random vector. $\mathbf{Q}^{\mathrm{H}} \mathbf{n}$ has the same statistical property as $\mathbf{n}$, and hence, $\mathbf{n}$ can be used directly to replace $\mathbf{Q}^{\mathrm{H}} \mathbf{n}$. As a result, Eq. (2.158) can be transformed into

$$\mathbf{x} = \mathbf{Rs} + \mathbf{n} \qquad (2.159)$$

If x_k and n_k are defined as the kth element of $\mathbf{x}$ and $\mathbf{n}$, the above equation can be expanded as follows:

$$\begin{bmatrix} x_1 \\ x_2 \\ \vdots \\ x_M \end{bmatrix} = \begin{bmatrix} r_{1,1} & r_{1,2} & \cdots & r_{1,M} \\ 0 & r_{2,2} & \cdots & r_{2,M} \\ \vdots & \vdots & \ddots & \vdots \\ 0 & 0 & \cdots & r_{M,M} \end{bmatrix} \begin{bmatrix} s_1 \\ s_2 \\ \vdots \\ s_M \end{bmatrix} + \begin{bmatrix} n_1 \\ n_2 \\ \vdots \\ n_M \end{bmatrix} \qquad (2.160)$$

Therefore, SIC detection can be carried out

$$x_M = r_{M,M} s_M + n_M$$

$$x_{M-1} = r_{M-1,M} s_M + r_{M-1,M-1} s_{M-1} + n_{M-1} \qquad (2.161)$$

$$\vdots$$

2. H is a thin matrix

The QR decomposition of $\mathbf{H}$ is

$$\mathbf{H} = \mathbf{QR}$$

$$= \mathbf{Q} \left. \begin{bmatrix} r_{1,1} & r_{1,2} & \cdots & r_{1,M} \\ 0 & r_{2,2} & \cdots & r_{2,M} \\ \vdots & \vdots & \ddots & \vdots \\ 0 & 0 & \cdots & r_{M,M} \\ 0 & 0 & \cdots & 0 \\ \vdots & \vdots & \vdots & \vdots \\ 0 & 0 & \cdots & 0 \end{bmatrix} \begin{array}{l} \left. \rule{0pt}{38pt} \right\} M \\ \\ \left. \rule{0pt}{38pt} \right\} N - M \end{array} \quad (2.162)$$

where $M < N$ and $\mathbf{Q}$ is an unitary matrix. We have $\mathbf{R} = [\bar{\mathbf{R}}^{\mathrm{T}} \ \mathbf{0}]^{\mathrm{T}}$, with $\bar{\mathbf{R}}$ denoting an $M \times M$ upper triangular matrix. According to Eq. (2.162), the received signal vector can be expressed as

$$\begin{bmatrix} x_1 \\ x_2 \\ \vdots \\ x_M \\ x_{M+1} \\ \vdots \\ x_N \end{bmatrix} = \begin{bmatrix} r_{1,1} & r_{1,2} & \cdots & r_{1,M} \\ 0 & r_{2,2} & \cdots & r_{2,M} \\ \vdots & \vdots & \ddots & \vdots \\ 0 & 0 & \cdots & r_{M,M} \\ 0 & 0 & \cdots & 0 \\ \vdots & \vdots & \vdots & \vdots \\ 0 & 0 & \cdots & 0 \end{bmatrix} \begin{bmatrix} s_1 \\ s_2 \\ \vdots \\ s_M \end{bmatrix} + \begin{bmatrix} n_1 \\ n_2 \\ \vdots \\ n_M \\ n_{M+1} \\ \vdots \\ n_N \end{bmatrix} \quad (2.163)$$

Furthermore,

$$x_N = n_N$$

$$\vdots$$

$$x_{M+1} = n_{M+1}$$

$$x_M = r_{M,M} s_M + n_M$$

$$x_{M-1} = r_{M-1,M} s_M + r_{M-1,M-1} s_{M-1} + n_{M-1}$$

$$\vdots \quad (2.164)$$

Since the received signal $\{x_{M+1}, x_{M+2}, \ldots, x_N\}$ does not contain any useful information, it can be ignored directly. On this basis, Eqs. (2.161) and (2.164) are identical in form, and thus, successive interference cancellation can be realized. First, s_M can be detected based on x_M.

$$\tilde{s}_M = \frac{x_M}{r_{M,M}}$$

$$= s_M + \frac{n_M}{r_{M,M}} \tag{2.165}$$

If $\mathcal{S} = \{s^{(1)}, s^{(2)}, \ldots, s^{(K)}\}$ is used as the K-QAM constellation symbol set of the signal, the detection expression of s_M is

$$\hat{s}_M = \arg \min_{s^{(k)} \in \mathcal{S}} |s^{(k)} - \tilde{s}_M|^2 \tag{2.166}$$

The above equation shows that since there is no interference term in the detection of s_M, the influence of s_M can be eliminated during the detection of s_{M-1}. This successive cancellation process can continue until all data signals are detected sequentially. In other words, the mth signal will be detected after the first $M - m$ signals are detected and the interference is eliminated, which can be described as

$$u_m = x_m - \sum_{q=m+1}^{M} r_{m,q} \hat{s}_q, \quad m \in \{1, 2, \ldots, M - 1\} \tag{2.167}$$

where $\hat{s}_q$ represents an estimated value of s_q detected from the received signal u_q. Assuming that there are no errors during all detection process, s_m can be estimated as

$$\hat{s}_m = \arg \min_{s^{(k)} \in \mathcal{S}} |s^{(k)} - \tilde{s}_m|^2 \tag{2.168}$$

where $\tilde{s}_m = \frac{u_m}{r_{m,m}} = s_m + \frac{n_m}{r_{m,m}}$.

Since the successive interference cancellation algorithm introduced above is based on the zero-forcing decision feedback equalizer (ZF-DFE), we call the algorithm a zero-forcing successive interference cancellation (ZF-SIC).[12,13] It should be noted that if the channel state matrix $\mathbf{H}$ is a fat matrix with $M > N$, which means the number of rows of the channel matrix is larger than the number of columns, then the successive interference cancellation algorithms cannot be used in this case due to the lack of an upper triangular array after QR decomposition.

In order to improve system performance, background noise should to be considered when performing the detection. To solve this problem, we need to employ a successive interference cancellation algorithm based on minimum mean square error decision equalizer (MMSE-DFE). And two implementation strategies of MMSE-SIC algorithm are introduced in this section.

Strategy 1: Define the extended channel matrix $\mathbf{H}_{\mathrm{ex}} = \left[\mathbf{H}^{\mathrm{T}} \sqrt{\frac{N_0}{E_s}}\mathbf{I}\right]^{\mathrm{T}}$, extended received signal $\mathbf{y}_{\mathrm{ex}} = [\mathbf{y}^{\mathrm{T}} \ \mathbf{0}^{\mathrm{T}}]^{\mathrm{T}}$, and extended background noise vector $\mathbf{n}_{\mathrm{ex}} = \left[\mathbf{n}^{\mathrm{T}} - \sqrt{\frac{N_0}{E_s}}\mathbf{s}^{\mathrm{T}}\right]^{\mathrm{T}}$. Through QR decomposition, we can get

$$\mathbf{H}_{\mathrm{ex}} = \mathbf{Q}_{\mathrm{ex}}\mathbf{R}_{\mathrm{ex}} \qquad (2.169)$$

where $\mathbf{Q}_{\mathrm{ex}}$ and $\mathbf{R}_{\mathrm{ex}}$ represent the unitary matrix and the upper triangular matrix, respectively. Replacing $\mathbf{y}$, $\mathbf{n}$, $\mathbf{Q}$, and $\mathbf{R}$ in Eq. (2.158) by $\mathbf{y}_{\mathrm{ex}}$, $\mathbf{n}_{\mathrm{ex}}$, $\mathbf{Q}_{\mathrm{ex}}$, and $\mathbf{R}_{\mathrm{ex}}$, we get

$$\mathbf{x}_{\mathrm{ex}} = \mathbf{Q}_{\mathrm{ex}}^{\mathrm{H}}\mathbf{y}_{\mathrm{ex}}$$
$$= \mathbf{R}_{\mathrm{ex}}\mathbf{s} + \mathbf{Q}_{\mathrm{ex}}^{\mathrm{H}}\mathbf{n}_{\mathrm{ex}} \qquad (2.170)$$

Based on Eq. (2.170), MMSE-SIC detection can be carried out according to Eqs. (2.158)–(2.168).

Strategy 2: Utilizing the minimum mean square error estimator (MMSE Estimator) directly, the MMSE estimator for signal s_1 can be expressed as

$$\mathbf{w}_{\mathrm{MMSE},1} = \arg \min_{\mathbf{w}} \mathrm{E}[|s_1 - \mathbf{w}^{\mathrm{H}}\mathbf{y}|^2]$$
$$= \left(\mathbf{H}\mathbf{H}^{\mathrm{H}} + \frac{N_o}{E_s}\mathbf{I}\right)^{-1}\bar{\mathbf{h}}_1 \qquad (2.171)$$

where $\bar{\mathbf{h}}_1$ represents the first column vector of $\mathbf{H}^{\mathrm{H}}$. The hard decision on symbol s_1 can be described as

$$\widehat{s}_{1,\mathrm{MMSE}} = \mathbf{w}_{\mathrm{MMSE},1}\mathbf{y} \qquad (2.172)$$

Assuming that s_1 can be detected correctly and its effect can be removed from $\mathbf{y}$, we can obtain

$$\mathbf{y}_1 = \sum_{m=2}^{M} \mathbf{h}_m s_m + \mathbf{n} \qquad (2.173)$$

According to $\mathbf{y}_1$, s_2 can be detected by the MMSE method. And the MMSE-SIC detection of s_m can be carried out by repeated interference cancellation and MMSE estimation.

2.4.3 *Simulation results*

As can be seen from Fig. 2.12, the optimal detector ML has obvious advantages compared with the MIMO linear detector (ZF, MMSE). However, the complexity which exponentially increases with the number of transmitting antennas makes it difficult to apply in practical systems. And although linear detectors (ZF, MMSE) have a relatively low complexity, their performance is not satisfactory. The SIC method can improve the performance of the linear detectors (ZF, MMSE) to a certain extent, but their performance is still not on par with ML.

2.5 Summary

How to utilize the optimal spatial signal combination and detection method effectively to improve the performance and spectrum efficiency of wireless communication systems is a key issue to be remembered when designing the next generation of wireless communication. The knowledge of spatial multidimensional signal combination and detection is first introduced in this chapter, and then the principle and basic concept of two typical multi-antenna systems, namely the array antenna system and the MIMO antenna system, which can improve the performance and spectrum efficiency of

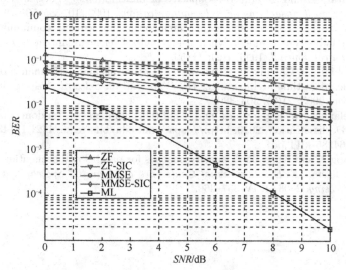

Fig. 2.12. The MIMO multiple detector error performance of a 4 × 4 MIMO system.

wireless communication system, are also introduced. In Chapter 3, we will elaborate on the principles and techniques of adaptive antennas based on the array antenna system introduced in this chapter.

References

1. Shannon CE. A Mathematical Theory of Communication. *Bell System Technical Journal*, 1948, 27(3): 379–423.
2. Janaswamy R. *Radio Wave Propagation and Smart Antenna for Wireless Communications.* Boston, MA: Kluwer Academic Publishers, 2000.
3. Simon MK and Alouini MS. *Digital Communications over Fading Channels: A Unified Approach to Performance Analysis.* New York: Wiley, 2000.
4. Proakis JG. *Digital Communications.* 4th edn. New York: McGraw-Hill, 2001.
5. Paulraj AJ, Nabar R and Gore D. *Introduction to Space–Time Wireless Communications.* Cambridge, UK: Cambridge University Press, 2003.
6. Gore DA, Sandhu S and Paulraj A. Delay diversity codes for frequency selective channels. *IEEE International Conference on Communications.* New York, 2002, 3: 1949–1953.
7. Godara LC. Applications of antenna arrays to mobile communications, Part II: Beamforming and direction-of-arrival considerations. *IEEE Proceedings*, 1997, 85(8): 1195–1245.
8. Foschini GJ and Gans MJ. On limits of wireless communications in a fading environment using multiple antennas. *Wireless Personal Communications*, 1998, 6(3): 311–335.
9. Telatar IE and Telatar IE. Capacity of multi-antenna Gaussian channels. *European Transactions on Telecommunications*, 1999, 10: 585–595.
10. Foschini GJ. Layered space–time architecture for wireless communications in a fading environment when using multiple-element antenna. *Bell Labs Technical Journal*, 1996, 1(2): 41–59.
11. Foschini GJ, Chizhik D, Gans MJ, *et al.* Analysis and performance of some basic space-time architectures. *IEEE Journal on Selected Areas Communication*, 2003, 21(3): 303–320.
12. Edelaman A. Eigenvalues and condition numbers of random matrices. Ph.D. dissertation, 2010. http://dspace.mit.edu/bitstream/1721.1/14322/2/21864285-MIT.pdf.
13. Zhang X and Kung SY. Capacity analysis for parallel and sequential MIMO equalizers. *IEEE International Conference on Acoustic, Speech, and Signal Processing.* 2003, 4: IV-357–360.

Chapter 3

Adaptive Antenna Array Theory and Technology

With the continuous growth of information in today's society, the rapid development of the global communications, and the rapid expansion of the personal mobile communication business, the contradiction between limited spectrum resources and increasing system capacity requirements is increasingly prominent. Meanwhile, problems such as multipath interference, multiple access interference, and channel fading widely exist in actual communication systems and also have a serious impact on system performance and capacity. The adaptive array antenna based on the wireless channel property and the array signal processing method can flexibly and efficiently utilize the spatial resources by controlling the antenna beam. It can resist fading and interference, improve spectrum utilization, and expand the system capacity while ensuring communication quality.

This chapter first explains the basic architecture and principle of adaptive antennas and then introduces three important issues of adaptive processing systems, namely adaptive correlation criterion, adaptive typical beamforming algorithm, and direction of arrival estimation algorithm. Finally, the array correction technology and system hardware architecture of the adaptive array antenna are explained.

3.1 The Basic Principle of Adaptive Antenna Array

The basic principle of the adaptive array antenna is to adaptively adjust the weight of the array antenna element excitation according to certain criteria and algorithms, so that the quality of the output signal is optimal with the adopted criteria after the array-received signals are weighted and superimposed. It is known that the array pattern, which is also called beam, is determined by the weight vector of the array. The effect of adjusting the weight is to make the main beam of the array pattern point to the useful signal and form a zero or lower sidelobe in the direction of the interference signal. Accordingly, different users or signals are spatially separated, and this is called "spatial filtering".

Figure 3.1 shows an adaptive antenna array containing M elements. And it can be seen that the adaptive antenna array includes an antenna array, a radio frequency and A/D conversion module, and a beamforming module. Signals from different users and different paths are first received on array elements and then converted to baseband digital signals by RF channels and A/D; therefore, the input beamformer signal will be a complex baseband vector. The beamformer module includes an adaptive weight-generation module and an array element signal weighting superposition module. The adaptive weight-generation module is the core of the entire adaptive antenna array system. It is an array signal processor that receives

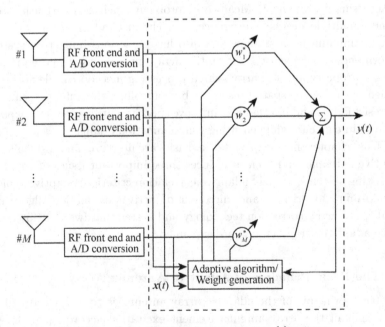

Fig. 3.1.   Adaptive antenna system architecture.

array signals from each array element and calculates a weight vector based on an adaptive algorithm. This weight vector is then input into the weighting superposition module, and the output of the entire adaptive antenna system will be obtained through weighting and superimposing the array signal vectors.

In order to better illustrate the principle of the adaptive antenna array, the baseband digital model of the received signal from the array antenna is introduced in the following, including the expression of the signal vector of the input beamformer and the statistical properties of the received signal. First, it is assumed that the signal meets the requirements of the narrowband model, whose bandwidth B of the signal is much smaller than the carrier frequency f_c. In fact, most of the communication system signals meet this requirement. In this model, the small delay of the incident signal between different elements can be replaced by phase shift, which means the response of the signal from different elements is only one phase difference for the same signal. It should be emphasized that the "narrowband" here is not the same as the narrowband concept in many communication system literatures. The latter generally means that the signal bandwidth is smaller than the channel bandwidth, but here the signal bandwidth is compared with the carrier frequency, referring in particular to the case where the transmission delay between the array elements is much shorter than the symbol length. Actually, general bandwidth communication systems, such as CDMA and OFDM, can satisfy the adaptive antenna narrowband model.

If the number of antenna elements is M, the M elements are denoted as antennas $\#1, \#2, \ldots, \#M$. Considering that only one signal is incident, the signal is represented as $s(t)$ at the transmitting end, the channel complex gain including amplitude and phase effects is $h(t)$, the incident angle is θ, and then the array vector $\mathbf{x}(t) = [\mathbf{x}_1(t), \mathbf{x}_2(t), \ldots, \mathbf{x}_M(t)]^{\mathrm{T}}$ of the received signal is

$$\mathbf{x}(t) = \mathbf{a}(\theta)h(t)s(t) + \mathbf{n}(t), \tag{3.1}$$

where $\mathbf{a}(\theta) = [1, \mathrm{e}^{-j\varphi_2(\theta)}, \ldots, \mathrm{e}^{-j\varphi_M(\theta)}]^{\mathrm{T}}$ is called the response space vector of the array space. $\varphi_i(\theta)$ represents the relative phase shift of the incoming signal between array element $\#i$ and array element $\#1$ (reference point), and the specific expression is determined by the relative geometric relationship between the array elements. If we take the linear equal-spaced array as shown in Fig. 3.2 as an example, it is easy to know

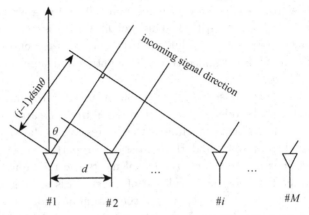

Fig. 3.2. Schematic diagram of phase difference of linear equal-spaced array elements.

$\varphi_i(\theta) = -(i-1)kd\sin\theta$, with k denoting the carrier propagation constant and d the array spacing. $\mathbf{n}(t) = [n_1(t), n_2(t), \dots, n_M(t)]^{\mathrm{T}}$ represents the array element noise vector, which is an independently distributed Gaussian signal.

The $\mathbf{a}(\theta)$ in Eq. (3.1) only reflects the effect of the array itself on signal reception. If the channel gain is included and $\mathbf{a}(\theta) = h(t)$ $[1, \mathrm{e}^{-\mathrm{j}\varphi_2(\theta)}, \dots, \mathrm{e}^{-\mathrm{j}\varphi_M(\theta)}]^{\mathrm{T}}$, then it is called the generalized array space response vector, which reflects the complete response of the array to a transmitted signal. And in this case

$$\mathbf{x}(t) = \mathbf{a}(\theta)\mathbf{s}(t) + \mathbf{n}(t) \tag{3.2}$$

The above equation is based on a continuous signal model. And for the discrete signal model, at the kth snapshot,

$$\mathbf{x}(k) = \mathbf{a}(\theta)\mathbf{s}(k) + \mathbf{n}(k) \tag{3.3}$$

Considering there are N signals that are incident on the array with angles $\theta_1, \theta_2, \dots, \theta_N$, the array-received signal at the kth snapshot is thus given as

$$\mathbf{x}(k) = \sum_{i=1}^{N} \mathbf{a}(\theta_i)s_i(k) + \mathbf{n}(k) = \mathbf{A}(k)\mathbf{s}(k) + \mathbf{n}(k), \tag{3.4}$$

where $\mathbf{A}(k) = [\mathbf{a}(\theta_1), \mathbf{a}(\theta_2), \ldots, \mathbf{a}(\theta_N)]$ and $\mathbf{s}(k) = [s_1(k), s_2(k), \ldots, s_N(k)]^T$. Eq. (3.4) is the array antenna-received signal model of the input beamformer.

The task of the beamformer is to process the received signal $\mathbf{x}(k)$ and generate a weight vector $\mathbf{W}(k) = [w_1(k), w_2(k), \ldots, w_N(k)]^T$ according to an adaptive algorithm to obtain the array output:

$$y(k) = \mathbf{W}^H \mathbf{x}(k) \tag{3.5}$$

This output is usually optimal under certain criteria. The optimal weight vector is always determined by the channel environment, which is reflected by the statistical properties of the received signal $\mathbf{x}(k)$, namely the distribution properties of $\mathbf{A}$ and noise. Under certain criteria, for $\mathbf{A}$ and noise distribution, there is always a certain optimal $\mathbf{W}$ vector solution denoted by $\mathbf{W}_{\text{opt}}$.

3.2 Optimal Filtering Criteria

Adaptive beam control can adaptively adjust the weight of the array antenna element excitation according to certain criteria and algorithm, so that the quality of the output signal is optimal under the adopted criteria after the array-received signals are weighted and superimposed. There are many criteria for measuring "optimal" such as minimum mean square error (MMSE) criterion, maximum signal to interference and noise ratio (Max-SINR) criterion, maximum likelihood estimation (ML) criterion, and minimum variance (MV) criterion. Different adaptive beam control criteria apply to different signals and reception environments. The optimal solutions can be decomposed into the product of the same linear matrix filter and a different scalar processor, and they all converge to the optimal Wiener solution. Several different criteria described above will be introduced in this section.

3.2.1 *Minimum mean square error criterion*

The minimum mean square error criterion requires the mean square error between the output signal and the reference signal to be minimized. As shown in Fig. 3.3, it is assumed that the desired signal arrives from angle θ_0 and the interference signals arrive from $\theta_1, \ldots, \theta_N$, respectively. They are all received by the M antenna arrays containing M weights and each received signal of array element M also includes additive Gaussian noise.

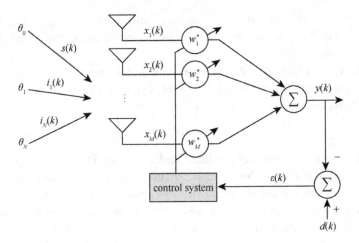

Fig. 3.3.   The mean square error adaptive system.

Time is measured by the kth sample. Therefore, the received signal

$$\mathbf{x}(k) = \mathbf{a}_0 s(k) + \sum_{i=1}^{N} \mathbf{a}(\theta_i) i_i(k) + \mathbf{n}(k)$$

$$= \mathbf{x}_s(k) + \mathbf{x}_i(k) + \mathbf{n}(k) = \mathbf{x}_s(k) + \mathbf{u}(k), \tag{3.6}$$

where $\mathbf{x}_s(k)$ represents the desired signal vector, $\mathbf{u}(k)$ represents the undesired signal vector, $\mathbf{x}_i(k)$ represents the interference signal vector, $\mathbf{n}(k)$ represents the zero-mean Gaussian noise of each channel, and $\mathbf{a}(\theta_i)$ represents the steering vector of antenna array of M array elements in the arrival direction θ_i.

Signal $d(k)$ is a reference signal, which is strongly correlated with the desired signal $s(k)$ while not correlated with the interference signal $i_i(k)$. If $s(k)$ is significantly the same as the interference signal, the minimum mean square error criterion will not work. Denote the error signal as $\varepsilon(k)$ with the expression

$$\varepsilon(k) = d(k) - \mathbf{W}^H \mathbf{x}(k) \tag{3.7}$$

The mean square error refers to the statistical expectation of $\varepsilon(k)$ square. Denote $\mathrm{E}\{\cdot\}$ as the expected operation, and then the expression of the mean square error is

$$\mathrm{E}\{|\varepsilon(k)|^2\} = \mathrm{E}\{|d(k)|^2\} - 2\mathbf{W}^H \mathbf{r}_{xd} + \mathbf{W}^H \mathbf{R}_{xx} \mathbf{W} \tag{3.8}$$

where $\mathbf{r}_{xd} = \mathrm{E}\{d^*(k)\mathbf{x}(k)\}$ and $\mathbf{R}_{xx} = \mathrm{E}\{\mathbf{x}(k)\mathbf{x}^{\mathrm{H}}(k)\}$, which is generally called the covariance matrix of the received signal. In order to obtain the optimal solution under the MMSE criterion to minimize the $\mathbf{W}$ in Eq. (3.8), the derivative of the equation about W only needs to be calculated. Let it equal zero, namely

$$\nabla_W(\mathrm{E}\{|\varepsilon(k)|^2\}) = -2\mathbf{r}_{xd} + 2\mathbf{R}_{xx}\mathbf{W}_{\mathrm{opt(MMSE)}} = 0 \qquad (3.9)$$

Then the optimal Wiener solution under the MMSE criterion can be obtained:

$$\mathbf{W}_{\mathrm{opt(MMSE)}} = \mathbf{R}_{xx}^{-1}\mathbf{r}_{xd} \qquad (3.10)$$

3.2.2 *Maximum signal-to-interference-and-noise ratio criterion*

The maximum signal-to-interference-and-noise ratio criterion requires the ratio of the power of the desired signal and the interference noise signal to be the largest for the output signal corresponding to the optimal weight vector.

For the desired signal, the weighted output power of antenna array is

$$\sigma_s^2 = \mathrm{E}\{|\mathbf{W}^{\mathrm{H}}\mathbf{s}(k)|^2\} = \mathbf{W}^{\mathrm{H}}\mathbf{R}_{ss}\mathbf{W} \qquad (3.11)$$

where $\mathbf{R}_{ss} = \mathrm{E}\{\mathbf{x}(k)\mathbf{x}^{\mathrm{H}}(k)\}$ represents the signal correlation matrix.

For the undesired signal, the weighted output power of the antenna array is

$$\sigma_u^2 = \mathrm{E}\{|\mathbf{W}^{\mathrm{H}}\mathbf{u}(k)|^2\} = \mathbf{W}^{\mathrm{H}}\mathbf{R}_{uu}\mathbf{W} \qquad (3.12)$$

where $\mathbf{R}_{uu} = \mathbf{R}_{ii} + \mathbf{R}_{nn}$ and $\mathbf{R}_{ii}$ represents the correlation matrix of the interference signal and $\mathbf{R}_{nn}$ represents the correlation matrix of noise.

SINR is defined as the ratio of the power of the desired signal and the undesired signal

$$\mathrm{SINR} = \frac{\sigma_s^2}{\sigma_u^2} = \frac{\mathbf{W}^{\mathrm{H}}\mathbf{R}_{ss}\mathbf{W}}{\mathbf{W}^{\mathrm{H}}\mathbf{R}_{uu}\mathbf{W}} \qquad (3.13)$$

By differentiating Eq. (3.13) with respect to $\mathbf{W}$ and equating it to zero, the maximum value of the SINR can be obtained. Harrington gave an overview of this optimization approach, and the following equation was obtained:

$$\mathbf{R}_{ss}\mathbf{W} = \text{SINR}\mathbf{R}_{uu}\mathbf{W} \tag{3.14}$$

or

$$\mathbf{R}_{uu}^{-1}\mathbf{R}_{ss}\mathbf{W} = \text{SINR}\mathbf{W} \tag{3.15}$$

Equation (3.15) is an eigenvector equation with an eigenvalue of SINR. The maximum SINR is equal to the maximum eigenvalue $\lambda_{\max}$ of the Hermitian matrix $\mathbf{R}_{uu}^{-1}\mathbf{R}_{ss}$. The eigenvector corresponding to the maximum eigenvalue is the optimal weight vector $\mathbf{W}_{\text{opt}}$.

Since the correlation matrix is defined as $\mathbf{R}_{ss} = \text{E}\{|\mathbf{s}(k)|^2\}\mathbf{a}_0\mathbf{a}_0^{\text{H}}$, the weight vector can be calculated by the optimal Wiener:

$$\mathbf{W}_{\text{opt(SINR)}} = \beta\mathbf{R}_{uu}^{-1}\mathbf{a}_0 \tag{3.16}$$

where

$$\beta = \frac{\text{E}\{|\mathbf{s}(k)|^2\}}{\lambda_{\max}}\mathbf{a}_0^{\text{H}}\mathbf{W}_{\text{opt(SINR)}} \tag{3.17}$$

3.2.3 *Maximum likelihood criterion*

In reality, there are many cases where no prior knowledge of useful signals is found to be applicable. Maximum likelihood criterion is proposed, which assumes that the desired signal $\mathbf{x}_s$ is unknown and the undesired signal $\mathbf{n}$ is subject to a zero-mean Gaussian distribution to define a likelihood function to estimate the desired signal.

The input signal vector is

$$\mathbf{x} = \mathbf{a}_0 s + \mathbf{n} = \mathbf{x}_s + \mathbf{n} \tag{3.18}$$

It is assumed that the total distribution obeys a Gaussian distribution, while the mean value is affected by the desired signal $\mathbf{x}_s$. The probability density function is described by the joint probability density $p(\mathbf{x}/\mathbf{x}_s)$, which can be considered as a likelihood function to estimate the parameter $\mathbf{x}_s$. The probability density function is expressed as

$$p(\mathbf{x}/\mathbf{x}_s) = \frac{1}{\sqrt{2\pi\sigma_n^2}}e^{-[(\mathbf{x}-\mathbf{a}_0 s)^{\text{H}}R_{nn}^{-1}(\mathbf{x}-\mathbf{a}_0 s)]} \tag{3.19}$$

where σ_n represents the noise standard deviation and $\mathbf{R}_{nn} = \sigma_n^2 I$ represents a noise correlation matrix.

By considering useful parameters in the exponent, it is easier to deal with the negative logarithm of the probability density function. And thus, it is called log-likelihood function. The log-likelihood function is defined as

$$L[\mathbf{x}] = -\ln[p(\mathbf{x}/\mathbf{x}_s)] = C(\mathbf{x} - \mathbf{a}_0 s)^H \mathbf{R}_{nn}^{-1}(\mathbf{x} - \mathbf{a}_0 s) \qquad (3.20)$$

where C is a constant and $\mathbf{R}_{nn} = \mathrm{E}\{\mathbf{n}\mathbf{n}^H\}$.

The estimate value $\hat{s}$ of the desired signal is defined and can be obtained by calculating the maximum value of the log-likelihood function. The maximum value of $L[\mathbf{x}]$ can be obtained by solving the partial derivative with respect to s and making it equal to zero. Thereafter,

$$\frac{\partial L[\mathbf{x}]}{\partial s} = -2\mathbf{a}_0^H \mathbf{R}_{nn}^{-1}\mathbf{x} + 2\hat{s}\mathbf{a}_0^H \mathbf{R}_{nn}^{-1}\mathbf{a}_0 = 0 \qquad (3.21)$$

and $\hat{s}$ can be solved by

$$\hat{s} = \frac{\mathbf{a}_0^H \mathbf{R}_{nn}^{-1}}{\mathbf{a}_0^H \mathbf{R}_{nn}^{-1}\mathbf{a}_0}\mathbf{x} = W_{\text{opt}}^H \mathbf{x} \qquad (3.22)$$

Finally,

$$\mathbf{W}_{\text{opt(ML)}}^H = \frac{\mathbf{a}_0^H \mathbf{R}_{nn}^{-1}}{\mathbf{a}_0^H \mathbf{R}_{nn}^{-1}\mathbf{a}_0} \qquad (3.23)$$

3.2.4 *Minimum variance criterion*

Sometimes there is no knowledge of the useful signal form and direction, such as in the case of radar photography, meteorological radar, and electrocardiogram. In order to better detect the useful signal and eliminate the clutter background, minimum variance criterion[1] is proposed, which assumes that the desired signal and the undesired signal have a zero mean to make the noise variance of the output signal minimum. The physical meaning of the criterion is that the smaller the total output power, the smaller the power of the noise and interference components, under the condition that the output of the useful signal is fixed.

Using the array structure of Fig. 3.4, the weighted antenna array output is

$$y = \mathbf{W}^H\mathbf{x} = \mathbf{W}^H\mathbf{a}_0 s + \mathbf{W}^H\mathbf{u} \qquad (3.24)$$

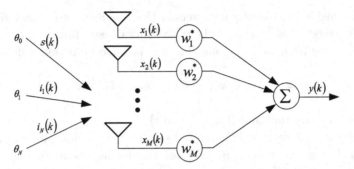

Fig. 3.4.   Single signal antenna array beamforming.

In order to obtain a response without distortion, constraints must also be added:

$$\mathbf{W}^H \mathbf{a}_0 = 1 \tag{3.25}$$

Substituting the constraint in to Eq. (3.24), the antenna array output is given as follows:

$$y = s + \mathbf{W}^H \mathbf{u} \tag{3.26}$$

Besides, if the mean value of the undesired signals is zero, then the desired value of the antenna array output is

$$\mathrm{E}\{y\} = s \tag{3.27}$$

The variance of y is

$$\sigma_y^2 = \mathrm{E}\{|\mathbf{W}^H \mathbf{x}|^2\} = \mathrm{E}\{|s + \mathbf{W}^H \mathbf{x}|^2\} = \mathbf{W}^H \mathbf{R}_{uu} \mathbf{W} \tag{3.28}$$

where $\mathbf{R}_{uu} = \mathbf{R}_{ii} + \mathbf{R}_{nn}$.

The Lagrangian multiplier method[2] is then used to find the minimum value of the variance. Since all antenna array weights are independent of each other, the constraints described by Eq. (3.25) are combined to define a modified performance criterion or cost function, which is a linear combination of variance and constraints:

$$J(\mathbf{W}) = \frac{\sigma_y^2}{2} + \lambda(1 - \mathbf{W}^H \mathbf{a}_0) = \frac{\mathbf{W}^H \mathbf{R}_{uu} \mathbf{W}}{2} + \lambda(1 - \mathbf{W}^H \mathbf{a}_0) \tag{3.29}$$

where λ is the Lagrangian multiplier and $J(\mathbf{W})$ is the cost function.

To find the minimum value of the cost function let Eq. (3.29) be equal to zero. Then we obtain the weight as

$$\mathbf{W}_{\text{opt(MV)}} = \lambda \mathbf{R}_{uu}^{-1} \mathbf{a}_0 \tag{3.30}$$

In order to determine the constant λ, substitute Eq. (3.25) into Eq. (3.30), to get

$$\lambda = \frac{1}{\mathbf{a}_0^{\text{H}} \mathbf{R}_{uu}^{-1} \mathbf{a}_0} \tag{3.31}$$

Finally, the optimal weight of the minimum variance is obtained:

$$\mathbf{W}_{\text{opt(MV)}} = \frac{\mathbf{R}_{uu}^{-1} \mathbf{a}_0}{\mathbf{a}_0^{\text{H}} \mathbf{R}_{uu}^{-1} \mathbf{a}_0} \tag{3.32}$$

Although the above criteria are completely different in principle, they are theoretically equivalent, and the optimal weight vectors obtained can be expressed as Wiener solutions. Adaptive beamforming based on these optimal criteria can yield a good array output performance. In practice, they can be used depending on different known conditions.

3.3 Adaptive Beamforming Algorithm

The best filtering criteria commonly used in beamforming as well as the expression of the optimal solution under various criteria were introduced in Section 3.2.4. In actual wireless communication, especially in the channel environment of mobile communication, channel conditions such as angle of arrival, signal amplitude, and phase change over time; thus, the corresponding optimal weight also changes. The adaptive antenna array continuously adjusts the weights so that it can quickly converge to the current optimal solution and track the changes of the channel, which is called adaptive beamforming. And the algorithm used to adjust the weight is called the adaptive beamforming algorithm. The adaptive beamforming algorithm is the core of the adaptive antenna array system and also the most important factor determining the performance of the system. It is also the focus and key problem of adaptive antenna array research.

First, it needs to know how to measure the performance of an adaptive algorithm. In general, the factors that measure the performance of an algorithm include the following aspects:

(1) **The convergence speed of the algorithm**: It refers to the number of iterations required of the algorithm to converge to the optimal solution in a static environment.

(2) **The tracking performance of the algorithm**: It refers to the ability of the algorithm to adaptively track the channel with the consideration of the change of channel.

(3) **The robustness of the algorithm**: It refers to whether the algorithm works normally when the input is ill, or under what conditions the algorithm can converge.

(4) **The computational complexity of the algorithm**: It is a very practical measurement criterion, which refers to the number of multiply and add operations required by the algorithm. It determines the hardware performance requirements and implementation costs of the algorithm.

There are several classifications of the adaptive beamforming algorithm. Generally, it is classified as non-blind algorithm and blind algorithm according to whether the algorithm requires an explicit training sequence. The non-blind algorithm refers to an algorithm that includes an explicit training sequence that is known at the receiving end in the transmitted signal and uses these training sequences for beamforming. These known training sequences are used to estimate the statistical properties of the signal at the receiving end in real time, thereby calculating the weight vector. It is well known that in many communication systems, some known training sequences are defined to be transmitted at the transmitting end, such as the mid-amble sequence in the GSM system, the preamble sequence in the 802.11a system and the pilot signal sequence in cdma2000. The commonly used non-blinded algorithms are least mean square (LMS), sample matrix inversion (SMI), and recursive least square (RLS). These methods are all based on the minimum mean square error criterion, which means the goal of generating weights is to make Eq. (3.8) tend to a minimum. For the principles of the methods, LMS is based on the steepest descent gradient estimation method, and both SMI and RLS are directly based on the Wiener optimal solution expression of Eq. (3.10). SMI directly deals with a data block, and there is no mutual iteration relationship between the new solution and the old solution. The conjugate gradient method is also a non-blind algorithm with fast convergence speed, which is derived from the minimization of a mean squared error expression. By the gradient search method, an optimal least squares solution is obtained in an iterative form.

A blind algorithm refers to an algorithm that does not need to transmit a training sequence, utilizes some characteristics inherent to the desired signal, or performs beamforming using the results of DOA estimation. The blind algorithm refers to an algorithm that does not need to transmit a training sequence and utilizes some inherent characteristics of the desired signal or the results of DOA estimation to perform beamforming. It does not need prior knowledge of training sequences, noise and interfering signal correlation characteristics, and complex array calibration. The commonly used blind algorithms are the constant modulus algorithm (CMA) and the least squares constant modulus Algorithm (LSCMA).

3.3.1 *Least mean square algorithm*

The least mean square algorithm is an iterative adaptive algorithm based on the steepest descent optimization method and has a wide range of applications in the field of adaptive equalization and adaptive beamforming. According to the gradient search method, the generated weight vector can be approximated to the Wiener optimal solution, and the iterative equation is

$$\mathbf{W}(k+1) = \mathbf{W}(k) + \frac{1}{2}\mu[-\nabla_{\mathbf{W}}(\mathrm{E}\{\varepsilon^2(k)\})]$$

$$= \mathbf{W}(k) + \mu[\mathbf{r}_{xd} - \mathbf{R}_{xx}\mathbf{W}(k)] \qquad (3.33)$$

where μ is a constant and is called a step factor. $\nabla_{\mathbf{W}}$ is the gradient of the performance surface. $\mathbf{r}_{xd}$ and $\mathbf{R}_{xx}$ are both statistics which need to be replaced by estimated values in practical use. The physical significance of the iterative formula is that on the performance surface of $\mathbf{W}$ corresponding to $\mathrm{E}\{\varepsilon^2(k)\}$, a new weight point can be found according to a given step size along the negative gradient direction of the performance surface of a certain weight point. And the search continues from the new weight point until the minimum point of the performance surface is found. (It is assumed that there is only one minimum point on the performance surface).

The principle of the LMS algorithm is to estimate $\mathbf{R}_{xx}$ and $\mathbf{r}_{xd}$ using the instantaneous sample values. At the kth snapshot, the estimated values of $\mathbf{R}_{xx}$ and $\mathbf{r}_{xd}$ are

$$\mathbf{R}_{xx}(k) = \mathbf{x}(k)\mathbf{x}^{\mathrm{H}}(k) \qquad (3.34)$$

$$\hat{\mathbf{r}}_{xd}(k) = d^*(k)\mathbf{x}(k) \qquad (3.35)$$

where $d(k)$ is a known training sequence. By substituting the above two equations into Eq. (3.33), we obtain

$$\begin{aligned}\mathbf{W}(k+1) &= \mathbf{W}(k) + \mu[\mathbf{x}(k)d^*(k) - \mathbf{x}(k)\mathbf{x}^{\mathrm{H}}(k)\mathbf{W}(k)] \\ &= \mathbf{W}(k) + \mu\mathbf{x}(k)[d^*(k) - y^*(k)] \\ &= \mathbf{W}(k) + \mu\mathbf{x}(k)\varepsilon^*(k)\end{aligned} \tag{3.36}$$

This is the iterative formula of the LMS algorithm.

In the LMS algorithm, the value of the step factor μ has a very important impact on the performance of the algorithm, including the stability, the convergence speed, the disturbance, and misadjustment of the algorithm. And in the following, the impact of μ on these three aspects is discussed.

3.3.1.1 *Algorithm stability*

Take the expectation of both sides of Eq. (3.36),

$$\begin{aligned}\mathrm{E}\{\mathbf{W}(k+1)\} &= \mathrm{E}\{\mathbf{W}(k)\} + \mu\mathrm{E}\{\mathbf{x}(k)\varepsilon^*(k)\} \\ &= \mathrm{E}\{\mathbf{W}(k)\} + \mu[\mathrm{E}\{\mathbf{x}(k)d^*(k)\} - \mathrm{E}\{\mathbf{x}(k)\mathbf{x}^{\mathrm{H}}(k)\mathbf{W}(k)\}]\end{aligned} \tag{3.37}$$

It is easy to know from Eq. (3.36) that the weight vector $\mathbf{W}(k)$ is only related to the input of the first $(k{-}1)$ moments. Assuming that the successive inputs are independent, $\mathbf{W}(k)$ and $\mathbf{x}(k)$ are independent of each other. On this basis, Eq. (3.37) can be simplified as

$$\begin{aligned}\mathrm{E}\{\mathbf{W}(k+1)\} &= \mathrm{E}\{\mathbf{W}(k)\} + \mu[\mathbf{r}_{xd} - \mathbf{R}_{xx}\mathrm{E}\{\mathbf{W}(k)\}] \\ &= (\mathbf{I} - \mu\mathbf{R}_{xx})\mathrm{E}\{\mathbf{W}(k)\} + \mu\mathbf{R}_{xx}\mathbf{W}_{\mathrm{opt}}\end{aligned} \tag{3.38}$$

where $\mathbf{W}_{\mathrm{opt}} = \mathbf{R}_{xx}^{-1}\mathbf{r}_{xd}$ is the Wiener filter solution. Defining the difference between the generated weight $\mathbf{W}(k)$ and the optimal weight $\mathbf{W}_{\mathrm{opt}}$ at the kth moment as a weight deviation vector and denoting it as $\mathbf{W}_d(k)$. We thus have

$$\mathbf{W}_d(k) = \mathbf{W}(k) - \mathbf{W}_{\mathrm{opt}} \tag{3.39}$$

Then Eq. (3.38) can be expressed as

$$\mathrm{E}\{\mathbf{W}_d(k+1)\} = (\mathbf{I} - \mu\mathbf{R}_{xx})\mathrm{E}\{\mathbf{W}_d(k)\} \tag{3.40}$$

Let $\mathbf{Q}$ be the orthogonal normalized matrix of $\mathbf{R}_{xx}$ and premultiply by $\mathbf{Q}^{-1}$ on both sides of the above equation. Denoting $\mathbf{W}_d = \mathbf{Q}\mathbf{W}_d'$, we can obtain

$$
\begin{aligned}
\mathrm{E}\{\mathbf{W}_d'(k+1)\} &= \mathbf{Q}^{-1}(\mathbf{I} - \mu\mathbf{R}_{xx})\mathbf{Q}\mathrm{E}\{\mathbf{W}_d'(k)\} \\
&= (\mathbf{I} - \mu\mathbf{Q}^{-1}\mathbf{R}_{xx}\mathbf{Q})\mathrm{E}\{\mathbf{W}_d'(k)\} \\
&= (\mathbf{I} - \mu\boldsymbol{\Lambda})\mathrm{E}\{\mathbf{W}_d'(k)\}
\end{aligned}
\tag{3.41}
$$

where $\boldsymbol{\Lambda}$ is a diagonal matrix composed of eigenvalues of $\mathbf{R}_{xx}$. It can be seen that decoupling between elements of vector $\mathbf{W}_d'$ is achieved, so the vector is called the principal deviation vector. Since $(\mathbf{I} - \mu\boldsymbol{\Lambda})$ is a diagonal array, it is easy to know that

$$
\mathrm{E}\{\mathbf{W}_d'(k)\} = (\mathbf{I} - \mu\boldsymbol{\Lambda})^k \mathrm{E}\{\mathbf{W}_d'(0)\}
\tag{3.42}
$$

If the algorithm is expected to converge to the Wiener optimal solution, then both the weight deviation vector $\mathrm{E}\{\mathbf{W}_d(k)\}$ and $\mathrm{E}\{\mathbf{W}_d'(k)\}$ need to tend to zero with k tending to infinity. From Eq. (3.42), if and only if $(\mathbf{I} - \mu\boldsymbol{\Lambda})^k$ tends to 0, the above requirements can be met, and according to the diagonal property of $(\mathbf{I} - \mu\boldsymbol{\Lambda})$,

$$
|1 - \mu\lambda_i| < 1, \quad i = 1, \ldots, M
\tag{3.43}
$$

then

$$
0 \le \mu \le \frac{2}{\lambda_{\max}}
\tag{3.44}
$$

In other words, in order to make the algorithm converge, the step factor must satisfy Eq. (3.44), where $\lambda_{\max}$ is the largest eigenvalue of $\mathbf{R}_{xx}$. The trace $\mathrm{tr}(\mathbf{R}_{xx})$ of $\mathbf{R}_{xx}$ is defined as the sum of all eigenvalues of $\mathbf{R}_{xx}$, and thus, $\mathrm{tr}(\mathbf{R}_{xx})$ must be not smaller than $\lambda_{\max}$. Therefore, in practical applications, the step factor is often selected to satisfy

$$
0 \le \mu \le \frac{2}{\mathrm{tr}(\mathbf{R}_{xx})}
\tag{3.45}
$$

3.3.1.2 *Algorithm convergence speed*

Regarding the convergence speed of the LMS algorithm, two problems will be discussed. First, what is the relationship between the convergence speed and the step factor μ for a particular signal environment? Second, how do the characteristics of the signal environment affect the convergence speed.

From Eq. (3.42), it can be found that the speed of the weight deviation vector tending to zero is determined by the common ratio matrix $(\mathbf{I} - \mu\mathbf{\Lambda})$. Intuitively, the ith element of $\mathbf{W}'_d$ is denoted as w'_{di}, then

$$w'_{\text{d}i}(k) = (1 - \mu\lambda_i)^k w'_{\text{d}i}(0) \tag{3.46}$$

In other words, the speed of each element in $\mathbf{W}'_d$ converging to zero is controlled by the corresponding common ratio $1 - \mu\lambda_i$. Assume that the signal environment is determined, which means all λ_i are determined. Then, when μ meets the requirements of Eq. (3.44), the larger the value is, the closer $1 - \mu\lambda_i$ is to 0 and the faster the convergence speed of the corresponding algorithm is. From the perspective of convergence speed, the value of μ should be as large as possible.

Next, the influence of the signal environment, namely the characteristics of $\mathbf{R}_{xx}$, on the convergence speed of the algorithm is discussed. It can be known from Eq. (3.46) that the convergence speed of the algorithm is determined by M common ratios $1 - \mu\lambda_i$ ($i = 1, \ldots, \text{M}$). When the distribution range of eigenvalues (the ratio between the maximum eigenvalue and the minimum eigenvalue) is large, the magnitude of the common ratio will also be large, while the convergence speed of the algorithm will become slow. It is a very important conclusion.

3.3.1.3 *Algorithm misadjustment*

From the perspective of convergence speed, the step factor μ should be as large as possible, but a larger value of μ will aggravate the algorithm's misadjustment. The LMS algorithm estimates the gradient using instantaneous sample values. Due to the influence of noise, the estimation error always exists, which will have a direct impact on the algorithm mainly including the algorithm's misadjustment. And the severity of misadjustment is directly related to the value of μ.

The misadjustment is due to the existence of the gradient estimation error, the mean square error is not infinitely close to the minimum value, but exhibits the characteristics of random fluctuation near the minimum value and the weight is also not infinitely close to the optimal value, but exhibits a random fluctuation near the optimal value when the algorithm converges. In the following, the misadjustment is defined mathematically and a qualitative measure of misadjustment performance in the LMS algorithm is given. We define the value of mean square error represented by Eq. (3.8) by considering the optimal weight, which is also called the minimum mean square error and is represented as $\xi_{\min}$. And define the mean square error after the kth iteration of the LMS algorithm as ξ_k and the excess mean square error as exc MSE, then

$$\text{exc MSE} = \mathrm{E}\{\xi_k - \xi_{\min}\} = \mathrm{E}\{\xi_k - \xi_{\min}\} = \mathrm{E}\{\mathbf{W}_d'^{\mathrm{H}}(k)\mathbf{\Lambda}\mathbf{W}_d'(k)\}$$

$$= \sum_{i=1}^{M} \lambda_i \mathrm{E}\{|w_{d,i}'(k)|^2\} \tag{3.47}$$

where $w_{d,i}'(k)$ is the ith element of vector $\mathbf{W}_d'(k) \cdot k$ is assumed to be large enough to make the algorithm converge, and then the misadjustment M_a is defined as $M_a = \text{exc MSE}/\xi_{\min}$, which can be evaluated only by calculating $\mathrm{E}\{|w_{d,i}'(k)|^2\}$. The misadjustment is caused by the gradient estimation noise, and $\hat{\nabla}_k$ is used to represent the gradient estimation in the kth iteration, which can be expressed as

$$\hat{\nabla}_k = \nabla_k + \mathbf{N}_k \tag{3.48}$$

where $\mathbf{N}_k$ expresses the gradient estimation noise. It is not difficult to conclude that with the consideration of gradient estimation noise, the iterative relation of the weight deviation vector is

$$\mathbf{W}_d(k+1) = (\mathbf{I} - \mu\mathbf{R}_{xx})\mathbf{W}_d(k) - \mu\mathbf{N}_k \tag{3.49}$$

Using the relationship $\mathbf{W}_d = \mathbf{Q}\mathbf{W}_d'$ to transform the above equation with respect to the principal axes system, we have

$$\mathbf{W}_d'(k+1) = (\mathbf{I} - \mu\mathbf{\Lambda})\mathbf{W}_d'(k) - \mu\mathbf{N}'_k \tag{3.50}$$

where $\mathbf{N}'_k = \mathbf{Q}^{-1}\mathbf{N}_k$ is called the principal gradient estimation noise. Calculating the covariance for both sides of the above equation and considering that k is large enough for the algorithm to converge, the covariance is independent of the number of iterations k, namely $\text{cov}\{\mathbf{W}_d'(k)\} = \text{cov}\{\mathbf{W}_d'(k+1)\}$:

$$\text{cov}\{\mathbf{W}_d'(k)\} = \frac{\mu}{8}(\mathbf{\Lambda} - \mu\mathbf{\Lambda}^2)^{-1}\text{cov}\{\mathbf{N}'(k)\} \tag{3.51}$$

For the LMS algorithm, ∇_k equals 0 when the algorithm converges, so

$$\mathbf{N}_k = \hat{\nabla}_k = -2\varepsilon^*(k)\mathbf{x}(k) \tag{3.52}$$

Thus,

$$\text{cov}\{\mathbf{N}_k\} = \mathrm{E}\{\mathbf{N}_k\mathbf{N}_k^{\mathrm{H}}\} = 4\mathrm{E}\{|\varepsilon(k)|^2\mathbf{x}(k)\mathbf{x}^{\mathrm{H}}(k)\} \tag{3.53}$$

and as $\nabla_k = -2\mathrm{E}\{\varepsilon^*(k)\mathbf{x}(k)\} = 0$, $|\varepsilon(k)|^2$ and $\mathbf{x}(k)$ are approximately uncorrelated, we have

$$\mathrm{cov}\{\mathbf{N}_k\} \approx 4\mathrm{E}\{|\varepsilon(k)|^2\}\mathrm{E}\{\mathbf{x}(k)\mathbf{x}^{\mathrm{H}}(k)\} \approx 4\xi_{\min}\mathbf{R}_{xx} \tag{3.54}$$

Transforming the above equation to the principal axes system, we have

$$\mathrm{cov}\{\mathbf{N}'_k\} \approx 4\xi_{\min}\mathbf{\Lambda} \tag{3.55}$$

Substituting Eq. (3.55) into Eq. (3.51), we obtain

$$\mathrm{cov}\{\mathbf{W}'_d(k)\} \approx \frac{\mu\xi_{\min}}{2}(\mathbf{\Lambda} - \mu\mathbf{\Lambda}^2)^{-1}\mathbf{\Lambda} \approx \frac{\mu\xi_{\min}}{2}\mathbf{\Lambda}^{-1}\mathbf{\Lambda} = \frac{\mu\xi_{\min}}{2} \tag{3.56}$$

The assumption that the diagonal elements of $\mu\mathbf{\Lambda}$ are generally much smaller than 1 is used in the above derivation. Substituting Eqs. (3.47) and (3.56) into $M_a = \mathrm{exc}\,\mathrm{MSE}/\xi_{\min}$, the misadjustment of the LMS algorithm can be obtained as

$$M_a \approx \frac{\mu}{2}\xi_{\min}\,\mathrm{tr}(\mathbf{R}_{xx}) \tag{3.57}$$

It can be seen from Eq. (3.57) that in order to reduce misadjustment, a smaller step factor needs to be set, but this will result in a lower convergence speed of the algorithm. They are contradictory, and thus, a compromise must be made between these two properties when considering the overall performance of the algorithm.

3.3.2 *Sample matrix inversion*

Sample matrix inversion (SMI) method, also known as direct matrix inversion (DMI),[3] estimates $\mathbf{R}_{xx}$ and $\mathbf{r}_{xd}$ in units of data blocks. The so-called data block divides the received signal vector sequence into a continuous data block in units of several sample lengths. Assuming that the sample length of each data block is N, the received signal sequence corresponding to the first data block is $[\mathbf{x}(0), \mathbf{x}(1), \ldots, \mathbf{x}(N-1)]$ and the sequence corresponding to the $(k+1)$th data block is $[\mathbf{x}(kN+0), \mathbf{x}(kN+1), \ldots, \mathbf{x}(kN+N-1)]$. On this basis, the statistic is estimated for each data block in turn, and the corresponding weight is generated, which is updated once for each data block. For the $(k+1)$th data block, the estimated values of $\mathbf{R}_{xx}$ and $\mathbf{r}_{xd}$ are $\hat{\mathbf{R}}_{xx}(k)$ and $\hat{\mathbf{r}}_{xd}(k)$, and the estimation equation is given as

$$\hat{\mathbf{R}}_{xx}(k) = \frac{1}{N} \sum_{i=0}^{N-1} \mathbf{x}(kN+i)\mathbf{x}^{H}(kN+i) \tag{3.58}$$

$$\hat{\mathbf{r}}_{xd}(k) = \frac{1}{N} \sum_{i=0}^{N-1} \mathbf{x}(kN+i)d(kN+i) \tag{3.59}$$

Replacing the corresponding statistic in Eq. (3.10) by the estimated value, the weight vector generated by the data block is obtained as

$$\mathbf{W}(k) = \hat{\mathbf{R}}_{xx}^{-1}(k)\hat{\mathbf{r}}_{xd}(k) \tag{3.60}$$

It should be noted that $\mathbf{W}(k)$ here is not the weight of the kth sampling moment, but the weight of the kth data block.

In the following, the SMI algorithm is explained from the perspective of the least squares solution of the linear equations. It is known that the goal of beamforming is to approximate the beamformer's output to the desired signal. In the known training sequence, it is necessary to approximate these training sequences. On this basis, the $\mathbf{W}(k)$ thus obtained is set as the solution of the following linear equations:

$$\begin{cases} \mathbf{x}^{H}(kN+0)\mathbf{W}(k) = d^{*}(kN+0) \\ \mathbf{x}^{H}(kN+1)\mathbf{W}(k) = d^{*}(kN+1) \\ \quad\vdots \\ \mathbf{x}^{H}(kN+N-1)\mathbf{W}(k) = d^{*}(kN+N-1) \end{cases} \tag{3.61}$$

Obviously, Eq. (3.60) is the least squares solution of Eq. (3.61), which is the solution to the following problem:

$$\min_{W} \left\{ \frac{1}{N} \sum_{i=0}^{N-1} |\mathbf{W}^{H}(k)x(kN+i) - d(kN+i)|^2 \right\} \tag{3.62}$$

Under time-varying channels, the main point of the SMI algorithm is to choose the appropriate size of the data block. For the case where the channel time-varying rate is slow, the channel has a relatively large time domain correlation for a long time. And in this case, the data block size can be set larger, because the larger the sampling length is, the higher the accuracy of $\hat{\mathbf{R}}_{xx}(k)$ and $\hat{\mathbf{r}}_{xd}(k)$ estimation is. However, for a fast time-varying channel, in order to quickly track the change of the channel, the speed of the weight update must be increased, and thus, the data block size should be set smaller.

There is no doubt that the SMI algorithm based on the least squares method converges much faster than the LMS algorithm based on the steepest descent search method. However, there are two major problems in the SMI algorithm limiting its application. The computational complexity of the algorithm is high, especially for the inverse operation. And although matrix dimensions are generally lower in beamforming applications than equalizer applications, the word length effect will introduce numerical instability to the inverse operation.

3.3.3 *Recursive least squares*

Different from SMI, which makes one-time estimation of statistics in a data block, recursive least-squares (RLS) does not divide the received signal vector sequence into data blocks but uses a data observation interval in the form of a sliding window. The estimation of $\mathbf{R}_{xx}$ and $\mathbf{r}_{xd}$ is updated every time a new sampled signal vector is received. For the kth sampling time, the mathematical expression is given as follows:

$$\hat{\mathbf{R}}_{xx}(k) = \sum_{i=1}^{k} \lambda^{k-i} \mathbf{x}(i)\mathbf{x}^{\mathrm{H}}(i) \tag{3.63}$$

$$\hat{\mathbf{r}}_{xd}(k) = \sum_{i=1}^{k} \lambda^{k-i} d^*(i)\mathbf{x}(i) \tag{3.64}$$

Comparing with the estimation method in SMI, a constant $\lambda(0 \le \lambda \le 1)$ called Forgetting Factor is introduced in the above equation.[4]

The estimation methods of the SMI algorithm and the RLS algorithm are compared in Fig. 3.5. The SMI algorithm independently performs statistical estimation and weight generation on different data blocks, and the weights before and after the update do not have any relationship with the data samples. However, RLS continuously expands the data observation interval to update the statistics and the generated weights. There is a correlation between the statistics and weights before and after the update, by which the operation of directly taking the inverse of the matrix can be replaced by an iterative operation.

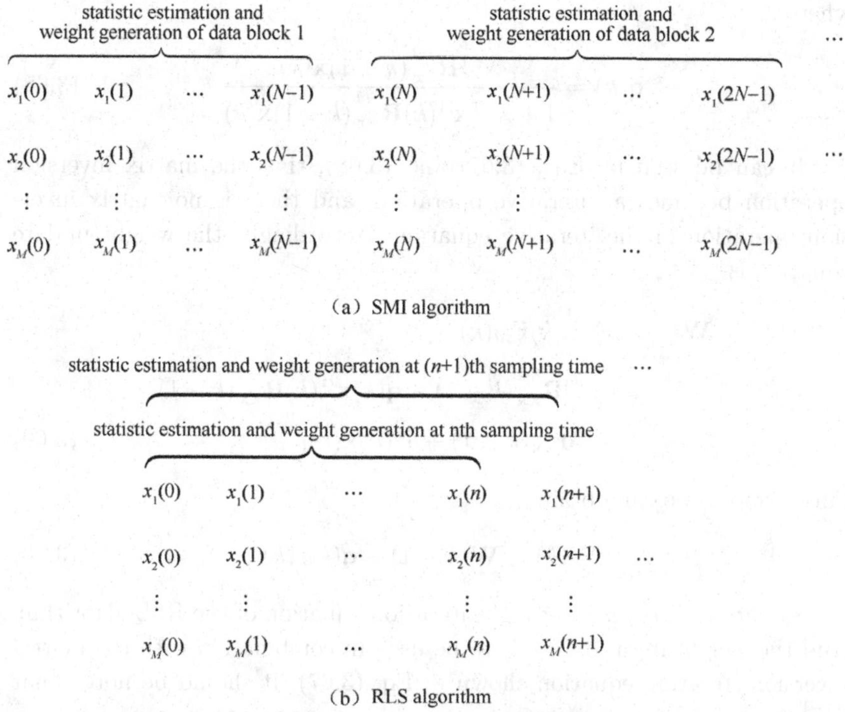

statistic estimation and
weight generation of data block 1

statistic estimation and
weight generation of data block 1

statistic estimation and
weight generation of data block 2   ...

$x_1(0)$	$x_1(1)$	...	$x_1(N-1)$	$x_1(N)$	$x_1(N+1)$	...	$x_1(2N-1)$	
$x_2(0)$	$x_2(1)$	...	$x_2(N-1)$	$x_2(N)$	$x_2(N+1)$	...	$x_2(2N-1)$	...
⋮	⋮		⋮	⋮	⋮		⋮	
$x_M(0)$	$x_M(1)$	...	$x_M(N-1)$	$x_M(N)$	$x_M(N+1)$	...	$x_M(2N-1)$	

(a) SMI algorithm

statistic estimation and weight generation at $(n+1)$th sampling time   ...

statistic estimation and weight generation at nth sampling time

$x_1(0)$	$x_1(1)$	...	$x_1(n)$	$x_1(n+1)$	
$x_2(0)$	$x_2(1)$	...	$x_2(n)$	$x_2(n+1)$	...
⋮	⋮		⋮	⋮	
$x_M(0)$	$x_M(1)$	...	$x_M(n)$	$x_M(n+1)$	

(b) RLS algorithm

Fig. 3.5.   Comparison of statistical estimation methods between SMI and RLS algorithms. (a) SMI algorithm. (b) RLS algorithm.

The sum of Eqs. (3.63) and (3.64) is divided into two terms, namely the sum of the first $i = k - 1$ terms and the last term $i = k$.

$$\hat{\mathbf{R}}_{xx}(k) = \lambda \sum_{i=1}^{k-1} \lambda^{k-1-i} \mathbf{x}(i)\mathbf{x}^H(i) + \mathbf{x}(k)\mathbf{x}^H(k) = \lambda\hat{\mathbf{R}}_{xx}(k-1) + \mathbf{x}(k)\mathbf{x}^H(k)$$

$$(3.65)$$

$$\hat{\mathbf{r}}_{xd}(k) = \lambda \sum_{i=1}^{k-1} \lambda^{k-i-1} d^*(i)\mathbf{x}(i) + d^*(k)\mathbf{x}(k) = \lambda\hat{\mathbf{r}}_{xx}(k-1) + d^*(k)\mathbf{x}(k)$$

$$(3.66)$$

Take the inverse of the two sides of Eq. (3.65) and use the Woodbury identity,[5]

$$\hat{\mathbf{R}}_{xx}^{-1}(k) = \lambda^{-1}[\hat{\mathbf{R}}_{xx}^{-1}(k-1) - \mathbf{q}(k)\mathbf{x}^H(k)\hat{\mathbf{R}}_{xx}^{-1}(k-1)]   (3.67)$$

where

$$\mathbf{q}(k) = \frac{\lambda^{-1}\hat{\mathbf{R}}_{xx}^{-1}(k-1)\mathbf{x}(k)}{1 + \lambda^{-1}\mathbf{x}^{\mathrm{H}}(k)\hat{\mathbf{R}}_{xx}^{-1}(k-1)\mathbf{x}(k)} \qquad (3.68)$$

It can be seen by Eqs. (3.67) and (3.68), that the matrix inversion operation becomes an iterative operation, and there is no matrix inversion operation in the iterative equation. Accordingly, the weight update equation is

$$\begin{aligned}
\mathbf{W}(k) &= \hat{\mathbf{R}}_{xx}^{-1}(k)\hat{\mathbf{r}}_{xd}(k) \\
&= \lambda^{-1}[\hat{\mathbf{R}}_{\mathbf{xx}}^{-1}(k-1) - \mathbf{q}(k)\mathbf{x}^{\mathrm{H}}(k)\hat{\mathbf{R}}_{\mathbf{xx}}^{-1}(k-1)] \\
&\quad \times [\lambda\hat{\mathbf{r}}_{\mathbf{xx}}(k-1) + d^*(k)\mathbf{x}(k)]
\end{aligned} \qquad (3.69)$$

Furthermore, we can obtain

$$\mathbf{W}(k) = \mathbf{W}(k-1) + \mathbf{q}(k)\varepsilon(k) \qquad (3.70)$$

Equation (3.70) is the weight iteration equation of the RLS algorithm. And the weight iteration needs to be used in combination with the matrix inversion iteration equation shown in Eq. (3.67). It should be noted that $\hat{\mathbf{R}}_{xx}^{-1}(k)$ must be initialized to the unit matrix I of $M \times M$ before the iteration begins. Meanwhile, it can be seen that Eq. (3.70) is very similar in form to the LMS algorithm weight iteration Eq. (3.36) with only $\mathbf{q}(k)$ replacing $\mu\mathbf{x}(k)$, where $\mathbf{q}(k)$ is called the filter gain vector. Figure 3.6 shows the signal processing flow of the RLS algorithm.

It is known that the classification method of sampling data in SMI can make the estimation of statistics reflect the current channel characteristics in real time and effectively track the channel changes. In RLS, the statistical calculation starts from 0 time. If the forgetting factor is not introduced,

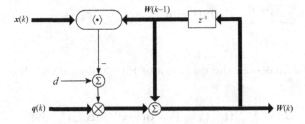

Fig. 3.6. RLS signal processing flow.

the contribution of all sampling data to the current statistic estimation is equal. And under the time-varying channel, it is obviously unreasonable. Because the sampling data are farther from the current time, the channel is less correlated with the current channel time domain. By introducing a value λ between 0 and 1, the contribution of the sampling data farther from the current time to the statistic estimation can be made to be smaller, thereby realizing effective tracking of the time-varying channel. In addition, by adjusting the magnitude of λ, the algorithm can be adapted to different channel time-varying rate environments. For example, when the channel time-varying rate is slow, a larger λ can be selected, and on the contrary, a smaller λ is selected.

Similar to SMI, the RLS algorithm converges much faster than LMS. The simulation results show that the convergence speed is one order of magnitude higher than that of the LMS algorithm when the signal-to-noise ratio is high. And compared with the SMI algorithm, the RLS algorithm has lower computational complexity and better numerical stability because it avoids direct matrix inversion.

3.3.4 *Conjugate gradient algorithm*

The conjugate gradient method (CGM) is similar to the SMI method. It also divides the received signal vector sequence into data blocks and then generates weights in each data block. However, different from the SMI method, the CGM does not directly generate the weights after $\mathbf{R}_{xx}$ and $\mathbf{r}_{xd}$ are estimated in each data block, but iteratively solves the least squares solution in the data block by the steepest descending gradient search iteration equation similar to the LMS algorithm.

First, Eq. (3.61) is modified for the $(k+1)$th data block, and the weight in the data block is defined as $\mathbf{W}_k$. The equation set to be solved is as follows:

$$\begin{cases} \mathbf{x}^{\mathrm{H}}(kN+0)\mathbf{W}_k = d^*(kN+0) \\ \mathbf{x}^{\mathrm{H}}(kN+1)\mathbf{W}_k = d^*(kN+1) \\ \quad\vdots \\ \mathbf{x}^{\mathrm{H}}(kN+N-1)\mathbf{W}_k = d^*(kN+N-1) \end{cases} \tag{3.71}$$

Define $\mathbf{X}_k = [\mathbf{x}(kN), \mathbf{x}(kN+1), \ldots, \mathbf{x}(kN+N-1)]$, $\mathbf{d}_k = [\mathbf{d}(kN), \mathbf{d}(kN+1), \ldots, \mathbf{d}(kN+N-1)]^{\mathrm{T}}$, and the error vector as

$$\mathbf{r}_k = \mathbf{d}_k^* - \mathbf{X}_k^{\mathrm{H}}\mathbf{W}_k \tag{3.72}$$

The goal of the conjugate gradient method is to minimize the error plane $\mathbf{r}_k^H \mathbf{r}_k$, and its solution is obtained by the steepest descent gradient method. First, $\mathbf{W}_k$ is initialized to $\mathbf{W}_k(0)$, and $\mathbf{W}_k(n)$ refers to the nth iteration result of the weight in the $(k+1)$th data block. After the weight is initialized, the following initial error vector is obtained:

$$\mathbf{r}_k(0) = \mathbf{d}_k^* - \mathbf{X}_k^H \mathbf{W}_k(0) \tag{3.73}$$

The initial pointing vector which actually refers to the gradient vector of the error plane $\mathbf{r}_k^H \mathbf{r}_k$ with respect to $\mathbf{W}_k$ is given as

$$\mathbf{g}_k(0) = \mathbf{X}_k \mathbf{r}_k(0) \tag{3.74}$$

Thereafter, the iteration is implemented according to the following equation:

$$\mathbf{W}_k(n+1) = \mathbf{W}_k(n) - \mu(n)\mathbf{g}_k(n) \tag{3.75}$$

where the step size is determined by the following equation:

$$\mu(n) = \frac{\mathbf{r}_k^H(n)\mathbf{X}_k\mathbf{X}_k^H\mathbf{r}_k(n)}{\mathbf{g}_k^H(n)\mathbf{X}_k\mathbf{X}_k^H\mathbf{g}_k(n)} \tag{3.76}$$

The Iterative equations for $\mathbf{r}_k(n)$ and $\mathbf{g}_k(n)$ are given as

$$\mathbf{r}_k(n+1) = \mathbf{r}_k(n) + \mu(n)\mathbf{X}_k^H\mathbf{g}_k(n) \tag{3.77}$$

$$\mathbf{g}_k(n+1) = \mathbf{X}_k\mathbf{r}_k(n+1) - \alpha(n)\mathbf{g}_k(n) \tag{3.78}$$

where

$$\alpha(n) = \frac{\mathbf{r}_k^H(n+1)\mathbf{X}_k\mathbf{X}_k^H\mathbf{r}_k(n+1)}{\mathbf{r}_k^H(n)\mathbf{X}_k\mathbf{X}_k^H\mathbf{r}_k(n)} \tag{3.79}$$

For an array of M-arys, the conjugate gradient method guarantees that the weight converges to the minimum point of the error plane $\mathbf{r}_k^H \mathbf{r}_k$ by at most M iterations. Compared with the LMS algorithm, the conjugate gradient method converges much faster. While compared with the SMI algorithm, the computational complexity of the conjugate gradient method is not necessarily advantageous because the algorithm requires multiple iterations in one data block. Besides, similar to the RLS algorithm, the conjugate gradient method avoids direct matrix inversion; therefore, its numerical stability is better than SMI.

3.3.5 *Constant modulus algorithm*

In 1983, Treichler and Agee *et al.*[6] proposed the constant modulus algorithm. The constant mode indicates that many common communication signals have constant envelope characteristics. In practical applications, after signals with a constant envelope, such as frequency modulation (FM), phase shift keying (PSK) and frequency shift keying (FSK), experience multipath fading, additive interference, or other unfavorable factors, they will produce amplitude disturbance thus destructing the constant modulus characteristic of the signal. Therefore, a "constant modulus criterion" can be defined to restore the constant modulus characteristic of the desired signal at the output of the beamformer. And thus, the following cost function is defined first:

$$J_{p,q}(k) = \mathrm{E}\{||y(k)|^p - \sigma^p|^q\} \qquad (3.80)$$

where $y(k) = \mathbf{W}^{\mathrm{H}}(k)\mathbf{x}(k)$ is the output signal of the beamforming. σ is a constant called constant modulus factor, which does not affect the performance of the algorithm, and its value is set as 1. p and q are positive real numbers and their value is generally set as 1 or 2. Different algorithms can be formed with different p and q, correspondingly recording them as $\mathrm{CMA}_{p,q}$.

Since the cost function of the constant modulus algorithm is nonlinear and cannot be solved directly, only the iterative method can be used to gradually approximate the optimal solution. The stochastic gradient descent constant modulus algorithm (SGD-CMA) is the earliest proposed constant modulus algorithm. It is based on the steepest descent gradient search method to optimize the constant modulus cost function. The iterative equation is given as follows:

$$\mathbf{W}(k+1) = \mathbf{W}(k) - \mu \nabla_{\mathbf{W}} J_{p,q}(k) \qquad (3.81)$$

where μ is the step factor and $\nabla_{\mathbf{W}}$ is the gradient operator. When p and q are determined, it can be seen that

$$\mathbf{W}(k+1) = \mathbf{W}(k) + \mu \mathbf{x}(k)\varepsilon^*(k) \qquad (3.82)$$

where

$$\mathrm{CMA}_{1,1} : \varepsilon(k) = \frac{y(k)}{2|y(k)|} \mathrm{sgn}(1 - |y(k)|) \qquad (3.83)$$

$$\mathrm{CMA}_{2,1} : \varepsilon(k) = y(k)\,\mathrm{sgn}(1 - |y(k)|^2) \qquad (3.84)$$

$$\text{CMA}_{1,2} : \varepsilon(k) = \frac{y(k)}{|y(k)|} - y(k) \tag{3.85}$$

$$\text{CMA}_{2,2} : \varepsilon(k) = 2y(k)\,\text{sgn}(1 - |y(k)|^2) \tag{3.86}$$

$\text{CMA}_{1,2}$ and $\text{CMA}_{2,2}$ are the most commonly used among the above equations. It is well known that the convergence performance of SGD-CMA is highly dependent on the initial value and the step size factor set by the algorithm. In general, the step size needs to be carefully regulated before being used in the algorithm. If the step size is too small, the convergence speed will be too slow, and if the step size is too large, the performance will be easily maladjusted.

Agee[7] proposed a fast convergence algorithm called nonlinear least squares (LS-CMA) algorithm using the nonlinear least squares method. The algorithm does not require a step factor and uses the extended Gaussian method to minimize the constant modulus cost function $\text{CMA}_{1,2}$. The cost function defined by the extended Gaussian method is

$$C(\mathbf{W}) = \sum_{k=1}^{K} |\phi_k(\mathbf{W})|^2 = \|\mathbf{\Phi}(\mathbf{W})\|_2^2 \tag{3.87}$$

where $\phi_k(\mathbf{W})$ represents the error of the kth data sample, $\mathbf{\Phi}(\mathbf{W}) = [\phi_1(\mathbf{W}), \phi_2(\mathbf{W}), \ldots, \phi_K(\mathbf{W})]^{\text{T}}$. K represents the number of data samples in a data block.

By using the Taylor series expansion for the part with a square sum form in Eq. (3.87), we have

$$C(\mathbf{W} + \Delta) = \|\mathbf{\Phi}(\mathbf{W}) + \mathbf{J}^{\text{H}}(\mathbf{W})\Delta\|_2^2 \tag{3.88}$$

where Δ denotes the offset vector when the weight is updated and $\mathbf{J}^{\text{H}}(\mathbf{W})$ is the complex Jacobian matrix of $\mathbf{\Phi}(\mathbf{W})$, which is given as

$$\mathbf{J}^{\text{H}}(\mathbf{W}) = [\nabla\phi_1(\mathbf{W}), \nabla\phi_2(\mathbf{W}), \ldots, \nabla\phi_k(\mathbf{W})] \tag{3.89}$$

Find the gradient for Eq. (3.89), and make it equal to 0. The offset of the smallest square error is

$$\Delta = -[\mathbf{J}(\mathbf{W})\mathbf{J}^{\text{H}}(\mathbf{W})]^{-1}\mathbf{J}(\mathbf{W})\mathbf{\Phi}(\mathbf{W}) \tag{3.90}$$

Adding the offset vector Δ and the weight vector $\mathbf{W}(n)$, the new weight vector that minimizes the cost function can be obtained as follows:

$$\mathbf{W}(n+1) = \mathbf{W}(n) - [\mathbf{J}(\mathbf{W}(n))\mathbf{J}^{\text{H}}(\mathbf{W}(n))]^{-1}\mathbf{J}(\mathbf{W}(n))\mathbf{\Phi}(\mathbf{W}(n)) \tag{3.91}$$

Note that n refers to the number of iterations, and do not confuse it with the sampling moment k.

Applying the above method to optimize the cost function of the constant modulus algorithm $CMA_{1,2}$,

$$C(\mathbf{W}) = \sum_{k=1}^{K} |\phi_k(\mathbf{W})|^2 = \sum_{k=1}^{K} ||y(k)| - 1|^2 = \sum_{k=1}^{K} ||\mathbf{W}^H x(k)| - 1|^2 \quad (3.92)$$

Comparing Eqs. (3.87) and (3.92), it can be known that

$$\phi_k(\mathbf{W}) = |\mathbf{W}^H x(k)| - 1 \quad (3.93)$$

Similar to the above derivation, the weight vector update equation can be obtained as follows:

$$\mathbf{W}(n+1) = \mathbf{W}(n) - [\mathbf{X}\mathbf{X}^H]^{-1}\mathbf{X}(y(n) - \mathbf{r}(n))^*$$
$$= \mathbf{W}(n) - [\mathbf{X}\mathbf{X}^H]^{-1}\mathbf{X}\mathbf{X}^H\mathbf{W}(n) + [\mathbf{X}\mathbf{X}^H]^{-1}\mathbf{X}\mathbf{r}^*(n)$$
$$= [\mathbf{X}\mathbf{X}^H]^{-1}\mathbf{X}\mathbf{r}^*(n) \quad (3.94)$$

where $\mathbf{r}^*(n)$ is the complex limiting output vector and

$$\mathbf{r}^*(n) = \left[\frac{\mathbf{W}^H(n)\mathbf{x}(1)}{|\mathbf{W}^H(n)\mathbf{x}(1)|}, \frac{\mathbf{W}^H(n)\mathbf{x}(2)}{|\mathbf{W}^H(n)\mathbf{x}(2)|}, \ldots, \frac{\mathbf{W}^H(n)\mathbf{x}(K)}{|\mathbf{W}^H(n)\mathbf{x}(K)|} \right]^H \quad (3.95)$$

The least squares constant modulus algorithm is divided into two types, namely static LS-CMA algorithm and dynamic LS-CMA algorithm. The static LS-CMA algorithm means that only one received data matrix X is needed during the whole iteration and the dynamic LS-CMA algorithm generates a new received data matrix X for every iteration. It can be used to generate a new weight vector. The greatest advantage of the least squares constant modulus algorithm is that the convergence speed is fast. Both the dynamic algorithm and the static algorithm can converge quickly, and the convergence speed is not affected by the size of the data block. However, the block size has an impact on weight value after convergence. Especially for static algorithms, under the conditions with too small data, the generated weights have a large fluctuation variance with respect to the Wiener optimal solution.

One of the advantages of the constant modulus algorithm is that there is no high requirement for carrier synchronization and sampling time. Compared to the non-blind algorithm which requires the amplitude phase information of the desired signal, its performance is heavily dependent on the accuracy of carrier synchronization and sampling time. However, the constant modulus algorithm also has several problems, which severely limits the practicability of the algorithm and prompts people to continuously improve the algorithm to solve these problems. The main problems include the following: (1) local minimum point problem. Different from the non-blind algorithm, the constant modulus algorithm cost function shown by Eq. (3.80) is not a pure convex function for $\mathbf{W}$. Therefore, the algorithm cannot guarantee the optimal solution that converges to the minimum point of the corresponding cost function, and it is likely to converge to the weight points corresponding to some local extremum. (2) Strong interference acquisition problems: The constant modulus algorithm only uses the constant modulus characteristic of the signal and does not care about the signal itself. Therefore, when there is a constant modulus interference signal, and the signal power is stronger than the desired signal, the algorithm is likely to converge to the interference signal. The solution is to use a multi-objective constant modulus algorithm to beamform all of the constant modulus signals and then sort out the desired signals from them. (3) Phase ambiguity problem: The constant modulus algorithm only requires the output signal to have constant modulus characteristics, but it does not guarantee the precise phase of the output signal. Although this problem does not affect the final beam pointing and the SINR, it will cause problems for subsequent processing (such as judgment) of the output signal, and thus, measures must be taken to solve it.

3.4 Direction of Arrival Estimation

The direction of arrival (DOA) technology is a signal processing technique that estimates the azimuth of a received signal. For many signal processing problems, the direction of the received signal needs to be estimated. For example, in mobile communications, radar, sonar, electronic surveillance, and seismic research, high-resolution DOA estimation techniques are needed to estimate the orientation of the signal source. The research work of DOA estimation began in the 1960s. Burg's maximum entropy spectrum estimation algorithm and Capon's maximum likelihood algorithm were applied in array signal processing. The array resolution performance has been greatly improved, breaking through the Rayleigh criterion limit and also marking the entering into the modern spectrum research stage. In the late 1970s, the eigen-structure subspace algorithms were proposed. Under the premise that the number of sensors is more than the number of sources, the algorithms propose the concept of dividing the observation space into signal subspace and noise subspace and use the orthogonality of the two subspaces to obtain the DOA. The multiple signal classification algorithm proposed by Schmidt and the rotation invariant method proposed by Roy *et al.*, are two examples. In the late 1980s, Vigerg *et al.*, proposed subspace fitting algorithms, among which the maximum likelihood algorithm and the weighted subspace fitting algorithm are significant. Some classic DOA estimation algorithms will be introduced in this section.

3.4.1 *Traditional spectral estimation method*

The classical spectral estimation algorithm estimates the DOA by calculating the spatial spectrum and then obtaining its local maximum. In 1958, Blackman and Tukey proposed a spectral estimation method (called BT method). The power spectrum estimation can be obtained by performing the same windowing processing on the self-delay data of the observed data, and its performance mainly depends on the selection of the window function. The Barlett method is similar to the BT method, which also processes the time series data, and its power spectrum expression is given as

$$P_B(\theta) = \frac{\mathbf{a}^H(\theta)\mathbf{R}\mathbf{a}(\theta)}{M^2} \tag{3.96}$$

where $\mathbf{a}(\theta)$ represents the direction vector of θ and M is the number of array elements.

Similar to the BT method, the periodogram method also uses the classical Fourier analysis method, so they both are called the linear spectrum estimation method. Theoretically, this algorithm will inevitably lead to a "leakage" phenomenon in frequency. Many scholars focus on choosing a special window function, but there is not much progress. Therefore, this method is only suitable for the case where the main lobe beam is wide, and this promotes the generation of new spectral estimation methods.

3.4.2 *Maximum entropy spectrum estimation*

The "entropy" in information theory comes from the "entropy" in thermodynamics and statistical mechanics, which indicates the degree of uncertainty of information and events. The maximum entropy method

(MEM) was proposed by Burg[8] in 1967. This method does not need to modify the autocorrelation function of the known data but extrapolates the autocorrelation function at the unknown delay point according to the principle of maximum entropy. And this means artificially increasing the number of sample data, so its resolution is much higher than the traditional spectral estimation method.

The spectral entropy of power spectrum $P_{\text{MEM}}(\theta)$ is defined as

$$H(P) = \int_0^{2\pi} \ln P_{\text{MEM}}(\theta)\, d\theta \qquad (3.97)$$

The maximum entropy spectrum method proposed by Burg can be expressed as follows: Find the power spectrum $P_{\text{MEM}}(\theta) > 0$ which makes the spectral entropy $P_{\text{MEM}}(\theta)$ defined by Eq. (3.97) to be largest when suffering the following constraint:

$$\mathbf{R}_{ij} = \int_0^{2\pi} P_{\text{MEM}}(\theta) \cos[2\pi \tau_{ij}(\theta)]\, d\theta \qquad (3.98)$$

where $\mathbf{R}_{ij}$ represents the correlation matrix between the detection values of the ith array element and the jth array element. $\tau_{ij}(\theta)$ represents the differential delay between the array element i and the array element j due to the direction θ. The solution is based on the Lagrangian multiplier method and finally gets

$$P_{\text{MEM}}(\theta) = \frac{1}{\tilde{\mathbf{W}}^{\mathrm{T}} \mathbf{q}(\theta)} \qquad (3.99)$$

where $\tilde{\mathbf{W}}^{\mathrm{T}}$ can be obtained by finding the minimum value of Eq. (3.100) as follows:

$$H(\mathbf{W}) = \int_0^{2\pi} \ln[\tilde{\mathbf{W}}^{\mathrm{T}} \mathbf{q}(\theta)]\, d\theta \qquad (3.100)$$

The constraint is

$$\begin{cases} \tilde{\mathbf{W}}^{\mathrm{T}} \mathbf{r} = 2\pi \\ \tilde{\mathbf{W}}^{\mathrm{T}} \mathbf{q}(\theta) > 0, \quad \forall \theta \end{cases} \qquad (3.101)$$

where $\mathbf{q}(\theta)$ and $\mathbf{r}$ are defined as

$$\mathbf{q}(\theta) = [1, \sqrt{2}\cos(2\pi f \tau_{12}(\theta)), \ldots]^{\mathrm{T}} \qquad (3.102)$$

$$\mathbf{r} = [\mathbf{R}_{11}, \sqrt{2}\mathbf{R}_{12}, \ldots]^{\mathrm{T}} \qquad (3.103)$$

3.4.3 *Multiple signal classification algorithm*

The multiple signal classification (MUSIC) algorithm is a high-resolution DOA estimation subspace algorithm proposed by Schmidt[9] in 1979, which uses the geometric properties of the array for parameter estimation. With the assumption that the signal is a narrowband signal, if N signals are incident on the M array elements of the array antenna, the received signal is

$$\mathbf{x}(t) = \sum_{i=1}^{N} \mathbf{a}(\theta_i) s_i(t) + \mathbf{n}(t) \tag{3.104}$$

Representing it in the matrix form, we have

$$\mathbf{x}(t) = \mathbf{A}\mathbf{s}(t) + \mathbf{n}(t) \tag{3.105}$$

where $\mathbf{s}(t) = [s_1(t), s_2(t), \ldots, s_N(t)]^{\mathrm{T}}$ is the incident signal vector, $\mathbf{n}(t) = [n_1(t), n_2(t), \ldots, n_M(t)]$ is the noise vector, and $\mathbf{a}(\theta_i)$ is the array direction vector corresponding to the ith signal.

The MUSIC algorithm needs to meet the following prerequisites:

(1) $M > N$, and the array direction vectors corresponding to different θ_i are linearly independent.
(2) $\mathrm{E}\{\mathbf{n}\} = 0$, $\mathrm{E}\{\mathbf{n}\mathbf{n}^{\mathrm{H}}\} = \sigma_n^2 \mathbf{I}$, $\mathrm{E}\{\mathbf{n}\mathbf{n}^{\mathrm{T}}\} = 0$, and these assumptions about noise are critical to the MUSIC algorithm.
(3) The matrix $\mathbf{P} = \mathrm{E}\{\mathbf{x}\mathbf{x}^{\mathrm{H}}\}$ is a non-singular positive definite matrix.

It is assumed that the input signal is not correlated with the noise in the MUSIC algorithm, and the autocorrelation matrix of the input signal is

$$\mathbf{R}_{xx} = \mathrm{E}\{\mathbf{x}\mathbf{x}^{\mathrm{H}}\} = \mathbf{A}\mathrm{E}\{\mathbf{s}\mathbf{s}^{\mathrm{H}}\}\mathbf{A}^{\mathrm{H}} + \mathrm{E}\{\mathbf{n}\mathbf{n}^{\mathrm{H}}\} = \mathbf{A}\mathbf{R}_{ss}\mathbf{A}^{\mathrm{H}} + \sigma_n^2 \mathbf{I} \tag{3.106}$$

where $\mathbf{R}_{ss}$ is the signal autocorrelation matrix. Make eigenvalue decomposition on $\mathbf{R}_{ss}$ and obtain M eigenvalues $\{\lambda_1, \lambda_2, \ldots, \lambda_M\}$ that satisfy $|\mathbf{R}_{xx} - \lambda_i \mathbf{I}| = 0$. Use the above equation to decompose and obtain

$$|\mathbf{A}\mathbf{R}_{ss}\mathbf{A}^{\mathrm{H}} + \sigma_n^2 \mathbf{I} - \lambda_i \mathbf{I}| = |\mathbf{A}\mathbf{R}_{ss}\mathbf{A}^{\mathrm{H}} - (\lambda_i - \sigma_n^2)\mathbf{I}| = 0 \tag{3.107}$$

Obviously, $\mathbf{A}\mathbf{R}_{ss}\mathbf{A}^{\mathrm{H}}$ is the eigenvalue of $(\lambda_i - \sigma_n^2)$. If the incident signals are uncorrelated, matrix $\mathbf{A}$ is a full rank matrix and the signal correlation matrix is also a full rank matrix.

Since the matrix $\mathbf{A}$ is a full rank matrix and $\mathbf{R}_{ss}$ is a non-singular matrix, when the number N of incident signals is smaller than the number

M of array antenna elements, the matrix $\mathbf{A}\mathbf{R}_{ss}\mathbf{A}^{\mathrm{H}}$ is semi-positive and its rank is M.

According to the basic knowledge of linear algebra, there are $(M-N)$ zeros among the eigenvalues v_i of the matrix $\mathbf{A}\mathbf{R}_{ss}\mathbf{A}^{\mathrm{H}}$. It can be seen from the above equation that there are $(M-N)$ eigenvalues equal to variance σ_n^2 of the noise.

However, in fact, since the autocorrelation matrix of the signal is estimated using a limited number of sample data, the eigenvalues corresponding to the noise power are not the same but are a set of relatively close values. As the number of samples increases, the variance representing the degree of dispersion decreases and becomes a set of very close values. Once the multiplicity K of the minimum eigenvalue is determined, the estimated number $\hat{N}$ of signals can be determined using the relationship $M = N + K$. So the estimated number of signals is

$$\hat{N} = M - K \tag{3.108}$$

In many DOA estimation algorithms, the number of signals needs to be determined. The eigenvector corresponding to the eigenvalue λ_i is $\mathbf{q}_i$ and satisfies

$$(\mathbf{R}_{xx} - \lambda_i \mathbf{I})\mathbf{q}_i = 0 \tag{3.109}$$

The eigenvectors corresponding to $(M - \hat{N})$ minimum eigenvalues satisfy

$$(\mathbf{R}_{xx} - \sigma_n^2 \mathbf{I})\mathbf{q}_i = \mathbf{A}\mathbf{R}_{ss}\mathbf{A}^{\mathrm{H}}\mathbf{q}_i + \sigma_n^2 \mathbf{I} - \sigma_n^2 \mathbf{I} = 0 \tag{3.110}$$

$$\mathbf{A}\mathbf{R}_{ss}\mathbf{A}^{\mathrm{H}}\mathbf{q}_i = 0 \tag{3.111}$$

Since the matrix $\mathbf{A}$ is a full rank matrix, the matrix $\mathbf{R}_{ss}$ is a non-singular matrix, and

$$\mathbf{A}^{\mathrm{H}}\mathbf{q}_i = 0 \tag{3.112}$$

The above equation can be written as

$$\begin{bmatrix} \mathbf{a}^{\mathrm{H}}(\theta_1)\mathbf{q}_i \\ \mathbf{a}^{\mathrm{H}}(\theta_2)\mathbf{q}_i \\ \vdots \\ \mathbf{a}^{\mathrm{H}}(\theta_N)\mathbf{q}_i \end{bmatrix} = \begin{bmatrix} 0 \\ 0 \\ \vdots \\ 0 \end{bmatrix} \tag{3.113}$$

The above equation shows that the eigenvectors of the $(M - \hat{N})$ minimum eigenvalues are orthogonal to the N directional steering vectors constituting the matrix $\mathbf{A}$, which is the core idea of the MUSIC algorithm.

The idea can be expressed as follows:

$$\{\mathbf{a}(\theta_1), \ldots, \mathbf{a}(\theta_N)\} \perp \{\mathbf{q}_N, \ldots, \mathbf{q}_{M-1}\} \tag{3.114}$$

The MUSIC algorithm is used to search for the array directional steering vectors that are the nearest orthogonal by finding the eigenvectors corresponding to those eigenvalues which are approximately equal to σ_n^2 of $\mathbf{R}_{xx}$. And thus, the directional steering vector related to the received signal is estimated, resulting in a DOA estimate of the signal.

Theoretical analysis shows that the eigenvectors of the covariance matrix belong to one of the two orthogonal subspaces, which are called the main principal eigensubspace and the non-principal eigensubspace. And the DOA can be determined by searching through all possible array directional steering vectors for those vectors that are orthogonal to the space formed by the non-primary eigensubspace.

In order to find the noise subspace, we need to construct a matrix containing the noise eigenvector:

$$\mathbf{S}_n = (\mathbf{q}_N, \mathbf{q}_{N+1}, \ldots, \mathbf{q}_{M-1}) \tag{3.115}$$

Since the directional steering vector corresponding to the signal component and the noise subspace eigenvector are orthogonal to each other, the DOA estimation values of multiple incident signals can be estimated by determining the peaks of the MUSIC spatial spectrum, and the peaks are determined by

$$P_{\text{MUSIC}}(\theta) = \frac{1}{\mathbf{a}^H(\theta)\mathbf{S}_n\mathbf{S}_n^H\mathbf{a}(\theta)} \tag{3.116}$$

or

$$P_{\text{MUSIC}}(\theta) = \frac{\mathbf{a}^H(\theta)\mathbf{a}(\theta)}{\mathbf{a}^H(\theta)\mathbf{S}_n\mathbf{S}_n^H\mathbf{a}(\theta)} \tag{3.117}$$

The orthogonality of $\mathbf{a}(\theta)$ and $\mathbf{S}_n$ makes the denominator reach a minimum, resulting in a peak of the MUSIC spectrum defined by the above equation.

The $\hat{N}$ maximum peaks in the MUSIC spectrum correspond to the DOA of the N signals incident on the array.

Once the DOA θ_i is determined from the MUSIC spectrum, the covariance matrix of the signal can be determined using the following equation:

$$\mathbf{R}_{ss} = (\mathbf{A}^H\mathbf{A})^{-1}\mathbf{A}^H(\mathbf{R}_{xx} - \lambda_{\min}\mathbf{I})\mathbf{A}(\mathbf{A}^H\mathbf{A})^{-1} \qquad (3.118)$$

By the above equation, the power of each input signal and their cross-correlation matrix can be obtained.

The basic steps of the MUSIC algorithm are briefly summarized as follows:

(1) Obtain the sample data $\mathbf{x}_k(k = 1,\ldots,K)$ of the input signal and estimate the covariance matrix of the input signal:

$$\hat{\mathbf{R}}_{xx} = \frac{1}{K}\sum_{k=1}^{K}\mathbf{x}_k\mathbf{x}_k^H \qquad (3.119)$$

(2) Make an eigenvalue decomposition on $\hat{\mathbf{R}}_{xx}$, that is,

$$\hat{\mathbf{R}}_{xx}\mathbf{S} = \mathbf{S}\mathbf{\Lambda} \qquad (3.120)$$

where $\mathbf{\Lambda} = \text{diag}\{\lambda_1,\lambda_2,\ldots,\lambda_M\}$, $\lambda_1 \geq \lambda_2 \geq \ldots \geq \lambda_M$ are the eigenvalues of $\hat{\mathbf{R}}_{xx}$, and $\mathbf{S} = (q_1, q_2,\ldots,q_M)$ is a matrix composed of eigenvectors corresponding to these eigenvalues.

(3) Estimate the number of signals using the multiplicity K of the minimum eigenvalues.

(4) Calculate the MUSIC spectrum.

(5) Find $\hat{N}$ maximum peaks of $\hat{P}_{\text{MUSIC}}(\theta)$ and obtain the estimate value of DOA.

From the above analysis, the MUSIC algorithm has a spectrum peak search process, and this process needs heavy computation. Therefore, various improvements are proposed for the basic MUSIC algorithm to reduce the amount of computation and at the same time improve the resolution and applicable scope of the algorithm. The main improvements are root MUSIC algorithm, constrained MUSIC algorithm, beam space MUSIC algorithm, and so on.

3.4.4 *Estimation of signal parameters via rotational invariance techniques*

The estimation of signal parameters via rotational invariance techniques (ESPRIT) algorithm was proposed by Roy *et al.*[10] in 1989 and is another typical algorithm in spatial spectrum estimation, which means using the rotation invariant subspace to estimate the signal parameters. When estimating the signal parameters, the geometry of the array is required to have the so-called invariance, which can be obtained by two means: one is that the array itself is of two or more identical sub-arrays; the other is that two or more identical sub-arrays are obtained by some transformation. For example, in practical applications, both equally spaced linear array and bilinear array can meet the requirements of the ESPRIT algorithm for arrays.

Consider an array antenna with $2M$ array elements and divide it into two sets with each having M array elements. The corresponding array elements of the two sets have the same translation Δx. For N incident signals, the phase difference between the two sets of array outputs is $\beta \Delta x \sin \theta_i (i = 1, 2, \ldots, N)$. Then the input signals of the two arrays are written in the matrix form as shown below:

$$\mathbf{x}_1(t) = [\mathbf{a}(\theta_1), \ldots, \mathbf{a}(\theta_N)] \begin{bmatrix} s_1(t) \\ s_2(t) \\ \vdots \\ s_M(t) \end{bmatrix} + \mathbf{n}_1(t) = \mathbf{A}\mathbf{s}(t) + \mathbf{n}_1(t) \quad (3.121)$$

$$\mathbf{x}_2(t) = \mathbf{A}\mathbf{\Phi}\mathbf{s}(t) + \mathbf{n}_2(t) \quad (3.122)$$

where $\mathbf{\Phi} = \mathrm{diag}\{e^{j\beta\Delta x \sin \theta_1}, e^{j\beta\Delta x \sin \theta_2}, \ldots, e^{j\beta\Delta x \sin \theta_M}\}$ is an $M \times M$ diagonal unitary matrix, with a phase shift between two pairs of arrays at each angle of arrival. $\mathbf{A}$ is the Vandermonde matrix of the steering vector of the subarray.

Consider all received signals under the action of two subarrays, which can be expressed as

$$\mathbf{x}(t) = \begin{bmatrix} \mathbf{x}_1(t) \\ \mathbf{x}_2(t) \end{bmatrix} = \bar{\mathbf{A}}\mathbf{s}(t) + \mathbf{n}(t) \quad (3.123)$$

where $\bar{\mathbf{A}} = \begin{bmatrix} \mathbf{A} \\ \mathbf{A}\mathbf{\Phi} \end{bmatrix}$, $\mathbf{n}(t) = \begin{bmatrix} \mathbf{n}_1(t) \\ \mathbf{n}_2(t) \end{bmatrix}$

The core idea of the ESPRIT algorithm is to derive the rotation invariance of the basic signal subspace by using the translation invariance of the array elements.

The two relevant subspaces contain the outputs $\mathbf{x}_1$ and $\mathbf{x}_2$ of two subarrays. We sample the output signal to obtain two sets of vectors $\mathbf{V}_1$ and $\mathbf{V}_2$, which form two identical subspaces, respectively.

The signal subspace is obtained from the subcorrelation matrix $\mathbf{R}_{uu} = \bar{\mathbf{A}}\mathbf{R}_{ss}\bar{\mathbf{A}} + \sigma_n^2\mathbf{I}$ of the input signal. If the number of signals is less than or equal to the number of antenna arrays, namely $N \leq 2M$, then $(2M - N)$ minimum eigenvalues of $\mathbf{R}_{uu}$ are equal to σ_n^2. The eigenvector $\mathbf{V}_s$ corresponding to the N largest eigenvalues satisfies

$$\text{Range}\{\mathbf{V}_S\} = \text{Range}\{\bar{\mathbf{A}}\} \tag{3.124}$$

where $\text{Range}\{\cdot\}$ represents the space formed by the vectors of the matrix.

Then there must exist a full rank matrix $\mathbf{T}$ such that $\mathbf{V}_s = \bar{\mathbf{A}}\mathbf{T}$. According to the invariance of the array structure, $\mathbf{V}_s$ can be decomposed into $\mathbf{V}_1 \in C^{M \times N}$ and $\mathbf{V}_2 \in C^{M \times N}$, which satisfy $\mathbf{V}_1 = \mathbf{A}\mathbf{T}$ and $\mathbf{V}_2 = \mathbf{A}\mathbf{\Phi}\mathbf{T}$.

Since $\mathbf{V}_1$ and $\mathbf{V}_2$ share a column space, the rank of $\mathbf{V}_{12} = [\mathbf{V}_1|\mathbf{V}_2]$ is N, and then

$$\text{Range}\{\mathbf{V}_1\} = \text{Range}\{\mathbf{V}_2\} = \text{Range}\{\mathbf{A}\} \tag{3.125}$$

According to the basic knowledge of the matrix, there must exist a unique matrix $\mathbf{F} \in \mathbf{C}^{2N \times N}$ with rank N, satisfying

$$0 = [\mathbf{V}_1|\mathbf{V}_2]\mathbf{F} = \mathbf{V}_1\mathbf{F}_1 + \mathbf{V}_2\mathbf{F}_2 = \mathbf{A}\mathbf{T}\mathbf{F}_1 + \mathbf{A}\mathbf{\Phi}\mathbf{T}F_2 \tag{3.126}$$

$\mathbf{F}$ forms the zero space of $\mathbf{V}_{12}$. Defining $\mathbf{\Psi} = -\mathbf{F}_1\mathbf{F}_2^{-1}$ the above equation can be rewritten as

$$\mathbf{A}\mathbf{T}\mathbf{\Psi} = \mathbf{A}\mathbf{\Phi}\mathbf{T} \tag{3.127}$$

$$\mathbf{A}\mathbf{T}\mathbf{\Psi}\mathbf{T}^{-1} = \mathbf{A}\mathbf{\Phi} \tag{3.128}$$

Obviously, the eigenvalue of $\mathbf{\Psi}$ must be equal to the diagonal element of the diagonal matrix $\mathbf{\Phi}$, namely $\lambda_1 = e^{j\beta\Delta x \sin\theta_1}$, $\lambda_2 = e^{j\beta\Delta x \sin\theta_2}, \ldots, \lambda_N = e^{j\beta\Delta x \sin\theta_N}$. And the column of $\mathbf{T}$ must be the eigenvector of $\mathbf{\Psi}$, which is the core idea of the ESPRIT algorithm. $\mathbf{\Psi}$ is a rotation operator, which rotates the signal subspace $\mathbf{V}_1$ into the signal subspace $\mathbf{V}_2$. Its eigenvalues are a series of nonlinear functions from which the DOA estimate of the signal can be obtained.

The basic steps of the above algorithm are summarized as follows:

(1) Obtain the estimated value $\hat{\mathbf{R}}_{uu}$ of the correlation matrix $\mathbf{R}_{uu}$ from the input signal.
(2) Make eigenvalue decomposition on $\hat{\mathbf{R}}_{uu}$, that is,

$$\hat{\mathbf{R}}_{uu} = \mathbf{V}\mathbf{\Lambda}\mathbf{V}^H \tag{3.129}$$

where $\mathbf{\Lambda} = \text{diag}\{\lambda_1, \lambda_2, \ldots, \lambda_M\}$ is the eigenvalue matrix and $\mathbf{V} = (\mathbf{q}_1, \mathbf{q}_2, \ldots, \mathbf{q}_M)$ is the eigenvector matrix.
(3) Estimate the number of signals using the number of minimum eigenvalues $\hat{N} = M - K$.
(4) Obtain the estimate $\hat{\mathbf{V}}_s$ of the signal subspace and decompose it into

$$\hat{\mathbf{V}}_s = \begin{pmatrix} \hat{\mathbf{V}}_1 \\ \hat{\mathbf{V}}_2 \end{pmatrix} \tag{3.130}$$

(5) Calculate eigenvalue decomposition $(\lambda_1 > \lambda_2 > \cdots > \lambda_{2\hat{N}})$ as follows:

$$\hat{\mathbf{V}}_{12}^H \hat{\mathbf{V}}_{12} = \begin{pmatrix} \hat{\mathbf{V}}_1^H \\ \hat{\mathbf{V}}_2^H \end{pmatrix} (\hat{\mathbf{V}}_1 \hat{\mathbf{V}}_2) = \mathbf{V}\mathbf{\Lambda}\mathbf{V}^H \tag{3.131}$$

Divide $\mathbf{V}$ into $\hat{N} \times \hat{N}$ subarrays.

$$\mathbf{V} = \begin{pmatrix} \mathbf{V}_{11} & \mathbf{V}_{12} \\ \mathbf{V}_{21} & \mathbf{V}_{22} \end{pmatrix} \tag{3.132}$$

(6) Calculate the eigenvalues $\lambda_1, \lambda_2, \ldots, \lambda_N$ of $\Psi = -\mathbf{V}_{12}\mathbf{V}_{22}^{-1}$.
(7) Estimate the DOA which is done as follows:

$$\hat{\theta}_i = \arcsin\left[\frac{\arg(\lambda_i)}{\beta\Delta x}\right], \quad i = 1, 2, \ldots, N \tag{3.133}$$

As can be seen from the above steps, the ESPRIT algorithm avoids many spectrum peak search processes required by many DOA estimation methods and directly estimates the DOA using the eigenvalues.

3.4.5 *Maximum likelihood algorithm*

The Bayesian estimation method is a classical method based on statistical theory and is suitable for the problem of parameter estimation. The maximum likelihood algorithm is a special case of the Bayesian estimation method, which is the Bayesian optimal estimation under the condition of known white noise. In spatial spectrum estimation, according to the model of the incident signal, the maximum likelihood algorithm is basically divided into two categories: deterministic maximum likelihood (DML) and random maximum likelihood (SML). The maximum likelihood algorithm derived when the incident signal obeys the Gaussian random distribution model is called the SML algorithm, whereas when the signal model is unknown, the maximum likelihood algorithm derived from the determined model is called the DML algorithm.

In order to derive the estimated value of the ML, the received signal of the antenna array is represented by a matrix as

$$\mathbf{X}(t) = \mathbf{A}(\theta)\mathbf{s}(t) + \mathbf{N}(t) \tag{3.134}$$

where $\mathbf{X} = [\mathbf{x}(1), \mathbf{x}(2), \ldots, \mathbf{x}(M)]$ is the $L \times M$-dimensional input data vector matrix, $\mathbf{A}(\theta) = [\mathbf{a}(\theta_1), \mathbf{a}(\theta_2), \ldots, \mathbf{a}(\theta_N)]$ is the $L \times N$-dimensional spatial eigenmatrix containing information about these target directions, and $\mathbf{N} = [n(1), n(2), \ldots, n(M)]$ is the $L \times N$-dimensional noise matrix. L represents the number of sampling points, M is the number of antenna array elements, and N is the number of incident signals.

For the above mathematical model, make the following assumptions: The number of signals is smaller than the number of array elements in the array, and the number of snapshots is bigger than the number of array elements; the noise covariance matrix between different snapshots is a zero matrix, and the noise received by each array element is overall distribution, and the noise power is σ^2; the signal covariance matrix $\mathbf{R}_s$ is positive definite (non-singular).

According to the above assumptions, the model is unknown for DML. Therefore, the first-order and second-order matrices of the observed data satisfy the following conditions:

$$\begin{cases} E\{\mathbf{x}(t_i)\} = \mathbf{A}(\theta)\mathbf{s}(t_i) \\ E\{[\mathbf{x}(t_i) - \bar{\mathbf{x}}(t_i)][\mathbf{x}(t_j) - \bar{\mathbf{x}}(t_j)]^{\mathrm{H}}\} = \sigma_n^2 \mathbf{I}\delta_{ij} \\ E\{[\mathbf{x}(t_i) - \bar{\mathbf{x}}(t_i)][\mathbf{x}(t_j) - \bar{\mathbf{x}}(t_j)]^{\mathrm{T}}\} = \mathbf{0} \end{cases} \tag{3.135}$$

According to Eq. (3.135), the joint probability density function of DML can be obtained. (The mean is the first equation, and the variance is the Gaussian distribution of the second equation.) Obviously, there is an observed vector L-time snapshot joint (conditional) probability density function (PDF):

$$f_{\text{DML}}\{X\} = \prod_{i=1}^{L} \frac{1}{\det(\pi\sigma_n^2\mathbf{I})} \exp\left(-\frac{1}{\sigma_n^2}|\mathbf{x}_i - \mathbf{A}\mathbf{s}_i|^2\right) \tag{3.136}$$

where $\det(\cdot)$ is the determinant of the matrix.

For SML, since its signal model is Gaussian random distribution, the observed data are zero mean, and the first- and second-order matrices satisfy the following equations:

$$\begin{cases} E\{\mathbf{x}(t_i)\} = \mathbf{0} \\ E\{\mathbf{x}(t_i)\mathbf{x}(t_j)^{\text{H}}\} = (\mathbf{A}(\theta)\mathbf{R}_{ss}\mathbf{A}^{\text{H}}(\theta) + \sigma_n^2\mathbf{I})\delta_{ij} \\ E\{\mathbf{x}(t_i)\mathbf{x}(t_j)^{\text{T}}\} = \mathbf{0} \end{cases} \tag{3.137}$$

Then the likelihood function of single observed data is

$$f_i(\mathbf{x}) = \frac{1}{\pi^M \det(\mathbf{R}_{xx})} \exp(\mathbf{x}_i^{\text{H}}\mathbf{R}_{xx}^{-1}\mathbf{x}_i) \tag{3.138}$$

L-time snapshot joint (conditional) probability density function is

$$f_{\text{SML}}\{\mathbf{X}\} = \prod_{i=1}^{L} \frac{1}{\pi^M \det(\mathbf{R}_x)} \exp(\mathbf{x}_i^{\text{H}}\mathbf{R}_{xx}^{-1}\mathbf{x}_i) \tag{3.139}$$

Taking negative logarithms on both sides of Eqs. (3.136) and (3.139),

$$-\ln f_{\text{DML}} = L\ln\pi + ML\ln\sigma_n^2 + \frac{1}{\sigma_n^2}\sum_{i=1}^{L}|\mathbf{x}_i - \mathbf{A}\mathbf{s}_i|^2 \tag{3.140}$$

$$-\ln f_{\text{SML}} = L[M\ln\pi + \ln(\det(\mathbf{R}_{xx})) + \text{tr}(\mathbf{R}_{xx}^{-1}\mathbf{R}_{xx})] \tag{3.141}$$

In order to obtain the maximum likelihood estimate of the parameter, the maximum value of the log-likelihood function in the parameter space should be obtained.

For DML, f in Eq. (3.140) is a function of the unknown parameters θ, σ_n^2, and $\mathbf{s}$. Therefore, the maximum likelihood estimation is to find a set of parameters that minimize the criterion of Eqs. (3.136) and (3.139).

The deterministic maximum likelihood estimation of unknown parameters σ_n^2 and $\mathbf{s}$ can be obtained from Eq. (3.140) as follows:

$$\begin{cases} \hat{\sigma}_{n,\,\mathrm{DML}}^2 = \dfrac{1}{M}\,\mathrm{tr}(P_{\mathbf{A}}^{\perp}\hat{\mathbf{R}}_{xx}) \\ \hat{\mathbf{s}}_{DML} = \mathbf{A}^{+}\mathbf{x} \end{cases} \tag{3.142}$$

The random maximum likelihood estimation of unknown parameters σ^2 and $\mathbf{R}_s$ can be obtained from Eq. (3.141) as follows:

$$\begin{cases} \hat{\sigma}_{n,\,\mathrm{SML}}^2 = \dfrac{1}{M-N}\,\mathrm{tr}(P_{\mathbf{A}}^{\perp}\hat{\mathbf{R}}_{xx}) \\ \hat{\mathbf{R}}_{ss,\mathrm{SML}} = \mathbf{A}^{+}(\hat{\mathbf{R}}_{xx} - \hat{\sigma}_{n,\,\mathrm{SML}}^2\mathbf{I})(\mathbf{A}^{+})^{\mathrm{H}} \end{cases} \tag{3.143}$$

The criterion of deterministic maximum likelihood (ignoring the constant term) is given by substituting Eq. (3.142) into Eq. (3.140), which means Eq. (3.140) is simplified to the estimate of the variable θ, that is,

$$\theta_{\mathrm{DML}} = \min[\mathrm{tr}(P_{\mathbf{A}}^{\perp}\hat{\mathbf{R}}_{xx})] = \max[\mathrm{tr}(P_{\mathbf{A}}\hat{\mathbf{R}}_{xx})] \tag{3.144}$$

where $\mathrm{tr}(\cdot)$ represents the trace which can be obtained by summing the diagonal elements of the matrix.

Similarly, the criterion of random maximum likelihood (ignoring the constant term) can be obtained by substituting Eq. (3.143) into Eq. (3.141), that is,

$$\theta_{\mathrm{SML}} = \min \ln[\det(\mathbf{A}\hat{\mathbf{R}}_{ss}\mathbf{A}^{\mathrm{H}} + \hat{\sigma}_{n,\,\mathrm{SML}}^2\mathbf{I})] = \min \ln[\hat{\sigma}_{n,\,\mathrm{SML}}^{2(M-N)}\det(\mathbf{A}^{+}\hat{\mathbf{R}}_{xx}\mathbf{A})] \tag{3.145}$$

3.4.6 *Subspace fitting algorithm*

There are numerous similarities between the weighted subspace fitting algorithm and the maximum likelihood algorithm. The maximum likelihood algorithm is equivalent to the fitting between the data (received data and actual signal data), and the weighted subspace fitting is equivalent to the fitting between the subspaces (the subspace of the received data and the subspace of the actual signal steering vector). Both the algorithms need to be solved through multidimensional search, so many of the solving processes used to implement the ML algorithm can be directly applied to the weighted subspace fitting algorithm. The subspace fitting problem consists of two parts: the fitting of the signal subspace and the fitting of the noise subspace.

3.4.6.1 *Signal subspace fitting*

The spatial domain formed by the signal subspace is the same space as the space formed by the array manifold, which means the signal subspace is a linear subspace of the array manifold, and only when the number of estimated signals is equal to the number of actual signals,

$$\text{Range}\{\mathbf{V}_S\} = \text{Range}\{\mathbf{A}(\theta)\} \qquad (3.146)$$

At the moment, there is a full rank matrix $\mathbf{T}$, so that

$$\mathbf{V}_S = \mathbf{A}(\theta)\mathbf{T} \qquad (3.147)$$

In addition, it can be known from the mathematical model in an ideal situation that

$$\mathbf{R}_{xx} = \mathbf{A}\mathbf{R}_{ss}\mathbf{A}^{\mathrm{H}} + \sigma_n^2\mathbf{I} = \mathbf{V}_S\lambda_S\mathbf{V}_S^{\mathrm{H}} + \sigma_n^2\mathbf{V}_n\mathbf{V}_n^{\mathrm{H}} \qquad (3.148)$$

According to the relationship between the noise subspace and the signal subspace, it can be obtained that

$$\mathbf{A}\mathbf{R}_{ss}\mathbf{A}^{\mathrm{H}} + \sigma_n^2\mathbf{I} = \mathbf{V}_S\lambda_S\mathbf{V}_S^{\mathrm{H}} + \sigma_n^2(\mathbf{I} - \mathbf{V}_S\mathbf{V}_S^{\mathrm{H}}) \qquad (3.149)$$

Namely, $\mathbf{A}\mathbf{R}_{ss}\mathbf{A}^{\mathrm{H}} + \sigma_n^2\mathbf{V}_S\mathbf{V}_S^{\mathrm{H}} = \mathbf{V}_S\lambda_S\mathbf{V}_S^{\mathrm{H}}$ and since $\mathbf{V}_S = \mathbf{A}(\theta)\mathbf{T}$ and $\mathbf{V}_S\mathbf{V}_S^{\mathrm{H}} = \mathbf{I}$, the ideal $\mathbf{T}$ can be obtained as follows:

$$\mathbf{T} = \mathbf{R}_{ss}\mathbf{A}^{\mathrm{H}}\mathbf{V}_S(\lambda_S - \sigma_n^2\mathbf{I})^{-1} \qquad (3.150)$$

When there is noise, the signal subspace is not equal to the space formed by the array manifold, so the above equation is not necessarily true. In order to solve this problem, we can find a matrix $\mathbf{T}$ that makes Eq. (3.147) hold by constructing a fitting relationship and also make the two fit best from the perspective of the least squares:

$$\theta, \hat{\mathbf{T}} = \min \|\mathbf{V}_S - \mathbf{A}\hat{\mathbf{T}}\|_F^2 \qquad (3.151)$$

The parameter we most care about in Eq. (3.151) is θ, and $\hat{\mathbf{T}}$ is just an auxiliary parameter. Therefore, for Eq. (3.151), the least squares solution of $\hat{\mathbf{T}}$ can be obtained when $\mathbf{A}$ is determined:

$$\hat{\mathbf{T}} = (\mathbf{A}^H\mathbf{A})^{-1}\mathbf{A}^H\mathbf{V}_S = \mathbf{A}^+\mathbf{V}_S \tag{3.152}$$

Substituting Eq. (3.152) into Eq. (3.151), we get

$$\theta = \min \|\mathbf{V}_S - \mathbf{A}\mathbf{A}^+\mathbf{V}_S\|_F^2$$
$$= \min \operatorname{tr}\{\mathbf{P}_\mathbf{A}^\perp\mathbf{V}_S\mathbf{V}_S^H\} = \max \operatorname{tr}\{\mathbf{P}_\mathbf{A}\mathbf{V}_S\mathbf{V}_S^H\} \tag{3.153}$$

Obviously, the optimization problem formed by Eq. (3.152) is the solution of the signal subspace fitting problem, namely the so-called signal subspace fitting DOA algorithm. A more general form of the weighted subspace fitting problem can be obtained by further generalization of Eq. (3.151) as follows:

$$\theta, \hat{\mathbf{T}} = \min \|\mathbf{V}_S\mathbf{W}^{1/2} - \mathbf{A}\hat{\mathbf{T}}\|_F^2 \tag{3.154}$$

Therefore, the solution for θ is given as

$$\theta = \min \operatorname{tr}\{\mathbf{P}_A^\perp\mathbf{V}_S\mathbf{W}\mathbf{V}_S^H\} = \max \operatorname{tr}\{\mathbf{P}_\mathbf{A}\mathbf{V}_S\mathbf{W}\mathbf{V}_S^H\} \tag{3.155}$$

3.4.6.2 *Noise subspace fitting*

For the noise subspace, the following relationship exists between the noise subspace of the signal and the array manifold:

$$\mathbf{U}_N^H\mathbf{A}(\theta) = 0 \tag{3.156}$$

By Eq. (3.156), the following fitting relationship can be obtained:

$$\theta = \min \operatorname{tr}\|\mathbf{U}_N^H\mathbf{A}(\theta)\|_F^2 = \min \operatorname{tr}\{\mathbf{U}_N^H\mathbf{A}(\theta)\mathbf{A}^H(\theta)\mathbf{U}_N\} \tag{3.157}$$

Similarly, the noise subspace fitting of Eq. (3.156) can be further extended to a weighted form, which means the following relationship exists between the noise subspace of the signal and the array manifold:

$$\mathbf{U}_N^H\mathbf{A}(\theta)\mathbf{W}^{1/2} = 0 \tag{3.158}$$

and then the noise subspace fitting formula shown in Eq. (3.157) should be rewritten as

$$\theta = \min \operatorname{tr}\|\{\mathbf{U}_N^H\mathbf{A}(\theta)\mathbf{W}^{1/2}\}\|_F^2 = \min \operatorname{tr}\{\mathbf{U}_N^H\mathbf{A}(\theta)\mathbf{W}\mathbf{A}^H(\theta)\mathbf{U}_N\}$$
$$= \min \operatorname{tr}\{\mathbf{W}\mathbf{A}^H(\theta)\mathbf{U}_N\mathbf{U}_N^H\mathbf{A}(\theta)\} \tag{3.159}$$

3.5 Adaptive Antenna Array Calibration

In an actual array system, it is very likely that the array response vector will not conform to the actual value alone according to the shape of the array. Only the antenna array and the RF circuit meet the ideal conditions, including the fact that the antenna elements are the same, the spatial arrangement is also strictly in accordance with the setting, and the RF circuits are also completely identical. In other words, only the respective array channels are completely identical, and the actual array response vector is equal to the response vector value determined according to the shape of the array. Various errors in actual implementation, such as manufacturing tolerances, assembly tolerances, circuit aging, and environmental factors such as temperature, make it impossible to achieve the above ideal conditions. This is called channel mismatch, or channel inconsistency. This mismatch includes both the mismatch of the RF circuits of each channel and the mismatch of the antenna elements of each channel.

The corresponding mathematical expressions are given below. The ideal response vector of the array is defined as $\mathbf{a}(\theta) = [1, e^{-j\varphi_2(\theta)}, \ldots, e^{-j\varphi_M(\theta)}]^T$ and the actual mismatch array response vector is $\mathbf{a}'(\theta)$. The relationship between them is given as follows:

$$\mathbf{a}'(\theta) = \text{diag}\{(\sigma_1, \sigma_2, \ldots, \sigma_M)\}\mathbf{a}(\theta) = \mathbf{\Gamma}\mathbf{a}(\theta) \qquad (3.160)$$

where $\mathbf{\Gamma} = \text{diag}\{(\sigma_1, \sigma_2, \ldots, \sigma_M)\}$, with σ_i indicating a plural number representing the amplitude and phase deviation due to mismatch in the ith array channel.

In many cases, the array mismatch affects the performance of the array. Therefore, an algorithm is needed to estimate the mismatch value σ_i of each channel and compensate it to eliminate the impact of channel mismatch. This process is called array calibration, or array channel calibration, and the corresponding algorithm is known as the channel calibration algorithm.

Before discussing the calibration algorithm, it is necessary to discuss under what circumstances the array needs to be calibrated In fact, in adaptive array antenna applications, array calibration is not always required. Generally, for an algorithm or application, according to the assumption that the actual array response vector is equal to the ideal response $\mathbf{a}(\theta) = [1, e^{-j\varphi_2(\theta)}, \ldots, e^{-j\varphi_M(\theta)}]^T$, the calibration is necessary. For example, if the MVDR beamformer is applied to the case where the desired signal DOA is known, then the desired signal channel response in the expression of the optimal solution is assumed to be ideal. Therefore, the channel mismatch must be estimated and compensated; otherwise, the beamforming output quality will be affected. Another situation where calibration is required is an adaptive beamforming algorithm which applies to beam space. In the beam space method, a spatial linear transform is used to convert the array element spatial signal into the beam space. For example, using DFT transformation, the effect is to form a number of orthogonal fixed beams, and then if the channel has a mismatch, the result of the transformation will be inconsistent with the expected one. Not only will the orthogonality of these fixed beams not be guaranteed but the beam shape will also be severely deformed. Meanwhile, applications such as array pattern synthesis and DOA estimation have a more direct relationship with the value of the array response, so array calibration must also be performed. The calibration algorithms can be divided into three categories: radio feed reference signal method, signal injection method, and blind signal calibration method.

3.5.1 *Radio feed reference signal method*

Since the RF channel contains both uplink and downlink, the corresponding channel calibration needs to be performed separately. The principle of using the radio feed reference signal method in the uplink (receiving antenna array) is shown in Fig. 3.7. The basic principle of the method is to transmit a known reference sequence from a known incident direction, and the amplitude and phase mismatch of each channel is calibrated in real time using the replica and array of the reference sequence for the complex correlation signal between the received sequences of signals. $s(n)$ denotes the sequence of the reference signal, and $.\theta$ denotes the direction of the incoming wave of the signal, and thus, the complex baseband received signal vector sequence expression of the array is given as as follows:

$$\begin{aligned} \mathbf{x}(n) &= a'(\theta)\mathbf{B}s(n) + \mathbf{n}(n) \\ &= \mathbf{\Gamma}\mathrm{diag}\{(b_1, b_2, \ldots, b_M)\}\mathbf{a}(\theta)s(n) + \mathbf{n}(n) \end{aligned} \qquad (3.161)$$

where $\mathbf{a}(\theta)s(n)$ is the complex baseband received signal free from the influence of mismatch, $\mathbf{\Gamma} = \mathrm{diag}\{\sigma_1, \sigma_2, \ldots, \sigma_M\}$, and σ_i $(i = 1, \ldots, M)$ represents the complex mismatch value that needs to be calibrated in each channel. $\mathbf{n}(n)$ is the additive white Gaussian noise vector on the array. A diagonal weighting matrix $\mathbf{B} = \mathrm{diag}\{(b_1, b_2, \ldots, b_M)\}$ is introduced in Eq. (3.161) of the signal model. As mentioned above, the calibration often needs to be performed online, which means during the calibration process,

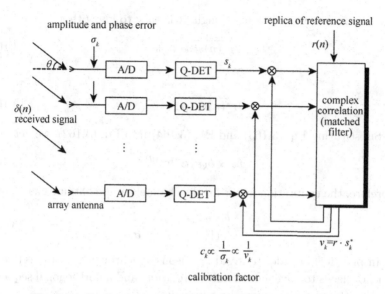

Fig. 3.7. Radio feed reference signal calibration (uplink).

the entire communication system is still operating normally and the array will still receive user signals from different directions. Therefore, measures must be taken to suppress these signals so that the received signal for calibration mainly contains the signal in the direction of the reference signal. For this purpose, it is necessary to construct lower sidelobes in directions other than the direction, and **B** plays such a role with the elements of real numbers.

In order to estimate the mismatch error σ_k in the kth channel, the correlation operation is performed on the received signal $x_k(n)$ of the channel and the replica of the reference signal $r(n)$. The correlation operation is performed by a sliding correlator, which is also called a matched filter. The reason why the sliding correlation is performed is because two sequences of the reference signal replica of the received signal are not synchronized. By moving correlation to observe the correlator output, when the peak occurs, the two sequences are considered to be synchronized, and the complex correlation outputs of $x_k(n)$ and $r(n)$ are denoted as follows:

$$v_k = \overline{r^*(n)x_k(n)} = \overline{r^*(n)[\sqrt{P}b_k\sigma_k e^{-j\varphi_k(\theta)}s(n) + n_k(n)]} \tag{3.162}$$

Assuming that $s(n)$ has a normalized variance, then P represents the received power of the reference signal arriving at the array. Assuming that the reference sequence is long enough, it is easy to know that

$$\overline{r^*(n)s(n)} = 1 \tag{3.163}$$

and

$$\overline{r^*(n)n_k(n)} = 0 \tag{3.164}$$

Substituting Eq. (3.163) and Eq. (3.164) into Eq. (3.162), we get

$$v_k \propto b_k \sigma_k e^{-j\varphi_k(\theta)} \tag{3.165}$$

Therefore, the calibration factor for the channel can be obtained as follows:

$$c_k = \frac{b_k v_k}{|v_k|^2} e^{-j\varphi_k(\theta)} \propto \frac{1}{\sigma_k} \tag{3.166}$$

In practice, in order to avoid erroneous synchronization, the reference sequence needs to have a good autocorrelation, and an orthogonal sequence based on the m sequence can be adopted.

For the calibration of the downlink (transmitting antenna array), the transmitting unit and the receiving unit are required to be completed together. According to the reference signal transmitted by the array antenna interfered by the channel mismatch information, the mismatch information is estimated at the receiving unit and the calibration factor is calculated. Figures 3.8 and 3.9 show the working principle models of the transmitting unit and the receiving unit, respectively.

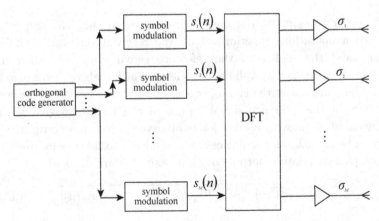

Fig. 3.8. Radio feed reference signal calibration (downlink transmitter structure).

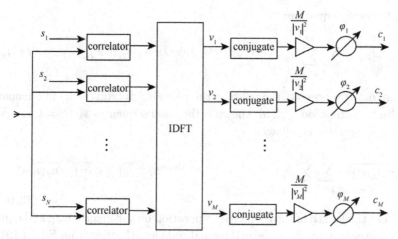

Fig. 3.9. Radio feed reference signal calibration (downlink receiver structure).

The algorithm uses a signal based on a synchronous orthogonal code to calculate a calibration factor. First, an Mlb$N$-way synchronous orthogonal code is generated at the transmitting end, denoted as $\{C_i(n),\ i = 1, 2, \ldots, M\text{lb}N\}$, where M is the number of antenna elements, and N is related to the modulation mode. For BPSK modulation, $N = 2$, and for QPSK, $N = 4$. All codes have a code length of L. And the orthogonal code means that the codes satisfy the following equations with each other:

$$\sum_{i=1}^{L} C_i(l)C_j(l) = \begin{cases} L, i = j \\ 0, i \neq j \end{cases} \tag{3.167}$$

By modulating $\{C_i\}$, an M-channel orthogonal complex signal sequence can be generated, denoted as $s_i(n),\ i = 1, \ldots, M$. This sequence is fed into a spatial DFT converter, which is equivalent to a fixed multi-beamformer, and the transformed output signal is transmitted through the RF circuit and the antenna unit, respectively. Due to the effect of channel mismatch, the transmitted signal of each channel is equivalent to a multiplier with a factor of σ_i.

The receiving antenna is a single antenna. The azimuth angle of the receiving antenna relative to the transmitting array is assumed to be θ, then the baseband signal received by the receiving antenna can be expressed by the following equation:

$$s(n) = \sum_{p=1}^{M} \sum_{q=1}^{M} [\sigma_p e^{-j\varphi_p(\theta)} e^{-j2\pi(p-1)(q-1)/M} s_q(n)] + n_r(n) \qquad (3.168)$$

where $n_r(n)$ represents the noise on the receiving antenna. $s(n)$ implements multiple correlation with all known orthogonal sequences s_k $(k = 1, \ldots, N)$ and is expressed as follows:

$$\overline{s(n)s_k^*(n)} = \sum_{p=1}^{M} \sum_{q=1}^{M} \sigma_p e^{-j\varphi_p(\theta)} e^{-j2\pi(p-1)(q-1)/M} \overline{s_q(n)s_k^*(n)} + \overline{n_r(n)s_k^*(n)}$$

$$(3.169)$$

Let the length of the correlation operation be sufficiently long and equal to an integer multiple of the orthogonal code length, then from Eq. (3.167), it can be known that

$$\overline{s_q(n)s_k^*(n)} = \begin{cases} 1, & q = k \\ 0, & q \neq k \end{cases} \qquad (3.170)$$

and

$$\overline{n_r(n)s_k^*(n)} = 0 \qquad (3.171)$$

Substituting Eqs. (3.170) and (3.171) into Eq. (3.169), we obtain

$$\overline{s(n)s_k^*(n)} = \sum_{p=1}^{M} \sigma_p e^{-j\varphi_p(\theta)} e^{-j2\pi(p-1)(q-1)/M} \qquad (3.172)$$

Equation (3.172) shows that $\{\overline{s(n)s_k^*(n)}, \quad k = 1, \ldots, M\}$ and $\{\sigma_p e^{-j\varphi_p(\theta)}, p = 1, \ldots, M\}$ are the Fourier transform pairs. Therefore, a spatial inverse DFT transform is carried out on $\overline{s(n)s_k^*(n)}$ to get

$$\sigma_p = \frac{e^{j\varphi_p(\theta)}}{N} \sum_{k=1}^{N} e^{j2\pi(p-1)(k-1)/M} \overline{s(n)s_k^*(n)} \qquad (3.173)$$

and the calibration factor is the reciprocal of the mismatch factor, that is,

$$c_p = \frac{1}{\sigma_p} \qquad (3.174)$$

Through these operations, the receiver completes the estimation of the transmit array channel mismatch and generates a calibration factor. On this basis, the transmitting antenna array channel can be calibrated by simply transmitting the calibration factor back to the transmit array and applying these calibration factors. In other words, the calibration of the downlink channel is a closed loop process, while the calibration of the uplink channel is an open loop process.

The main parts of the uplink and downlink of the calibration algorithm can be operated in parallel, and finally, the calibration factors of each channel can be obtained at the same time. A relatively high calibration speed can be achieved even in the case of a large number of array elements. The performance of the algorithm is mainly limited by the channel noise of the reference signal in the spatial propagation process. Using a long orthogonal code, a better calibration performance can be obtained even in the case of a low carrier-to-noise ratio.

3.5.2 *Signal injection method*

Similar to the radio feed reference signal method, the signal injection method also inputs a reference signal to the array (the uplink and downlink are similar). And the channel mismatch parameter is estimated by comparing the channel output of the signal with the reference signal through the array. However, the reference signal in the radio feed reference signal method is transmitted by the test antenna and received by the array through the radio channel, and in the signal injection method, the test antenna is not required. The reference signal is directly fed into each channel of the array by the feeder without the transmission of the radio channel and the antenna unit.

Figure 3.10 shows a system configuration scheme which uses the signal injection method to calibrate. In this scheme, the calibration signal generating unit generates a calibration signal having the same carrier frequency and the same code rate as the actual signal in the reverse link, and sequentially injects it into the RF circuit of each channel through a multiplexer. After the transmission through the mismatched RF circuit, the signal is despread and compared to the output of the calibration signal generator to obtain the amplitude and phase deviation caused by the RF circuit, and then the calibration factor can be calculated. The specific calculation method is similar to the radio feed reference signal method.

When the signal injection method is applied, the amplitude and phase transformation of each RF circuit during calibration can be ignored. In order to avoid affecting the normal operation of the system, the power

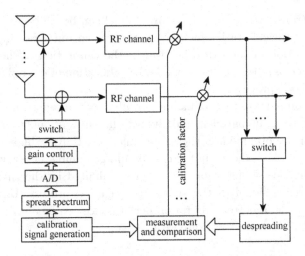

Fig. 3.10.   Signal injection calibration (uplink).

of the input calibration signal should be controlled. The signal injection method can be implemented at any time when calibration is required, and it does not require test antennas, but at the same time increases the complexity of the array antenna system itself.

3.5.3 *Blind signal calibration method*

Whether it is a radio feed reference signal method or a signal injection method, a reference sequence needs to be introduced. For communication systems operating online, the reference signal is an interference to the user signal, and the user signal also affects the calibration using the reference signal. Therefore, the researchers proposed a blind signal calibration method that does not require the use of reference sequences.

The uplink and downlink calibrations are still discussed separately. Figure 3.11 shows the schematic diagram of the uplink channel calibration. As can be seen in the figure, the signals received by each array element get into a combiner through a bypass generated by a directional coupler before entering the RF channel. The combiner multiplexes the signals into one channel, and the combined signal enters a channel called calibration receiver. Assuming that the channel factor is 1, the corresponding baseband output signal can be denoted as

$$y(n) = L[\mathbf{r}(n)] + \mathbf{n}_c(n) \tag{3.175}$$

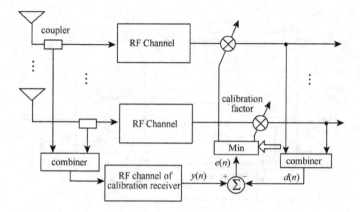

Fig. 3.11. Blind signal calibration method (uplink).

where $\mathbf{r}(n)$ represents the received signal vector which is not affected by the mismatch, $L[\cdot]$ corresponds to a linear combination operator, and $\mathbf{n}_c(n)$ represents the noise sequence of the channel output.

The channel output vector of the array itself can be expressed as follows considering the channel mismatch:

$$\mathbf{x}(n) = \boldsymbol{\Gamma}\mathbf{r}(n) + \mathbf{n}(n) \tag{3.176}$$

To eliminate the mismatch, introduce the calibration factor to each channel. Denote $\mathbf{c} = [c_1, c_2, \ldots, c_M]^{\mathrm{T}}$ as the vector formed by the calibration factor, then output vector after calibration is given as

$$\mathbf{x}'(n) = \mathrm{diag}(\mathbf{c})\mathbf{x}(n) = \mathrm{diag}(\mathbf{c})\boldsymbol{\Gamma}\mathbf{r}(n) + \mathrm{diag}(\mathbf{c})\mathbf{n}(n) \tag{3.177}$$

and then the same combination operation as described above is applied to $\mathbf{x}'(n)$ to construct a reference signal:

$$d(n) = L[\mathbf{x}'(n)] \tag{3.178}$$

It is worth noting that the two combination operations should be identical. The task below is to adjust the calibration factor to minimize the mean square error between $y(n)$ and $d(n)$. Here, the calibration factor is adjusted by the NLMS algorithm, and the equation is obtained as follows:

$$\mathbf{c}(n+1) = \mathbf{c}(n) + \mu(n)e^*(n)\mathbf{x}'(n) \tag{3.179}$$

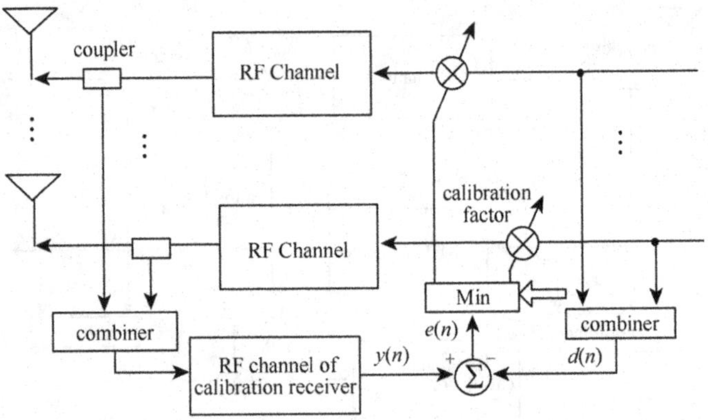

Fig. 3.12. Blind signal calibration method (downlink).

where

$$e(n) = d(n) - y(n) \tag{3.180}$$

$$\mu = \frac{\mu_0}{\mathbf{x}'^{H}(n)\mathbf{x}'(n)} \tag{3.181}$$

The downlink calibration is shown in Fig. 3.12. The output of the adaptive antenna unit is combined into a reference signal $d(n)$ before calibration, and the signals before the antenna array is transmitted are combined into $y(n)$, and then the weight is updated with the same algorithm as in the uplink to minimize the error $e(n)$. This calibration algorithm has fast convergence characteristics, and because it does not require a reference sequence, it does not affect the system operation. This method is very suitable for online calibration requirements.

3.6 Adaptive Antenna System Hardware Architecture

At present, all countries in the world pay great importance to the role of adaptive antenna technology in various communication fields in the future and have launched a large number of theoretical- and experimental-based researches. The main function of the adaptive antenna array system is divided into two parts: One is to estimate the DOA of the multipath radio waves from the mobile station and perform spatial filtering to suppress interference from other mobile stations. The other one is to perform digital beamforming on the signal transmitted by the base station to enable the base station to transmit signals back to the mobile station along the

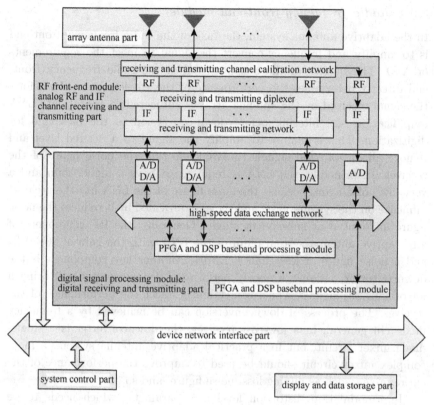

Fig. 3.13. Adaptive antenna radio base station system reference architecture.

DOA of the mobile wave, thereby reducing the transmission power and reducing the signal interference to other mobile stations. Figure 3.13 shows an adaptive antenna radio base station system reference architecture,[11] including the array antenna part, the analog RF and IF channel receiving and transmitting parts (including channel amplitude phase calibration channel), the digital receiving and transmitting parts, the system control part, the device network interface part, and the optional display and data storage parts according to the requirements. Algorithms such as core array signal processing, modulation and demodulation, code decoding, user data packing and splitting are implemented in FPGA and DSP. In order to implement the reconfiguration of algorithms and functions, each baseband signal processing module is provided with an external data interface such as program memory, embedded controller, and network.

3.6.1 *Radio frequency front-end module*

In the adaptive antenna system, the task of the radio frequency front-end is to amplify and frequency-convert the signal to meet the requirements of A/D. The quality of the output signal of the radio frequency front-end directly determines the performance of the whole system. Therefore, the signal received by the antenna array is subjected to appropriate LNA amplification and filtering before down-conversion to the baseband for digitization. This is mainly to amplify the signal to a desired level and remove all out-of-band signals to avoid affecting the noise figure of the receiver. In principle, the LNA is required to have a higher gain and a very low noise figure because the noise figure of the LNA has the greatest influence on the system noise, and the gain provided by it reduces the noise figure introduced at subsequent stages. Generally, the RF component of an adaptive antenna system requires the LNA with the gain of 20–30 dB and a noise figure of less than 1–1.5 dB. Another key component is the downconverter, because a poorly performing downconverter will bring a lot of spurious signals, which can seriously affect the performance of the receiver. The process of downconversion can be achieved by a frequency mixer. In general, in a low-cost receiver, the downconverter is a single-diode mixer circuit, but in a practical adaptive antenna system, a more complex mixer circuit should be used to improve the performance of the entire mixer, such as mixing loss, noise figure, and so on.

Intermodulation distortion level is a parameter which needs to be mainly considered. When the RF signal is small, the IF signal power increases linearly with the RF input power, but when the RF power increases beyond a certain range, the linear relationship becomes nonlinear, resulting in intermodulation distortion. The RF signal contains two or more components with close frequencies (such as mobile communication within a cell), and correspondingly the IF output contains many needless IF components that fall within the IF bandwidth. The results of cross-modulation are as follows: the IF filtering cannot be filtered out, and the distortion caused by the third-order intermodulation is significant. A high-gain LNA can cause severe distortion, so a balance between sensitivity and dynamic range is required. In practical systems, an attenuator is typically inserted between the LNA and the mixer to ensure that the power of the RF input mixer is small enough to avoid intermodulation distortion. Another method is to add a feedforward circuit to the system to superimpose the two signals in reverse to cancel the intermodulation, which has been currently adopted in many active linear power amplifiers.

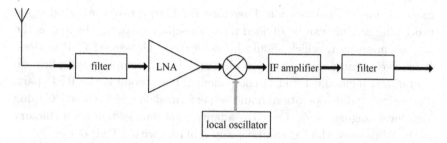

Fig. 3.14. RF front-end working principle.

Considering that the adaptive antenna system is very sensitive to errors, it is necessary to ensure the consistency of the amplitude and phase of each branch of the RF front-end. The typical principle of the RF front-end is shown in Fig. 3.14.

3.6.2 *Data signal processing module*

In adaptive antenna systems, the digital signal processing module plays an important role. Its performance of hardware and software directly determines the performance of the system. By executing the appropriate instructions in the software of the system, the digital signal processing module can enhance the desired signal while minimizing the effects of interference and transmission delays. If the adaptive algorithm used is appropriate, the digital signal processing module can output an almost interference-free desired signal in real time at the adaptive antenna output.

The implementation of the algorithm mainly includes a beamforming function and a weight update function. The beamforming function generates the desired output of the adaptive antenna by using and reusing the updated available weights, and the weight update function derives a new set of optimal weights from the most recently adopted received values. In order to achieve a quick response, output beamforming and weight update need to be performed in parallel as two separate tasks. Moreover, since data transmission is fast, the calculations related to beamforming must be done at high speed. Since each new snapshot of the data sample is updated repeatedly, it is necessary to enable the beamforming software to execute efficiently with the assembly instructions even during the R&D phase. In addition, the weight update is slower mainly because the actual mobile environment remains basically unchanged within 1–2 ms and even if you choose a relatively simple algorithm, the weight update operation is also very complicated, so it is worth writing the weight update software with more advanced language code. Therefore, the hardware of the digital signal processing module can be divided into two separate parts. The first is the beamforming part, which should be done using high-speed DSP devices. It involves a large number of complex signals and complex multiplication operations, including I and Q components. The second is the R&D part. The weight update operation should be performed on a high-speed PC using high-level language code. Once the adaptive antenna system is satisfactory in the laboratory, the PC can be easily replaced with a DSP device.

3.6.3 *Parallel digital beamforming*

With the continuous development of the digital signal processing hardware, the speed at which digital signal processors execute instructions is already very high, making data reading and transmission easy. However, the researchers found that after the adaptive multi-beam is adopted, the speed of beamforming is often a bottleneck, especially when the number of beams is large.

Digital beamforming performs a weighted summation process on the received signals of the array elements to form a beam. The main beam is aligned with the desired user direction, and the beam zero is aligned with the interference direction. According to the degree of beamforming, there are two ways to realize smart antennas: array space processing and beam space processing.

Array space processing method (all adaptive array processing)

After performing weighted summation processing on the received signal samples of each array element directly, an array output is formed, so that the main pattern of the array pattern is aligned with the arrival direction of the user signal. And each array element participates in adaptive weighting adjustment.

Beam space processing (partial adaptive array processing)

It contains a two-stage processing process. The first stage performs fixed weight summation on each array element signal to form multiple beams pointing in different directions and the second stage adaptively strengthens and adjusts the beam output of the first stage to obtain an array output. This scheme does not adaptively process all the array elements from the perspective of the overall optimal calculation weighting coefficient, but only adaptively processes some of the array elements. This structure has

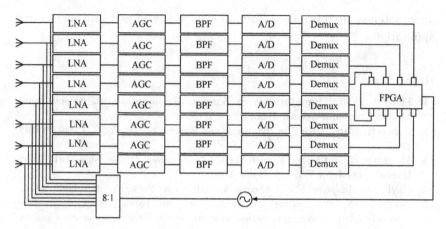

Fig. 3.15. **Hardware structure of the 8-channel adaptive antenna system.**

advantages of small computational complexity, fast convergence, and good beam conformal performance.

Parallel digital beamforming mainly emphasizes parallel processing as much as possible for data transmission and processing. For example, for 8 channels, there must be at least 8 parallels in the ADC. The data and weight combinations for each channel should be parallel and for multiple beams working at the same time, and parallel processing should also be performed as much as possible. Figure 3.15 shows the hardware structure link of an 8-channel adaptive antenna system with calibration.

3.7 Summary

Although antennas are used to transmit and receive radio waves, different from conventional antennas, adaptive antennas rely on the combination of multiple antenna arrays. By combining the feeding signals of each unit antenna and according to different environments and application requirements, the receiving and transmitting direction characteristics are dynamically adjusted through a sophisticated array-processing algorithm to achieve intelligent beam performance. The basic architecture of the adaptive array antenna is introduced in this chapter, and the adaptive correlation criteria, adaptive beamforming algorithm, and DOA estimation algorithm of the adaptive processing system are discussed in detail. Finally, the array calibration technology and system hardware architecture in adaptive array antenna are introduced from the perspective of practical engineering applications.

References

1. Litva J. *Digital Beamforming in Wireless Communications*. Artech House Mobile Communications, 1996.
2. Cohen H. *Mathematics for Scientists and Engineers*. New York: Prentice Hall, 1992.
3. Monzingo R. and Miller T. *Introduction to Adaptive Arrays*. New York: Wiley Interscience, John Wiley & Sons, 1980.
4. Haykin S. *Adaptive Filter Theory*. 4th edn. New York: Prentice Hall, 2002.
5. Godard DN. Self-recovering equalization and carrier tracking in two-dimensional data communication system. *IEEE Transactions on Communications*, 1980, 28(11): 1867–1875.
6. Treichler JR. and Agee BG. A new approach to multipath correction of constant modulus signals. *IEEE Transactions on Acoustics, Speech and Signal Processing*, 1983, 31(4): 459–472.
7. Agee B. The least-squares CMA: A new technique for rapid correction of constant modulus signals. *IEEE International Conference on ICASSP'86*, 1986, 11: 953–936.
8. Burg JP. Maximum entropy spectral analysis. *Society of Exploration Geophysicists*, 37th Annual Meeting, Oklahoma City, 1967.
9. Schmidt RO. Multiple emitter location and signal parameter estimation. *IEEE Transactions on Antenna and Propagation*, 1986, 34(3): 276–280.
10. Roy R, Paulraj A. and Kailath T. Esprit-A subspace rotation approach to estimation of parameters of cissoids in noise. *IEEE Transactions on Acoustics, Speech and Signal Processing*, 1986, 34(5): 1340–1342.
11. Namkyu R, Yun Y, Choi S, *et al.* Smart antenna base station open architecture for SDR networks. *IEEE Wireless Communications*, 2006, 13(3): 58–69.

Chapter 4

MIMO Multi-Antenna Theory and Technology

With the rapid development of multimedia communication using wireless Internet, the demand for broadband high-speed data communication services is growing. The capacity of conventional single-antenna transmitting and receiving communication systems is far from being able to meet the needs of actual use, and its reliability needs to be improved. MIMO technology is one of the key technologies to realize high-speed broadband wireless communication in the future. Its core concept is to improve the transmission capacity and spectrum efficiency of wireless communication systems by utilizing the spatial freedom provided by multiple transmitting antennas and multiple receiving antennas.

This chapter first introduces the channel model of the MIMO system and analyzes the channel capacity improvement of the MIMO system. On this basis, MIMO space–time coding technology is introduced, including space–time trellis code, space–time block code, and layered space–time code. Second, the single-user and multi-user beamforming methods in MIMO beamforming technology are introduced. Third, the design of the MIMO antenna is discussed, which involves mutual coupling between multiple antennas, spatial correlation, and multi-antenna mutual coupling suppression. Finally, the application of massive MIMO systems, channel hardening in large sizes, and some technical challenges faced by large-scale MIMO systems are discussed.

4.1 MIMO Channel Model

An MIMO communication system is a communication system having multiple antenna channels at both the transmitting end and the receiving end. The typical structure of an MIMO system is shown in Fig. 4.1 with M_T representing transmitting antennas and M_R representing receiving antennas. Denote $h_{i,j}(\tau,t)$ as the time-varying channel impulse response between the jth $(j = 1,2,\ldots,M_T)$ transmitting antenna and the ith $(i = 1,2,\ldots,M_R)$ receiving antenna at the time with delay τ, namely the response at time t of the pulse transmitted at time $(\tau - t)$.

The channel response of an MIMO system can be represented by an $M_R \times M_T$ matrix $\mathbf{H}(\tau,t)$:

$$\mathbf{H}(\tau,t) = \begin{bmatrix} h_{1,1}(\tau,t) & \cdots & h_{1,M_T}(\tau,t) \\ h_{2,1}(\tau,t) & \cdots & h_{2,M_T}(\tau,t) \\ \vdots & & \vdots \\ h_{M_R,1}(\tau,t) & \cdots & h_{M_R,M_T}(\tau,t) \end{bmatrix} \tag{4.1}$$

The jth column vector $[h_{1,j}(\tau,t), h_{2,j}(\tau,t),\ldots,h_{M_R,j}(\tau,t)]^T$ in the matrix represents the space–time signal characteristics of the jth transmitting antenna to the receiving antenna array. Assuming that the transmitted signal of the jth antenna is denoted as $x_j(t)$, the received signal of the ith receiving antenna is given as

$$y_i(t) = \sum_{j=1}^{N} h_{i,j}(\tau,t)x_j(t) + n_i(t), \quad i = 1,2,\ldots,M_T \tag{4.2}$$

where $n_i(t)$ represents additive noise at the receiver.

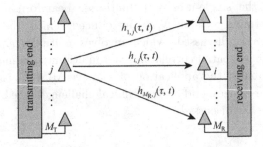

Fig. 4.1. **The MIMO multi-antenna system structure.**

According to the physical scattering model, an MIMO physical channel model can be constructed. Assuming that the system is a narrow-band array, the receiving antenna array has a linear array with element spacing d, and the wavefront of the incident signal is incident on the receiving antenna array with angle θ.

Assuming that the bandwidth of the incident signal is B, $x(t)$ can be expressed as

$$x(t) = \alpha(t)e^{j\omega t} \tag{4.3}$$

where $\alpha(t)$ is the complex envelope of the signal and ω is the carrier frequency (radian). With the assumption of the narrowband array, the signal bandwidth B is much smaller than the reciprocal of the time T of the incident signal wavefront passing through the antenna array, namely $B \ll 1/T$. If $y_1(t)$ is used to express the received signal of the first antenna, then the received signal of the ith antenna is

$$y_i(t) = y_1(t)e^{-(i-1)j2\pi \cos(\theta)(d/\lambda)} \tag{4.4}$$

where λ is the wavelength of the incident signal, and the signals received on the two antennas are identical in all aspects, except phase. Consider the single-reflection scattering model in Fig. 4.2, for a scatterer with an aperture angle θ relative to the receiving antenna, an aperture angle φ relative to the transmitting antenna array, and a delay τ, the complex envelope is $S(\theta, \tau)$. If the geometric position of the transmitting and receiving antenna arrays is given, then the other variable can be determined by any two of the (θ, φ, τ) variables. Therefore, the impulse response of the MIMO channel can be expressed as

$$\mathbf{H}(\tau) = \int_{-\pi}^{\pi} \int_0^{\tau_{\max}} S(\theta, t)\mathbf{a}(\theta)\mathbf{b}^{\mathrm{T}}(\varphi)g(\tau - t)\mathrm{d}t\,\mathrm{d}\theta \tag{4.5}$$

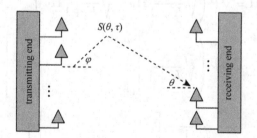

Fig. 4.2. Single reflection scattering model.

where $\tau_{\max}$ is the maximum delay spread of the channel and $g(\tau)$ represents the sum of the responses of the transmitter pulseformer and the receiver matched filter. $\mathbf{a}(\theta)$ and $\mathbf{b}(\varphi)$ are the direction vectors of the receiving and transmitting antenna arrays, respectively.

The above channel model based on the single-reflection scattering model has many limitations, and it does not reflect the complete impact of the channel. The assumption of multiple reflections is made in a more general model, which means the signal passes through multiple scatterers from the transmitting end to the receiving end. In this case, the three parameters (θ, φ, τ) will be independent of each other. According to the assumption of the narrowband array with $B \ll 1/\tau_{\max}$, Eq. (4.5) can be expressed as

$$\mathbf{H}(\tau) = \left(\int_{-\pi}^{\pi} \int_{0}^{\tau_{\max}} S(\theta, t)\mathbf{a}(\theta)\mathbf{b}^{\mathrm{T}}(\varphi)\mathrm{d}t\,\mathrm{d}\theta \right) g(\tau) = \mathbf{H}g(\tau) \qquad (4.6)$$

If we further assume the response $g(\tau) = \delta(\tau)$, then we only need to care about the nature of $\mathbf{H}$ for Eq. (4.6). When the antenna array pattern and the array geometry are appropriately selected, for the multi-scattering model, the element of $\mathbf{H}$ can be considered as a cyclic symmetric complex Gaussian random variable obeying zero mean and variance of 1, namely $[\mathbf{H}]_{i,j} \sim \mathcal{CN}(0,1)$. In this case, the MIMO channel is an independently and identically distributed Rayleigh fading channel, denoted by $\langle x, y \rangle = E\{xy^*\}$. For a scattering-rich NLOS environment, $\mathbf{H} = \mathbf{H}_w$ is true if the spacing between the transmitting and receiving antenna elements is sufficiently large and the polarization mode is the same. If there is an LOS component in the channel environment, the mean of the channel matrix is no longer zero, and the element in this case obeys the Rician distribution, which can be expressed as

$$\mathbf{H} = \sqrt{P}\left(\sqrt{\frac{K}{K+1}}\mathbf{H}_{\mathrm{F}} + \sqrt{\frac{1}{K+1}}\mathbf{H}_{\mathrm{V}} \right)$$

$$= \sqrt{P}\left(\sqrt{\frac{K}{K+1}} \begin{bmatrix} e^{j\varphi_{11}} & \cdots & e^{j\varphi_{1M_{\mathrm{T}}}} \\ \vdots & \ddots & \vdots \\ e^{j\varphi_{M_{\mathrm{R}}1}} & \cdots & e^{j\varphi_{M_{\mathrm{R}}M_{\mathrm{T}}}} \end{bmatrix} \right.$$

$$\left. + \sqrt{\frac{1}{K+1}} \begin{bmatrix} a_{11} & \cdots & a_{1M_{\mathrm{T}}} \\ \vdots & \ddots & \vdots \\ a_{M_{\mathrm{R}}1} & \cdots & a_{M_{\mathrm{R}}M_{\mathrm{T}}} \end{bmatrix} \right) \qquad (4.7)$$

where $\mathbf{H}_F$ is a fixed LOS component matrix with elements $e^{j\varphi_{ij}}$ and $\mathbf{H}_V$ represents the NLOS component matrix with its element a_{ij}, which is a complex Gaussian random variable. P is the sum of the power of the fixed component and the random component, and $K = P_{\mathrm{LOS}}/P_{\mathrm{NLOS}}$ is the Rician distribution factor, which represents the power ratio of the two components.

In the actual environment, it is not guaranteed that the statistical properties of $\mathbf{H}$ will always be subject to the $\mathbf{H}_W$ independent distribution. For example, if the spacing between the antennas is not large enough or when small scattering leads to a spatial fading correlation, then the presence of the LOS component in the channel will cause the Rician fading, and different polarization modes will cause gain imbalance between the elements. All these will have a great impact on the characteristics of the MIMO channel.

Therefore, if the spatial correlation of the channel is considered, the spatial complex correlation coefficient between one transmitting antenna M_{T} and the two receiving antennas $M_{\mathrm{R}1}$ and $M_{\mathrm{R}2}$ can be expressed as

$$\rho_{M_{\mathrm{R}1}M_{\mathrm{R}2}} = \left\langle \alpha_{M_{\mathrm{R}1}M_{\mathrm{T}}}^{(\tau)}, \alpha_{M_{\mathrm{R}2}M_{\mathrm{T}}}^{(\tau)} \right\rangle \tag{4.8}$$

where $\alpha_{M_{\mathrm{R}1}M_{\mathrm{T}}}^{(\tau)}$ represents the complex transmission coefficient between the transmitting antenna M_{T} and the receiving antenna $M_{\mathrm{R}1}$. $\langle x, y \rangle = \mathrm{E}\{xy^*\}$ and τ represent the delay. If the transmitting antenna is compactly placed and has the same radiation pattern, the spatial correlation function at the receiving end is independent of the transmitting antenna M_{T}. It can also define the spatial complex correlation coefficient between the two antennas $M_{\mathrm{T}1}$ and $M_{\mathrm{T}2}$ at the transmitting end:

$$\rho_{M_{\mathrm{T}1}M_{\mathrm{T}2}} = \left\langle \alpha_{M_{\mathrm{R}}M_{\mathrm{T}1}}^{(\tau)}, \alpha_{M_{\mathrm{R}}M_{\mathrm{T}2}}^{(\tau)} \right\rangle \tag{4.9}$$

We define the symmetric correlation matrix between the receiving end and the transmitting end according to Eqs. (4.8) and (4.9) as follows:

$$\mathbf{R}_{\mathrm{R}} = [\rho_{M_{\mathrm{R}_i}M_{\mathrm{R}_j}}]_{M_{\mathrm{R}} \times M_{\mathrm{R}}}, \quad \mathbf{R}_{\mathrm{T}} = [\rho_{M_{\mathrm{T}_i}M_{\mathrm{T}_j}}]_{M_{\mathrm{T}} \times M_{\mathrm{T}}} \tag{4.10}$$

Similarly, the correlation coefficients between two pairs of transmitting and receiving antennas can also be defined as follows:

$$\rho_{M_{\mathrm{T}2}M_{\mathrm{R}2}}^{M_{\mathrm{T}1}M_{\mathrm{R}1}} = \left\langle \alpha_{M_{\mathrm{T}1}M_{\mathrm{R}1}}^{(\tau)}, \alpha_{M_{\mathrm{T}2}M_{\mathrm{R}2}}^{(\tau)} \right\rangle, \quad M_{\mathrm{T}1} \neq M_{\mathrm{T}2}, \quad M_{\mathrm{R}1} \neq M_{\mathrm{R}2} \tag{4.11}$$

If the radiating patterns of the transmitting and receiving antenna elements are the same, $\rho_{M_{\mathrm{R}_i}M_{\mathrm{R}_j}}$ and $\rho_{M_{\mathrm{T}_i}M_{\mathrm{T}_j}}$ are independent of M_{T} and

M_R, respectively, then the above equation can be further expressed as

$$\rho_{M_{T2}M_{R2}}^{M_{T1}M_{R1}} = \rho_{M_{R_i}M_{R_j}}\rho_{M_{T_i}M_{T_j}} \tag{4.12}$$

The covariance matrix of an MIMO channel can be treated as the Kronecker product of the correlation matrix $\mathbf{R}_T$ at the transmitting end and the correlation matrix $\mathbf{R}_R$ at the receiving end, namely

$$\mathbf{R} = \mathbf{R}_T \otimes \mathbf{R}_R \tag{4.13}$$

And this allows an appropriate model to be established for the spatial correlation of the MIMO channel.

The distribution of the scatterer, the geometry of the antenna, and the pattern of the elements together determine the correlation of the $\mathbf{H}$ elements. The calculation of the complex correlation coefficient is mainly based on the power azimuth spectrum (PAS) distribution and the angular spread (AS). Uniform distribution, Gaussian distribution, and Laplacian distribution are the commonly used PAS. If the relevant parameters such as PAS, AS, and average angle-of-arrival (AOA) are determined, the corresponding complex correlation coefficient can be calculated.

For convenience, we often assume that the channels between the antennas are uncorrelated and that the channel matrix is a full-rank matrix with each element obeying an independent complex Gaussian distribution. This is a very ideal case. If a more accurate channel model needs to be established, the specific propagation of radio waves in the environment must be considered, and at the same time, it is necessary to consider the shape of the transmitting and receiving antenna arrays, the spacing between the antennas, the polarization of the antennas, and the angular spread of the received signal, which makes it more realistic.

4.2 MIMO Channel Capacity

System capacity is one of the most important indicators to express the performance of a communication system. In the case that the error probability of the receiving end can be arbitrarily small, the maximum information transmission rate that the communication link can reach is called the channel capacity. The channel capacity is the upper bound of the information transmission rate between both the sides under the given channel conditions. According to the Shannon Information Theory,[1] for continuous channels, if the channel bandwidth is B and is interfered by additive white Gaussian noise, the theoretical equation for channel capacity is

$$C = B\text{lb}\left(1 + \frac{S}{\sigma^2}\right) \tag{4.14}$$

where σ^2 is the average power of the additive white Gaussian noise (AWGN), S is the average power of the signal, S/σ^2 is the signal-to-noise ratio, and B is the channel bandwidth. Although increasing the signal-to-noise ratio can improve the efficiency of spectrum use, in actual communication systems, it is not recommended to increase the transmission power of the transmitting end in consideration of actual conditions such as electromagnetic pollution, performance of radio frequency circuits, and interference between users. The noise power σ^2 is related to the channel bandwidth B. If the noise unilateral power spectral density is n_0, the Shannon equation can also be expressed as

$$C = B\text{lb}\left(1 + \frac{S}{n_0 B}\right) \tag{4.15}$$

when the bandwidth $B \to \infty$, then

$$\lim_{B \to \infty} C = \lim_{B \to \infty} \left[\frac{n_0 B}{S}\text{lb}\left(1 + \frac{S}{n_0 B}\right)\right]\left(\frac{S}{n_0}\right) = \frac{S}{n_0}\text{lb}\, e \approx 1.44\frac{S}{n_0} \tag{4.16}$$

It can be seen that when S and n_0 are determined, the channel capacity increases with the increase of the bandwidth B when B is limited. However, when $B \to \infty$, the noise power also tends to infinity, and C cannot be increased without limitation.

The channel capacity can be increased significantly with MIMO multi-antenna technology without the need for additional power and bandwidth. Assuming that the number of transmitting antennas is M_T, the number of receiving antennas is M_R, the channel is interfered by the additive white Gaussian noise, and the transmitted signal vector is $\mathbf{x}$, then the received signal vector $\mathbf{y}$ can be expressed as

$$\mathbf{y} = \mathbf{Hx} + \mathbf{n} \tag{4.17}$$

where $\mathbf{H}$ is an $M_R \times M_T$ complex matrix, vector $\mathbf{n}$ is a zero-mean complex Gaussian additive white noise, and the real and imaginary parts are independently and identically distributed with the same variance. The autocorrelation matrix satisfies $E\{\mathbf{nn}^H\} = \sigma^2 \mathbf{I}_{M_R}$, which means the noise on the different receiving antennas is independent of each other. In the following, the capacities of the deterministic MIMO channel and the random MIMO channel are discussed, and the capacities of the SISO, SIMO, MISO, and MIMO channels under the condition of equally distributed transmitted power are compared.

4.2.1 *Deterministic channel capacity*

For a deterministic channel matrix $\mathbf{H}$, the capacity C of the channel is equal to the maximum value of the average mutual information $\mathbf{I}(\mathbf{x}; \mathbf{y})$ of the channel input $\mathbf{x}$ and the output $\mathbf{y}$.

$$C = \max_{f(x)} \mathbf{I}(\mathbf{x}; \mathbf{y}) \tag{4.18}$$

where $f(\mathbf{x})$ is the probability distribution of the transmitted signal vector $\mathbf{x}$.

For the channel model of Eq. (4.17), the mutual information of the channel is

$$\mathbf{I}(\mathbf{x}; \mathbf{y}) = H(\mathbf{y}) - H(\mathbf{y}|\mathbf{x}) \tag{4.19}$$

where $H(\mathbf{y})$ is the differential entropy of the vector $\mathbf{y}$ and $H(\mathbf{y}|\mathbf{x})$ is the conditional differential entropy of $\mathbf{y}$ when x is given:

$$H(\mathbf{y}) = \mathrm{lb}[\det(\pi e \mathbf{R}_{yy})] \tag{4.20}$$

$$H(\mathbf{n}) = \mathrm{lb}[\det(\pi e \sigma^2 \mathbf{I}_{M_{\mathrm{R}}})] \tag{4.21}$$

where $\mathbf{R}_{yy} = \mathrm{E}\{\mathbf{y}\mathbf{y}^{\mathrm{H}}\} = \mathbf{H}\mathbf{R}_{xx}\mathbf{H}^{\mathrm{H}} + \sigma^2 \mathbf{I}_{M_{\mathrm{R}}}$ and $\mathbf{R}_{xx} = \mathrm{E}\{\mathbf{x}\mathbf{x}^{\mathrm{H}}\}$.

If $\mathbf{y}$ and $\mathbf{x}$ are independent of each other, namely $H(\mathbf{y}|\mathbf{x}) = H(\mathbf{n})$, then

$$\mathbf{I}(\mathbf{x}; \mathbf{y}) = H(\mathbf{y}) - H(\mathbf{n}) \tag{4.22}$$

Since $H(\mathbf{n})$ is a constant, maximizing $\mathbf{I}(\mathbf{x}; \mathbf{y})$ is equivalent to maximizing $H(\mathbf{y})$. When $\mathbf{y}$ obeys a cyclic symmetric complex Gaussian distribution, the entropy $H(\mathbf{y})$ of $\mathbf{y}$ is the largest, provided $\mathbf{x}$ also obeys the cyclic symmetric complex Gaussian distribution.

If $\mathbf{x}$ has a zero mean and the covariance matrix is $\mathbf{R}_{xx} = \mathrm{E}\{\mathbf{x}\mathbf{x}^{\mathrm{H}}\} = \mathbf{Q}$, then $\mathbf{y}$ also has zero mean with covariance matrix $\mathbf{R}_{yy} = \mathrm{E}\{\mathbf{y}\mathbf{y}^{\mathrm{H}}\} = \mathbf{H}\mathbf{Q}\mathbf{H}^{\mathrm{H}} + \sigma^2 \mathbf{I}_{M_{\mathrm{R}}}$. In this case, the mutual information can be expressed as

$$\mathbf{I}(\mathbf{x};\, \mathbf{y}) = \text{lb det}\left(\mathbf{I}_{M_R} + \frac{1}{\sigma^2}\mathbf{HQH}^H\right) \tag{4.23}$$

Therefore, when $\mathbf{H}$ is determined, the capacity of the MIMO channel can be expressed as

$$C = \max_{\text{tr}(\mathbf{Q}) \le P} \text{lb det}\left(\mathbf{I}_{M_R} + \frac{1}{\sigma^2}\mathbf{HQH}^H\right) \tag{4.24}$$

where P is the total transmitted power of the transmitter. Let $\text{E}\{\mathbf{x}^H - \mathbf{x}\} \le P$ ensuring that the entire transmitted power is not increased by the increase of the transmitting antenna. Where we exchange the expectation and trace operation, we can get $\text{tr}(\text{E}\{\mathbf{xx}^H\}) \le P$, namely $\text{tr}(\mathbf{Q}) \le P$.

If the status information of the channel of the transmitting end is unknown, the transmitted power can be equally distributed on the M_T transmitting antennas. Assuming that the transmitted signals of the respective transmitting antennas are independent of each other, we have

$$\mathbf{Q} = \mathbf{R}_{xx} = \text{E}\{\mathbf{xx}^H\} = \frac{P}{M_T}\mathbf{I}_{M_T} \tag{4.25}$$

Therefore, the channel capacity when the power of each antenna is transmitted equally at the transmitting end is given as

$$C = \text{lb det}\left(\mathbf{I}_{M_R} + \frac{1}{M_T\sigma^2}\mathbf{HH}^H\right),\ M_T \le M_R \tag{4.26}$$

If the channel information of the transmitting end is known, the channel capacity of the MIMO can be further improved by performing reasonable power allocation on each antenna while maintaining the total transmitted power.

If singular value decomposition is performed on the channel matrix $\mathbf{H}$, then

$$\mathbf{H} = \mathbf{UDV}^H \tag{4.27}$$

where $\mathbf{U}$ and $\mathbf{V}$ are unitary matrices, with $\mathbf{U} \in \mathbb{C}^{M_R \times M_R}$, $\mathbf{V} \in \mathbb{C}^{M_T \times M_T}$, $\mathbf{U} = (u_1, u_2, u_3, \dots, u_{M_R})$, $\mathbf{V} = (v_1, v_2, v_3, \dots, v_{M_T})$. $\mathbf{D}(M_R \times M_T)$ is a non-negative diagonal matrix where $\mathbf{D} = \text{diag}\{\sigma_1, \sigma_2, \sigma_3, \dots, \sigma_{M_T}\}$ with

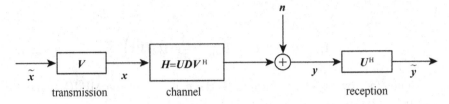

Fig. 4.3. SVD decomposition of the channel.

$\sigma_1 \geq \sigma_2 \geq \sigma_3 \geq \ldots \geq \sigma_m > \sigma_{m+1} = \ldots = \sigma_{M_T} = 0$ and σ_i is the ith singular value of $\mathbf{H}$. Then Eq. (4.17) is rewritten as

$$\mathbf{y} = \mathbf{UDV}^H \mathbf{x} + \mathbf{n} \tag{4.28}$$

Define $\tilde{\mathbf{y}} = \mathbf{U}^H \mathbf{y}$, $\tilde{\mathbf{x}} = \mathbf{V}^H \mathbf{x}$ (or $\mathbf{x} = \mathbf{V}\tilde{\mathbf{x}}$), and $\tilde{\mathbf{n}} = \mathbf{U}^H \mathbf{n}$, which is equivalent to multiplying the transmitted signal vector by the matrix $\mathbf{V}$ before transmission and multiplying the received signal by the matrix $\mathbf{U}^H$. And then the channel can be equivalent to

$$\tilde{\mathbf{y}} = \mathbf{D}\tilde{\mathbf{x}} + \mathbf{n} \tag{4.29}$$

The SVD decomposition of the channel is shown in Fig. 4.3.

For a unitary matrix $\mathbf{VV}^H = \mathbf{I}$, it does not affect the power of the transmitted signal without changing the geometric length of the vector, $\mathrm{E}\{\tilde{\mathbf{x}}^H\tilde{\mathbf{x}}\} = \mathrm{E}\{\mathbf{x}^H\mathbf{x}\}$, namely $\mathrm{tr}(\tilde{\mathbf{Q}}) = \mathrm{tr}(\mathbf{Q})$. Note that $\mathbf{U}$ and $\mathbf{V}$ are both invertible, and $\mathbf{n}$ and $\tilde{\mathbf{n}}$ have the same distribution which means $\mathrm{E}\{\tilde{\mathbf{n}}^H\tilde{\mathbf{n}}\} = \mathbf{I}_M$. And since the rank of $\mathbf{H}$ satisfies $\mathrm{rank}(\mathbf{H}) \leq \min\{M_T, M_R\}$, the number of non-zero singular values is at most $\min\{M_T, M_R\}$. Assume $M_T \leq M_R$, $\mathrm{rank}(\mathbf{H}) = m$, $1 \leq m \leq M_T$, and non-zero singular values are $(\sigma_1, \sigma_2, \sigma_3, \ldots, \sigma_m)$, then the component of $\tilde{\mathbf{y}}$ is given as follows:

$$\tilde{y}_i = \sigma_i \tilde{x}_i + \tilde{n}_i, \quad 1 \leq i \leq m \tag{4.30}$$

The other components ($m < i < M_R$) of $\tilde{\mathbf{y}}$ are the components of noise $\tilde{\mathbf{n}}$.

In this way, the MIMO channel can be regarded as m parallel SISO subchannels, and the gain of each subchannel is also the corresponding singular value, as shown in Fig. 4.4. For the case where the number of antennas at the transmitting end is larger than the number of antennas at the receiving end, the analysis method is the same as above.

The channel capacity of the MIMO system through the above transformation is equal to the sum of the capacities of the m SISO subchannels,

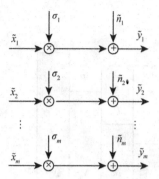

Fig. 4.4. Schematic diagram of parallel subchannels.

namely

$$C = \sum_{i=1}^{m} \text{lb}\left(1 + \frac{\lambda_{\mathbf{x},i}}{\sigma^2}\lambda_{\mathbf{H},i}\right) \qquad (4.31)$$

where $\lambda_{x,i}$ and $\lambda_{\mathbf{H},i}$ are the autocorrelation matrices $\mathbf{R}_{\tilde{x}\tilde{x}}$ of the transmitted signal vector and the ith eigenvalue of $\mathbf{H}^{\mathbf{H}}\mathbf{H}$, respectively, and here it is assumed that the transmitting signals of the respective antennas are independent of each other and still satisfy the constraint condition that the total transmitted power is constant. Under the condition that the total transmitted power is constant, using the known channel information, the water-filling algorithm[2] can be used to allocate different powers to different subchannels at the transmitting end and allocate more energy on a subchannel with a larger gain and less energy on a subchannel with a smaller gain. For the attenuated subchannel, no energy is allocated, so that the transmitted power can be fully used to achieve the maximum total capacity of the MIMO system, namely

$$C = \max_{\sum_{i=1}^{m} \lambda_{x,i} = P} \sum_{i=1}^{m} \text{lb}\left(1 + \frac{\lambda_{\mathbf{x},i}}{\sigma^2}\lambda_{\mathbf{H},i}\right) \qquad (4.32)$$

Using the Lagrangian operator, the optimal power allocation scheme for the water-filling algorithm can be obtained as follows:

$$\lambda_{\mathbf{x},i}^{\text{opt}} = \left(\Psi - \frac{\sigma^2}{\lambda_{\mathbf{H},i}}\right)^{+}, \quad i = 1, 2, \dots \qquad (4.33)$$

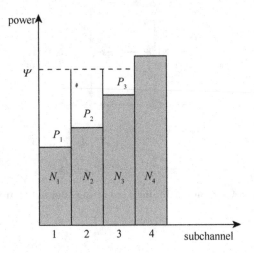

Fig. 4.5. **Schematic diagram of the water-filling algorithm.**

where $\lambda_{\mathbf{x},i}^{\text{opt}}$ satisfies $\sum_{i=1}^{m} \lambda_{\mathbf{x},i}^{\text{opt}} = P$ and Ψ is a constant, which ensures that the total transmitted power is constant. $(s)^{+} = \begin{cases} s, \ s > 0 \\ 0, \ s \leq 0 \end{cases}$ and $\lambda_{\mathbf{x},i}^{\text{opt}}$ can be obtained by the iterative algorithm.

Set $N_i = \frac{\sigma^2}{\lambda_{\mathbf{H},i}}$, $\lambda_{\mathbf{x},i} = P_i$ and according to Eq. (4.33), $P_i = (\Psi - N_i)^{+}$ and $\sum_i P_i = P$ can be obtained. Figure 4.5 shows the schematic diagram of the water-filling algorithm, where P_i represents the power allocated on the ith subchannel.

After the optimal subchannel power allocation scheme is determined, we can obtain the covariance matrix of the optimal transmitting signal $\tilde{\mathbf{x}}$ as follows:

$$\mathbf{R}_{\tilde{x}\tilde{x}} = \text{diag}\{\lambda_{\tilde{x},1}^{\text{opt}}, \lambda_{\tilde{x},2}^{\text{opt}}, \ldots, \lambda_{\tilde{x},m}^{\text{opt}}\} \tag{4.34}$$

Since $\tilde{\mathbf{x}} = \mathbf{V}\tilde{\mathbf{x}}$, the optimal covariance matrix of $\mathbf{x}$ is $\mathbf{R}_{xx} = \mathbf{V}\mathbf{R}_{\tilde{x}\tilde{x}}\mathbf{V}^{\text{H}}$.

As two special cases of MIMO, the SIMO and MISO channel capacities can be given according to the previously derived MIMO capacity equation. For the SIMO channel, $M_{\text{T}} = 1$, the rank of channel $\mathbf{H}$ is 1, and there is only one spatial subchannel ($m = 1$). Therefore, the capacity of the SIMO channel is

$$C = \text{lb}\left(1 + \frac{P\|\mathbf{H}\|_{\text{F}}^2}{\sigma^2}\right) \tag{4.35}$$

where $\|\mathbf{H}\|_F$ represents the F norm of $\mathbf{H}$. If $|h_{i,j}|^2 = 1$, then $\|\mathbf{H}\|_F^2 = M_R$ and Eq. (4.35) can be written as

$$C = \mathrm{lb}\left(1 + \frac{PM_R}{\sigma^2}\right) \qquad (4.36)$$

Since there is only one spatial subchannel in the SIMO channel, the channel information at the transmitting end does not contribute to the increase in capacity.

And for the MISO channel, $M_R = 1$. When there is no channel information at the transmitting end, the signal is transmitted with equal power at each antenna, namely $\mathbf{R}_{xx} = \frac{P}{M_T}\mathbf{I}_{M_T}$. So the channel capacity of MISO is

$$C = \mathrm{lb}\left(1 + \frac{P\|\mathbf{H}\|_F^2}{M_T\sigma^2}\right) \qquad (4.37)$$

Similarly, when $|h_{i,j}| = 1$ and $\|\mathbf{H}\|_F^2 = M_T$, Eq. (4.37) is rewritten as

$$C = \mathrm{lb}\left(1 + \frac{P}{N_0}\right) \qquad (4.38)$$

It can be seen that, in the case $\mathbf{H}$ is constant, if the channel information is unknown to the transmitting end, the channel capacity of MISO is the same as that of SISO (in fading environment, it is better than SISO), but smaller than that of SIMO. This is because the SIMO system can utilize the array gain at the receiving end. Similarly, for the MISO channel, if the channel information is known at the transmitting end, all the transmitted power can be concentrated on one spatial subchannel. At this time, for the same channel transmission coefficient, the channel capacity of MISO is the same as SIMO, namely

$$C = \mathrm{lb}\left(1 + \frac{P\|\mathbf{H}\|_F^2}{\sigma^2}\right) \qquad (4.39)$$

Their capacity logarithmically increases with the number of antennas.

4.2.2 *Random MIMO channel capacity*

For random channels, the capacity of an MIMO system is also a random value, which is usually described by the ergodic capacity and the outage capacity. For the Rayleigh fading case, the elements of $\mathbf{H}$ are assumed to be independent zero-mean complex Gaussian random variables with independent real and imaginary parts. The phase of the elements obeys the uniform distribution and the amplitude obeys the Rayleigh distribution.

Then, the ergodic capacity of a random channel MIMO system can be expressed as

$$\bar{C} = \mathrm{E}\{C\} = \mathrm{E}\left\{ \mathrm{lbdet}\left(\mathbf{I}_{M_{\mathrm{R}}} + \frac{1}{\sigma^2}\mathbf{H}\mathbf{Q}\mathbf{H}^{\mathrm{H}} \right) \right\} \tag{4.40}$$

when channel information is known at the transmitting end and equal power transmission is performed, the corresponding capacity equation is obtained according to Eq. (4.26) as follows:

$$\bar{C} = \mathrm{E}\left\{ \sum_{i=1}^{m} \mathrm{lb}\left(1 + \frac{P\lambda_i}{\sigma^2 M_{\mathrm{T}}} \right) \right\} \tag{4.41}$$

when the channel information is unknown at the transmitting end, the transmitting end performs power allocation using the water-filling algorithm. According to Eq. (4.32),

$$\bar{C} = \mathrm{E}\left\{ \sum_{i=1}^{m} \mathrm{lb}\left(1 + \frac{\lambda_{x,i}^{\mathrm{opt}}}{\sigma^2}\lambda_{\mathbf{H},i} \right) \right\} \tag{4.42}$$

The channel's outage capacity $C_{\mathrm{out},q}$ satisfies

$$P(C \leq C_{\mathrm{out},q}) = q\%$$

where $C_{\mathrm{out},q}$ indicates that the communication system can guarantee that it is greater than this capacity value with the probability of $(100 - q)\%$. If the channel information is known at the transmitting end, the system's outage capacity can be increased with the same outage probability.

4.2.3 *Comparison of MIMO channel capacity for average power allocation*

It is assumed that the analysis model of the channel capacity is a complex baseband linear system, the number of transmitting antennas is M_{T}, the number of receiving antennas is M_{R}, the channel state information of the transmitting end is unknown, the total transmitted power is P, the power of each transmitting antenna is P/M_{T}, the total power received by the receiving antenna is equal to the total transmitting power, the channel is interfered by additive white Gaussian noise, the noise power of each receiving antenna is σ^2, the bandwidth of the transmitted signal is sufficiently narrow and the frequency response of the channel can be considered flat. The channel matrix is represented by an $M_R \times M_T$ complex matrix H, and the (i, j)th element $h_{i,j}$ of H represents the channel attenuation coefficient of the ith transmitting antenna to the jth receiving antenna.

4.2.3.1 *SISO channel capacity*

It is a communication system that uses a single antenna to transmit and a single antenna to receive (1×1). For a deterministic SISO channel, $M_R = M_T = 1$, the channel matrix degenerates to a single channel coefficient $H = h = 1$. According to the Shannon equation, the normalized capacity of the channel can be expressed as[3]

$$C = \text{lb}\left(1 + \frac{P}{\sigma^2}\right) \tag{4.43}$$

This capacity is generally not limited by the complexity of the coding or signal design, which means as long as the signal-to-noise ratio is increased by 3 dB, the channel capacity is increased by 1 bit/Hz/s. Considering the influence of channel fading, if h is used to represent the complex Gaussian channel amplitude ($H = h$) of unit power at the time of observation, the normalized channel capacity is expressed as

$$C = \text{lb}\left(1 + \frac{P}{\sigma^2}|h|^2\right) \tag{4.44}$$

4.2.3.2 *MISO channel capacity*

A communication system which uses M_T antennas to transmit and a single antenna to receive, namely an MISO channel, is equivalent to transmit diversity. The channel matrix becomes vector $\mathbf{H} = (h_1, h_2, \ldots, h_{M_T})^H$, where, h_i represents the channel amplitude of the ith antenna from the transmitting side to the receiving side. If the amplitude of the channel is fixed, the capacity of the channel[4] can be expressed as

$$C = \text{lb}\left(1 + \mathbf{H}\mathbf{H}^H \frac{P}{\sigma^2 M_T}\right)$$

$$= \text{lb}\left(1 + \sum_{i=1}^{M_T} |h_i|^2 \frac{P}{\sigma^2 M_T}\right)$$

$$= \text{lb}\left(1 + \frac{P}{\sigma^2}\right) \tag{4.45}$$

where $\sum_{i=1}^{M_T} |h_i|^2 = M_T$. It is because the coefficients of the channel are assumed to be fixed and subject to normalization, and the channel capacity does not increase as the number of transmitting antennas increases.

If the amplitude of the channel coefficients varies randomly, the channel capacity can be expressed as

$$C = \text{lb}\left(1 + \chi^2_{2M_T} \frac{P}{\sigma^2 M_T}\right) \tag{4.46}$$

where $\chi^2_{2M_T}$ is an χ-square random variable with $2M_T$ degrees of freedom and $\chi^2_{2M_T} = \sum_{i=1}^{M_T} |h_i|^2$. Obviously, the channel capacity is also a random variable.

4.2.3.3 *SIMO channel capacity*

A communication system which uses M_R antennas to transmit and a single antenna to receive, namely an SIMO channel, is equivalent to reception diversity. The channel can be regarded as consisting of M_R different coefficients, namely $\mathbf{H} = [h_1, h_2, \ldots, h_{M_R}]$, where h_j represents the channel coefficient of the jth antenna from the transmitting side to the receiving side. If the amplitude of the channel coefficient is fixed, the channel capacity[4] can be expressed as

$$
\begin{aligned}
C &= \text{lb}\left(1 + \mathbf{H}^H \mathbf{H} \frac{P}{\sigma^2}\right) \\
&= \text{lb}\left(1 + \sum_{j=1}^{M_R} |h_j|^2 \mathbf{H}^H \frac{P}{\sigma^2}\right) \\
&= \text{lb}\left(1 + M_R \frac{P}{\sigma^2}\right)
\end{aligned}
\tag{4.47}
$$

where $\sum_{j=1}^{M_R} |h_j|^2 = M_R$ because the channel system is normalized. It can be seen from the equation of the channel capacity that the SIMO channel obtains M_R times diversity gain compared with the SISO channel.

If the amplitude of the channel coefficients varies randomly, the channel capacity can be expressed as

$$C = \text{lb}\left(1 + \chi^2_{2M_R} \frac{P}{\sigma^2}\right) \tag{4.48}$$

where $\chi^2_{2M_R}$ is an χ-square random variable with $2M_R$ degrees of freedom and $\chi^2_{2M_R} = \sum_{j=1}^{M_R} |h_j|^2$. The channel capacity is also a random variable.

4.2.3.4 MIMO channel capacity

A communication system that uses M_R antennas to receive and M_T antennas to transmit is called an MIMO channel. Under the condition that the state information of transmission channel is unknown, if the amplitude of the channel is fixed, the channel capacity can be expressed as

$$C = \mathrm{lb}\left[\det\left(\mathbf{I}_{\min} + \frac{P}{M_T\sigma^2}\mathbf{Q}\right)\right] \tag{4.49}$$

where min is the minimum value of M_T and M_R. The definition of matrix $\mathbf{Q}^5$ is as follows:

$$\mathbf{Q} = \begin{cases} \mathbf{H}^H\mathbf{H}, & M_R < M_T \\ \mathbf{H}\mathbf{H}^H, & M_R > M_T \end{cases} \tag{4.50}$$

(1) MIMO system with 1 channel matrix

For the MIMO system with 1 channel matrix, namely $h_{i,j} = 1 (i = 1, 2, \ldots, M_T; j = 1, 2, \ldots, M_R)$, if the receiving end adopts the coherent detection combining technique, then the signals on each antenna after processing should have the same frequency and phase. In this case, it can be considered that the signals from the M_T transmitting antenna are the same, namely $s_i = s(i = 1, 2, \ldots, M_T)$. The signal received by the jth antenna can be represented as $r_j = M_T s_i = M_T s$, and the power received by the antenna can be expressed as $M_T^2(P/M_T) = M_T P$, and thus, the equivalent signal-to-noise ratio obtained on each receiving antenna is $M_T P/\sigma^2$. Therefore, the total signal-to-noise ratio at the receiving end is $M_R M_T P/\sigma^2$. The multi-antenna system at this time is equivalent to a single-antenna system, but this single-antenna system achieves $M_R M_T$ times diversity gain compared to the original, pure, single-antenna system, and the channel capacity can be expressed as

$$C = \mathrm{lb}\left(1 + M_R M_T \frac{P}{\sigma^2}\right) \tag{4.51}$$

If the receiving end adopts the non-coherent detection combining technique, since the signals on each antenna after processing are not the same, the signal-to-noise ratio obtained on each receiving antenna is still

P/σ^2, and the total signal-to-noise ratio obtained by the receiving end is $M_{\rm R}P/\sigma^2$. At this time, the equivalent single-antenna system obtains $M_{\rm R}$ times diversity gain compared to the original pure single-antenna system, and the channel capacity is expressed as

$$C = \mathrm{lb}\left(1 + M_{\rm R}\frac{P}{\sigma^2}\right) \tag{4.52}$$

(2) MIMO system with orthogonal transmission subchannel

For an MIMO system with orthogonal transmission subchannels, which means parallel subchannels composed of multiple antennas are orthogonal to each other, there is no mutual interference between the individual channels. For convenience, assume that the number of antennas at both ends is the same ($M_{\rm R} = M_{\rm T} = M$). And the channel matrix can be expressed as $\mathbf{H} = \sqrt{M}\mathbf{I}_M$, where, $\mathbf{I}_M$ is an $M \times M$ unit matrix and the coefficient $\sqrt{M}$ is introduced to meet the requirements of power normalization. By Eq. (4.49), we can obtain

$$\begin{aligned}
C &= \mathrm{lb}\left[\det\left(\mathbf{I}_M + \frac{P}{M\sigma^2}\mathbf{H}\mathbf{H}^{\rm H}\right)\right] \\
&= \mathrm{lb}\left[\det\left(\mathbf{I}_M + \frac{P}{M\sigma^2}M\mathbf{I}_M\right)\right] \\
&= \mathrm{lb}\left[\det\left(\mathrm{diag}\left(1 + \frac{P}{\sigma^2}\right)\right)\right] \\
&= \mathrm{lb}\left[1 + \frac{P}{\sigma^2}\right]^M = M\,\mathrm{lb}\left[1 + \frac{P}{\sigma^2}\right]
\end{aligned} \tag{4.53}$$

Compared to the original single-antenna system, the channel capacity achieves M times gain due to the decoupling between the sub-channels of the individual antennas.

If the amplitude of the channel coefficient changes randomly, the capacity of the MIMO channel is a random variable, and its average value[6] can be expressed as

$$C = \mathrm{E}\left\{\mathrm{lb}\left[\det\left(\mathbf{I}_r + \frac{P}{M_{\rm T}\sigma^2}\mathbf{Q}\right)\right]\right\} \tag{4.54}$$

where r is the rank of channel matrix $\mathbf{H}$ and $r \leq \min(M_{\rm T}, M_{\rm R})$.

(3) Ultimate capacity of the MIMO channel

When the number of transmitting antennas and receiving antennas is large, the calculation of Eq. (4.54) becomes complicated, but it can be estimated by means of the Lagrangian polynomial

$$C = \int_0^\infty \text{lb}\left(1 + \frac{P}{M_T\sigma^2}\lambda\right) \sum_{k=0}^{m-1} \frac{k}{(k+n+m)!} [L_k^{(n-m)}(\lambda)]^2 \lambda^{n-m} \, e^{-\lambda} \, d\lambda$$

(4.55)

where $m = \min(M_T, M_R)$, $n = \max(M_T, M_R)$, and $L_k^{(n-m)}(x)$ is a k-order Lagrangian polynomial. If $\lambda = m/n$, which means when the number of antennas (M_T, M_R) increases, their ratio λ remains constant, and the channel capacity expression normalized by m can be derived as

$$\lim_{n\to\infty} \frac{C}{n} = \frac{1}{2\pi} \int_{v_1}^{v_2} \text{lb}\left(1 + \frac{mP}{M_T\sigma^2}v\right) \sqrt{\left(\frac{v_2}{v} - 1\right)} \sqrt{\left(1 - \frac{v_1}{v}\right)} dv \quad (4.56)$$

where $v_2 = (\sqrt{\tau} + 1)^2$, and $v_1 = (\sqrt{\tau} - 1)^2$. Under the condition of fast Rayleigh fading, set $m = n = M_T = M_R$ and $v_1 = 0$, $v_2 = 4$ can be obtained. Asymptotic channel capacity Eq. (4.56) becomes

$$\lim_{n\to\infty} \frac{C}{n} = \frac{1}{\pi} \int_0^4 \text{lb}\left(1 + \frac{P}{\sigma^2}v\right) \sqrt{\left(\frac{1}{v} - \frac{1}{4}\right)} dv$$

$$\geq \frac{1}{\pi} \int_0^4 \text{lb}\left(\frac{P}{\sigma^2}v\right) \sqrt{\left(\frac{1}{v} - \frac{1}{4}\right)} dv$$

$$\geq \text{lb}\left(\frac{P}{\sigma^2}\right) - 1 \quad (4.57)$$

Equation (4.57) shows that the ultimate channel capacity increases linearly with the number of antennas (n) and increases logarithmically with the signal-to-noise ratio (P/σ^2).

4.3 MIMO Space–Time Coding Technology

The concept of space–time coding is based on the pioneering work of Wintersong in the mid-1980s on antenna diversity for wireless communication capacity. Space–time coding is a signal coding technique which can obtain a higher data transmission rate. It combines spatial signal transmission with time signal transmission to achieve a two-dimensional combination of space and time. In space, by setting up multiple antennas at the transmitting end and the receiving end, respectively, the multi-capacity spatial diversity technology is used to increase the capacity of the system. In time, the diversity gain is obtained at the receiving end by using the same antenna to transmit different signals in different time slots. In this way, the space–time coding technique can simultaneously obtain diversity gain and coding gain and can implement parallel multipath transmission in the transmission channel to improve band utilization.

4.3.1 *Space–time coding and coding guidelines*

For a multi-antenna system, assume that the transmitter uses M_T transmitting antennas and the receiver uses M_R receiving antennas. As shown in Fig. 4.6, the input information data are divided into M_T sub-data streams through space–time coding. Through pulse shaping and modulation, the M_T signals are transmitted simultaneously from M_T different antennas to produce a codeword matrix $\mathbf{C}$ with M_T rows.

The element of the ith row and the tth column of $\mathbf{C}$ is denoted by c_t^i, which represents a signal transmitted by the ith antenna at time slot t, $1 \leq i \leq M_T$. It is assumed that the channel is flat quasi-static fading which means the fading coefficient $h_{i,j}$ remains unchanged in one frame of data, $h_{i,j}$ is independent of each frame, and the bilateral variance is 0.5. The constellation diagram has been normalized so that the average energy of the constellation is 1. The signal received on the ith secondary receiving antenna in the time slot t is

$$y_t^i = \sum_{j=1}^{M_T} h_{i,j} c_t^j \sqrt{E_S} + n_t^i, \quad i = 1, 2, \ldots, M_R \tag{4.58}$$

where E_S is the average energy of each signal point in the constellation. n_t^i is the zero-mean additive complex Gaussian white noise received by the ith

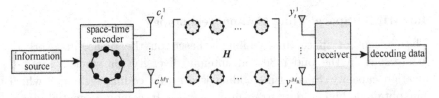

Fig. 4.6. The space–time coding MIMO system.

secondary receiving antenna in the tth slot, and the bilateral power spectral density is $\sigma^2/2$.

The codewords transmitted in L time slots are considered to be $\mathbf{c} = c_1^1 c_1^2 \ldots c_1^{M_T} c_2^1 c_2^2 \cdots c_2^{M_T} \cdots c_L^1 c_L^2 \cdots c_L^{M_T}$, and the receiver misjudges the codewords as $\mathbf{e} = e_1^1 e_1^2 \cdots e_1^{M_T} e_2^1 e_2^2 \cdots e_2^{M_T} \cdots e_L^1 e_L^2 \cdots e_L^{M_T}$ by maximum likelihood detection. Assuming that the channel state information is known at the receiving end, the error probability of misjudging $\mathbf{c}$ as $\mathbf{e}$ can be approximated as

$$P(\mathbf{c} \to \mathbf{e}|h_{i,j}, \ i = 1,2,\ldots, M_R; j = 1,2,\ldots, M_T) \leq \exp[-d^2(\mathbf{c,e})E_s/4\sigma^2] \tag{4.59}$$

where

$$d^2(\mathbf{c,e}) = \sum_i^{M_R} \sum_t^L \left| \sum_j^{M_T} h_{i,j}(c_t^j - e_t^j) \right|^2 \tag{4.60}$$

Defining $\mathbf{\Omega}_i = (h_{i,1}, h_{i,2}, \ldots, h_{i,M_T})$, Eq. (4.60) can be rewritten as

$$d^2(\mathbf{c,e}) = \sum_i^{M_R} \sum_{j_2}^{M_T} \sum_{j_1}^{M_T} h_{i,j_1} h_{i,j_2}^* \sum_t^L (c_t^{j_1} - e_t^{j_1})(c_t^{j_2} - e_t^{j_2})^*$$

$$= \sum_t^{M_R} \mathbf{\Omega}_i \mathbf{A}(\mathbf{c,e}) \mathbf{\Omega}_i^H \tag{4.61}$$

where matrix $\mathbf{A}(\mathbf{c,e})$ is

$$\mathbf{A}(\mathbf{c,e})_{i,j} = \sum_t^L (c_t^i - e_t^i)(c_t^j - e_t^j)^* \tag{4.62}$$

The difference matrix $\mathbf{B}(\mathbf{c,e})$ is defined as

$$\mathbf{B}(\mathbf{c,e}) = \begin{pmatrix} e_1^1 - c_1^1 & e_2^1 - c_2^1 & \cdots & e_L^1 - c_L^1 \\ e_1^2 - c_1^2 & e_2^2 - c_2^2 & \cdots & e_L^2 - c_L^2 \\ \vdots & \vdots & & \vdots \\ e_1^{M_T} - c_1^{M_T} & e_2^{M_T} - c_2^{M_T} & \cdots & e_L^{M_T} - c_L^{M_T} \end{pmatrix} \tag{4.63}$$

Matrix $\mathbf{A}(\mathbf{c,e})$ can then be expressed as $\mathbf{A}(\mathbf{c,e}) = \mathbf{B}(\mathbf{c,e})\mathbf{B}(\mathbf{c,e})^H$, where, $\mathbf{B}(\mathbf{c,e})$ is the square root of $\mathbf{A}(\mathbf{c,e})$.

Then the error probability can be written as

$$P(\mathbf{c} \to \mathbf{e} | h_{i,j}, i = 1, 2, \ldots, M_{\mathrm{R}}; j = 1, 2, \ldots, M_{\mathrm{T}})$$

$$\leq \prod_i^{M_{\mathrm{R}}} \exp[-\boldsymbol{\Omega}_i \mathbf{A}(\mathbf{c}, \mathbf{e}) \boldsymbol{\Omega}_i^{\mathrm{H}} E_s / 4\sigma^2] \qquad (4.64)$$

$\mathbf{A}(\mathbf{c}, \mathbf{e})$ is a Hermite matrix whose n eigenvalues $\lambda_i (i = 1, 2, \ldots, n)$ are non-negative real numbers. According to the matrix eigen decomposition theory, there must be a unitary matrix $\mathbf{V}$ and a real diagonal matrix $\mathbf{D}$, which satisfy

$$\mathbf{V}\mathbf{A}(\mathbf{c}, \mathbf{e})\mathbf{V}^{\mathrm{H}} = \mathbf{D} \qquad (4.65)$$

The diagonal element of matrix $\mathbf{D}$ is the eigenvalue of $\mathbf{A}(\mathbf{c}, \mathbf{e})$.

Next, the eigenvalue of the matrix $\mathbf{A}(\mathbf{c}, \mathbf{e})$ is used to represent $d^2(\mathbf{c}, \mathbf{e})$ and set

$$(\beta_{i,1}, \beta_{i,2}, \ldots, \beta_{i,M_{\mathrm{T}}}) = \boldsymbol{\Omega}_i \mathbf{V}^{\mathrm{H}} \qquad (4.66)$$

Then from Eq. (4.61), it can be obtained that

$$\boldsymbol{\Omega}_i \mathbf{A}(\mathbf{c}, \mathbf{e}) \boldsymbol{\Omega}_i^{\mathrm{H}} = \sum_{j=1}^{M_{\mathrm{T}}} \lambda_j |\beta_{i,j}|^2 \qquad (4.67)$$

Since $h_{i,j}$ are complex Gaussian random variables independent of each other and $\mathbf{V}^{\mathrm{H}}$ is a unitary matrix, $\beta_{i,j}$ are also a complex Gaussian random variables independent of each other. $\mathrm{E}\{h_{i,j}\}$ is assumed to be the mean of $h_{i,j}$. Set $\mathbf{E}_\Omega = (\mathrm{E}\{h_{i,1}\}, \mathrm{E}\{h_{i,2}\}, \ldots, \mathrm{E}\{h_{i,M_{\mathrm{T}}}\})$, then the mean of $\beta_{i,j}$ is $\mathrm{E}\{\beta_{i,j}\} = \mathbf{E}_\Omega \cdot \mathbf{v}_i$ with $\mathbf{v}_i$ representing the column vector of matrix $\mathbf{V}^{\mathrm{H}}$. Set $K_{i,j} = |\mathrm{E}\{\beta_{i,j}\}|^2 = |\mathbf{E}_\Omega \cdot \mathbf{v}_i|^2$, then the bilateral variance is $\sigma^2/2$.

For $|\beta_{i,j}| \geq 0$, $|\beta_{i,j}|$ obeys an independent Rician distribution whose probability density is given as

$$p(|\beta_{i,j}|) = 2|\beta_{i,j}| \exp(-|\beta_{i,j}|^2 - K_{i,j}) I_0(2|\beta_{i,j}| \sqrt{K_{i,j}}) \qquad (4.68)$$

where $I_0(\cdot)$ is a modified zero-order Bessel function of the first kind.

According to the probability density function of the variable $|\beta_{i,j}|$, the mean of the upper limit $\prod_i^{M_{\mathrm{R}}} \exp(-E_S/4\sigma^2) \sum_{j=1}^{M_{\mathrm{T}}} \lambda_j |\beta_{i,j}|^2$ of the error probability can be calculated and

$$P(\mathbf{c} \to \mathbf{e}) \le \prod_{i=1}^{M_R} \left[\prod_{j=1}^{M_T} \frac{1}{1 + \frac{E_S}{4\sigma^2}\lambda_j} \exp\left(-\frac{K_{i,j} \frac{E_S}{4\sigma^2}\lambda_j}{1 + \frac{E_S}{4\sigma^2}\lambda_j} \right) \right] \qquad (4.69)$$

Therefore, in the case of Rayleigh fading, the inequality (4.69) can be written as

$$P(\mathbf{c} \to \mathbf{e}) \le \left[\frac{1}{\prod_{i=1}^{M_T} \left(1 + \lambda_i E_S/4\sigma^2 \right)} \right]^{M_R} \qquad (4.70)$$

Assume rank $(\mathbf{A}) = r$, then $\mathbf{A}$ has r non-zero eigenvalues $\lambda_1, \lambda_2, \ldots, \lambda_r$. So the above inequality can be written as

$$P(\mathbf{c} \to \mathbf{e}) \le \left(\prod_{i=1}^{M_T} \lambda_i \right)^{-M_R} (E_S/4\sigma^2)^{-rM_R} \qquad (4.71)$$

The diversity gain is the index of the SNR in the error probability expression, and the coding gain is the gain obtained by the system compared to the uncoded system with a certain diversity gain. As can be seen from the above equation, the diversity gain obtained is rM_R and the coding gain obtained is $(\lambda_1 \lambda_2 \ldots \lambda_r)^{1/r}$ with $\lambda_1 \lambda_2 \ldots \lambda_r$ representing the absolute value of the determinant sum of all $r \times r$-order principal and complement minors. It can be seen that there are two parameters for measuring space–time coding performance: one is the diversity gain obtained by transmitting and receiving with multiple antennas; the other is the coding gain obtained by coding. In this way, it gives two design criteria for Rayleigh fading down-space coding.

(1) Rank Criterion: To obtain the maximum diversity gain $M_R M_T$, the difference matrix $\mathbf{B}(\mathbf{c}, \mathbf{e})$ must be full rank for any codewords $\mathbf{c}$ and $\mathbf{e}$. For two different sets of codewords, if the minimum rank of the difference matrix $\mathbf{B}(\mathbf{c}, \mathbf{e})$ is $r(r \le M_T)$, the obtained diversity gain is rM_R.

(2) Determinant Criterion: Assuming that the diversity gain rM_R is fixed, the coding gain depends on the determinant sum of all $r \times r$-order principal and complement minors of the matrix $\mathbf{A}(\mathbf{c}, \mathbf{e})$. By making its minimum value maximize, the maximum coding gain can be obtained. $\mathbf{A}(\mathbf{c}, \mathbf{e})$ is able to contain all codeword pairs $\mathbf{c}$ and $\mathbf{e}$. If the diversity gain is to reach $M_R M_T$ and the maximum coding gain is to be obtained,

the minimum value of the determinant of matrix $\mathbf{A}(\mathbf{c}, \mathbf{e})$ must be maximized.

4.3.2 *Space–time trellis code*

In 1998, Tarokh *et al.*[7] of AT&T Lab proposed the space–time trellis code (STTC), which is based on trellis code modulation and uses transmission diversity and channel coding to improve the anti-fading performance of the system. It has a high coding gain and diversity gain and can use multi-ary modulation to increase the transmission rate of the system.

For a space–time trellis code encoder, the next output state depends on its current state and the current input information bits. If the modulation method uses a constellation of size 2^q, there is a q bit input trellis encoder at each moment k, and the encoder determines its M_T outputs according to the generator polynomial and simultaneously transmits them through M_T antennas. Corresponding to the encoded trellis diagram, the encoder selects an output branch based on the current state and the currently input bit sequence.

The diagram of the 8PSK-8 state space–time trellis code with two transmitting antennas is shown in Fig. 4.7. The upper left corner of the

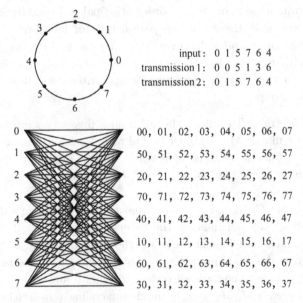

Fig. 4.7. **8PSK-8 state space–time trellis with two antennas.**

figure is a constellation diagram of 8PSK, and the constellation points are represented by numbers 0–7.

The trellis diagram represents the transition between the states of the space–time trellis encoder, and the left column of data in the trellis diagram represents the state of the encoder. The right number of the trellis diagram indicates the encoder output of each transition state from the current state to another state, where the first number represents the constellation point number of the signal transmitted from the first sub-transmitting antenna and the second number represents the constellation point number of the signal transmitted from the second sub-transmitting antenna.

For 8PSK, the input bit string of the space–time encoder is divided into a group of 3 bits corresponding to one of the 8 constellation points. Assume that there are 3 bits $d_k b_k a_k$ for the input encoder at the kth moment. At the moment, the encoder state is determined by the input bits at the $(k-1)$th and the $(k-2)$th time. At the kth time, the output of the encoder is

$$
\begin{aligned}
(x_1^k, x_2^k) = {} & d_{k-1}(4,0) + b_{k-1}(2,0) \\
& + a_{k-1}(5,0) + d_k(0,4) + b_k(0,2) + a_k(0,1)
\end{aligned}
\tag{4.72}
$$

Figure 4.8 shows the corresponding encoder structure. The numbers in the figure are weighting coefficients, and the adder performs the addition in modulo 8. The memory capacity of the encoder is determined by the number of encoder states.

If the number of states is increased, the free distance of any two coding paths in the state trellis diagram can be increased, and a larger coding gain

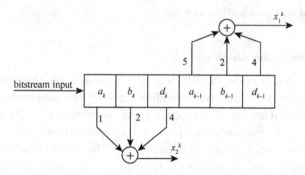

Fig. 4.8. The 8PSK-8 state encoder structure.

can be obtained, and the performance is better. However, as the number of encoder states increases, the complexity increases.

The space–time trellis code adopts the trellis coding method, so the Viterbi decoding algorithm can be used for decoding at the receiving end. Assume that the decoder knows the ideal channel state information $h_{i,j}(i = 1, 2 \ldots M_\mathrm{R}; j = 1, 2 \ldots M_\mathrm{T})$, r_t^i is the signal received by the receiving antenna i at time t, and the branch metric of the transmission branch labeled $q_t^1 q_t^2 \ldots q_t^{M_\mathrm{R}}$ is given as

$$\sum_{i=1}^{M_\mathrm{R}} \left| r_t^i - \sum_{j=1}^{M_\mathrm{T}} h_{i,j} q_t^j \right|^2 \tag{4.73}$$

If the encoded data are recovered by a minimum error probability, the path with the smallest cumulative metric can be selected as the output of the decoder by the add–compare–select method in the Viterbi decoding algorithm.

The design of the space–time trellis code can first maximize the diversity gain and then optimize the coding gain based on this according to the criteria in Section 4.3.1. Using exhaustive search, some better performing space–time trellis codes can be obtained. Reference 8 proves that space–time trellis code modulation can achieve the best compromise between code complexity and transmission rate. It is an optimal code, so there is no block code modulation method whose performance exceeds the space–time trellis code but is less complex than the space–time trellis code. However, when the diversity order and transmission rate increase, the decoding of space–time trellis codes will become very complicated, which is the main reason for limiting the application of space–time trellis codes in practical communication systems.

4.3.3 *Space–time block code*

Space–time block code (STBC) effectively overcomes the shortcomings of the space–time trellis code decoding, making the maximum likelihood decoding algorithm at the receiving end very simple. Although there is loss in performance compared to the space–time trellis code, the decoding complexity is much smaller than the space–time trellis code. Moreover, increasing the number of transmitting antennas or increasing the transmission rate does not have a large impact on its decoding complexity.

In 1998, Alamouti[9] proposed a simple two-branch transmit diversity scheme. When two transmitting antennas and one receiving antenna are used, the diversity gain obtained by this transmit diversity scheme is the same as the diversity gain obtained by using one transmitting antenna and two receiving antennas using maximum ratio combining (MRC). Moreover, this kind of transmit diversity scheme can be easily extended to the case of two transmitting antennas and M_R receiving antennas, and the diversity gain can be obtained as $2M_R$.

The Alamouti transmit diversity scheme of a typical two transmitting antenna and one receiving antenna is given as follows. Figure 4.9 shows the structure of the transmit diversity scheme.

At time t, two signals are simultaneously transmitted from two transmitting antennas, antenna 0 transmits signal s_0, and antenna 1 transmits signal s_1. Assuming that the symbol period is T, at the next time $t+T$, antenna 0 transmits signal $-s_1^*$, and antenna 1 transmits signal s_0^*. Table 4.1 shows the corresponding space–time coding scheme.

At time t, the channel gain between the transmitting antenna 0 and the receiving antenna is represented by a complex number $h_0(t)$, and the channel gain between the transmitting antenna 1 and the receiving antenna is represented by a complex number $h_1(t)$. Assume that the fading remains

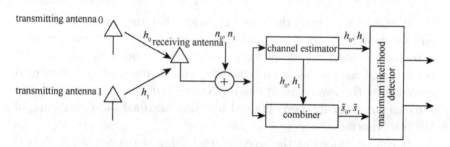

Fig. 4.9. **Structure of the transmit diversity scheme.**

Table 4.1. **Transmit diversity coding and transmission sequence with two antennas.**

Time	Transmitting antenna 0	Transmitting antenna 1
t	s_0	s_1
$t+T$	$-s_1^*$	s_0^*

constant for two consecutive symbol periods, namely

$$\begin{cases} h_0(t) = h_0(t+T) = h_0 = \alpha_0 \, e^{j\theta_0} \\ h_1(t) = h_1(t+T) = h_1 = \alpha_1 \, e^{j\theta_1} \end{cases} \tag{4.74}$$

The signals received at time t and time $t + T$ can be represented as

$$\begin{cases} r_0 = r(t) = h_0 s_0 + h_1 s_1 + n_0 \\ r_1 = r(t+T) = -h_0 s_1^* + h_1 s_0^* + n_1 \end{cases} \tag{4.75}$$

where n_0 and n_1 represent the noise and interference at the receiving end, respectively.

The combiner at the receiving end in Fig. 4.9 sends the following two combined signals to the maximum likelihood detector:

$$\begin{cases} \tilde{s}_0 = h_0^* r_0 + h_1 r_1^* \\ \tilde{s}_1 = h_1^* r_0 - h_0 r_1^* \end{cases} \tag{4.76}$$

Substituting Eqs. (4.74) and (4.75) into Eq. (4.76),

$$\begin{cases} \tilde{s}_0 = h_0^* r_0 + h_1 r_1^* = (\alpha_0^2 + \alpha_1^2) s_0 + h_0^* n_0 + h_1 n_1^* \\ \tilde{s}_1 = h_1^* r_0 - h_0 r_1^* = (\alpha_0^2 + \alpha_1^2) s_1 - h_0 n_1^* + h_1^* n_0 \end{cases} \tag{4.77}$$

It can be seen from the above equation that the combined signal $\tilde{s}_i$ and the combined signal using maximal ratio combining the two receiving antennas are identical except for the phase of the noise component, and the actual signal-to-noise ratio is not affected. Therefore, the diversity gain obtained by the two-transmit-one-receive transmit diversity scheme is the same as the diversity gain obtained by using maximal ratio combining of the two branches.

It can be judged at the receiving end using the maximum likelihood criterion. Assume that the decision signals are s_{0i} and s_{1i}, respectively, if and only if $i \neq k$,

$$d^2(r_0, h_0 s_{0i} + h_1 s_{1i}) + d^2(r_1, -h_0 s_{1i}^* + h_1 s_{0i}^*) \leq d^2(r_0, h_0 s_{0k} + h_1 s_{1k})$$
$$+ d^2(r_1, -h_0 s_{1k}^* + h_1 s_{0k}^*) \tag{4.78}$$

where

$$d^2(x, y) = (x - y)(x - y)^* \tag{4.79}$$

Equation (4.78) can be equivalent to

$$
\begin{cases}
(\alpha_0^2 + \alpha_1^2 - 1)|s_{0i}|^2 + d^2(\tilde{s}_0, s_{0i}) \\
\quad \leq (\alpha_0^2 + \alpha_1^2 - 1)|s_{0k}|^2 + d^2(\tilde{s}_0, s_{0k}), \quad \forall i \neq k \\
(\alpha_0^2 + \alpha_1^2 - 1)|s_{1i}|^2 + d^2(\tilde{s}_1, s_{1i}) \\
\quad \leq (\alpha_0^2 + \alpha_1^2 - 1)|s_{1k}|^2 + d^2(\tilde{s}_1, s_{1k}), \quad \forall i \neq k
\end{cases}
\tag{4.80}
$$

For PSK signal, $|s_i|^2 = |s_k|^2$, $\forall i, k$. Therefore, s_0 and s_1 are judged as s_{0i} and s_{1i} if and only if the following equation holds:

$$
\begin{cases}
d^2(\tilde{s}_0, s_{0i}) \leq d^2(\tilde{s}_0, s_{0k}), \quad \forall i \neq k \\
d^2(\tilde{s}_0, s_{0i}) \leq d^2(\tilde{s}_0, s_{0k}), \quad \forall i \neq k
\end{cases}
\tag{4.81}
$$

This two-transmitting–one-receiving transmit diversity scheme is also easily extended to two transmitting antennas and M_R receiving antennas, where the diversity order is $2M_R$. The Alamouti transmit diversity method does not require information feedback from the receiving end to the transmitting end, and its computational complexity is similar to that of the MRC. If the total transmitted power is the same, the Alamouti method distributes energy to the two transmitting antennas, resulting in a 3-dB performance loss compared to the MRC.

Tarokh *et al.* extended the two-antenna transmit diversity scheme proposed by Alamouti to any number of transmitting antennas and applied orthogonal design theory to propose orthogonal space–time block codes. The orthogonal space–time block code requires the space–time block coding matrix $\mathbf{G}$ to satisfy the orthogonal condition, namely

$$
\mathbf{G}\mathbf{G}^H = \alpha \mathbf{I}_n
\tag{4.82}
$$

where $\alpha = |c_1|^2 + |c_2|^2 +, \ldots, +|c_n|^2$, $c_1, c_2, \ldots, c_n$ is the codeword transmitted within a certain time slot. $\mathbf{I}_n$ is an $n \times n$ unit matrix. This orthogonality is reflected in the space and time domains. For matrix $\mathbf{G} = [g_{i,j}]_{m \times n}$, the element $g_{i,j}$ of the ith row and the jth column represents the signal transmitted on the jth transmitting antenna at the time slot i. For space–time block coding $(p \geq k)$ that uses p time slots to transmit k characters, the rate is defined by $R = k/p$.

The Alamouti transmit diversity transmission scheme introduced above is a 2×2 orthogonal space–time block code, and the transmission matrix is

$$
\mathbf{S} = \begin{pmatrix} s_1 & -s_2^* \\ s_2 & s_1^* \end{pmatrix}
\tag{4.83}
$$

This is the simplest orthogonal block space–time code, and its coding ratio is $R = k/p = 1$.

Two sets of space–time block codes of multiple transmitting antennas ($n \geq 2$) are given below, and their rates are 1/2 and 3/4, respectively.

For a space–time block code with rate $R = 1/2$, four symbols are transmitted in eight time slots. If three transmitting antennas are used, the corresponding orthogonal space–time block code matrix can be designed as

$$\mathbf{C} = \begin{pmatrix} c_1 & -c_2 & -c_3 & -c_4 & c_1^* & -c_2^* & -c_3^* & -c_4^* \\ c_2 & c_1 & c_4 & -c_3 & c_2^* & c_1^* & c_4^* & -c_3^* \\ c_3 & -c_4 & c_1 & c_2 & c_3^* & -c_4^* & c_1^* & c_2^* \end{pmatrix} \tag{4.84}$$

If four transmitting antennas are used, the orthogonal space–time block code matrix is given as

$$\mathbf{C} = \begin{pmatrix} c_1 & -c_2 & -c_3 & -c_4 & c_1^* & -c_2^* & -c_3^* & -c_4^* \\ c_2 & c_1 & c_4 & -c_3 & c_2^* & c_1^* & c_4^* & -c_3^* \\ c_3 & -c_4 & c_1 & c_2 & c_3^* & -c_4^* & c_1^* & c_2^* \\ c_4 & c_3 & -c_2 & c_1 & c_4^* & c_3^* & -c_2^* & c_1^* \end{pmatrix} \tag{4.85}$$

For a space–time block code with rate $R = 3/4$, three symbols are transmitted in four time slots. If three transmitting antennas are used, the corresponding orthogonal space–time block code matrix can be designed as

$$\mathbf{C} = \begin{pmatrix} c_1 & -c_2^* & \frac{1}{\sqrt{2}}c_3^* & \frac{1}{\sqrt{2}}c_3^* \\ c_2 & c_1^* & \frac{1}{\sqrt{2}}c_3^* & -\frac{1}{\sqrt{2}}c_3^* \\ \frac{1}{\sqrt{2}}c_3 & \frac{1}{\sqrt{2}}c_3^* & \frac{1}{2}(-c_1 - c_1^* + c_2 - c_2^*) & \frac{1}{2}(c_1 - c_1^* + c_2 + c_2^*) \end{pmatrix} \tag{4.86}$$

If four transmitting antennas are used, the orthogonal space–time block code matrix is

$$\mathbf{C} = \begin{pmatrix} c_1 & -c_2^* & \frac{1}{\sqrt{2}}c_3^* & \frac{1}{\sqrt{2}}c_3^* \\ c_2 & c_1^* & \frac{1}{\sqrt{2}}c_3^* & -\frac{1}{\sqrt{2}}c_3^* \\ \frac{1}{\sqrt{2}}c_3 & \frac{1}{\sqrt{2}}c_3^* & -\frac{1}{2}(c_1 + c_1^* - c_2 + c_2^*) & \frac{1}{2}(c_1 - c_1^* + c_2 + c_2^*) \\ \frac{1}{\sqrt{2}}c_3 & -\frac{1}{\sqrt{2}}c_3 & \frac{1}{2}(c_1 - c_1^* - c_2 - c_2^*) & -\frac{1}{2}(c_1 + c_1^* + c_2 - c_2^*) \end{pmatrix} \tag{4.87}$$

The decoding of the orthogonal space–time block code can use the maximum likelihood detection method. Assume that the path gain $h_{i,j}$ of the fading channel can be accurately estimated at the receiving end. According to Eq. (4.58), the receiving end can use the maximum likelihood decoding algorithm to calculate all the codewords $c_1^1 c_1^2 \cdots c_1^n c_2^1 c_2^2 \cdots c_2^n \cdots c_p^1 c_p^2 \cdots c_p^n$ by the following equation and find the smallest codeword as the correct codeword to complete the decoding:

$$\sum_{t=1}^{p} \sum_{i=1}^{M} \left| y_t^i - \sum_{j}^{N} h_{i,j} c_t^j \right|^2 \tag{4.88}$$

By changing the definition of the received signal vector, an orthogonal channel matrix can be constructed by using the orthogonal transmission matrix and the detection and decision can be separately made for each symbol at the receiving end, which requires only some linear processing, thereby further simplifying the maximum likelihood detection decoding algorithm. This orthogonal space–time block code can obtain the whole diversity gain provided by multiple transmitting and receiving antennas.

4.3.4 *Layered space–time code*

Bell Lab's layered space–time structure (BLAST) was originally a space–time coding scheme proposed by Foschini of Bell Labs. It uses multiple antennas to simultaneously transmit parallel data streams in the same frequency band. In a propagation environment with a rich multipath, each data stream can be separated at the receiving end. Therefore, the layered space–time code has a very high frequency band utilization, which can increase the capacity linearly with the number of antennas. It is one of the solutions for high-speed wireless communication in the MIMO system.

Figure 4.10 shows the structure of layered space–time coding. The original high-speed data stream is demultiplexed and separated into M sub-data streams of the same rate and input into M parallel channel encoders for independent coding. These encoders can be conventional convolutional encoders or can output signals directly without any coding. Spatial layered coding maps the output of the parallel encoder to the transmitting antenna, which is transmitted after modulation. Since all sub-streams are transmitted using the same frequency band, the spectrum usage is very efficient.

Layered space–time coding (LSTC) can be divided into horizontal layered space–time coding (HLSTC), vertical layered space–time coding (VLSTC), and diagonal layered space–time coding (DLSTC) according to

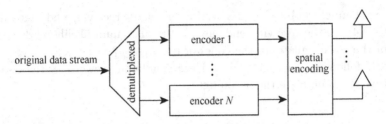

Fig. 4.10. Structure of a layered space–time code system.

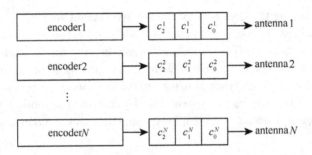

Fig. 4.11. Horizontal layered space–time code.

the mapping way from parallel encoder output data flow to transmission antenna.

The coding process of horizontal space–time coding is shown in Fig. 4.11 and the structure of HLST is relatively simple. The output of the ith $(i = 1, 2, \ldots, N)$ channel coder is directly transmitted by the ith antenna. The encoder and the antenna maintain a fixed correspondence. Here, the output of the kth encoder at time $\tau(\tau = 0, 1, \ldots)$ is represented by c_τ^k.

The diagonal layered space–time structure (DLST) is a better performance layered structure. Figure 4.12 shows the coding structure of three antenna diagonal layered space–time codes. In the DLST structure, for a particular encoder, its output is not always transmitted through a specific antenna, but is sent to M_T transmitting antennas for cyclic transmission instead. The output of the encoder is arranged on the diagonal of the transmit matrix. Compared to the signal transmitted by the first antenna, the time at which the ith antenna transmits the signal is delayed by $i - 1$ unit time.

Assuming that the rate of the sub-encoder is fixed, regardless of the number of transmitting antennas, the data rate provided by the LST is proportional to the number of transmitting antennas M_T, which

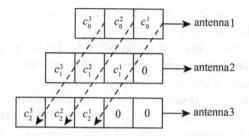

Fig. 4.12. Diagonal layered space–time code.

greatly improves the spectrum utilization. From the perspective of diversity, the output of each HLST encoder always experiences a specific fading channel, which may cause performance degradation of a layer and result in congestion of the communication link. However, the DLST is transmitted circularly by different antennas, so that the output of each sub-encoder goes through M_T different paths to the receiving end. The introduction of spatial diversity can obtain more diversity gain than HLST and is superior to HLST in anti-fading performance. However, since the initial position needs to be filled in the lower corner of the transmit matrix, there will be some loss in spectral efficiency, especially when the data block length is relatively short, and the impact is obvious.

4.3.5 *Other space–time coding*

The space–time block code and the space–time trellis code are introduced above, and they need to know the channel state information at the receiving end when decoding. When the channel changes faster or the number of transmitting antennas is large, it is very difficult or even impossible to obtain the channel information by channel estimation at the receiving end. The following discussion briefly introduces two kinds of space–time coding which do not require channel information at the receiving end: unitary space–time coding (USTC) and differential space–time coding (DSTC).

For an ideal Rayleigh fast-fading channel environment, it is assumed that the channel fading factor remains constant for a period of time (T symbol intervals). For M_T transmitting antennas, the transmitted codeword matrix $\mathbf{C}$ of unitary space–time code is a $T \times M_T$ unitary matrix satisfying $\mathbf{C}^H \mathbf{C} = \mathbf{I}_{M_T}$. The design criteria for USTC are also different from the space–time codes introduced before. It is no longer used to optimize the Euclidean distance between any two codeword matrices but is used to optimize the norm $\|C_i^* C_j\|_F$ of the correlation matrix between any two codeword matrices in order to minimize it.

Differential space–time coding proposed by Tarokh extends the single-antenna differential detection technique to multi-antenna systems. It is based on Alamouti's transmit diversity scheme and still uses two transmitting antennas. The transmit code matrix has complex orthogonality, and there is no need to know the channel state information at both the transmitting end and the receiving end. Differential space–time coding can achieve the same diversity gain as the Alamouti orthogonal space–time block code, can achieve full-rate transmission, and also has a low decoding complexity at the receiving end.

In addition, better performance can be achieved if the space–time coding is cascaded with other coding methods or combined with beamforming. The Turbo code is developed based on the convolutional code. It combines the convolutional code with the random interleaver to implement random coding and uses an iterative decoding algorithm at the receiving end. Compared with the traditional convolutional code, the Turbo code is a coding and decoding method which approximates the Shannon limit and has good coding gain. Space–time coding has a high diversity gain, but the coding gain is not high. If the Turbo code and the space–time code are cascaded to obtain a space–time Turbo code, it can obtain both the coding and the transmit diversity gain. The method uses the Turbo encoder as the outer encoder and the space–time encoder as the inner encoder. The receiving end performs joint decoding of the inner code and the outer code according to the iterative decoding method of the Turbo code.

The combination of STBC and antenna beamforming is to form a new transmitted codeword matrix by premultiplying a beamforming matrix by the original STBC coding matrix. At low SNR, traditional beamformer performance is better than STBC, but with the increase of SNR, STBC performance will exceed beamforming. However, the integrated scheme of STBC + beamforming always achieves better performance than separate beamforming or STBC. The optimal value of the weight matrix for beamforming is obtained from the correlation between the true value and the estimated value of the channel information.

With the development of the multi-antenna technology, in order to obtain greater diversity gain and coding gain, the combination of the coding technology and the modulation technology, the application of the precoding technology and space–time coding in OFDM, and space–time-frequency three-dimensional coding have been the research hotspots. In a word, multi-antenna space–time coding technology will have great potential in future mobile communications and will be widely used.

4.4 MIMO Beamforming Technology

Problems such as channel fading, multipath interference, and multiple access interference will seriously affect the communication performance of the future high-rate wireless transmission systems. Therefore, how to improve system capacity while resisting channel fading and interference is an urgent problem to be solved for communication systems in the future. As an effective means to suppress interference and reduce noise damage, beamforming technology has gradually attracted attention in the field of mobile communications with the rapid development of large-scale and ultra-large-scale integrated circuits and digital signal processing technologies. Smart antenna technology based on beamforming technology has been applied as a key technology in 3G standard TD-SCDMA.

By appropriately weighting the signals transmitted by the antennas in the antenna array, beamforming can generate a directional virtual beam. And thus the goals of enhancing the desired signal while suppressing interference and improving communication capacity and quality can be achieved.[10] Although the beamforming technology of MIMO system is derived from the antenna array beamforming technology, the MIMO system can adopt the corresponding beamforming strategy to improve the diversity or multiplexing gain of the system since the parallel subchannels of the MIMO system can be considered as independent.[11] In this section we will focus on the MIMO beamforming technology.

Assume that the number of transmitting antennas is M_T and the number of receiving antennas is M_R. The corresponding MIMO system model is shown in Fig. 4.13, where channel $\mathbf{H}$ is an $M_R \times M_T$ matrix, the transmitted signal $\mathbf{s}$ is an $M_T \times 1$ vector, and the receiving signal $\mathbf{y}$ is an $M_R \times 1$ vector.

For convenience, we assume that the channel is Rayleigh stationary fading, then the receiving signal can be written as

$$\mathbf{y} = \mathbf{Hs} + \mathbf{n} \tag{4.89}$$

where $\mathbf{n}$ is the additive white Gaussian noise, $\mathrm{E}\{\mathbf{n}^H\mathbf{n}\} = N_0\mathbf{I}$ with N_0 representing the noise single-sideband power spectral density. When the transmitter knows the channel information, it usually uses equal power transmission, which means the signal power of each antenna is P_s/M_T with

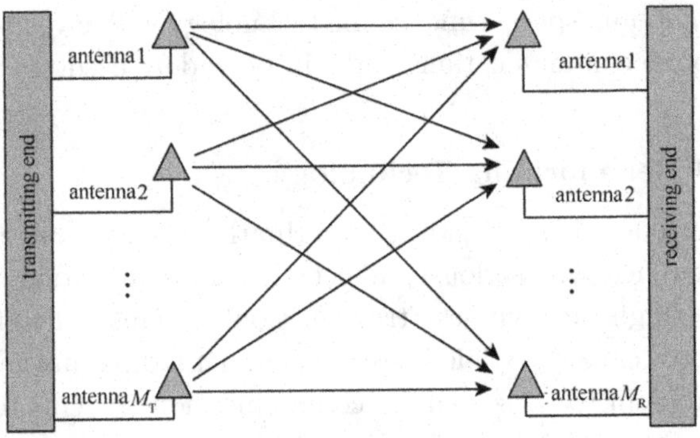

Fig. 4.13. Schematic diagram of the MIMO system.

P_s being the total power. The transmitting signal covariance matrix is

$$\mathbf{R}_s = \frac{P_s}{M_T}\mathbf{I}_M \qquad (4.90)$$

It can be seen that the channel capacity of the system is expressed as

$$C = \max_{\mathrm{Tr}(\mathbf{R}_s)=P_s} \mathrm{lb}\det\left(\mathbf{I}_K + \frac{P_s}{MN_0}\mathbf{H}\mathbf{R}_s\mathbf{H}^{\mathrm{H}}\right) \qquad (4.91)$$

When the transmitter knows the channel state information, the channel capacity can be optimized by rationally designing the covariance matrix $\mathbf{R}_s$. For single-user beamforming, the required beam is mainly obtained by processing the channel matrix $\mathbf{H}$. And for multi-user systems, beamforming is mainly used to implement space division multiple access. Specifically, each antenna of the base station can add different weight vectors when transmitting signals to different users. When the receiver receives the signal, each user only receives the signal transmitted to itself and does not need to receive the signal transmitted to other users. Therefore, the signal interference between users can be reduced or eliminated, and thus, the purpose of using the same frequency resource by multiple users can be realized. In the following, we will introduce the single-user beamforming technology and multi-user beamforming technology in detail.

4.4.1 *Single-user beamforming*

The state information is known at the transmitting end and we can usually implement eigen beamforming to achieve single-user beamforming.[12] In the single-user MIMO system shown in Fig. 4.14, it is assumed that the

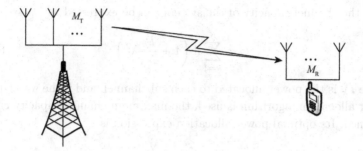

Fig. 4.14. The single-user MIMO system.

channel matrices $\mathbf{H}$ are known at the transmitting end, and the singular value decomposition (SVD) is obtained for the channel matrix.

$$\mathbf{H} = \mathbf{U}\boldsymbol{\Sigma}\mathbf{V}^{\mathrm{H}} \tag{4.92}$$

where $\mathbf{U}$ is an $M_{\mathrm{R}} \times K$ unitary matrix, $\mathbf{V}$ is an $M_{\mathrm{T}} \times K$ unitary matrix, and $\boldsymbol{\Sigma}$ is a $K \times K$ diagonal matrix. They can be expressed as

$$
\begin{aligned}
\mathbf{U} &= [\mathbf{u}_1, \mathbf{u}_2, \ldots, \mathbf{u}_K], \\
\mathbf{V} &= [\mathbf{v}_1, \mathbf{v}_2, \ldots, \mathbf{v}_K], \\
\boldsymbol{\Sigma} &= \begin{bmatrix} \lambda_1 & 0 & \cdots & 0 \\ 0 & \lambda_2 & \vdots & \vdots \\ \vdots & \vdots & \ddots & 0 \\ 0 & \cdots & 0 & \lambda_K \end{bmatrix}
\end{aligned} \tag{4.93}
$$

where $\lambda_1 \geq \lambda_2 \geq \lambda_K$, which means the diagonal elements are singular values arranged in descending order, and K is the rank of the channel matrix. Using $\mathbf{V}$ and $\mathbf{U}^{\mathrm{H}}$ as the transmit beamforming and receive beamforming matrices at the transmitting end and the receiving end, respectively, the received signal is given as

$$
\begin{aligned}
\hat{\mathbf{y}} &= \mathbf{U}^{\mathrm{H}}(\mathbf{HVs} + \mathbf{n}) = \mathbf{U}^{\mathrm{H}}\mathbf{U}\boldsymbol{\Sigma}\mathbf{V}^{\mathrm{H}}\mathbf{Vs} + \mathbf{U}^{\mathrm{H}}\mathbf{n} \\
&= \boldsymbol{\Sigma}\mathbf{s} + \hat{\mathbf{n}}
\end{aligned} \tag{4.94}
$$

It can be seen that the MIMO transmission channel is converted into K parallel scalar channels, and the gain of the kth channel is λ_k. At this time, the channel capacity of the system can be expressed as

$$C = \sum_{k=1}^{K} \text{lb}\left(1 + \frac{P_k}{N_0}\lambda_k^2\right) \tag{4.95}$$

where P_k is the power allocated to each subchannel, and if the water-filling power allocation algorithm is used, the maximum channel capacity can be obtained. Its optimal power allocation expression is

$$P_i^{\text{opt}} = \left(L - \frac{N_0}{\lambda_i^2}\right)_+ \tag{4.96}$$

where $(A)_+$ denotes $\max(A, 0)$. By selecting L, the power allocation can satisfy the constraint $\sum_{i=1}^{K} P_i^{\text{opt}} = P_{\text{total}}$, which can be realized by the Lagrangian multiplier method.

This method is a typical MIMO beamforming method. For a single user, it has high performance, but the transmitting end needs to know the user's channel information, so the user needs to estimate and use the uplink feedback channel information, which increases the overhead of the uplink. In order to reduce the overhead of the uplink, how to perform channel quantization becomes a hot issue in this research. Its main purpose is to achieve a compromise between uplink overhead and system performance, which means minimizing the amount of information required for feedback while achieving a specific performance.

4.4.2 *Multi-user beamforming*

When multiple users exist in the system, in order to fully utilize the potential degrees of freedom, multiple users are allowed to access the channel simultaneously. To achieve this goal, most transmit beamforming schemes need to estimate user channel information and feed back the user channel information to the base station. The base station designs a weight matrix based on the channel information to avoid inter-user interference, thereby increasing the signal-to-noise ratio at the receiving end and improving system performance.[13] Of course, there are also a few beamforming schemes which do not require the user channel information, such as opportunistic beamforming. MIMO multi-user beamforming mainly consists of nonlinear and linear processing. Nonlinear pre-processing is represented by dirty paper coding, and linear processing mainly includes zero-forcing beamforming and block diagonal beamforming. Here, we will briefly introduce several multi-user beamforming methods such as dirty

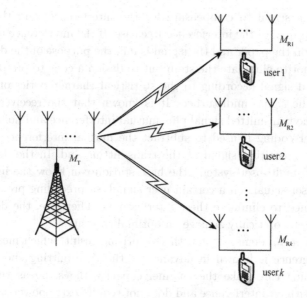

Fig. 4.15.   Multi-user MIMO system.

paper coding, zero-forcing beamforming, block diagonal beamforming, and opportunistic beamforming.

4.4.2.1 *Multi-user MIMO system model*

Considering the configuration of M_T antennas at the transmitting end and the MIMO system supporting K users, the number of antennas of the kth user is M_{Rk}, as shown in Fig. 4.15.

Assuming that the channel is a slow-fading Rayleigh channel, the received signal of the kth user can be written as

$$\mathbf{y}_k = \mathbf{H}_k\mathbf{s}_k + \sum_{j \neq k}\mathbf{H}_k\mathbf{s}_j + \mathbf{n}_k \tag{4.97}$$

where $\mathbf{H}_k$ represents the $M_{Rk} \times M_T$ channel matrix from the base station to the kth user, $\mathbf{s}_k$ represents the $M_T \times 1$ signal transmitted by the base station to the kth user, and $\mathbf{n}_k$ expresses the additive white Gaussian noise.

4.4.2.2 *Dirty paper coding*

Dirty paper coding is a nonlinear technique. The basic idea is that if the transmitting end knows the interference between channels in advance, it can precode the signal to compensate for the interference, and the channel capacity is equal to the interference-free case. If the interference is regarded as a stain on the paper and the signal is ink, the purpose of the dirty paper coding is not to eliminate the stain but to design a code to pre-process the transmitted signal according to the statistical characteristics of the stain to make the signal undisturbed. It is known that the received signal is equal to the transmitted signal plus mutual interference and noise, and the dirty paper coding is used to subtract the mutual interference and noise from the transmitted signal at the transmitting end. In the downlink of the MIMO multi-user system, the base station can know the interference of other user signals on a certain user signal, so precoding processing can be performed to eliminate these interferences. Therefore, the dirty paper coding can theoretically achieve an optimal capacity.

Costa *et al.*, demonstrated this surprising result, which means that if the interference is known in advance at the transmitting end, the dirty paper coding can make the channel capacity the same as the channel capacity without interference and does not require extra power to eliminate the interference. However, the method proposed by Costa *et al.* has only theoretical significance and does not propose a realistic and feasible engineering implementation scheme. The encoder and decoder construction of the dirty paper coding method is very complicated, and obtaining complete channel information is difficult in practical wireless systems. On the contrary, the less complex linear precoding method is more feasible, so this book will not discuss the dirty paper coding in depth.

4.4.2.3 *Zero-forcing beamforming*

Zero-forcing beamforming is also called channel inversion. In the case of fully known channel state information, zero-forcing beamforming uses the generalized inverse matrix of the channel matrix as a beamforming matrix to beamform the transmitted signal. By inverting the channel matrix, the final result is that the precoding realizes the diagonalization of the channel. In this case, each user is equivalent to a set of single-input and single-output channels, thereby eliminating interference between users. Zero-forcing beamforming can achieve approximate performance of dirty paper coding as the number of users increases. However, the requirements for full diagonalization are strict which requires that the number of transmitting antennas not be less than the sum of the number of receiving antennas of all communication users.

4.4.2.4 *Block diagonal beamforming*

Another common method of MIMO multi-user beamforming is block diagonalization. The block diagonalization pre-processing method is used to find a modulation matrix $\mathbf{W}$ which makes $\mathbf{HW}$ a block diagonal matrix, thereby forming multiple independent, parallel, equivalent, single-user MIMO channels[14] and making the interference between users zero. The equivalent single-user MIMO channel has the same characteristics as the traditional single-user MIMO channel, so the signal detection technology of the traditional single-user MIMO system can also be used. For example, methods such as V-BLAST, maximum likelihood detection, and singular value decomposition can be used for each user. Increasing the number of base station transmitting antennas will increase the number of transmitting antennas for all users' equivalent MIMO channels. And with the increase in the number of transmitting antennas, the total number of users that the system can accommodate will also increase in the case of guaranteeing the capacity of a single-user channel.

Block diagonalization is actually a generalization of channel inversion. The difference is that block diagonalization optimizes the allocated transmitted power over a set of antennas of an equivalent single-user MIMO channel, while channel inversion is for the allocated power of every antenna. Therefore, compared to channel inversion, the condition for block diagonalization is not that strict. Block diagonalization requires two conditions: (1) The number of transmitting antennas is not less than the sum of the number of receiving antennas of any user, which is the dimension condition; (2) in order to simultaneously transmit data to multiple users, block diagonalization must also avoid space division multiplexing for users with high channel correlation, which is the channel independence condition. Therefore, in the case where other multiplexing methods are not used at the same time, the number of multiple users will be limited. When using other multiple access methods, such as TDMA and FDMA, the limitations of these conditions are not that strict. Considering the case where a base station is equipped with fewer antennas but there are a large number of users in the service area, a feasible method is to combine SDMA with other multiple access methods. For example, users are grouped so that users within each group meet dimensional conditions. SDMA can be used between user groups, and different frequency bands or time slots are allocated between groups. And the channel-independent condition requires that two users with a strong spatial correlation should not be included in the same group as much as possible. In the following, we will introduce the detailed process of block diagonal beamforming.

Considering the MIMO multi-user system model described in Eq. (4.97), the combined processed signal for user k can be expressed as follows:

$$\mathbf{y}_k = \mathbf{H}_k \mathbf{W}_k \mathbf{s}_k + \sum_{j \neq k} \mathbf{H}_k \mathbf{W}_j \mathbf{s}_j + \mathbf{n}_k \tag{4.98}$$

where $\mathbf{W}_k$ is the transmit beamforming matrix of user k. The first term in the above equation is the desired signal of user k, and the second term is the interference signal of other users. Set $\tilde{\mathbf{W}}_k = [\mathbf{W}_1, \ldots, \mathbf{W}_{k-1}, \mathbf{W}_{k+1}, \ldots, \mathbf{W}_K]$ and $\tilde{\mathbf{s}}_k = [\mathbf{s}_1^H, \ldots, \mathbf{s}_{k-1}^H, \mathbf{s}_{k+1}^H, \ldots, \mathbf{s}_K^H]$, then the above equation can be expressed as

$$\mathbf{y}_k = \mathbf{H}_k \mathbf{W}_k \mathbf{s}_k + \mathbf{H}_k \tilde{\mathbf{W}}_k \tilde{\mathbf{s}}_k + \mathbf{n}_k \tag{4.99}$$

When the base station knows the channel state information $\mathbf{H}_k$ of each user, the transmitter can design $\mathbf{W}_k$ to make $\mathbf{H}_k \tilde{\mathbf{W}}_k \tilde{\mathbf{s}}_k = 0$, namely $\mathbf{H}_k \mathbf{W}_j = \mathbf{0}\,(k \neq j)$, so that the interference of other users to the user k is zero. Then, according to the water-filling definition, the multi-user MIMO channel is equivalent to the parallel single-user MIMO channel, so that the space resources can be fully utilized, and the system capacity and spectrum utilization are greatly improved without increasing the system bandwidth and the transmission power.

For a system with a single antenna at the user end, the channel diagonalization must be completed by the transmitter, and only when the number of transmitting antennas is not less than the sum of the users, namely $n_T \geq K$, it is possible to complete the channel inversion. For a system with multiple antennas at the user end, since each user can use joint detection on its own received signal vector, it can be seen that full diagonalization is not optimal.

$\mathbf{W}_k$ can be solved by block diagonalization as follows:

$$\mathbf{W} = [\mathbf{W}_1, \mathbf{W}_2, \ldots, \mathbf{W}_K] = \underset{0 < \operatorname{tr}(\mathbf{W}_k \mathbf{W}_k^H) \leq P_k, k=1,\ldots,K}{\arg} \mathbf{H}_k \tilde{\mathbf{W}}_k \tilde{\mathbf{s}}_k = 0,$$

$$k = 1, \ldots, K$$

We define $\tilde{\mathbf{H}}_k = [\mathbf{H}_1^H, \ldots, \mathbf{H}_{k-1}^H, \mathbf{H}_{k+1}^H, \ldots, \mathbf{H}_K^H]^H$. It can be seen from the above equation that $\mathbf{W}_k$ must fall in the null space of $\tilde{\mathbf{H}}_k$, and thus, the dimensional condition that all users satisfy the interference forcing zero constraint can be obtained. When the null space dimension of $\tilde{\mathbf{H}}_k$ is greater than zero, the signal can be transmitted to user k, which can also be expressed as $\text{rank}(\tilde{\mathbf{H}}_k) < M_T$:

$$\max[\text{rank}(\tilde{\mathbf{H}}_k), \ldots, \text{rank}(\tilde{\mathbf{H}}_K)] < M_T \qquad (4.100)$$

when Eq. (4.100) is satisfied, block diagonalization is possible.

Assume that all users meet the above dimensional conditions and define

$$A_k = \text{rank}(\tilde{\mathbf{H}}_k) \leq M_R - M_{Rk}$$

where $M_R = \sum_k^K M_{Rk}$ and make SVD decomposition on $\tilde{\mathbf{H}}_k$, namely $\tilde{\mathbf{H}}_k = \tilde{\mathbf{U}}_k \tilde{\boldsymbol{\Sigma}}_k \tilde{\mathbf{V}}_k^H$. Define $\tilde{\mathbf{V}}_k = [\tilde{\mathbf{V}}_k^{(1)}, \tilde{\mathbf{V}}_k^{(0)}]$, with $\tilde{\mathbf{V}}_k^{(1)}$ containing the first A_k right singular value vectors and $\tilde{\mathbf{V}}_k^{(0)}$ containing the last $M_T - A_k$ right singular value vectors. It can be seen that $\tilde{\mathbf{V}}_k^{(0)}$ constitutes the null space orthogonal basis of matrix $\tilde{\mathbf{H}}_k$, and its columns constitute the beamforming matrix $\mathbf{W}_k$ of user k.

Assuming that the total transmitted power of the system is P_s, the block diagonal beamforming algorithm can be summarized as follows:

(1) For the kth $(k(k = 1, \ldots, K))$ user, calculate the right null space $\tilde{\mathbf{V}}_k^{(0)}$ of $\tilde{\mathbf{H}}_k$ and calculate the singular value decomposition as follows:

$$\tilde{\mathbf{H}}_k \tilde{\mathbf{V}}_k^{(0)} = \mathbf{U}_k \begin{bmatrix} \boldsymbol{\Sigma}_k & 0 \\ 0 & 0 \end{bmatrix} [\mathbf{V}_k^{(1)}, \mathbf{V}_k^{(0)}]^H \qquad (4.101)$$

(2) Water-fill the diagonal elements of $\boldsymbol{\Sigma}$ and determine the power weighting matrix $\boldsymbol{\Lambda}$ considering the total power constraint. $\boldsymbol{\Lambda} = \text{diag}(\lambda_1, \ldots, \lambda_K)$ with λ_k representing the power allocated to user k which can be obtained by water-filling of the diagonal elements of $\boldsymbol{\Sigma} = \text{diag}(\boldsymbol{\Sigma}_1, \ldots, \boldsymbol{\Sigma}_K)$.
(3) Calculate the beamforming matrix for each user as follows:

$$\mathbf{W} = [\tilde{\mathbf{V}}_1^{(0)} \mathbf{V}_1^{(1)}, \tilde{\mathbf{V}}_2^{(0)} \mathbf{V}_2^{(1)}, \ldots, \tilde{\mathbf{V}}_K^{(0)} \mathbf{V}_K^{(1)}] \boldsymbol{\Lambda}^{1/2} \qquad (4.102)$$

Through the above steps, when the transmitter knows the channel state information of the user, the block diagonalization precoding algorithm can be successfully completed, and the interference between users is eliminated. On this basis, the multi-user MIMO channel is converted into the parallel single-user MIMO channel. Although block diagonal beamforming cannot achieve the upper limit of the capacity of dirty paper coding, it is important in practical applications due to its relatively low complexity.

4.4.2.5 *Opportunistic beamforming*

The beamforming previously introduced is required to know all or part of the channel state information. Users need to estimate and feed back the amplitude and phase of each antenna channel. Especially in the case of fast time-varying FDD, the feedback amount will be large, which greatly increases the expenses of the systems. When the number of users is large, it is almost impossible for the base station to obtain all channel state information from the users, so a system which only needs limited channel state information will be more practical. When the channel environment is slow fading, the signal correlation is large, which does not have the characteristics of realizing multi-user diversity. At this time, the opportunity beamforming technique can be used to utilize the random fluctuation generated by multiple antennas to weight the signal, so that the slow-changing channel exhibits fast-fading characteristics. Therefore, better multi-user diversity can be achieved and system capacity can be increased.[15]

In a multi-user MIMO system, optimal beamforming techniques can be used if the amplitude and phase of the channel gain of all transmitting antennas to the users can be tracked and fed back. However, if the feedback is limited, the real sense of optimal beamforming will not be realized. In systems with many users, the probability that the instantaneous amplitude and phase of some user channel gains match the amplitude and phase of the transmitting antenna is relatively large, so opportunistic beamforming techniques are considered. Opportunistic beamforming can approximate the performance of optimal beamforming with limited feedback when the number of users is large.

(1) Traditional opportunistic beamforming

Assuming that the base station knows the reachability rate of each user and the necessary power allocation scheme, the base station selects the optimal user from the feedback information and serves it. Since the system only serves one user at a time, Eq. (4.97) can be rewritten as

$$\mathbf{y}_k = \mathbf{H}_k \mathbf{s}_k + \mathbf{n}_k \tag{4.103}$$

Perform SVD decomposition on the channel matrix $\mathbf{H}_k$,

$$\mathbf{H}_k = \mathbf{U}_k \mathbf{\Sigma}_k \mathbf{V}_k^{\mathrm{H}} \tag{4.104}$$

Set the beamforming matrix as $\mathbf{W}_k \in \mathbb{C}^{n_T \times n_T}$ which satisfies $\mathbf{W}_k^H \mathbf{W}_k = \mathbf{I}$, and use $\mathbf{W}_k$ to process the signal $\mathbf{s}_k$, then the received signal can be expressed as

$$\mathbf{y}_k = \mathbf{U}_k \mathbf{\Sigma}_k \mathbf{V}_k^H \mathbf{W}_k \mathbf{s}_k + \mathbf{n}_k \tag{4.105}$$

If $\mathbf{V}_k^H \mathbf{W}_k = \mathbf{I}$, then user k uses optimal beamforming to completely eliminate interference from other antennas. It is equivalent to know the complete channel information at the base station and the signal is processed with matrix $\mathbf{V}_k$.

Set $\mathbf{H}_{\mathrm{eq},k} = \mathbf{U}_k \mathbf{\Sigma}_k \mathbf{V}_k^H \mathbf{W}_k$ as the equivalent channel matrix of user k, Eq. (4.105) can be rewritten as

$$\mathbf{y}_k = \mathbf{H}_{\mathrm{eq},k} \mathbf{s}_k + \mathbf{n}_k \tag{4.106}$$

Since there is no correlation between the $\mathbf{s}_k$ elements, the problem can be regarded as the case where the base station transmits data to the user k on the multiple access channel with M_T independent users, and the transmitted power limitation of the base station can be equivalent to the limitation of the sum of the M_T user powers. Therefore, the maximum rate of user k is equivalent to the sum of the multiple access channel capacities under the limitation of the sum of the powers.

Define $\mathbf{H}_{\mathrm{eq},k} = [\mathbf{h}_1, \mathbf{h}_2, \ldots, \mathbf{h}_{M_T}]$ and $\mathbf{s}_k = [s_k(1), s_k(2), \ldots, s_k(M_T)]^T$, then Eq. (4.106) can be rewritten as

$$\mathbf{y}_k = \sum_{j=1}^{M_T} \mathbf{h}_j s_k(j) + \mathbf{n}_k \tag{4.107}$$

The maximum rate of user k can be obtained by solving the optimization problem of Eq. (4.108):

$$\max \left(\mathrm{lb} \left| \sum_{k=1}^{M_T} P_k \mathbf{h}_k \mathbf{h}_k^H + \mathbf{I} \right| \right) \tag{4.108}$$

Its constraint is $\sum_{k=1}^{M_T} P_k \leq P_s$, $P_k \geq 0$ with P_s being the total power. The above optimization problem can be solved effectively by using the iterative water-filling algorithm, and P_k can be calculated by the following steps:

(a) for any user, initialize $P_k^{(0)} = 0$;

(b) in the first iteration, the interference between equivalent users is treated as noise and the effective channel is generated as

$$\mathbf{h}_k^{\mathrm{eq}} = \left(\mathbf{I} + \sum_{j=1, j \neq k} P_k \mathbf{h}_j \mathbf{h}_j^{\mathrm{H}} \right)^{-1/2} \mathbf{h}_k \qquad (4.109)$$

Regard all valid channels as parallel uninterrupted channels and perform the water-filling algorithm to obtain a new set of power allocation values:

$$P_j^{(t)} = \arg \left(\max_{Q_1, \ldots, Q_n} \sum_{k=1}^{M_{\mathrm{T}}} \mathrm{lb}(1 + Q_k \| \mathbf{h}_k^{\mathrm{eq}} \|^2) \right), \quad j = 1, \ldots, M_t \quad (4.110)$$

where $Q_k \geq 0$ and $\sum_{k=1}^{M_{\mathrm{T}}} Q_k \leq P_{\mathrm{s}}$;

(c) repeat step (b) until the accuracy requirement is reached.

In summary, the opportunistic beamforming algorithm for multi-user MIMO systems can be summarized as follows:

(1) The base station multiplies the training sequence by the opportunistic beamforming matrix $\mathbf{W}_k$ and broadcasts it to all users.

(2) Each user estimates the equivalent channel $\mathbf{H}_{\mathrm{eq},k}$ by the received known training sequence and calculates the respective maximum rate using an iterative water-filling algorithm.

(3) Each user feeds back the respective rate to the base station.

(4) The base station selects the user with the largest rate and broadcasts to all users.

(5) The selected user feeds back power to the allocation scheme.

(6) The base station transmits data to the selected user by a power allocation scheme fed back by the user.

(7) The user uses joint interference cancellation to receive multiple data streams.

(8) Repeat steps (1)–(7) for each channel.

(2) Multi-beam opportunistic beamforming

In conventional opportunistic beamforming, beamforming performance is not ideal with a small number of users. In order to overcome the problem of poor performance of the opportunity beamforming in the case of a small number of users, two solutions can be employed. One is to combine opportunistic beamforming with receiving antenna selection techniques. Assuming that each user has multiple receiving antennas and one RF chain and the user can track the SNR of each antenna and feed back the optimal SNR to the base station, the multi-antenna at the receiving end can be equivalent to the effective user of the downlink. Thereby, the same performance as the opportunistic beamforming in the case of multiple users can be achieved, and there is no need to increase the system complexity at the base station side. However, in actual use, more cases with the terminal having only one antenna are seen. Even if there are multiple receiving antennas, the subchannel between them cannot be independent fading, so this method is not very practical. Another more practical solution is multi-beam opportunistic beamforming using spatial subchannel selection. In the following, we will detail the implementation of opportunistic beamforming based on spatial subchannel selection.

Using the diagram of the multi-user MIMO system as in Fig. 4.15, the base station has M_T transmitting antennas, and each base station has K users. For convenience, we assume that each user's receiving end is equipped with a single antenna, namely $M_{Rk} = 1$.

Then in the qth time slot, the transmitted signal can be written as $\mathbf{s}(t) = [s_1(t), s_2(t), \ldots, s_{M_T}(t)]^T$. The signal received by user k is

$$\mathbf{r}_k(t) = \sqrt{\rho}\mathbf{H}_k(q)\mathbf{s}(t) + \mathbf{n}(t), \quad t \in [(q-1)T, qT] \tag{4.111}$$

where $\mathbf{H}_k(q) = [h_{1,k}(q), h_{2,k}(q), \ldots, h_{M_T,k}(q)]$, with $h_{i,k}(q)$ representing the channel response coefficient of the ith antenna of the base station to the receiver of user k in the time slot q. $\mathbf{n}(t)$ is the Gaussian white noise. Transmit M_t data substreams use $M_t(1 < M_t < M_T)$ random beamforming vectors, and in this case $\mathbf{s}(t)$ can be expressed as

$$\mathbf{s}(t) = \mathbf{B}(q)\sqrt{1/M_t}\mathbf{x}(t) \tag{4.112}$$

where $\mathbf{x}(t) = [x_1(t), x_2(t), \ldots, x_{M_t}(t)]^T$, $\mathbf{B}(q)$ is the M_t columns selected from the $M_T \times M_T$ unitary matrix randomly generated from each time slot, and $\mathbf{B}(q) = [\mathbf{b}_1(q), \mathbf{b}_2(q), \ldots, \mathbf{b}_{M_t}(q)]^T$ with $\mathbf{b}_i(q)$ satisfying $\|\mathbf{b}_i(q)\|_F = 1$. At this time, the signal received by user k is

$$\mathbf{r}_k(t) = \sqrt{\rho/M_t}\sum_{i=1}^{M_t}\tilde{h}_{i,k}(q)x_i(t) + n(t) \tag{4.113}$$

where $\tilde{h}_{i,k}(q)$ is the projection of $\mathbf{H}_k(q)$ on the beamforming vector $\mathbf{b}_i(q)$. The system capacity in the case of $1 < M_t < M_T$ is discussed below. Since the transmitting end simultaneously transmits multiple substreams, mutual interference may exist between the multiple substreams when the spatial multiplexing method is adopted, and the channel quality metric is changed from the signal-to-noise ratio to the signal-to-interference ratio. For user k, its user throughput rate is $C_k(q) = \sum_{m=1}^{M_t} \mathrm{lb}[1 + \gamma_{m,k}(n)]$, and then the channel is assigned to the best user. Through the scheduling of the base station, the mth substream channel is assigned to the user $k_m^*(q)$, $k_m^*(q) = \underset{k=1,2,\dots,K}{\arg\max} \{\gamma_{m,k}(q)\}$, and thus, the throughput rate of the system can be written as

$$C^*(q) = \sum_{m=1}^{M_t} \mathrm{lb}(1 + \gamma_{m,k_m^*(q)}) \tag{4.114}$$

This scheme can transmit multiple signal substreams simultaneously and achieve higher throughput rate, and the throughput can be significantly increased with the number of users. When the number of users is large, its performance is close to the block diagonalization algorithm in which the base station fully knows the channel state information. Compared with the block diagonalization algorithm, the opportunistic beamforming algorithm only needs to feed back partial channel state information, and the overhead of the uplink does not increase linearly with the increase of the number of users. The above advantages are beyond those obtained by the block diagonalization algorithm in which the number of users increases sharply as the amount of feedback increases.

In a word, the principle of multi-beam opportunistic beamforming is very simple. From the analysis of the opportunity beamforming, it can be seen that the more the users, the greater the probability that the randomly generated beam matches a certain user channel parameter, and the greater the throughput of the system. In the case of a small number of users, it is due to the decrease in the probability of such a match, resulting in a decrease in system throughput. It can be seen that if the randomly generated beam and the channel parameter of a certain user can have a high matching probability when the number of users is small, the throughput of the system can be greatly increased. The multi-beam opportunistic beamforming based on spatial subchannel selection is good at this. In the pilot time slot, the base station randomly generates multiple weighting coefficients simultaneously to form multiple beams, and each user feeds back the maximum signal-to-noise gain (or channel gain) and the corresponding beam sequence number considering multiple beams. By this way, it provides multiple selectable beams for each user, thereby increasing the multi-user diversity gain. This method greatly increases the probability of matching channel parameters in the case of a small number of users. Transforming the case of a small number of users to that of a large number of users can significantly improve system throughput and improve system performance. Its main drawback is the increase of pilot overhead.

In the above, we introduce the channel capacity and beamforming methods of the MIMO system from the theoretical level, and the engineering implementation of the MIMO system is closely related to its antenna technology. In the following, we will discuss the design methods of transmitting and receiving multiple antennas in an MIMO system.

4.5 MIMO Multi-antenna Technology

Transmitting and receiving multi-antenna systems are an important part of the MIMO wireless system, and their performance directly affects the performance of MIMO channels. The signals from multiple antennas are mixed and scattered together in the wireless channel. After the data are received by multiple antennas at the receiving end, the system separates and recovers the transmitted data by a space–time processing algorithm, and its performance depends on the degree of independence of the received signals of each antenna unit, namely the correlation. And the correlation between multiple antennas is closely related to the design of the antenna unit, the number of array units, the array structure, and the way the array is placed. Therefore, the high performance of the MIMO wireless systems depends on the richness of the multipath propagation and the rational design of multiple antennas.

4.5.1 *Mutual coupling of multiple antenna units*

With the increasing number of antenna units and the continued miniaturization of the antenna systems, the spacing of antenna units is decreasing, and mutual coupling of antennas has become another important factor affecting the performance of the MIMO wireless channels. Figure 4.16 shows an equivalent network model for a receiving multi-antenna system, in which $Z_{L1}, \ldots, Z_{LM_R}$ are the load impedances, $Z_{A1}, \ldots, Z_{AM_R}$ are the impedances of the antenna (the self-impedance). The illumination of the

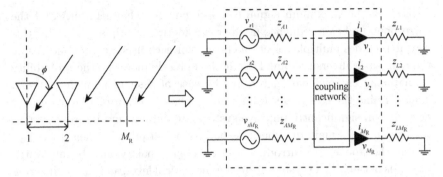

Fig. 4.16. Equivalent network model for receiving multiple antennas.[16]

receiving antenna array by the DOA is equivalent to the application of the additional signal source $(v_{s1}, \ldots, v_{sM_R})$ to the array antenna unit. Due to the limited spacing of the antenna units, the mutual coupling effect between them cannot be ignored. The signal voltage and current of the feed point are as shown in the figures. According to the circuit theory, the feed point voltage can be expressed as

$$
\begin{cases}
v_1 &= -i_1 z_{11} - i_2 z_{12} - \cdots - i_{M_R} z_{1M_R} + v_1^{\mathrm{o}} \\
v_2 &= -i_1 z_{21} - i_2 z_{22} - \cdots - i_{M_R} z_{jM_R} + v_2^{\mathrm{o}} \\
\vdots \\
v_{M_R} &= -i_1 z_{M_R 1} - i_2 z_{M_R 2} - \cdots - i_{M_R} z_{M_R M_R} + v_{M_R}^{\mathrm{o}}
\end{cases}
\tag{4.115}
$$

where $v_j^{\mathrm{o}} (j = 1, \ldots, M_R)$ represents the open-circuit voltage of the feed point, namely the voltage at which the feed point is open. According to circuit theory

$$
v_j = i_j z_{Lj}, \quad j = 1, \ldots, M_R
\tag{4.116}
$$

Substituting Eq. (4.116) into Eq. (4.115), we get

$$
\mathbf{v}^{\mathrm{o}} = (\mathbf{I}_{M_R} + \mathbf{Z_L}^{-1} \mathbf{Z}) \mathbf{v}
\tag{4.117}
$$

where $\mathbf{v}^{\mathrm{o}}$ is the feed point open-circuit voltage vector, $\mathbf{v}$ is the feed point voltage vector, $\mathbf{I}_{M_R}$ is the M_R-dimensional unit matrix, $\mathbf{Z}$ is the mutual impedance matrix, and $\mathbf{Z}_L$ is the diagonal matrix with the diagonal element representing the load impedance. The receiving signal voltage vector can be written as

$$\mathbf{v}_r = (\mathbf{I}_{M_R} + \mathbf{Z}_L^{-1}\mathbf{Z})^{-1}\mathbf{v}^\circ \tag{4.118}$$

Assume $\mathbf{C}_r$ to be the matrix of the coupling coefficient between the antenna units, and assume

$$\mathbf{v}_r^c = \mathbf{C}_r\mathbf{v}_r^{nc} \tag{4.119}$$

$$\mathbf{v}_r^{nc} = (\mathbf{I}_{M_R} + \mathbf{Z}_L^{-1}\mathbf{Z}_A)^{-1}\mathbf{v}^\circ \tag{4.120}$$

where $\mathbf{Z}_A$ is a diagonal matrix whose diagonal elements are antenna impedances $z_{A1}, z_{A2}, \ldots, z_{AM_R}$. Consider $\mathbf{v}_r^{nc}$ as the receiving signal voltage vector without mutual coupling. And according to Eq. (4.118),

$$[\mathbf{C}_r - (\mathbf{I}_{M_R} + \mathbf{Z}_L^{-1}\mathbf{Z})^{-1}(\mathbf{I}_{M_R} + \mathbf{Z}_L^{-1}\mathbf{Z}_A)]\mathbf{v}^\circ = 0 \tag{4.121}$$

From Eq. (4.121), the matrix of the coupling coefficients can be calculated as

$$\mathbf{C}_r = \text{diag}(\text{Rand}) \cdot (\mathbf{I}_{M_R} + \mathbf{Z}_L^{-1}\mathbf{Z})^{-1}(\mathbf{I}_{M_R} + \mathbf{Z}_L^{-1}\mathbf{Z}_A) \tag{4.122}$$

where diag(Rand) is a random diagonal matrix. If there is a constraint; the matrix of coupling coefficients is a unit matrix without considering mutual coupling, then

$$\mathbf{C}_r = (\mathbf{I}_{M_R} + \mathbf{Z}_L^{-1}\mathbf{Z})^{-1}(\mathbf{I}_{M_R} + \mathbf{Z}_L^{-1}\mathbf{Z}_A) \tag{4.123}$$

If both the load impedance and the self-impedance of each antenna unit are equal, namely $\mathbf{Z}_L = z_L\mathbf{I}_{M_R}$ and $\mathbf{Z}_A = z_A\mathbf{I}_{M_R}$, then $\mathbf{C}_r$ can be simplified as

$$\mathbf{C}_r = (z_L + z_A)(\mathbf{Z}_L + \mathbf{Z})^{-1} \tag{4.124}$$

It is worth noting that Eq. (4.123) gives a more general form of the coupling coefficient matrix, which is especially convenient for mutual coupling analysis between different antenna units.

4.5.2 *Spatial correlation coefficient*

In the MIMO propagation environment, the divergence angle of the receiving signal is Δ, and the arrival is parallel incident to two antenna units with a distance D in the ϕ_m direction. The model is shown in Fig. 4.17.

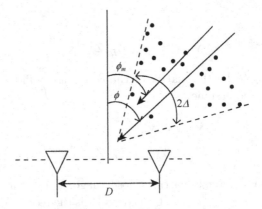

Fig. 4.17. Schematic diagram of two antennas receiving the scatter signal.

If the mutual coupling effect between the two antennas is not considered, the receiving signal can be expressed as follows:

$$\mathbf{r}(\phi) = \begin{bmatrix} \sum_m g_1(\phi_m) a_m \, \mathrm{e}^{\mathrm{j}\beta_m} \sqrt{p(\phi_m)} \\ \sum_m g_2(\phi_m) b_m \, \mathrm{e}^{\mathrm{j}\beta_m} \mathrm{e}^{\mathrm{j}\tau_m} \sqrt{p(\phi_m)} \end{bmatrix} = \begin{bmatrix} r_1(\phi) \\ r_2(\phi) \end{bmatrix} \tag{4.125}$$

where the signal amplitudes a_m and b_m are subject to the Rayleigh distribution, the phase β_m is uniformly distributed, and the multi-antenna receiving signal is subject to the Nakagami distribution. $\tau_m = 2\pi D \sin(\phi_m)/\lambda$ is the delay of the two units receiving signals, λ is the signal wavelength, and m is the number of arrivals. g_1 and g_2 are the patterns of the two antenna units, and for the omnidirectional antenna, both of them are one. Set the power angle spectrum of the arrival to $p(\phi)$ and define the voltage correlation coefficient of the as follows:

$$R_A = R = R_{xx} + jR_{xy} = R_{yy} - jR_{yx}$$

$$= \frac{1}{\sqrt{P_1 P_2}} \int_{-\pi+\phi_0}^{\pi+\phi_0} r_2(\phi) r_1^*(\phi) p(\phi) d\phi \tag{4.126}$$

where P_1 and P_2 are the average powers of the two antenna receiving signals, R_{xx} is the normalization coefficients between the real part and the real part, and R_{xy} is the normalization coefficient between the real part and the imaginary part of the receiving signal voltage. The signal envelope correlation coefficient is defined as

$$R_p = R_{A^2}(z) = |R_A|^2 = R_{xx}^2 + R_{xy}^2 \tag{4.127}$$

If the phase of the voltage correlation coefficient is ignored (in engineering), then

$$R_A = \sqrt{R_{A^2}(z)} \tag{4.128}$$

Substituting Eq. (4.125) into Eq. (4.126), we obtain

$$R_{xx} = \mathrm{Re}\left\{ \frac{1}{\sqrt{P_1 P_2}} \int_{-\pi+\phi_0}^{\pi+\phi_0} g_2(\phi) b_\phi g_1^*(\phi) a_\phi^* \, \mathrm{e}^{\mathrm{j}2\pi D/\lambda \sin(\phi)} p(\phi) \mathrm{d}\phi \right\} \tag{4.129}$$

$$R_{xy} = \mathrm{Im}\left\{ \frac{1}{\sqrt{P_1 P_2}} \int_{-\pi+\phi_0}^{\pi+\phi_0} g_2(\phi) b_\phi g_1^*(\phi) a_\phi^* \, \mathrm{e}^{\mathrm{j}2\pi D/\lambda \sin(\phi)} p(\phi) \mathrm{d}\phi \right\} \tag{4.130}$$

Here, the average power is defined as follows:

$$P_1 = \sum_m |g_1(\phi_m)|^2 a_m^2 p(\phi_m) = \int_{-\pi+\phi_0}^{\pi+\phi_0} |g_1(\phi)|^2 a_\phi^2 p(\phi) \mathrm{d}\phi \tag{4.131}$$

$$P_2 = \sum_m |g_2(\phi_m)|^2 b_m^2 p(\phi_m) = \int_{-\pi+\phi_0}^{\pi+\phi_0} |g_2(\phi)|^2 b_\phi^2 p(\phi) \mathrm{d}\phi \tag{4.132}$$

In the case of the arrival with an equal power incident on the omnidirectional antenna unit, namely $g_1 = g_2 = 1$, $a_m = b_m$, the normalized voltage coefficient can be simplified as

$$R_{xx} = \int_{-\pi+\phi_0}^{\pi+\phi_0} \cos[2\pi D/\lambda \sin(\phi)] p(\phi) \mathrm{d}\phi \tag{4.133}$$

$$R_{xy} = \int_{-\pi+\phi_0}^{\pi+\phi_0} \sin[2\pi D/\lambda \sin(\phi)] p(\phi) \mathrm{d}\phi \tag{4.134}$$

when the spacing between the two antenna units is less than half the wavelength, the mutual coupling effect of the two antenna units needs to be considered. And the receiving signal obtained by using the principle of multiplication of the pattern is given as

$$
\mathbf{r}^c(\phi) = \mathbf{Y}\begin{bmatrix} r_1(\phi) \\ r_2(\phi) \end{bmatrix} = \begin{bmatrix} 1 + \frac{Z_{11}}{Z_L} & \frac{Z_{12}}{Z_L} \\ \frac{Z_{21}}{Z_L} & 1 + \frac{Z_{22}}{Z_L} \end{bmatrix}^{-1}
$$
$$
\times \begin{bmatrix} \sum_m g_1(\phi_m) a_m\, e^{j\beta_m}\sqrt{p(\phi_m)} \\ \sum_m g_2(\phi_m) b_m\, e^{j\beta_m}\, e^{j\tau_m}\sqrt{p(\phi_m)} \end{bmatrix} \quad (4.135)
$$

where Z_{11} and Z_{22} are the self-impedances of the antenna unit, Z_{12} and Z_{21} are mutual impedances, and Z_L is the load impedance. Define $\mathbf{Y} = \begin{bmatrix} a & b \\ b & a \end{bmatrix}$, then the receiving signal can be expressed as

$$
\mathbf{r}^c(\phi) = \begin{bmatrix} a & b \\ b & a \end{bmatrix}\begin{bmatrix} \sum_m g_1(\phi_m) a_m\, e^{j\beta_m}\sqrt{p(\phi_m)} \\ \sum_m g_2(\phi_m) b_m\, e^{j\beta_m}\, e^{j\tau_m}\sqrt{p(\phi_m)} \end{bmatrix} \quad (4.136)
$$

By substituting Eq. (4.136) into Eq. (4.126) and setting $\tau(\phi) = \sin(\phi)2\pi D/\lambda$, the general equation of the voltage correlation coefficient[17] can be obtained as follows:

$$
R^c = R^c_{xx} + jR^c_{xy}
$$
$$
= \frac{\int_{-\pi+\phi_0}^{\pi+\phi_0}\{[bg_1(\phi)a_\phi + ag_2(\phi)b_\phi\, e^{j\tau(\phi)}][ag_1(\phi)a_\phi + bg_2(\phi)b_\phi\, e^{j\tau(\phi)}]^*\}}{\sqrt{\int_{-\pi+\phi_0}^{\pi+\phi_0}|g_1(\phi)|^2 a_\phi^2 p(\phi)\mathrm{d}\phi\int_{-\pi+\phi_0}^{\pi+\phi_0}|g_2(\phi)|^2 b_\phi^2 p(\phi)\mathrm{d}\phi}} \;\; p(\phi)\mathrm{d}\phi
$$
$$
= \frac{\int_{-\pi+\phi_0}^{\pi+\phi_0}\left\{\begin{array}{l} a^*b|g_1(\phi)|^2 a_\phi^2 + ab^*|g_2(\phi)|^2 b_\phi^2 + |a|^2 a_\phi b_\phi^* \cdot \\ \left[g_1^*(\phi)g_2(\phi)e^{j\tau(\phi)} + \left|\frac{b}{a}\right|^2 g_1(\phi)g_2^*(\phi)e^{-j\tau(\phi)}\right] \end{array}\right\} p(\phi)\mathrm{d}\phi}{\sqrt{\int_{-\pi+\phi_0}^{\pi+\phi_0}|g_1(\phi)|^2 a_\phi^2 p(\phi)\mathrm{d}\phi\int_{-\pi+\phi_0}^{\pi+\phi_0}|g_2(\phi)|^2 b_\phi^2 p(\phi)\mathrm{d}\phi}}
$$
$$
(4.137)
$$

In the case of the arrival with an equal power incident on the omnidirectional antenna unit, its normalized correlation coefficient can be simplified as

$$
R = \int_{-\pi+\phi_0}^{\pi+\phi_0}\{[b + a\, e^{j\tau(\phi)}][a + b\, e^{j\tau(\phi)}]^* p(\phi)\}\mathrm{d}\phi \quad (4.138)
$$

Therefore, the voltage correlation coefficient under the effect of mutual coupling can be written as

$$R_{xx}^c = (|a|^2 + |b|^2)R_{xx} + 2\operatorname{Re}(ab^*) \tag{4.139}$$

$$R_{xy}^c = (|a|^2 - |b|^2)R_{xy} \tag{4.140}$$

It can be seen that mutual coupling has different effects on R_{xx} and R_{xy}. If mutual coupling is not considered, only $a = 1$ and $b = 0$ in Eq. (4.137) are required.

Only the correlation between the two antenna units are considered above, and for the multi-antenna unit system, the correlation between each two antenna units is obtained by the same method, and the correlation matrix is formed to analyze the performance of the MIMO system and guide the multi-antenna design of the MIMO system.

4.5.3 *Spatial correlation and MIMO channel*

Ignoring the effects of antenna mutual coupling, the received signal vector can be expressed as

$$\mathbf{r}^{nc}(\phi) = [g_1(\phi), g_2(\phi)\,\mathrm{e}^{\mathrm{j}\tau(\phi)}, \ldots, g_{M_R}(\phi)\mathrm{e}^{\mathrm{j}\tau(\phi)(M_R-1)}]^{\mathrm{T}} \tag{4.141}$$

where $g_j(\phi)(j = 1, \ldots, M_R)$ is the pattern of each antenna unit, the delay between two adjacent antenna elements is $\tau(\phi) = 2\pi D \sin(\phi)/\lambda$, d is the antenna element spacing, λ is the wavelength, and ϕ is the angle between the arrival direction of the wave and the normal of the array.

If the antenna mutual coupling effect is considered, the received signal can be written as

$$\mathbf{r}^c(\phi) = \mathbf{C}_r \cdot \mathbf{r}^{nc}(\phi) \tag{4.142}$$

where $\mathbf{C}_r$ is the coupling coefficient matrix. Since the antenna unit is passive and reciprocal, for the binary receiving array, we set the coupling coefficient matrix as $\mathbf{C}_r = \begin{bmatrix} a & b \\ b & a \end{bmatrix}$. Substituting Eq. (4.141) into Eq. (4.142), we get

$$\mathbf{r}^c(\phi) = \begin{bmatrix} (a + bg_2(\phi)\mathrm{e}^{\mathrm{j}\tau(\phi)}/g_1(\phi))g_1(\phi) \\ (a + bg_1(\phi)\mathrm{e}^{-\mathrm{j}\tau(\phi)}/g_2(\phi))g_2(\phi)\mathrm{e}^{\mathrm{j}\tau} \end{bmatrix} \tag{4.143}$$

Comparing Eq. (4.141) with Eq. (4.143), the effect of mutual coupling of the antenna is equivalent to distorting the pattern of the antenna unit as

$$\begin{bmatrix} g_1^c(\phi) \\ g_2^c(\phi) \end{bmatrix} = \begin{bmatrix} ag_1(\phi) + bg_2(\phi)e^{j\tau(\phi)} \\ ag_2(\phi) + bg_1(\phi)e^{-j\tau(\phi)} \end{bmatrix} \tag{4.144}$$

If the antenna unit is omnidirectional, namely $g_1 = g_2 = 1$, the distorted element pattern is simplified to

$$\begin{bmatrix} g_1^{omn-c}(\phi) \\ g_2^{omn-c}(\phi) \end{bmatrix} = \begin{bmatrix} a + be^{j\tau(\phi)} \\ a + be^{-j\tau(\phi)} \end{bmatrix} \tag{4.145}$$

Set the power spectrum of the DOA signal as $p(\phi)$ and define the correlation coefficient of the received signals of the two antenna units as follows:

$$\rho_{12} = R_{xx} + jR_{xy} = \frac{1}{\sqrt{P_1 P_2}} \int_{-\pi+\phi_0}^{\pi+\phi_0} r_1(\phi)r_2^*(\phi)p(\phi)\mathrm{d}\phi \tag{4.146}$$

where P_1 and P_2 are the average power received by the two antenna units and are defined as follows:

$$P_1 = \int_{-\pi+\phi_0}^{\pi+\phi_0} |r_1(\phi)|^2 p(\phi)\mathrm{d}\phi \tag{4.147}$$

$$P_2 = \int_{-\pi+\phi_0}^{\pi+\phi_0} |r_2(\phi)|^2 p(\phi)\mathrm{d}\phi \tag{4.148}$$

The signal envelope correlation coefficient is defined as

$$\rho_{env} = |\rho_{12}|^2 = R_{xx}^2 + R_{xy}^2 \tag{4.149}$$

Assuming that the antenna units are omnidirectional and do not consider mutual coupling and substituting Eq. (4.141) into Eqs. (4.146)–(4.148), the spatial correlation coefficient obtained is as follows:

$$\rho_{12}^{omn-nc} = R_{xx}^{omn-nc} + jR_{xy}^{omn-nc} = \int_{-\pi+\phi_0}^{\pi+\phi_0} e^{-j\tau(\phi)}p(\phi)\mathrm{d}\phi \tag{4.150}$$

Assuming that the antenna units are directional, considering mutual coupling, and substituting Eq. (4.142) into Eqs. (4.145)–(4.147), the common spatial correlation coefficient is given as

$$\rho_{12}^c = \frac{1}{\sqrt{P_1^c P_2^c}} \int_{-\pi+\phi_0}^{\pi+\phi_0} [ag_1(\phi) + bg_2(\phi)e^{j\tau(\phi)}]$$
$$\times [bg_1(\phi) + ag_2(\phi)e^{j\tau(\phi)}]^* p(\phi)d\phi \tag{4.151}$$

The average power received by the antenna unit in Eq. (4.151) is

$$P_1^c = \int_{-\pi+\phi_0}^{\pi+\phi_0} |ag_1(\phi) + bg_2(\phi)e^{j\tau(\phi)}|^2 p(\phi)d\phi \tag{4.152}$$

$$P_2^c = \int_{-\pi+\phi_0}^{\pi+\phi_0} |bg_1(\phi) + ag_2(\phi)e^{j\tau(\phi)}|^2 p(\phi)d\phi \tag{4.153}$$

Defining $c = b/a$, Eqs. (4.151)–(4.153) can be simplified as

$$P_1^c = |a|^2 \int_{-\pi+\phi_0}^{\pi+\phi_0} [|g_1(\phi)|^2 + |c|^2 |g_2(\phi)|^2$$
$$+ 2\text{Re}(cg_1^*(\phi)g_2(\phi)e^{j\tau(\phi)})]p(\phi)d\phi \tag{4.154}$$

$$P_2^c = |a|^2 \int_{-\pi+\phi_0}^{\pi+\phi_0} [|g_2(\phi)|^2 + |c|^2 |g_1(\phi)|^2$$
$$+ 2\text{Re}(cg_2^*(\phi)g_1(\phi)e^{-j\tau(\phi)})]p(\phi)d\phi \tag{4.155}$$

$$\rho_{12}^c = \frac{|a|^2}{\sqrt{P_1^c P_2^c}} \int_{-\pi+\phi_0}^{\pi+\phi_0} \begin{bmatrix} c|g_2(\phi)|^2 + c^*|g_1(\phi)|^2 + |c|^2(g_2(\phi)g_1^*(\phi)e^{j\tau(\phi)}) \\ + (g_2^*(\phi)g_1(\phi)e^{-j\tau(\phi)}) \end{bmatrix}$$
$$p(\phi)d\phi \tag{4.156}$$

If the antenna unit is omnidirectional, the average power received and the correlation coefficient can be further simplified as

$$P_1^{omn-c} = |a|^2 [1 + |c|^2 + 2\text{Re}(c)R_{xx}^{omn-nc} + 2\text{Im}(c)R_{xy}^{omn-nc}] \tag{4.157}$$

$$P_2^{omn-c} = |a|^2 [1 + |c|^2 + 2\text{Re}(c)R_{xx}^{omn-nc} - 2\text{Im}(c)R_{xy}^{omn-nc}] \tag{4.158}$$

$$\rho_{12}^{omn-c} = \frac{[2\text{Re}(c) + (1 + |c|^2)R_{xx}^{omn-nc} + j(1 - |c|^2)R_{xy}^{omn-nc}]}{\sqrt{[1 + |c|^2 + 2\text{Re}(c)R_{xx}^{omn-nc}]^2 - 4[\text{Im}(c)R_{xy}^{omn-nc}]}} \tag{4.159}$$

Its envelope correlation coefficient can be written as

$$\rho_{\text{env\_12}}^{omn\text{-}c} = \frac{\begin{aligned}(1 + |c|^2)^2 \rho_{\text{env\_12}}^{omn\text{-}nc} + 4\text{Re}(c)^2 + 4\text{Re}(c) \\ \times (1 + |c|^2) R_{xx}^{omn\text{-}nc} - 4|c|^2 (R_{xy}^{omn\text{-}nc})^2\end{aligned}}{\begin{aligned}4\text{Re}(c)^2 \rho_{\text{env\_12}}^{omn\text{-}nc} + (1 + |c|^2)^2 + 4\text{Re}(c) \\ \times (1 + |c|^2) R_{xx}^{omn\text{-}nc} - 4|c|^2 (R_{xy}^{omn\text{-}nc})^2\end{aligned}} \qquad (4.160)$$

The analytical equation of the correlation coefficient is given above. The results show that if mutual coupling is considered, the correlation between the antenna units needs to be corrected, and this correction is jointly determined by the coupling coefficient and the correlation coefficient without considering mutual coupling. For the omnidirectional radiating antenna unit, when the normalized coupling coefficient c is a pure imaginary number and the correlation coefficient without considering the mutual coupling condition is a real number, the mutual coupling has no effect on the correlation coefficient.

From Eqs. (4.157) and (4.158), the difference in the average power received by the two omnidirectional antenna elements due to mutual coupling of the antennas (power imbalance) is obtained as follows:

$$\Delta P_{12}^{omn\text{-}c} = 4|a|^2 \text{Im}(c) R_{xy}^{omn\text{-}nc} \qquad (4.161)$$

Equations (4.154) and (4.155) show that the actual average power received by the antenna units is related to the antenna element pattern, element spacing, mutual coupling coefficient, and the arrival spectrum. And Eq. (4.161) indicates that the average power difference is determined by the imaginary part of the normalized coupling coefficient and the imaginary part of the correlation coefficient without considering the mutual coupling condition, which means when c is a real number or the correlation coefficient without considering mutual coupling is a real number, the power is balanced. For example, when the arrival is evenly distributed over the entire azimuth plane, it can be known from Eq. (4.150) that the correlation coefficient without considering the mutual coupling is a real number as follows (zero-order Bessel function):

$$\rho_{12,\text{uni}}^{omn\text{-}nc} = \frac{1}{2\pi} \int_{-\pi + \phi_0}^{\pi + \phi_0} e^{-j\tau(\phi)} d\phi = J_0(2\pi D/\lambda) \qquad (4.162)$$

At this time, if the mutual coupling effect is considered, the average power received by the two antenna units is still balanced, and the correlation coefficient can be expressed as

$$\rho_{12,\text{uni}}^{omn-c} = \frac{2\text{Re}(c) + (1 + |c|^2)\rho_{12,\text{uni}}^{omn-nc}}{1 + |c|^2 + 2\text{Re}(c)\rho_{12,\text{uni}}^{omn-nc}} \qquad (4.163)$$

When c is a pure imaginary number, mutual coupling has no effect on the correlation. Substituting the parameter c into Eq. (4.163), the correlation coefficient of the arrival distributed evenly over the entire azimuth plane can be obtained as follows:

$$\rho_{12,\text{uni}}^{omn-c} = \frac{2\text{Re}(a^*b) + (|a|^2 + |b|^2)J_0(2\pi D/\lambda)}{|a|^2 + |b|^2 + 2\text{Re}(a^*b)J_0(2\pi D/\lambda)} \qquad (4.164)$$

If both the mutual coupling and the spatial correlation between the receiving antenna units are considered, the equivalent MIMO channel matrix $\mathbf{H}$ can be expressed as

$$\mathbf{H} = \mathbf{C}_r\mathbf{R}_r^{1/2}\mathbf{H}_W \qquad (4.165)$$

where $\mathbf{R}_r$ is the spatial correlation matrix of the receiving array without considering the mutual coupling of the antenna, and its element is the spatial correlation coefficient between the array elements without considering the mutual coupling. $\mathbf{H}_W$ is a Gaussian matrix whose elements are spatially independent and follows a Gaussian distribution. If the spatial correlation coefficient has considered the mutual coupling effect and the correlation matrix is $\mathbf{R}_{rc}$, then

$$\mathbf{H} = \mathbf{R}_{rc}^{1/2}\mathbf{H}_W \qquad (4.166)$$

In the case where the transmitting end equally distributes the transmitted power, the instantaneous information capacity of the MIMO system is

$$C = \text{lb}\left[\det\left(\mathbf{I}_{M_R} + \frac{\rho}{M_T}\mathbf{H}\mathbf{H}^H\right)\right] \text{ (bit/s/Hz)} \qquad (4.167)$$

where ρ is the average signal-to-noise ratio of each receiving antenna unit and M_T is the number of transmitting antenna units. Substituting Eq. (4.166) into Eq. (4.167), the effect of mutual coupling on MIMO channel capacity can be evaluated.

4.5.4 *MIMO multi-antenna decoupling*

The electromagnetic coupling between MIMO antennas mainly has two important effects. First, strong electromagnetic coupling will affect the port characteristics of multiple antennas. It not only destroys the original matching state of each port but also causes the energy between the ports to leak. The transmission coefficient between each port is large, and the efficiency of the antenna is greatly reduced, and even completely unusable. Second, strong electromagnetic coupling will change the surface current distribution on the radiating element, resulting in a large difference between the radiation pattern and the ideal situation. In order to reduce the electromagnetic coupling between MIMO antennas, many experts and scholars have carried out in-depth research and obtained a lot of decoupling techniques. In summary, they can be divided into the following five methods: (1) decoupling technology with parasitic radiating elements; (2) decoupling technology using a separate ground-plane structure; (3) decoupling technology using a special planar structure; (4) decoupling technique using filter mechanism; and (5) decoupling technology using an additional decoupling network.

4.5.4.1 *Decoupling technology with parasitic radiating elements*

In theory, the antenna design problem can be equivalent to the design with a specific current distribution radiator. The various electrical performance parameters of the antenna (input impedance and radiation pattern, etc.) are determined by the current distribution across the radiator. Similarly, the electromagnetic coupling phenomenon between MIMO antennas can be treated as a current distribution of mutual coupling between the antennas. Mark *et al.* have conducted in-depth research on the current distribution problem of multi-antenna coupling and gave a decoupling technology model using parasitic elements,[18] as shown in Fig. 4.18. The basic idea of the decoupling technique using parasitic elements is to add one or more parasitic elements between the multiple antennas which originally had strong coupling, resulting in new electromagnetic coupling. If the newly generated coupling and the originally existing coupling can cancel each other out, the ideal decoupling effect is achieved.

In Fig. 4.18(a), when the parasitic element is not added, the initial excitation current on the dipole A is set to I_{Excited}. Since the distance between the two dipoles is very close, a strong electromagnetic coupling

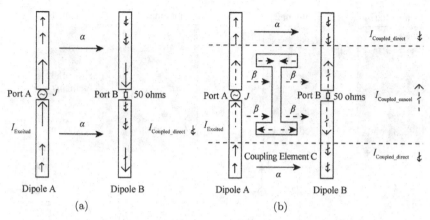

Fig. 4.18. **Decoupling technology model with parasitic elements. (a) Without parasitic elements. (b) With parasitic elements.**

will inevitably occur and finally a coupling current will be generated on the dipole B, which is set to $I_{Coupled\_direct}$. Assume the coupling coefficient at this time is α, then the relationship between the excitation current $I_{Excited}$ on dipole A and the coupling current $I_{Coupled\_direct}$ on dipole B is

$$I_{Coupled\_direct} = \alpha I_{Excited} \tag{4.168}$$

In Fig. 4.18(b), after the parasitic element is added, the parasitic element will also be related to the electromagnetic coupling between the two dipoles. Due to the symmetry of the structure, the coupling coefficient from dipole A to the parasitic element and from the parasitic element to dipole B is β, and the new coupling current $I_{Coupled\_cancel}$ from dipole A to dipole B through the parasitic element is

$$I_{Coupled\_cancel} = \beta^2 I_{Excited} \tag{4.169}$$

Considering the coexistence of two coupling currents, the final coupling current $I_{Coupled\_all}$ on dipole B is

$$I_{Coupled\_all} = I_{Coupled\_direct} + I_{Coupled\_cancel} = (\alpha + \beta^2)I_{Excited} \tag{4.170}$$

If $(\alpha + \beta^2) = 0$, the effective decoupling effect can be achieved. In a word, the key decoupling technique using parasitic radiating elements is to make the existing coupling current and the coupling current generated by the parasitic radiating element cancel each other, so that they satisfy the conditions of equal amplitude and opposite phase.

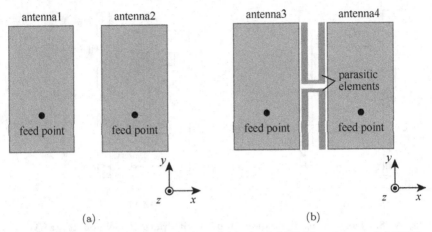

Fig. 4.19. **Double-rectangular microstrip patch MIMO antenna. (a) Without parasitic elements. (b) With parasitic elements.**

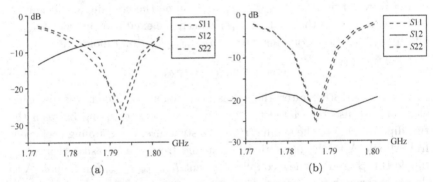

Fig. 4.20. **Comparison of S parameters. (a) Without parasitic elements. (b) With parasitic elements.**

According to the main idea of the parasitic unit decoupling technology, Chen *et al.*[19] of Shanghai Jiao Tong University designed several small-pitch rectangular microstrip MIMO antennas suitable for handheld mobile terminals, as shown in Fig. 4.19. The MIMO antenna of the parallel structure consists of double-rectangular microstrip patch antennas with the gap of 1/16 working wavelength. Two U-shaped parasitic elements are inserted between the two antennas to improve the isolation. The corresponding port reflection coefficient and port isolation are shown in Fig. 4.20.

4.5.4.2 *Separate ground-plane structure decoupling*

The separate ground-plane structure means that the multiple antennas on the same dielectric substrate each have their own separate ground planes, which means the ground planes are not physically connected together. Although the separate ground-plane structure can effectively cut off the conduction current between the ground planes, due to the presence of high-frequency electromagnetic coupling, there will still be an induced current causing a high degree of coupling between the ports of the multiple antennas on the same substrate. However, low mutual coupling can be achieved by using the separate ground-plane structure and by arranging the relative positions between multiple antennas reasonably.

Mohammad *et al.*[20] designed an electrical MIMO antenna for mobile terminals, and its structural model is shown in Fig. 4.21. As can be seen, the MIMO antenna consists of two zigzag line antennas which are integrated on the same dielectric substrate but have separate ground planes. In order to reduce the size of the antenna, the radiating element is designed to fold back and forth in a zigzag line shape in a certain period. At the same time, in order to obtain a higher degree of isolation, it not only adopts a separate ground-plane structure but also extends a suitably sized microstrip line at the edges of the two separate ground planes. After optimization, the double zigzag line-shaped MIMO antenna can work in the frequency band of 760–886 MHz and has a low coupling degree.

4.5.4.3 *Special ground-plane structure decoupling technology*

When the antenna radiates electromagnetic waves, it will generate a large ground current distribution on the ground plane, which means the ground current will also participate in the radiation process of the antenna, affecting the characteristic parameters of the antenna, such as the input impedance and the radiation pattern. For the electromagnetic coupling phenomenon between MIMO antennas, a large ground current is also induced on the ground plane, causing a high mutual coupling between antennas. How to reduce the induced ground current on the ground plane is the key to successful decoupling. Many experts and scholars have conducted in-depth research on this and have achieved many research results. The defect ground structure (DGS) changes the ground current distribution by changing different shapes on the ground plane, thereby changing the various properties of the antenna. It has great guiding significance on how

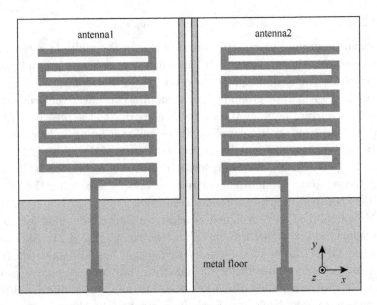

Fig. 4.21. Electrically small MIMO antenna with zigzag line shape.

to decouple between MIMO antennas. As long as a special ground-plane structure greatly reduces the current distribution of the coupled ground, effective decoupling can be achieved.

Hong *et al.*,[21] designed an ultra-wideband MIMO antenna for PDA, and its structural model is shown in Fig. 4.22. The MIMO antenna consists of two Y-shaped radiating elements and a ground plane with a three-microstrip branching structure. The antenna was printed on an FR4 dielectric substrate with a thickness of 1.6 mm and was fed by a microstrip line. In order to obtain the characteristics of an ultra-wideband, the radiation unit is designed in a Y shape. In order to reduce the coupling, three microstrip lines are projected on the ground plane between the two Y-shaped radiating elements, where the microstrip branches 1 and 2 are symmetrically distributed with respect to the microstrip branch 3. Effective decoupling can be achieved by selecting a microstrip branch line of the appropriate length.

4.5.4.4 *Filter mechanism decoupling*

The electromagnetic band gap (EBG) structure is a periodic structure with high impedance and band resistance, which can be applied to

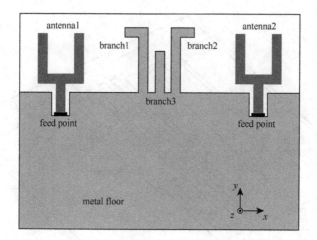

Fig. 4.22.   The ultra-wideband MIMO antenna.

the decoupling problem between multiple antennas. However, due to its structural complexity and high production cost, the scope of the application is greatly limited. Chiu *et al.*,[22] designed a ground-plane structure that is simple but can be effectively decoupled based on the filter mechanism. Generally, it is formed by digging out some periodic rectangular gaps in the middle of a complete ground plane. The part between two gaps can be equivalent to the capacitance C, and the narrow microstrip of the intermediate connection gap can be equivalent to the inductance L. Therefore, this ground plane equivalently forms a parallel LC filter. This filter has a band-stop characteristic, which can effectively prevent the coupling current from flowing on the ground plane, thereby achieving decoupling between MIMO antennas. Figure 4.23 shows the structural model of an MIMO antenna based on this decoupled ground plane. It is composed of two planar inverted-F antennas and a ground plane containing periodic gaps.

4.5.4.5 *Additional decoupling network*

When using the previous decoupling methods to decouple multiple antennas, the antenna design must be considered simultaneously with the decoupling structure, and joint optimization needs to be used to obtain satisfactory performance indicators. This is because in the presence of induced currents of various decoupling structures when decoupling, the decoupling structure also acts as an antenna radiating element. When

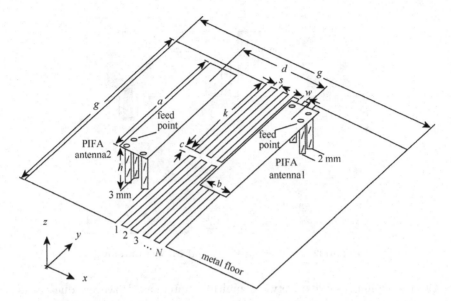

Fig. 4.23. MIMO antenna with the decoupling ground plane.

various decoupling structures are added, the radiation characteristics of the original antenna unit will inevitably change. When various decoupling structures are added, the radiation characteristics of the original antenna unit will inevitably change. The biggest advantage of the decoupling method with the additional decoupling network and the previous methods is that the design of the decoupling network can be separated from the design of the antenna unit. The core idea of this method is to consider the coupling as a circuit parameter, while introducing new circuit components to counteract the effects of coupling. However, the biggest drawback is that a large number of operations are required in the isolation design, and designing a usable feed network is also a problem for the calculation results which have been completed. Chen *et al.*,[23] gave a schematic diagram of a dual-antenna system when decoupling with a decoupling network, as shown in Fig. 4.24. In a two-antenna system with good matching but strong mutual coupling, the coupling between the two antennas is greatly reduced by decoupling the network. However, the matching effect of the antenna is very poor at this time. After the decoupling network, two matching networks are, respectively, added, so that the purpose of achieving good matching and high port isolation can be achieved. The decoupling network generally consists of two segments of normalized electrical length

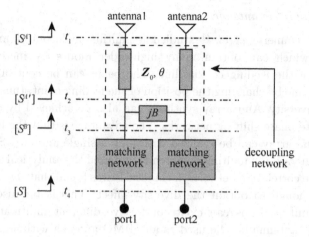

Fig. 4.24. Diagram of the decoupling network in a dual-antenna system.

L, a characteristic impedance of Z_0, and a parallel-equivalent inductive or capacitive component. The normalized electrical length L is selected such that the transconductance at the reference plane t_2 becomes a pure-imaginary number and the parallel inductive or capacitive element acts to eliminate the transconductance at the reference plane t_3, causing it to become zero. On this basis, effective decoupling is achieved. The matching network can be implemented either by lumped elements or by a microstrip transmission line. In practical applications, sometimes the decoupling network and the matching network are organically combined, and the functions of decoupling and matching are completed at the same time.

4.5.5 *MIMO multi-antenna selection*

In the early stage, MIMO antennas were typically designed using conventional antenna designs such as the printed dipole antenna and microstrip antennas. Later, the design ideas of many new antennas were gradually proposed and steadily put into practical use. The current trend in researching MIMO antennas is to explore high-performance, low-cost antenna unit designs and layouts.

4.5.5.1 *Multimode antenna*

In 1998, Demmerle *et al.*,[24] studied a multimode biconical multi-beam antenna, which can obtain many high-order modes by increasing the diameter of the feeding coaxial line. The beam can be controlled in the azimuth plane by changing the position of the feeding point, thus achieving angular diversity. And array synthesis can also be achieved by combining appropriate phase-shifting networks. The advantage is that the function of the antenna array can be realized with only a single antenna. Svantesosn further analyzed the multimode antenna and used the analytical solution to express the correlation between the modes. It was found that the correlation was low enough to obtain the diversity effect. This is because different antenna unit patterns can excite or receive different multipath signals. Multimode antenna can be used as an MIMO antenna without occupying too much space.

4.5.5.2 *Switched parasitic antenna*

In 1999, Vauhgna studied a switched parasitic antenna with an active antenna unit connected to a transceiver and a parasitic antenna unit connected to terminating impedance. There is strong coupling between the parasitic unit and the active unit. By controlling the connection between the parasitic unit and the termination impedance (i.e. turn on and off, change the current distribution of the parasitic antenna unit), the antenna pattern can be changed to achieve angle diversity. SPA is similar to an antenna array with several fixed beams, but the former is smaller and more suitable for some portable mobile devices. In order to reduce the influence of the switching state of the parasitic unit on the impedance of the active unit, the parasitic unit is usually placed symmetrically around it. This antenna scheme is simpler than a conventional diversity antenna, which typically uses a multiplexer to connect all antenna elements. In 2001, Wennstrom *et al.*,[25] proposed using SPA for MIMO systems and pointed out that the correlation between signal modes was low enough to obtain diversity gain. It also shows that the channel capacity using SPA can be compared with the channel using the antenna array. Although the former has a loss in signal-to-noise ratio, SPA can save costs with only one transceiver compared to fact that each antenna in the diversity antenna array is connected to a transceiver.

4.5.5.3 *Printed antenna array such as the fractal antenna and the planar inverted-F antenna*

The fractal antenna has the characteristics of large bandwidth, small size, low sidelobes, and easy conformality and is one of the candidate methods for the MIMO antenna unit. Similarly, planar inverted-F antennas (PIAFs) have significant characteristics, such as compact size, low profile, and easy adjustment and processing, and are also commonly used in portable wireless devices. Karaboikis *et al.*[26] studied the use of fractal antennas and planar inverted-F printed antennas for MIMO terminal equipment and pointed out that placing two, three, four, or six fractal units or planar inverted F-printed antennas on a portable terminal can satisfy the diversity requirements.

4.5.5.4 *High dielectric antenna array*

In MIMO antenna design, it is important to reduce the size of the antenna unit. The use of high dielectric materials such as ceramics can reduce the antenna size and improve some properties such as deresonance resistance, radiation efficiency, and multiple resonances in some designs to improve bandwidth. Therefore, high dielectric antenna is another important choice for MIMO antenna design. High dielectric antennas have three basic forms: dielectric loaded antenna (dielectric is not used as a radiator but used only to reduce antenna size), dielectric resonator antennas (the dielectric resonator above the conductive floor is an excited radiator, with medium bandwidth), and wideband dielectric monopole antennas (the dielectric resonator is an excited radiator, but the metal floor underneath the resonator is removed, with ultra-wideband).

4.5.5.5 *Photonic band gap/electromagnetic band gap substrate antenna array*

Photonic band gap (PBG) is a phenomenon in optics. Periodically, some small holes are placed on the photonic substrate. If the period of the small holes is equal to or close to the wavelength of the illumination light, the light waves in the band gap are absorbed without being propagated. EBG materials are based on the PBG phenomenon of this periodic structure, namely the introduction of periodic disturbances (such as holes and dielectric columns) on the substrate. At present, many EBG structures have been proposed for the use as planar antenna array substrates. Both simulation and testing show that the EBG substrate antenna has excellent characteristics, such as suppressing surface waves, reducing the coupling effect between antenna elements, and improving the gain and isolation performance of the antenna unit. Therefore, EBG materials have outstanding advantages in MIMO terminal antenna design. Research also shows that the use of a high dielectric substrate combined with EBG structure to design the MIMO multi-antenna can further improve the performance of the antenna unit, such as reducing the size of the antenna unit, suppressing surface waves, and improving the isolation performance between units.

4.5.5.6 *Compact cube layout antenna array*

In 1965, Gilbert proposed the concept of energy-intensive antennas, in which a vertically polarized electric field and two horizontally polarized magnetic fields, respectively, received by a vertically polarized electric dipole and two horizontal polarized dipoles in a multipath propagation environment were independent of each other. Therefore, the magnetic field component is also a good source of diversity, also known as field component diversity. In 2002, Andersen *et al.* pointed out that the antenna structure for designing the MIMO systems was equivalent to designing low correlation diversity systems based on the propagation environment and proposed a miniature cubic layout antenna array, which was to place 12 electric dipoles on each side of parallel cubes. It has polarization diversity and a spatial diversity effect and is especially suitable for indoor environment with arbitrary polarization.

4.5.5.7 *Three-dimensional orthogonal layout monopole antenna array*

In 2002, Jungnikcel *et al.* pointed out that for MIMO systems, the arranged multi-antenna array should receive scattered signals as much as possible, and each antenna unit should receive signals from different directions. A good example is fixing the receiving antenna to a hemispherical metal surface. Therefore, Jungnikcel *et al.*[27] proposed a three-dimensional orthogonal layout monopole antenna array in which a quarter-wave monopole antenna perpendicular to its corresponding floor is placed in the center of three mutually perpendicular metal floors to form a mutually orthogonal monopole antenna array. According to the need for MIMO systems, more identical forms of monopole antenna arrays can be constructed. This layout allows for independent sampling of the three components of the electric field vector at one location. Since the spacing of the monopole antenna elements is large enough, the coupling between them is less than $-20\,\text{dB}$. The measurement results show that in the indoor environment, the actual channel is close to the iid channel, and even if the antenna is used in an outdoor environment, a large capacity can be obtained. The antenna array is obviously superior to other array forms.

Only some typical design solutions are given above. They are based on the basic technical requirements of the MIMO system for antenna design and the characteristics of MIMO antennas and indicate the current status and research direction of MIMO antenna design, which mainly includes three aspects: research on multi-antenna unit design, new materials, and multi-antenna layout. This is because in an actual MIMO antenna design, a low-profile antenna unit with a simple feed network is best suited for MIMO systems, and none of the antennas can provide an ideal single diversity. Usually, several diversity methods are used together. The isolation between antenna elements is crucial for the diversity of MIMO systems. For example, EBG materials can be used to suppress surface waves to improve isolation performance. The layout of multi-antenna elements also has an important impact on diversity performance.

4.6 Massive MIMO Technology

In existing MIMO systems, only a small number of antennas are used (for example, 4 or 8 antennas in a 4G system), which only plays a small part in the benefits of the MIMO technology, and the spectral efficiency obtained is only about 15 bit/s/Hz, or even less. However, if we use a large number of antennas in the communication terminal, more benefits will be obtained. For example, in an MIMO system with hundreds of antennas, gigabit rate transmission can be achieved with a high spectral efficiency of several hundred bits/s/Hz. In 2010, Marzetta[28] of Bell Labs proposed to set up a large-scale antenna on the base station side instead of the existing multi-antenna. The number of base station antennas is much larger than the number of single-antenna mobile terminals which they can simultaneously serve, thereby forming a massive MIMO wireless communication system.

4.6.1 *Massive MIMO system application prospects*

The use of the multi-antenna technology will bring many benefits. First, the more antennas are used, the more degrees of freedom are generated in the airspace. This has many uses, such as increasing the data transmission rate without increasing the bandwidth and improving the reliability of the link through spatial diversity. More specifically, in a point-to-point MIMO communication system, M_T represents the number of transmitting antennas and M_R represents the number of receiving antennas, and the probability of link interruption is

$$P_{\text{outage}} \propto \text{SNR}^{-M_T M_R} \tag{4.171}$$

Therefore, under the premise that M_T and M_R are large, the bit error rate of the MIMO link decreases exponentially with the increase of SNR. In addition, the achievable rate scale is

$$\min(M_T, M_R)\text{lb}(1 + \text{SNR}) \tag{4.172}$$

The above equation shows the possibility of achieving a high data rate without increasing the bandwidth on the premise that M_T and M_R is large.

The system architecture of massive MIMO systems varies with the application environment, which includes point-to-point MIMO architecture and multi-user MIMO architecture. In a point-to-point MIMO structure, the number of transmitting antennas in the transmitter, M_T, and the number of receiving antennas in the receiver, M_R, can be very large. A high-speed wireless backhaul connection between base stations using the multi-antenna technology is a typical application of the point-to-point massive MIMO architecture. In multi-user MIMO architecture, the architecture of single point to multi-point (such as downlink in cellular systems) and multi-point to single point (such as uplink in cellular systems) is common. Communication takes place between a single station and multiple user terminals, which may be small devices such as mobile phones and smart phones, or medium-sized devices such as notebook computers, set-top boxes, and televisions. In a user terminal such as a smartphone, only a limited number of antennas can be installed due to space constraints and in a user terminal such as a notebook computer, a set top box, or a television, more antennas can be installed. Regardless of the size of the user terminal and the number of antennas that can be installed, it is relatively easy to use hundreds or thousands of antennas in a base station of a multi-user MIMO architecture. Figure 4.25 shows the actual antenna layout scenario for several massive MIMO system base stations.[29] In this case, the degree of spatial freedom provided by the large-scale antenna configuration of the base station is utilized to improve the multiplexing capability of the

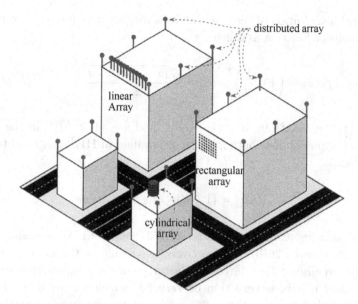

Fig. 4.25. Scenario of the massive MIMO base station antenna layout.

spectrum resources between multiple users and the spectrum efficiency of each user link, thereby greatly improving the overall utilization rate of the spectrum resources. At the same time, using the diversity gain and array gain provided by the large-scale antenna configuration of the base station, the power efficiency of communication between each user and the base station can be further significantly improved.

4.6.2 *Channel Hardening under large sizes*

The most obvious advantages of the massive MIMO systems are the increase of data rates and diversity gain. In addition, its large size can also produce the advantage that small MIMO systems do not have, which is that as the dimension $M_R \times M_T$ of channel matrix $\mathbf{H}$ becomes larger (for example, increase M_R and M_T simultaneously and keep their proportions constant), its singular value distribution becomes insensitive to the actual distribution of the channel matrix elements (as long as the channel matrix elements are independent and identically distributed). This is the result of the Marcenko–Pastur theorem. It shows that for an $M_R \times M_T$ matrix $\mathbf{H}$, when $M_R, M_T \to \infty$ and $M_R/M_T \to \beta$, if the elements in $\mathbf{H}$ satisfy the zero mean independent and identical distribution and the variance is $1/M_R$, then the empirical distribution of the eigenvalues is roughly determined to converge to the density function as follows:

$$f_\beta(x) = \left(1 - \frac{1}{\beta}\right)^+ \delta(x) + \frac{\sqrt{(x-a)^+(b-x)^+}}{2\pi\beta x} \qquad (4.173)$$

where $(z)^+ = \max(z, 0)$, $a = (1 - \sqrt{\beta})^2$, and $b = (1 + \sqrt{\beta})^2$. In the same way, the empirical distribution of the eigenvalues of $\mathbf{HH}^H$ can be obtained as follows:

$$\tilde{f}_\beta(x) = (1 - \beta)\delta(x) + \beta f_\beta(x) \qquad (4.174)$$

The images represented by Eqs. (4.173) and (4.174) are shown in Figs. 4.26(a) and 4.26(b),[30] respectively, depending on the value of β.

The premise of the Marcenko–Pastur theorem being effective is that the channel matrix is very thin or very fat, which can be derived from $\beta = 0.2$ and $\beta = 10$ in Fig. 4.26, such that the non-zero eigenvalues of $\mathbf{H}^H\mathbf{H}$ and $\mathbf{HH}^H$ are far from zero. The Marcenko–Pastur's theorem also shows that the "hardening" of a channel means that a single eigenvalue distribution converges to the average asymptotic eigenvalue distribution. In this sense, as the number of antennas increases, the channel becomes more and more certain. Figure 4.27 depicts the large-scale channel hardening behavior, which shows the intensity maps of $\mathbf{H}^H\mathbf{H}$ at $M_R = M_T = 8, 32, 96,$ and 256, where the elements of $\mathbf{H}$ are Gaussian terms with zero mean unit variance and independent distribution. It can be seen that as the dimension of $\mathbf{H}$ increases, the magnitude of the value on the diagonal of $\mathbf{H}^H\mathbf{H}$ is larger than that of the non-diagonal.

Channel hardening has many advantages for large-scale signal processing. For example, using a zero-forcing (ZF) detector and a minimum mean square error detector requires an operational matrix inversion. It is very advantageous to use the series expansion method to solve the inverse solution of large random matrices. Due to channel hardening, it is very efficient to solve the inverse solution of the large-dimensional approximation matrix by series expansion and deterministic approximation based on limit distribution. Channel hardening allows superior performance to be achieved with a simple algorithm at large size and this low-complexity detection algorithm is suitable for large-size channel systems.

4.6.3 *Technical challenges faced by large-scale MIMO*

Large-scale MIMO wireless communication increases the spectrum efficiency of the system by significantly increasing the number of antennas to explore the wireless resources that benefit the spatial dimension. The problem involved is how to break through the "bottleneck" of the wireless transmission technology caused by the significant increase in the number

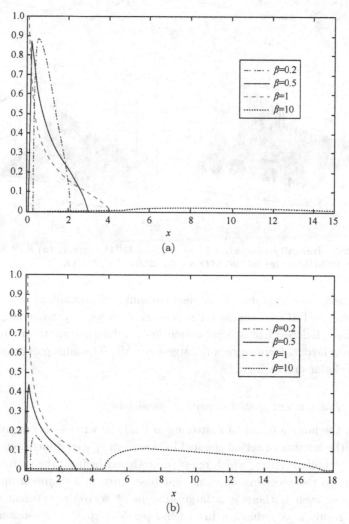

Fig. 4.26.   Marcenko–Pastur density function. (a) $H^H H$. (b) HH^H.

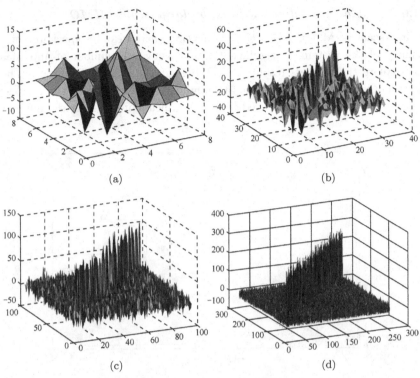

Fig. 4.27. Intensity diagram of the channel $H^H H$ matrix. (a) 8×8 MIMO. (b) 32×32 MIMO. (c) 96×96 MIMO. (d) 256×256 MIMO.

of antennas, and explore the wireless transmission technology suitable for large-scale MIMO communication scenarios. Some key technologies are as follows: independent spatial dimension availability, multi-antenna and RF chain layout, low-complexity large-scale MIMO signal processing, and multi-cellular processing.

4.6.3.1 *Independent spatial dimension availability*

Due to the large amount of scattering around the wireless communication nodes, the number of actual channel-independent spatial dimensions is limited. The pinhole effect, which refers to all the paths from the transmitting antenna to the receiving antenna that pass through a common aperture, can occur even if there is a large amount of scattering present. These effects result in a reduction in the independent spatial dimensions (e.g. a low rank channel matrix). In addition, the spacing between the antennas of the communication terminals is also crucial to determine the number of independent spatial dimensions. If the spacing between the antenna elements is too close, it will cause spatial correlation and reduce the capacity of the MIMO channel. Conversely, if there is sufficient spacing between the antenna elements, many antennas can be installed in the medium and large communication terminals. For a space-limited user terminal, installing a larger number of antenna elements requires a miniaturized antenna array.

There is usually a large amount of scattering in typical indoor and outdoor urban environments. The measurement of the hierarchical structure and statistical characteristics of large-scale MIMO channels requires dense channel measurements in different physical environments (indoor, outdoor, urban, suburban, rural, etc.) and different communication bands (such as 2.5 GHz, 5 GHz, 11 GHz, etc.). It is worth noting that some large-scale MIMO channel measurements show that although the theoretical full rank channel model is significantly different from the experimentally measured channel model, most of the theoretical performance gains of large-scale antenna arrays are available.

4.6.3.2 *Multi-antenna and RF chain layout*

It is a problem to place multiple antennas when the communication terminal is relatively small in size. Keeping the antenna space constant, increasing the number of antennas will reduce the spacing between units, which will increase the spatial correlation and in turn reduce the channel capacity of MIMO. As a rule of thumb, if the antenna elements are considered to be almost uncorrelated, then the spacing between the antenna elements is at least $\lambda/2$ (λ is the carrier wavelength). The following methods can help to reduce the difficulty of antenna and RF chain layout.

- **Use higher carrier frequency:** Since the higher the carrier frequency is, the shorter the carrier wavelength is, so that a larger number of antennas can be placed in the same antenna space. In addition, in terms of antenna layout, carrier frequencies at 11 GHz, 30 GHz, and 60 GHz are attractive.
- **Make full use of antenna space:** The antenna layout is not only in one or two dimensions (such as a line array, a planar array) but also in a compact volume which is called an MIMO cube antenna for short.
- **Compact antenna array:** A compact antenna array refers to the antenna element spacing that is less than half the wavelength. The design of a compact antenna array requires that the unit mutual

coupling and radiation efficiency be used under acceptable conditions to solve the layout problem of the antenna in a large-scale MIMO system. PIFA antenna is a typical antenna unit.

- **Spatial modulation:** Spatial modulation is a relatively new modulation method suitable for multi-antenna communication, which can reduce the number of transmitting RF chains in MIMO transmitters without reducing the efficiency. It reduces the hardware complexity, size, and cost of transmitting the RF chain.

4.6.3.3 *Low-complexity large-scale MIMO signal processing*

Low-complexity signal processing algorithms for synchronization, signal detection, precoding, channel estimation, and channel decoding are critical for the implementation of large-scale MIMO systems.

- **MIMO detection:** The MIMO detector of the receiver is used to recover signals transmitted from multiple transmit antennas simultaneously, which is usually a bottleneck of the overall performance and complexity of the system. The optimal detector based on the maximum likelihood or maximum *a posteriori* probability (MAP) criterion has an exponential relationship with the number of transmitting antennas. And in large-scale MIMO systems, high complexity should be avoided. The existing detectors either have good performance and high complexity (such as sphere decoders) or have low complexity and poor performance (such as ZF detectors, MMSE detectors). However, channel hardening of large matrices has proven to be very useful. Some low-complexity algorithms based on local search, metaheuristic, backpropagation (BP), and sampling techniques have shown their performance and complexity to be suitable for large-scale MIMO systems. They have the same complexity as linear detectors, but exhibit near-optimal performance, especially for large-scale signal detection.

- **LDPC code:** One of the main aspects of using the message passing algorithm detection (such as large-scale backpropagation) is that the graph model algorithm can be well combined with the Turbo or LDPC decoding algorithm to achieve joint processing of detection/decoding in a large-scale MIMO system. This joint algorithm requires an LDPC code designed for a large-scale MIMO channel, especially an LDPC code matched with a large-scale MIMO channel, which can be designed by detecting/decoding combined with the external information transfer method. In large-scale MIMO channels, this specially designed LDPC code performs much better than some existing LDPC codes.

- **Spatial modulation:** It is a relatively new modulation method for multi-antenna communication, which is suitable for large-scale MIMO systems. Due to the permission of the use of fewer RF chains than the number of transmitting antennas without sacrificing efficiency, in large-scale MIMO systems, it reduces the complexity, size, and cost of the RF hardware. The novelty of this modulation is that in addition to traditional modulation (such as QAM) transmission of information, information can also be transmitted by antenna selection.

- **Single-carrier communication:** Due to the higher peak-to-average ratio of multi-carrier systems, single-carrier communication techniques are becoming more popular than multi-carrier techniques such as OFDM/OFDMA. The LTE standard has used Single-Carrier Frequency Division Multiple Access (SC-FDMA) in the uplink. Similarly, SC-FDMA is also applicable to the downlink of multi-user MIMO. Although SC-FDMA provides better peak-to-average ratio and performance than OFDMA, SC-FDMA receivers are more complex than OFDMA receivers for the sake of equilibrium.

- **Channel estimation:** The channel estimation method plays an important role in MIMO receivers (for signal detection) and transmitters (for precoding). In pilot-assisted channel estimation, the number of training slots for pilot transmission increases linearly with the number of transmitting antennas, which results in the reduction of data throughput. However, in the case of large channel coherence time, such pilot transmission-based throughput reduction can be reduced in slow-fading channels, such as fixed wireless channels. In the channel estimation and frequency division duplex systems in high-mobility scenarios, the transmitter sends a large amount of feedback of channel estimation coefficients to the receiver, which needs to be studied in a large-scale MIMO system environment.

- **Precoding:** Applying channel state information (CSI) at the transmitter requires precoding the signal at the transmitter. Since there are a large number of antennas at the base station for downlink multi-user communication, some available spatial degrees of freedom can also be used to design simple precoding and reduce the peak-to-average power ratio.

4.6.3.4 *Multi-cellular processing*

In addition to the different wireless link-level issues discussed above, some system-level issues cannot be ignored in large-scale MIMO systems. An important aspect is that multi-cellular processing, including the size of the cell, the frequency between cells, resource allocation, general interference processing, and especially inter-cell interference processing, will bring new challenges to the layout of large-scale MIMO systems. Base station cooperation is a new and effective method to solve the multi-cell problem. For example, a multi-cellular precoding method by base station cooperation is an effective method of handling inter-cell interference. And the LTE wireless standard has adopted base station cooperation, such as coordinated multipoint transmission (COMP), which can dynamically coordinate the transmission and reception of different base stations. Base station cooperation is expected to play a significant role in large-scale MIMO systems. Pilot pollution is another prominent problem in multi-cellular processing. It is an inter-cell interference problem that occurs in multi-cellular systems where non-orthogonal pilot sequences are used for uplink channel estimation, and base station cooperation can be used to overcome this problem.

Although various technical challenges are discussed in Section 4.6.3, in the literatures,[31, 32] large-scale MIMO test platforms have begun to appear. These test platforms use different sizes of MIMO structures, different numbers of antennas, different bands and bandwidths and are placed in different physical environments for testing (e.g. indoors, outdoors). However, in fact, all of these test platforms have shown that high spectral efficiency benefits from the use of a large number of antennas and the specific implementation of the MIMO systems.

4.7 Summary

MIMO technology is one of the key technologies to realize high-speed broadband wireless communication in the future. This chapter introduces the channel model of the MIMO system in turn, analyzes the determined and the random MIMO channel capacity, and compares the SIMO, SOMI, and MIMO channel capacity of the average power allocation. First, the MIMO space–time coding technology is introduced, including the space–time trellis code, space–time block code, and layered space–time code. Second, MIMO beamforming technology is introduced for single-user and multi-user technology. Third, for antenna, an important part of the MIMO system, the design of the MIMO system antenna including multi-antenna mutual coupling, spatial correlation, and multi-antenna mutual coupling suppression is expounded. Finally, for the development of future MIMO systems, some technical challenges faced by large-scale MIMO system applications, large-scale channel hardening, and large-scale MIMO systems are discussed.

References

1. Shannon CE. A mathematical theory of communication. *The Bell System Technical Journal*, 1948, 27(7): 379–423.
2. Jang J, Lee KB, and Lee YH. Transmit power and bit allocations for OFDM systems in a fading channel. *IEEE Global Telecommunications Conference*, San Francisco, USA, 2003.
3. Proakis JG. *Digital Communications*, (3rd edn.). New York: McGraw-Hill, 1995.
4. Foschini GJ and Gans MJ. On limits of wireless communications in a fading environment when using multiple antennas. *Wireless Personal Communications*, 1998, 6(3): 311–335.
5. Vucetic B and Yuan J. *Space-Time Coding*. England: John Wiley & Sons Ltd., 2003.
6. Gesbert D, Boelcskei H, Gore D, *et al.* MIMO wireless channels: Capacity and performance prediction. *IEEE Global Telecommunications Conference*, San Francisco, CA, 2000.
7. Tarokh V, Seshadri N, and Calderbank AR. Space-time codes for high data rate wireless communication: Performance analysis and code construction. *IEEE Transactions on Information Theory*, 1998, 44(2): 744–765.
8. Vahid T, Nambi S, and Calderbank AR. Space-time codes for high data rate wireless communications: Performance criterion and code construction. *IEEE Transactions on Information Theory*, 1998, 44: 744–765.
9. Alamouti SM. A simple transmit diversity technique for wireless communications. *IEEE Journal on Selected Areas in Communications*, 1998, 16: 1451–1458.
10. Palomar DP, Cioffi JM, and Lagunas MA. Joint Tx-Rx beamforming design for multicarrier MIMO channels: A unified framework for convex optimization. *IEEE Transactions on Signal Process*, 2003, 51(9): 2381–2401.
11. Wiesel A, Eldar YC, and Shamai S. Linear precoding via conic optimization for fixed MIMO receivers. *IEEE Transactions on Signal Process*, 2006, 54(1): 161–176.
12. Love DJ and Heath RW. Equal gain transmission in multiple-input multiple output wireless systems. *IEEE Transactions on Communication*, 2003, 51(7): 1102–1110.
13. Spencer QH, Peel CB, Swindlehurst AL, *et al.* An introduction to the multiuser MIMO downlink. *IEEE Communications Magazine*, 2004, 42(10): 60–67.

14. Shen Z, Chen R, Andrews JG, *et al.* Low complexity user selection algorithms for multiuser MIMO systems with block diagonalization. *IEEE Transactions Signal Process*, 2006, 54(9): 3658–3663.

15. Chung J, Hwang CS, and Kim K. A random beamforming technique in MIMO systems exploiting multiuser diversity. *IEEE Journal on Selected Areas in Communications*, 2003, 21(5): 848–855.

16. Li X. Research on MIMO Channel Modeling and Multi-antenna Design in Next Generation Wireless Communication Systems. University of Electronic Science and Technology of China, 2005.

17. Li X and Nie ZP. Evaluating the spatial correlation of fading signals in MIMO channels. *Acta Electronica Sinica*, 2004, 32(12): 82–86.

18. Mak ACK, Rowell CR, and Murch RD. Isolation enhancement between two closely packed antennas. *IEEE Transactions on Antennas and Propagation*, 2008, 56: 3411–3419.

19. Chen N, Geng JP, Ye S, *et al.* An isolation technology of a reverse phase coupling for strongly coupled antennas. *Journal of CAEIT*, 2011, 5: 537–540.

20. Mohammad SS, Yanal SF, and Sheikh SI. Design and fabrication of a dual electrically small MIMO antenna system for 4G terminals. *German Microwave Conference (GeMIC)*, Darmstadt, 2011, 1–4.

21. Hong S, Lee J, and Choi J. Design of UWB diversity antenna for PDA applications. *10th International Conference on Advanced Communication Technology*, Gangwon-Do, 2008, 1: 583–585.

22. Chiu CY, Cheng CH, Corbett RD, *et al.* Reduction of mutual coupling between closed-packed antenna elements. *IEEE Transactions on Antennas and Propagation*, 2007, 55: 1732–1939.

23. Chen SC, Wang YS, and Chung SJ. A decoupling technique for increasing the port isolation between two strongly coupled antennas. *IEEE Transactions on Antennas and Propagation*, 2008, 56: 3650–3658.

24. Demmerle F and Wiesbeek W. A biconical multibeam antenna for space-division multiple access. *IEEE Transactions on Antennas and Propagation*, 1998, 46(6): 782–787.

25. Wennstrom M and Svantesson T. Antenna solution for MIMO channels: The switched parasitic antenna. *12th IEEE International Symposium on Personal, Indoor and Mobile Radio Communications*, San Diego, USA, 2001, 1: 159–163.

26. Karaboikis M, Soras C, Tsachtsiris G, *et al.* Compact dual-printed inverted-F antenna diversity systems for portable wireless devices. *IEEE Antennas and Wireless Propagation Letters*, 2004, 3(1): 9–14.

27. Jungniekel V, Pohl V, Nguyen H, *et al.* High capacity antennas for MIMO radio systems. *5th International Symposium on Wireless Personal Multimedia Communications*, 2002, 2: 407–411.

28. Marzetta TL. Noncooperative cellular wireless with unlimited numbers of base station antennas. *IEEE Transactions on Wireless Communications*, 2010, 9(11): 2590–3600.

29. Larsson EG. Massive MIMO for next generation wireless systems. *IEEE Communications Magazine*, 2014, 2: 186–195.

30. Chockalingam A and Rajan BS. *Large MIMO Systems*. England: Cambridge University Press, 2014.

31. Nishimori K, Kudo R, Honma N, *et al.* 16 × 16 multiuser MIMO testbed employing simple adaptive modulation scheme. *IEEE 69th Vehicular Technology Conference*, 2009, 1–5.

32. Suzuki H, Matthews J, Kendall R, *et al.* Highly spectrally efficient Ngara rural wireless broadband access demonstrator. *International Symposium on Communications and Information Technologies (ISCIT)*, 2012, 914–919.

Chapter 5

Spatial Multidimensional Signal Reception and Iterative Processing

In Chapters 2 and 4, we introduced the basic principle of the uncoded MIMO system and the signal transmitting and receiving technology. For the receiver signal detection of MIMO, although the conventional MIMO signal detection methods have been stated in Chapter 2, it is still difficult to achieve a good compromise between performance and complexity. Moreover, it is difficult for the uncoded MIMO system to reach or approach the theoretical channel capacity that the MIMO system can provide. Therefore, the study of multidimensional signal iterative reception processing technology with low complexity and high performance has great significance for the practical application of the MIMO system.

In this chapter, for the uncoded MIMO system, first we introduce how to achieve high performance with low complexity for the lattice reduction-based MIMO signal detection technology; second, in order to reach the theoretical channel capacity, a further introduction of the iterative decode basic principle of bit-interleaved coded modulation (BICM) system and the best maximum a posteriori probability (MAP) iterative signal processing detection methods are stated in this chapter. On this basis, in order to avoid high complexity of the MAP method, low-complexity and high-performance detection methods based on random sampling and bit filtering are also discussed, and a comparative analysis is made with the MAP method in terms of complexity and performance.

5.1 MIMO Detection Technology Based on Lattice Theory[a]

As a key technology for low-complexity and high-performance signal detection in MIMO systems, the lattice reduction (LR) method can transform a set of substrates in space into a set of quasi-orthogonal substrates in polynomial time. When we consider the received signal of the MIMO system as the lattice of the vector space formed by the basis of its channel matrix, we can apply the LR method to the quasi-orthogonal transformation of the substrate. Therefore, the anti-interference ability of the spatial combined signal can be greatly improved with lower computational complexity. In terms of lattice decoding and the recent search for the Euclidean vector, LR has been widely used. In this section, we introduce LR-based signal detection methods to achieve a low-complexity, high-performance, and full-reception diversity gain signal detection in high-dimensional MIMO systems. A MIMO signal detector using LR technology is generally called an LR-based MIMO detector.[1]

5.1.1 *Lattice mathematical basis*

According to the lattice theory, the lattice Λ is defined as an M-dimensional discrete subset of the n-dimensional real set $\mathbf{R}^n$, namely

$$\Lambda = \left\{ \mathbf{u} | \mathbf{u} = \sum_{m=1}^{M} \mathbf{b}_m z_m, \ z_m \in \mathbb{Z} \right\} \tag{5.1}$$

where $\mathbf{b}_m \in \mathbf{B} = \{\mathbf{b}_1, \mathbf{b}_2, \ldots, \mathbf{b}_M\}$, $\mathrm{rank}(\mathbf{B}) = M, M \leq n$, $\mathbf{B}$ is called the base of the lattice Λ, and Λ is called the lattice formed by $\mathbf{B}$. It is worth noting that the same lattice can be formed by different substrates. First, recall the MIMO system model,

$$\mathbf{y} = \mathbf{H}\mathbf{s} + \mathbf{n} \tag{5.2}$$

If the channel matrix $\mathbf{H}$ is regarded as a set of substrates, the receiving signal $\mathbf{y}$ becomes a column of vectors in the lattice formed by the base $\mathbf{H}$. It is known from the definition of the lattice that the $\mathbf{s}$ element in Eq. (5.2) should be an integer, and $\mathbf{H}$ and $\mathbf{y}$ should be composed of real numbers.

According to the transformation relationship between the complex matrix and the real matrix, we can transform $\mathbf{H}$ into a set of matrices

---

[a]Reprinted/adapted by permission from Springer Nature Customer Service Centre GmbH: Springer *"Low Complexity MIMO Detection"* by Bai L and Choi J, 2012.

composed of real bases. The transformation method is

$$\begin{bmatrix} \Re(\mathbf{y}) \\ \Im(\mathbf{y}) \end{bmatrix} = \begin{bmatrix} \Re(\mathbf{H}) & -\Im(\mathbf{H}) \\ \Im(\mathbf{H}) & \Re(\mathbf{H}) \end{bmatrix} \begin{bmatrix} \Re(\mathbf{s}) \\ \Im(\mathbf{s}) \end{bmatrix} + \begin{bmatrix} \Re(\mathbf{n}) \\ \Im(\mathbf{n}) \end{bmatrix} \tag{5.3}$$

where $\Re(\cdot)$ and $\Im(\cdot)$ represent the real and imaginary parts, respectively. Accordingly, we can define the $2N \times 1$ real receiving signal vector $\mathbf{y}_r = [\Re(\mathbf{y})^T \Im(\mathbf{y})^T]^T$, $2M \times 1$ real transmitting signal vector $\mathbf{s}_r = [\Re(\mathbf{s})^T \Im(\mathbf{s})^T]^T$, $2N \times 1$ noise vector $\mathbf{n}_r = [\Re(\mathbf{n})^T \Im(\mathbf{n})^T]^T$, and $2N \times 2M$ real channel matrix $\mathbf{H}_r = \begin{bmatrix} \Re(\mathbf{H}) & -\Im(\mathbf{H}) \\ \Im(\mathbf{H}) & \Re(\mathbf{H}) \end{bmatrix}$. Thus, Eq. (5.3) can be written as

$$\mathbf{y}_r = \mathbf{H}_r \mathbf{s}_r + \mathbf{n}_r \tag{5.4}$$

where the real channel matrix $\mathbf{H}_r$ can be used as a set of substrates of the lattice. Next, the transmitting signal $\mathbf{s}_r$ is transformed onto a continuous integer field by using translation and scaling. Although initially people considered the lattice space on the real base $\mathbf{H}_r$, further studies have shown that the lattice space can be obtained by the complex channel matrix $\mathbf{H}$, and the complex lattice reduction can reduce the complexity of MIMO detection.

Taking the complex-valued MIMO system model as an example, the MIMO detection method based on lattice reduction is introduced. Since $\mathbf{s}$ is a non-contiguous integer domain, $\mathbf{s}$ needs to be properly translated and scaled before the lattice reduction to transform $\mathbf{s}$ to a continuous integer domain. For QAM modulation,

$$\{\alpha \mathbf{s} + \beta\} \subseteq \mathbb{C}, \quad \mathbf{s} \in \mathcal{S} \tag{5.5}$$

where α and β represent the scaling and translation parameters, respectively. For K-QAM modulation, the symbol set can be obtained as follows:

$$\mathcal{S} = \{s = a + jb | a, b \in \{-(2P-1)A, \ldots, -3A, -A, A,$$

$$3A, \ldots, (2P-1)A\}\} \tag{5.6}$$

where $P = \frac{\log K}{2}$, and $A = \sqrt{\frac{3E_s}{2(K-1)}}$ represents the symbolic energy. The parameters for scaling and translation which make Eq. (5.5) true are

$$\begin{cases} \alpha = \frac{1}{2A} \\ \beta = \frac{2P-1}{2}(1 + j) \end{cases} \tag{5.7}$$

It should be noted here that the values of α and β are not unique. The MIMO system model based on the lattice reduction is

$$
\begin{aligned}
\tilde{\mathbf{y}} &= \tilde{\mathbf{H}}\tilde{\mathbf{s}} + \mathbf{n} \\
&= \tilde{\mathbf{H}}(\alpha \mathbf{s} + \beta \mathbf{I}) + \mathbf{n} \\
&= \frac{\mathbf{H}}{\alpha}\alpha \mathbf{s} + \frac{\mathbf{H}}{\alpha}\beta \mathbf{I} + \mathbf{n} \\
&= \mathbf{H}\mathbf{s} + \mathbf{n} + \frac{\mathbf{H}}{\alpha}\beta \mathbf{I} \\
&= \mathbf{y} + \frac{\mathbf{H}}{\alpha}\beta \mathbf{I}
\end{aligned}
\tag{5.8}
$$

In other words, at the receiving end, the receiving signal $\mathbf{y}$ needs to be processed as follows:

$$
\tilde{\mathbf{y}} = \mathbf{y} + \frac{\mathbf{H}}{\alpha}\beta \mathbf{I}
\tag{5.9}
$$

It equivalently transforms $\mathbf{s}$ to a continuous integer domain.

Now, the LR-based MIMO system model can be written as follows:

$$
\tilde{\mathbf{y}} = \tilde{\mathbf{H}}\tilde{\mathbf{s}} + \mathbf{n}
\tag{5.10}
$$

Considering that a lattice space can be obtained from different bases or channel matrices, in order to eliminate noise and interference between multiple signals, we can find a matrix whose base can form the same space as the base of the original channel matrix, and the column vectors are approximately orthogonal between each other. This technology is LR. LR can improve the performance of the MIMO sub-optimal detection method in the MIMO system, and the corresponding detection method is called the LR-based MIMO detection method.

5.1.2 *MIMO detection based on lattice reduction*

If there are two sets of substrates $\mathbf{H}$ and $\mathbf{G}$, they can form the same lattice space and the column vector of each set of bases is a linear combination of integral coefficients of another set of base column vectors. For example,

$$
\mathbf{H} = \begin{bmatrix} 1 & 2 \\ 1 & 1 \end{bmatrix}
\tag{5.11}
$$

and

$$
\mathbf{G} = \begin{bmatrix} 1 & 0 \\ 0 & 1 \end{bmatrix}
\tag{5.12}
$$

and Eq. (5.13) can be easily obtained as follows:

$$\begin{bmatrix} 1 \\ 1 \end{bmatrix} = \begin{bmatrix} 1 \\ 0 \end{bmatrix} + \begin{bmatrix} 0 \\ 1 \end{bmatrix} \tag{5.13}$$

and

$$\begin{bmatrix} 2 \\ 1 \end{bmatrix} = 2 \times \begin{bmatrix} 1 \\ 0 \end{bmatrix} + \begin{bmatrix} 0 \\ 1 \end{bmatrix} \tag{5.14}$$

Therefore, the substrates $\mathbf{H}$ and $\mathbf{G}$ can form the same space. We can also obtain

$$\mathbf{H} = \mathbf{GU} \tag{5.15}$$

where $\mathbf{U}$ is a unimodular matrix. Therefore, the received signal can be rewritten as

$$\begin{aligned} \mathbf{y} &= \mathbf{GUs} + \mathbf{n} \\ &= \mathbf{Gc} + \mathbf{n} \end{aligned} \tag{5.16}$$

where $\mathbf{c} = \mathbf{Us}$. The elements in the unimodular matrix $\mathbf{U}$ are all integers. If $\mathbf{s} \in \mathbb{C}^M$, then we can obtain $\mathbf{c} \in \mathbb{C}^M$. However, since $\mathbf{s}$ is composed of QAM symbols, namely s_k, the real and imaginary parts of s_k can be transformed to continuous integer domains by scaling and translating parameters.

According to Eq. (5.16), since the received signal can be regarded as a point in the lattice space formed by the base (for example, $\mathbf{H}$ or $\mathbf{G}$), for the MIMO system established based on this, we can utilize the traditional low-complexity detection methods (such as linear or SIC methods) to detect $\mathbf{c}$. Here, we should note that if the ML detection method is applied to the matrix after the lattice reduction, there will be no performance improvement because the traditional ML detection method has already achieved the best performance. In the following, we introduce the LLL algorithm for finding an approximate orthogonal matrix.

5.1.2.1 *LLL algorithm*

The Lenstra–Lenstra–Lovasz (LLL), complex value algorithm can perform LR on a MIMO system with an M base and an $N \times M(N \geq M)$ channel matrix. The LLL algorithm was originally designed for real-valued matrices, and later it was extended to the complex-valued matrices, namely the complex Lenstra–Lenstra–Lovasz (CLLL) algorithm. In this section, we first introduce the real-valued LLL algorithm of LR in the MIMO system.

We derive the $2N \times 2M$ real-valued matrix $\mathbf{H_r}$ from the $N \times M$ complex-valued matrix $\mathbf{H}$, so that the LLL algorithm can transform a given base $\mathbf{H_r}$ into a new matrix $\mathbf{G_r}$ consisting of quasi-orthogonal base vectors. QR decomposition of $\mathbf{G_r}$ yields

$$\mathbf{G_r} = \mathbf{Q_r}\mathbf{R_r} \tag{5.17}$$

where, $\mathbf{Q_r}$ is a $2N \times 2N$ unitary matrix ($\mathbf{Q_r^T}\mathbf{Q_r} = \mathbf{I}_N$) and $\mathbf{R_r}$ is a $2N \times 2M$ upper triangular matrix. The $2N \times 2M$ real-valued matrix $\mathbf{G_r}$ can be regarded as the matrix after the LLL reduction. The elements of $\mathbf{R_r}$ after QR decomposition satisfy the inequality

$$\left| [\mathbf{R_r}]_{\ell,\rho} \right| \leq \frac{1}{2} \left| [\mathbf{R_r}]_{\ell,\ell} \right|, 1 \leq \ell < \rho \leq 2M \tag{5.18}$$

and

$$\delta [\mathbf{R_r}]_{\rho-1,\rho-1}^2 \leq [\mathbf{R_r}]_{\rho,\rho}^2 + [\mathbf{R_r}]_{\rho-1,\rho}^2, \rho = 2,\ldots,2M \tag{5.19}$$

where $[\mathbf{R_r}]_{p,q}$ represents the (p, q) element of $\mathbf{R_r}$. The value of the parameter δ plays a key role in the compromise of the performance and complexity of the algorithm. In LLL and CLLL algorithms, the range of δ is usually $(\frac{1}{4}, 1)$ and $(\frac{1}{2}, 1)$, respectively. And selecting $\delta = \frac{3}{4}$ can better meet the compromise requirement between performance and complexity.

The process of generating the matrix $\mathbf{G_r}$ after LLL reduction from the real-valued matrix $\mathbf{H_r}$ by the LLL algorithm is summarized as follows, where $\{\mathbf{H_r}\}$ and $\{\mathbf{Q_r}, \mathbf{R_r}, \mathbf{T_r}\}$ are the input and output, respectively.

INPUT:$\{\mathbf{H_r}\}$
OUTPUT:$\{\mathbf{Q_r}, \mathbf{R_r}, \mathbf{T_r}\}$
(1) $[\mathbf{Q_r}\mathbf{R_r}] \leftarrow \mathrm{qr}(\mathbf{H_r})$
(2) $\zeta \leftarrow \mathrm{size}(\mathbf{H_r}, 2)$
(3) $\mathbf{T_r} \leftarrow \mathbf{I}_\zeta$
(4) while $\rho \leq \zeta$
(5)   for $\ell = 1:\rho - 1$
(6) $\mu \leftarrow \lceil (\mathbf{R_r}\,(\rho - \ell, \rho)/\mathbf{R_r}\,(\rho - \ell, \rho - \ell)) \rfloor$
(7)   if $\mu \neq 0$
(8) $\mathbf{R_r}(1: \rho - \ell, \rho) \leftarrow \mathbf{R_r}(1: \rho - \ell, \rho) - \mu\mathbf{R_r}(1: \rho - \ell, \rho - \ell)$
(9) $\mathbf{T_r}(:, \rho) \leftarrow \mathbf{T_r}(:, \rho) - \mu\mathbf{T_r}(:, \rho - \ell)$
(10)   end if
(11)   end for
(12)   if $\delta(\mathbf{R_r}(\rho - 1, \rho - 1))^2 > \mathbf{R_r}(\rho, \rho)^2 + \mathbf{R_r}(\rho - 1, \rho)^2$
(13) Swap the $(\rho - 1)$th and ρth columns in $\mathbf{R_r}$ and $\mathbf{T_r}$

(14) $\Theta = \begin{bmatrix} \alpha & \beta \\ -\beta & \alpha \end{bmatrix}, \alpha = \frac{\mathbf{R}_r(\rho-1,\rho-1)}{\|\mathbf{R}_r(\rho-1:\rho,\rho-1)\|} \quad \beta = \frac{\mathbf{R}_r(\rho,\rho-1)}{\|\mathbf{R}_r(\rho-1:\rho,\rho-1)\|}\|$

(15) $\mathbf{R}_r(\rho-1:\rho,\rho-1:\zeta) \leftarrow \Theta \mathbf{R}_r(\rho-1:\rho,\rho-1:\zeta)$

(16) $\mathbf{Q}_r(:,\rho-1:\rho) \leftarrow \mathbf{Q}_r(:,\rho-1:\rho)\Theta^T$

(17) $\rho \leftarrow \max\{\rho-1,2\}$

(18) else

(19) $\rho \leftarrow \rho+1$

(20) end if

(21) end while

The matrix $\mathbf{G}_r = \mathbf{H}_r\mathbf{T}_r$ after the LLL reduction can be obtained from the output. And an LR-based MIMO detector can be implemented using the matrix $\mathbf{G}_r$ after reduction and the corresponding integer unimodular matrix $\mathbf{T}_r$.

Here, orthogonal deficiency (OD) can be used to compare the orthogonality of the original matrix and the matrix after LLL reduction.

$$\text{Orthogonal resolution} \begin{cases} \mathbf{H}_r : 1 - \dfrac{\det(\mathbf{H}_r^H\mathbf{H}_r)}{\displaystyle\prod_{i=1}^{8}\|\mathbf{h}_i\|^2} = 0.999\,5 \\[2em] \mathbf{G}_r : 1 - \dfrac{\det(\mathbf{G}_r^H\mathbf{G}_r)}{\displaystyle\prod_{i=1}^{8}\|\mathbf{g}_i\|^2} = 0.305\,6 \end{cases} \tag{5.20}$$

From Eq. (5.20), it can be seen that the highly correlated matrix $\mathbf{H}_r$ is transformed into a quasi-orthogonal matrix $\mathbf{G}_r$ through LR.

As mentioned above, the CLLL algorithm can directly perform LR on the complex-valued matrix. Compared with the LLL algorithm, the CLLL algorithm can reduce the complexity by about half while providing the same performance. Therefore, in terms of reducing complexity, people prefer to apply the CLLL algorithm for LR transformation.

Performing the QR decomposition on matrix $\mathbf{G}$ which is obtained by CLLL algorithm from an $N \times M$ matrix $\mathbf{H}$, we can get $\mathbf{G} = \mathbf{QR}$, where $\mathbf{Q}$ is a unitary matrix and $\mathbf{R}$ is an upper triangle matrix. If $\mathbf{R}$ satisfies the following conditions, then $\mathbf{G}$ is the matrix after CLLL reduction:

$$\begin{aligned} \left|\Re([\mathbf{R}]_{\ell,\rho})\right| &\leq \tfrac{1}{2}\left|\Re([\mathbf{R}]_{\ell,\ell})\right| \\ \left|\Im([\mathbf{R}]_{\ell,\rho})\right| &\leq \tfrac{1}{2}\left|\Re([\mathbf{R}]_{\ell,\ell})\right|, 1 \leq \ell < \rho \leq M \end{aligned} \tag{5.21}$$

and

$$\delta \left| [\mathbf{R}]_{\rho-1,\rho-1} \right|^2 \leq \left| [\mathbf{R}]_{\rho,\rho} \right|^2 + \left| [\mathbf{R}]_{\rho-1,\rho} \right|^2, \rho = 2, \ldots, M \qquad (5.22)$$

where $[\mathbf{R}]_{p,q}$ represents the (p, q) element of $\mathbf{R}$. Set $\delta = (\frac{1}{2}, 1)$, and the CLLL algorithm can be summarized as follows, where $\{\mathbf{H}\}$ and $\{\mathbf{Q}, \mathbf{R}, \mathbf{T}\}$ are the input and output, respectively.

INPUT:$\{\mathbf{H}\}$
OUTPUT:$\{\mathbf{Q}, \mathbf{R}, \mathbf{T}\}$
(1) $[\mathbf{Q}\ \mathbf{R}] \leftarrow \mathrm{qr}(\mathbf{H})$
(2) $\zeta \leftarrow \mathrm{size}(\mathbf{H}, 2)$
(3) $\mathbf{T} \leftarrow \mathbf{I}_\zeta$
(4) while $\rho \leq \zeta$
(5)   for $\ell = 1{:}\rho - 1$
(6) $\mu \leftarrow \lceil (\mathbf{R}(\rho - \ell, \rho) / \mathbf{R}(\rho - \ell, \rho - \ell)) \rfloor$
(7)   if $\mu \neq 0$
(8) $\mathbf{R}(1{:}\rho - \ell, \rho) \leftarrow \mathbf{R}(1{:}\rho - \ell, \rho) - \mu\mathbf{R}(1{:}\rho - \ell, \rho - \ell)$
(9) $\mathbf{T}(:,\rho) \leftarrow \mathbf{T}(:,\rho) - \mu\mathbf{T_r}(:,\rho - \ell)$
(10)   end if
(11)   end for
(12)   if $\delta \left| (\mathbf{R}(\rho - 1, \rho - 1)) \right|^2 > \left| \mathbf{R}(\rho, \rho) \right|^2 + \left| \mathbf{R}(\rho - 1, \rho) \right|^2$
(13)
(14) $\mathbf{\Theta} = \begin{bmatrix} \alpha^* & \beta \\ -\beta & \alpha \end{bmatrix}, \alpha = \frac{\mathbf{R}(\rho-1,\rho-1)}{\|\mathbf{R}(\rho-1{:}\rho,\rho-1)\|}\ \ \beta = \frac{\mathbf{R}(\rho,\rho-1)}{\|\mathbf{R}(\rho-1{:}\rho,\rho-1)\|}$
(15) $\mathbf{R}(\rho - 1{:}\rho, \rho - 1{:}\zeta) \leftarrow \mathbf{\Theta}\mathbf{R}(\rho - 1{:}\rho, \rho - 1{:}\zeta)$
(16) $\mathbf{Q}(:,\rho - 1{:}\rho) \leftarrow \mathbf{Q}(:,\rho - 1{:}\rho)\mathbf{\Theta}^H$
(17) $\rho \leftarrow \max\{\rho - 1, 2\}$
(18)   else
(19) $\rho \leftarrow \rho + 1$
(20)   end if
(21) end while

The CLLL algorithm differs from the LLL algorithm in three aspects: the rounding operation in step (6) is performed for a complex integer; in step (12), the absolute value operation is used; the unitary matrix Θ is performed for a complex integer.

Applying the complex-valued unimodular matrix $\mathbf{T}$ and the matrix $\mathbf{G} = \mathbf{HT}$ after CLLL reduction, the LR-based linear and SIC detectors can be used to estimate $\mathbf{c}$. It should be noted here that in order to transform $\mathbf{c}$ to $\mathbf{s}$, it is necessary to perform the corresponding translation and scaling of the real and imaginary parts.

5.1.2.2 *Linear detection based on LR*

Using the CLLL algorithm to perform a lattice reduction on the channel matrix $\tilde{\mathbf{H}}$, the matrix after the lattice reduction is

$$\mathbf{G} = \tilde{\mathbf{H}}\mathbf{T} \tag{5.23}$$

where $\mathbf{T}$ is an integer unimodular matrix. And then Eq. (5.10) can be written as

$$\begin{aligned} \tilde{\mathbf{y}} &= \tilde{\mathbf{H}}\tilde{\mathbf{s}} + \mathbf{n} \\ &= \mathbf{G}\mathbf{T}^{-1}\tilde{\mathbf{s}} + \mathbf{n} \\ &= \mathbf{G}\mathbf{c} + \mathbf{n} \end{aligned} \tag{5.24}$$

where $\mathbf{c} = \mathbf{T}^{-1}\tilde{\mathbf{s}}$. In this case, when performing MIMO detection, $\hat{\mathbf{c}}$ can be detected first to obtain $\hat{\tilde{\mathbf{s}}}$, and furthermore, $\mathbf{s}$ is obtained by inverse scaling and by translating. At this time, the LR-based zero-forcing detector is

$$\mathbf{W}_{\mathrm{LR-ZF}} = \mathbf{G}(\mathbf{G}^H\mathbf{G})^{-1} \tag{5.25}$$

The detected value of $\hat{\mathbf{c}}$ is

$$\begin{aligned} \hat{\mathbf{c}}_{\mathrm{LR-ZF}} &= \mathbf{W}_{\mathrm{LR-ZF}}^H \tilde{\mathbf{y}} \\ &= (\mathbf{G}^H\mathbf{G})^{-1}\mathbf{G}^H\tilde{\mathbf{y}} \end{aligned} \tag{5.26}$$

and

$$\hat{\tilde{\mathbf{s}}}_{\mathrm{LR-ZF}} = \mathbf{T}\lfloor\hat{\mathbf{c}}_{\mathrm{LR-ZF}}\rceil \tag{5.27}$$

After scaling and translating, $\hat{\mathbf{s}}_{\mathrm{LR-ZF}}$ is obtained.

    MMSE linear filter is given as follows:

$$\begin{aligned} \mathbf{W}_{\mathrm{LR-MMSE}} &= \arg \min_{\mathbf{W}_{\mathrm{LR-MMSE}}} \mathrm{E}\left[\left\|(\mathbf{c} - \mathrm{E}(\mathbf{c})) - \mathbf{W}^H(\tilde{\mathbf{y}} - \mathrm{E}(\tilde{\mathbf{y}}))\right\|^2\right] \\ &= \mathbf{G}\left(\mathbf{G}^H\mathbf{G} + \frac{N_0}{E_{\mathbf{s}}}\mathbf{I}\right)^{-1} \end{aligned} \tag{5.28}$$

The detected value of $\hat{\mathbf{c}}$ is thus given as follows:

$$\hat{\mathbf{c}}_{\mathrm{LR-MMSE}} = \mathbf{W}_{\mathrm{LR-MMSE}}^H(\tilde{\mathbf{y}} - \mathrm{E}(\tilde{\mathbf{y}})) + \mathrm{E}(\mathbf{c}) \tag{5.29}$$

and,

$$\hat{\tilde{\mathbf{s}}}_{\mathrm{LR-MMSE}} = \mathbf{T}\lceil\hat{\mathbf{c}}_{\mathrm{LR-MMSE}}\rfloor \tag{5.30}$$

After scaling and translating, $\hat{\mathbf{s}}_{\mathrm{LR-MMSE}}$ is obtained.

5.1.2.3 *Performance evaluation*

In this section, we derive the error probability of LR-based MIMO detection to verify LR-based detection performance, where the elements of the channel matrix $\mathbf{H}$ are zero-mean CSCG random variables with a variance of σ_h^2. The noise vector $\mathbf{n}$ can also be considered as a zero-mean CSCG random vector with $\mathrm{E}\left[\mathbf{nn}^H\right] = \mathbf{N}_0\mathbf{I}$.

Define an $N \times M$ matrix $\mathbf{H} = [\mathbf{h}_1, \ldots, \mathbf{h}_M]$, whose orthogonal resolution is defined as

$$\mathcal{OD}_M\left(\mathbf{H}\right) = 1 - \frac{\det\left(\mathbf{H}^H\mathbf{H}\right)}{\prod\limits_{i=1}^{M}\|\mathbf{h_i}\|^2} \tag{5.31}$$

LR can find a new channel matrix with better orthogonality (or lower orthogonal resolution) than the original matrix. Then the system model can be rewritten as

$$\mathbf{y} = \mathbf{GUs} + \mathbf{n} \tag{5.32}$$

where $\mathbf{U}$ is a unimodular matrix, and the CLLL algorithm is used to transform $\mathbf{H}$ to $\mathbf{G}$. According to Eq. (5.21) and Eq. (5.22),

$$\left|[\mathbf{R}]_{\ell,\ell}\right|^2 \geq \delta\left|[\mathbf{R}]_{\ell-1,\ell-1}\right|^2 - \left|[\mathbf{R}]_{\ell-1,\ell}\right|^2$$

$$\geq \left(\delta - \frac{1}{2}\right)\left|[\mathbf{R}]_{\ell-1,\ell-1}\right|^2 \tag{5.33}$$

and thus,

$$\left|[\mathbf{R}]_{\ell,\ell}\right|^2 \leq \left(\delta - \frac{1}{2}\right)^{\ell-\rho}\left|[\mathbf{R}]_{\rho,\rho}\right|^2 \tag{5.34}$$

where $1 \leq \ell < \rho \leq M$. If $\mathbf{r}_\rho$ represents the ρth column of $\mathbf{R}$, then

$$\|\mathbf{r}_\rho\|^2 = \left|[\mathbf{R}]_{\rho,\rho}\right|^2 + \sum_{\ell=1}^{\rho-1}\left|[\mathbf{R}]_{\ell,\rho}\right|^2$$

$$\leq \left|[\mathbf{R}]_{\rho,\rho}\right|^2 + \sum_{\ell=1}^{\rho-1}\frac{1}{2}\left|[\mathbf{R}]_{\ell,\ell}\right|^2$$

$$\leq \left|[\mathbf{R}]_{\rho,\rho}\right|^2 + \sum_{\ell=1}^{\rho-1}\frac{1}{2}\left(\rho - \frac{1}{2}\right)^{\ell-\rho}\left|[\mathbf{R}]_{\rho,\rho}\right|^2 \tag{5.35}$$

If $\zeta = \frac{2}{2\rho-1}$, then $\zeta \in (2, \infty)$ due to $\rho = (\frac{1}{2}, 1)$. Therefore, Eq. (5.35) can be rewritten as

$$\|\mathbf{r}_\rho\|^2 \leq \left(\frac{1}{2} + \frac{1-\zeta^\rho}{2(1-\zeta)} \right) \left| [\mathbf{R}]_{\rho,\rho} \right|^2$$

$$\leq \frac{1}{2} \zeta^\rho \left| [\mathbf{R}]_{\rho,\rho} \right|^2 \qquad (5.36)$$

Then, for an $N \times M$ matrix $\mathbf{G}$ after reduction, the orthogonal resolution satisfies

$$\mathcal{OD}_M(\mathbf{G}) = 1 - \frac{\det(\mathbf{H}^H\mathbf{H})}{\prod\limits_{i=1}^{M} \|\mathbf{h}_i\|^2}$$

$$= 1 - \frac{\prod\limits_{i=1}^{M} \left| [\mathbf{R}]_{i,i} \right|^2}{\prod\limits_{i=1}^{M} \|\mathbf{r}_i\|^2}$$

$$\leq 1 - \frac{\prod\limits_{i=1}^{M} \left| [\mathbf{R}]_{i,i} \right|^2}{\prod\limits_{i=1}^{M} \frac{1}{2}\zeta^i \left| [\mathbf{R}]_{i,i} \right|^2}$$

$$\leq 1 - 2^M \zeta^{-\frac{M(M+1)}{2}}$$

$$= 1 - 2^M \left(\frac{2}{2\rho-1} \right)^{-\frac{M(M+1)}{2}} \qquad (5.37)$$

It can be found that

$$\sqrt{1 - \mathcal{OD}_M(\mathbf{G})} \geq 2^{\frac{M}{2}} \left(\frac{2}{2\delta-1} \right)^{-\frac{M(M+1)}{4}} := c_\delta \qquad (5.38)$$

The derivation of LLL (real value) can give the same result, then through LLL/CLLL-LR (i.e. LR uses LLL or CLLL algorithm), $\mathcal{OD}_M(\mathbf{G})$ is limited to $1 - c_\delta^2$.

Theorem 5.1. *For an $N \times M(N \geq M)$ MIMO system, LR-based linear detection can achieve maximum reception diversity gain, namely N.*

Proof: In order to obtain the diversity gain, we calculate the error probability $P_{e,LR}$ for the LR-based linear detection method. LR-based MMSE detection and LR-based ZF detection have the same error probability.

For, convenience, we assume that LR-based ZF is applied in MIMO detection. Define $\mathbf{x} = \mathbf{G}^{\dagger}\mathbf{y}$ representing the output of the LR-based ZF detection, where $\mathbf{G}^{\dagger}$ denotes the pseudo-inverse of $\mathbf{G}$, so we can obtain that

$$\mathbf{x} = \mathbf{U}\mathbf{s} + \mathbf{G}^{\dagger}\mathbf{n} \tag{5.39}$$

Then the estimate of $\mathbf{s}$ is

$$\hat{\mathbf{s}} = 2\mathbf{U}^{-1}\left\lfloor \frac{1}{2}(\mathbf{x} - \mathbf{U}(1+\mathrm{j})\mathbf{1}) \right\rceil + (1+\mathrm{j})\mathbf{1}$$

$$= \mathbf{s} + 2\mathbf{U}^{-1}\left\lfloor \frac{1}{2}\mathbf{G}^{\dagger}\mathbf{n} \right\rceil \tag{5.40}$$

Since the correct detection of $\mathbf{s}$ can be obtained when $\lfloor \frac{1}{2}\mathbf{G}^{\dagger}\mathbf{n} \rceil = 0$, the upper bound of the error probability of detecting $\mathbf{s}$ for a given $\mathbf{H}$ is

$$P_{e,LR|\mathbf{H}} \leq 1 - \Pr\left(\left\lfloor \frac{1}{2}\mathbf{G}^{\dagger}\mathbf{n} \right\rceil = 0 \,\middle|\, \mathbf{H} \right) \tag{5.41}$$

Define $\mathbf{G}^{\dagger} = [\hat{\mathbf{g}}_1 \dots \hat{\mathbf{g}}_M]^{\mathrm{T}}$ with $\hat{\mathbf{g}}_i^{\mathrm{T}}(i = 1, 2, \dots, M)$ representing the ith column of $\mathbf{G}^{\dagger}$ and $\mathbf{G} = [\mathbf{g}_1 \dots \mathbf{g}_M]$ with $\mathbf{g}_i$ representing the ith column of $\mathbf{G}$. Therefore, Eq. (5.41) can be rewritten as

$$P_{e,LR|\mathbf{H}} \leq \Pr\left(\max_{1 \leq i \leq M} |\hat{\mathbf{g}}_i^{\mathrm{T}}\mathbf{n}| \geq 1 \,\middle|\, \mathbf{H} \right) \tag{5.42}$$

According to Eqs. (5.21), (5.22), and (5.38), we can get the inequality

$$\max_{1 \leq i \leq M} \|\hat{\mathbf{g}}_i^{\mathrm{T}}\| \leq \frac{1}{\sqrt{1 - \mathcal{OD}_M(\mathbf{G})} \cdot \min\limits_{1 \leq i \leq M} \|\mathbf{g}_i\|} \tag{5.43}$$

We have

$$\max_{1 \leq i \leq M} \|\hat{\mathbf{g}}_i^{\mathrm{T}}\mathbf{n}\| \leq \max_{1 \leq i \leq M} \|\hat{\mathbf{g}}_i^{\mathrm{T}}\| \cdot \|\mathbf{n}\|$$

$$\leq \frac{\|\mathbf{n}\|}{\sqrt{1 - \mathcal{OD}_M(\mathbf{G})} \cdot \min\limits_{1 \leq i \leq M} \|\mathbf{g}_i\|} \tag{5.44}$$

The upper bound of $P_{e,LR|\mathbf{H}}$ can be further expressed as

$$P_{e,LR|\mathbf{H}} \leq \Pr\left(\frac{\|\mathbf{n}\|}{\sqrt{1 - \mathcal{OD}(\mathbf{G})} \cdot \min\limits_{1 \leq i \leq M} \|\mathbf{g}_i\|} \geq 1 \Big| \mathbf{H}\right) \tag{5.45}$$

According to Eq. (5.38), $\sqrt{1 - \mathcal{OD}_M(\mathbf{G})} \geq c_\delta$. Use $\mathbf{h}_{\min}$ to represent the non-zero vector with the smallest norm in all vectors in the space formed by $\mathbf{H}$, and because $\mathbf{H}$ and $\mathbf{G}$ form the same space, it is easy to get

$$\|\mathbf{h}_{\min}\| \leq \min\limits_{1 \leq i \leq M} \|\mathbf{g}_i\| \tag{5.46}$$

From Eqs. (5.41) and (5.45), we can obtain the following:

$$P_{e,LR|\mathbf{H}} \leq \Pr\left(\max\limits_{1 \leq i \leq M} |\hat{\mathbf{g}}_i^{\mathrm{T}} \mathbf{n}| \geq 1 \Big| \mathbf{H}\right)$$

$$\leq \Pr\left(\frac{\|\mathbf{n}\|}{\sqrt{1 - \mathcal{OD}_M(\mathbf{G})} \cdot \min\limits_{1 \leq i \leq M} \|\mathbf{g}_i\|} \geq 1 \Big| \mathbf{H}\right)$$

$$\leq \Pr\left(\|\mathbf{n}\| \geq c_\delta \|\mathbf{h}_{\min}\| \Big| \mathbf{H}\right) \tag{5.47}$$

In addition, the upper bound of the symbol average error probability is

$$E_{\mathbf{H}}[P_{e,LR|\mathbf{H}}] \leq E_{\mathbf{H}}\left[\Pr\left(\|\mathbf{n}\|^2 \geq c_\delta^2 \|\mathbf{h}_{\min}\|^2 \Big| \mathbf{H}\right)\right]$$

$$= E_n\left[\Pr\left(\|\mathbf{h}_{\min}\|^2 \leq \frac{\|\mathbf{n}\|^2}{c_\delta^2} \Big| \mathbf{n}\right)\right] \tag{5.48}$$

Use $\mathbf{b}$ to represent a non-zero $M \times 1$ vector whose elements belong to a complex integer coefficient set, and denote $\mathbf{u}_b = \mathbf{Hb}$ as an $N \times 1$ vector in space Λ formed by $\mathbf{H}$, then we have

$$\|\mathbf{h}_{\min}\|^2 = \arg \min\limits_{\mathbf{u}_b \in \Lambda, \mathbf{u}b \neq 0} \|\mathbf{u}_b\|^2 \tag{5.49}$$

Since the elements in $\mathbf{H}$ are independent and satisfy the distribution $\mathcal{CN}(0,1)$, we see that $\mathbf{u}_b$ satisfies the distribution $\mathcal{CN}(0, \|\mathbf{b}\|^2)$, and $2\frac{\|\mathbf{u}_b\|^2}{\|\mathbf{b}\|^2}$ is a $2N$-dof central chi-square distribution. Therefore, if $\kappa = \frac{\|\mathbf{n}\|^2}{c_\delta^2}$, then the upper bound of the probability of $\|\mathbf{u}_b\|^2 \leq \kappa$ is given as follows:

$$\Pr\left(\|\mathbf{u}_b\|^2 \leq \kappa\right) = 1 - e^{-\frac{\kappa}{\|\mathbf{b}\|^2}} \sum_{n=0}^{N-1} \frac{\left(\frac{\kappa}{\|\mathbf{b}\|^2}\right)^n}{n!}$$

$$= e^{-\frac{\kappa}{\|\mathbf{b}\|^2}} \sum_{n=N}^{\infty} \frac{\left(\frac{\kappa}{\|\mathbf{b}\|^2}\right)^n}{n!}$$

$$\leq \left(\frac{1}{\|\mathbf{b}\|^2}\right)^N \kappa^N \qquad (5.50)$$

Define $\mathcal{H}_W$ as the wth case of $\mathbf{u}_b$ when $w \in [1, \infty)$, and $\mathcal{H}_{\min} = \|\mathbf{h}_{\min}\|^2$. Based on the cumulative distribution function $\mathcal{H}_{\min}$, we have

$$\Pr(\mathcal{H}_{\min} < v) = 1 - \Pr(\mathcal{H}_{\min} \geq v)$$

$$= 1 - \lim_{W \to \infty} \int_v^{\infty} d\mathcal{H}_1 \int_v^{\infty} d\mathcal{H}_2$$

$$\cdots \int_v^{\infty} f(\mathcal{H}_1, \mathcal{H}_2, \ldots, \mathcal{H}_W) d\mathcal{H}_W \qquad (5.51)$$

The probability density function of $\mathcal{H}_{\min}$ can thus be obtained as follows:

$$f(v) = \lim_{W \to \infty} \sum_{w=1}^{W} \int_v^{\infty} d\mathcal{H}_1 \int_v^{\infty} d\mathcal{H}_{w-1} \int_v^{\infty} d\mathcal{H}_{w+1}$$

$$\cdots \int_v^{\infty} f(\mathcal{H}_1, \ldots, \mathcal{H}_{w-1}, v, \mathcal{H}_{w+1}, \ldots, \mathcal{H}_W) d\mathcal{H}_W$$

$$\leq \sum_{w=1}^{\infty} f_{\mathcal{H}_W}(v) \qquad (5.52)$$

where $f_{\mathcal{H}_W}(v)$ represents the probability density function of $\mathcal{H}_W$. Thereafter, according to Eqs. (5.50) and (5.52), we can obtain

$$\Pr\left(\|\mathbf{h}_{\min}\|^2 \leq \kappa\right) \leq \int_0^{\kappa} \sum_{w=1}^{\infty} f_{\mathcal{H}_W}(v) dv$$

$$\leq \sum_{t=1}^{\infty} \sum_{\forall \|\mathbf{b}\|^2 = t} \left(\frac{1}{\|\mathbf{b}\|^2}\right)^N \kappa^N \qquad (5.53)$$

and thus when

$$\Pr\left(\|\mathbf{h}_{\min}\|^2 \le \kappa\right) \le c_{NM}\kappa^N, \tag{5.54}$$

there is a finite constant c_{NM} dependent on M and N, even if $N = M$.

In addition, since $\|\mathbf{b}\|^2 = t$ is a hypersphere with radius $\sqrt{t}$ in $2M$-dimensional space, the number of integer vectors $\mathbf{b}$ is limited to this hypersphere under $\|\mathbf{b}\|^2 = t$ condition. Therefore, the upper bound of $\Pr\left(\|\mathbf{h}_{\min}\|^2 \le \kappa\right)$ is further obtained as follows:

$$\Pr\left(\|\mathbf{h}_{\min}\|^2 \le \kappa\right) \le \sum_{t=1}^{\infty}\left(\frac{2\pi^M t^{M-\frac{1}{2}}}{(M-1)!}\left(\frac{1}{t}\right)^N\right)\kappa^N$$

$$= \left(\sum_{t=1}^{\infty}\frac{1}{t^{N-M+\frac{1}{2}}}\right)\frac{2\pi^M}{(M-1)!}\kappa^N \tag{5.55}$$

where the right side of the inequality converges to a finite constant when $N > M$.

In short, according to Eqs. (5.48) and (5.54), the upper bound of the average error probability is

$$E_{\mathbf{H}}[P_{e,LR|\mathbf{H}}] \le E_{\mathbf{n}}\left[\Pr\left(\|\mathbf{h}_{\min}\|^2 \le \frac{\|\mathbf{n}\|^2}{c_\delta^2}\,|\mathbf{n}\right)\right]$$

$$\le E_{\mathbf{n}}\left[c_{NM}\left(\frac{1}{c_\delta^2}\right)^N\|\mathbf{n}\|^{2N}\right]$$

$$= c_{NM}\left(\frac{1}{c_\delta^2}\right)^N\frac{(2N-1)!}{(N-1)!}\left(\frac{1}{N_0}\right)^{-N} \tag{5.56}$$

Since the upper bound of $P_{e,LR|\mathbf{H}}$ in Eq. (5.56) is an N-order moment of the chi-square random variable $\|\mathbf{n}\|^2$, it can be seen that the reception diversity gain of the LR-based linear detector is greater than or equal to N. It is worth noting that N is also the maximum reception diversity gain of the $N \times M$ MIMO system. Therefore, an LR-based linear detector can achieve a full-reception diversity gain N.   □

5.1.3 *Simulation results*

Figure 5.1 shows the error performance of multiple MIMO detectors in a 4×4 MIMO system. It can be seen from the figure that the optimal detector

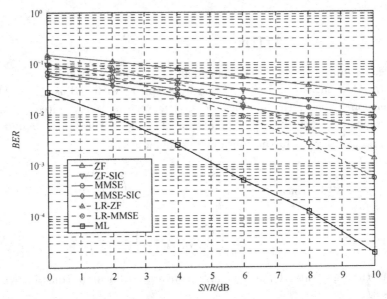

Fig. 5.1. Error performance of multiple MIMO detectors in a 4 × 4 MIMO system.

ML has obvious advantages compared with MIMO linear detectors (ZF, MMSE), but its exponentially increasing complexity makes it difficult for application in practical systems. However, although it has less complexity, the performance of linear detectors (ZF, MMSE) is not satisfying. The LR-based signal detection method can obtain the approximate performance of ML with a lower complexity, which means that the full-reception diversity gain can be obtained. Therefore, the LR-based signal detection method can achieve a good compromise between performance and complexity.

5.2 Iterative Detection and Decoding Basic Principle and Optimal MAP Detection[b]

In Section 5.1, we introduced signal detection methods based on lattice reduction for uncoded MIMO systems, but uncoded MIMO systems cannot achieve or approximate the theoretical channel capacity of the system. To solve this problem, people began to consider the BICM-ID system. By using

[b]Reprinted/adapted by permission from Springer Nature Customer Service Centre GmbH: Springer *"Low Complexity MIMO Receivers"* by Bai L, Choi J and Yu Q, 2014.

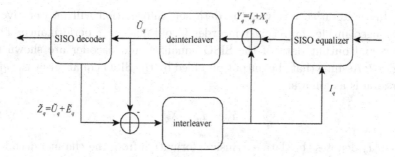

Fig. 5.2. Schematic diagram of the BICM receiver.

the BICM-ID system, channel decoding and signal detection can be jointly processed iteratively to further improve the system performance.

5.2.1 *BICM-ID system*

For the receiver, when a (channel) code sequence is transmitted through a noisy channel, for equalization and detection, it can be assumed that the transmitted signal is an uncoded signal. After signal equalization or demodulation, the information bit sequence is extracted using a channel decoder. However, in order to improve system performance, we can consider using feedback to design the iterative receiver. For the design of an iterative receiver, a random bit interleaver is an important component, and the resulting transmission scheme is called a BICM structure. Generally, the BICM receiver consists of an SISO equalizer (or demodulator), an SISO decoder, a (bit) interleaver, and a de-interleaver as shown in Fig. 5.2.

If the time is t, the discrete time baseband signal on the flat fading channel is given as

$$y_t = h_t s_t + n_t, \qquad (5.57)$$

where h_t denotes the channel gain, $s_t \in S$ is the transmission symbol, n_t represents the additive white Gaussian noise with a variance of N_0. After the BICM-ID-based iterative receiver receives the encoded signal, the SISO equalizer will first calculate the *a priori* information of the encoded signal and provide it to the SISO decoder. The channel decoder feeds back the decoded bit information to the channel equalizer to further suppress noise and fading so that the equalizer can provide more reliable information to the channel decoder at the next iteration. By iteration, more reliable information is exchanged between the equalizer and the decoder. When noise and fading are completely suppressed, the best equalized signal will be provided to the channel decoder to achieve the desired performance.

In an iterative receiver, the data soft information will be iteratively exchanged inside the receiver in order to obtain better performance. The input and output data of the SISO equalizer and decoder are shown in Fig. 5.2. Assume that the output provided by the SISO equalizer at the qth iteration is as follows:

$$Y_q = I_q + X_q \tag{5.58}$$

where I_q denotes the data-extrinsic information from the channel decoder, and X_q denotes the information from the receiving signal data. In general, X_q is dependent on I_q. If the SISO equalizer can provide more reliable information X_q for the data sequence, the channel decoder can get a higher credible I_q. With a higher credible I_q, the decoded bit information is closer to the information transmitted by the transmitter. Note that Y_q, X_q, and I_q refer to the data at this time, which will be defined in detail later.

The output of the channel decoder can be written as

$$\widetilde{Z}_q = \widetilde{U}_q + \widetilde{E}_q \tag{5.59}$$

where $\widetilde{U}_q$ denotes the information of the input channel decoder and $\widetilde{E}_q$ denotes the extrinsic information obtained from the channel decoder. The variables with symbol $\sim$ represent the variables after deinterlacing, and the variables without symbol $\sim$ represent the variables after interlacing. For example, $\widetilde{U}_q$ refers to the output of the de-interleaver and U_q refers to the input. According to Fig. 5.2, U_q becomes X_q as follows:

$$\begin{aligned} U_q &= Y_q - I_q \\ &= X_q \\ \widetilde{U}_q &= \widetilde{X}_q \end{aligned} \tag{5.60}$$

then in the next iteration, we have

$$\begin{aligned} I_{q+1} &= E_q \\ \widetilde{Z}_{q+1} &= \widetilde{X}_{q+1} + \widetilde{E}_{q+1} \end{aligned} \tag{5.61}$$

By iteration, the extrinsic information of the coded bits is exchanged between the SISO equalizer and the SISO decoder, and the performance of the BICM-ID can be continuously improved by iteration.

Note that due to the accumulation of information, it is important to subtract the extrinsic information from each iteration to avoid deviations.

Assuming the extrinsic information is not subtracted, then

$$I_{q+1} = X_q + I_q + E_q$$
$$\tilde{Z}_{q+1} = \left(\tilde{X}_{q+1} + \tilde{I}_{q+1}\right) + \tilde{E}_{q+1}$$
$$= \tilde{X}_{q+1} + \tilde{X}_q + \tilde{I}_q + \tilde{E}_q + \tilde{E}_{q+1} \tag{5.62}$$

Obviously, when $q \to \infty$, the $\sum_{k=0}^{q} \tilde{X}_k$, and the $\sum_{k=0}^{q} \tilde{E}_k$ in cumulative item $\tilde{Z}_q$ will derivate, which is expressed by $\tilde{I}_q$. At this time, the BICM-ID will deviate.

In the following, we will define the variables X_q, I_q, and E_q. For the SISO equalizer, Y_q refers to the logarithmic posterior probability, and X_q and I_q refer to the log-likelihood ratio and Log-ratio of *a priori* probability (LAPRP), respectively. For a given bit b in s_t and the receiving signal y_t, we can obtain

$$\underbrace{\log \frac{\Pr(b = +1|y_t)}{\Pr(b = +1|y_t)}}_{=Y} = \underbrace{\log \frac{\Pr(y_t|b = +1)}{\Pr(y_t|b = -1)}}_{=X} + \underbrace{\log \frac{\Pr(b = +1)}{\Pr(b = -1)}}_{=I} \tag{5.63}$$

With a symbol and a receiving signal under a noisy channel provided, we can define Y_q, X_q, and I_q in the same way. In this case, we apply MAP detection to the SISO equalization. MAP channel decoding is well suited to provide the output in Eq. (5.59).

Denote $b_t(m)$ as the mth most significant bit in the s_t mapping bit, and the log-ratio of *a posteriori* probability (LAPP) will be given by

$$L(b_t(m)) = \log \frac{\Pr(b_t(m) = +1|y_t)}{\Pr(b_t(m) = -1|y_t)} \tag{5.64}$$

If the *a priori* probability (APRP) is represented by $\Pr(b_t(m))$, the input log-likelihood ratio (LLR) of the channel decoder can be given as follows:

$$\begin{aligned}
\text{LLR}(b_t(m)) &= \log \frac{f(y_t|b_t(m) = +1)}{f(y_t|b_t(m) = -1)} \\
&= \log \frac{\Pr(b_t(m) = +1|y_t)/\Pr(b_t(m) = +1)}{\Pr(b_t(m) = -1|y_t)/\Pr(b_t(m) = -1)} \\
&= L(b_t(m)) - \log \frac{\Pr(b_t(m) = +1)}{\Pr(b_t(m) = -1)}
\end{aligned} \tag{5.65}$$

where $\log \frac{\Pr(b_t(m)=+1)}{\Pr(b_t(m)=-1)}$ is the log-ratio of *a priori* probability (LAPRP).

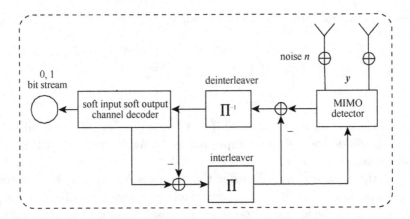

Fig. 5.3. **Schematic diagram of the MIMO channel iterative receiver.**

5.2.2 *MIMO iterative receiver-optimal MAP detection*

For coded MIMO systems, bit-interleaved coded modulation (BICM) can be used on MIMO channels to achieve a good performance with data rate close to channel capacity. Meanwhile, the MIMO-BICM system does not bring high computational overhead to the transmitter and receiver. When a soft-input–soft-output (SISO) channel decoder is used in an MIMO-BICM system, based on the Turbo principle, iterative decoding and detection (IDD) can be used to improve the system performance. In MIMO-BICM-ID, MAP detection can achieve optimal detection performance.

The structure of the MIMO channel iterative receiver is shown in Fig. 5.3, where the LLR of the data symbols is constantly exchanged between the MIMO detector and the channel decoder. The principle of the iterative receiver is the same as that of the BICM-ID system discussed in Section 5.2.2. Considering an MIMO system with N_t transmitting antennas and N_r receiving antennas, the system model is

$$\mathbf{y} = \mathbf{Hs} + \mathbf{n} \tag{5.66}$$

where $\mathbf{H}$, $\mathbf{s} = [s_1, \ldots, s_{N_t}]^T$, and $\mathbf{n}$ represents $N_r \times N_t$ channel matrix, $N_t \times 1$ data symbol vector, and $N_r \times 1$ zero mean CSCG vector with covariance matrix $N_0 \mathbf{I}$. Define $s_k \in A$ with A representing the alphabetic symbol and $|A| = 2^M$. It is assumed that the average transmitted power of each antenna is normalized to $E_s \triangleq \frac{1}{|A|} \sum_{s_k \in A} |s_k|^2 = 1$.

In this chapter, we assume that a random bit interleaver is used in BICM transmitters, and channel coding uses convolutional coding with a code rate of R_c. After convolutional coding, successive sets of M (interleaved) coded bits $\{b_{k,1}, b_{k,2}, \ldots, b_{k,M}\}$ are, respectively, modulated into 2M-ary transmitting signal s_k and transmitted through the kth transmitting antenna, where $b_{k,l} \in \{\pm 1\}$ is the lth bit of s_k. The transmitted symbol s consists of $N_t M$ coded bits. Since random bit interleaving is used, we assume that s_k and $b_{k,l}$ are independent of each other.

In an MIMO-BICM-ID receiver, the MIMO detector first provides a soft decision of the coded bits to the SISO channel decoder, and after the SISO channel decoder performs soft decoding, the bit-extrinsic information is fed back to the MIMO detector. This information is utilized by the MIMO detector as *a priori* information for transmitting data symbols in subsequent iterations. The MIMO-BICM-ID system can improve the system performance by iteratively utilizing the soft bit extrinsic information exchanged between the detector and the decoder.

In MAP detection, the output is soft bit information and the exact LLR of $b_{k,l}$ is given by

$$L_E(b_{k,l}) = \log \frac{\sum_{s \in A_{k,l}^+} \Pr(\mathbf{s}|\mathbf{y})}{\sum_{s \in A_{k,l}^-} \Pr(\mathbf{s}|\mathbf{y})} - L_A(b_{k,l}) \tag{5.67}$$

where $A_{k,l}^\pm$ denotes a subset of A^{N_t} which satisfies the lth bit of s_k which is ± 1. $L_A(b_{k,l}) = \log \frac{\Pr(b_{k,l}=+1)}{\Pr(b_{k,l}=-1)}$ is the LAPRP provided by the SISO decoder as *a priori* information. $\Pr(b_{k,l}|\mathbf{y})$ and $\Pr(\mathbf{s}|\mathbf{y})$ represent APPs of $b_{k,l}$ and the APPs of s when y is given, respectively.

Set

$$L_{\mathrm{app}}(b_{k,l}) \triangleq \log \frac{\sum_{\mathbf{s} \in A_{k,l}^+} \Pr(\mathbf{s}|\mathbf{y})}{\sum_{\mathbf{s} \in A_{k,l}^-} \Pr(\mathbf{s}|\mathbf{y})} \tag{5.68}$$

Since the noise n is a CSCG vector, according to the Bayesian criterion,

$$L_{\mathrm{app}}(b_{k,l}) = \log \frac{\sum_{\mathbf{s} \in A_{k,l}^+} e^{-\frac{1}{N_0}\|\mathbf{y}-\mathbf{Hs}\|} \Pr_{\mathrm{api}}(\mathbf{s})}{\sum_{\mathbf{s} \in A_{k,l}^-} e^{-\frac{1}{N_0}\|\mathbf{y}-\mathbf{Hs}\|} \Pr_{\mathrm{api}}(\mathbf{s})} \tag{5.69}$$

where

$$\text{Pr}_{\text{api}}(\mathbf{s}) = \exp\left(\frac{1}{2}\sum_{k=1}^{N_t}\sum_{l=1}^{M} b_{k,l;\mathbf{s}} L_A(b_{k,l;\mathbf{s}})\right) \tag{5.70}$$

where $b_{k,l;\mathbf{s}}$ in Eq. (5.70) represents the (k,l)th bit with $\mathbf{s}$ given.

Set

$$\mathbf{s}_{k,l}^{\pm} = \arg\max_{s \in A_{k,l}^{\pm}} \left\{ -\frac{1}{N_0}\|\mathbf{y} - \mathbf{Hs}\|^2 + \sum_{k=1}^{N_t}\sum_{l=1}^{M} b_{k,l;\mathbf{s}} L_A(b_{k,l}) \right\} \tag{5.71}$$

According to $L_{k,l}^{\pm} \triangleq \frac{\|\mathbf{y}-\mathbf{Hs}_{k,l}^{\pm}\|^2}{N_0} + \sum_{k=1}^{N_t}\sum_{l=1}^{M} b_{k,l;\mathbf{s}_{k,l}^{\pm}} L_A(b_{k,l})$, we can rewrite the maximum logarithm of Eq. (5.67) as[1]

$$L_E(b_{k,l}) \approx \frac{1}{2}(L_{k,l}^{+} - L_{k,l}^{-}) - L_A(b_{k,l}) \tag{5.72}$$

As can be seen from $A_{k,l}^{\pm}$ in Eq. (5.67) or Eq. (5.72), the computational complexity of MAP increases exponentially with N_t. Therefore, low-complexity suboptimal methods in MIMO systems have been extensively studied to estimate LLR with near precision.

5.3 Detection and Decoding Technology Based on Random Sampling

In order to avoid the exponential growth complexity of the optimal MAP detection, a random sampling-based detection and decoding technique is proposed.[2] Random sampling is based on random successive interference cancellation (SIC) detection, where *a priori* information (API) information is considered in the list generation process, and a list of candidate solution vectors with high a posteriori information can be generated. In order to reduce the complexity of obtaining the API in the LR domain, the random sampling detection algorithm also uses a joint Gaussian distribution to estimate the API, so that random sampling detection can find multiple high posteriori probabilities (APP) with candidate solution vectors possessing a lower computational complexity.

5.3.1 *System model*

In this section, we will first use an equivalent real-valued system model. Set $n_t = 2N_t, n_r = 2N_r$. $\mathcal{S}$ represents a finite set of real-valued transmitted signals corresponding to $\mathcal{A}$. Define $\mathbf{y}_r = [\Re\{y\ \Im\{y\}\}]^T, \mathbf{s}_r = [\Re\{s\ \Im\{s\}\}]^T, \mathbf{n}_r = [\Re\{n\ \Im\{n\}\}]^T$, and

$$\mathbf{H}_r = \begin{bmatrix} \Re\{H\} & -\Im\{H\} \\ \Im\{H\} & \Re\{H\} \end{bmatrix} \in \mathbb{R}^{n_r \times n_t} \tag{5.73}$$

where $\mathbf{y}_r \in \mathbb{R}^{n_r}, \mathbf{n}_r \in \mathbb{R}^{n_r}$, and $\mathbf{s}_r \in \mathcal{S}^{n_t}$. Then the system model is

$$\mathbf{y}_r = \mathbf{H}_r \mathbf{s}_r + \mathbf{n}_r \tag{5.74}$$

where $\mathbf{s}_r = [s_1, \ldots, s_{n_t}]^T$.

5.3.2 *LR-based sampling list generation method*

By the LLL algorithm, we can also find an approximately orthogonal set of basis vectors $\mathbf{G}_r = \mathbf{H}_r \mathbf{T}_r$, where $\mathbf{T}_r$ is a complex-valued integer unimodular matrix. By defining $\mathbf{u}_r = \mathbf{T}_r^{-1}\mathbf{s}_r$, we can obtain

$$\mathbf{y}_r = \mathbf{G}_r \mathbf{u}_r + \mathbf{n}_r \tag{5.75}$$

and combining with the QR decomposition of $\mathbf{G}_r$, $\mathbf{G}_r = \mathbf{Q}_r \mathbf{R}_r$ can be obtained with $\mathbf{Q}_r$, the unitary matrix, and $\mathbf{R}_r$, the upper triangular matrix. Premultiplying $\mathbf{y}_r$ by $\mathbf{Q}_r^H$, we have

$$\mathbf{x}_r = \mathbf{Q}_r^H \mathbf{y}_r = \mathbf{R}_r \mathbf{u}_r + \mathbf{n}_r \tag{5.76}$$

Since the statistical properties of $\mathbf{Q}_r^H \mathbf{n}_r$ and $\mathbf{n}_r$ are the same, $\mathbf{Q}_r^H \mathbf{n}_r$ can be replaced by $\mathbf{n}_r$. Therefore, based on the LR-based complex-valued SIC, the nth symbol detection is given as

$$\mathbf{u}_{r,n} = \frac{1}{\alpha}\left(\lfloor \tilde{\mathbf{u}}_{r,n} \rceil - (\beta + j\beta)t_n \mathbf{1}\right) \tag{5.77}$$

where $\tilde{\mathbf{u}}_{r,n} = \alpha\,\mathbf{u}_r + (\beta + j\beta)t_n \mathbf{1}$ and $\mathbf{u}_r = (\mathbf{x}_{r,n} - \sum_{j=n+1}^{N_t} \mathbf{r}_{n,j}\hat{\mathbf{u}}_j)/\mathbf{r}_{n,n}, t_n = [\mathbf{T}^{-1}]_{(n,1:N_t)}$.

In order to improve the performance of the list generation method for near MAP detection, the API of each bit should be considered after the first iteration. If an enumeration search is used, its complexity will increase exponentially with the number of transmitting antennas. Therefore, in the process of list generation, we use a Gaussian estimation to obtain the API of $\mathbf{u}_r$, and then use a suitable sampling distribution to select a candidate solution of high APP for the list according to the list generation algorithm.

5.3.2.1   *Gaussian estimation in the LR domain*

In order to obtain the API of $\mathbf{u}_r$, if all the vectors in the LR domain are generated according to the method in Ref. 3, the computational complexity will be $O(2^{MN_t})$. Therefore, in the following, we will introduce a low-complexity LR domain API estimation method, which uses the Gaussian distribution of $\mathbf{u}_r$ to estimate the API of $\mathbf{u}_r$.

Consider that $\mathbf{u}_r$ is a linear combination of $\mathbf{s}_r$ and assume that the statistical properties of $\mathbf{s}_r$ can be obtained from the SISO decoder. Thus, the mean vector and covariance matrix of $\mathbf{u}_r$ are

$$\bar{\mathbf{u}}_r = \mathrm{E}[\mathbf{T}_r^{-1}\mathbf{s}_r] = \mathbf{T}_r^{-1}\mathrm{E}[\mathbf{s}_r] \tag{5.78}$$

and

$$\begin{aligned} \mathbf{Q}_r &= \mathrm{E}[\mathbf{u}_r\mathbf{u}_r^{\mathrm{T}}] - \bar{\mathbf{u}}_r\bar{\mathbf{u}}_r^{\mathrm{T}} \\ &= \mathbf{T}_r^{-1}\mathrm{E}[\mathbf{s}_r\mathbf{s}_r^{\mathrm{T}}]\mathbf{T}_r^{-\mathrm{T}} - \bar{\mathbf{u}}_r\bar{\mathbf{u}}_r^{\mathrm{T}} \end{aligned} \tag{5.79}$$

It should be noted that each individual symbol u_k of $\mathbf{u}_r$ is composed of independent elements of $\mathbf{s}_r$. In addition, each individual symbol s_k has a finite mean and variance. Therefore, according to the central limit theorem, $\mathbf{u}_r = [u_1, u_2, \ldots, u_{n_t}]^{\mathrm{T}}$ can be modeled by n_t random variables of joint Gaussian distribution with a mean of $\bar{\mathbf{u}}_r$ and a covariance of $\mathbf{Q}_r$. In other words, when n_t is large enough, it can be seen that

$$\mathbf{u}_r \sim \mathcal{N}(\bar{\mathbf{u}}_r, \mathbf{Q}_r) \tag{5.80}$$

The detected symbols and the symbols to be detected at the nth layer of the SIC detection are represented by $\mathbf{u}_{r,D}^{(n)} = [u_{n+1}, \ldots, u_{n_t}]$ and $\mathbf{u}_{r,ND}^{(n)} = [u_1, u_2, \ldots, u_n]^{\mathrm{T}}$. Note that $\mathbf{Q}_r$ is not necessarily a diagonal matrix here. Therefore, the API of $\mathbf{u}_{r,ND}^{(n)}$ depends on $\mathbf{u}_{r,D}^{(n)}$, and when given $\mathbf{u}_{r,D}^{(n)}$, the conditional distribution of $\mathbf{u}_{r,ND}^{(n)}$ also needs to be taken into account.

For a given $\mathbf{u}_{r,D}^{(n)}$, denote $\bar{\mathbf{u}}_r^{(n)}$ and $\mathbf{Q}_r^{(n)}$ as the conditional expectation and covariance matrix of $\mathbf{u}_{r,ND}^{(n)}$, respectively, namely $\mathbf{Q}_r^{(n_t)} = \mathbf{Q}_r, \bar{\mathbf{u}}_r^{(n_t)} = \bar{\mathbf{u}}_r$. And then

$$\bar{\mathbf{u}}_r^{(n+1)} = \begin{bmatrix} \bar{\mathbf{u}}_{r,1}^{(n+1)} \\ \bar{u}_{r,2}^{(n+1)} \end{bmatrix} \tag{5.81}$$

where $\bar{\mathbf{u}}_{\mathrm{r}}^{(n+1)} \in \mathbb{R}^{n+1}, \bar{\mathbf{u}}_{\mathrm{r},1}^{(n+1)} = [\bar{\mathbf{u}}_{\mathrm{r},1}^{(n+1)}]_{(1:n,1)}$, and

$$
\mathbf{Q}_{\mathrm{r}}^{(n+1)} = \begin{bmatrix} \mathbf{Q}_{\mathrm{r},1}^{(n+1)} & \mathbf{q}_{\mathrm{r},2}^{(n+1)} \\ \mathbf{q}_{\mathrm{r},3}^{(n+1)} & q_{\mathrm{r},4}^{(n+1)} \end{bmatrix} \tag{5.82}
$$

where $\mathbf{Q}_{\mathrm{r}}^{(n+1)} \in \mathbb{R}^{(n+1)\times(n+1)}$, $\mathbf{Q}_{\mathrm{r},1}^{(n+1)} = [\mathbf{Q}_{\mathrm{r}}^{(n+1)}]_{(1:n,1:n)}$, $\mathbf{q}_{\mathrm{r},2}^{(n+1)} = [\mathbf{Q}_{\mathrm{r}}^{(n+1)}]_{(1:n,n+1)}$, and $\mathbf{q}_{\mathrm{r},3}^{(n+1)} = [\mathbf{Q}_{\mathrm{r}}^{(n+1)}]_{(n+1,1:n)}$. Thus, when $\mathbf{u}_{\mathrm{r},D}^{(n)}$ is given, the conditional Probability Density Function (PDF) of $\mathbf{u}_{\mathrm{r},ND}^{(n)}$ is

$$
f(\mathbf{u}_{\mathrm{r},ND}^{(n)}|\mathbf{u}_{\mathrm{r},D}^{(n)}) \propto \mathcal{N}(\bar{\mathbf{u}}_{\mathrm{r}}^{(n)}, \mathbf{Q}_{\mathrm{r}}^{(n)}) \tag{5.83}
$$

where $\bar{\mathbf{u}}_{\mathrm{r},n} = (\bar{\mathbf{u}}_{\mathrm{r},1}^{(n+1)} + \frac{\mathbf{q}_{\mathrm{r},2}^{(n+1)}}{q_{\mathrm{r},4}^{(n+1)}}(\hat{u}_{\mathrm{r},(n+1)} - \bar{u}_{\mathrm{r},2}^{(n+1)})$ and $\mathbf{Q}_{\mathrm{r}}^{(n)} = \mathbf{Q}_{\mathrm{r},1}^{(n+1)} - \frac{\mathbf{q}_{\mathrm{r},2}^{(n+1)}\mathbf{q}_{\mathrm{r},3}^{(n+1)}}{q_{\mathrm{r},4}^{(n+1)}}$.

In the nth layer of SIC detection, since $\mathbf{R}_{\mathrm{r}}$ is the upper triangle, the API for estimating $u_{\mathrm{r},n}$ with the edge pdf $f(\mathbf{u}_{\mathrm{r},ND}^{(n)}|\mathbf{u}_{\mathrm{r},D}^{(n)})$ is

$$
f(u_{\mathrm{r},n}|\mathbf{u}_{\mathrm{r},D}^{(n)}) \propto \left(-\frac{(u_{\mathrm{r},n} - \widehat{u}_{\mathrm{r},n}^{(n)})^2}{2\sigma^2} \right) \tag{5.84}
$$

where $\sigma = \sqrt{\sigma_4(n)}$. Therefore, Eqs. (5.82) and (5.83) can be used to obtain the distribution of *a priori* probability and a posterior probability at the nth layer of the LR-based SIC detection. By API estimation, we can generate a list of candidate solution vectors with high APP in the LR domain.

5.3.2.2 *LR-based random IDD*

On the $\mathcal{S}^{n_{\mathrm{t}}}$, when the candidate list is generated, the API information can be utilized to obtain better detection performance through the determined iterative tree search (ITS) method. However, for LR-based IDD, obtaining the exact bit information by ITS in the LR domain requires a high computational complexity. Since the *a priori* information in the LR domain cannot be generated by the original bit soft information LLR, it is difficult to utilize the API when using the ITS method. According to the API Gaussian estimation in Section 5.3.2, we can find candidate solutions with high APP in the LR domain with low complexity by random sampling. In addition, in the nth layer of the LR-based SIC detection, by using an appropriate distribution to sample vectors close to $\tilde{u}_{\mathrm{r},n}$ or $(\alpha\bar{u}_{\mathrm{r},n}^{(n)} + \beta t_n \mathbf{1})$, it is also possible to avoid enumerating the symbols in the LR domain.

Table 5.1. Random sampling algorithm pseudo code.

```
(1) function Rand_SCI_ρ(x,R)
(2)   for i = n_t to 1 do
(3)     c_i ← r²_{i,i}logρ/ min_{1≤i≤n_t} |r²_{i,i}|²
(4)     û_j ← Rand_Round_{c_i} (( x_i − Σ_{j=i+1}^{n} r_{i,j}û_j ) /r_{i,i} )
(5)   end for
(6)   return û
(7) end function
```

In LR-based IDD random sampling detection, obtaining an appropriate sampling distribution is critical to the performance of the list generation method. For LR-based detection methods in non-IDD systems, the sampling algorithm in Ref. 4 enables the distribution described by Eq. (5.85) to round $\tilde{u}_n$ to integer z, thereby obtaining performance close to ML detection. This distribution can be expressed as

$$\mathrm{Pr}_{\mathrm{cond},n}(Z = z) = \frac{\exp(-c(\tilde{u}_{\mathrm{r},n} - z)^2)}{s(c)} \tag{5.85}$$

where for the nth detection of SIC, $s(c) = \sum_{z=-\infty}^{\infty} \exp(-c(\tilde{u}_{\mathrm{r},n} - z)^2)$ and $c = \frac{\log\rho}{\min_{1\leq i\leq n_t} |r_{i,i}|^2}|r_{n,n}|^2$. For the convenience of the reader, the sampling algorithm in Ref. 4 is given in Table 5.1.

Although the original sample distribution in Eq. (5.84) can find the ML candidate solution vector with a higher probability, for the IDD system, its performance is not comparable to MAP because the API is not considered. In order to obtain a candidate solution vector of high APP by random sampling, the Gaussian distribution in Eq. (5.86) can be used. Define

$$\mathrm{Pr}_{\mathrm{api},n}(Z = z) \propto \exp\left[-\frac{(\bar{u}'_{\mathrm{r},n} - z)^2}{2w_n^2}\right] \tag{5.86}$$

where $\bar{u}'_{\mathrm{r},n} = \alpha\bar{u}_{\mathrm{r},n}^{(n)} + \beta t_n \mathbf{1}$ and $\omega_n = \sqrt{|\alpha^2\sigma^2|}$. Since the APP distribution of $\mathbf{s}_\mathrm{r}$ is the product of $\mathrm{Pr}(\mathbf{y}_\mathrm{r}|\mathbf{s}_\mathrm{r})$ and $\mathrm{Pr}_{\mathrm{api}}(\mathbf{s}_\mathrm{r})$, $\bar{u}'_{\mathrm{r},n}$ and $\tilde{u}_{\mathrm{r},n}$ can be regarded as the LR-based likelihood and soft decisions of *a priori* information in the nth layer SIC detection, respectively. Therefore, the sampling distribution for the nth layer SIC detection can be corrected to

$$\mathrm{Pr}_n(Z = z) = C_n\mathrm{Pr}_{\mathrm{cond},n}(Z = z)\mathrm{Pr}_{\mathrm{api},n}(Z = z) \tag{5.87}$$

where C_n is a normalized constant. According to the distribution in Eq. (5.86), SIC detection of each layer can perform random SIC (Rand-SIC) sampling in the lattice domain. Through K parallel Rand-SIC samples, we can get a list with high APP candidate solution vectors. Obviously, the probability of sampling to the MAP solution will increase as K increases. In the following, we demonstrate its sampling performance through a lemma.

Lemma 1. *Define* $\mathbf{u_r} = [u_{r,1}, \ldots, u_{r,n_t}]^T$ *in the LR domain,* $A = \log\rho / \min_{1 \leq i \leq n_t} |r_{i,i}|^2$, *and* $S = \prod_{i=1}^{n_t} s(A|r_{i,i}|^2)$ *and set* $\mathbf{y}$ *as the vector of* $\mathbb{R}^{n_r}$. *For* ρ *that can make* $AN_0 > 1$, *the bound of the probability that Rand-SIC finds* $\mathbf{u_r}$ *is given as*

$$\mathrm{Pr}_{\mathrm{samp}}(\mathbf{u_r}) \geq \frac{1}{S} \left(e^{-\frac{1}{N_0} \|\mathbf{y_r} - \mathbf{G_r u_r}\|^2} \mathrm{Pr}_{\mathrm{api}}(\mathbf{u_r}) \right)^{AN_0} \tag{5.88}$$

where $\mathrm{Pr}_{\mathrm{api}}(\mathbf{u_r})$ represents the prior probability of $\mathbf{u_r}$.

Proof: Using Eqs. (5.84), (5.85), and (5.86), the probability of sampling to u_i at the ith layer SIC is greater than

$$\frac{C_i}{s(A|r_{i,i}|^2)} e^{-A\left(x_i - \sum_{j=i+1}^{n_t} r_{i,j} u_j\right)^2} \mathrm{Pr}_{\mathrm{api}}(u_{r,i}) \tag{5.89}$$

where $\mathrm{Pr}_{\mathrm{api}}(u_{r,i}) = \mathrm{Pr}(u_{r,i}|\mathbf{u}_{r,D}^{(i)})$ is the edge conditional probability of $u_{r,i}$ for a given $\mathbf{u}_{r,D}^{(i)}$. According to the conditional probability product rule, it can be obtained by Eq. (5.82) that $\qquad\qquad\square$

$$\mathrm{Pr}_{\mathrm{samp}}(\mathbf{u_r}) \geq \frac{e^{-A\|\mathbf{x_r} - \mathbf{R_r u_r}\|^2}}{S} \prod_{i=1}^{n_t} \mathrm{Pr}_{\mathrm{api}}(u_{r,i})$$

$$= \frac{e^{-A\|\mathbf{x} - \mathbf{Ru}\|^2}}{S} \prod_{i=1}^{n_t} \mathrm{Pr}(u_{r,i}|\mathbf{u}_{r,D}^{(i)})$$

$$= \frac{1}{S} e^{-A\|\mathbf{x_r} - \mathbf{R_r u_r}\|^2} \mathrm{Pr}_{\mathrm{api}}(\mathbf{u_r}) \tag{5.90}$$

when ρ is large enough, $AN_0 > 1$ and in this case

$$\mathrm{Pr}_{\mathrm{samp}}(\mathbf{u_r}) \geq \frac{1}{S} \left(e^{-\frac{1}{N_0} \|\mathbf{x_r} - \mathbf{R_r u_r}\|^2} \mathrm{Pr}_{\mathrm{api}}(\mathbf{u_r}) \right)^{AN_0} \tag{5.91}$$

According to the literature in Ref. 4, we know that the decoding radius of a non-IDD system can be maximized by optimizing the parameter ρ.

For LR-based MAP detection, it is also necessary to optimize the parameter ρ to maximize the decoding radius of the SIC detection in the IDD system. Setting $\rho > 1$, we obtain

$$\prod_{i=1}^{n_t} s(c_i) < \exp\left(\frac{2n_t}{\rho}(1 + g(\rho))\right) \tag{5.92}$$

where $g(\rho) = \rho^{-3}/(1 - \rho^{-5})$ and $c_i = A|r_{i,i}|^2$. Combining Eq. (5.89), the lower bound of the probability of $\mathbf{u}_r$ is

$$\Pr_{\text{samp}}(\mathbf{u}_r) > e^{-\frac{2n_t}{\rho}(1+g(\rho))}\left(e^{-\frac{1}{N_0}\|\mathbf{y}_r - \mathbf{G}_r\mathbf{u}_r\|^2}\Pr_{\text{api}}(\mathbf{u}_r)\right)^{AN_0} \tag{5.93}$$

Define $\mathbf{u}_{r,K}$ as the vector in LR domain, and $\Pr_{\text{samp}}(\mathbf{u}_{r,K}) > 1/K$. Through K times Rand-SIC, the probability that $\mathbf{u}_{r,K}$ is not in the list is lower than $(1 - \frac{1}{K})^K$. When ρ is large enough, $g(\rho)$ can be ignored. Therefore, based on the following estimates

$$e^{-\frac{1}{2n_t}}\left(e^{-\frac{1}{N_0}\|\mathbf{y}_r - \mathbf{G}_r\mathbf{u}_r\|^2}\Pr_{\text{api}}(\mathbf{u}_r)\right)^{AN_0} \approx \frac{1}{K} \tag{5.94}$$

we can get

$$\|\mathbf{y}_r - \mathbf{G}_r\mathbf{u}_r\|^2 - N_0\log\Pr_{\text{api}}([u_r]) \approx N_0 R_{\text{LRMAP}}(\rho) \tag{5.95}$$

where

$$R_{\text{LRMAP}}(\rho) = \frac{\min_i|r_{i,i}|^2}{N_0\log\rho}\left(\log K - \frac{2n_t}{\rho}\right) \tag{5.96}$$

It can be seen from Eq. (5.92) that $R_{\text{LRMAP}}(\rho)$ is the effective value of the square of the MAP detection radius. Therefore, Rand-SIC can find the MAP solution with high probability by maximizing $R_{\text{LRMAP}}(\rho)$. Setting $\frac{\partial R_{\text{LRMAP}}(\rho)}{\partial \rho} = 0$, we obtain $\log K = \frac{2n_t}{\rho}\log(e\rho)$ with $\rho > 1$. Therefore, when $AN_0 > 1$, the optimal value of ρ is

$$\rho = \max\left\{e^{\frac{1}{N_0}\min_{1 \le i \le n_t}|r_{i,i}|^2}, \rho_0\right\} \tag{5.97}$$

where ρ is the numerical solution of $K = (e\rho)^{2n_t/\rho_0}$. In most practical cases, the value of ρ is large enough such that $g(\rho)$ can be ignored.

In summary, the real-valued LR-based randomized list generation algorithm (RLR-RLGA) based on LR is summarized in Table 5.2. It should be noted that since the Kth sampling of Rand-SIC can be performed independently, this method is suitable for parallel implementation.

For efficient rounding, we limit the sampling candidate integer solution to $2N$ nearest integers of $\tilde{u}_{r,n}$. At the same time, since the sampled point

Table 5.2. Real-valued LR-based random list generation algorithm.

---

(1) Preprocessing. Set $A = \log \rho / \min_i |r_{i,i}|^2$

(2) Random list generation

for $k = 1:1:K$ do

$\mathbf{Q}^{(n_t)} = \mathbf{Q}$

$\overline{\mathbf{u}}^{(n_t)} = \overline{\mathbf{u}}$

for $n = n_t : -1 : 1$ do

Update $\hat{\mathbf{u}}^{(n)}$ and $\mathbf{Q}^{(n)}$

$c = A|r_{n,n}|^2$

$$u = \left(x_n - \sum_{j=n+1}^{n_t} r_{i,j} \hat{u}_j \right) / r_{i,i}$$

$\tilde{u}_n = \alpha u + \beta \mathbf{t}_n \mathbf{1}$

$\hat{u}_{n'} = \alpha \hat{u}_n + \beta \mathbf{t}_n \mathbf{1}$

$w_n = \sqrt{\alpha^2 v_4^{(n)}}$

for $z = \lfloor \tilde{u}_n \rfloor - N + 1 : 1 : \lfloor \tilde{u}_n \rfloor + N$

$\mathrm{Pr}_{\mathrm{cond},n}(Z = z) \propto \exp(-c(\tilde{u}_n - z)^2)$

$\mathrm{Pr}_{\mathrm{api},n}(Z = z) \propto \exp(-c(\bar{u}_{n'} - z)^2 / (2w_n^2))$

$\mathrm{Pr}_n(Z = z) \propto \mathrm{Pr}_{\mathrm{cond},n}(Z = z)\mathrm{Pr}_{\mathrm{api},n}(Z = z)$

end for

Generate an integer Z by the distribution of $\mathrm{Pr}_n(Z = z)$

$\hat{u}_n = (Z - \beta \mathbf{t}_n \mathbf{1}) / \alpha$

end for

$\hat{\mathbf{s}}^{(k)} = \mathbf{T}\hat{\mathbf{u}}$

If necessary, limit $\hat{\mathbf{s}}^{(k)}$ to the original constellation

end for

(3) Calculate LLR using $\{\hat{\mathbf{s}}^{(1)}, \ldots, \hat{\mathbf{s}}^{(K)}\}$ for each bit

---

may not belong to the point on the original modulation constellation, in this case, we can directly assign it to the constellation point closest to the point. In addition, since the sampling of the LR-RLGA is random, there is basically no case where the K candidate solutions are smaller than the APP of the conventional SIC solution. However, in order to improve the sampling detection performance, we still use the traditional LR-based SIC results for the first iteration to extend the list of candidate solution vectors.

5.3.2.3 *Complex-valued LR-based list generation*

The real-valued random sampling algorithm actually extends the system's dimension and then performs RLR-RLGA based on the system model after the extended dimension. In order to reduce the computational complexity caused by this, we study the complex-valued LR-based randomized list generation algorithm (CLR-RLGA).

By the complex-valued LLL algorithm, we can also find an approximately orthogonal set of basis vectors $\mathbf{G} = \mathbf{HT}$, where $\mathbf{T}$ is a complex-valued integer unimodular matrix. Defining $\mathbf{u} = \mathbf{T}^{-1}\mathbf{s}$, we have

$$\mathbf{y} = \mathbf{Gu} + \mathbf{n} \tag{5.98}$$

Combining the QR decomposition of $\mathbf{G}$, we get $\mathbf{G} = \mathbf{QR}$ with $\mathbf{Q}$ being the unitary matrix and $\mathbf{R}$ denoting the upper triangular matrix. Premuliplying $\mathbf{y}$ by $\mathbf{Q}^{\mathrm{H}}$, we have

$$\mathbf{x} = \mathbf{Q}^{\mathrm{H}}\mathbf{y} = \mathbf{Ru} + \mathbf{n} \tag{5.99}$$

It is worth noting that since the statistical properties of $\mathbf{Q}^{\mathrm{H}}\mathbf{n}$ and $\mathbf{n}$ are the same, $\mathbf{Q}^{\mathrm{H}}\mathbf{n}$ can be replaced by $\mathbf{n}$. Now, the nth symbol detection of complex-valued LR-based SIC is given as follows:

$$\mathbf{u}_n = \frac{1}{\alpha}(\lfloor \tilde{\mathbf{u}}_n \rceil - (\beta + \mathrm{j}\beta)t_n \mathbf{1}) \tag{5.100}$$

where, $\tilde{\mathbf{u}}_n = \alpha\mathbf{u} + (\beta + \mathrm{j}\beta)t_n\mathbf{1}$ and $\mathbf{u} = (\mathbf{x}_n - \sum\limits_{j=n+1}^{N_t} r_{n,j}\hat{\mathbf{u}}_j)/r_{n,n}, t_n = [\mathbf{T}^{-1}]_{(n,1:N_t)}$. Based on $\mathbf{s} = \mathbf{Tu}$, the mean vector and covariance matrix of $\mathbf{u}$ are obtained as follows:

$$\mathbf{u} = \mathrm{E}[\mathbf{T}^{-1}\mathbf{s}] = \mathbf{T}^{-1}\mathrm{E}[\mathbf{s}] = \mathbf{T}^{-1}\mathrm{E}[\mathbf{s}] \tag{5.101}$$

and

$$\begin{aligned}
\mathbf{Q} &= \mathrm{E}[\mathbf{uu}^{\mathrm{H}}] - \mathbf{uu}^{\mathrm{H}} \\
&= \mathbf{T}^{-1}\mathrm{E}[\mathbf{ss}^{\mathrm{T}}]\mathbf{T}^{-\mathrm{H}} - \mathbf{uu}^{\mathrm{H}}
\end{aligned} \tag{5.102}$$

Assume that each element of the LR domain symbol vector $\mathbf{u}$ is a CSCG random variable. Based on the central limit theorem, we get

$$\mathbf{u} \sim \mathcal{CN}(\mathbf{u}, \mathbf{Q}) \tag{5.103}$$

As RLR-RLGA, define $\mathbf{u}_D^{(n)}, \mathbf{u}_{ND}^{(n)}$, and $\mathbf{u}^{(n)}$. Set $\mathbf{Q}^{(N_t)} = \mathbf{Q}$ and $\mathbf{u}^{(N_t)} = \mathbf{u}$, and then

$$\mathbf{u}^{(n+1)} = \begin{bmatrix} \mathbf{u}_1^{(n+1)} \\ \bar{\mathbf{u}}_2^{(n+1)} \end{bmatrix} \tag{5.104}$$

where $\mathbf{u}^{(n+1)} \in \mathbb{C}^{n+1}, \mathbf{u}_1^{(n+1)} = [\mathbf{u}^{(n+1)}]_{(1:n,1)}$, and

$$\mathbf{Q}^{(n+1)} = \begin{bmatrix} \mathbf{Q}_1^{(n+1)} & \mathbf{q}_2^{(n+1)} \\ \mathbf{q}_3^{(n+1)} & q_4^{(n+1)} \end{bmatrix} \tag{5.105}$$

where $\mathbf{Q}^{(n+1)} \in \mathbb{C}^{(n+1)\times(n+1)}$, $\mathbf{u}_1^{(n+1)} = [\mathbf{Q}^{(n+1)}]_{(1:n,1:n)}$, $\mathbf{q}_2^{(n+1)} = [\mathbf{Q}^{(n+1)}]_{(1:n,n+1)}$, and $\mathbf{q}_3^{(n+1)} = [\mathbf{Q}^{(n+1)}]_{(n+1,1:n)}$.

Since each element of the LR domain symbol $\mathbf{u}$ is a CSCG random variable, the conditional probability density function of the nth layer of the SIC is

$$f(\mathbf{u}_{ND}^{(n)}|\mathbf{u}_D^{(n)}) \propto \mathcal{CN}(\mathbf{u}^{(n)}, \mathbf{u}^{(n)}) \tag{5.106}$$

where $\mathbf{u}_n = \mathbf{u}_1^{(n+1)} + \frac{\mathbf{q}_2^{(n+1)}}{q_4^{(n+1)}}(\hat{\mathbf{u}}_{(n+1)} - \bar{\mathbf{u}}_2^{(n+1)})$ and $\mathbf{Q}^{(n)} = \mathbf{Q}_1^{(n+1)} - \frac{\mathbf{q}_2^{(n+1)}\mathbf{q}_3^{(n+1)}}{q_4^{(n+1)}}$.

For RLR-RLGA, random sampling is performed with real-valued integers. In CLR-RLGA, in order to take Gaussian random sampling for complex-valued list generation, we make the real and imaginary variances of the same complex-valued signal the same. Some statistics may be lost due to mandatory CSCG assumptions, but the simulation results show that the performance degradation from CLR-RLGA to RLR-RLGA is small and its computational complexity is lower than RLR-RLGA.

5.3.3 *Complexity analysis*

In this section, we analyze the complexity of the LR-RLGA detector and compare it with the existing methods in terms of performance and complexity. For convenience, we use average floating point numbers (FLOPs) to measure the complexity.

5.3.3.1 *Complexity analysis and reduction*

In addition to the LLL algorithm, LR-RLGA has a fixed computational complexity, which has obvious advantages over the unfixed computational complexity of spherical decoding detectors.[5,6] With the consideration of $N_t = N_r$, the complexity of the CLR-RLGA algorithm is analyzed below.

In this section, we analyze the computational complexity based on the following three aspects of the CLR-RLGA algorithm: (1) the calculation and update of API in the LR domain; (2) random rounding; and (3) using the candidate solution list to calculate the LLR.

For the calculation of the API, the complexity of $\mathbf{u}$ is first to be calculated as $O(N_t^2)$. Since $E[\mathbf{ss}^H]$ is symmetric, the number of complex multiplications to obtain $E[\mathbf{ss}^H]$ is $\frac{1}{2}N_t^2$, and the complexity of calculating Q is $O(N_t^3)$. Therefore, the complexity level of API initialization is N_t^3.

For the SIC detection of the nth layer, the computational complexity order of $\mathbf{u}^{(n)}$ and $\mathbf{Q}^{(n)}$ is both $O((n+1)^2)$. And thus, the complexity order of the parallel Rand-SIC algorithm based on the API update is $O\left(\frac{1}{3}N_t^3\right)$.

The complexity of random rounding is $O(KN_t^2)$.[4] When the length of the list is K, the complexity order of LLR calculation is $O(KN_t^2)$. Therefore, when the list length is K, the complexity of CLR-RLGA is given as follows:

$$O(N_t^3) + O\left(\frac{K}{3}N_t^3\right) + O(KN_t^2) + O(KN_t^2)$$
$$= O\left(KN_t^2\left(\frac{K}{3}+1\right)N_t^3\right) \tag{5.107}$$

The complexity of each API update is $O\left(\frac{K}{3}N_t^3\right)$, which can reduce the complexity of API updates by considering the relevance of $\mathbf{u}$. Since the value is determined by its covariance matrix $\mathbf{Q}$, when the lattice reduction is not performed, $\mathbf{Q}$ is a diagonal matrix and $\mathbf{u}$ is irrelevant. However, when combining lattice reduction, since the lattice reduction transformation matrix $\mathbf{T}$ is generally not diagonal, $\mathbf{Q}$ is not diagonal and $\mathbf{u}$ becomes cross-correlated. Although the process of the API update is necessary for a cross-correlated matrix, if some channel correlation is weak, then the API updates can be ignored to reduce the computational complexity. Therefore, if the elements of $\mathbf{u}$ are mutually uncorrelated, the API can only be estimated from the edge distribution of $\mathbf{u}_n$ in the nth layer SIC detection. The simulation results provided below will also show that the performance of the CLR-RLGA detector is degraded slightly when API updates are not used. Therefore, the complexity order of the CLR-LRGA can be reduced to $O(K + N_t)N_t^2$.

5.3.3.2 *Complexity comparison*

In this section, we will compare the computational complexity of the following seven different MIMO-BICM detectors by the average number of FLOPs:

(1) RLR-RLGA, with API updates.
(2) CLR-RLGA, with API updates.
(3) RLR-RLGA, without API updates.
(4) CLR-RLGA, without API updates.
(5) Fixed candidate algorithm (FCA) in Ref. 7.

(6) Minimum mean square error parallel interference cancellation (MMSE-PIC) in Ref. 8.

(7) MAP detector.

For MAP and FCA detectors, since the subsequent iterations require only a small amount of complexity, we only consider the number of FLOPs for the first iteration of the two detectors. For the LR-RLGA and MMSE-PIC detectors, since the computational complexity of each iteration is the same, we consider the average number of FLOPs per iteration. Table 5.3 shows the average number of FLOPs per iteration for a single vector symbol.

It can be seen from the table that the complexity order of the LR domain-based list generation algorithm is independent of the modulation index M. Conversely, the complexity of the FCA grows with M because its list generation is done in the original modulation constellation. Since the FCA only needs to generate a list at the first iteration and then use this list for the next iteration, it has lower computational complexity. However, in terms of performance, LR-RLGA has a significant advantage over FCA because the list generation algorithm in FCA does not consider API.

Although MMSE-PIC can achieve a full-reception diversity gain by a fixed complexity when generating LLR, the MMSE-PIC is relatively poor in performance because the list is not used. In addition, by adjusting K, LR-RLGA can also provide a performance-complexity compromise as demonstrated by the simulation results in Section 5.3.4.

Table 5.3. **Average FLOPs for different IDD detectors in an MIMO-BICM system.**

| $\{M, N_t, N_r, K\}$ | Average FLOPs ($\times 10^4$) | | | | | | |
	I	II	III	IV	V	VI	VII
$\{2, 4, 4, 10\}$	1.91	1.49	1.33	1.16	1.21	1.36	9.83
$\{2, 4, 4, 20\}$	3.20	2.62	2.05	2.01	2.09	1.36	9.83
$\{2, 4, 4, 30\}$	4.50	3.86	2.89	2.82	3.02	1.36	9.83
$\{2, 4, 4, 60\}$	8.39	7.26	5.44	5.40	5.82	1.36	9.83
$\{4, 4, 4, 10\}$	1.92	1.50	1.35	1.17	2.08	1.39	838.86
$\{4, 4, 4, 20\}$	3.21	2.64	2.05	2.02	3.72	1.39	838.86
$\{4, 4, 4, 30\}$	4.52	3.87	2.89	2.83	5.35	1.39	838.86
$\{4, 4, 4, 60\}$	8.42	7.30	5.46	5.42	10.25	1.39	838.86
$\{2, 8, 8, 10\}$	10.82	7.01	6.52	4.71	4.29	10.37	3 355.44
$\{2, 8, 8, 20\}$	17.62	12.45	9.02	7.75	8.51	10.37	3 355.44
$\{2, 8, 8, 30\}$	24.43	17.60	11.51	10.83	13.36	10.37	3 355.44
$\{2, 8, 8, 60\}$	44.83	33.14	20.14	19.95	28.91	10.37	3 355.44

In addition, when K is large, the complexity of the CLR-RLGA is much lower than that of the RLR-RLGA for LR-RLGA and CLR-RLGA detectors without API updates. In terms of the performance and based on the simulation results in Section 5.3.4, we can see that the performance degradation from CLR-RLGA to RLR-RLGA is small irrespective of whether API is updated or not.

5.3.4 *Simulation results*

In this section, we analyze the bit error rate (BER) performance of LR-RLGA through MATLAB simulation. It is assumed that each element of the channel matrix satisfies $h_{n,k} \sim \mathcal{CN}(0, 1/N_{\mathrm{r}})$ and is independent of each other, and each symbol vector corresponds to an independent **H**. QAM is used as the modulation method, and (5, 7) half-rate convolutional code is adopted for channel coding, and random interleaving is applied to ensure that bits is independent of each other. Here, the length of the uncoded information sequence is set to be 2^{10}, and for LR, we use the LLL algorithm and set $\delta = 0.75$, and the signal-to-noise ratio SNR is defined as $E_b/N_0 = 1/(MN_0 R_c)$ with $R_c = \frac{1}{2}$.

For comparison, we simulated FCA in Ref. 7, MMSE-PIC in Ref. 8, and LSD in Ref. 9 to illustrate the performance based on LR random sampling. Figure 5.4 shows the BER performance of different IDD detectors for 4-QAM MIMO modulation in 4×4 MIMO systems. For this system, the full list length is $4^4 = 256$, and the generated length of all lists is set to $K = 10$. It can be seen from the figure that the performance of the LR-based random sampling algorithm after the first iteration has significant advantages over the FCA and MMSE-PIC detectors. After 3 iterations, both LR-RLGA and MMSE-PIC are close to optimal performance. However, there is still a significant performance gap between FCA and MAP. It can also be seen that the RLR-RLGA detector has a small performance degradation compared to the CLR-RLGA with or without API updates. Although MMSE-PIC has a comparable complexity to LR-RLGA (see Table 5.3), MMSE-PIC has a large gap in performance with LR-RLGA. In addition, LR-based random sampling can also be adjusted by adjusting K to achieve a balance between performance and complexity.

Figure 5.5 shows the BER performance of FCA and RLR-RLGA at different K values for $E_b/N_0 = 5\,\mathrm{dB}$ in MIMO systems with 4-QAM modulation. With an increase to $K = 20$ (which is small enough compared to the full list length $K = 256$), the performance of the RLR-RLGA detector

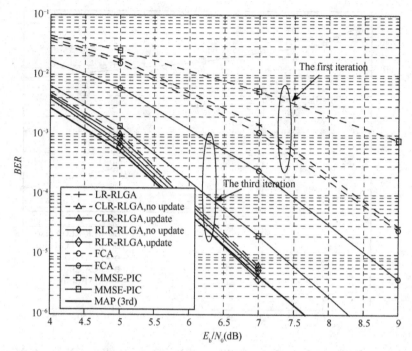

Fig. 5.4. **BER performance of different IDD receivers at 4-QAM, $N_t=N_r = 4$ and $K=10$.**

can almost reach the performance of the MAP. In addition, compared to RLR-RLGA, the performance of FCA decreases rapidly as K increases, because API information is not considered when generating lists in FCA. In fact, even if the list length of the FCA is $K = 45$, its performance is still worse than that of the RLR-RLGA with $K = 10$, and the total complexity of their three iterations is equivalent (see Table 5.3). It can be seen that by adjusting K, LR-RLGA provides a compromise between performance and complexity.

5.4 Bit Filtering-Based Detection and Decoding Technology

In Section 5.3.4, we introduced a detection and decoding technique based on random sampling, which can sample candidate vector solutions with high APP by random sampling. In addition, bit filtering-based detection and decoding techniques can achieve better performance with lower computational complexity. Compared to random sampling-based detection and

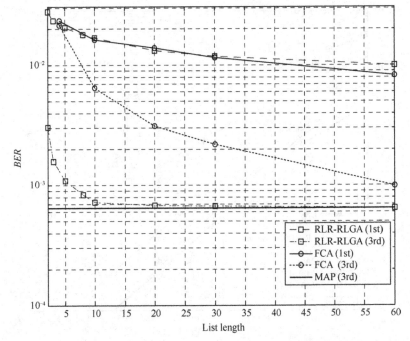

Fig. 5.5. BER performance of different K values at $N_t = N_r = 4$, $M = 2$, and $E_b/N_0 = 5\,\text{dB}$.

decoding techniques, bit filtering LR combines bit level detection and integer perturbation list generation method to improve performance. In order to find candidate vectors with high APP using the API, we also studied LR-based bit-level MMSE filters. In addition, in order to reduce the performance degradation caused by the LR detector quantization and rounding, we will also introduce an integer perturbation list generation method with small detection radius and low complexity.[10]

5.4.1 *LR-based IDD and bit-level combination and list generation*

5.4.1.1 *Design of bit-level MMSE filter based on LR*

According to the system model in Section 5.3.1, it is considered that the modulation constellation can be divided into two subsets, namely $\mathcal{A}^+_{k,l}$ and $\mathcal{A}^-_{k,l}$ representing $+1$ or -1 set of the lth bit of the kth symbol, respectively.

Therefore, an LR-based bit-level MMSE filter can be designed by combining the API generated by the SISO decoder in the IDD for estimating $\mathbf{s}_{k,l}^{\pm}$.

For $b_{k,l}$, it can be defined as

$$\tilde{\mathcal{A}}_{k,l}^{\pm} = \{\tilde{\mathbf{s}} | \tilde{\mathbf{s}} \in \tilde{\mathcal{A}}^{N_t}, b_{k,l;\tilde{\mathbf{s}}} = \pm 1\} \tag{5.108}$$

and

$$\mathcal{U}_{k,l}^{\pm} = \{\mathbf{u} | \mathbf{u} = \mathbf{T}^{-1}\tilde{\mathbf{s}}, \tilde{\mathbf{s}} \in \tilde{\mathcal{A}}^{N_t}, b_{k,l;\tilde{\mathbf{s}}} = \pm 1\} \tag{5.109}$$

In addition, in order to derive the LR-MMSE filter, it is also required to give the statistical information for $\mathbf{u}$ in the case of $b_{k,l}$. Therefore, set

$$\mathbf{u}_{k,l}^{\pm} = \mathbf{T}^{-1}\tilde{\mathbf{s}}_{k,l}^{\pm} \tag{5.110}$$

$$\mathbf{m}_{k,l}^{\pm} = \mathrm{E}\{\mathbf{u}_{k,l}^{\pm}\} = \mathbf{T}^{-1}\mathrm{E}\{\tilde{\mathbf{s}}_{k,l}^{\pm}\} \tag{5.111}$$

$$\mathbf{R}_{k,l}^{\pm} = \mathrm{Cov}(\mathbf{u}_{k,l}^{\pm}, \mathbf{u}_{k,l}^{\pm}) = \mathbf{T}^{-1}\mathrm{Cov}(\tilde{\mathbf{s}}_{k,l}^{\pm}, \tilde{\mathbf{s}}_{k,l}^{\pm})\mathbf{T}^{-\mathrm{H}} \tag{5.112}$$

where $\tilde{\mathbf{s}}_{k,l}^{\pm}$ is assumed to be a random vector as follows:

$$\tilde{\mathbf{s}}_{k,l}^{\pm} \in \{[\tilde{s}_1, \ldots, \tilde{s}_{k-1}, \tilde{s}_{k,l}^{\pm}, \tilde{s}_{k+1}, \ldots, \tilde{s}_{N_t}]^{\mathrm{T}}\} \tag{5.113}$$

where $\tilde{s}_{k,l}^{\pm}$ is the kth element of $\tilde{\mathbf{s}}_{k,l}^{\pm}$, which consists of a subset of the lth element with -1 symbol of $\tilde{\mathcal{A}}$. Besides, since the symbols transmitted by each antenna are statistically independent, we assume $\tilde{s}_m \in \tilde{\mathcal{A}}, m \neq k$ and each element of $\tilde{\mathbf{s}}_{k,l}^{\pm}$ is independent. Therefore, $\mathrm{Cov}(\tilde{\mathbf{s}}_{k,l}^{\pm}, \tilde{\mathbf{s}}_{k,l}^{\pm})$ is a diagonal matrix.

In order to obtain the estimate of $\tilde{\mathbf{s}}_{k,l}^{\pm}$, we assume that the soft estimate of $\mathbf{u}_{k,l}^{\pm}$ following LR-MMSE filtering is

$$\hat{\mathbf{u}}_{k,l}^{\pm} = \mathbf{W}_{k,l}^{\pm}(\tilde{\mathbf{y}} - \mathbf{Gm}) + \mathbf{m}_{k,l}^{\pm} \tag{5.114}$$

where $\mathbf{W}_{k,l}^{\pm}$ represents the LR-MMSE filter matrix for detecting $\tilde{\mathbf{s}}_{k,l}^{\pm}$. If the receiving signal is $\tilde{\mathbf{y}} = \mathbf{Gu}_{k,l}^{\pm} + \mathbf{n}$ with $\mathbf{u}_{k,l}^{\pm}$ expressing a vector to be estimated and detected, then when using MMSE criteria we can obtain the following equation with the condition $\frac{\partial \mathrm{E}\{\|\mathbf{u}_{k,l}^{\pm} - \hat{\mathbf{u}}_{k,l}^{\pm}\|\}}{\partial \mathbf{W}_{k,l}^{\pm}} = 0$:

$$\mathbf{W}_{k,l}^{\pm}(\mathbf{G}\mathbf{Q}_{k,l}^{\pm}\mathbf{G}^{\mathrm{H}} + N_0\mathbf{I}) = \mathbf{R}_{k,l}^{\pm}\mathbf{G}^{\mathrm{H}} \qquad (5.115)$$

where

$$\mathbf{Q}_{k,l}^{\pm} = \mathrm{E}\{\mathbf{u}_{k,l}^{\pm}(\mathbf{u}_{k,l}^{\pm})^{\mathrm{H}}\} - \mathbf{m}(\mathbf{m}_{k,l}^{\pm})^{\mathrm{H}} - \mathbf{m}_{k,l}^{\pm}\mathbf{m}^{\mathrm{H}} + \mathbf{m}\mathbf{m}^{\mathrm{H}} \qquad (5.116)$$

On this basis, we can get

$$\mathbf{W}_{k,l}^{\pm} = \mathbf{R}_{k,l}^{\pm}\mathbf{G}^{\mathrm{H}}(\mathbf{G}\mathbf{Q}_{k,l}^{\pm}\mathbf{G}^{\mathrm{H}} + N_0\mathbf{I})^{-1} \qquad (5.117)$$

Finally, the estimate of $\tilde{\mathbf{s}}_{k,l}^{\pm}$ is

$$\hat{\mathbf{s}}_{k,l}^{\pm} = \alpha \mathcal{Q}_{\tilde{A}_{k,l}^{\pm}}\left\{\lfloor \mathbf{T}\hat{\mathbf{u}}_{k,l}^{\pm}\rceil\right\} - \alpha\beta\mathbf{1} \qquad (5.118)$$

It is worth noting that there are two different mean vectors in Eq. (5.114) ($\mathbf{m}$ and $\mathbf{m}_{k,l}^{\pm}$), where the first vector $\mathbf{m}$ is used for soft cancellation and the second mean vector $\mathbf{m}_{k,l}^{\pm}$ can be used for obtaining the soft estimation of $\mathbf{u}_{k,l}^{\pm}$ after LR-MMSE filtering.

The above bit-level filter requires matrix inversion for each bit, which results in a higher computational complexity. However, it should be noted that when the API is sufficiently reliable, $\mathbf{m}_{k,l}^{+}$ or $\mathbf{m}_{k,l}^{-}$ can be close to $\mathbf{m}$ and $\mathrm{E}\{\mathbf{u}_{k,l}^{+}(\mathbf{u}_{k,l}^{+})^{\mathrm{H}}\}$ or $\mathrm{E}\{\mathbf{u}_{k,l}^{\pm}(\mathbf{u}_{k,l}^{\pm})^{\mathrm{H}}\}$ can be close to $\mathrm{E}\{\mathbf{u}\mathbf{u}^{\mathrm{H}}\}$. Therefore, it can be assumed that $\mathbf{m}_{k,l}^{+} \approx \mathbf{m}$ and $\mathrm{E}\{\mathbf{u}_{k,l}^{+}(\mathbf{u}_{k,l}^{+})^{\mathrm{H}}\} \approx \mathrm{E}\{\mathbf{u}\mathbf{u}^{\mathrm{H}}\}$. Based on this, $\mathbf{R} = \mathrm{E}\{\mathbf{u}\mathbf{u}^{\mathrm{H}}\} - \mathbf{m}\mathbf{m}^{\mathrm{H}}$ can be used for the estimation of $\mathbf{Q}_{k,l}^{+}$. However, when the API is sufficiently reliable, the effect of the approximation on the $\hat{\mathbf{s}}_{k,l}^{-}$ estimate can be ignored, thus reducing its impact on the LLR calculation and making the detection more accurate. In addition, it is also worth noting that $\mathbf{R}$ and $\mathbf{Q}_{k,l}^{\pm}$ are the same at the first iteration, and API information is not needed. Therefore, it is reasonable to estimate $\mathbf{Q}_{k,l}^{\pm}$ by $\mathbf{R}$, and this only requires a matrix inversion. Since $\mathbf{R}$ and $\{k,l\}$ are independent, there is an obvious advantage to using $\mathbf{R}$ over $\mathbf{Q}_{k,l}^{\pm}$ or the traditional soft cancellation filter matrix generation method.

For convenience, the bit-level LR-MMSE filtering method in Eq. (5.117) is called LR-IDD-1, and the filtering method using $\mathbf{R}$ is called LR-IDD-2. Through complexity and simulation analysis, we will prove that the complexity of LR-IDD-2 is significantly lower than that of LR-IDD-1, and the detection performance of both methods is close. In the following, we will introduce the list generation method of LR-IDD-2.

5.4.1.2 *Generating the integer perturbation list*

In the following, we introduce a low-complexity list generation method in the LR domain. The core idea is to make an integer perturbation of the estimated decision to improve the performance of the bit-level LR-MMSE filtering. Of course, the list can also be obtained by iterative tree search[5,6,9,11] or enumeration list,[3] but these methods may have higher computational complexity because they do not utilize the quasi-orthogonal basis vector after the lattice reduction.

Define

$$\dot{\mathbf{u}}_{k,l}^{\pm} = \mathbf{T}^{-1} \mathcal{Q}_{\tilde{A}_{k,l}^{\pm}} \left\{ \lfloor \mathbf{T}\hat{\mathbf{u}}_{k,l}^{\pm} \rceil \right\} \tag{5.119}$$

If the Sphere Decoder is used to estimate $\mathbf{u}_{k,l}^{\pm}$, the optimal candidate solution set is given as

$$\mathcal{C}_{\mathbf{u}_{k,l}^{\pm}} = \{\tilde{\mathbf{u}}_{k,l}^{\pm} : \| \tilde{\mathbf{u}}_{k,l}^{\pm} - \dot{\mathbf{u}}_{k,l}^{\pm} \|_{\mathbf{G}^{\mathrm{H}}\mathbf{G}}^2 < r\} \tag{5.120}$$

The search radius r here is predefined. Since $\mathbf{G}$ is nearly orthogonal due to the use of lattice reduction, $\mathbf{G}^{\mathrm{H}}\mathbf{G}$ is the nearly diagonal matrix. Therefore, $\mathcal{C}_{\mathbf{u}_{k,l}^{\pm}}$ can be approximated as

$$\mathcal{C}_{\mathbf{u}_{k,l}^{\pm}} = \{\tilde{\mathbf{u}}_{k,l}^{\pm} : \| \tilde{\mathbf{u}}_{k,l}^{\pm} - \dot{\mathbf{u}}_{k,l}^{\pm} \|^2 < r\} \tag{5.121}$$

For the detection radius $r < \sqrt{2}$, when the quantization error is within an acceptable range, the radius is sufficiently large such that the elements in $\mathcal{C}_{\mathbf{u}_{k,l}^{\pm}}$ can be obtained only by increasing or decreasing the value of $\dot{\mathbf{u}}_{k,l}^{\pm}$ in each dimension.

Set the list length to be

$$K = 4 \sum_{m=1}^{\mathcal{M}} N_m \tag{5.122}$$

where $N_m \in \{0,1,2\}$, $\mathcal{M} \in \mathbb{Z}^+$, and $\mathcal{M} \leq N_t$. Denote $[\dot{\mathbf{u}}_{k,l}^{\pm}]_m$ as the mth element of $\dot{\mathbf{u}}_{k,l}^{\pm}$. The resulting list generation algorithm can be summarized as follows:

(1) Calculate the Euclidean module of each column of $\mathbf{G}$, where the set of $\mathcal{M}$ shortest column vectors is as follows:

$$\mathcal{G} = \{\mathbf{g}^{(1)}, \mathbf{g}^{(2)}, \ldots, \mathbf{g}^{(\mathcal{M})}\} \tag{5.123}$$

where $\mathbf{g}^{(m)}$ denotes the mth shortest column vector of $\mathbf{G}$.

(2) Define

$$\{P_1, P_2, \ldots, P_8\} = \{1, -1, j, -j, 1+j, 1-j, -1+j, -1-j\}$$

$$\dot{\mathbf{s}}_{k,l}^{\pm} = \mathcal{Q}_{\tilde{\mathcal{A}}_{k,l}^{\pm}} \left\{ \lfloor \mathbf{T}\hat{\mathbf{u}}_{k,l}^{\pm} \rceil \right\} \tag{5.124}$$

For $\mathbf{g}^{(m)}$, $1 \le m \le \mathcal{M}$, $N_m \in \{0, 1, 2\}$, and $1 \le j \le 4N_m$, the additional candidate solutions are as follows:

$$\dot{\mathbf{s}}_{k,l}^{(\pm,m,j)} = \mathcal{Q}_{\tilde{\mathcal{A}}_{k,l}^{\pm}} \left\{ \dot{\mathbf{s}}_{k,l}^{\pm} + [\mathbf{T}]_m (P_j + [\dot{\mathbf{u}}_{k,l}^{\pm}]_m) \right\} \tag{5.125}$$

where $[\mathbf{T}]_m$ denotes the mth column of $\mathbf{T}$.

(3) Define

$$\tilde{\mathcal{A}}_{k,l}^{(\pm,K)} = \dot{\mathbf{s}}_{k,l}^{\pm} \cup \left\{ \dot{\mathbf{s}}_{k,l}^{(\pm,m,n)} \right\}$$

$$= \left\{ \mathbf{s}_{k,l}^{(\pm,1)}, \mathbf{s}_{k,l}^{(\pm,2)}, \ldots, \mathbf{s}_{k,l}^{(\pm,K+1)} \right\} \tag{5.126}$$

Define

$$\mathcal{L}_{k,l}^{(\pm,K)} = \max_{\mathbf{s} \in \mathcal{A}_{k,l}^{(\pm,K)}} \left\{ -\frac{1}{N_0} \parallel \mathbf{y} - \mathbf{Hs} \parallel^2 + \sum_{k=1}^{N_t} \sum_{l=1}^{M} b_{k,l;\mathbf{s}} L_A(b_{k,l}) \right\} \tag{5.127}$$

The LLR estimation of $b_{k,l}$ can thus be obtained as follows:

$$L_E(b_{k,l}) \approx \frac{1}{2}(\mathcal{L}_{k,l}^{+} - \mathcal{L}_{k,l}^{-}) - L_A(b_{k,l}) \tag{5.128}$$

Since the LLR of different bits can be obtained simultaneously, the bit-level LR-MMSE can implement parallel computing, which is a significant advantage. In addition, it is also worth noting that although the additional candidate solutions satisfying $r \ge \sqrt{2}$ can be obtained using multidimensional integer perturbations, the single-dimensional integer perturbation can achieve near-optimal performance with lower computational complexity since the channel matrix becomes nearly orthogonal after the lattice reduction.

Furthermore, if LR is not performed, the performance of the above list generation algorithm may be severely affected when the detection radius is small, since the lattice vectors may not be nearly orthogonal at this time. In fact, if the lattice vector after LR is not used, then the LSD method can also be used to generate the list, but its computational complexity will increase significantly.

5.4.2 *Complexity analysis*

In this section, we first analyze the complexity order based on the bit filtering method and then discuss the complexity based on the LLL lattice-reduction. For convenience, set $N_t = N_r$, and then consider the complexity order of the operation: (1) looking for LR-MMSE filter; (2) generating the list; (3) calculating the LLR of the candidate solution list.

In order to obtain the MMSE filter matrix of LR-IDD-1, it is necessary to perform a matrix inversion for each bit individually, which requires $O(N_t^3)$ complexity for each bit. Therefore, the complexity of LR-IDD-1 is mainly composed of matrix inversion and its complexity in looking for the LR-MMSE filter is $O(MN_t^4)$. In addition to matrix inversion, since for each bit $\mathbf{Q}_{k,l}^{\pm}$ and $\mathbf{R}_{k,l}^{\pm}$ are different, finding an LR-MMSE filter also requires matrix multiplication.

Conversely, LR-IDD-2 requires much less computational complexity when looking for LR-MMSE filters. Since $\mathbf{R}$ and (k,l) are independent,

$$\mathbf{G}^H(\mathbf{G}^H\mathbf{R}\mathbf{G} + N_0\mathbf{I})^{-1}(\mathbf{y} - \mathbf{G}\mathbf{m}) \qquad (5.129)$$

can be obtained at initialization time. Thereafter, only one matrix vector multiplication is needed to estimate $\mathbf{s}_{k,l}^{\pm}$. Therefore, the complexity of finding a bit-level LR-MMSE filter depends primarily on the process of getting $\mathbf{R}_{k,l}^{\pm}$. Since $\mathrm{Cov}(\tilde{\mathbf{s}}_{k,l}^{\pm}, \tilde{\mathbf{s}}_{k,l}^{\pm})$ is a diagonal matrix, this process only requires the complexity of a single matrix multiplication. Therefore, the LR-IDD-2 complexity order of the LR-MMSE filtering is $O(MN_t^4)$.

In the process of list generation, since integer perturbations are added only to each dimension of $\dot{\mathbf{s}}_{k,l}^{\pm}$, only one vector–scalar multiplication is required for each candidate solution in the original constellation. Therefore, for MN_t bits of each symbol vector, the complexity of the list generation on the LR domain is $O(MKN_t^2)$. In this section, we only consider the case (through the simulation in Section 5.5.3), where the above method can also reach the matched filter bound (MFB) under the condition $K \approx N_t^2$. Now, the complexity of the integer perturbation list generation method is $O(MN_t^4)$.

When calculating LLR, at initialization time it needs to calculate

$$\{[\tilde{\mathbf{H}}]_m \tilde{s} | 1 \leq m \leq N_t, \tilde{s} \in \tilde{\mathcal{A}}\} \qquad (5.130)$$

where $[\tilde{\mathbf{H}}]_m$ represents the mth column of $\tilde{\mathbf{H}}$. Considering that the complexity of calculating the LLR is about $O(2^M N_t^2)$, it can be obtained that when $N_t \geq 4$, the complexity is not dominant compared with the complexity of obtaining the LR-MMSE filter.

Since LR-IDD-2 requires only one matrix inversion, and LR-IDD-1 requires MN_t times matrix inversion, the complexity of LR-IDD-2 can be significantly less than the complexity of LR-IDD-1. For LR-IDD-1, the overall computational complexity of the LR-MMSE filter is

$$O(\varepsilon MN_t^4) \tag{5.131}$$

where $\varepsilon > 1$ represents the complexity increase brought about by LR-IDD-2. Simulation shows that the performance difference between LR-IDD-1 and LR-IDD-2 is small, while the complexity of LR-IDD-2 is much lower than that of LR-IDD-1.

5.4.3 *Simulation results*

In this section, the performance of LR-IDD-1 and LR-IDD-2 is shown through simulation results. Assume that the elements of the channel matrix are independent and $[\mathbf{H}]_{n,k} \sim \mathcal{CN}(0, 1/N_r)$. Each individual symbol vector corresponds to an independent channel matrix $\mathbf{H}$ and uses 4-QAM modulation. The channel coding method is a $\frac{1}{2}$ rate convolutional code which generates the polynomial $(5, 7)$. Assume that the length of the uncoded information sequence is 2^{10}. For the lattice reduction, we use the LLL algorithm and set $\delta = 0.75$. Define the SNR as $E_b/N_0 = E_s/(MN_0R_c = 1/MN_0R_c)$ with $R_c = \frac{1}{2}$.

For comparative analysis, we also conducted the simulation by the LSD in Ref. 9, the MCMC in Ref. 12, and the MMSE-SC in Ref. 8. For LSD, the adopted list length of a 4×4 MIMO system is $N_{cand} = 64$ and $N_{cand} = 128$, $N_{cand} = 128$; $N_{cand} = 256$, $N_{cand} = 512$, and $N_{cand} = 1024$ are applied to an 8×8 MIMO system. In addition, for MCMC, six parallel Gibbs samplers are used, each of which uses six samples.

5.4.3.1 *Comparison of LR-IDD-1 and LR-IDD-2*

As described above, since LR-IDD-2 is an approximate estimate of LR-IDD-1, we first compare the performance of LR-IDD-1 and LR-IDD-2. Figure 5.6 shows the BER performance of LR-IDD-1 and LR-IDD-2 in a 4×4 MIMO system with $E_b/N_0 = 5$ dB. We can see that there is almost no performance difference between LR-IDD-1 and LR-IDD-2, which also proves that LR-IDD-2 is a reasonable approximation for LR-IDD-1.

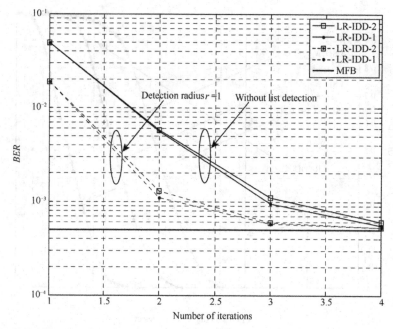

Fig. 5.6. **Performance comparison of LR-IDD-1 and LR-IDD-2 in a 4 × 4 MIMO system.**

Furthermore, to illustrate the effect of the list generation method on the performance of the bit filtering, Fig. 5.6 also shows the performance comparison of the bit filtering method with or without the list generation method. When using the list generation method, set the detection radius $x = 1$. As can be seen from Fig. 5.6, after using the integer perturbation list generation method, the performance of the bit filtering is greatly improved. Note that since the complexity caused by the list generation is small in the LR-IDD detection, it can be seen from Fig. 5.6 that the LR-IDD detector can achieve significant performance improvement through list generation with lower additional complexity overheads.

5.4.3.2 *Complexity comparison*

In this section, we compare the computational complexity of different iterative detectors for 8 × 8 MIMO systems by means of average floating point calculations (FLOPs). Since some detectors have floating computational complexity, for the sake of fairness, we use the average FLOPs cumulative distribution function (CDF) of single transmitting and receiving data to

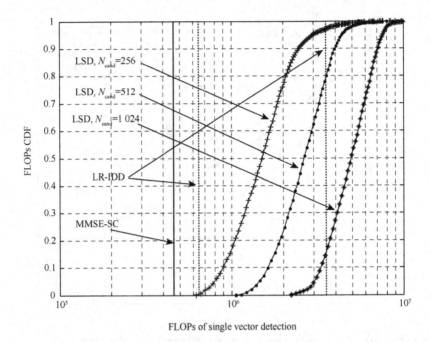

Fig. 5.7. **CDF of an 8 × 8 MIMO system FLOPs at $E_b/N_0 = 5\,\mathrm{dB}$.**

measure the complexity of different detectors. For 8 × 8 MIMO systems, we consider three iterations and set the detection radius $r = 1$.

As can be seen from Fig. 5.7, in the 8 × 8 MIMO system, LR-IDD-2 has a lower computational complexity than LR-IDD-1, but is similar to MMSE-SC. It should be noted that although the complexity of LSD is usually variable, the complexity is still too high even in its best case (i.e., at its lowest complexity); the complexity of bit filtering is deterministic and is independent of the actual channel and SNR, which is also a significant advantage of the bit filtering described in this section over LSD detectors.

Although LR-IDD-2 has a complexity similar to the MMSE-SC detector, further simulations show that LR-IDD-2 can achieve a performance similar to LSD detectors.

5.4.3.3 *Convergence analysis*

The convergence behavior of IDD can be analyzed by the extrinsic information transfer (EXIT) map. EXIT was originally proposed by Brink[13] to analyze the convergence of iterative decoders.

Assume that the mutual information between the transmission bit $b_{k,l}$ and the external information $L_A(b_{k,l})$ of the SISO decoder is $I_{in} = I(L_A(b_{k,l}; b_{k,l})$, and assume that the mutual information between the transmission bit $b_{k,l}$ and the external information $L_E(b_{k,l})$ input to the SISO decoder is defined as $I_{out} = I(L_E(b_{k,l}; b_{k,l})$. For a given SNR, the transfer function between I_{in} and I_{out} is $I_{out} = f(I_{in}, E_b/N_0)$ with $0 \leq I_{in}, I_{out} \leq 1$. Define $b = b_{k,l}$ and $L_A = L_A(b_{k,l})$, then the mutual information I_{in} of the equal-probability binary input bits is

$$
\begin{aligned}
I_{in} &= H(b) - H(L_A|b) \\
&= H(b) - H(L_A; b) + H(L_A) \\
&= \frac{1}{2} \sum_{b \in \{\pm 1\}} \int_{-\infty}^{\infty} f_{L_A|b}(l_A|b) \text{lb} f_{L_A|b}(l_A|b) \mathrm{d}l_A \\
&\quad - \int_{-\infty}^{\infty} f_{L_A}(l_A) \text{lb} f_{L_A}(l_A) \mathrm{d}l_A
\end{aligned}
\tag{5.132}
$$

where $f_{L_A}(l_A) = \frac{1}{2} \sum_{b \in \{\pm 1\}} f_{L_A|b}(l_A|b)$. Define $L_E = L_E(b_{k,l})$, then

$$
\begin{aligned}
I_{out} &= \frac{1}{2} \sum_{b \in \{\pm 1\}} \int_{-\infty}^{\infty} f_{L_E|b}(l_A|b) \text{lb} f_{L_E|b}(l_E|b) \mathrm{d}l_E \\
&\quad - \int_{-\infty}^{\infty} f_{L_E}(l_E) \text{lb} f_{L_E}(l_E) \mathrm{d}l_E
\end{aligned}
\tag{5.133}
$$

And the EXIT function $I_{out} = f(I_{in}, E_b/N_0)$ can be obtained through experimental simulation.

Figure 5.8 shows the EXIT curve for an 8×8 MIMO system at 6 dB. Since the convergence behavior of IDD is independent of the mapping rules and the channel coding used,[14,15] we use the same convolutional code and mapping rules in this simulation. In addition, since the EXIT map is independent of channel coding, the convergence behavior of the system depends only on different iterative detectors. In general, the higher the EXIT curve, the better the performance achieved by the detector. Note that the corresponding larger I_{in} value in the curve represents the performance of the detector iteration in the later period, while the smaller I_{out} value corresponds to the performance of the iteration in the early period. As can be seen from Fig. 5.8, the performance of the bit filtering-based method is similar to that of the LSD, and the performance of the MMSE-SC is worse

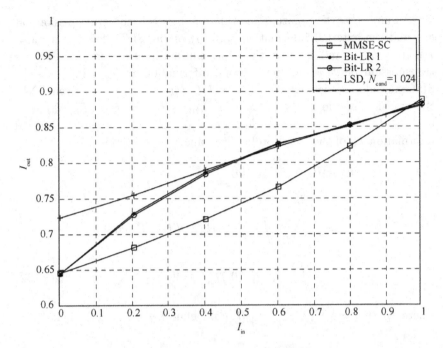

Fig. 5.8. EXIT curve of an 8 × 8 MIMO system.

than the other methods. In addition, it can also be seen that the bit filtering-based method has a lower area of the EXIT curve corresponding to the smaller I_{in} value than the MAP, which indicates that the bit filtering-based method does not provide near-MAP performance in the early period of the iteration. It is because the API obtained in the early period of the iteration is not very reliable. However, after several iterations, the bit filtering-based method can approach the performance of MAP detection.

5.4.3.4 *BER performance*

In this section, we present the BER performance of multiple detectors in a 4×4 MIMO system, as shown in Fig. 5.9. For bit filtering-based detectors, $r = 1$ is still set to maintain low complexity. As analyzed above, the MMSE-SC detector has the weakest performance but it has a lower complexity. The LR-IDD-2 detector provides performance similar to BER, LSD, and MCMC detectors, and its complexity is close to that of the MMSE-SC

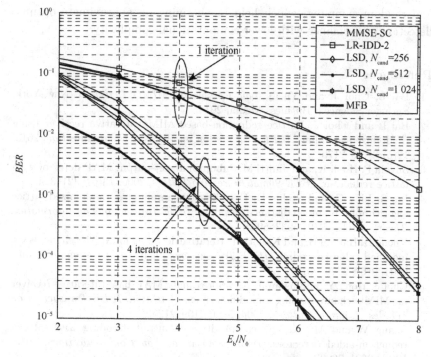

Fig. 5.9. BER performance of a 4 × 4 MIMO system.

detector, which further shows the high performance and low complexity of LR-IDD.

5.5 Summary

Spatial multidimensional signal iterative reception processing technology is one of the key technologies for wireless communication in the future. This chapter first introduces the signal detection method based on lattice reduction for uncoded MIMO systems and theoretically analyzes that it can obtain the full-reception diversity gain. On this basis, in order to further achieve or close to the theoretical system capacity that the MIMO system can provide, this chapter discusses IDD-based iterative decoding and detection techniques in MIMO coding systems. Finally, in order to avoid the exponential complexity of optimal MAP detection, this chapter also introduces two detection methods based on bit filtering and random sampling, which help in obtaining an approximate optimal detection performance with lower computational complexity.

References

1. Bai L, Choi J, and Yu Q. *Low Complexity MIMO Detection*. New York, Springer Science+ Business Media, 2014.
2. Bai L and Choi J. Lattice reduction-based MIMO iterative receiver using randomized sampling. *IEEE Transaction on Wireless Communication*, 2013, 12(5): 2160–2170.
3. Silvola P, Hooli K, and Juntti M. Suboptimal soft-output MAP detector with lattice reduction. *IEEE Signal Processing Letters*, 2006, 13(6): 321–324.
4. Liu S, Ling C, and Stehle D. Decoding by sampling: A randomized lattice algorithm for bounded distance decoding. *IEEE Transactions on Information Theory*, 2011, 57(9): 5933–5945.
5. Vikalo H, Hassibi B, and Kailath T. Iterative decoding for MIMO channels via modified sphere decoding. *IEEE Transactions on Wireless Communications*, 2004, 3(6): 2299–2311.
6. Choi J, Hong Y, and Yuan J. An approximate MAP based iterative receiver for MIMO channels using a modified sphere detection. *IEEE Transaction on Wireless Communications*, 2006, 5(8): 2199–2126.
7. Zhang W and Ma X. Low-complexity soft-output decoding with lattice-reduction-aided detectors. *IEEE Transactions on Communications*, 2010, 58(9): 2621–2629.
8. Wang X and Poor HV. Iterative (turbo) soft interference cancellation and decoding for coded CDMA. *IEEE Transactions on Communications*, 1999, 47(7): 1046–1061.
9. Hochwald B and Brink ST. Achieving near-capacity on a multiple antenna channel. *IEEE Transactions on Communications*, 2003, 51(3): 389–399.
10. Li QY, Zhang J, Bai L, *et al.* Lattice reduction-based approximation MAP detection with bit-wise combining and integer perturbed list generation. *IEEE Transaction on Communications*, 2013, 61(8): 3259–3269.
11. Hagenauer J, Offer E, and Papke L. Iterative decoding of binary block and convolutional codes. *IEEE Transactions on Information Theory*, 1996, 42(2): 429–445.
12. Farhang-Boroujeny B, Zhu H, and Shi Z. Markov chain Monte Carlo algorithms for CDMA and MIMO communication systems. *IEEE Transactions on Signal Processing*, 2006, 54(5): 1896–1909.
13. Brink ST. Convergence behavior of iteratively decoded parallel concatenated codes. *IEEE Transactions on Communications*, 2001, 49(10): 1727–1737.
14. Chindapol A and Ritcey JA. Design, analysis, and performance evaluation for BICM-ID with square QAM constellations in Rayleigh fading channels. *IEEE Journal on Selected Areas Communications*, 2001, 19(5): 944–957.
15. Fabregas AG, Martinez A, and Caire G. *Bit-Interleaved Coded Modulation*. Boston, Now Publishers Inc., 2008.

Chapter 6

Ground-Based Cooperative Transmission System

Since the concept of mobile communication was proposed by Bell Labs in the United States in 1947, ground-based mobile communication system has achieved rapid development in the past 30 years and is being widely used in more and more countries and regions. In this chapter, we will first state the characteristics of the ground-based wireless communication system and its development process. Key technologies such as multidimensional joint resource scheduling, multi-user cooperative transmission, multi-cell cooperative transmission, and anti-interference methods in the new generation ground-based cooperative transmission system, and massive MIMO in the future 5G communication system will be emphatically introduced.

6.1 Ground-Based Transmission System Overview

Since the end of the 20th century, wireless mobile communication based on terrestrial cellular systems is gradually having an impact in changing people's lives and has become an indispensable part of human society. According to the 2011 final report released by the International Telecommunication Union, the number of mobile phone users worldwide has reached 5.9 billion, the overall permeability is about 87%, and the permeability of developing countries is also 79%. Mobile communication has become one of the main means of communication in modern communication networks.[1]

6.1.1 *Development of ground-based wireless communication systems*

6.1.1.1 *Wireless communication system in the early stages*

In 1978, Bell Labs successfully tested the first cellular mobile communication system in Chicago, namely the advanced mobile phone service (AMPS),[2] and put it into commercial application in 1983. AMPS divided the entire coverage area into several cells. Adjacent cells use different frequency resources to achieve frequency reuse and enable users to automatically access the public switched telephone network (PSTN) in the coverage area. Subsequently, AMPS developed rapidly in the United States. At the same time, the United Kingdom established an extended omnidirectional communication system, and Japan established a narrowband full-access communication system. Both were analog frequency division multiple access (FDMA) system, which belongs to the first-generation (1G) mobile communication system.

The 1G system adopted technologies such as cellular networking and frequency reuse to achieve large-area coverage, support for handoff of uninterrupted communication of mobile terminals, and effectively improve spectrum utilization. However, 1G systems also had limitations, including that there was no public interface between different national systems, global roaming could not be achieved, digital services could not be provided, and the security was low. Therefore, analog cellular mobile communication was gradually replaced by digital cellular mobile communication, but the system architecture adopted by 1G was used in subsequent systems.

The second-generation (2G) cellular mobile communication system based on digital communication technology was introduced in the early 1990s. The global system for mobile communications (GSM), which was established in Europe in 1992, was the first digital cellular mobile communication network[3] and then Japanese digital cellular (JDC)[4] and US IS-95[5] had also been put into use one after the other. GSM and JDC use time division multiple access (TDMA), while IS-95 uses the code division multiple access (CDMA) technology. These systems used digital modulation technology to transmit voice and low-speed data services, belonging to 2G technology.

Compared with the 1G system, the 2G system had a higher spectrum utilization, stronger confidentiality, and better voice quality. With years of development, the 2G system standards were also relatively complete, and the technology was relatively mature. However, with the development of data services, there was a need for a stronger system to support high-speed mobile communications.

6.1.1.2 *The third-generation wireless communication system*

The concept of the third-generation (3G) mobile communication was first proposed by the ITU in 1985, which was called the future public land mobile telecommunications system (FPLMTS). In 1996, it was renamed the international mobile telecommunications 2000 (IMT-2000) system, and operated in the 2000-MHz band and could provide data rates up to 2000 kbit/s.

According to the overall goal of the ITU, the third-generation mobile communication system had the following characteristics:

(1) providing high-rate and multi-rate support for multiple services; supporting multimedia services from voice to packet data; providing the necessary bandwidth as needed especially the Internet; the minimum wireless transmission requirements are shown in Table 6.1;

(2) global coverage and global seamless roaming, global use of common frequency bands (1885–2025 MHz, 2110–2200 MHz); however, the systems are not required to have the same internal technologies in the wireless transmission equipment and the network, and only require uniformity in network interface, interworking, and service capabilities;

(3) high spectral efficiency;

(4) high quality of service. Long-distance voice quality and data service with a bit error rate less than 10^{-6};

(5) the core network transitions from circuit switching to packet switching and eventually evolves to an all-IP network;

(6) good commercial features such as low cost, low power consumption, small size, and high security.

Since 1996, the study of the 3G standardization systems entered a substantive phase. In April 1997, the ITU began to collect technical solutions for wireless transmission in IMT-2000.[6] In 1999, the interface

Table 6.1. Minimum transmission requirements for
3G mobile communication systems.

Fast-moving environment	Maximum rate up to 114 kbit/s
Walking environment	Maximum rate up to 384 kbit/s
Indoor environment	Maximum rate up to 2 Mbit/s

technical specifications of the 3G system were approved, including five technologies as well as the CDMA and TDMA, which are as follows:

(1) CDMA technology

1) **IMT-2000 CDMA DS:** universal terrestrial radio access (UTRA)/ WCDMA and direct sequence (DS) cdma2000;
2) **IMT-2000 CDMA MC:** multicarrier (MC) cdma2000;
3) **IMT-2000 CDMA TDD:** time division-synchronous code division multiple access (TD-SCDMA) and UTRA/TDD (also known as WCDMA TDD);

(2) TDMA technology

1) **IMT-2000 TDMA SC:** UWC136;
2) **MT-2000 TDMA MC:** DECT.

where North American cdma2000,[7] European WCDMA,[8,9] and China's TD-SCDMA[10] are the currently available main 3G technologies. Cdma2000 and WCDMA can work in the frequency division duplexing (FDD) mode. In FDD mode, the uplink and downlink use different frequency bands. The parameters of cdma2000 and WCDMA FDD are shown in Table 6.2.

WCDMA and TD-SCDMA technologies can adopt time division duplexing (TDD) mode. The uplink and downlink use the same frequency band, and one time period is divided into multiple time slots, and each time slot can be allocated to different users. The comparison of parameters between TD-SCDMA and WCDMA TDD is shown in Table 6.3.

6.1.1.3 *The fourth-generation wireless communication system*

Since 2004, the 3rd-generation partnership project (3GPP) organization has started research on long-term evolution (LTE).[11] LTE is a transition from 3G to fourth-generation (4G) technologies. It improves and enhances the 3G air access technology and adopts orthogonal frequency division multiplexing (OFDM) and multiple-input multiple-output (MIMO) as the standard for wireless networks. Nokia–Siemens successfully developed the world's first LTE phone in September 2009.[12]

Since the preliminary definition of the framework and objectives of the IMT-2000, a subsequent evolution system was made in 2003,[13,14] and the ITU officially defined the evolution system as IMT-Advanced in October 2005, which was the so-called 4G mobile communication system. The World Radio Conference in 2007 allocated spectrum for IMT-Advanced

Table 6.2. Parameters of the 3G system in FDD mode.

System	Occupied bandwidth (MHz)	Chip rate (Mchip/s)	Spread spectrum	Multiple access method
cdma2000	$1.25N$, $N \in \{1,3,6,9,12\}$	$1.2288N$, $N \in \{1,3,6,9,12\}$	Downlink: Walsh code and quasi-orthogonal code. Uplink: Walsh code and long code.	Multi-carrier mode: MC-CDMA. Single-carrier mode: DS-CDMA
WCDMA FDD	5	3.84	OVSF, spread-spectrum coefficient: Downlink: 4–512 Uplink: 4–256	DS-CDMA

Table 6.3. Parameters of the 3G system in TDD mode.

System	Occupied bandwidth (MHz)	Chip rate (Mchip/s)	Spread spectrum	Number of slots
TD-SCDMA	1.6	1.28	DS, spread-spectrum coefficient: 1/2/4/8/16	7 regular time slots + 3 feature time slots
WCDMAFDD	5	3.84	DS, spread-spectrum coefficient: 1/2/4/8/16	15 identical time slots

and in March 2008 issued a circular for the collection of IMT-Advanced standards. By October 2009, a total of six candidates were recruited[15–20] The proposal was divided into two major categories, LTE-Advanced[21] and IEEE 802.16m[22] of 3GPP. Some of the parameters are shown in Table 6.4. LTE-Advanced is an evolution of LTE and maintains backward compatibility with LTE, supported by 3GPP, ETSI, etc. And IEEE802.16m is a standard of the IEEE802.16 series, which is mainly supported by forums such as IEEE and WiMAX and its partners.

Under the guidance of the ITU Working Group, 14 independent evaluation teams around the world are conducting rigorous evaluation and standard integration work on 4G proposals. The global core standard

Table 6.4. Comparison of some of the parameters of LTE-Advanced and IEEE 802.16m in the 4G system

System	LTE-Advanced	IEEE 802.16m
Peak rate	Downlink 1000 Mbit/s, uplink 500 Mbit/s	Static 1000 Mbit/s, moving 100 Mbit/s
Support bandwidth (MHz)	1.25–20	5–20
Multiple access method	Downlink OFDMA, uplink SC-FDMA	OFDMA
Interference cancellation technique	Soft spectrum reuse, base station cooperative scheduling, cooperative multipoint transmission.	Interference randomization, interference-aware base station cooperation scheduling, transmission beamforming.
Compatibility	Compatible with early 3GPP systems.	Compatible with early WiMAX systems.

of the first version of IMT-Advanced was completed in October 2011, and the technical framework of the official IMT-Advanced was basically determined.

The characteristics of IMT-Advanced are as follows:

(1) achieve high-speed versatility worldwide, while maintaining cost-effective conditions and supporting a wide range of services and applications;
(2) high-quality mobile services;
(3) user terminals are suitable for global use;
(4) the ability to support IMT services and fixed network services;
(5) worldwide roaming capabilities;
(6) enhanced peak rates to support new services and applications, such as multimedia services.

Therefore, the requirements proposed by the IMT-Advanced system include the following: indoor (moving speed 0–10 km/h) peak rate per unit bandwidth of downlink data service is up to 3 bit/s/Hz and uplink is 2.25 bit/s/Hz; the microcellular (moving speed is 10–30 km/h) downlink is

2.6 bit/s/Hz and the uplink is 1.8 bit/s/Hz; the urban area (30–120 km/h) downlink is 2.2 bit/s/Hz and the uplink is 1.4 bit/s. /Hz; the high-speed mobile (120–350 km/h) downlink is 1.1 bit/s/Hz and uplink is 0.7 bit/s/Hz; flexible support for different carriers such as 1.25 MHz, 1.4 MHz, 2.5 MHz, 3 MHz, 5 MHz, 10 MHz, 15 MHz, 20 MHz, 40 MHz; call setup delay is less than 100 ms in idle mode and less than 50 ms in sleep mode. Table 6.5 compares the key parameters of 3G and 4G.

6.1.1.4 *The future wireless communication system development trend*

From 1G to 4G, its core technologies are mainly FDMA, TDMA, CDMA, and OFDMA, which use frequency, time, and symbols to improve the spectrum efficiency of the system. However, there is still a broad space for development in the use of space resources. The International Telecommunication Union (ITU) ITU standardizes Beyond IMT-Advanced as the B4G mobile communication standard. B4G mobile communication standards include multi-point transmission spatial signal combining technology, cooperative network transmission, interference coordination technology, home base station transmission mode, massive MIMO technology, cognitive radio, and Internet of Things. The reasonable use of space resources and the development of the corresponding multi-antenna technology will become important technical means for B4G performance improvement. At the same time, reasonable resource scheduling, multi-user collaboration, multi-cell cooperation, and anti-interference methods have become essential for supporting the development of B4G.

Table 6.5. Comparison of key parameters of 3G and 4G.

System	3G	4G
Network architecture	Based on extensive cellular	Integrated WLAN and WAN
Bit rate	384–2 084 kbit/s	20–100 Mbit/s in moving mode
Frequency bandwidth	1800–2 400 MHz	2–8 GHz
Bandwidth	5–20 MHz	100 MHz or higher
Exchange	Circuit switching and data exchange	Data packet exchange
IP	One of many air interface protocols	All IP (IPv6.0)

6.1.2 *Characteristics of ground-based wireless communication systems*

Ground-based mobile communication systems have the following main characteristics compared to other communication means.

(1) **Using wireless channels to transmit information:** The wireless channel is different from the media transmission channel of constant parameters, and its important characteristics are multipath and time varying.[23] In mobile communication, the signal sent by the transmitter will reach the receiver in any of the following ways: direct reflection, diffraction, scatter, and other ways. This multipath transmission causes the receiver to receive multiple superimposed signals of the same signal, thus affecting the receiving signal stability. In addition, when the transmitter or receiver is in motion, the channel state will change with time, and the carrier frequency of the signal will also produce a frequency shift, namely the Doppler shift. This requires that the mobile communication system must have the ability to resist time-varying multipath fading, thereby ensuring communication quality.

(2) **Working under interference conditions:** Mobile communication systems are subject to various interferences from the outside world, such as natural or artificial white noise interference,[24] narrowband interference,[25] short-term interference,[26] and so on. In addition, the mobile communication system itself will also generate interference, including intermodulation interference,[27] adjacent channel interference,[28] co-channel interference,[29] multiple access interference between different users[30] and so on. This requires that the wireless communication system must have some anti-interference ability.

(3) **Limited spectrum resources:** Different mobile communication systems generally require operation in a specific frequency range. China has planned a public mobile communication frequency of 525 MHz, and the spectrum available for mobile communication is extremely limited. In order to meet the increase in the user demand, spectrum utilization can be improved only within the existing limited frequency band, which requires an appropriate radio resource management and allocation scheme to increase the transmission rate of the system under a given bandwidth.

(4) **Demanding equipment:** Since the mobile device is in an unfixed position for a long time, external vibrations and collisions may affect the device, which requires the device to have a strong adaptability. In addition, in order to meet the needs of different businesses and different

groups of people, mobile devices should have a simple and practical interface and operation mode, which brings a great challenge to the research and development of mobile devices.

Considering the above characteristics of mobile communication, in order to provide users with anytime and anywhere, fast and reliable communication services, various theories and related technologies have been extensively studied to overcome bottlenecks of mobile communication.

6.2 Multidimensional Joint Resource Management of Ground-Based Wireless Communication System

With the rapid development of the Internet, the fusion of multiple wireless communication networks and the Internet certainly will form a ubiquitous heterogeneous network characterized by a "core-access-terminal" hierarchical structure in the future. These hierarchical and heterogeneous network characteristics will also bring a huge challenge to future radio resource management, and the traditional cellular network-based radio resource management architecture can no longer meet this challenge. In this section, we introduce the space–time–frequency joint radio resource management architecture from the perspective of functional models and implementation architectures.[1]

6.2.1 *Radio resource management model based on a two-layer cognitive loop*

Since Dr. Mitola proposed the concept of cognitive radio (CR)[31] in 1999, cognitive technology has been widely used in various fields of wireless communication research. The purpose of cognition is to improve the intelligence of wireless communication systems, and the fundamental way to solve the complex problems of multidimensional radio resource allocation and heterogeneous network environment faced by future radio resource management systems is to improve the intelligence of the system. Therefore, in this section we mainly introduce an intelligent radio resource management model based on two-layer cognitive loop.

6.2.1.1 *Demand analysis*

Before introducing the intelligent radio resource management model based on the two-layer cognitive loop, let us analyze the design requirements of the future radio resource management architecture.

(1) Support the "core-access-terminal" hierarchical network structure, which can realize the organic combination of network-centralized, network-distributed, terminal decision-making multiple radio resource management modes.
(2) Support the heterogeneous network environment, which can not only realize the resource management of the unique radio access technology (RAT) but also coordinate the radio resource scheduling between different RATs.
(3) Support the effective use of airspace resources and realize the joint optimization configuration of multidimensional radio resources such as space, time, frequency, code, power, and rate.
(4) Support cognitive functions, realize intelligent radio resource management with learning ability, and acquire the relevant knowledge of radio resource management through data collection and mining.

It should be noted that the above demand analysis mainly focuses on some added functional demands of the future radio resource management relative to the traditional radio resource management and does not represent the design demands of the entire radio resource management system, which is also a major factor considered in the next design. Let us first introduce the design basis of the future radio resource management architecture, i.e., the two-layer cognitive loop model.

6.2.1.2 *Two-layer cognitive loop model*

Cognitive loops are the basic model of cognitive behavior and have been extensively studied in the field of wireless communications. In Ref. 32, Thomas *et al.* pointed out that for cognitive networks, the design of cognitive loops can be based on the observe–orient–decide–act (OODA) loop, which was proposed by Boyd and applied to military command. So far, OODA loops have been adopted in most cognitive loop designs. Balamuralidhar *et al.* applied the OODA-loop model to the wireless communication scenario,[33] and divided the whole cognitive process into five parts, including sense–analyze–decide–reconfigure–communicate (SADRC). At the same time, Fortuna *et al.* proposed their own cognitive loop model,[34] including sense–plan–decide–act–learn–policy (SPDALP) six states. It is important to note that the most significant model in cognitive networks is the observe–orient–plan–decide–act–learn (OOPDAL), a loop model of six links proposed by Mitola and Maguire.[31] The OOPDAL loop introduces the acquisition and application of knowledge into the loop and is used to describe the cognitive behavior of cognitive radio.

From a practical point of view, in wireless communication systems, especially in hierarchical heterogeneous networks (such as mobile Internet), entities with different roles or different tasks need to work together to achieve a certain goal. Some entities configured in the mobile Internet management and control plane, including transmission control entities, service control entities, and network management entities, which can operate in a unified plane, can usually easily obtain global information in the network. Therefore, the management and control entity is more suitable to make global optimization decisions based on global interests, including overall user preferences, network situation, and other information. The terminal is closer to the user side and can grasp the needs of different users and the real-time details in the application scenario. Therefore, it is more suitable to adaptively adjust the communication parameters and communication modes in real time through cooperative methods under the suggestion of the control and management entity. However, due to the differences in geographical location, service functions, hardware, and software, the functions of these entities will be limited by different conditions. Based on the above analysis, the single-loop cognitive model cannot accurately and fully abstract the cognitive behavior of different entities in the mobile internet. And it is in desperate need of a clearer, more accurate cognitive model to characterize cognitive behavior in complex network scenarios. Based on this, a hierarchical cognitive structure, a two-layer cognitive loop model,[35] was proposed to match the cognitive behavior of different entities in the mobile Internet in the process of management, role division, and interaction.

As shown in Fig. 6.1, the two-layer cognitive loop model includes decision loops: OOPDAL loop and execution loop (OODA loop), where the OOPDAL loop can run on the centralized management platform and play the role of the "brain" in the management and control system to provide intelligent strategies and guidance. At the same time, based on the strategy delivered by OOPDAL and the scene information collected in the actual application, the OODA loop completes the adaptive parameter reconfiguration. The results of the two-layer cognitive loop include the adjustment of the state, or the execution of the operation will eventually act on the external world and receive corresponding feedback from the external world. In this way, the operation of the entire loop is continuously adjusted, so that the system can get better benefits.

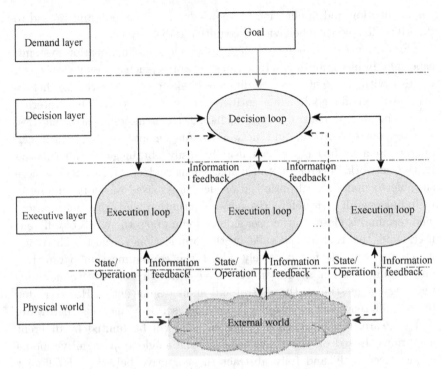

Fig. 6.1.   Two-layer cognitive loop model.

From a systemic point of view, the two-layer cognitive loop model can be considered as an open system, which means that the system can exchange information with the outside world at any time, including network status, manager's intention, and so on. In this open system, all information from the outside world is treated as an input parameter. At the same time, network operation commands issued from the decision entity are treated as output parameters. Once a request from the demand layer is received, the decision platform will develop an optimal strategy based on the collected information and historical communication rules. In some scenarios, a decision component can provide optimization decisions to multiple execution components simultaneously. It is generally considered that two different loops will undertake different tasks, and the two loops will also exhibit different characteristics. This chapter compares the characteristics of the execution loop with the decision loop, as shown in Table 6.6.

Table 6.6.   Comparison of characteristics between the decision loop and the execution loop

Decision loop	Execution loop
Qualitative description	Quantitative description
Develop strategies	Optimize control with strategy as a guide.
The process of generating a strategy is quasi-real time; the process of learning is not real time.	Real-time control
Human–machine (network) combination, people in the loop.	Autocomplete by machine
Smart, learning	Adaptive, agile
Relatively active	Relatively passive

(1) Decision loop

Table 6.6 shows that the decision loop uses learning as a means to develop a macro-strategy for the execution loop and plays the role of the source of intelligent mobile Internet intelligence. The decision loop can abstractly manage and control cognitive behavior in the platform entity, including network management entities, transmission control entities, service control entities, and so on. From Table 6.6, the operation of the decision loop will be a human–machine (network) combination process. On the one hand, people can generalize knowledge and even input expert knowledge into the rule base. On the other hand, through the machine to mine the massive data in the network, valuable communication rules will be obtained. These long-term statistical rules will provide further knowledge support for future communication to improve the user experience in the mobile Internet. Generally, from the perspective of practical application, the learning process of massive data in the decision loop is offline and relatively active. In order to provide more flexibility and adaptability to the execution loop, the policy set developed by the decision-making entity is basically a qualitative description and is issued in the form of a regular representation that the execution entity can understand. Based on the cognitive loop model

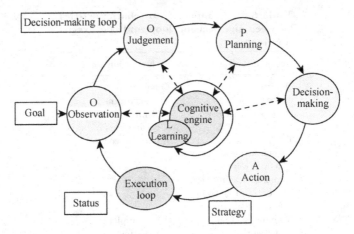

Fig. 6.2. Decision-making loop model OOPDAL.

proposed in Ref. 31, the decision loop model is designed as the OOPDAL model shown in Fig. 6.2.

The core component of the OOPDAL loop is a cognitive engine based on artificial intelligence technology. Different from the cognitive model in Ref. 31, the OOPDAL loop separates the learning process into an independent part. The main reason is that in the face of complex application backgrounds in the mobile Internet, massive communication data and complex network status will inevitably make the learning process impossible to complete in real time. And the decision-making process requires the strategy to be a quasi-real-time process; therefore, it is necessary to set the learning process to an independent offline mode. In addition, the independent extraction of the learning session will highlight the "brain" status of the cognitive engine component in the decision-making loop and form a unique cognitive source. The OOPDAL loop consists of six parts: observation, judgment, planning, decision-making, action, and learning. Detailed introduction and analysis will be shown in the following points:

- **Observation:** The observation component is treated as the information input to the open system. The input information includes the intention of the network administrator, the real-time resource status of the entire network, the information feedback of the user side, the status of collecting the execution loop report, and actively collecting the required information and storing it in the database.

- **Judgment:** The judgment component will pre-process the received information and form a global situation under the current scene based on the pre-processed information and the knowledge support of the cognitive engine (CE).
- **Planning:** Based on the global situation, combined with the knowledge support of the established input target and the cognitive engine, the planning component will formulate a set of possible strategies.
- **Decision-making:** Based on the rules of the cognitive engine and the preferences of the user, the decision-making component prioritizes the decision set and determines the final policy output.
- **Action:** The action component will deliver the final set of policies to the relevant entities which execute the loop.
- **Learning:** Learning component is the core part of the decision-making loop and will influence the entire decision process, including observation, positioning, planning, and decision-making.

The most important learning methods in the decision-making loop include artificial intelligence methods such as data mining, learning, and reasoning techniques. The learning component, on the one hand, will reduce the dimension of massive data and, on the other hand, will help CE understand the data. By extracting relevant information, the CE will form the current user requirements and globally optimal knowledge or rules in the network scenario. In the following, the structure of the cognitive engine will be emphatically introduced. The cognitive engine includes four major components: database, learning machine, inference engine, and knowledge base. At the same time, it strengthens the status of the item human in the loop, as shown in Fig. 6.3.

- **Database:** The database stores all historical data related to the communication process,[36] including user information, service request level (VIP or common user), scenario information, network status, network resource distribution, user feedback, and so on. In practical applications, database design and application are closely related, and the entries of the database must be consistent with the characteristics of the communication scene.
- **Learning machine:** The learning machine will be used for inductive reasoning. The main processes include learning task modeling, historical data mining, and acquiring relevant knowledge or rules.
- **Knowledge Base:** The knowledge base will be used to store formatting rules obtained through inductive reasoning. At the same time, the

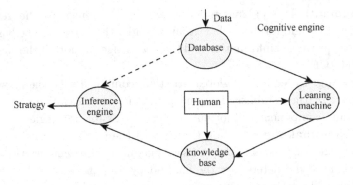

Fig. 6.3. Structure of the cognitive engine.

professional experience of human (experts) will also be added to the knowledge base as a practical rule.

- **Inference engine:** The inference engine will be used for deductive reasoning. According to the rules in the knowledge base and the current network status and user information, the inference engine predicts and outputs the relevant execution strategy by associating effective rules.

- **Human:** Human occupies a relatively special position in the cognitive engine. On the one hand, for special learning tasks, human will assist the learning machine to model the learning process, which is an important manifestation of the combination of man and machine. On the other hand, when the intelligence of the cognitive engine is not perfect or the engine is started at one initial stage, human inputs the expert knowledge into the rule base, and at the same time corrects the current rule according to his own prior knowledge. Therefore, the role of human in the cognitive engine is to better improve the cognitive engine. And as the intelligence of the cognitive engine increases, the role of human will gradually weaken until the cognitive engine runs autonomously, and then exits.

(2) Execution loop

Under the guidance of the macro-policy of the decision-making loop, the execution loop executes the delivered policy in an adaptive manner. Therefore, the execution loop remains agile and flexible. The execution loop can run on related entities such as routers, base stations, and terminals. These entities can perform optimization strategies in a distributed manner, change

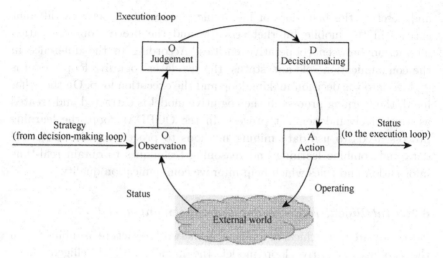

Fig. 6.4. Execution loop model OODA.

the state of the network, and respond to the external environment, and finally adaptively achieve the desired quality of service. The execution loop usually consists of an observation component, a positioning component, a decision component, and an action component, as shown in Fig. 6.4.

- **Observation:** The observation component will receive the policy delivered by the decision-making loop and collect real-time external environment information of the execution entity.
- **Judgment:** Carry out an analysis and inference of the external environment state, and obtain a relative objective operation.
- **Decision-making:** Take the strategy delivered by the upper decision-making loop from the policy library, perform optimization according to the optimization target, and determine the operation and parameters of the corresponding entity.
- **Action:** The action component outputs the most appropriate configuration parameters to specific execution entities, such as routers and base stations, and reports the status to the decision-making loop.

Comparing the two-layer cognitive loop model with the OOPDAL cognitive loop proposed by Mitola, the primary difference is that the single-loop structure is extended to a generalized hierarchical structure. In addition, the two-loop cognitive model has two main different characteristics. On the one hand, the two-layer cognitive loop model can accurately abstract and describe the behaviors of hierarchical cooperation between different entities in the mobile Internet scenario and the process of information interaction between cooperative entities. According to the difference in the communication role and status, the two-layer cognitive loop model is divided into the decision-making loop and the execution loop. On the other hand, the learning process in the cognitive model is extracted and treated as a relatively independent process. In the OOPDAL loop, the learning process needs to use data mining methods to process massive historical data and combine learning and reasoning techniques to obtain real-time information and rules which help improve communication quality.

6.2.2 *Intelligent radio resource management model*

For the future hierarchical heterogeneous network structure, combined with the two-layer cognitive loop model, the model of the intelligent radio resource management should adopt a hierarchical structure, namely the core layer, the access layer, and the terminal layer, as shown in Fig. 6.5. The core layer refers to the public management entity in the core network, including the advanced radio resource management (ARRM) functional entity and the cognitive engine functional entity. The access layer refers to the radio resource management entity in the access network, including the local radio resource management (LRRM) functional entity. The terminal layer is a radio resource management entity on the terminal side, including the terminal decision management (TDM) functional entity.

The ARRM entity is mainly used for admission control and load balancing between heterogeneous networks. Preemptive traffic control can be achieved through admission control, thus effectively preventing network

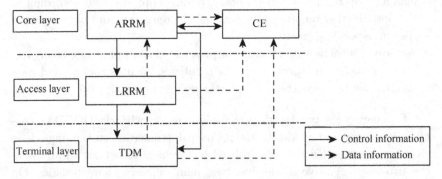

Fig. 6.5. Intelligent radio resource management system model.

congestion. The ARRM can generate the radio resource management policy and the radio access network selection policy of different radio access networks according to the relevant knowledge in the CE and send the LRRM and the TDM in a recommended form, and then the LRRM and the TDM make the final decision according to the delivered policy. It can effectively deal with some unexpected events in this way. The CE entity can collect and store a large amount of related data of the terminal and the radio access network and learn and mine the data to form related domain knowledge to guide the generation of the ARRM policy. The LRRM entity mainly determines the allocation scheme of radio resources, such as space, time, and frequency, according to the ARRM delivery policy. The TDM entity makes a decision according to the radio access network selection policy generated by the ARRM and performs reconfiguration of the waveform parameters on the terminal according to the decision.

In the following, we will make a detailed introduction of the functions of the functional entities in the intelligent radio resource management model and their relationship, as shown in Fig. 6.6.

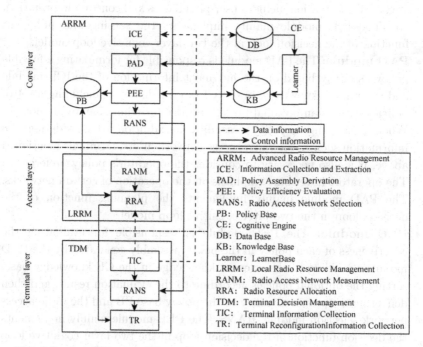

Fig. 6.6. Intelligent radio resource management function architecture.

6.2.2.1 *Advanced radio resource management*

ARRM mainly includes five functional modules: information collection and extraction (ICE), policy assembly derivation (PAD), policy efficiency evaluation (PEE), radio access network selection (RANS), and policy base (PB).

- **ICE module**: The ICE module is responsible for collecting network information of each radio access network (RAN), including the network load, coverage, and so on. The information can be collected periodically by LRRM or by way of inquiry. According to the collection of RAN information, ICE will determine whether the network load exceeds the threshold, whether the load between RANs is balanced, whether switching is required, and so on. In addition, the ICE module will also accept the network access requests from the terminal TDM and collect relevant terminal and user information. Terminal information includes terminal capabilities (mainly refers to the access mode supported by the terminal), terminal status (terminal location, mobile speed, currently available network, etc.), and the quality of service (QoS) requirements, etc.; user information includes user preferences and contract information, etc. The ICE module mainly implements the sensing and judgment function of the decision loop in the two-layer cognitive loop model.

- **PAD module:** The PAD module is responsible for formulating a feasible policy assembly based on the judgment information of the ICE module and the related knowledge in the CE knowledge base, including a set of policies such as an optional target network for admission and handover. When generating a policy assembly, in addition to considering the information such as the radio access network, users, terminals mentioned above, it is also necessary to consider the operator's policy preferences. The operators have some emphasis on the operation of certain networks. The PAD module mainly implements the planning function of the decision loop in the two-layer cognitive loop model.

- **PEE module:** The PEE module is responsible for evaluating the effectiveness of each policy in the policy assembly generated by the PAD module according to the relevant knowledge in the CE knowledge base, sorting the optional policies according to the evaluation result, and then delivering the proposed policy to the policy base PB and the radio access network selection module, RANS. The PEE module mainly implements the decision function of the decision loop in the two-layer cognitive loop model.

- **RANS module:** The RANS module is responsible for making a suggestion to the policy for issuing the corresponding module of the terminal. The RANS module mainly implements the action function of the decision loop in the two-layer cognitive loop model.
- **PB:** The PB is responsible for storing the radio resource management policy generated by PEE and delivering the corresponding policy according to the radio resource allocation request of the radio access network.

6.2.2.2 *Cognitive engine*

The cognitive engine mainly includes three functional modules: data base (DB), Learner, and knowledge base (KB).

- **DB:** DB is responsible for storing all kinds of raw data, including different levels of data such as radio access network, terminal, and user as mentioned above. In addition, the DB also stores data such as user-returned quality of experience (QoE) and network performance of the radio access network feedback as a goal for further learning.
- **Learner:** The Learner is responsible for offline learning and data mining of the data in DB, forming expert domain knowledge, and storing knowledge in the knowledge base. The Learner can adopt a mechanism of regular learning. The timescale used for regular learning is much larger than the timescale used by the underlying adaptive radio resource allocation. The Learner can also use an event-triggered learning mechanism. For example, when the database is updated, it can trigger the Learner to learn new data.
- **KB:** KB is responsible for storing the knowledge gained from learning and issuing corresponding knowledge according to the requests of PAD and PEE in ARRM for guiding judgment and decision-making.

6.2.2.3 *Local radio resource management*

LRRM mainly includes two functional modules: radio access network measurement (RANM) and radio resource allocation (RRA).

- **RANM:** The RANM module is responsible for collecting various information on the access network and reporting the information to the ICE module in the ARRM and the database in the CE. The RANM module mainly implements the observation function of the execution loop in the two-layer cognitive loop model.

- **RRA:** The RRA module first determines whether to accept the recommendation according to the policy issued by the ARRM. If accepted, the RRA formulates a resource allocation scheme according to the observation information of the RANM and the corresponding policy. And if not accepted, the resource allocation scheme is directly formulated based on the observation information of the RANM. The resource allocation scheme includes the specific allocation of multidimensional resources such as space, time, frequency, and code. The RRA module mainly implements the judgment and decision function of the execution loop in the two-layer cognitive loop model.

6.2.2.4 *Terminal decision management*

TDM mainly includes three functional modules: terminal information collection (TIC), access network selection (RANS), and terminal reconfiguration (TR).

- **TIC:** The TIC module collects information on the terminal side, including terminal information and user information, and reports the information to the ICE module and database of ARRM. The TIC is also responsible for feeding back the user's QoE information for CE learning. TIC module mainly implements the observation function of the execution loop in the two-layer cognitive loop model.
- **RANS:** The RANS module is responsible for making decisions based on the recommendations issued by the RANS in the ARRM. The decision needs to be based on the user's preferences. For example, some users prefer to make their own access network selection decisions. This module mainly reflects the radio resource management mode of the terminal decision and implements the decision function of the execution loop in the two-layer cognitive loop model.
- **TR:** The TR module is responsible for implementing the reconfiguration of the terminal waveform parameters according to the access network selection policy issued by the RANS and the corresponding access network resource allocation scheme, so as to access the corresponding target network. The TR function requires terminal support, and the reconfiguration capability is also an important indicator for future heterogeneous network terminals. The TR module mainly implements the action function of the execution loop in the two-layer cognitive loop model.

In summary, the intelligent radio resource management model is based on a two-layer cognitive loop, fully considers the radio resource management requirements of future heterogeneous networks, and achieves the design goals proposed at the beginning of this section. The ARRM and CE functional entities perform coarse-grained, large-time-scale cooperation, and management of radio resource intelligence among heterogeneous networks, mainly implementing the corresponding functions of the decision-making loop in the two-layer loop, and implementing recommendations on the execution loop in the form of strategies. The LRRM and TR functional entities perform fine-grained and small-time-scale adaptive allocation of radio resources in the access network, mainly implementing the corresponding functions of the execution loop in the two-layer cognitive loop model, and feed back the results to the decision-making loop.

6.2.3 *Service-oriented radio resource management implementation architecture*

Traditional radio resource management architectures are tightly coupled structures, and the connections within the system depend on predefined languages, platforms, and interfaces. In a heterogeneous network environment, this tightly coupled architecture obviously cannot handle the complex radio resource management interaction problems between different manufacturers and different operators. In response to this problem, this section will introduce a loosely coupled implementation architecture for service-oriented radio resource management.

Service-oriented architecture (SOA)[37] is a software-style architecture which is a new phase of process-oriented, object-oriented, component-oriented software development and integration. It has been widely used in the development and integration of heterogeneous systems between enterprises. SOA-based systems consist of loosely coupled, platform-independent, and well-defined interfaces that can be flexibly combined to form applications through a Web-based publish/subscribe mechanism. As shown in Fig. 6.7, SOA has three main roles as follows: service registry, service provider, and service consumer. The service provider publishes the provided service description to the service registry for the service consumer. When the service consumer finds the required service in the service registry, the service can be binded and called according to the service description file. Such a service provider and service consumer can make a loosely coupled relationship through indirect addressing by a third party (service registry), which ensures the independence of service development and integration, and improves component reusability and system flexibility. Loose coupling is also the most prominent characteristic of SOA.

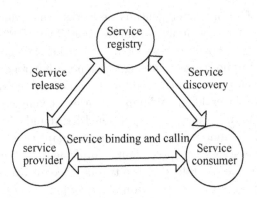

Fig. 6.7. Service-oriented architecture (SOA).

With the softwarization of various radio functions, the radio architecture and software architecture continue to align, and the software communication architecture (SCA) is the product of the development of software architecture to componentization. At present, the software architecture has evolved into a service-oriented phase, and thus, the service-oriented radio architecture (SORA)[38] came into being. SORA is an open distributed radio architecture which uses the design principles in SOA for the development and integration of wireless systems.

SORA is a service-oriented encapsulation of wireless system function modules based on Web service standards and uses the above principles to design and integrate the system, thereby improving the flexibility of the wireless system. There are two problems that need to be noted here. First, SORA is open, which means SORA adopts a series of open Web service standards, and it will facilitate system scalability and innovation. Second, SORA is distributed, and system components can be distributed on the network. System integration through indirect and remote calls to form a virtual radio system breaks through the traditional radio architecture and improves the reusability and loose coupling of system components.

6.2.4 *MIMO–OFDM system radio resource scheduling*

MIMO technology and orthogonal frequency division multiplexing (OFDM) are recognized as two key technologies in the physical layer of 4G systems. OFDM technology can effectively resist-multipath interference by using subcarrier transmission to convert frequency selective fading into flat fading, and MIMO technology can provide multiple subchannels for parallel transmission by using the multipath structure of the channel, which can greatly improve system capacity. The combination of MIMO and OFDM technology will become a powerful air interface technology for wireless communication systems in the future and can effectively improve spectrum utilization through rational allocation of multidimensional wireless resources. In the following, we will classify MIMO–OFDM technology into five categories and then introduce the related radio resource management strategies.

6.2.4.1 *Spatial multiplexing-based OFDM technology*

First, we introduce OFDM technology based on spatial multiplexing. It transmits multiple symbols simultaneously on multiple transmitting antennas by the spatial multiplexing technique, and the number of receiving antennas is greater than the number of transmitting antennas. The objectives of the optimization include the optimization of power efficiency, the quality of service for each user, the fairness of each user's service, and the generality of different multi-user detection algorithms.

6.2.4.2 *OFDM technology based on space–time coding/space–frequency coding/space–time–frequency coding*

We know that encoding MIMO–OFDM systems in time, frequency, and space can improve the reliability and robustness of information transmission. Therefore, we compare the OFDM techniques based on space–time coding/space–frequency coding/space–time–frequency coding and find that OFDM technology based on space–time coding has the lowest decoding complexity. OFDM technology based on space–frequency coding can minimize inter-user interference, and OFDM technology based on space–time–frequency coding can achieve end-to-end maximum diversity gain.

6.2.4.3 *Beamforming-based OFDM technology*

The beamforming-based OFDM technology mainly includes two types: one is an adaptive beamforming MIMO–OFDM system and the other is an eigen beamforming MIMO–OFDM system. The adaptive beamforming MIMO–OFDM system mainly adjusts the beamforming scheme to perform adaptive modulation and adaptive frequency domain power allocation according to the channel state. The eigen beamforming MIMO–OFDM system mainly utilizes the eigen beamforming technology to decompose the MIMO channel into multiple parallel subchannels. Under the premise of constraining the packet error rate, bit rate, and total transmitted power, the purpose of maximizing the total transmission rate is achieved by the dynamic subcarrier and bit allocation.

6.2.4.4 *OFDM technology based on antenna selection*

The OFDM technology based on antenna selection includes three types: the first type is an end-to-end single- input and single-output (SISO) antenna selection system; the second type is an end-to-end single-input and multi-output (SIMO) antenna selection system and a multi-input and single-output (MISO) antenna selection system; the third type is the end-to-end MIMO antenna selection system. The end-to-end SISO antenna selection system refers to selecting one antenna at the transmitting end and the receiving end to maximize the gain of the channel. The end-to-end SIMO antenna selection system selects an antenna at the transmitting end and uses the antenna array for maximum ratio combining reception at the receiving end. For different antenna selection schemes, we select the transmitting antenna with the largest signal-to-noise ratio at the receiving end. The end-to-end MISO antenna selection system uses transmitting beamforming at the transmitting end and an antenna at the receiving end. For different antenna selection schemes, we select the receiving antenna that maximizes the signal-to-noise ratio of the receiving end. For the end-to-end MIMO antenna selection system, we select antennas based on two aspects. The transmitting antenna group and the receiving antenna group which can provide the maximum beamforming gain can be selected, and the transmitting antenna group and the receiving antenna group which can provide the most parallel subchannels can also be selected. The former option mainly improves the reliability, and the latter option mainly improves the effectiveness of the system.

6.2.4.5 *Multi-user MIMO–OFDM technology*

The multi-user MIMO–OFDM technology mainly combines multi-user beamforming techniques of MIMO, such as zero-forcing beamforming, to optimize the MIMO–OFDM system while reducing inter-user interference.

It is also worth noting that the radio resource management technology of the MIMO–OFDM system mainly concentrates on the physical layer and the MAC layer, which belong to the dynamic resource allocation problem on a small timescale. These problems are generally at a lower level in the joint radio resource management architecture, and the resource allocation is performed in an adaptive manner, including adaptive allocation of multiple dimensions such as the subcarrier, subspace, rate, and power.

6.3 Multi-User Cooperative Transmission Method

The ground-based cooperative transmission system is a wireless communication system which serves multiple users. When considering the simultaneous access of multiple users, how to reasonably utilize the channel differences of different users to maximize the acquisition of space resources is the key to improving the overall performance of future wireless communication systems. This section describes how to use the multi-user cooperative transmission method to improve the overall performance and spectrum efficiency of the ground-based multi-user access system, focusing on key technologies such as orthogonal beamforming, multi-user relay beamforming, and multi-user selection.

6.3.1 *Orthogonal beamforming technology*

6.3.1.1 *System model*

Consider a scenario in which both multiple mobile communication users and fixed communication users access a channel, where the base station is equipped with N_t antennas, and the downlink has M subcarriers. A group is the group where the mobile users are located, and the B group is the group where the fixed users are located. The user priority in A is higher than that in B, which means the group B users cannot affect group A when accessing.

On subcarrier m, the base station broadcasts the combined signal $\mathbf{s}_m = \mathbf{s}_{A,m} + \mathbf{s}_{B,m}$ to all users, and

$$
\begin{aligned}
\mathbf{s}_{A,m} &= \mathbf{w}_{A,m} a_m \\
\mathbf{s}_{B,m} &= \mathbf{w}_{B,m} b_m
\end{aligned}
\tag{6.1}
$$

where a_m and b_m are the original signals transmitted to the group A users and the group B users respectively. $\mathbf{w}_{A,m}$ and $\mathbf{w}_{B,m}$ are the normalized beamforming vectors transmitted to group A and group B users, respectively, and $\|\mathbf{w}_{A,m}\| = \|\mathbf{w}_{B,m}\| = 1$. Define the signal power as $P_A = \mathrm{E}[|a_{m,q}|^2]$ and $P_B = \mathrm{E}[|b_m|^2]$. Assuming that the number of users in group A is K, the signal received by user k_m is

$$
x_{m,k_m} = \mathbf{h}_{m,k_m}^{\mathrm{H}} (\mathbf{s}_{A,m} + \mathbf{s}_{B,m}) + n_{m,k_m}
\tag{6.2}
$$

where $\mathbf{h}_{m,k_m}$ is the channel vector from the base station to user k_m in group A, n_{m,k_m} is a Gaussian white noise obeying the $\mathcal{CN}(0,\sigma^2)$ distribution with $k_m = 1, 2, \ldots, K$. Similarly, assuming that the number of users of group B is R, the user r_m in group B receives the signal as

$$y_{m,r_m} = \mathbf{g}_{m,r_m}^{\mathrm{H}}(\mathbf{s}_{\mathrm{I},m} + \mathbf{s}_{\mathrm{II},m}) + n_{m,r_m} \tag{6.3}$$

where $\mathbf{g}_{m,r_m}$ is the channel vector from the base station to user r_m in group **B**, n_{m,r_m} is a Gaussian white noise obeying the $\mathcal{CN}(0,\sigma^2)$ distribution with $r_m = 1, 2, \ldots, R$.

The transmitting beamforming system is shown in Fig. 6.8. Assume that there are actually Q users accessing in group A during a time period, and $Q \leq K$. At the same time, select one user from R users of group B and ensure that group B users reach the maximum throughput without affecting the normal communication of group A users.

Suppose you select Q user transmitting signals from group A, then

$$\mathbf{s}_{\mathrm{A},m} = \sum_{q=1}^{Q} \mathbf{w}_{\mathrm{A},m,q} a_{m,q} \tag{6.4}$$

$$\mathbf{s}_{\mathrm{B},m} = \mathbf{w}_{\mathrm{B},m} b_m$$

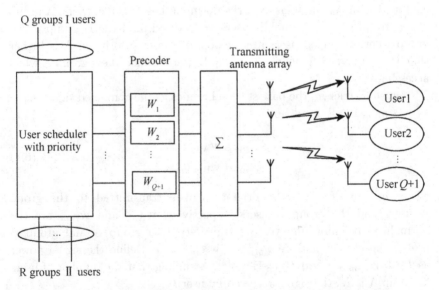

Fig. 6.8. **Block diagram of the transmitting beamforming system.**

6.3.1.2 *The user selection of group A*

Based on the methods of Refs. 39 and 40, the system performance is improved by selecting users whose channels are approximately orthogonal to each other to access the system. And then

$$1 - \frac{|\mathbf{h}_{m,k_m^i}^{\mathrm{H}} \mathbf{h}_{m,k_m^j}|^2}{\|\mathbf{h}_{m,k_m^i}\|^2 \|\mathbf{h}_{m,k_m^j}\|^2} > 1 - \varepsilon, \quad i,j = 1,2,\ldots,Q \quad (6.5)$$

where $\mathbf{h}_{m,k_m^q}$ is the channel vector of the qth user with $q = 1,2,\ldots,Q$. Assuming that the selected user channels are orthogonal to each other, namely

$$\begin{aligned} \mathbf{h}_{m,k_m^i} \perp \mathbf{h}_{m,k_m^j}, \quad &\forall m = 1,\ldots,M, \\ &i,j = 1,\ldots,Q, \\ &i \neq j \end{aligned} \quad (6.6)$$

Therefore, the beamforming matrix of the group A users can be expressed as

$$\mathbf{W}_{\mathrm{A},m} = \left[\frac{\mathbf{h}_{m,k_m^1}}{\|\mathbf{h}_{m,k_m^1}\|}, \ldots, \frac{\mathbf{h}_{m,k_m^Q}}{\|\mathbf{h}_{m,k_m^Q}\|} \right] \quad (6.7)$$

6.3.1.3 *Orthogonal beamforming*

The set of Q users in the group A selected on the subcarrier m is defined as $\mathcal{U}_m$, and the receiving SINR of the user k_m^q on the subcarrier m can be expressed as

$$\mathrm{SINR}_{\mathrm{A},m,k_m^q} = \frac{|\mathbf{h}_{m,k_m^q}^{\mathrm{H}} \mathbf{w}_{\mathrm{A},m,q}|^2 P_{\mathrm{A}}}{\sum\limits_{i=1,i\neq q}^{Q} |\mathbf{h}_{m,k_m^q}^{\mathrm{H}} \mathbf{w}_{\mathrm{A},m,i}|^2 P_{\mathrm{A}} + |\mathbf{h}_{m,k_m^q}^{\mathrm{H}} \mathbf{w}_{\mathrm{B},m,q}|^2 P_{\mathrm{B}} + \sigma^2} \quad (6.8)$$

where $\mathbf{h}_{m,k_m^i} \perp \mathbf{h}_{m,k_m^j}$, $\forall m = 1,\ldots,M, i \neq j$. For user k_m^q, the optimal beamforming vector which maximizes SINR can be expressed as

$$\mathbf{w}_{\mathrm{A},m,q} = \frac{\mathbf{h}_{m,k_m^q}}{\|\mathbf{h}_{m,k_m^q}\|} \quad (6.9)$$

The receiving SINR of user r_m in group B is

$$\mathrm{SINR}_{\mathrm{B},m,r_m} = \frac{|\mathbf{g}_{m,r_m}^{\mathrm{H}} \mathbf{w}_{\mathrm{B},m}|^2 P_{\mathrm{B}}}{\sum\limits_{i=1}^{Q} |\mathbf{g}_{m,r_m}^{\mathrm{H}} \mathbf{w}_{\mathrm{A},m,i}|^2 P_{\mathrm{A}} + \sigma^2} \quad (6.10)$$

In Eq. (6.10), in the case where $\mathbf{w}_{A,m,i}$ is known, the maximization of SINR can be realized by maximizing $|\mathbf{g}_{m,r_m}^{\mathrm{H}} \mathbf{w}_{B,m}|$, then the optimization problem of maximizing SINR under orthogonal constraints can be expressed as

$$
\begin{aligned}
&\text{maximize} \quad |\mathbf{g}_{m,r_m}^{\mathrm{H}} \mathbf{w}_{B,m}| \\
&\text{subject to} \quad \mathbf{w}_{B,m} \perp \mathbf{h}_{m,k_m^i}, \quad \forall i = 1, \ldots, Q \\
&\qquad\qquad\quad \mathbf{h}_{m,k_m^i} \perp \mathbf{h}_{m,k_m^j}, \quad i, j = 1, \ldots, Q, \ i \neq j
\end{aligned}
\tag{6.11}
$$

In order to simplify the above optimization problem, we omit all subscripts, then the problem can be restated as

$$
\begin{aligned}
&\text{maximize} \quad |\mathbf{g}^{\mathrm{H}} \mathbf{w}| \\
&\text{subject to} \quad \mathbf{w} \perp \mathbf{h}_i, \quad \forall i = 1, \ldots, Q \\
&\qquad\qquad\quad \mathbf{h}_i \perp \mathbf{h}_j, \quad i, j = 1, \ldots, Q, \ i \neq j
\end{aligned}
$$

Assume that $\mathbf{v}$ is an arbitrary $L \times 1$-dimensional vector, and vector $\mathbf{v} - \frac{\mathbf{h}_i}{\|\mathbf{h}_i\|} \frac{\mathbf{h}_i^{\mathrm{H}} \mathbf{v}}{\|\mathbf{h}_i\|}$ is a vector perpendicular to $\mathbf{h}_i$. By subtracting $\mathbf{v}$ from the projection of $\mathbf{v}$ in multiple perpendicular directions, a vector perpendicular to the subspace formed by the set of orthogonal vectors is obtained, namely

$$
\mathbf{v} - \sum_{i=1}^{Q} \frac{\mathbf{h}_i}{\|\mathbf{h}_i\|} \frac{\mathbf{h}_i^{\mathrm{H}} \mathbf{v}}{\|\mathbf{h}_i\|}
\tag{6.12}
$$

By traversing $\mathbf{v}$, we can get all the vectors perpendicular to the subspace composed of vector $\mathbf{h}_i$, then the domain $\mathbf{w}$ of the optimization problem can be represented by $\mathbf{v}$ as follows:

$$
\begin{aligned}
\mathbf{w} &= \mathbf{v} - \sum_{i=1}^{Q} \frac{\mathbf{h}_i}{\|\mathbf{h}_i\|} \frac{\mathbf{h}_i^{\mathrm{H}} \mathbf{v}}{\|\mathbf{h}_i\|} \\
&= \left(\mathbf{I} - \sum_{i=1}^{Q} \frac{\mathbf{h}_i \mathbf{h}_i^{\mathrm{H}}}{\|\mathbf{h}_i\|^2} \right) \mathbf{v}
\end{aligned}
\tag{6.13}
$$

and the conditional constraint of $\|\mathbf{w}\| = 1$ is achieved by adjusting $\mathbf{v}$.

The objective function $|\mathbf{g}^{\mathrm{H}} \mathbf{w}|$ is transformed to

$$
|\mathbf{g}^{\mathrm{H}} \mathbf{w}| = \left| \mathbf{g}^{\mathrm{H}} \left(\mathbf{I} - \sum_{i=1}^{Q} \frac{\mathbf{h}_i \mathbf{h}_i^{\mathrm{H}}}{\|\mathbf{h}_i\|^2} \right) \mathbf{v} \right|
\tag{6.14}
$$

and thus,

$$\mathbf{w} = \left(\mathbf{I} - \sum_{i=1}^{Q} \frac{\mathbf{h}_i \mathbf{h}_i^{\mathrm{H}}}{\|\mathbf{h}_i\|^2} \right) \mathbf{v}$$

$$= \left(\mathbf{I} - \sum_{i=1}^{Q} \frac{\mathbf{h}_i \mathbf{h}_i^{\mathrm{H}}}{\|\mathbf{h}_i\|^2} \right) \left(\mathbf{I} - \sum_{i=1}^{Q} \frac{\mathbf{h}_i \mathbf{h}_i^{\mathrm{H}}}{\|\mathbf{h}_i\|^2} \right)^{\mathrm{H}} \mathbf{g} \qquad (6.15)$$

Since matrix $\mathbf{X} = \left(\mathbf{I} - \sum_{i=1}^{Q} \frac{\mathbf{h}_i \mathbf{h}_i^{\mathrm{H}}}{\|\mathbf{h}_i\|^2} \right)$ has the characteristics of $\mathbf{X}^{\mathrm{H}} = \mathbf{X}$ and $\mathbf{X}^n = \mathbf{X}$ $(n = 1, 2, \dots)$ Eq. (6.15) can be further simplified as

$$\mathbf{w} = \left(\mathbf{I} - \sum_{i=1}^{Q} \frac{\mathbf{h}_i \mathbf{h}_i^{\mathrm{H}}}{\|\mathbf{h}_i\|^2} \right) \mathbf{g}$$

Normalize the vector to get the final form as

$$\hat{\mathbf{w}}_{\mathrm{B},m} = \left(\mathbf{I} - \sum_{i=1}^{Q} \frac{\mathbf{h}_{m,k_m^i} \mathbf{h}_{m,k_m^i}^{\mathrm{H}}}{\|\mathbf{h}_{m,k_m^i}\|^2} \right) \mathbf{g}_{m,r_m}$$

$$= \left(\mathbf{I} - \sum_{i=1}^{Q} \mathbf{w}_{\mathrm{A},m,k_m^i} \mathbf{w}_{\mathrm{A},m,k_m^i}^{\mathrm{H}} \right) \mathbf{g}_{m,r_m}$$

$$= (\mathbf{I} - \mathbf{W}_{\mathrm{A},m} \mathbf{W}_{\mathrm{A},m}^{\mathrm{H}}) \mathbf{g}_{m,r_m} \qquad (6.16)$$

where $\mathbf{W}_{\mathrm{A},m} = [\mathbf{w}_{\mathrm{A},m,1}, \mathbf{w}_{\mathrm{A},m,2}, \dots, \mathbf{w}_{\mathrm{A},m,Q}]$.

In summary, the group B user beamforming vector which makes Eq. (6.11) reach the optimal solution is

$$\mathbf{w}_{\mathrm{B},m} = \frac{1}{\|\hat{\mathbf{w}}_{\mathrm{B},m}\|} \hat{\mathbf{w}}_{\mathrm{B},m} \qquad (6.17)$$

6.3.2 *Beamforming technology for multi-user relay systems*

In order to enable the relay system to serve multiple users at the same time, each user can only occupy one orthogonal frequency division multiplexing subcarrier. Although this can avoid inter-user interference, the system's spectrum resource utilization is low. Considering the space diversity gain of the MIMO technology, the spectrum resource utilization of the OFDM system can be further improved. Multiple users can use a certain beamforming method to simultaneously transmit information on the same subcarrier with MIMO space diversity.

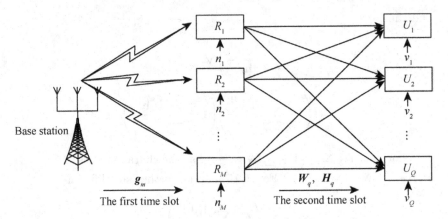

Fig. 6.9. Block diagram of the multi-user relay system.

Consider that the base station has N antennas and transmits mixed signals to Q users through M relays with $N > M$, and assume that both the relay and the user are equipped with a single antenna. All relays use a 2-slot amplify-and-forward strategy. The system model is shown in Fig. 6.9.

In the first time slot, using the MIMO space diversity technology, the base station transmits signal s_q to each relay, and the signal y_m received by relay m can be expressed as

$$y_m = \mathbf{g}_m \sum_{q=1}^{Q} \mathbf{b}_q s_q + n_m, \quad m = 1, 2, \ldots, M \tag{6.18}$$

where $\mathbf{g}_m$ is the channel vector from the base station to the relay m, $\mathbf{b}_q$ is the beamforming vector transmitted by the base station, and n_m is the noise around the relay m.

In the second time slot, the relay uses beamforming technology to forward the signal to the user, and the signal received by the qth user is

$$r_q = \mathbf{H}_q \mathbf{W}_q \mathbf{y} + v_q$$

$$= \mathbf{H}_q \mathbf{W}_q \mathbf{G} s_q + \mathbf{H}_q \mathbf{W}_q \mathbf{G} \sum_{i \neq q}^{Q} s_i + \mathbf{H}_q \mathbf{W}_q \mathbf{n} + v_q, \quad q = 1, 2, \ldots, Q$$

$$\tag{6.19}$$

where $\mathbf{H}_q$ is the channel matrix of all relays to user q, $\mathbf{W}_q$ is the beamforming vector for all relays to user q, $\mathbf{y}$ is the signal vector received by all relays with $\mathbf{y} = [y_1, y_2, \ldots, y_M]^{\mathrm{T}}$, v_q is the noise near the user q, $\mathbf{G}$ is the channel matrix from the base station to all relays with $\mathbf{G} = [\mathbf{g}_1, \mathbf{g}_2, \ldots, \mathbf{g}_M]^{\mathrm{T}}$, and $\mathbf{n}$ is the noise near all relays with $\mathbf{n} = [n_1, n_2, \ldots, n_M]^{\mathrm{T}}$.

The SINR received by user q is

$$\mathrm{SINR}_q = \frac{P_s^q}{P_s^q + P_n^q}$$

$$= \frac{P_q |\mathbf{H}_q \mathbf{W}_q \mathbf{G}|^2}{\sum\limits_{i=1, i \neq q}^{Q} P_i |\mathbf{H}_q \mathbf{W}_q \mathbf{G}|^2 + |\mathbf{H}_q \mathbf{W}_q|^2 N + N_q} \tag{6.20}$$

where $P_q = \mathrm{E}[|s_q|^2]$, $P_i = \mathrm{E}[|s_i|^2]$, $i \neq q$, and N and N_q represent the noise power of n_m and v_q, namely $n_m \sim \mathcal{CN}(\mathbf{I}, N)$, $v_q \sim \mathcal{CN}(\mathbf{I}, N_q)$.

By this model, the following typical optimization problem is considered:

$$\min_{\mathbf{W}_q} \sum_{m=1}^{M} P_m$$

$$\text{subject to } \mathrm{SINR}_q \geq \mathrm{SINR}_q^*, \quad q = 1, 2, \ldots, Q \tag{6.21}$$

where SINR_q^* is the received SNR limitation of user q.

For the maximization problem of worst user received SNR under relay power constraints, its constraints can be divided into two categories as follows:

(1) Total power constraint of the relay

$$\max_{\mathbf{W}_q} \min_{q} \mathrm{SINR}_q$$

$$\text{subject to } \sum_{m=1}^{M} P_m \leq P_t, \quad m = 1, 2, \ldots, M \tag{6.22}$$

where P_t is the total power constraint of the relay.

(2) Individual power constraint of each relay

$$\max_{\mathbf{W}_q} \min_{q} \ \mathrm{SINR}_q$$

$$\text{subject to } P_m \leq P_m^*, \ m = 1, 2, \ldots, M \tag{6.23}$$

where P_m^* is the individual power constraint of each relay.

Both optimization problems can be solved by the convex optimization method such as SDP. Zheng and Blosttein[41] studied the scenario in which a multi-antenna base station transmits signals to multiple users through a relay system and proposed an iterative algorithm for jointly optimizing the base station precoding matrix and the relay beamforming matrix. It preliminarily explores the scenario where there is a relay user interference signal, but it only considers how to minimize the total power consumed by the base station and the relay in the case of user SINR limitation. However, for multi-user systems, the problem of maximizing the SINR of the worst user under power constraints and the optimal design of the antenna selection matrix in the multi-antenna base station have not been effectively solved.

6.3.3 Multi-user selection strategy[a]

In some cases, we need to select a set of optimal users from multiple candidate users to access the MIMO channel at the same time. For this problem, we focus on how to select a multi-user selection strategy for selecting a set of optimal users to access the system simultaneously from multiple candidate users.[42]

6.3.3.1 System model

It is assumed that in a multi-user MIMO system, Q users transmit signals to the base station through the uplink, where each user is equipped with P transmitting, antennas, and the base station is equipped with N receiving antennas. The user's signal length is L, $\mathbf{H}_q$ and $\mathbf{S}_q$, respectively, represent the $N \times P$-dimensional channel matrix and $P \times L$-dimensional signal matrix of each user with $q = 1, 2, \ldots, Q$. Different MIMO detectors are used at the base station to detect signals from various users. We assume that all users share the uplink channel and assume that the number of users who can simultaneously access is $(K \leq \lfloor \frac{N}{P} \rfloor)$.

Assuming that the MIMO channel is a block-fading channel, if $Q = 9$ and $K = 4$ in a certain time slot, the first, fourth, sixth, and seventh users are selected to access the channel at the same time, as shown in Fig. 6.10.

There are many factors affecting user selection, such as transmission optimization,[43] information flow status, and user priority.[44, 45] Due to space limitation, we will only discuss the options for user selection based on channel conditions.

(1) Exhaustive selection strategy

User selection based on ML and linear detection: According to the system model, assuming that the length of the signal transmitted by each user is

---

[a]Reprinted/adapted by permission from Springer Nature Customer Service Centre GmbH: Springer "Low Complexity MIMO Detection" by Bai L and Choi J, 2012.

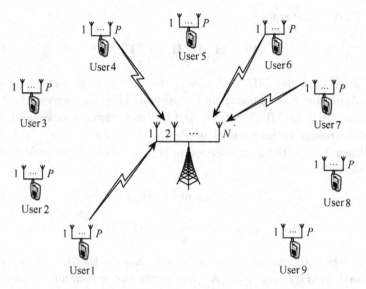

Fig. 6.10. User selection for a multi-user MIMO system.

$L = 1$, the signal received by the base station can be expressed as

$$\mathbf{y}_\mathcal{Q} = \mathbf{H}_\mathcal{Q}\mathbf{s}_\mathcal{Q} + \mathbf{n} \tag{6.24}$$

where $\mathcal{Q}$ is the selected user serial number set $\mathcal{Q} = \{q_{(1)}, q_{(2)}, \ldots, q_{(k)}\}$, with $q_{(k)}$ representing the number of the kth selected user in all candidate users ($\mathcal{Q} = \{q_{(1)}, q_{(2)}, q_{(3)}, q_{(4)}\} \subseteq \{1, 4, 6, 7\}$). $\mathbf{H}_\mathcal{Q} = [\mathbf{H}_{q_{(1)}}, \mathbf{H}_{q_{(2)}}, \ldots, \mathbf{H}_{q_{(K)}}]$ denotes an $N \times KP$-dimensional combined channel matrix, $\mathbf{s}_\mathcal{Q} = [s_{q_{(1)}}, s_{q_{(2)}}, \ldots, s_{q_{(k)}}]^T$ denotes a $KP \times 1$-dimensional combined transmission signal vector, and $\mathbf{n}$ denotes an $N \times 1$-dimensional Gaussian white noise.

For simplicity, we omit the user number $\mathcal{Q}$, and then the estimated signals for ML detection and linear detection can be written as follows:

$$\hat{\mathbf{s}} = \arg \min_{\mathbf{s} \in \mathcal{S}^{KP}} \|\mathbf{y} - \mathbf{H}\mathbf{s}\|^2 \tag{6.25}$$

and

$$\hat{\mathbf{s}} = \mathbf{W}^H \mathbf{y} \tag{6.26}$$

In Eq. (6.26), the ZF detector is

$$\mathbf{W} = \mathbf{H}(\mathbf{H}^H\mathbf{H})^{-1} \tag{6.27}$$

MMSE detector is

$$\mathbf{W} = \mathbf{H}\left(\mathbf{H}^H\mathbf{H} + \frac{N_0}{E_s}\mathbf{I}\right)^{-1} \tag{6.28}$$

For a particular MIMO detector, the detection performance mainly depends on the channel matrix in the system. Therefore, we use the MDist or ME strategy for ML detection. And for linear detection, we need to use the ME strategy for user selection.

When $K > 1$, the user selection policy based on MDist or ME can be expressed as

$$\mathcal{Q}_{\text{MDist}} = \arg\max_{\mathcal{Q}} \mathcal{D}(\mathbf{H}_{\mathcal{Q}}) \tag{6.29}$$

$$\mathcal{Q}_{\text{ME}} = \arg\max_{\mathcal{Q}} \lambda_{\min}(\mathbf{H}_{\mathcal{Q}}^H\mathbf{H}_{\mathcal{Q}}) \tag{6.30}$$

where $\mathcal{D}(\mathbf{H}_{\mathcal{Q}})$ represents the lattice of the shortest length non-zero vector produced by $\mathbf{H}_{\mathcal{Q}}$, and $\lambda_{\min}(\mathbf{A})$ represents the minimum eigenvalue of matrix $\mathbf{A}$. When using the ML detector, the MDist selection strategy is used to select K users with the lowest bit error rate and the ME strategy is used to select K users with the highest SNR.

By the LR transformation based on the CLLL algorithm, the user number in Eq. (6.24) can be expressed as follows:

$$\begin{aligned}\mathbf{G} &= \mathbf{H}\mathbf{U}^{-1} \\ \mathbf{c} &= \mathbf{U}\mathbf{s}\end{aligned} \tag{6.31}$$

where $\mathbf{G}$ is a matrix with approximately orthogonal column vectors, $\mathbf{U}$ is a unitary matrix. Equation (6.24) can then be rewritten as follows:

$$\mathbf{y} = \mathbf{G}\mathbf{c} + \mathbf{n} \tag{6.32}$$

Using $\mathbf{W}$ to represent the linear filter of matrix $\mathbf{G}$, the judgment of $\mathbf{c}$ is expressed as

$$\hat{\mathbf{c}} = \lfloor \mathbf{W}^H\mathbf{y} \rceil \tag{6.33}$$

where LR-ZF filter is

$$\mathbf{W}^H = (\mathbf{G}^H\mathbf{G})^{-1}\mathbf{G}^H \tag{6.34}$$

LR-MMSE filter is

$$\mathbf{W}^H = \left(\mathbf{G}^H\mathbf{G} + \frac{N_0}{E_s}\mathbf{U}^{-H}\mathbf{U}^{-1}\right)^{-1}\mathbf{G}^H \tag{6.35}$$

For LR-based ZF-SIC detection, QR decomposition of matrix $\mathbf{G}$ in Eq. (6.32) is performed:

$$\mathbf{G} = \mathbf{QR} \qquad (6.36)$$

where $\mathbf{Q}$ is a unitary matrix, $\mathbf{R}$ is an upper triangular matrix, and Eq. (6.32) is rewritten as

$$\mathbf{y} = \mathbf{QRc} + \mathbf{n} \qquad (6.37)$$

Multiply $\mathbf{Q}^H$ on both sides of Eq. (6.37), then

$$\mathbf{Q}^H\mathbf{y} = \mathbf{Rc} + \mathbf{Q}^H\mathbf{n} \qquad (6.38)$$

Since $\mathbf{Q}^H\mathbf{n}$ and $\mathbf{n}$ have the same statistical properties, Eq. (6.38) can be rewritten as

$$\mathbf{Q}^H\mathbf{y} = \mathbf{Rc} + \mathbf{n} \qquad (6.39)$$

For LR-based MMSE-SIC detection, Eq. (6.24) can be extended as

$$\mathbf{y}_{\text{ex}} = \mathbf{H}_{\text{ex}}\mathbf{s} + \mathbf{n}_{\text{ex}} \qquad (6.40)$$

where $\mathbf{y}_{\text{ex}} = \begin{bmatrix} \mathbf{y} \\ \mathbf{0} \end{bmatrix}$, $\mathbf{H}_{\text{ex}} = \begin{bmatrix} \mathbf{H} \\ \sqrt{\dfrac{N_0}{E_\text{s}}}\mathbf{I} \end{bmatrix}$, $\mathbf{n}_{\text{ex}} = \begin{bmatrix} \mathbf{n} \\ -\sqrt{\dfrac{N_0}{E_\text{s}}}\mathbf{s} \end{bmatrix}$

After the LR transformation,

$$\mathbf{H}_{\text{ex}} = \mathbf{G}_{\text{ex}}\mathbf{U}_{\text{ex}} \qquad (6.41)$$

where $\mathbf{U}_{\text{ex}}$ is the unimodular matrix, and performing on QR decomposition on $\mathbf{G}_{\text{ex}}$, we get

$$\mathbf{G}_{\text{ex}} = \mathbf{Q}_{\text{ex}}\mathbf{R}_{\text{ex}} \qquad (6.42)$$

where $\mathbf{Q}_{\text{ex}}$ is a unitary matrix, $\mathbf{R}_{\text{ex}}$ is an upper triangular matrix. Eq. (6.40) can then be rewritten as

$$\mathbf{y}_{\text{ex}} = \mathbf{Q}_{\text{ex}}\mathbf{R}_{\text{ex}}\mathbf{U}_{\text{ex}}\mathbf{s} + \mathbf{n}_{\text{ex}} \qquad (6.43)$$

Multiply $\mathbf{Q}_{\text{ex}}^H$ on both sides,

$$\mathbf{Q}_{\text{ex}}^H\mathbf{y}_{\text{ex}} = \mathbf{R}_{\text{ex}}\mathbf{U}_{\text{ex}}\mathbf{s} + \mathbf{Q}_{\text{ex}}^H\mathbf{n}_{\text{ex}}$$
$$= \mathbf{R}_{\text{ex}}\tilde{\mathbf{c}} + \tilde{\mathbf{n}} \qquad (6.44)$$

where, $\tilde{\mathbf{c}} = \mathbf{U}_{\text{ex}}\mathbf{s}$, $\tilde{\mathbf{n}} = \mathbf{Q}_{\text{ex}}^H\mathbf{n}_{\text{ex}}$.

So far, the signals $\mathbf{c}$ and $\tilde{\mathbf{c}}$ can be detected using the SIC method according to Eqs. (6.39) and (6.44). The ME standard for LR linear detector can be expressed as

$$\mathcal{Q}_{\mathrm{ME}} = \arg\max_{\mathcal{Q}} \lambda_{\min}(\mathbf{G}_{\mathcal{Q}}^{\mathrm{H}}\mathbf{G}_{\mathcal{Q}}) \tag{6.45}$$

Similarly, the MD standard for LR-SIC-based detection is

$$\mathcal{Q}_{\mathrm{MDist}} = \arg\max_{\mathcal{Q}} \left\{ \min_l |r_{l,l}^{(\mathcal{Q})}| \right\} \tag{6.46}$$

where $r_{l,l}^{(\mathcal{Q})}$ is $\mathbf{R}$ in Eq. (6.39) or the (l,l)th element of $\mathbf{R}_{\mathrm{ex}}$ in Eq. (6.44).

Since the above methods exhaustively list all possible combinations of K users among Q candidate users and select a set of optimal users, the above user selection strategy also becomes an exhaustive selection strategy.

(2) Greedy selection strategy

Since the computational complexity of the method described in (1) increases sharply with the increase of K or Q, the complexity is extremely high and it is not practical. So we need to find a low-complexity multi-user selection strategy that can be applied to actual systems.

In order to reduce the complexity of the LR exhaustive selection strategy, consider the lattice reduction-based greedy (LRG) user selection algorithm.

For the LRG user selection algorithm based on LR detection, let $k = 1$, $\bar{\mathcal{Q}} = \{1, 2, \ldots, Q\}$, the algorithm can then be expressed in the following three steps:

• Step 1:

$$q_{(1)} = \arg\max_{q \in \mathcal{Q}} \lambda_{\min}(\mathbf{G}_q^{\mathrm{H}}\mathbf{G}_q) \tag{6.47}$$

According to Eq. (6.47), the first selected user number can be obtained. If LR-ZF detection is used, $\mathbf{G}_q$ is the matrix of $\mathbf{H}_q$ after lattice reduction. And if LR-MMSE detection is used, $\mathbf{G}_q$ is the matrix of $\mathbf{H}_{\mathrm{ex},q} = \begin{bmatrix} \mathbf{H}_q \\ \sqrt{\frac{N_0}{E_{\mathrm{s}}}}\mathbf{I} \end{bmatrix}$ after lattice reduction. Since the number of user antennas $P = 1$, it can be seen that $\mathbf{H}_q$ degenerates into a vector, so no LR operation is required, and thus, Eq. (6.47) can be replaced with

$$q_{(1)} = \arg\max_{q \in \mathcal{Q}} \lambda_{\min}(\mathbf{H}_q^{\mathrm{H}} \mathbf{H}_q) \tag{6.48}$$

So far, the first user has been selected, and then we implement the following steps:

○ add $q_{(1)}$ to the selected user number set $\mathcal{Q}$;
○ remove the selected $\{q_{(1)}\}$ from $\bar{\mathcal{Q}}$, namely $\bar{\mathcal{Q}} \leftarrow \bar{\mathcal{Q}} \backslash \{q_{(1)}\}$;
○ $\mathbf{H}_{(1)} = \mathbf{H}_{q_{(1)}}$.

• **Step 2:** Define $k \leftarrow k+1$, $\mathbf{H}_{(k),q} = [\mathbf{H}_{(k-1)}, \mathbf{H}_q]$, where $q \in \bar{\mathcal{Q}}$. At this time, the number of the kth selected user is

$$q_{(k)} = \arg\max_{q \in \mathcal{Q}} \lambda_{\min}(\mathbf{G}_{(k),q}^{\mathrm{H}} \mathbf{G}_{(k),q}) \tag{6.49}$$

Similarly, for LR-ZF, $\mathbf{G}_{(k),q}$ is the matrix of $\mathbf{H}_{(k),q}$ after lattice reduction. And for LR-MMSE, $\mathbf{G}_{(k),q}$ is the matrix of $\mathbf{H}_{\mathrm{ex},q} = \begin{bmatrix} \mathbf{H}_q \\ \sqrt{\frac{N_0}{E_s}}\mathbf{I} \end{bmatrix}$ after lattice reduction. In this way, we can select the kth user and then implement the following steps:

○ add $q_{(k)}$ to the selected user number set $\mathcal{Q}$;
○ remove the selected $\{q_{(k)}\}$ from $\bar{\mathcal{Q}}$, namely $\bar{\mathcal{Q}} \leftarrow \bar{\mathcal{Q}} \backslash \{q_{(k)}\}$;
○ $\mathbf{H}_{(k)} = \mathbf{H}_{(k),q_{(k)}}$.

• **Step 3:** If $k = K$, stop the algorithm, otherwise go to Step (2).

For the LRG user selection algorithm based on LR-SIC detection, set $k = 1$, $\bar{\mathcal{Q}} = \{1, 2, \ldots, Q\}$. The algorithm steps are given as follows:

• **Step 1:** As mentioned above, for LR-ZF-SIC, $\mathbf{G}_q$ is the matrix of $\mathbf{H}_q$ after lattice reduction. And for LR-MMSE-SIC, $\mathbf{G}_q$ is the matrix of $\mathbf{H}_{\mathrm{ex},q} = \begin{bmatrix} \mathbf{H}_q \\ \sqrt{\frac{N_0}{E_s}}\mathbf{I} \end{bmatrix}$ after lattice reduction. Perform QR decomposition on $\mathbf{G}_q$, namely $\mathbf{G}_q = \mathbf{Q}_q \mathbf{R}_q$ with $\mathbf{Q}_q$ a unitary matrix and $\mathbf{R}_q$ an upper triangular array. The number of the first selected user is

$$q_{(1)} = \arg\max_{q \in \mathcal{Q}} \left\{ \min_l |r_{l,l}^{(q)}| \right\} \tag{6.50}$$

where $r_{l,l}^{(q)}$ represents the (l,l)th element of the matrix $\mathbf{R}_q$. Similarly, since the number of antennas $P = 1$, $\mathbf{H}_q$ degenerates into a vector which means that LR or QR operations are no longer required, so Eq. (6.50) can be replaced by Eq. (6.48). After selecting the number of the first user, we implement the following steps:

○ add $q_{(1)}$ to the selected user number set $\mathcal{Q}$;
○ remove the selected $\{q_{(1)}\}$ from $\bar{\mathcal{Q}}$, namely $\bar{\mathcal{Q}} \leftarrow \bar{\mathcal{Q}} \backslash \{q_{(1)}\}$;
○ $\mathbf{H}_{(1)} = \mathbf{H}_{q_{(1)}}$.

• **Step 2:** Set $k \leftarrow k+1$, $\mathbf{H}_{(k),q} = [\mathbf{H}_{(k-1)}, \mathbf{H}_q]$ with $q \in \bar{\mathcal{Q}}$. For LR-ZF-SIC or LR-MMSE-SIC detection, $\mathbf{G}_{(k),q}$ is the matrix of $\mathbf{H}_{(k),q}$ or $\mathbf{H}_{\mathrm{ex},(k),q}$ after lattice reduction. Perform QR decomposition on $\mathbf{G}_{(k),q}$, namely $\mathbf{G}_{(k),q} = \mathbf{Q}_{(k),q} \mathbf{R}_{(k),q}$ with $\mathbf{Q}_{(k),q}$ a unitary matrix and $\mathbf{R}_{(k),q}$ an upper triangular array. The number of the kth selected user is

$$q_{(k)} = \arg \max_{q \in \mathcal{Q}} \left\{ \min_l |r_{l,l}^{(k),q}| \right\} \tag{6.51}$$

where $r_{l,l}^{(k),q}$ represents the (l,l)th element of the matrix $\mathbf{R}_{(k),q}$. After selecting the number of the kth user, we implement the following steps:

○ add $q_{(k)}$ to the selected user number set $\mathcal{Q}$;
○ remove the selected $\{q_{(k)}\}$ from $\bar{\mathcal{Q}}$, namely $\bar{\mathcal{Q}} \leftarrow \bar{\mathcal{Q}} \backslash \{q_{(k)}\}$;
○ $\mathbf{H}_{(k)} = \mathbf{H}_{(k),q_{(k)}}$.

• **Step 3:** If $k = K$, stop the algorithm, otherwise go to Step (2).

In the above two algorithms, the complex-valued matrix $\mathbf{H}_{(k)}$ represents the $N \times kP$-dimensional joint channel matrix of k selected users. $\mathbf{H}_{q_{(k)}}$ represents the $N \times P$-dimensional channel matrix of the kth candidate user, whose number is $q_{(k)}$, and $q_{(k)} \in \bar{\mathcal{Q}}$, $\bar{\mathcal{Q}} = \{1, 2, \ldots, Q\} \backslash \{q_{(1)}, q_{(2)}, \ldots, q_{(k-1)}\}$.

6.3.3.2 *LR base iterative method*

In the above LRG user selection strategy, all column vectors of each new channel matrix are subjected to LR operations. If we can use the results of the first $(k-1)p$ LBR vectors, it is possible to perform LR operations only on the newly added p column vectors, which greatly reduces the computational complexity. We can design a method that can perform local LR operations using the base after lattice reduction. We call this algorithm the LR-based lattice reduction (UBLR).

The UBLR algorithm is implemented based on the CLLL algorithm. The CLLL algorithm transforms a given base into a new base with a base vector that is nearly orthogonal, namely

$$\mathcal{L}(\mathbf{G}_{(k)}) = \mathcal{L}(\mathbf{H}_{(k)}) \leftrightarrow \mathbf{G}_{(k)} = \mathbf{H}_{(k)}\mathbf{U}_{(k)} \tag{6.52}$$

where $\mathbf{U}_{(k)}$ is a unimodular matrix. Perform QR decomposition on $\mathbf{G}_{(k)}$,

$$\mathbf{G}_{(k)} = \mathbf{Q}_{(k)}\mathbf{R}_{(k)} \tag{6.53}$$

where $\mathbf{Q}_{(k)}$ is a unitary matrix and $\mathbf{R}_{(k)}$ is an upper triangular matrix. If $\mathbf{R}_{(k)}$ satisfies the following inequality[46]

$$|\Re([\mathbf{R}]_{i,j})| \le \frac{1}{2}|[\mathbf{R}]_{i,i}| \text{ 且 } |\Im([\mathbf{R}]_{i,j})| \le \frac{1}{2}|[\mathbf{R}]_{i,i}|, \quad 1 \le i < j \le kP \tag{6.54}$$

and

$$\delta|[\mathbf{R}]_{j-1,j-1}|^2 \le |[\mathbf{R}]_{j,j}|^2 + |[\mathbf{R}]_{j-1,j}|^2, \quad j = 2, 3, \dots, kP \tag{6.55}$$

$\mathbf{G}_{(k)}$ can be called the lattice reduction under δ Where $[\mathbf{R}]_{i,j}$ represents the (i,j)th element in matrix $\mathbf{R}_{(k)}$ and δ is the equalization parameter between algorithm complexity and performance.[47] Reference 46 shows that for the CLLL algorithm, it can be chosen between $(1/2, 1)$. Here, we assume $\delta = 3/4$.

(1) CLLL algorithm

In the CLLL algorithm, the channel matrix $\mathbf{H}_{(k)}$ produces a nearly orthogonal matrix $\mathbf{G}_{(k)}$ and a unimodular matrix $\mathbf{U}_{(k)}$. Perform QR decomposition on $\mathbf{H}_{(k)}$,

$$\mathbf{H}_{(k)} = \tilde{\mathbf{Q}}_{(k)}\tilde{\mathbf{R}}_{(k)} \tag{6.56}$$

where $\tilde{\mathbf{Q}}_{(k)}$ is a unitary matrix and $\tilde{\mathbf{R}}_{(k)}$ is an upper triangular matrix. Define the set $\tilde{\mathcal{M}}_{(k)}$ as

$$\tilde{\mathcal{M}}_{(k)} = \{\tilde{\mathbf{Q}}_{(k)}, \tilde{\mathbf{R}}_{(k)}, \tilde{\mathbf{T}}_{(k)}\} \tag{6.57}$$

where $\tilde{\mathbf{T}}_{(k)} = \mathbf{I}_{mP}$. If the set $\tilde{\mathcal{M}}_{(k)}$ is the input of the CLLL algorithm, the output is

$$\mathcal{M}_{(k)} = \{\mathbf{Q}_{(k)}, \mathbf{R}_{(k)}, \mathbf{T}_{(k)}\} \tag{6.58}$$

and the LBR matrix $\mathbf{G}_{(k)}$ can be written as

$$\mathbf{G}_{(k)} = \mathbf{Q}_{(k)}\mathbf{R}_{(k)} = \mathbf{H}_{(k)}\mathbf{T}_{(k)} \tag{6.59}$$

Table 6.7. CLLL algorithm.

	INPUT: $\{\tilde{\mathbf{Q}}_{(k)}, \tilde{\mathbf{R}}_{(k)}, \tilde{\mathbf{T}}_{(k)}\}$
	OUTPUT: $\{\mathbf{Q}_{(k)}, \mathbf{R}_{(k)}, \mathbf{T}_{(k)}\}$
(1)	$\gamma = \text{size}(\tilde{\mathbf{T}}_{(k)}, 2)$
(2)	$\mathbf{Q}_{(k)} \leftarrow \tilde{\mathbf{Q}}_{(k)}, \ \mathbf{R}_{(k)} \leftarrow \tilde{\mathbf{R}}_{(k)}, \ \mathbf{T}_{(k)} \leftarrow \tilde{\mathbf{T}}_{(k)}$
(3)	while $j \leq \gamma$
(4)	for $i = 1 : j - 1$
(5)	$\mu \leftarrow \lfloor \mathbf{R}_{(k)}(j - i, j) / \mathbf{R}_{(k)}(j - i, j - i) \rfloor$
(6)	if $\mu \neq 0$
(7)	$\mathbf{R}_{(k)}(1 : j - i, j) \leftarrow \mathbf{R}_{(k)}(1 : j - i, j) - \mu \mathbf{R}_{(k)}(1 : j - i, j - i)$
(8)	$\mathbf{T}_{(k)}(:, j) \leftarrow \mathbf{T}_{(k)}(:, j) - \mu \mathbf{T}_{(k)}(:, j - i)$
(9)	end if
(10)	end for
(11)	if $\delta \lvert \mathbf{R}_{(k)}(j - 1, j - 1) \rvert^2 > \lvert \mathbf{R}_{(k)}(j, j) \rvert^2 + \lvert \mathbf{R}(j - 1, j) \rvert^2$
(12)	Exchange the $(j - 1)$th column and the jth column in $\mathbf{R}_{(m)}$ and $\mathbf{T}_{(m)}$ respectively.
(13)	$\boldsymbol{\Theta} = \begin{bmatrix} \alpha^* & \beta \\ -\beta & \alpha \end{bmatrix}, \ \alpha = \dfrac{\mathbf{R}_{(k)}(j - 1, j - 1)}{\lVert \mathbf{R}_{(k)}(j - 1 : j, j - 1) \rVert}, \ \beta = \dfrac{\mathbf{R}_{(k)}(j, j - 1)}{\lVert \mathbf{R}_{(k)}(j - 1 : j, j - 1) \rVert}$
(14)	$\mathbf{R}_{(k)}(j - 1 : j, j - 1 : \gamma) \leftarrow \boldsymbol{\Theta} \mathbf{R}_{(k)}(j - 1 : j, j - 1 : \gamma)$
(15)	$\mathbf{Q}_{(k)}(:, j - 1 : j) \leftarrow \mathbf{Q}_{(k)}(:, j - 1 : j) \boldsymbol{\Theta}^{\mathrm{T}}$
(16)	$j \leftarrow \max\{j - 1, 2\}$
(17)	else
(18)	$j \leftarrow j + 1$
(19)	end if
(20)	end while

Since the CLLL algorithm is an iterative algorithm, input the initial parameters $\mathbf{Q}_{(k)} \leftarrow \tilde{\mathbf{Q}}_{(k)}$, $\mathbf{R}_{(k)} \leftarrow \tilde{\mathbf{R}}_{(k)}$, $\mathbf{T}_{(k)} \leftarrow \tilde{\mathbf{T}}_{(k)}$ to the CLLL algorithm. Set $j = 2$, and the algorithm can be summarized in Table 6.7.

In the LRG user selection strategy, when the kth user is selected, we have

$$\mathbf{H}_{(k)} = [\mathbf{H}_{(k-1)}, \mathbf{H}_{(k)}] \tag{6.60}$$

When selecting the $(k - 1)$th user, the CLLL algorithm has been implemented on the matrix $\mathbf{H}_{(k-1)}$ and the corresponding lattice reduction matrix $\mathbf{G}_{(k-1)}$ is obtained. If we can use the information of $\mathbf{G}_{(k-1)}$ to get $\mathbf{G}_{(k)}$, then the complexity will be greatly reduced. We call this algorithm the UBLR algorithm.

(2) UBLR algorithm

The UBLR algorithm utilizes a known set of matrices $\mathcal{M}_{(k-1)} = \{\mathbf{Q}_{(k-1)}, \mathbf{R}_{(k-1)}, \mathbf{T}_{(k-1)}\}$ to increase the efficiency of transforming $\mathbf{H}_{(k)}$ into a lattice reduction matrix $\mathbf{G}_{(k)}$. When selecting the $(k-1)$th user, the generated lattice reduction matrix is

$$\mathbf{G}_{(k-1)} = \mathbf{Q}_{(k-1)}\mathbf{R}_{(k-1)}$$
$$= \mathbf{H}_{(k-1)}\mathbf{T}_{(k-1)} \tag{6.61}$$

where $\mathbf{R}_{(k-1)}$ satisfies Eqs. (6.54) and (6.55) and $\mathbf{T}_{(k-1)}$ is a unimodular matrix, which is used for the column vector exchange of the CLLL algorithm.

Using the known $\mathcal{M}_{(k-1)}$, the UBLR algorithm can start operations from the $(j = (k-1)P + 1)$th column to reduce the number of iterations. Perform QR decomposition on matrix $\mathbf{H}_{(k-1)}$,

$$\mathbf{H}_{(k-1)} = \tilde{\mathbf{Q}}_{(k-1)}\tilde{\mathbf{R}}_{(k-1)} \tag{6.62}$$

where $\tilde{\mathbf{Q}}_{(k-1)}$ is a unitary matrix and $\tilde{\mathbf{R}}_{(k-1)}$ is an upper triangular matrix. When $\tilde{\mathbf{T}}_{(k-1)} = \mathbf{I}_{(k-1)}$, the matrix set can be written as

$$\tilde{\mathcal{M}}_{(k-1)} = \{\tilde{\mathbf{Q}}_{(k-1)}, \tilde{\mathbf{R}}_{(k-1)}, \tilde{\mathbf{T}}_{(k-1)}\} \tag{6.63}$$

Since $\tilde{\mathbf{R}}_{(k-1)}$ is an $(N \times (k-1)P)$-dimensional upper triangular matrix and $\tilde{\mathbf{R}}_{(k)}$ is an $(N \times kP)$-dimensional upper triangular matrix, we have

$$\tilde{\mathbf{R}}_{(k-1)} = \tilde{\mathbf{R}}_{(k)}(:, 1 : (k-1)P) \tag{6.64}$$

which means that the reduction and column transformation operations performed in the first $(k-1)P$ columns of the matrix $\tilde{\mathbf{R}}_{(k)}$ are the same as those performed in $\tilde{\mathbf{R}}_{(k-1)}$. Set $\mathcal{M}_{(k)} \leftarrow \tilde{\mathcal{M}}_{(k)}$. Substituting the value of $\mathbf{R}_{(k-1)}$ into $\mathbf{R}_{(k)}$, we get

$$\mathbf{R}_{(k)}(:, 1 : (k-1)P) \leftarrow \mathbf{R}_{(k-1)} \tag{6.65}$$

It can be seen that the first $(k-1)P$ columns of $\mathbf{R}_{(k)}$ satisfy the Eqs. (6.54) and (6.55). Similarly, we can substitute the value of

$\{\mathbf{Q}_{(k-1)}, \mathbf{T}_{(k-1)}\}$ into $\{\mathbf{Q}_{(k)}, \mathbf{T}_{(k)}\}$ to achieve low-complexity updates, namely

$$\mathbf{Q}_{(k)} \leftarrow \mathbf{Q}_{(k-1)}$$
$$\mathbf{T}_{(k)}(1{:}(k-1)P, 1{:}(k-1)P) \leftarrow \mathbf{T}_{(k-1)} \tag{6.66}$$

The algorithm for updating the above base is shown in Table 6.8.

So far, we have completed the update operations on the matrices $\mathbf{Q}_{(k)}$ and $\mathbf{T}_{(k)}$ using $\mathbf{Q}_{(k-1)}$ and $\mathbf{T}_{(k-1)}$. However, the update of $\mathbf{R}_{(k)}(1{:}(k-1)$ $P, (k-1)P+1{:}kP)$ has not been considered in line (8) of Table 6.8. Since the CLLL algorithm is implemented directly on $\mathbf{H}_{(k)}$, $\mathbf{R}_{(k)}(1{:}(k-1)$ $P, (k-1)P+1{:}kP)$ is updated accordingly, thereby we need to perform some additional recovery operations on the $\mathbf{R}_{(k)}(1{:}(k-1)P, (k-1)P+1{:}kP)$ item in $\mathcal{M}_{(k)}$. Define

$$\mathcal{A}_{(k-1)} = \{\Theta_{(k-1)}, \varphi_{(k-1)}, \xi_{(k-1)}\} \tag{6.67}$$

where

$$\Theta_{(k-1)} = \{\Theta_{(k-1,1)}, \Theta_{(k-1,2)}, \ldots, \Theta_{(k-1,\xi)}\}$$
$$\varphi_{(k-1)} = \{\varphi_{(k-1,1)}, \varphi_{(k-1,2)}, \ldots, \varphi_{(k-1,\xi)}\} \tag{6.68}$$
$$\xi_{(k-1)} = \xi$$

where $\Theta_{(k-1)}$ is used to store the operations of exchanging $\mathbf{Q}_{(k-1)}$ and $\mathbf{R}_{(k-1)}$, $\varphi_{(k-1)}$ is used to store its exchanged vectors, and $\xi_{(k-1)}$ is used to store its number of exchanges. According to the information in $\mathcal{A}_{(k-1)}$, Table 6.9 shows the update algorithm for $\mathbf{R}_{(k)}(1{:}(k-1)P, (k-1)P+1{:}kP)$, where $i = kP$.

Table 6.8. Base update algorithm in UBLR algorithm (Part 1).

(6)	$\mathbf{T}_{(k)}(1{:}(k-1)P, 1{:}(k-1)P) \leftarrow \mathbf{T}_{(k-1)}$
(7)	$\mathbf{Q}_{(k)} \leftarrow \mathbf{Q}_{(k-1)}$
(8)	$\mathbf{R}_{(k)}(:, 1{:}(k-1)P) \leftarrow \mathbf{R}_{(k-1)}$

Table 6.9. Base update algorithm in UBLR algorithm (Part 2).

(9)	for $i = 1{:}\xi_{(k-1)}$
(10)	$\mathbf{R}_{(k)}(\varphi_{(k-1,i)} - 1{:}\varphi_{(k-1,i)}, (m-1)P+1{:}\gamma) \leftarrow \Theta_{(k-1,i)}\mathbf{R}_{(k)}(\varphi_{(k-1,i)} - 1{:}\varphi_{(k-1,i)}, (m-1)P+1{:}\gamma)$
(11)	end for

Table 6.10. The UBLR algorithm for selecting the kth user (based on CLLL).

INPUT: $\{\mathcal{M}_{(k-1)}, \mathcal{A}_{(k-1)}, \mathbf{H}_{(k-1)}, \mathbf{H}_{q_{(k)}}\}$

OUTPUT: $\{\mathcal{M}_{(k)}, \mathcal{A}_{(k)}\}$

(1) $\mathbf{H}_{(k)} \leftarrow [\mathbf{H}_{(k-1)}, \mathbf{H}_{q_{(k)}}]$

(2) $\omega \leftarrow \text{size}(\mathbf{H}_{(k-1)}, 2)$

(3) $\gamma \leftarrow \text{size}(\mathbf{H}_{(k)}, 2)$

(4) $[\mathbf{Q}_{(k)}, \mathbf{R}_{(k)}] \leftarrow \text{qr}(\mathbf{H}_{(k)})$

(5) $\mathbf{T}_{(k)} \leftarrow \mathbf{I}_{\gamma}$

$\vdots$

Perform the first part of the base update (see Table 6.8)

$\vdots$

Perform the second part of the base update (see Table 6.9)

$\vdots$

(12) $j \leftarrow \omega + 1$

(13) $\xi_{(k)} \leftarrow 0$

$\vdots$

Perform the CLLL algorithm (see Table 6.7)

According to the base update method shown in Tables 6.8 and 6.9, the UBLR algorithm can efficiently update $\mathcal{M}_{(k)}$. Thereafter, we can use the CLLL algorithm to generate the lattice reduction matrix $\mathbf{G}_{(k)}$.

Based on the different parts of the algorithm provided in Tables 6.8 and 6.9, Table 6.10 summarizes the UBLR algorithm for selecting the kth user.

If a real-valued LR algorithm, namely the LLL algorithm, is used, the UBLR algorithm can also be implemented on a real channel matrix. In a multi-user MIMO system, the user selection strategy using the LLL algorithm has the same performance as the user selection strategy using the CLLL algorithm.

6.4 Multi-cell Cooperative Transmission and Anti-Interference Method

In Section 6.3.2, we introduced a multi-user cooperative transmission method in a single cell. However, when the user is at the cell edge, it will be strongly interfered by neighboring cells, causing the edge user's quality of service and throughput to degrade drastically. In this section, we will introduce multi-cell cooperative transmission and anti-interference methods for addressing the problems that service quality and throughput are degraded due to strong mutual interference of cell edge users.

6.4.1 *Multi-cell cooperative transmission*

The same-frequency networking mode in the LTE system severely limits the quality of service and throughput of edge users, and thus inter-cell interference becomes the main interference. How to reduce inter-cell interference and improve the performance of the same-frequency networking is a major problem which needs to be solved in the LTE-Advanced system.

Coordinated multiple points (CoMP) is considered to be an effective technique for reducing inter-cell interference and improving cell edge throughput and system throughput.[48] Its core idea is that the cell edge user can simultaneously receive and transmit signals with multiple cells and coordinate the signals. In the downlink communication process, if the transmission signals from multiple cells can be coordinated to avoid interference between each other, the performance of the downlink communication can be greatly improved. And in uplink communication, signals are jointly received and combined by multiple cells. If coordinated scheduling is performed on multiple cells at the same time, inter-cell interference can be suppressed, and the SNR of the received signal can be improved.

CoMP includes uplink reception and downlink transmission. Uplink CoMP reception improves the cell edge user throughput by jointly receiving user data through multiple cells. And the downlink CoMP transmission is based on whether the service data are acquired at multiple coordinated points to adopt two coordinated modes of "cooperative scheduling/beamforming" (CS/CB) and "joint processing (JP)".[49]

6.4.1.1 *Cooperative schedule/beamforming (CS/CB)*

Cooperative scheduling/beamforming refers to dynamic information interaction between multiple cells and coordination of the corresponding scheduling and transmission weights to minimize the mutual interference between multiple cells. As shown in Fig. 6.11, the serving cells of user 1 and user 2 are cell 1 and cell 2, respectively, and the data received by user 1 and user 2 are from cell 1 and cell 2, respectively. When the geographical positions of terminals of different cells are relatively close (if they are all at

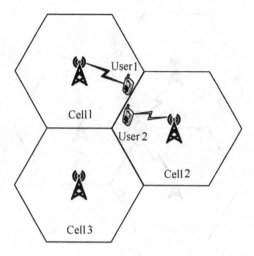

Fig. 6.11. **Schematic diagram of cooperative scheduling/beamforming.**

the edge of their respective cells), it is highly probable that the signals of the two terminals interfere with each other. At this time, the data transmission of the two terminals can be allocated to different time–frequency resources by using the cooperative beamforming technology, and the same time–frequency resources are allocated to other non-adjacent terminals. This type of scheduling coordination can minimize interference to users of neighboring cell edges.

6.4.1.2 *Joint processing (JP) technology*

Joint processing means that multiple cells work together for the terminal in a coordinated manner, and the joint processing technology can be further divided into joint transmission (JT) and dynamic cell selection (DCS) technologies. In joint processing, multiple transmission points can simultaneously transmit data to the terminal. All cells in the coordinated set transmit the same or different data to the terminal under the same time–frequency resource, which refers to multiple coordinated cells transmitting data to the same user at the same time. As shown in Fig. 6.12, the serving cell of the user 1 is a coordinated cell set of cells 1, 2, and 3. The three cells simultaneously transmit data for the user 1 in cooperation. In this way, the gains from two aspects will be obtained. First, the signals of the cells participating in the cooperation are all useful signals, which can reduce the total interference received by the terminal. Second, the signals of the cells

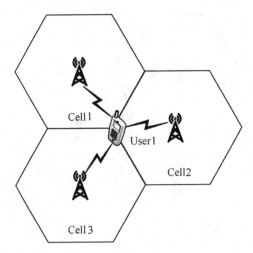

Fig. 6.12. Schematic diagram of multi-cell joint processing.

participating in the cooperation are superimposed on each other, and the power level of the signals received by the terminal can be improved.

Since the user's data are simultaneously transmitted by multiple cell base stations in the joint processing mode, the serving cell shares the data addressed to the terminal to other coordinated cells. Compared with the cooperative scheduling/beamforming method, not only the channel information and the scheduling information need to be exchanged between the base stations but also the data information needs to be shared, so the joint processing has higher requirements on the rate and delay of the connection between the cells. In addition, the upper limit of the performance of the joint processing scheme is the use of global precoding, and the global precoding has higher requirements for information feedback.

As a key technology of LTE-A, CoMP effectively improves the average throughput of the system and the SNR of users at the edge of the cell. Although CoMP increases the complexity of the system, it has an advantage in increasing system capacity and coverage gain.

Actually, in the process of coordinated multi-cell transmission, eliminating or reducing interference of cell edge users is of great significance for improving multi-cell cooperative transmission performance. Therefore, in Section 6.4.3, we will detail the multi-cell anti-interference method.

6.4.2 *Geometric modeling of multi-cell interference system*

The ground-based cellular system was originally designed to alleviate the limited frequency of wireless communications and increase the capacity of wireless communication systems. In a traditional multi-cell system, cells with a certain distance use the same frequency, while neighboring cells use different frequencies to reduce inter-cell interference. However, with the development of wireless communication, the sharp increase of mobile users, and the higher requirements of users on data rates and service types, spectrum resources have become more and more inadequate and the traditional multi-cell structure has been unable to meet the current needs. In order to solve this problem, the related research proposes the concept of full-frequency reuse, which means all cells will reuse all frequencies to improve spectrum utilization and cell capacity. In addition, due to the wide application of the OFDM technology in LTE, the frequency interference among cells can be better suppressed by the OFDM technology, which causes the interference received by the user mainly from the co-channel interference among cells. In particular, considering the development trend of miniaturization and flattening of the network in the future, the probability that the user is at the edge of the cell increases, and thus is more susceptible to interference from neighboring cells. Therefore, multi-cell co-channel interference has become a bottleneck restricting the capacity and quality of future communication systems.

First, we establish a geometric model of the multi-cell interference system[50] (shown in Fig. 6.13) to illustrate the mutual interference problem between multi-cell users. Set the coordinates of the central cell base station as the origin, and the radius of the cell be R, then the coordinates of each base station can be determined. For example, the coordinates of the base station 2 are $(1.5R, 0.86R)$.

Taking each base station as the origin and making a square with side length $2R$, the user is randomly and evenly distributed in the square to obtain the user coordinate value (x, y). And the cell with a regular hexagon is equivalent to a circle with a radius of R, as shown in Fig. 6.13. When the user coordinate value (x, y) falls within a circle with a radius R, it indicates that the user is an internal user of the cell, as shown by the black dot in Fig. 6.14. And when the user coordinate (x, y) falls outside the circle with the radius R and is in the square with the side length $2R$, it indicates that the user is the cell edge user, as shown by the white point in Fig. 6.14.

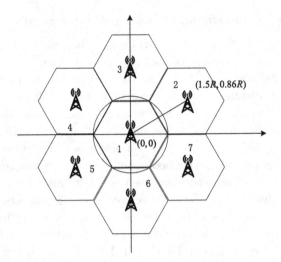

Fig. 6.13. Schematic diagram of a multi-cell system.

Since the user in the cell center is relatively close to the base station and far away from the interference signal source of other cells, its SINR is relatively large. However, for a cell edge user, whose distance from the user to the base station is greater than R, since the user occupying the same carrier resource in the neighboring cell has a relatively large interference, and the distance from the base station is far away, its SINR is relatively small. As a result, although the overall throughput of the cell is high, the cell edge user has poor service quality and low throughput. Therefore, in order to improve the quality of service at the cell edge, it is very important to use inter-cell interference suppression technology for edge users.

6.4.3 *Multi-cell system anti-interference technology*

In order to suppress interference between cells and improve the quality of the service of edge cells, various anti-interference technologies have been widely studied, including interference randomization, interference cancellation, and interference coordination/avoidance. In the following, we will introduce these anti-interference techniques.[50]

6.4.3.1 *Interference randomization*

Interference randomization is the randomization of interference signals by artificial signal superposition. This randomization method cannot reduce

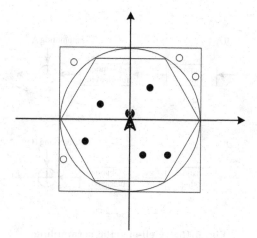

Fig. 6.14. Schematic diagram of user selection in a single cell.

the energy of the interference, but can make the interference signal close to the white noise, and then use the white noise processing method to perform interference suppression at the terminal. At present, the main methods of interference randomization are as follows:

(1) Cell-specific scrambling

The signals of each cell are scrambled by using different pseudo-random scrambling codes after channel coding and channel interleaving to obtain the effect of interference white noise, as shown in Fig. 6.15.

Cells A and B adopt different channel coding and interleaving modes. The specific interference signal is scrambled at the transmitting end of the cell A, so that the interference signal from cell B becomes white noise in the view of the receiving user in cell A. And the interference signal from cell B is suppressed by using a matched filter at the receiving end in cell A. Performing the same operation on cell B can improve the receiving signal quality of each cell.

(2) Cell-specific interleaving

The signals of each cell are channel-interleaved with different interleaving patterns after channel coding to obtain an interference white noise effect, also called interleave-division multiple access (IDMA). Similar to cell-specific scrambling, a specific interleaving pattern is added after the

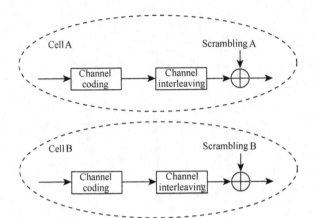

Fig. 6.15.   Cell-specific scrambling.

transmission data channel coding, and the receiving end of each cell uses a known receiving pattern to solve the signal it needs.

For interference randomization, the performance achieved by cell-specific scrambling and cell-specific interleaving is close. In addition, using different frequency-hopping patterns in different cells to obtain interference randomization effects can also be considered.

6.4.3.2 *Interference cancellation*

Interference cancellation can demodulate and decode the cell interference signal by using different spreading codes, and then reconstruct and delete the interference signal from the cell. There are two main methods for implementing interference cancellation between cells.

(1) Traditional signal joint detection

Interference cancellation is performed by using the multi-antenna space suppression method at the receiving end. The related detection algorithms such as LR method and iterative received signal processing have been widely used in MIMO research (see Chapter 5).

(2) IDMA-based deletion

If IDMA is used to cancel the inter-cell interference, similar to the CDMA spreading mode, the cell is regarded as a user, and the IDMA can generate different interleaving patterns by the pseudo-random interleaver to allocate to different cells. And then the receiver uses the corresponding interleaving pattern to de-interleave, and the target signal and the interference signal can be, respectively, solved. Furthermore, by using the idea of serial interference cancellation, the interference signal is subtracted from the total receiving signal, thereby effectively improving the SINR of the receiving signal.

The advantage of interference cancellation between cells is that there is no restriction on the frequency resources at the cell edge, and the neighboring cells can use the same frequency resource even at the cell edge to obtain a higher cell edge spectrum efficiency and total spectrum efficiency. However, the limitation is that the cells must be kept in synchronization, and the target cell must know the pilot structure of the interfering cell to perform channel estimation on the interference signal, which requires the transmission mechanism of the user signal and the control signaling to be considered in the multi-cell cooperation system scheme. For users who want to perform cell interference cancellation, they must be assigned the same frequency resource.

6.4.3.3 *Interference coordination/avoidance*

The core idea of interference coordination/avoidance is to restrict available resources of a cell by inter-cell coordination to lower the interference of the cell to neighboring cells. On this basis, the SNR of the neighboring cells on these resources and the data transmission rate of the cell edge users are improved.

6.4.4 *Multi-cell system cooperative interference suppression*

In addition to multi-cell interference technology, multi-point cooperation, cooperative relay, smart antenna, and other cooperative technologies can also effectively suppress inter-cell interference. Thereby, the coverage capability of the cell, the stability of the user switching over cells, and the call quality of the cell edge user are improved.

In the multi-cell cooperative communication system, one of the cooperative base stations can be selected as the primary base station to collect and release control information and transmit data. Optimized configuration of resources is implemented within this cooperative cluster, while other base stations are degraded to radio remote units (RRU). Under this structure, since the inter-cluster interference is greatly suppressed due to the long geographical distance, the interference of the system mainly comes from the co-channel interference in the cooperative cluster. Moreover, since the time–frequency resources of the uplink and downlink in the cooperative cluster are optimally configured, the transmission delay of the signaling will be effectively improved, and the data information can be simultaneously transmitted to the user from multiple access points, thereby effectively suppressing the intra-cluster interference problem.

The multi-cell cooperative technology mainly utilizes multi-base station cooperation to reduce intra-cluster interference, thereby expanding the coverage area and improving the total system capacity and user communication quality. Currently available cooperative key technologies are listed below:[51]

(1) **Smart association:** The user terminal (UE) can automatically search for an access point with the smallest path loss for access under the cooperative signaling mechanism. The cooperative multi-cell controller can determine the corresponding access points or select multiple access points to jointly send multiple users according to the reference information reported by each access point.

(2) **Station load balancing technology:** Multiple stations need to be allocated by the eNodeB to properly share the service load of the coverage area, so that the wireless resources can be reasonably utilized and can meet the load requirements of the network hardware devices, furthermore proving the total system capacity and performance.

(3) **Multi-antenna cooperative MIMO technology:** Multiple access points, that are present in a region can be used for joint beamforming of multiple users under the deployment of a base station controller to improve the spectrum utilization of the system, making it possible to differentiate users in the case of occupying the same time–frequency resources to increase the system capacity.

(4) **Cooperative station selection technology:** The base station scheduling technology is used to reasonably select the number and location of cooperative base stations to reduce the complexity of cooperation and improve the overall performance.

(5) **Dynamic multi-cell interference cooperative technology:** In the cooperative multi-cell system, the optical communication between the base stations enables high-speed and accurate transmission of the interaction information required for cooperation between the base stations, thereby realizing dynamic multi-cell interference cooperation.

(6) **Cooperative relay technology:** The multi-cell cooperative system combined with the cooperative relay technology can further expand the coverage and improve the transmission quality of the wireless link. Multi-point relay and relay power are both hot research topics.

We will take the cooperative scheduling and joint transmission cooperative interference suppression technology in LTE-A system as an example to describe its cooperative anti-interference principle.

As shown in Fig. 6.16, downlink multi-cell cooperation generally uses joint transmission to suppress co-channel interference. The number of cooperative base stations is M, the number of antennas configured by each base station is n_t, the number of users is M, and the number of antennas configured by each user is n_r, which constitutes an $n_tM \times n_rM$ virtual MIMO system.

Define the normalized complex Gaussian gain channel from base station to user k as

$$\mathbf{H}_k = \mathbf{G}_k\mathbf{F}_k \tag{6.69}$$

where $\mathbf{G}_k$ is the decomposition matrix and $\mathbf{F}_k$ is the received power.

$$\mathbf{F}_k = \mathrm{diag}\{\sqrt{P_{k,1}}, \sqrt{P_{k,2}}, \ldots, \sqrt{P_{k,n_tM}}\} \tag{6.70}$$

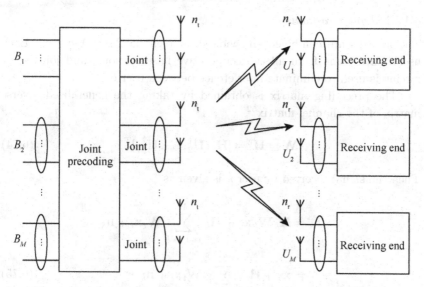

Fig. 6.16. Downlink multi-cell cooperation based on precoding.

The total channel matrix is

$$\mathbf{H} = [\mathbf{H}_1, \mathbf{H}_2, \ldots, \mathbf{H}_M]^{\mathrm{T}} \tag{6.71}$$

If $\mathbf{s}_k = [s_{k,1}, s_{k,2}, \ldots, s_{k,l}]^{\mathrm{T}}$ represents the data transmitted by user k, the total transmitted data are $\mathbf{s} = [\mathbf{s}_1, \mathbf{s}_2, \ldots, \mathbf{s}_M]^{\mathrm{T}}$. Assuming that the precoding matrix of user k is $\mathbf{W}_k \in \mathbb{C}^{n_t M \times l}$, the signal processed by the precoding matrix is

$$\mathbf{x} = \sum_{k=1}^{M} \mathbf{W}_k \mathbf{s}_k = \mathbf{W}\mathbf{s} \tag{6.72}$$

where $\mathbf{W} = [\mathbf{W}_1, \mathbf{W}_2, \ldots, \mathbf{W}_M]$ is the total precoding matrix, and then the signal received by user k can be expressed as

$$\mathbf{r}_k = \mathbf{H}_k \sum_{i=1}^{M} \mathbf{W}_i \mathbf{s}_i + \mathbf{n}_k \tag{6.73}$$

In multi-cell systems, the design criterion for joint transmission is to minimize interference between multiple cells, which can be realized by joint zero-forcing, joint diagonalization, and joint dirty paper coding.

6.4.4.1 *Joint zero-forcing*

The M cells are combined and viewed as a virtual MIMO system. Each user's data come from all the cooperative base stations, and joint zero-forcing is used to eliminate interference between user data.

The precoding matrix is obtained by taking the generalized inverse matrix of the channel matrix[52]

$$\mathbf{W} = \mathbf{H}^{\dagger} = [\mathbf{H}_1^{\dagger}, \mathbf{H}_2^{\dagger}, \ldots, \mathbf{H}_M^{\dagger}]^{\mathrm{T}} \tag{6.74}$$

Then the signal received by user k is given as

$$\mathbf{r}_k = \mathbf{H}_k \mathbf{W}_k \mathbf{x}_k + \mathbf{H}_k \sum_{i=1, i \neq k}^{M} \mathbf{W}_i \mathbf{x}_i + \mathbf{n}_k$$

$$= \mathbf{x}_k + \mathbf{H}_k \sum_{i=1, i \neq k}^{M} \mathbf{W}_i \mathbf{x}_i + \mathbf{n}_k \tag{6.75}$$

6.4.4.2 *Joint diagonalization*

(1) Construct zero space of the user channel matrix[53]

The augmented matrix corresponding to user k is

$$\tilde{\mathbf{H}}_k = [\mathbf{H}_1, \ldots, \mathbf{H}_{k-1}, \mathbf{H}_{k+1}, \ldots, \mathbf{H}_M]^{\mathrm{T}} \qquad (6.76)$$

We perform a singular value decomposition on $\tilde{\mathbf{H}}_k$ and obtain

$$\tilde{\mathbf{H}}_k = \tilde{\mathbf{U}}_k \begin{bmatrix} \tilde{\mathbf{\Sigma}}_k & \mathbf{0} \\ \mathbf{0} & \mathbf{0} \end{bmatrix} \begin{bmatrix} \tilde{\mathbf{V}}_k^{(1)} & \tilde{\mathbf{V}}_k^{(0)} \end{bmatrix}^{\mathrm{H}} \qquad (6.77)$$

where $\tilde{\mathbf{\Sigma}}_k$ is a diagonal matrix and $\tilde{\mathbf{V}}_k^{(1)}$ is a left singular value vector containing non-zero singular values of $\tilde{\mathbf{H}}_k$. $\tilde{\mathbf{V}}_k^{(0)}$ is a right singular value vector containing non-zero singular values of $\tilde{\mathbf{H}}_k$ and thus $\tilde{\mathbf{V}}_k^{(0)}$ is an orthogonal basis of $\tilde{\mathbf{H}}_k$ zero space. Then the precoding matrix can be expressed as

$$\mathbf{W} = [\mathbf{B}_1, \mathbf{B}_2, \ldots, \mathbf{B}_M] = [\hat{\tilde{\mathbf{V}}}_1^{(0)}, \hat{\tilde{\mathbf{V}}}_2^{(0)}, \ldots, \hat{\tilde{\mathbf{V}}}_M^{(0)}] \qquad (6.78)$$

Through precoding matrix processing in Eq. (6.78), the user channel matrix can be diagonalized, thereby completely eliminating the interference between users.

(2) ZF is used internally by the users to eliminate traffic interference

We perform a singular value decomposition on the equivalent channel matrix of user k and obtain

$$\mathbf{H}_k \hat{\tilde{\mathbf{V}}}^{(0)} = \mathbf{U}_k \begin{bmatrix} \mathbf{\Sigma}_k & \mathbf{0} \\ \mathbf{0} & \mathbf{0} \end{bmatrix} \begin{bmatrix} \mathbf{V}_k^{(1)} & \mathbf{V}_k^{(0)} \end{bmatrix}^{\mathrm{H}} \qquad (6.79)$$

Therefore, a complete precoding matrix of user k can be obtained.

$$\mathbf{W}_k = \hat{\tilde{\mathbf{V}}}_k^{(0)} \mathbf{V}_k^{(1)} \qquad (6.80)$$

Finally, the precoding matrix of the entire system is

$$\mathbf{W} = [\mathbf{W}_1, \mathbf{W}_2, \ldots, \mathbf{W}_M] = [\hat{\tilde{\mathbf{V}}}_1^{(0)} \mathbf{V}_1^{(1)}, \hat{\tilde{\mathbf{V}}}_2^{(0)} \mathbf{V}_2^{(1)}, \ldots, \hat{\tilde{\mathbf{V}}}_M^{(0)} \mathbf{V}_M^{(1)}] \qquad (6.81)$$

6.4.4.3 *Joint dirty paper coding*

Dirty paper coding,[54] is expanded to multiple cells, which can be expressed as follows:

(1) Perform QR decomposition on $\mathbf{H}^H$,

$\mathbf{H}^H = \mathbf{QR}$, and thus $\mathbf{H} = \mathbf{Q}^H \mathbf{R}^H$. We define $\mathbf{L} = \mathbf{R}^H$ as the lower triangular array, $\mathbf{F} = \mathbf{Q}^H$, and the following matrix is thus established:

$$\mathbf{W} = \text{diag} \left(\frac{1}{r_{1,1}}, \ldots, \frac{1}{r_{Mn_t, Mn_t}} \right) \mathbf{L} \qquad (6.82)$$

At the transmitting end, $\mathbf{W}$ is used as the precoding matrix, and loop iteration is used to eliminate the interference. The transmitted signal can be expressed as follows:

$$
\begin{aligned}
x_1 &= a_1 \\
x_2 &= a_2 - b_{21} x_1 \\
&\vdots \\
x_k &= a_k - \sum_{i=1}^{k-1} b_{kj} x_j
\end{aligned}
\qquad (6.83)
$$

and then the kth channel receiving data are given as

$$
\begin{aligned}
r_k &= \sum_{i=1}^{k} b_{kj} x_k + n_k \\
&= a_k - \sum_{i=1}^{k-1} b_{kj} x_j + \sum_{i=1}^{k-1} b_{kj} x_k + n_k \\
&= a_k + n_k
\end{aligned}
\qquad (6.84)
$$

The DPC principle can be used to eliminate the interference between multiple channels.

(2) Maximize capacity by water injection method

Make decomposition on $\mathbf{H}$,

$$\mathbf{H} = \mathbf{LU} \qquad (6.85)$$

where $\mathbf{L}$ is the lower triangular matrix and $\mathbf{U}$ is the orthogonal matrix. If the diagonal elements of $\mathbf{L}$ are expressed as l_{ii} and both are positive numbers, then the decomposition is uniquely determined. Assume that the transmitted power of each data stream is p_i, then

$$p_i = \left\lfloor \zeta - \frac{N_0}{|l_{ii}|^2} \right\rfloor^+ \tag{6.86}$$

where $\lfloor A \rfloor^+ = \max(A, 0)$ and ζ is the water injection line. The power of each substream should satisfy

$$\sum_{i=1}^{ML_s} p_i = P_t \tag{6.87}$$

Therefore, its system capacity can be expressed as

$$C = \sum_{i=1}^{ML_s} \mathrm{lb} \left(1 + \frac{p_i |l_{ii}|^2}{N_0} \right) \tag{6.88}$$

6.5 The Massive MIMO System

In Chapter 4 of this book, we briefly introduced massive MIMO technologies in terms of channel characteristics, application prospects, and technical challenges. In this section, we will further discuss the basic principles of the massive MIMO for system mathematical models.

6.5.1 *Review of the basic concepts of a massive MIMO System*

With the rapid development of wireless communication, the traditional MIMO technology can no longer meet the exponentially rising data communication needs. At the end of 2010, Bell Labs scientist Thomas L. Marzetta proposed to set up a large-scale antenna at the base station instead of the existing multi-antenna. The number of base station antennas is much larger than the number of single-antenna mobile terminals that can be simultaneously served, thereby forming a massive MIMO (massive MIMO, large-scale antenna system full-dimension MIMO) wireless communication system.[55] As shown in Fig. 6.17, the basic feature of a massive MIMO system is that it can obtain a more accurate beam-steering capability than the traditional MIMO systems (with no more than 8 antennas) by configuring a large number of antennas (from tens to

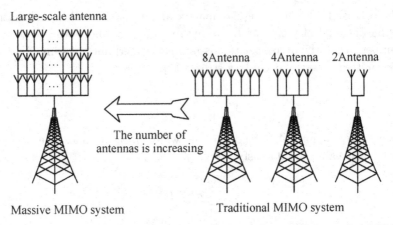

Fig. 6.17. **Comparison of a traditional MIMO system and a massive MIMO system.**

thousands) at the base station. Through spatial multiplexing technology, more users are served on the same time–frequency resource to improve the spectrum efficiency of the wireless communication system, so as to meet the transmission requirements of massive information in the future 5G wireless system. In addition, when the number of base station antennas tends to infinity, thermal noise and inter-cell interference, which seriously affect the performance of the communication system, are negligible. And the simplest beamforming can also become an optimal beamforming solution, such as the maximum ratio combining receiver (MRC Receiver). Compared with LTE, the cell throughput of massive MIMO can reach 1200 Mbit/s and the spectrum utilization reaches an unprecedented 60 bit/s/Hz/cell with the same 20-MHz bandwidth. Therefore, compared with the existing wireless communication technology, the massive MIMO technology has the following incomparable advantages, and it has become the core technology of the future 5G communication system. The characteristics of a massive MIMO system can be summarized as follows:

(1) Compared to the traditional method of increasing the system capacity by reducing the cell size,[56] a massive MIMO can increase the system capacity by directly increasing the number of antennas of the base station. A massive MIMO system increases the antenna aperture, and the coherent combining can reduce the transmission power required for uplink and downlink, which meets the requirements of future "green communication".[57]

(2) Literature in Ref. 58 has proved that in multi-cell MIMO systems, when a certain QoS is guaranteed and there is ideal Channel State Information (CSI), the transmission power of the user is inversely proportional to the number of antennas of the base station. And when the CSI is not ideal, it is inversely proportional to the square of the number of base station antennas.

(3) Taking advantage of uplink and downlink channel reciprocity, the cost of channel training is only related to the number of users in each cell and does not depend on the number of the base station antennas. Therefore, when the number of base station antennas tends to infinity, it does not increase the feedback overhead of the system. The literature in Ref. 59 has proved that the extra antenna is beneficial to the performance improvement.

(4) Different from previous interference coordination, massive MIMO can average inter-cell interference and thermal noise through a large number of transmitting and receiving antennas. This is because as the number of base station antennas increases, the inner product growth rate of the desired user channel vector and interfering user channel vector is lower than that of the desired user channel vector and its own. Therefore, thermal noise and inter-cell interference, which usually affect system performance, can be ignored.

In the following, with regard to the above advantages of massive MIMO, we further discuss the basic principles and characteristics of a massive MIMO on the basis of three cases which are single-user, multi-user, and multi-cell.

6.5.2 *Single-user massive MIMO*

For single-user massive MIMO, assuming that the number of antennas equipped by the base station is M and the number of antennas equipped by users is N, the signal received by the user can be expressed as

$$\mathbf{y} = \sqrt{p_d}\, \mathbf{Hs} + \mathbf{n} \tag{6.89}$$

where $\mathbf{H}$ is an $N \times M$-dimensional complex Gaussian channel matrix, $\mathbf{s}$ is an $M \times 1$ dimensional signal vector, $\mathbf{n}$ is an $N \times 1$-dimensional complex Gaussian noise, and p_d is the transmission power of the base station. Assuming that the user side knows the full channel information $\mathbf{H}$, the received signal-to-noise ratio can be expressed as

$$\text{SNR} = \frac{p_d \|\mathbf{H}\|^2}{N_0} = p_d \|\mathbf{H}\|^2 \tag{6.90}$$

(1) When the number of transmitting antennas is greater than the number of receiving antennas, the capacity of the receiving end can be expressed as

$$C = \text{lb}\det\left(\mathbf{I}_N + \frac{p_d}{M}\mathbf{H}\mathbf{H}^{\mathrm{H}}\right) \tag{6.91}$$

where

$$\frac{1}{M}\mathbf{H}\mathbf{H}^{\mathrm{H}} = \frac{1}{M}\begin{bmatrix} \|\mathbf{h}_1\|^2 & \mathbf{h}_1\mathbf{h}_2^{\mathrm{H}} & \cdots & \mathbf{h}_1\mathbf{h}_N^{\mathrm{H}} \\ \mathbf{h}_2\mathbf{h}_1^{\mathrm{H}} & \|\mathbf{h}_2\|^2 & \cdots & \mathbf{h}_2\mathbf{h}_N^{\mathrm{H}} \\ \vdots & \vdots & \ddots & \vdots \\ \mathbf{h}_N\mathbf{h}_1^{\mathrm{H}} & \mathbf{h}_N\mathbf{h}_2^{\mathrm{H}} & \cdots & \|\mathbf{h}_N\|^2 \end{bmatrix} \tag{6.92}$$

It can be seen that when the number of base station antennas M approaches infinity, there exists

$$\frac{\|\mathbf{h}_i\|^2}{M} = \frac{|h_1^i|^2 + |h_2^i|^2 + \cdots + |h_2^i|^2}{M} \approx \underbrace{\text{Var}[h]}_{1} + \underbrace{(\text{E}[h])}_{0} = 1$$

$$\frac{\mathbf{h}_i\mathbf{h}_j^{\mathrm{H}}}{M}_{(i\neq j)} = \frac{1}{M}\left(\underbrace{h_1^i h_1^{j*}}_{\text{Gaussian}} + \underbrace{h_2^i h_2^{j*}}_{\text{Gaussian}} + \cdots + \underbrace{h_M^i h_M^{j*}}_{\text{Gaussian}}\right) \approx \text{E}[h] = 0 \tag{6.93}$$

As can be known from Eqs. (6.92) and (6.93),

$$\frac{1}{M}\mathbf{H}\mathbf{H}^{\mathrm{H}} \approx \mathbf{I}_N \tag{6.94}$$

Therefore, when the number of base station antennas is much larger than the number of user antennas, namely, $M \gg N$, Eq. (6.91) can be further expressed as

$$C \approx \mathrm{lb} \det(\mathbf{I}_N + p_d \mathbf{I}_N)$$

$$= \mathrm{lb} \det \left(\begin{bmatrix} 1+p_d & 0 & \cdots & 0 \\ 0 & 1+p_d & \cdots & 0 \\ \vdots & \vdots & \ddots & \vdots \\ 0 & 0 & \cdots & 1+p_d \end{bmatrix}_{N \times N} \right)$$

$$= N \mathrm{lb}(1+p_d) \tag{6.95}$$

It can be seen from Eq. (6.95) that in the case of $M \gg N$, the system capacity is independent of the number M of transmitting antennas and linearly increases as the number of receiving antennas N increases.

(2) When the number of transmitting antennas is smaller than the number of receiving antennas, the capacity of the receiving end can be expressed as

$$C = \mathrm{lb} \det \left(\mathbf{I}_M + \frac{p_d}{M} \mathbf{H}^\mathrm{H} \mathbf{H} \right) \tag{6.96}$$

where

$$\frac{1}{M} \mathbf{H}^\mathrm{H} \mathbf{H} = \frac{N}{M} \frac{1}{N} \begin{bmatrix} \|\mathbf{h}_1\|^2 & \mathbf{h}_1 \mathbf{h}_2^\mathrm{H} & \cdots & \mathbf{h}_1 \mathbf{h}_M^\mathrm{H} \\ \mathbf{h}_2 \mathbf{h}_1^\mathrm{H} & \|\mathbf{h}_2\|^2 & \cdots & \mathbf{h}_2 \mathbf{h}_M^\mathrm{H} \\ \vdots & \vdots & \ddots & \vdots \\ \mathbf{h}_M \mathbf{h}_1^\mathrm{H} & \mathbf{h}_M \mathbf{h}_2^\mathrm{H} & \cdots & \|\mathbf{h}_M\|^2 \end{bmatrix} \tag{6.97}$$

When the number of antennas N at the receiving end tends to infinity, there also exists

$$\frac{\|\mathbf{h}_i\|^2}{N} = \frac{|h_1^i|^2 + |h_2^i|^2 + \cdots + |h_2^i|^2}{N} \approx \underbrace{\mathrm{Var}[h]}_{1} + \underbrace{(\mathrm{E}[h])}_{0} = 1$$

$$\frac{\mathbf{h}_i \mathbf{h}_j^\mathrm{H}}{N_{(i \neq j)}} = \frac{1}{N} \left(\underbrace{h_1^i h_1^{j*}}_{\text{Gaussian}} + \underbrace{h_2^i h_2^{j*}}_{\text{Gaussian}} + \cdots + \underbrace{h_N^i h_N^{j*}}_{\text{Gaussian}} \right) \approx \mathrm{E}[h] = 0 \tag{6.98}$$

It can be known from Eqs. (6.97) and (6.98) that

$$\frac{N}{M} \frac{1}{N} \mathbf{H}^\mathrm{H} \mathbf{H} \approx \frac{N}{M} \mathbf{I}_M \tag{6.99}$$

Therefore, when the number of antennas at the receiving end is much larger than the number of antennas at the transmitting end, namely $N \gg M$, Eq. (6.96) can be further expressed as

$$C \approx \mathrm{lb}\det\left(\mathbf{I}_M + \frac{Np_d}{M}\mathbf{I}_N\right)$$

$$= \mathrm{lb}\det\left(\begin{bmatrix} 1 + \dfrac{Np_d}{M} & 0 & \cdots & 0 \\ 0 & 1 + \dfrac{Np_d}{M} & \cdots & 0 \\ \vdots & \vdots & \ddots & \vdots \\ 0 & 0 & \cdots & 1 + \dfrac{Np_d}{M} \end{bmatrix}_{M \times M}\right)$$

$$= M\mathrm{lb}\left(1 + \frac{Np_d}{M}\right) \tag{6.100}$$

As can be seen from Eq. (6.100), in the case of $N \gg M$, the system capacity has an exponential relationship with the number of receiving antennas.

6.5.3 *Multi-user massive MIMO*

6.5.3.1 *Massive MIMO downlink channel*

Considering the multi-user MIMO system model shown in Fig. 6.18, it is assumed that there are M antennas at the base station and there are K users with single antennas in the cell.

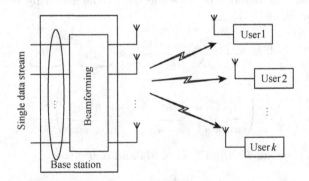

Fig. 6.18. Multi-user MIMO system model.

$\mathbf{h}_k$ represents the channel vector from the base station to the kth user, $\mathbf{w}_k$ is the beamforming vector of the kth user, and the signal received by the user can be expressed as

$$y = \sqrt{p_d}\,\mathbf{Hx} + \mathbf{n} + \sqrt{p_d}\,\mathbf{HWs} + \mathbf{n} \qquad (6.101)$$

where $\mathbf{H} \triangleq [\mathbf{h}_1, \mathbf{h}_2, \ldots, \mathbf{h}_K]$, $\mathbf{W} \triangleq [\mathbf{w}_1, \mathbf{w}_2, \ldots, \mathbf{w}_K]$, and beamforming meets the total power constraints, namely $E[\|\mathbf{x}\|^2] = \mathrm{tr}(\mathbf{W}^H\mathbf{W}) \le P$, $n_i \sim \mathcal{CN}(0,1)$.

We consider two traditional linear pre-processing methods, MRT and ZFBF, in which the filter matrix of MRT is $\mathbf{W} = \mathbf{H}^H$ and the filter matrix of ZFBF is $\mathbf{W} = \mathbf{H}^H(\mathbf{HH}^H)^{-1}$. The signal received by user k can be expressed as

$$y_k = \underbrace{\sqrt{p_d}\,\mathbf{h}_k\mathbf{w}_k s_k}_{\text{Desired signal}} + \underbrace{\sqrt{p_d}\,\sum_{i=1,i\neq k}^{K}\mathbf{h}_k\mathbf{w}_i s_i}_{\text{Interference signal}} + \underbrace{\mathbf{n}}_{\text{Noise}} \qquad (6.102)$$

It can be known from Eq. (6.102) that the signal-to-interference-and-noise ratio of the kth user can be expressed as

$$\mathrm{SINR}_k = \frac{p_d|\mathbf{h}_k\mathbf{w}_k|^2}{p_d\sum\limits_{i=1,i\neq k}^{K}|\mathbf{h}_k\mathbf{w}_i|^2 + 1} \qquad (6.103)$$

The rate of the kth user can be expressed as

$$R_k = \mathrm{lb}(1 + \mathrm{SINR}_k) \qquad (6.104)$$

The system's resultant rate is

$$R_{\mathrm{sum}} = \sum_{k=1}^{K} E\{R_k\} \qquad (6.105)$$

It is assumed that the number of base station antennas and the number of users tend to be infinite, namely $M, K \to \infty$ and $M/K = \alpha$, we can determine the expressions of SINR_k and R_{sum}. First consider MRT precoding, since $|\mathbf{h}_k\mathbf{h}_i^H|^2 \sim \chi_M^2$, it is known that

$$\frac{1}{K}\sum_{i=1,i\neq k}^{K}|\mathbf{h}_k\mathbf{h}_i^H|^2 \approx \mathrm{E}\{|\mathbf{h}_k\mathbf{h}_i^H|^2\} = M \qquad (6.106)$$

Then the SINR of the kth user can be expressed as

$$\mathrm{SINR}_k^{\mathrm{MRT}} = \frac{\frac{p_d}{\gamma}|\mathbf{h}_k\mathbf{h}_k^H|^2}{\frac{p_d}{\gamma}\sum\limits_{i=1,i\neq k}^{K}|\mathbf{h}_k\mathbf{h}_i^H|^2 + 1} \approx \frac{p_d\alpha}{p_d+1} \qquad (6.107)$$

where $\gamma = \|\mathbf{H}^H\|_F^2 \approx KM$. From Eq. (6.105), the resultant rate of the system is

$$R_{\mathrm{sum}}^{\mathrm{MRT}} = K\mathrm{lb}\left(1 + \frac{p_d\alpha}{p_d+1}\right) \qquad (6.108)$$

Considering the case of using ZFBF, since $1/\mathrm{tr}((\mathbf{H}^H\mathbf{H})^{-1}) = \frac{M-K}{K}$, which is the diversity order of ZFBF, the SINR of the kth user can be expressed as

$$\mathrm{SINR}_k^{\mathrm{ZF}} = \frac{p_d}{\mathrm{tr}((\mathbf{H}^H\mathbf{H})^{-1})} \approx p_d(\alpha - 1) \qquad (6.109)$$

Then the resultant rate of the system is

$$R_{\mathrm{sum}}^{\mathrm{ZF}} = K\mathrm{lb}(1 + p_d(\alpha - 1)) \qquad (6.110)$$

6.5.3.2 *Massive MIMO upstream channel*

In the following, we analyze the uplink channel of a massive MIMO system, as shown in Fig. 6.19.

The signal received by the base station can be expressed as

$$\mathbf{y} = \sqrt{p_u}\mathbf{G}\mathbf{x} + \mathbf{n} \qquad (6.111)$$

where $\mathbf{y}$ represents the $M \times 1$-dimensional signal vector received by the base station, $\mathbf{G} = \mathbf{H}\mathbf{D}^{1/2}$, $\mathbf{H} \triangleq [\mathbf{h}_1, \mathbf{h}_2, \ldots, \mathbf{h}_K]$, $\mathbf{D} \triangleq (\beta_1, \beta_2, \ldots, \beta_K)$, and $\mathrm{E}[|x_k|^2] = 1$.

Here, we use the simplest Maximum Ratio Combining (MRC) linear detector, namely $\mathbf{A} = \mathbf{G}$, then the processed received signal can be

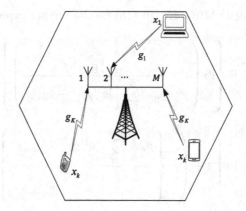

Fig. 6.19. Block diagram of the massive MIMO uplink system.

expressed as

$$\mathbf{r} = \sqrt{p_u}\mathbf{A}^{\mathrm{H}}\mathbf{G}\mathbf{x} + \mathbf{A}^{\mathrm{H}}\mathbf{n} \tag{6.112}$$

The received signal of the kth user can be further expressed as

$$r_k = \sqrt{p_u}\mathbf{a}_k^{\mathrm{H}}\mathbf{G}\mathbf{x} + \mathbf{a}_k^{\mathrm{H}}\mathbf{n}$$

$$= \underbrace{\sqrt{p_u}\mathbf{a}_k^{\mathrm{H}}\mathbf{g}_k x_k}_{\text{Desired signal}} + \underbrace{\sqrt{p_u}\sum_{i=1,i\neq k}^{K}\mathbf{a}_k^{\mathrm{H}}\mathbf{g}_i x_i}_{\text{Interference signal}} + \underbrace{\mathbf{a}_k^{\mathrm{H}}\mathbf{n}}_{\text{Noise}} \tag{6.113}$$

The kth user's SINR is

$$\mathrm{SINR}_k = \frac{p_u|\mathbf{a}_k^{\mathrm{H}}\mathbf{g}_k|^2}{p_u\sum_{i=1,i\neq k}^{K}|\mathbf{a}_k^{\mathrm{H}}\mathbf{g}_i|^2 + \|\mathbf{a}_k\|^2} \tag{6.114}$$

The uplink reachable rate of the kth user is

$$R_{P,k} = E\{\mathrm{lb}(\mathrm{SINR}_k)\}$$

$$= E\left\{\mathrm{lb}\left(1 + \frac{p_u|\mathbf{a}_k^{\mathrm{H}}\mathbf{g}_k|^2}{p_u\sum_{i=1,i\neq k}^{K}|\mathbf{a}_k^{\mathrm{H}}\mathbf{g}_i|^2 + \|\mathbf{a}_k\|^2}\right)\right\} \tag{6.115}$$

when the detector is MRC, Eq. (6.115) can be further expressed as

$$
R_{P,k}^{\mathrm{MRC}} = \mathrm{E}\left\{ \mathrm{lb}\left(1 + \frac{p_u\|\mathbf{g}_k\|^4}{p_u\sum\limits_{i=1,i\neq k}^{K}|\mathbf{g}_k^{\mathrm{H}}\mathbf{g}_i|^2 + \|\mathbf{g}_k\|^2} \right)\right\}
$$

$$
\geq \mathrm{lb}\left(1 + \left(\mathrm{E}\left\{ \frac{p_u\sum\limits_{i=1,i\neq k}^{K}|\mathbf{g}_k^{\mathrm{H}}\mathbf{g}_i|^2 + \|\mathbf{g}_k\|^2}{p_u\|\mathbf{g}_k\|^4} \right\} \right)^{-1} \right)
$$

$$
= \mathrm{lb}\left(1 + \frac{p_u(M-1)\beta_k}{p_u\sum\limits_{i=1,i\neq k}^{K}\beta_i + 1} \right) \triangleq \tilde{R}_{P,k}^{\mathrm{MRC}} \tag{6.116}
$$

Define $p_u = E_u/M$, then

$$
\tilde{R}_{P,k}^{\mathrm{MRC}} = \mathrm{lb}\left(1 + \frac{\dfrac{E_u}{M}(M-1)\beta_k}{\dfrac{E_u}{M}\sum\limits_{i=1,i\neq k}^{K}\beta_i + 1} \right) \tag{6.117}
$$

when the number of base station antennas $M \to \infty$,

$$
\tilde{R}_{P,k}^{\mathrm{MRC}} = \mathrm{lb}(1 + \beta_k E_u) \tag{6.118}
$$

It can be seen that when the number of base station antennas $M \to \infty$, both small-scale fading and inter-user interference disappear, and the transmission power is inversely proportional to the number of antennas.

6.5.4 *Multi-cell massive MIMO*

In the following, we will discuss massive MIMO technology in the case of multiple cells. For convenience, we will only discuss the two-cell case using the MRT precoder, as shown in Fig. 6.20. We analyze the interference between cells for user 1, and user 2, and the same analysis method can be used.

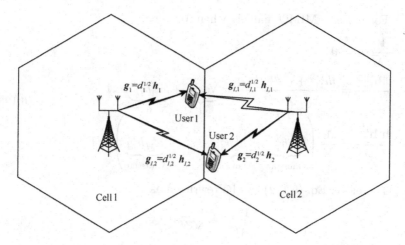

Fig. 6.20. Schematic diagram of multi-cell massive MIMO.

After being processed by the MRT precoder, the transmitting signals of base stations 1 and 2 can be expressed as

$$
\begin{aligned}
x_1 &= \frac{1}{\sqrt{\gamma_1}} \mathbf{h}_1^H \tilde{x}_1 \\
x_2 &= \sqrt{\gamma_2} \mathbf{h}_2^H \tilde{x}_2
\end{aligned}
\tag{6.119}
$$

when the number of base station antennas M is large, Eq. (6.119) can be further written as

$$
\begin{aligned}
x_1 &\approx \frac{1}{\sqrt{M}} \mathbf{h}_1^H \tilde{x}_1 \\
x_2 &\approx \frac{1}{\sqrt{M}} \mathbf{h}_2^H \tilde{x}_2
\end{aligned}
\tag{6.120}
$$

Then the signal received by user 1 can be expressed as

$$
y_1 \approx \sqrt{\frac{p_d}{M}} d_1^{1/2} \mathbf{h}_1 \mathbf{h}_1^H \tilde{x}_1 + \sqrt{\frac{p_d}{M}} d_{I,1}^{1/2} \mathbf{h}_{I,1} \mathbf{h}_2^H \tilde{x}_2 + n_1
\tag{6.121}
$$

When we scale the received y_1 by $1/\sqrt{M}$, we obtain

$$
\frac{1}{\sqrt{M}} y_1 \approx \sqrt{p_d} d_1^{1/2} \frac{\mathbf{h}_1 \mathbf{h}_1^H}{M} \tilde{x}_1 + \sqrt{p_d} d_{I,1}^{1/2} \frac{\mathbf{h}_{I,1} \mathbf{h}_2^H}{M} \tilde{x}_2 + \frac{1}{\sqrt{M}} n_1
\tag{6.122}
$$

For massive MIMO, namely when $M \to \infty$,

$$\frac{1}{\sqrt{M}}n_1 = 0$$

$$\frac{\|\mathbf{h}_i\|^2}{M} = \frac{|h_1^i|^2 + \cdots + |h_M^i|}{M} \approx \underbrace{\text{Var}[h]}_{1} + \underbrace{(\text{E}[h])^2}_{0} = 1 \qquad (6.123)$$

$$\frac{\mathbf{h}_i \mathbf{h}_j^{\text{H}}}{M_{(i \neq j)}} = \frac{1}{M} \left(\underbrace{h_1^i h_1^{j*}}_{\text{Gaussian}} + \underbrace{h_2^i h_2^{j*}}_{\text{Gaussian}} + \cdots + \underbrace{h_M^i h_M^{j*}}_{\text{Gaussian}} \right) = \text{E}[h] = 0$$

Therefore, Eq. (6.122) can be rewritten as

$$\frac{1}{\sqrt{M}}y_1 \approx \sqrt{p_d}d_1^{1/2}\tilde{x}_1 \qquad (6.124)$$

Therefore, the signal y_1 received by user 1 can be further expressed as

$$y_1 = \sqrt{p_d M}d_1^{1/2}\tilde{x}_1 \qquad (6.125)$$

It can be seen from Eq. (6.125) that when M is very large, there is no inter-cell interference and noise interference in the equation, and in the case where the received power is kept constant, the transmitted power decreases as M increases.

6.6 Summary

This chapter first outlines its development history and characteristics for ground-based transmission systems. On this basis, aiming at the problems faced by the future radio resource management architecture, the radio resource management model based on the two-layer cognitive loop and the radio resource management implementation architecture based on SORA are studied to improve the utilization efficiency of multi-layer wireless resources such as space, time, and frequency in ground-based wireless communication systems. In addition, as a key component of the access layer in the cognitive loop architecture, this chapter also introduces multi-user cooperative transmission technology and multi-cell coordinated transmission anti-interference technology to utilize the limited spectrum resources to improve the system performance and increase the system capacity.

References

1. Bai L, Li Y, Huang Q, Dong X and Yu Q. Spatial Signal Combining Theories and Key Technologies. Posts&Telecom Press, Beijing, 2013.
2. Young WR. Advanced mobile phone service: Introduction, background, and objectives. *Bell System Technical Journal*, 1979, 58: 1–14.
3. Groupe Speciale Mobile (GSM). Recommendations, 1988.
4. RCR STD 27-B. Personal digital cellular telecommunication system, 1995.
5. TIA/EIA/IS-95 Interim Standard. Mobile station-base station compatibility standard for dual mode wideband spread spectrum cellular system, 1993.
6. ITU-R Recommendation M.1457. Detailed Specifications of the Radio Interfaces of International Mobile Telecommunications-2000 (IMT-2000), 2000.
7. 3GPP2 C.S0002-D, Version 1.0. Physical Layer Standard for cdma 2000 Spread Spectrum Systems, 2004.
8. 3GPP TS 25.211 V4.2.0. Physical Channels and Mapping of Transport Channels onto Physical Channels (TDD), 2001.
9. 3GPP TS 25.211-840. Physical Channels and Mapping of Transport Channels onto Physical Channels (FDD), 2001.
10. Peng MG and Wang WB. *TD-SCDMA Mobile Communication System*. 2nd edn. Beijing: Mechanical Industry Press, 2007.
11. Holma H and Toskala A. *LTE for UMTS-OFDMA and SC-FDMA Based Radio Access*. Chippenham, UK: Wiley-Blackwell, 2009.
12. Nokia Siemens Networks successfully completed the world's first LTE handover test, 2009. http://www.cnki.com.cn/Article/CJFDTOTAL-DXJS2009 11039.htm.
13. ITU-R M.2038. Technology trends, 2004.
14. ITU-R M.1645. Framework and overall objectives of the future development of IMT-2000 and systems beyond IMT-2000, 2004.
15. ITU-R IMT-ADV/4-E. Acknowledgement of Candidate Submission from CHINA Under Step 3 of the IMT-Advanced Process (3GPP Technology), 2009.
16. ITU-R IMT-ADV/4-E. Acknowledgement of Candidate Submission from IEEE Under Step 3 of the IMT-Advanced Process (IEEE Technology), 2009.
17. ITU-R IMT-ADV/5-E. Acknowledgement of Candidate Submission from JAPAN Under Step 3 of the IMT-Advanced Process (IEEE Technology), 2009.
18. ITU-R IMT-ADV/6-E. Acknowledgement of Candidate Submission from JAPAN Under Step 3 of the IMT-Advanced Process (3GPP Technology), 2009.
19. ITU-R IMT-ADV/7-E. Acknowledgement of Candidate Submission from TTA Under Step 3 of the IMT-Advanced Process (IEEE Technology), 2009.
20. ITU-R IMT-ADV/8-E. Acknowledgement of Candidate Submission from 3GPP Proponent Under Step 3 of the IMT-Advanced Process (3GPP Technology), 2009.

21. 3GPP TR 36.913 v.8.0.1. Requirements for Further Advancements for E-UTRA, Tech.rep, 3rd Generation Partnership Project, 2009.

22. IEEE P802.16m/D3. Part 16: Air interface for broadband wireless access systems, advanced air interface, 2009.

23. Saleh A and Valenzuela R. A statistical model for indoor multipath propagation. *IEEE Journal on Selected Areas Communication*, 1987, 5(2): 128–137.

24. Bergmans P. A simple converse for broadcast channels with additive white Gaussian noise. *IEEE Transactions Information Theory*, 1974, 20(2): 279–280.

25. Saulnier GJ. Suppression of narrowband jammers in a spread-spectrum receiver using transform-domain adaptive filtering. *IEEE Journal on Selected Areas Communications*, 1992, 10(4): 742–749.

26. Redundancy JW. The discrete Fourier transform, and impulse noise cancellation. *IEEE Transactions on Communication*, 1983, 31(3): 458–461.

27. Babcock WC. Intermodulation interference in radio systems. *Bell Systems Technical Journal*, 1953, 32: 63–73.

28. Kahn LR. Reduction of adjacent channel interference, 1980, US Patent 4, 192, 970.

29. Suehiro N. A signal design without co-channel interference for approximately synchronized CDMA systems. *IEEE Journal on Selected Areas Communication*, 1994, 12(5): 837–841.

30. Moshavi S. Multi-user detection for DS-CDMA communications. *IEEE Communication Magazine*, 1996, 34(10): 124–136.

31. Mitola J and Maguire GQ. Cognitive radio: Making software radios more personal. *IEEE Personal Communication*, 1999, (6): 13–18.

32. Thomas RW and Friend H. Cognitive networks: adaptation and learning to achieve end-to-end performance objectives. *IEEE Communication Magazine*, 2006, 44(12): 51–57.

33. Balamuralidhar P and Prasad R. A context driven architecture for cognitive radio nodes. *Wireless Personal Communications*, 2008, 45(3): 423–434.

34. Fortuna C and Mohorcic C. Trends in the development of communication networks: Cognitive networks. *Computer Networks*, 2009, (53): 1354–1376.

35. Dong X, Li Y, and Wei SQ. Design and Implementation of a Cognitive Engine Functional Architecture. *Chinese Science Bulletin*, 2012, 57(12):1067–1073.

36. Liu J, Li J, Liu C, *et al.* Discover dependencies from data-a review. *IEEE Transactions on Knowledge and Data Engineering*, 2009, (99): 38–45.

37. Yu J and Han YB. *Service-Oriented Computing-Principles and Applications.* Beijing: Tsinghua University Press, 2006.

38. Dong X, Wei S, and Li Y. Service-oriented radio architecture: A novel M2M network architecture for cognitive radio systems. *International Journal of Distributed Sensor Networks*, 2012, 2012: 1–8.

39. Huang K, Anderews JG, and Heath RW. Performance of orthogonal beamforming for SDMA with limited feedback. *IEEE Transactions on Vehicular Technology*, 2009, 58(1): 152–164.

40. Yoo T, Jindal N, and Goldsmith A. Multi-antenna downlink channels with limited feedback and user selection. *IEEE Journal on Selected Areas in Communications*, 2007, 25(7): 1478–1491.

41. Zheng Y and Blostein S. Downlink distributed beamforming through relay networks. *IEEE Global Telecommunication Conference*, 2009, 1–6.

42. Bai L, Chen C, Choi J, *et al.* Greedy user selection using a lattice reduction updating method for multiuser MIMO systems. *IEEE Transactions on Vehicular Technology*, 2011, 60(1): 136–147.

43. Nam S and Lee K. Transmit power allocation for an extended V-BLAST system. *IEEE Personal, Indoor and Mobile Radio Communications*, 2002, (2): 843–848.

44. Lau VKN. Proportional fair space-time scheduling for wireless communications. *IEEE Transactions on Communication*, 2005, 53(4): 1353–1360.

45. Yang L, Kang M, and Alouini MS. On the capacity-fairness tradeoff in multiuser diversity systems. *IEEE Transactions on Vehicular Technology*, 2007, 56(4): 1901–1907.

46. Ma X and Zhang W. Performance analysis for MIMO systems with lattice-reduction aided linear equalization. *IEEE Transactions on Communications*, 2008, 56(2): 309–318.

47. Lenstra AK, Lenstra HW, and Lovasz L. Factoring polynomials with rational coefficients. *Math Annual*, 1982, (261): 515–534.

48. 3GPP R1-083069 LTE-Advanced Coordinated Multipoint Transmission/ Reception. Ericsson.

49. 3GPP TR36.814 V9.0.0-2010 Further Advancements for E-UTRA Physical Layer Aspects, 2010.

50. Liu YD. Research on Cooperative Scheduling and Interference Suppression Technology in Multi-cell MIMO Systems. University of Electronic Science and Technology of China, 2010.

51. Sun HX. Network evolution and interference in coordinated multi-point communication system. *ZTE Com Tec*, 2010.

52. Spencer QH, Swindlehurst AL and Haardt M, *et al.* Zero-forcing methods for downlink spatial multiplexing in multi-user MIMO channels. *IEEE Transactions on Signal Processing*, 2004, 52: 22–24.

53. Zhang J, Chen RH, Andrews JG, *et al.* Coordinated multi-cell MIMO system with cellular block diagonalization. *Conference Record of the Forty-First Asilomar Conference on Signals, Systems and Computers*, Pacific Grove, CA, 2007, 1669–1673.

54. Costa MHM. Writing on dirty paper. *IEEE Transactions on Information Theory*, 1983, 29(5): 439–441.

55. Marzetta TL. Noncooperative cellular wireless with unlimited numbers of base station antennas. *IEEE Transactions on Wireless Communications*, 2010, 9(11): 3590–3600.

56. Andrews JG, Claussen H, Dohler M, *et al.* Femtocells: Past, present, and future. *IEEE Journal on Selected Areas in Communications*, 2012, 30(3): 497–508.

57. Li GY, Xu ZK, Xiong C, *et al.* Energy-efficient wireless communication: Tutorial, survey, and open issues. *IEEE Wireless Communications*, 2011, 18(6): 28–35.
58. Ngo HQ, Larsson EG, and Marzetta TL. Energy and spectral efficiency of very large multiuser MIMO systems. *IEEE Transactions on Communications*, 2012, 61(4): 1436–1449.
59. Marzetta TL. How much training is required for multiuser MIMO? *Fortieth Asilomar Conference on Signal, Systems and Computers*, Pacific Grove, CA, 2006, 359–363.

Chapter 7

Air-Based Cooperative Transmission System

With the continuous development of network services, the defects of traditional ground cellular communication systems on coverage and transmission rate are more obvious. The new air-based transmission system, as an important supplement to the ground-based transmission system, has gradually attracted widespread attention. High-altitude platform station (HAPS) is considered to be an air-based broadband wireless access method with good potential application value, and it may become the third wireless communication system after the ground-based wireless communication system and the satellite-based communication system. It can achieve high mobility and high data rate of users and can complete wide-area coverage with less base stations and faster deployment. From the perspective of the air-based system and employing the cooperative transmission method, this chapter first introduces the background of the high-altitude platform communication system, including Google's Project Loon. Considering that the flexible beamforming of the antenna array is the core means of high-altitude platform implementation and cell coverage optimization, this chapter then introduces the array-based air-based transmission system and discusses the air-based beamforming technology based on two-dimensional filtering. Furthermore, the high-altitude platform cell planning method is given, and the efficient transmission mechanism between high-altitude platforms is introduced finally.

7.1 Overview of Air-Based Transmission Technology

Different from ground-based communication systems, base stations for air-based communication systems are high-altitude platforms which float in low-altitude areas. Therefore, the frequency band selection and cell planning of the air-based transmission system are significantly different from those of the ground-based systems. This section will provide an overview of the high-altitude platform communication system and provide a detailed introduction to Google's Project Loon.

7.1.1 *Introduction to the high-altitude platform communication system*

The high-altitude platform communication system is a space station operating at a height of 17–22 km in synchronization with the Earth. It is a new communication means with the advantages of microwave relay and satellite communication systems. It can be used in communication systems with ground control equipment, entry equipment, and a variety of wireless users in the main frequency bands of 47/48 GHz and 28/31 GHz. The high-altitude platform communication system is particularly suitable for temporary services in limited areas, remote areas, and emergency situations. The platform can move everywhere with its own power system, and it can maintain a stable position and return to the ground. The distance between the platforms can reach 500 km or so. As a separate mobile communication hub, the coverage can reach hundreds of square kilometers, and it is easy to manage and use. It can provide a wider broadband network for areas that cannot be fully covered by communication networks. Therefore, it is particularly suitable for developing countries.

Figure 7.1 shows the scenario of the high-altitude platform service, which consists of the sky end and the ground end. The sky end mainly consists of a platform (aircraft) and airborne communication equipment in the stratosphere. And the high-altitude communication platform consists of a huge balloon and control system,[1] causing the stability of the stratosphere to be a major problem. According to the measured data, the long-term average wind level is 30–40 m/s, and the high-altitude platform cannot bear the sudden fierce wind, which causes the loss of temporary communication. Although the wind direction of the stratosphere is relatively stable, the platform still needs to cope with wind direction changes. Recently, the advances in composite materials, the updates of computers and navigation systems, the studies of low-speed and high-altitude aerodynamics, and the

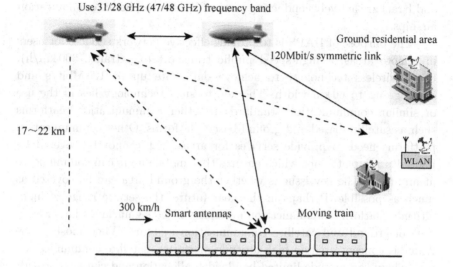

Use 31/28 GHz (47/48 GHz) frequency band

Ground residential area

120Mbit/s symmetric link

17~22 km

WLAN

300 km/h Smart antennas

Moving train

Fig. 7.1. High-altitude platform communication scenario.

propulsion systems consisting of internal combustion engines and solar energy have made the platform possible to hold its position. The platform is kept stationary relative to the ground by wind and its own power and cannot be separated from the atmosphere, so it needs to be supervised by the national aviation and telecommunications sector.[2] Since fossil energy is not easy to carry, the energy used by the platform is solar energy, and the atmosphere is thin, which is very suitable for designing solar panels with a large surface area. The key to the technology is the need for a durable, efficient, and lightweight integrated solar/fuel cell power supply which can store the energy needed for one night. Therefore, the regenerative fuel cell (RFC) is the most suitable choice. It is not only light but also has a high storage capacity. During the day, hydrogen and oxygen react electrochemically to generate electricity and water. At night, hydrogen and oxygen electrolyze and release the stored electricity from water.[3] In many countries, communication airships have been developed. For example, the balloon of the platform system which has been reported has a mass of 6000 kg, a load of 5000 kg, and a volume of 1700 m^3. The outer surface of the balloon is composed of 4 layers of materials. It has the ability of high strength, lightweight, and UV resistance, and it uses GPS positioning. The upper surface is covered with solar cells, which can provide 520 kW of power. At present, countries such as the United States, Canada, Japan, and Israel are actively conducting research on stratospheric communication airships.

The purpose of HAPS is to provide effective network services for users in remote areas or high-speed public transport (e.g. trains, 300 km/h), using wireless technology to achieve data rate up to 120 Mbit/s and coverage up to 60 km width. The key to such technology lies in the use of similar communication standards to other communication platforms such as satellite-based and ground-based platforms. Other communication platforms need to provide services for areas that cannot be covered by high-altitude platforms, which ensures that mobile users can communicate at any time. The key issue is whether the ground area can be covered as much as possible. Perhaps in the near future, the service range of high-altitude platform communication systems will be significantly larger than that of ground and satellite communication systems. When most of the traffic is concentrated on high-altitude platforms, satellite communication technology can provide limited bandwidth allocation and can also provide diverse broadcast content (such as videos) for very remote areas. And ground communications can provide high-capacity peer-to-peer services and seamlessly connect to other networks. In the near future, the traditional space-based communication mode will be replaced by the space–air-based communication mode.[4]

- The high-altitude platform communication system is designed to achieve a high transmission rate of 120 Mbit/s so that the high-quality standard is mainly based on G.1010 and Y.1541 standards of the International Telecommunication Union-Telecommunication Standardization Sector (ITU-T). The protocol used is still universal TCP/IP, and in addition to the basic services, some special cases need to be included. For example,
  - provide a private network (such as a corporate LAN) which is independent of the core network,
  - point-to-point backbone connections between core networks (such as internet service provider [ISP] backbone connections),
  - multiple users can access the core network at the same time.

It can be seen that integration and automation services and maintenance become very important when mobile users access the network.

By the combination of multiple platforms, it is possible to provide multiaspect services for a wide range of public areas, while adding more and faster services to overlapping areas, where they use the same frequency allocation. This technology is mainly based on the direction of the user's antenna. And when the user selects one of the platforms, other platforms have little impact on the link used by the user. Therefore, at the beginning, you can deploy one platform first, and then expand to multiple platforms after obtaining a certain income to form a complete joint service group. For frequency allocation, the main frequency band currently used is 31/28 GHz or 47/48 GHz.

The antenna system is a key part of the HAPS system. Due to the simultaneous presence of multiple accesses and the repeated use of information, the antenna system must support extremely high spectrum utilization. In order to ensure interconnection with the existing communication systems, the International Telecommunication Union has defined a HAPS standard based on CDMA systems that uses digital beamforming techniques to reduce the attenuation caused by adjacent links and increase the capacity of CDMA systems. At present, countries are working on research and development of multi-beam antennas for HAPS, and Japan and South Korea have proposed preliminary design schemes.[5,6] The design of HAPS mainly considers antenna operating frequency, sidelobe limitations, system capacity, platform functionality, and stability and reliability.[5]

The relatively fixed ground system adopts the traditional cellular network, and the coverage is mainly determined by the design of the antenna array. Each cell has a certain bandwidth, and the entire system is maximized by reasonable allocation. The HAPS system can provide mobile cellular coverage or fixed wireless services, and through the combination with ground telecommunication networks, real-time communication throughout the region can be realized. Platform network (backhaul) and platform communication can use optical communication. Optical communication systems have higher data transmission rates than millimeter-wave band communications, so optical backhaul can greatly expand wireless links without cloud coverage and is particularly suitable for transmitting data without strict time requirements. However, high communication rates (at least 14 Gbit/s) are required between platforms, and traditional methods are more difficult to implement, while optical communication can best meet this requirement. Since the platform location is higher than the cloud, internal communication is not affected by weather factors. This method can be used to establish an air network without requiring particularly complicated and expensive ground equipment in remote areas.

From August to October 2004, a platform test was conducted in the British town of Pershore, and the following demonstration was successfully carried out using a spherical circulator at a height of 300 m:

- fixed users use broadband fixed wireless access (BFWA) at 28 GHz;
- end-to-end network connection;
- high-speed network services and video on demand;
- optical communication from HAP to the ground.

This experiment and more attempts in the future are testing the indicators of high-altitude platform communication in a step-by-step manner. The load weight limitations of stratospheric aircraft, the use of the 28/29-GHz and the 28/31-GHz millimeter bands, the single-beam coverage of the ground range, the design of the embedded antenna, and the modulation and coding of the signals have been verified. By the use of nano-laser, the platform-to-ground station can transmit up to 270 Mbit/s video signals.

Providing communication support for users at high speeds is also a goal of high-altitude platform services. In the following, a description of some on-board WLANs based on trains is given.[4]

HAPS networks need to be seamlessly integrated with the existing communication networks, so it is necessary to consider specific requirements and specific environments on the basis of the existing development standards. The survey shows that the relatively mature broadband standards cannot meet the requirements of future HAPS high-speed communication. The main reason may be that the frequency band is not suitable. The IEEE 802.16 series of standards still under development is likely to become the standard for future high-speed communications. However, the millimeter-band signal propagation between HAP and mobile vehicles is seriously affected by precipitation attenuation and scattering, and the influence of the Doppler effect also needs to be considered. The amount of transmission at different times and the use of a buffer can optimize the attenuation caused by precipitation. Signal modulation and demodulation are also critical, and methods such as quadrature phase shift keying (QPSK), orthogonal frequency division multiplexing (OFDM), and convolutional coding can be extended to train WLAN networks. Emerging MIMO wireless communication technology can also be applied to high-altitude platform networks, and finally, a feasible digital signal processing (DSP) platform is used to implement a HAPS-based on-vehicle WLAN network. However, the high-speed and frequent interleaving of vehicles is a major challenge for resource allocation, and providing efficient spectrum utilization and adequate quality of service is currently the key to exploration. Antennas used in vehicles need to consider efficiency, flexibility, and cost efficiency. Based on various requirements, advanced beamforming techniques must be applied as soon as possible.

The high-altitude platform communication system is a new communication method that has emerged in recent years. It has a good application prospect in both civil and military fields. The International Telecommunication Union also has a designated dedicated spectrum to study the multiplexing methods of spectrum resources. In recent years, the success of various experiments has pointed the way for the development of the HAPS system. Section 7.1.2 provides a brief introduction to Google's high-altitude platform service program — Project Loon.

7.1.2 *Introduction to Project Loon*

Project Loon is an experimental program of Google Inc., which is run by Google X Labs. It aims to provide cheap and stable network connectivity for developing countries, especially relatively backward rural areas, by setting up hot air balloons and establishing network connections. Because two-thirds of the world's people can't afford expensive broadband charges, when they encounter natural disasters, the network is always vulnerable, resulting in communication disruption.

The project scenario is shown in Fig. 7.2. The hot air balloon used is made of polyethylene plastic and its fully deployed height is 12 m, which can withstand more pressure than ordinary meteorological air balloons. There is a solar panel in the middle, and an electronic device below which transmits and receives signals. The hot air balloon, which relies on solar remote control, will move more than 20 km above the stratosphere, avoiding

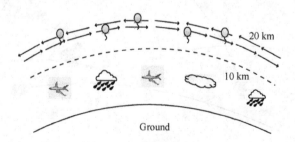

Fig. 7.2. Project Loon.

clouds and aircraft navigation within 10 km of the Earth's surface. In other words, it is much higher than the altitude of many airplanes. Working in a manner similar to satellite networks, the balloon transmits signals to and from special antennas and receivers on the ground. The wind direction in the stratosphere has obvious stratification. Project Loon uses software to calculate the flight direction of the balloon and lets it fly to a specific layer, and then form a huge high-altitude network. After the balloon receives the network signal from the ground in the air, the signal is then transmitted to nearby balloons and other receiving sides on the ground. By constantly transmitting and receiving, the network signal is transmitted to more places.

The most obvious problem for this project is that the upper atmosphere is always moving, and Google temporarily said that it will use "some complex algorithms and a large amount of computing" to solve this problem. The specific plan is still under further exploration. Because this plan requires new wireless transmission and as it is also better to use the new spectrum, it is subject to strict supervision by countries, making it difficult to implement.

The communication scenario is shown in Fig. 7.3. The interconnection between the platforms forms a large communication network. The "balloon" receives a network signal from the ground in the air and transmits it to nearby balloons and other receiving sides on the ground. The network signal is transmitted to more places by constantly transmitting and receiving. And the utilization of spectrum resources can be optimized by reasonable

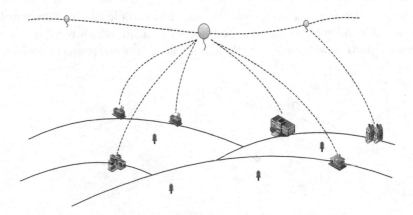

Fig. 7.3. Project Loon communication scenario.

allocation of ground users, which ensures that the users can enjoy faster network services.

Project Loon's first pilot was launched in New Zealand in June 2013. Local villagers provided the feedback that "the access speed and quality of hot air balloon network are much better than the dial-up network that is currently used". At present, Google is also looking for partners for the next stage, hoping that the future rural roaming service can be solved by a single balloon.

7.2 Array-Based and Air-Based Transmission System

The high-altitude platform can provide line of sight (LOS) links to a large number of users in a large area and can also reduce the use of infrastructure relative to terrestrial networks. Such systems use a cell structure to provide overall channel capacity, and the cell is served by a number of spot beams on the HAP.

In 1989, Lee described the function of the terrestrial cellular structure.[7] In order to provide a wide coverage area, the cells are divided and in order to control co-channel interference, different channels are allocated to neighboring cells based on the frequency, time slot, and coding. Typically, three, four, or seven cells are aggregated into groups and the overall frequency allocation is made among them. The more the number of cells in the group, the larger the multiplexing distance and the larger the carrier-to-interference ratio (CIR), but the fewer the number of channels per cell, which is a basic compromise in most mobile communication systems. Fixed channel allocation in a non-attenuating environment can provide the highest channel capacity, but dynamic allocation can achieve higher channel capacity when the communication load of each cell changes.[8-10] And dynamic channel allocation is also useful when the environment or communication load is unpredictable.[11-13]

The high-altitude platform communication system and the terrestrial communication system are the same in some aspects while differing in other aspects. The multiplexing scheme is still available (fixed or dynamic), but the main difference is how the interference is generated and how it decays with distance. In a high-altitude platform system, interference is caused by the antenna providing service over the same channel, resulting from main lobe or sidelobe overlap. In this section, we will explain the relationship between the number of antennas sharing the same channel and the distribution of CIR on the ground.

The ideal antenna beam illuminates the corresponding cell with uniform power above the cell, and the power fading outside the cell is zero, in which case the antenna is actually a spatial filter. In practice, the achievable spot beams do not meet the ideal criteria, especially in the millimeter wave band, where array beamforming techniques are difficult. The most viable antenna for this application may be the aperture type, whose radiation characteristics have been perfectly established. In order to minimize interference, very low sidelobes and steep main lobe drop beams are very advantageous. While the sidelobe suppression can be realized by the design of the corrugated horn,[14] the rate of descent is mainly affected by the width of the main lobe, namely the directivity. If very high directionality is chosen, the edge of the cell will suffer from excessive power attenuation, and if very low directivity is chosen, too much power will exceed the range of the cell. For HAPS frequency allocation, such as 48 GHz, limited available transmission capacity and rain attenuation increase the edge link budget, especially at the edge of the cell. In this section, we present an optimized directionality rule based on maximizing power at the edge of each cell. It is in contrast to similar work,[15] where those cells are defined to be within the range of the half power beamwidth.

In wireless communication networks at high-altitude platforms, co-channel interference is a function of antenna beamwidth, angular separation, and sidelobe levels. When millimeter waves are applied to a HAPS serving cell, the array aperture antenna type on the platform is a feasible method. We present a method for predicting co-channel interference based on curve fitting approximation for the radiation pattern of elliptical beams, which illustrates the optimal power at the cell edge and an optimal beamwidth estimating method for the cell of a common hexagonal layout. And this method is applied to a building with 121 cells, where the sidelobes are modeled to be flat and below the peak 40 dB level, the carrier-to-interference ratio (CIRs) of a cell group with four cells varies from 15 dB at the cell edge to 27 dB at the cell center, and these numbers will increase between 19 dB and 30 dB in the case of the group with seven cells. By reducing the level of sidelobes, CIR can be improved.

This section will first describe a simple model for calculating the antenna beam pattern. Thereafter, the power and ground CIR levels are obtained by calculating the beamwidth and the pointing angle required for the hexagonal cells of the same conventional layout size, and the results of the calculation are given. Our intention is to establish a system planning method for multiple antenna beams by using simple building blocks.[16]

7.2.1 *Mathematical model of the antenna beam*

The aperture antenna and the high directivity coefficient can be obtained by approximating the main lobe model from the nth power of the cosine function:[17]

$$D = D_{\max}(\cos \theta)^n \qquad (7.1)$$

where θ represents the angle with respect to the antenna boresight and n represents the roll-off factor of the model. As shown in Fig. 7.4, it is a typical curve of a corrugated horn radiation pattern.

The curve fits the main lobe very well before the pattern changes to $-26\,\text{dB}$ of the peak. In addition, because the curve does not produce new sidelobe structures, the low-flat sidelobe structure is more suitable for model simulation.[18] As shown in Fig. 7.4, when the sidelobe level is very low, the peak directivity coefficient can be approximated by the following equation:[19]

$$D_{\max} = \frac{32 \log 2}{\theta^2_{3\,\text{dB}} + \phi^2_{3\,\text{dB}}} \qquad (7.2)$$

where $\theta_{3\,\text{dB}}$ and $\phi_{3\,\text{dB}}$ represent the 3-dB beamwidth of two orthogonal planes. Since a uniform circular beam is adopted, both values are equal

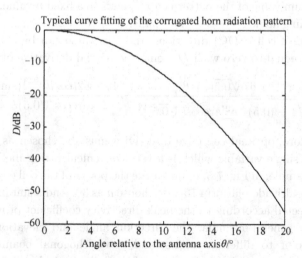

Fig. 7.4. **Typical curve fitting of the corrugated horn radiation pattern** $((\cos\theta)^n$ with $n = 208$).

and the directivity coefficient of the antenna is further approximated by

$$D = (\cos \theta)^n \frac{32 \log 2}{2\theta_{3\,\mathrm{dB}}^2} \tag{7.3}$$

The 3-dB beamwidth is a function of n, and the directivity coefficient now is half of its maximum, then

$$\cos \left(\frac{\theta_{3\,\mathrm{dB}}}{2} \right)^n = 0.5 \tag{7.4}$$

and thus

$$\theta_{3\,\mathrm{dB}} = 2 \arccos \left(\sqrt[n]{\frac{1}{2}} \right) \tag{7.5}$$

Therefore, the directivity coefficient can only be expressed as a function of θ and n:

$$D = (\cos \theta)^n \frac{32 \log 2}{2 \left(2 \arccos \left(\sqrt[n]{\dfrac{1}{2}} \right) \right)^2} \tag{7.6}$$

Let's assume that $\theta = \theta_{\mathrm{edge}}$ making D fixed at the edge of the cell, and n is a variable. As shown in Fig. 7.5, for a given angle at the edge of the cell, the maximum value of the pattern corresponds to a fixed n value. When the corresponding angle increases, the smaller n can obtain the maximum value of the edge of cell (EOC) direction. And this value can be calculated by making D' equal to zero with D' being the partial derivative of n, that is,

$$\frac{\partial D}{\partial n} = \frac{-1.67 \sqrt[n]{0.5}(\cos \theta)^n}{\sqrt{1 - (0.5)^{\frac{2}{n}}} n^2 [\arccos(\sqrt[n]{0.5})]^3} - \frac{4n \log 2 (\cos \theta)^{n-1} (\sin \theta)}{(\arccos \sqrt[n]{0.5})^2} \tag{7.7}$$

Therefore, optimal cell edge directivity must be chosen as this curve has only a single variable which is a very convenient fitting method.

For example, in Fig. 7.5, to maximize the power of the cell edge pointing to the high-altitude platform 15°, we choose n as 30. And a suitable antenna is then selected according to the peak directivity coefficient of Eq. (7.2).

In the general formula, the direction angle and elevation angle of the cell point to different angles, and two orthogonal beamwidths are generated while optimizing the power of the cell edge in both planes of the elliptical beam. Elliptical beam antenna techniques that produce optimized

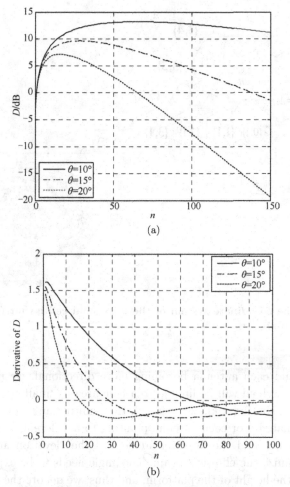

Fig. 7.5. Directivity coefficient of the cell edge 16. (a) As a function of n.
(b) Derivative with respect to n.

geographic coverage are also discussed in Ref. 20. The effects of CIR will
be given subsequently.

7.2.2 *Efficient algorithm for predicting co-channel*
interference

The number of cells is generally between 100 and 200, because the demand
for the total aperture area of the antenna increases rapidly as the cell
size decreases. Due to the need for generating more cells (meaning more

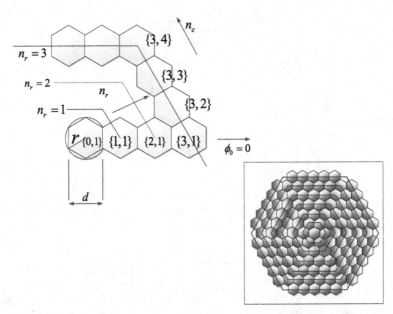

Fig. 7.6. The coordinate system of the hexagonal cell layout (illustration: 121 cell layouts).

antennas) and each antenna becoming more directional, we predict that the HeliNet payload will be limited to a hole area as small as m^2.[21]

For a cell sharing a known channel, the pointing angle of the antenna is first calculated. For each antenna pointing to a different cell, the above method is used, and the direction angle and the elevation angle can be used to optimize the elliptical beam. The angle needs to be expressed as a function of the height of the platform, and thus, we denote the coordinates of the cell as $\{n_r, n_c\}$ with n_r representing the cylinder number of coaxial hexagonal cells and n_c representing the number of cells of the coaxial ring. The cell distribution on the first side of the third ring is also shown in Fig. 7.6.[6]

The direction angle and elevation angle are formed by pointing to the center of any cell from the high-altitude platform and can be calculated by

$$\theta_0 = \arctan \frac{g}{h} \tag{7.8}$$

$$\phi_0 = \arcsin \frac{(c' - 1)d \sin \frac{\pi}{3}}{g} + (n_s - 1)\frac{\pi}{3} \tag{7.9}$$

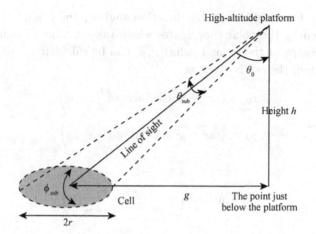

Fig. 7.7. HAP and cell geometry.

where d is the width of the hexagonal cell. As shown in Fig. 7.7, if h is the height of the high-altitude platform and g is the distance from the high-altitude platform to the center of the cell, then

$$g = \sqrt{(n_r d)^2 + ((c'-1)d)^2 - 2n_r d^2(c'-1)\cos\left(\frac{\pi}{3}\right)} \qquad (7.10)$$

Since the result is the same on each side of the hexagonal cell, c' is used to indicate the cell location on each side relative to the first cell:

$$c' = n_c - (n_s - 1)n_r \qquad (7.11)$$

where n_s is an integer between 1 and 6, representing the different sides of the hexagon:

$$n_s = 1 + \text{floor}\left[\frac{n_c - 1}{n_r}\right] \qquad (7.12)$$

where floor represents the rounded down operator. The direction angle and height angle pointing to the cell with radius r can be calculated by the following equation:

$$\theta_{\text{sub}} = \arctan\left(\frac{g+r}{h}\right) - \arctan\left(\frac{g-r}{h}\right) \qquad (7.13)$$

$$\phi_{\text{sub}} = 2\arctan\frac{r}{\sqrt{g^2 + h^2}} \qquad (7.14)$$

For each antenna beam, the direction angle θ_a and height angle ϕ_a are represented by the polar coordinates which take the line of sight as axis, and the energy at the ground point (x, y) can be calculated. The variation of azimuth of the cell is given as

$$x_0 = \sqrt{x^2 + y^2} \cos\left(\arctan\frac{y}{x} - \phi_0\right) \tag{7.15}$$

$$y_0 = \sqrt{x^2 + y^2} \sin\left(\arctan\frac{y}{x} - \phi_0\right) \tag{7.16}$$

and then

$$\theta_a = \arctan\left(\frac{\sqrt{x_a^2 + y_0^2}}{h\cos\theta_0 + x_0\sin\theta_0}\right) \tag{7.17}$$

$$\phi_a = \arctan\frac{y_0}{x_a} \tag{7.18}$$

where x_a is the projection of x_0 on a plane perpendicular to the line of sight, as shown in Fig. 7.8,[16] and is given as

$$x_a = (x_0 - h\tan\theta_0)\cos\theta_0 \tag{7.19}$$

In this condition, the direction angle is a function of a cell coordinate (n_r, n_c) with variables h and d, so it can be quickly generated according to the h and d of the high-altitude platform. The elliptical beam curves

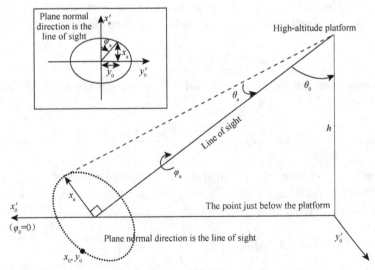

Fig. 7.8. Derivation of the antenna directivity of a point on the ground (illustration: φ_a is the angle from normal to the radial direction).

applicable to Eq. (7.1) are represented by n_θ and n_ϕ, respectively, and are adapted to optimize the directionality θ_{sub} and ϕ_{sub} of the cell edge. And thus the directivity coefficient of the point $\{x, y\}$ is

$$D = D_{\max}\{\cos(\theta_a \cos \phi_a)\}^{n_\theta} \{\cos(\theta_a \sin \phi_a)\}^{n_\phi} \tag{7.20}$$

at the same time,

$$D_{\max} = \frac{32 \log 2}{\left\{2 \arccos\left(^{n_\theta}\sqrt{\frac{1}{2}}\right)\right\}^2 + \left\{2 \arccos\left(^{n_\phi}\sqrt{\frac{1}{2}}\right)\right\}^2} \tag{7.21}$$

Therefore, we can get a $\{x, y, \text{power}\}$ data column, where power represents the antenna directivity coefficient at point $\{x, y\}$ on the ground minus the extra free space loss for the sub-platform. (Since CIR is not a function of free space loss, it is very useful to include a power source that allows the power variation in the service area to be in the proper range.)

According to the space solution, the size of each beam data column is generally 10^4. Utilizing the data columns obtained, the magnitude of co-channel interference can be calculated as follows:

$$\text{CIR}(x, y) = \frac{P_{\max}(x, y)}{-P_{\max}(x, y) + \sum_{i=1}^{n_{cc}} P_i(x, y)} \tag{7.22}$$

where n_{cc} represents the number of cells in the same channel. At each point $\{x, y\}$, all data columns $\{x, y, \text{power}\}$ are detected to find the maximum power $P_{\max}(x, y)$, which is the payload. The denominator in the above equation is the sum power of all other beams, namely the interference. Therefore, for each cell group, a new sequence $\{x, y, \text{CIR}\}$ can be further obtained, and then the geographic coverage feature can be quantified by setting different threshold values. In the following, the effect of the antenna beam we discussed above can be illustrated by some representative conclusions.

7.2.3 *121 cell structure results*

Previous studies on HAP cellular structures[21, 22] were often assumed to be circularly symmetric beams, and here, we will show that elliptical beams can produce better coverage. In some in-depth studies, the structure is a traditional hexagonal cell layout, with 121 cells of 6.3-km diameter serving a coverage of 60 km in diameter.[23] When four channels are selected for

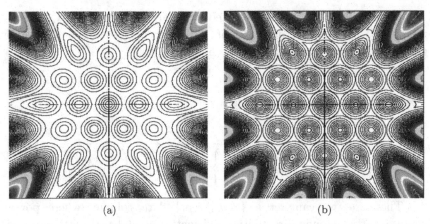

(a)   (b)

Fig. 7.9.   Four-channel CIR profile. (a) Circular beam. (b) Optimal elliptical beam.

transmission, the adjacent cells are numbered 1, 2, 3, 4. And then we divide the 121 cells into four groups, namely three groups of 30 cells and a further group of 31 cells. The CIR mode of the group with 31 cells is shown in Fig. 7.9,[16] and the sidelobes are modeled at the flat −40-dB level. The HAP height is 20 km.

The CIR coverage comparison of the circular beam and the elliptical beam is shown by the contours in Fig. 7.9 with a 10-dB spacing. In the former, the azimuth pointing to each HAP cell has been chosen to obtain a 3-dB circular beamwidth. In this case, the beamwidth is bigger than it is in the elevation plane because the pitch angle to each cell in the HAP is smaller than the azimuth (except for the centrally located cell because it is directly below the HAP). The resulting CIR pattern shows a considerable deformation of the cells, which is often radioactive further away from their intended location. Conversely, when an optimized elliptical beam is employed, the region of high CIR will have a better geographic location and exhibit a higher CIR. The geographic coverage in both cases is quantified in Fig. 7.10 as a partial area co-channel cell group serving a given CIR threshold.[16] For a given CIR, the optimized elliptical beam provides a distinct advantage. In this multiplexing scheme, the other three cell groups closely follow the same trend.

Through further processing of the data set, the geographic relationship between the coverage of the four cell groups can be described. The difference in coverage will be displayed in the selected CIR threshold. Considering the overlap of regions, the CIR coverage trend (quality of service) is worse

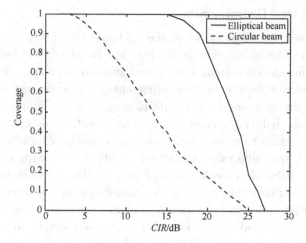

Fig. 7.10. Coverage of the four channels.

at the center when the CIR threshold is 18 dB and the geographic overlap
between channels 1, 2, and 3 is 10 dB, and coverage is available even beyond
the expected 60-km-diameter circle. It shows that it is beneficial to use a
fixed multiplexing scheme to control the difficulty of geographic coverage.

An intuitive conclusion is that the edges of the cell tend to accept
multiple channels coverage. It is useful for increasing the channel capacity
at the edge of the cell where the CIR and power budget of the primary
channel are the weakest.

7.2.4 *Conclusions*

Many of the issues related to the broadband service cellular plans from HAP
have been explored. A key factor is the shape of the antenna beams and their
effect on the CIR mode which can be found. The work is not specific to any
RF frequency, but the focus is on the approximate curve fitting method for
bandwidth and aperture antenna radiation patterns between 28 GHz and
48 GHz. Elliptical beams provide an advantage by optimizing power at the
edge of the cell, which is most important when the RF link budget is critical.
By cropping the beamwidth of each antenna to the pointing angle of its
corresponding cell, the array antenna is used to serve the selected coverage
area. Although these physical demonstrations have not been provided for
these beams, the form of beam modeling is both realistic and easy to handle
for the description of cellular services.

7.3 Air-Based Beamforming

With the mathematical model of the air-based transmission system, the application of smart antenna technology is a novel method based on the HAP communication system. First, smart antenna technology can generate multiple narrow beams, concentrating energy in a defined area (cell), which can provide space division multiplexing access for improving spectral efficiency and reducing communication equipment. Second, the ability of the smart antenna to resist interference can reduce or eliminate co-channel interference, thus improving the signal quality and allowing transmission power to be reduced. A method of implementing the smart antenna is based on digital beamforming, pointing the main beam to the direction of the target user (specified by the azimuth estimate) while adjusting the inactive portion of the signal or the low-level sidelobes pointing to other users or sources of interference.[24] The main challenge in implementing digital beamforming based on HAP communication systems is that it requires a large number of array elements (including antenna elements, amplifiers, I-Q downconverters, and AD converters) which result in a high complexity and high cost of the system.

To implement an HAP communication system, we introduce a digital beamforming scheme which significantly reduces the number of array elements without any performance penalty.[26] With this scheme, the complexity and cost of the system are reduced, thus improving the adaptability of the HAP system. In addition, the proposed digital beamforming scheme can specify both the narrowband main beamwidth and the low level of the sidelobes. Our proposed digital beamformer, the two-dimensional spatial interpolation beamformer (2D SIB), is an updated version of the spatially interpolated beamformer for uniform planar arrays discussed in Ref. 25. The 2D SIB shown in Fig. 7.11 consists of a cascade structure with two beamformers (or two spatial filters). The first beamformer is called the two-dimensional spatial shaping filter (2D SSF), which is based on the performance of a conventional beamformer (conventional beamforming or cone beamforming[26]), where the internal cell spacing is replaced by Ld, d is the internal beam spacing of the conventional beamformer, and L is an integer called the Expansion Factor. The second beamformer is called a spatial masking filter (2D SMF) and is used at the 2D SMF output to attenuate the grating lobes due to changes in array spacing. Therefore, a beam pattern with a narrower main beamwidth (because of the increased spacing) and a lower sidelobe level (due to the attenuation of the 2D SMF) can be obtained without increasing

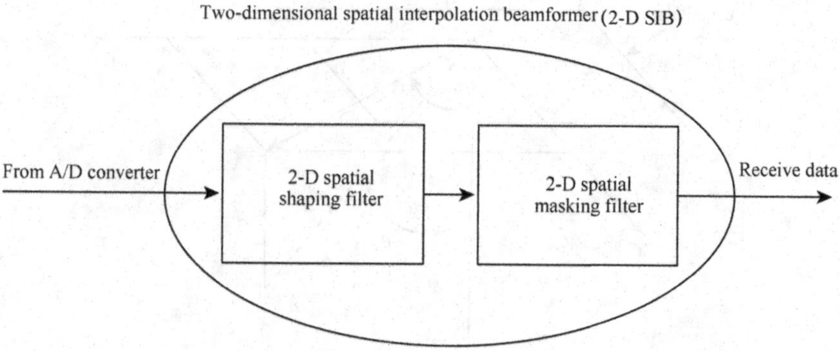

Two-dimensional spatial interpolation beamformer (2-D SIB)

Fig. 7.11. **Two-dimensional spatial interpolation beamformer.**

the array elements. In other words, we can reduce the number of array elements while still maintaining the same main beamwidth and sidelobe levels as conventional beamforming methods which require more array elements.

This section will focus on beamforming techniques based on two-dimensional filtering.

7.3.1 *Two-dimensional spatial interpolation beamformer (2D SIB)*

7.3.1.1 *Two-dimensional prototype beamformer*

A conventional cone beamformer which uses a uniform rectangular array is called a two-dimensional prototype beamformer and the antenna unit is placed in the x–y plane as shown in Fig. 7.12. If there is case where the incident wave is incident on the array in the direction of the pitch angle $\theta(-90° \leq \theta \leq 90°)$ and the azimuth angle $\phi(0° \leq \phi \leq 360°)$, according to the literature in Ref. 27, a rectangular array can be thought of as a linear array with N identical elements $w_{\mathrm{pr},m}^{(1)}$. And each element is a linear array with M elements (along the x-axis). The array factor in the far-field condition can be expressed as

$$F_{\mathrm{pr}}^{(1)}(\phi, \theta) = \sum_{m=0}^{M-1} w_{\mathrm{pr},m}^{(1)} \mathrm{e}^{-\mathrm{j}kmd_x \cos\phi \sin\theta} \tag{7.23}$$

where the mth element has a complex weight of magnitude and is phase oriented to the x-axis, which is expressed as

$$w_{\mathrm{pr},m}^{(1)} = W_{\mathrm{pr},m}^{(1)} \mathrm{e}^{\mathrm{j}kmd_x \cos\phi_0 \sin\theta_0} \tag{7.24}$$

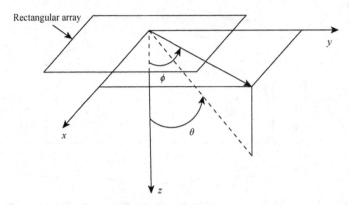

Fig. 7.12. Rectangular array in x–y plane.

where $W_{\text{pr},m}^{(1)}$ is the magnitude of the complex weight, $k = \frac{2\pi}{\lambda}$ is the phase propagation factor, d_x is the internal element spacing in x direction, and ϕ_0 and θ_0 are the desired azimuth and elevation angles, respectively. From Eq. (7.23), we can obtain

$$F_{\text{pr}}^{(1)}(\phi, \theta) = \sum_{m=0}^{M-1} W_{\text{pr},m}^{(1)} e^{-jkmd_x(\cos\phi\sin\theta - \cos\phi_0\sin\theta_0)} \qquad (7.25)$$

The array factor of the linear array with N elements is given as follows:

$$F_{\text{pr}}^{(2)}(\phi, \theta) = \sum_{n=0}^{N-1} w_{\text{pr},n}^{(2)} e^{-jknd_y\cos\phi\sin\theta} \qquad (7.26)$$

The complex weight $w_{\text{pr},n}^{(2)}$ of the nth element is oriented on the y-axis and is given as follows:

$$w_{\text{pr},n}^{(2)} = W_{\text{pr},n}^{(2)} e^{jknd_y\cos\phi_0\sin\theta_0} \qquad (7.27)$$

d_y is the internal element spacing in the y direction. From Eq. (7.26), it is seen that

$$F_{\text{pr}}^{(2)}(\phi, \theta) = \sum_{m=0}^{N-1} W_{\text{pr},n}^{(2)} e^{-jknd_y(\cos\phi\sin\theta - \cos\phi_0\sin\theta_0)} \qquad (7.28)$$

For convenience, we define the (normalized) spatial frequencies as

$$\begin{aligned} \mu &= kd_x(\cos\phi\sin\theta - \cos\phi_0\sin\theta_0), \\ \nu &= kd_y(\cos\phi\sin\theta - \cos\phi_0\sin\theta_0) \end{aligned} \qquad (7.29)$$

Replacing the exponential terms in Eqs. (7.25) and (7.28) with

$$z_x = e^{jkd_x(\cos\phi\sin\theta - \cos\phi_0\sin\theta_0)} = e^{j\mu}$$
$$z_y = e^{jkd_y(\cos\phi\sin\theta - \cos\phi_0\sin\theta_0)} = e^{j\nu}$$

(7.30)

We have

$$F_{\mathrm{pr}}^{(1)}(\mu) = \sum_{m=0}^{M-1} W_{\mathrm{pr},m}^{(1)} z_x^{-m}$$

$$F_{\mathrm{pr}}^{(2)}(\nu) = \sum_{n=0}^{N-1} W_{\mathrm{pr},n}^{(2)} z_y^{-n}$$

(7.31)

According to the principle of multiplication of the pattern, the complete array factor of the 2D prototype beamformer is

$$F_{\mathrm{pr}}(\mu,\nu) = F_{\mathrm{pr}}^{(1)}(\mu) F_{\mathrm{pr}}^{(2)}(\nu)$$

(7.32)

7.3.1.2 *2D SSF and 2D SMF*

The 2D SSF is based on the two-dimensional prototype beamformer and replaces the internal element spacing d_x and d_y with $L_x d_x$ and $L_y d_y$. L_x and L_y are integers called the expansion factors of the x direction and the y direction, respectively. Replacing z_x and z_y in Eqs. (7.31) and (7.32) with $z_x^{L_x}$ and $z_y^{L_y}$, the 2D SSF array factor can be obtained as follows:

$$F_{\mathrm{sh}}(\mu,\nu) = F_{\mathrm{sh}}^{(1)}(\mu) F_{\mathrm{sh}}^{(2)}(\nu)$$

$$= \sum_{m=0}^{M-1} W_{\mathrm{pr},m}^{(1)} z_x^{-mL_x} \sum_{n=0}^{N-1} W_{\mathrm{pr},n}^{(2)} z_y^{-nL_y}$$

(7.33)

The design of the two-dimensional spatial filter mainly considers three parameters: (1) the 3-dB main lobe width of the target beamformer in ϕ_0 and θ_0 directions (the corresponding 3-dB spatial frequency is μ_{d-3} and ν_{d-3}); (2) the main lobe width of the target beamformer from zero to zero in the ϕ_0 and θ_0 directions (the corresponding zero-to-zero spatial frequency is μ_{d-0} and ν_{d-0}); and (3) target beamformer sidelobe level value (SLL_d).

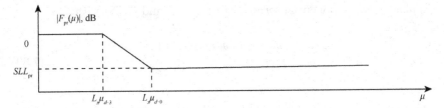

Fig. 7.13. **Two-dimensional prototype beamformer** ($\mu_{\text{pr}-3} = L_x \mu_{d-3}, \mu_{d-0} = L_x \mu_{d-0}, \text{SLL}_{\text{pr}} = \text{SLL}_d$).

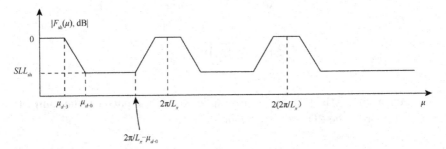

Fig. 7.14. **2D SSF** ($\mu_{\text{sh}-3} = \mu_{d-3}, \mu_{\text{sh}-0} = \mu_{d-0}, \text{SLL}_{\text{sh}} = \text{SLL}_d$).

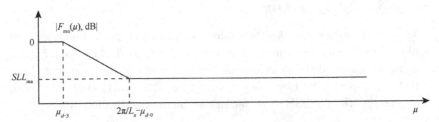

Fig. 7.15. **2D SMF** ($\mu_{\text{ma}-3} = \mu_{d-3}, \mu_{\text{ma}-0} \leq ((2\pi)/L) - \mu_{d-0}, \text{SLL}_{\text{ma}} = \text{SLL}_d$).

Figures 7.13 and 7.14 show the amplitude response and the corresponding design parameters of the two-dimensional prototype beamformer and 2D SSF with respect to spatial frequency μ, respectively. As expected, the L_x times expansion of the spatial spacing results in an L_x times compression of the 2D SSF pattern, as shown in Fig. 7.14, but in the filter, the grating lobes will appear at the point of $\frac{2\pi}{\lambda}$ integer multiples of the μ-axis. If we connect a 2D spatial masking filter (2D SMF) behind the 2D SSF (as shown in Fig. 7.15), the grating lobes are attenuated to obtain a beamformer[26] with a frequency response as shown in Fig. 7.16.

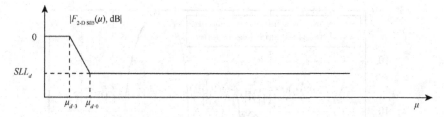

Fig. 7.16. 2D SIB.

The 2D SSF and 2D SMF can provide the same conclusion for the spatial frequency ν. By the principle of multiplication of the pattern, the final array factor 2D SSF and 2D SMF can be obtained. The cascade structure of 2D SSF and 2D SMF is called a 2D SIB, and its pattern is

$$|F_{2\text{D SIB}}(\mu,\nu)| = |F_{\text{ah}}(\mu,\nu)||F_{\text{ma}}(\mu,\nu)| \qquad (7.34)$$

where $|F_{\text{ah}}(\mu,\nu)|$ is the amplitude response of 2D SSF, and $|F_{\text{ma}}(\mu,\nu)|$ is the amplitude response of 2D SMF.

7.3.2 *Design example of two-dimensional spatial interpolation filter*

As an example, we design a narrowband beamformer which meets the following requirements:

- the antenna array gain G is 25 dB;
- the main lobe points in a direction with a pitch angle of 30° and an azimuth angle of 45°;
- The 3-dB main lobe width in both the azimuth and vertical directions is 8° and the SLL is below −75 dB. The main lobe width and SLL should meet the requirements of ITU R-221.

We first design a two-dimensional prototype beamformer adopting a uniform rectangular array with an internal element spacing $d_x = d_y = \frac{\lambda}{2}$ of the array plane. In order to obtain a 3-dB main lobe width with 8° in the azimuth and vertical directions, this two-dimensional prototype beamformer should have a 3-dB main lobe width with 27.5° in the vertical direction and 21° in the azimuth direction. The Dolph–Chebyshev window should have 21×21 elements. Thus, a 2D SSF can be obtained by replacing d_x and d_y with $L_x d_x$ and $L_y d_y$, respectively.

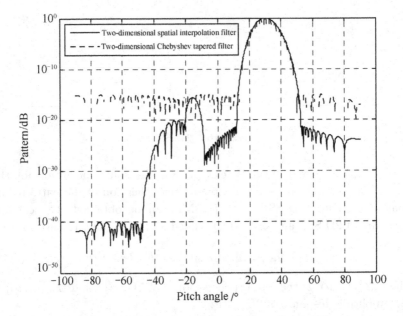

Fig. 7.17. Direction of the pitch angle at 30°.

In the following, a 2D SMF is designed to reduce the SSL to $-75\,\mathrm{dB}$ to attenuate the grating lobes which appear in the range of $-90° \leq \theta \leq 90°$ and $0° \leq \phi \leq 360°$ due to the increase in the internal element spacing. The same as the design of the 2D SSF, the 2D SMF main lobe still points to the direction whose pitch angle θ_0 is 30° and azimuth ϕ_0 is 45°. The Dolph–Chebyshev window can obtain a 2D SMF with 22×22 elements. And this 2D SMF cascades to the 2D SSF to form a 2D SIB.

Figure 7.17 shows a 2D SIB beam pattern with a 3-dB main lobe width of 7.25° in the vertical direction. And the 2D SIB beam pattern with a 3-dB main lobe width of 8.75° in the azimuth direction is shown in Fig. 7.18. Figure 7.17 compares the 2D SIB of 21×21 elements with the traditional Dolph–Chebyshev tapered beamformer (2D DCTB). In order to obtain the same main lobe width and SSL value (less than $-75\,\mathrm{dB}$) for the 2D SIB of 21×21 elements, the total number of elements of the 2D DCTB should be 63×63.

Therefore, by the 2D SIB, the number of digital beamformer array elements (antenna elements, receiving modules, A/D converters, etc.) is significantly reduced. According to the above example, the number of array elements is reduced from 63×63 to 21×21, yet having the same

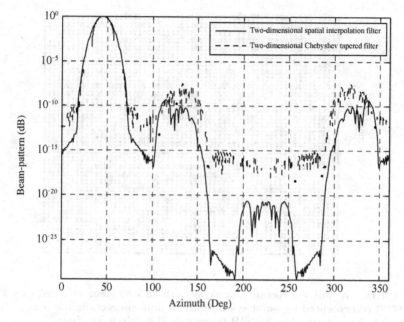

Fig. 7.18. Direction of the azimuth angle at 45°.

performance as a conventional tapered beamformer. Figure 7.19 shows a
uniform rectangular array (represented by dot symbol) of 63×63 elements
used as a 2D DCTB and a uniform rectangular array of 21×21 elements
used as a 2D SIB (represented by circle symbol) in the x–y plane. For the
sake of clarity, two overlapping uniform rectangular arrays are displayed,
and the dot symbol and the circle symbol indicate the position of the
antenna elements in the two uniform rectangular arrays. The internal
element spacing of the 2D DCTB URA is $\frac{\lambda}{2}$ and the internal element spacing
of the 2D SIB URA is $\frac{3\lambda}{2}$.[26]

Digital beamforming schemes based on two-dimensional spatial interpolation have many advantages. First, the number of array elements (antenna
elements, receiving modules, A/D converters, etc.) is greatly reduced.
At the same time, the main beamwidth and sidelobe levels obtained remain
the same as those under the conventional beamforming method requiring
more array elements. Therefore, the complexity and cost of the system
can be reduced. Second, this new beamforming scheme can produce very
narrow main lobe widths and very low SSL, and the main lobe width and
SSL can be determined independently without the requirement of a balance
between them.

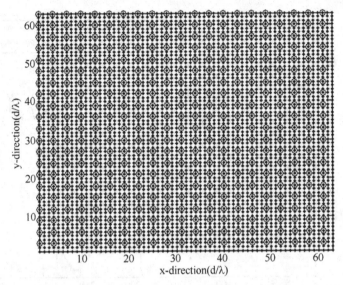

Fig. 7.19. A uniform rectangular array with 63 × 63 elements used as a 2D DCTB (represented by point symbol) and a uniform rectangular array with 21 × 21 elements used as 2D SIB (represented by circle symbol).

7.4 High-Altitude Platform Cell Planning

The high-altitude platform can be mainly divided into the integrated terrestrial–HAP–satellite system and the terrestrial–HAP system, as shown in Fig. 7.20. The same as traditional terrestrial cellular communication systems, cell planning for high-altitude platforms is also a critical technology. This section will focus on the cell planning strategies in three different communication scenarios, analyze the performance of the wireless link, and provide some theoretical basis for the engineering implementation of the high-altitude platform communication system.

7.4.1 *Coverage and cell partition of high-altitude platforms*

7.4.1.1 *Coverage of high-altitude platforms*

The altitude and coverage of the high-altitude platform are in a certain proportional relationship. The relationship between the minimum communication pitch angle α and the diameter d of the coverage can be

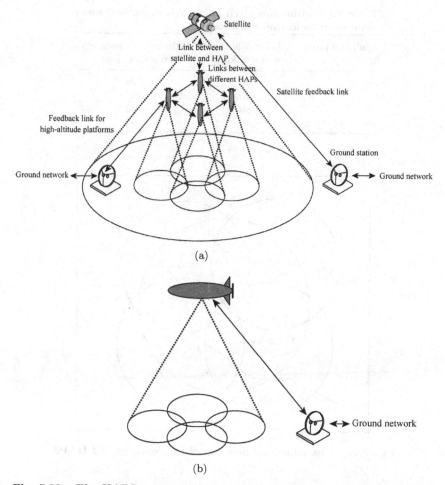

Fig. 7.20. The HAPS communication system structure. (a) An integrated terrestrial-HAP satellite system. (b) An integrated terrestrial-HAP system.

expressed by

$$d = 2R \left(\cos^{-1} \left(\frac{R}{R+h} \cos(\alpha) \right) - \alpha \right) \tag{7.35}$$

where R represents the radius of the earth. Table 7.1 shows the relationship between the minimum communication pitch angle and the diameter of the coverage when the altitude of the high-altitude platform is 22 km.[28]

Table 7.1. Minimum pitch angle, coverage, and maximum communication distance.

Minimum pitch angle (°)	Diameter of the coverage (km)	Maximum communication distance (km)
0	1056	529
5	420	212
15	160	83
30	76	44

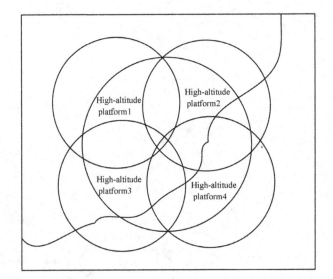

Fig. 7.21. The schematic diagram of the coverage of 4 HAPS.

As can be seen from Table 7.1, the high-altitude platform at a height of 22 km in the air has a circular coverage area of 1056-km diameter. Considering terrain masking, the quality of communication is guaranteed when the minimum communication pitch angle is 5°. We can also find that a high-altitude platform can cover a range of 420 km in diameter, provided that the lowest pitch angle is 5°. In order to cover a wide range, more high-altitude platforms will be used to form a network system. For example, in order to seamlessly cover a circular area of 600 km in diameter, Fig. 7.21 shows the need for four high-altitude platforms covering a diameter of 430 km to form a network system.

7.4.1.2 *Cell partition*

Cell partition is one of the key technologies for high-altitude platform communication, and three cell partition methods[28] are provided below and discussed. Taking the ground mobile communication system as a reference, the first method is to divide into hexagonal cells of the same size. Figures 7.22 and 7.23 illustrate the coverage of a partitioned cell as a hexagon. The advantage of the first method is that the cell is easy

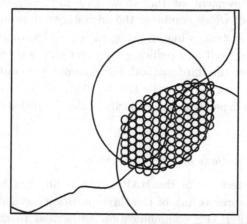

Fig. 7.22. Coverage diagram (the radius of the plot is 2 km and the diameter of the coverage is 43 km).

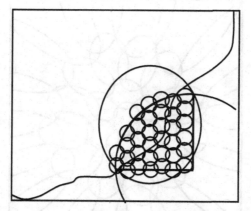

Fig. 7.23. Coverage diagram (the radius of the plot is 3 km and the diameter of the coverage is 43 km).

to manage. In addition, the difficulty it brings is the beamforming of the antenna and the interference of the beam.

The second method is an elliptical cell. When the beam of the antenna is fixed, the formation of the elliptical cell divides the coverage of the HAP. The advantage of the second method is the simple antenna implementation. However, the result of the outer large-area elliptical cell method and the inner small-area elliptical cell method easily leads to the lack of channel capacity.

As an improvement of the above two methods, we give a third partition method, which combines the advantages of ground and satellite communication systems while avoiding their disadvantages by enhancing the inner elliptical cell and reducing the outer elliptical cell. Figures 7.24 and 7.25 illustrate the third method. For example, from outside to the half of the inside beamwidth, it can be 15°, 15°, 15°, 10°, 10°, respectively. The size of the beam depends on the capacity of the channel and the number of antennas.

7.4.1.3 *The calculations of wireless connection*

Different characteristics of the HAPS wireless link can be compared by calculating the wireless link of the three partition methods. The channel characteristics of HAPS communication are similar to those of satellite communication, and both show LOS propagation with small multipath

Fig. 7.24. Ellipse cell.

Fig. 7.25. Five-layer elliptical cell.

Table 7.2. System parameters.

Parameter	Value
Bandwidth (MHz)	3.84
Data rate (Mbit/s)	3.84
Carrier frequency (GHz)	2
Coverage area diameter (km)	43
EIRP (dBw) transmitted by the terminal	0.5
Minimum transmission distance from the earth (km)	22
Maximum transmission distance from the earth (km)	31

effects and shadow effects. For example, Table 7.2 illustrates the system parameters for HAPS communication.

Assuming that the HAPS use a circular aperture antenna, the gain of the antenna is

$$G = \eta \left(\frac{\pi D}{\lambda} \right)^2 = \eta \left(\frac{\pi f D}{c} \right)^2 \tag{7.36}$$

where η, D, λ are the efficiency of the antenna, the diameter of the antenna, and the wavelength, respectively. Half-power beamwidth is

$$\theta = 72.7 \frac{\lambda}{D} = 72.7 \frac{c}{fD} \tag{7.37}$$

Therefore, the relationship between the antenna gain and the half-power beamwidth is given as

$$G = \eta \left(\frac{72.7\pi}{\theta} \right)^2 \tag{7.38}$$

In the sun, the carrier-to-noise ratio C/N can be calculated from

$$\frac{C}{N} = \left(\frac{\text{EIRP}}{LI} \right) \left(\frac{G}{T} \right) \left(\frac{1}{kB} \right) \tag{7.39}$$

where EIRP is the carrier power, L is the loss of the atmosphere, I is the loss of free space, and G is the gain of the antenna. T is the system noise temperature, k is the Boltzmann constant, and B is the bandwidth of the noise. EIRP can be calculated by

$$\text{EIRP} = P \times G \tag{7.40}$$

The carrier-to-noise ratio C/N can be written in the form of dB as follows:

$$\frac{C}{N} = \text{EIRP(dB w)} - L(\text{dB}) - I(\text{dB}) + \frac{G}{T}(\text{dB/K})$$
$$- k(\text{dB w/K-Hz}) - B(\text{dBHz}) \tag{7.41}$$

Assume that the HAP has a transmitted power of $2\,\text{W}$ and an atmospheric loss of $L = 1\,\text{dB}$. The C/N of the uplink three cell partition methods can be obtained from Table 7.3 to Table 7.6.

The three cell partition methods have different carrier-to-noise ratios, and the center carrier-to-noise ratio is $3\,\text{dB}$ from the edge of the hexagonal cell. Therefore, the first cell partition method will be applied to the regional average service load. The carrier-to-noise ratio of the elliptical cell is $16\,\text{dB}$ at the center compared with the edge. Due to the large outer coverage area and the small inner coverage area, the second and third cell partition methods will be applied to provide loads to centralized areas (such as cities) and to areas with fewer services (such as rural areas).

7.4.2 *Conclusions*

This section focuses on coverage performance, wireless link performance, and HAPS multi-spot beam cell partition scheme. Three cell partition strategies are given for three scenarios of high-altitude platform communication systems. Through numerical calculations and computer simulation

Table 7.3. C/N of the cell center with an uplink radius of 3 km.

Parameter	EIRP	Free-space loss	G/T	Boltzmann constant	Noise bandwidth	Atmosphere loss	C/N
Value	−3 dBw	125.3 dB	−14.4 dB/K	−228.6 dBw/K-Hz	66 dB-Hz	1 dB	18.9 dB
Explanation	$P = 0.5$ W	$d = 22$ km	$T = 300$ K		$B = 3.84$ MHz		

Table 7.4. C/N of the cell edge with an uplink radius of 3 km.

Parameter	EIRP	Free-space loss	G/T	Boltzmann constant	Noise bandwidth	Atmosphere loss	C/N
Value	−3 dBw	128.3 dB	−14.4 dB/K	−228.6 dBw/K-Hz	66 dB-Hz	1 dB	15.9 dB
Explanation	$P = 0.5$ W	$d = 31$ km	$T = 300$ K		$B = 3.84$ MHz		

Table 7.5. C/N of the uplink ellipse cell center.

Parameter	EIRP	Free-space loss	G/T	Boltzmann constant	Noise bandwidth	Atmosphere loss	C/N
Value	−3 dBw	125.3 dB	−3.4 dB/K	−228.6 dBw/K-Hz	66 dB-Hz	1 dB	29.9 dB
Explanation	$P = 0.5$ W	$d = 22$ km	$T = 300$ K		$B = 3.84$ MHz		

Table 7.6. C/N of the edge of the uplink elliptic cell.

Parameter	EIRP	Free-space loss	G/T	Boltzmann constant	Noise bandwidth	Atmosphere loss	C/N
Value	−3 dBw	128.3 dB	0.2 dB/K	−228.6 dBw/K-Hz	66 dB-Hz	1 dB	13.5 dB
Explanation	$P = 0.5$ W	$d = 31$ km	$T = 300$ K		$B = 3.84$ MHz		

analysis, we present the performance of the wireless link and the appropriate scenario for each cell partition strategy. The content of this section is very important in terms of the engineering implementation of the high-altitude platform communication system. At present, a range of technologies are being used and developed to meet the growing demand for high data rate communications, where 2.5G and 3G networks, wireless local area networks, and satellites have been widely used to provide communication services. However, bandwidth services which provide low transmission delay while covering a wide range of applications have always been a dream of communication engineers developing wireless network systems. With some of their outstanding features and the ability to provide a wide range of services beyond communication, HAPS seems to represent the dream of communications engineers working in "ideal wireless systems". With the advantages of many ground and satellite systems and the potential to provide broadband communications in a cost-effective manner, HAPS does not replace the existing technology, but complements them. We hope that in the next few years, we will hope to realize some of these projects and we believe the usefulness of HAPS and the first network may begin to build in the air.

7.5 High-Altitude Platform Transmission Mechanism

In the previous sections, we discussed the key technologies used in communication between high-altitude platforms and the ground. This section focuses on the communication methods between high-altitude platforms. In terms of the current technical means, millimeter-wave communication (MMWC) is a suitable wireless communication mode between high-altitude platforms. In the case of a millimeter-wave array antenna configured above the high-altitude platform communication, the core challenge of achieving a high-speed connection between the two platforms is mutual alignment, which refers to how to set a vector for beamforming. And this section will discuss this problem in detail.

7.5.1 *The introduction of related technologies*

In the communication between high-altitude platforms, in order to compensate for propagation attenuation, it is common to use phased-array antenna beamforming to obtain array gain.[28, 29] In order to effectively obtain high array gain, the antenna weight vectors (AWVs) at the receiving and transmitting ends need to be correctly set before the signal transmission, which is called joint transmit/receive beamforming. If the channel state information (CSI) is known to both the receiving and transmitting ends, then the best AWVs are derived directly based on well-known channel performance evaluation criteria, which is the maximum received SNR criterion. Unfortunately, due to the large number of antennas, channel estimation for millimeter-wave communications will be very time consuming. In addition, because of the need to utilize matrix decomposition, namely SVD decomposition, the computational complexity will become very high. For these reasons, the beamforming training method is very advantageous for finding antenna weight vectors because of its low computational complexity.[30–32] There are generally two types of joint beamforming training methods. One is based on fixed dictionary-based switching beamforming training.[33] The dictionary includes a series of predefined AWVs. Beamforming training at the transmitting end and the receiving end needs to be checked in a certain order, and then the antenna weight vector pair which obtains the maximum SNR is selected. The other is adaptive beamforming training, which does not require a dictionary. The antenna weight vector expected by the receiving end and the transmitting end is obtained by real-time joint iterative training. It can be clearly seen from the above description that the switching beamforming method is relatively simple, and the adaptive method is relatively complicated.

Most adaptive beamforming training uses the same optimal method, where the iterative training method without *a priori* CSI is used to find the best singular vector at both the receiving end and the transmitting end.[34,35] This singular value vector-based training method (SGV) requires that both the amplitude and phase of the antenna weight vector be adjusted. Furthermore, in practical millimeter-wave communication, phased arrays are typically designed such that only the phase is adjustable and the amplitude is set to a fixed value, which simplifies the design and reduces the energy losses.[30,33,34] In fact, even in a general MIMO system, the gain is fixed and the phase is adjustable, which can significantly reduce the complexity of the engineering practice.[36,37] In these examples, the SGV method is no longer applicable due to the fixed gain of the phased array. The training methods proposed in Refs. 36, 37 are also not suitable for this case, because these methods only require full or quantized *a priori* CSI beamforming transmitted at the transmitting end. And for joint beamforming, *a priori* CSI information is not required for either the transmitter or the receiver.

In this section, we introduce a steering vector-based joint beamforming training method (STV) which takes advantage of the directional characteristics of the millimeter-wave communication channel.[38] Performance evaluations show that for LOS channels, both STV and SGV have fast convergence rates and achieve ideal array gain. And for non-LOS channels, STV converges faster than SGV, but the array gain is also reduced. Of course, the STV can still achieve the desired array gain. In summary, the STV is able to achieve faster convergence rates and near-ideal array gains in both LOS and non-LOS channels, making it have a high engineering practical value.

7.5.2 *System and channel model*

Without loss of generality, we believe that the normalized distance between the individual antenna elements of the high-altitude platform communication system is half its wavelength. The number of array elements at the transmitting end is M, and the number of array elements at the receiving side is N. The ULA is a phased array, which means that only the phase can be controlled. A single RF path refers to the path connecting the devices at the receiving and transmitting ends. Based on the millimeter-wave communication channel test results in Ref. 28,39, since the millimeter-wave wavelength is relatively small, the most important ones in multipath cells (MPCs) are reflection effects, and the scattering and diffraction effects are negligible. Therefore, MPCs in millimeter-wave communication have directional characteristics, which means different MPCs have different signal transmission steering angles ϕ_{tl} and signal receiving steering angles ϕ_{rl}. Therefore, the channel model expression is given as follows:[40, 41]

$$\mathbf{H} = \sqrt{NM} \sum_{l=0}^{L-1} \lambda_l \mathbf{g}_l \mathbf{h}_l^{\mathrm{H}} \qquad (7.42)$$

where L is the number of multipath units, $(\cdot)^{\mathrm{H}}$ is the conjugate transpose operator, λ_l is the coefficient of the channel, and $\mathbf{g}_l$ and $\mathbf{h}_l$ are the steering vectors of the receiving and transmitting ends,[40, 41] with expressions $\mathbf{g}_l = \{e^{j\pi(n-1)\Omega_{rl}}/\sqrt{N}\}_{n=1,2,\ldots,N}$ and $\mathbf{h}_l = \{e^{j\pi(m-1)\Omega_{tl}}/\sqrt{M}\}_{m=1,2,\ldots,M}$. Ω_{rl} and Ω_{tl} represent the cosine of the transmitting and receiving angle of the 1st MPC.

Assuming that the transmitting AWV $\mathbf{t}$ and the receiving AWV $\mathbf{r}$ satisfy $\|\mathbf{t}\| = \|\mathbf{r}\| = 1$, the expression of the received signal $\mathbf{y}$ is $\mathbf{y} = \mathbf{r}^{\mathrm{H}}\mathbf{H}\mathbf{t}s + \mathbf{r}^{\mathrm{H}}\mathbf{n}$

with **s** denoting the transmitted symbol and **n** indicating the noise vector. The purpose of beamforming training is to find suitable transmitting and receiving AWVs so that a high received SNR can be obtained. The received SNR is defined as $\gamma = |\mathbf{r}^H \mathbf{H} \mathbf{t}|^2 / \sigma^2$, with σ^2 being the noise energy.

7.5.3 *Singular vector-based training method*

Let us first introduce the SGV method. It is well known that in order to maximize γ, the ideal AWVs should be the largest singular vector of the channel matrix **H**. Perform the SVD decomposition on **H**,

$$\mathbf{H} = \mathbf{U} \mathbf{\Sigma} \mathbf{V}^H = \sum_{k=1}^{K} \rho_k \mathbf{u}_k \mathbf{v}_k^H \tag{7.43}$$

where **U** and **V** are unitary matrices with their columns $\mathbf{u}_k$ and $\mathbf{v}_k$, respectively. $\mathbf{\Sigma}$ is an $N \times M$ diagonal matrix whose elements are non-negative real-valued ρ_k with $\rho_1 \geq \rho_2 \geq \cdots \geq \rho_K \geq 0$ and $K = \min(\{M, N\})$. The ideal AWVs requires $\mathbf{t} = \mathbf{v}_1$ and $\mathbf{r} = \mathbf{u}_1$.

Generally, **H** is not available, so iterative methods are needed for beamforming training to find the ideal AWVs. Based on Refs. 31, 32, $\mathbf{H}^{2m} \triangleq (\mathbf{H}^H \mathbf{H})^m = \sum_{k=1}^{K} \rho_k^{2m} \mathbf{v}_k \mathbf{u}_k^H$, which can be obtained by utilizing the directionality of the communication channel through m iterations. When m is large, $\mathbf{H}^{2m} \approx \rho_1^{2m} \mathbf{v}_1 \mathbf{v}_1^H$, therefore, the ideal transmitting and receiving AWVs can be obtained by normalizing $\mathbf{H}^{2m} \mathbf{t}$ and $\mathbf{H} \times \mathbf{H}^{2m} \mathbf{t}$, respectively.

The SGVs training method is as follows:

1. **Initialization:** An initial transmitting AWV vector **t** is selected at the transmitting end, and the selection of the AWV can be random.
2. **Iteration:** Iterate ε times as follows and then stop.

   Use the same AWV vector **t** for continuous transmission in N slots, and simultaneously use the unit matrix $\mathbf{I}_N$ as the AWV vector of the receiving end, which refers to the nth column of $\mathbf{I}_N$ which is taken as the nth slot of the received AWV. And thus the received vector $\mathbf{r} = \mathbf{I}_N^H \mathbf{H} \mathbf{t} + \mathbf{I}_N^H \mathbf{n}_r = \mathbf{H} \mathbf{t} + \mathbf{n}_r$ can be obtained with $\mathbf{n}_r$ representing the noise vector, and thus, **r** is normalized.

   Use the same AWV vector **t** for continuous transmission in M slots of the receiving end and simultaneously use the unit matrix $\mathbf{I}_M$ as the AWV vector of the transmitting end. A new received vector $\mathbf{t} = \mathbf{I}_M^H \mathbf{H}^H \mathbf{r} + \mathbf{I}_M^H \mathbf{n}_t = \mathbf{H}^H \mathbf{t} + \mathbf{n}_t$ can be obtained with $\mathbf{n}_t$ being the noise vector.

3. **Result:** $\mathbf{t}$ is the AWV of the transmitting end, and $\mathbf{r}$ is the AWV of the receiving end.

It can be seen that the number ε of iterations is based on the actual channel response, which will be explained later in this section. Obviously, although the SGV training method is very effective, it requires the amplitude and phase of AWVs to be adjusted. In a constant-amplitude phased array, this condition cannot be satisfied.

7.5.4 *Steering vector-based training method*

In fact, the SGV training method is a common method for any channel, which does not take advantage of the characteristics of the millimeter-wave communication channel. In millimeter-wave communication, the channel has a directional characteristic, which means $\mathbf{H}$ can naturally be expressed by Eq. (7.44), and Eqs. (7.44) and (7.45) are very similar. The difference is that $\{\mathbf{g}_l\}$ and $\{\mathbf{h}_l\}$ in Eq. (7.44) are constant-amplitude steering vectors rather than orthogonal bases, and $\{\mathbf{u}_k\}$ and $\{\mathbf{v}_k\}$ in Eq. (7.45) are strictly non-gain fixed orthogonal bases. In addition, according to Ref. 41 Tse and Viswanath, if $|\Omega_{rm} - \Omega_{rn}| \geq 1/N$ and $|\Omega_{tm} - \Omega_{tn}| \geq 1/M$, then $|\mathbf{g}_m^H \mathbf{g}_n|$ and $|\mathbf{h}_m^H \mathbf{h}_n|$ will be approximately equal to 0. This means that the receiving and transmitting angles can now be decomposed by the antenna array, which is very common in millimeter-wave communications. As a suboptimal method, the steering vector of the MPC in the strongest direction can be used as the AWVs transmitted and received by the transmitting end and the receiving end. Therefore, we propose the STV training method. The advantage of STV is that the elements of the steering vector have a fixed gain, which is very suitable for phased arrays with constant amplitude. Furthermore, although both the receiving and transmitting angles can be decomposed by the array in subsequent analyses, the STV training method can also be used even when the angle is indecomposable. The reason is that multiple MPCs have very close angles that are indistinguishable; hence, they can be thought of as a single MPC.

Assuming $\mathbf{H}$ is in advance, the STV is deduced as follows. By the use of the directional characteristics of millimeter-wave communication, we can get $\mathbf{H}^{2m} \approx \sum_{l=1}^{L} |\sqrt{MN}\lambda_l|^{2m} \mathbf{h}_l \mathbf{h}_l^H$, where m is a positive real number. The kth MPC is assumed to be the strongest, and for $l \neq k$, $|\lambda_l|^{2m}/|\lambda_k|^{2m}$ is exponentially decreasing, which means that the contribution of the other $L - 1$ MPCs to the vector $\mathbf{H}^{2m}$ is exponentially decreasing compared to the strongest MPC. Thereby, we can know that for a given large enough m and any initial transmitted AWVt, we can get $\lim_{m\to\infty} \mathbf{H}^{2m} = |\sqrt{MN}\lambda_k|^{2m}\mathbf{h}_k\mathbf{h}_k^H$ and get the following expression:

$$\mathbf{H}^{2m}\mathbf{t} = |\sqrt{MN}\lambda_k|^{2m}\mathbf{h}_k\mathbf{h}_k^H\mathbf{t} = (|\sqrt{MN}\lambda_k|^{2m}\mathbf{h}_k^H\mathbf{t})\mathbf{h}_k \qquad (7.44)$$

It can be thought of as $\mathbf{h}_k$ multiplied by a complex coefficient. It is worth noting that $\mathbf{h}_k$ is a constant-amplitude steering vector, so the expected estimate of the transmitted AWV is $e_t = \exp(j\angle(\mathbf{H}^{2m}\mathbf{t}))/\sqrt{M}$, with $\angle$ representing the radians of the angle vector. In fact, the estimate is derived from the normalization of $\mathbf{H}^{2m}\mathbf{t}$.

In addition, it can be obtained that

$$\mathbf{H} \times \mathbf{H}^{2m}\mathbf{t} = (\lambda_k\sqrt{MN}|\lambda_k\sqrt{MN}|^{2m}\mathbf{h}_k^H\mathbf{t})\mathbf{g}_k \qquad (7.45)$$

Therefore, it is possible to use the estimate $\mathbf{e}_t = \exp(j\angle(\mathbf{H} \times \mathbf{H}^{2m}\mathbf{t}))/\sqrt{M}$ to obtain the desired received AWV.

Obviously, for a given CSI, AWVs is available along the direction of the strongest MPC at the transceiver. In actual millimeter-wave communication, $\mathbf{H}$ is basically unknown to the transceiver, and thus, we give the beamforming training of STV joint iteration with the detailed process as follows:

1. **Initialization:** An initial transmitting AWV vector $\mathbf{t}$ is selected at the transmitting end, and the selection of the AWV can be random.
2. **Iteration:** Iterate ε times as follows and then stop.

   Use the same AWV vector $\mathbf{t}$ for continuous transmission in N slots and simultaneously use the DFT matrix $\mathbf{F}_N$ as the AWV vector of the receiving end, which refers to the nth column of $\mathbf{F}_N$ which is taken as the nth slot of the received AWV. It is noted that the unit matrix $\mathbf{I}_N$ cannot be used here because each of its terms does not have a constant gain characteristic, but other unitary matrices with constant gain can be used. And thus the received vector is $\mathbf{r} = \mathbf{F}_N^H\mathbf{H}\mathbf{t} + \mathbf{F}_N^H\mathbf{n}_r$ with $\mathbf{n}_r$ the noise vector. For $\mathbf{e}_r$, it is calculated by $\mathbf{e}_r = \exp(j\angle(\mathbf{F}_N\mathbf{r}))/\sqrt{N}$, and then assign $\mathbf{e}_r$ to $\mathbf{r}$.

   Use the same AWV vector $\mathbf{t}$ for continuous transmission in M slots for the receiving end and simultaneously use the DFT matrix $\mathbf{F}_M$ as the AWV vector of the transmitting end. The received vector $\mathbf{t} = \mathbf{F}_M^H\mathbf{H}^H\mathbf{r} + \mathbf{F}_M^H\mathbf{n}_t$ can be obtained with $\mathbf{n}_t$ the noise vector. For $\mathbf{e}_t$, it is calculated by $\mathbf{e}_t = \exp(j\angle(\mathbf{F}_M\mathbf{t}))/\sqrt{M}$ and then assign $\mathbf{e}_t$ to $\mathbf{t}$.

3. **Result:** t is the AWV of the transmitting end, and r is the AWV of the receiving end.

In practice, the number of iterations depends on the channel response. And based on the simulation results in the fifth part, ε equals 2 and 3 can ensure convergence. It is noted that the STV is based on SGV and is a specialized method for millimeter-wave communication with a constant-amplitude phased array, thus leading STV and SGV to have the same characteristics. The SGV discovers the maximum eigenvector of channel matrix **H**, which is ideal and achievable for any channel, while the STV is a constant-width steering vector used to find the strongest MPC which utilizes the directional characteristic of millimeter-wave communication. It is a sub-optimal method and is only available under the millimeter-wave communication channel. In other words, the STV needs to estimate the constant-width steering vector of the strongest MPC in every iteration. At the same time, in order to make the STV easy to implement for the constant-amplitude phased array, it uses the DFT matrix in the training of the transceiver by considering that the DFT matrix has constant-amplitude characteristics.

7.5.5 *Performance evaluation*

In this part, we use simulation to evaluate the performance of the STV from both the array gain and the convergence speed and compare it with the corresponding performance of the SGV. In all simulations, the channel is normalized to $E(\sum_{l=1}^{L} |\lambda_l|^2) = 1$, the SNR of the transmission sequence is $\gamma_t = 1/\sigma^2$, and the array gain which is the ratio of the received SNR and the transmitted SNR is given as $\eta = \gamma/\gamma_t = |\mathbf{r}^H \mathbf{H} \mathbf{t}|^2$. The initial selection rule for transmitting AWVs is to ensure that the transmitted energy can be projected evenly onto the M base vectors of the receiving matrix, namely $\mathbf{I}_m$ and $\mathbf{F}_m$. For STV, it is necessary to use a normalized constant-length zero autocorrelation code sequence, and for SGV, it is $\mathbf{I}_M/\sqrt{M}$.

Empirically, the array gain is achieved by implementing 1000 times the calculations of the ratio of the received SNR and the transmitted SNR. Furthermore, the upper bound of the SVD is derived from the mean square of the largest singular value of the 1000 operations. The channel implementation is the LOS and NLOS channels under the Rayleigh and Rice distribution models, and for the LOS channel, the MPC energy is $|\lambda_k|^2 = 0.769\,2$, while the average MPC channel energy is given as $E(\{|\lambda_l|^2\}_{l=2,3,4}) = [0.076\,9, 0.076\,9, 0.076\,9]$ for the NLOS channel.

For the NLOS channel $E(\{|\lambda_l|^2\}_{l=1,2,3,4}) = [0.25, 0.25, 0.25, 0.25]$, the steering angles of the transmitting end and the receiving end are randomly distributed on $[0, 2\pi)$ every time it is implemented.

Figure 7.26 shows the array gain for SGV and STV with different iteration numbers of LOS and NLOS, where $M = N = 16$. Figure 7.26(a) compares the convergence speed of SGV and STV with higher SNR (25 dB) for LOS and NLOS channels, where the cases of $M = N = 16$ and $M = N = 32$ are considered. It can be seen that under the LOS channel, both training methods achieve a very fast convergence speed and an ideal array gain, which is the upper bound of the SVD. However, under the NLOS channel, both training methods have a slower convergence speed. And compared with SGV, STV achieves a faster convergence speed under relatively reduced array gain. Of course, the gain of the STV eventually reaches the upper bound of the SVD. The conclusions in Fig. 7.26 are applicable irrespective of whether the number of antenna arrays is large or small.

The meaning of these conclusions is as follows: In the LOS channel, there is only one strong MPC, and its steering vector is almost ideal AWVs, so that the STV can obtain the ideal array gain. However, for the NLOS channel with multiple MPCs and different steering angles, one of them, which is not optimal, is obtained as the AWV by the STV training method, causing the STV to not achieve the desired array gain. On the contrary, since SGV is based on the maximum singular vector method, once it able to converge, it will certainly reach the SVD upper limit.

In addition, the ability of the STV to achieve faster convergence in the NLOS channel indicates better robustness in each STV iteration, while the AWV estimate of the SGV is more sensitive to noise.

In short, although the STV is designed for a millimeter-wave communication device with constant amplitude, the SGV is more versatile. STV and SGV have approximate convergence rates and array gains under the LOS and NLOS channels. On the other hand, it should be noted that $M + N$ training slots will be consumed for a single iteration, which will significantly reduce the system efficiency, especially when the antenna array is relatively large. In other words, when there is no constant gain limit, the STV is more effective with the iteration number of 1 or 2 because the STV achieves a higher array gain under these conditions, as can be seen in Fig. 7.26.

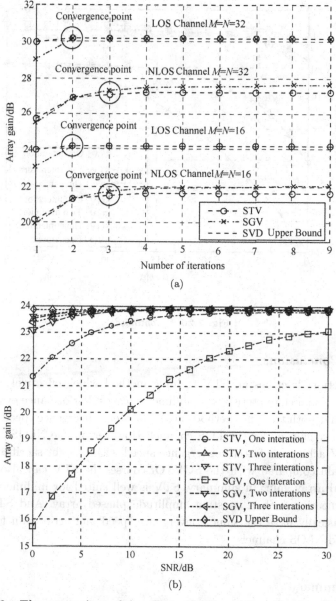

Fig. 7.26. The comparison of the effects of different iterations on the gain of SGV and STV arrays when the number of transceiver arrays is $M = N = 16$ under the LOS and NLOS channels, and the comparison of the convergence speed of SGV and STV. (a) Comparison of convergence speed between SGV and STV. (b) LOS. (c) LOS.

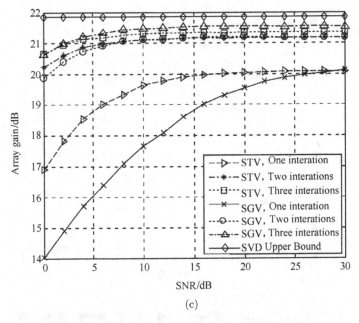

(c)

Fig. 7.26. (*Continued*)

7.5.6 *Conclusions*

This section describes an STV training method which effectively utilizes the directional characteristics of millimeter waves. Performance evaluation shows that both training methods achieve faster convergence speed and an ideal array gain under the LOS channel. However, in the NLOS channel, the STV achieves a faster convergence speed with a slight sacrifice of the array gain compared with the SGV. Of course, the STV can also obtain the ideal array gain. In summary, STV is well suited for millimeter-wave communication with a constant-amplitude phased array. And STV and SGV basically have the same convergence speed and array gain for both LOS and NLOS channels.

7.6 Summary

Wireless communication services are provided in two established systems: ground-based systems and satellite-based systems. In ground-based systems, signal transmission and communication range are limited due to signal scattering and multipath effects. In addition, because the spectrum resources are very limited, the ground-based system contains a large number of antenna towers, base stations, and microwave links scattered in the ground area. Satellite-based systems can provide a wide range of communication coverage when ground facilities are much less than those in ground-based systems. However, because of the large communication distance, the system complexity is high, communication delays are large, and the user terminals are expensive.

For future wireless communication systems, the high-altitude platform-based system described in this chapter is a very promising alternative. HAP systems are superior to ground-based systems and satellite-based systems and overcome their disadvantages. In order to provide overall channel capacity, the HAP system uses a cell structure with concomitant co-channel interference as a function of antenna beamwidth, angular separation, and sidelobe levels. In Section 7.2, a method for predicting co-channel interference based on curve fitting approximation is presented for the radiation pattern of elliptical beam. It shows that the cell with regular hexagonal layout is a method to achieve optimal cell edge power. In addition to the regular hexagonal cell layout pattern, other cell partitioning strategies are given in Section 7.4.

The ideal antenna beam illuminates the corresponding cell with uniform power above the cell and is zero power fading outside the cell. In this sense, the antenna acts as a spatial filter. The digital beamforming technique based on two-dimensional spatial filters discussed in Section 7.3 can significantly reduce the number of antenna elements and the corresponding receiver modules such as A/D converters without any performance loss. Therefore, system complexity and system cost can be reduced, and the adaptability of the HAP system can be improved. However, in practice, array beamforming techniques in the millimeter-wave band are very difficult. The joint beamforming training method based on the steering vector (STV) among the high-altitude platforms discussed in Section 7.5 utilizes the directional characteristics of the millimeter-wave communication channel.[38] For the LOS channel, the STV has a fast convergence rate and can achieve the desired array gain.

References

1. Mansoor S, Hashimoto H, Umehira M, *et al.* Wireless communication in the twenty-first century: A perspective. *Proceeding of the IEEE*, 1997, 85(10): 1622–1638.

2. ITU-D/2/049-E. Operational and Technical Characteristics for a Terrestrial IMT-2000 System Using High Altitude Platform Stations (Technical Information Document), 1998.

3. Cushman R and Deronck H. Progress of regenerative fuel cell technology in the United States of America. *Proceedings of the Second Stratospheric Platform Systems Workshop.* 2000, 99–107.

4. Grace D, Capstick MH, Mohorcic M, *et al.* Integrating users into the broadband network via high altitude platforms. *IEEE Wireless Communications,* 2005, 12(5): 98–105.

5. Wu G, Miura R, and Hase Y. A broadband wireless access system using stratospheric platform. *IEEE Global Telecommunications Conference,* San Francisco, CA, 2000, 1: 225–230.

6. Ku BJ, *et al.* Conceptual design of multibeam antennas (MBA) and user antenna for stratospheric communication system (SCS). *Proceedings of the Second Stratospheric Platform Systems Workshop.* 2000, 163–170.

7. Lee WCY. Spectrum efficiency in cellular. *IEEE Transactions on Vehicular Technology,* 1989, 38(2): 69–75.

8. Grace D, Tozer TC, and Burr AG. Reducing call dropping in distributed dynamic channel assignment algorithms by incorporating power control in wireless ad hoc networks. *IEEE Journal on Selected Areas in Communications,* 2000, 18(11): 2417–2428.

9. Cheng MM and Chuang JC. Performance evaluation of distributed measurement-based dynamic channel assignment in local wireless communications. *IEEE Journal on Selected Areas in Communications,* 1996, 14(4): 698–710.

10. Chuang JC. Performance issues and algorithms for dynamic channel assignment. *IEEE Journal on Selected Areas in Communications,* 1993, 11(6): 955–963.

11. Cimini LJ, Foschini GJ, Chik-Lin I, *et al.* Call blocking performance of distributed algorithms for dynamic channel allocation in microcells. *IEEE Transactions on Communications,* 1994, 42(8): 2600–2607.

12. Zander J. Performance of optimum transmitter power control in cellular radio systems. *IEEE Transactions on Vehicular Technology,* 1992, 41(1): 57–62.

13. Chang LF, Noerpal AR, and Ranade A. Performance of personal access communications system — unlicensed B. *IEEE Journal on Selected Areas in Communications,* 1996, 14(4): 718–727.

14. Olver AD, Clarricoats PJB, Kishk AA, *et al. Microwave Horns and Feeds.* IEE Press, New York, 1994.

15. El-Jabu B and Steele R. Cellular communications using aerial platforms. *IEEE Transactions on Vehicular Technology,* 2001, 50(3): 686–700.

16. Thornton J, Grace D, Capstick MH and Tozer TC. Optimizing an array of antennas for cellular coverage from a high altitude platform. *IEEE Transactions on Wireless Communications,* 2003, 2(3): 484–492.

17. Balanis CA. *Antenna Theory, Analysis and Design,* 2nd edn. New York: Wiley, 1997, 812–813.

18. *Instruments and Components Catalogue* U.K.: Flann Microwave Instruments Ltd., 1998.
19. Balanis CA. *Antenna Theory, Analysis and Design*, 2nd edn. New York: Wiley, 1997, 48–49.
20. Adatia N, Watson BK, and Ghosh S. Dual polarized elliptical beam antenna for satellite application. *Antennas and Propagation Society International Symposium*. 1981, 19: 488–491.
21. Grace D, Thornton J, Konefal T, *et al.* Broadband communications from high altitude platforms — the HeliNet solution. *Wireless Personal Multimedia Communications*. WPMC 2001, Aalborg, Denmark, 2001.
22. Daly NE, Tozer TC, Grace D, *et al.* Frequency reuse from high altitude platforms. *Wireless Personal Multimedia Communications* (WPMC 2000). Bangkok, 2000.
23. Thornton J, Grace D, Spillard C, *et al.* Broadband communications from high altitude platforms: The European HeliNet programme. *Electronics & Communication Engineering Journal*, 2001, 13(3): 138–144.
24. Godara LC. Applications of antenna arrays to mobile communications, part I: performance improvement, feasibility, and system considerations. *Proceedings of the IEEE*, 1997, 85(7): 1031–1060.
25. Do-Hong T and Russer P. A new design method for digital beamforming using spatial interpolation. *IEEE Antennas and Wireless Propagation Letters*, 2003, 2(1): 177–181.
26. Do-Hong T, Olbrich G, and Russer P. Smart antenna technology for high-altitude-platform based wireless communication systems. *15th International Microwaves, Radar and Wireless Communications*, 2004, 2: 645–648.
27. Litva I and Kwok-Yeung Lo T. Digital Beamforming in Wireless Communications. Massachusetts, Anech House Publishers, 1999.
28. Guan M, Yuan F, and Guo Q. Performance of coverage and wireless link for HAPS communication. *International Conference on Wireless Communications & Signal Processing* (WCSP 2009), 2009, 1–4.
29. Xiao Z. Suboptimal spatial diversity scheme for 60 GHz millimeter wave WLAN. *IEEE Communications Letters*, 2013, 17(9): 1790–1793.
30. Wang J, Lan Z, Pyo C, *et al.* Beam codebook based beamforming protocol for multi-gbps millimeter-wave WPAN systems. *IEEE Journal on Selected Areas in Communications*, 2009, 27(8): 1390–1399.
31. Xia P, Yong S, Oh J, *et al.* A practical SDMA protocol for 60 GHz millimeter wave communications. *42nd Asilomar Conference on Signals, Systems and Computers*. Pacific Grove, CA, 2008, 2019–2023.
32. Tang Y, Vucetic B, and Li Y. An iterative singular vectors estimation scheme for beamforming transmission and detection in MIMO systems. *IEEE Communications Letters*, 2005, 9(6): 505–507.
33. Valdes-Garcia A, Nicolson ST, Lai J-W, *et al.* A fully integrated 16-element phased-array transmitter in SiGe BiCMOS for 60-GHz communications. *IEEE Journal of Solid-State Circuits*, 2010, 45(12): 2757–2773.
34. Cohen E, Jakobson C, Ravid S, *et al.* A thirty two element phased-array transceiver at 60GHz with RF-IF conversion block in 90nm flip chip CMOS

process. *2010 IEEE Radio Frequency Integrated Circuits Symposium (RFIC)*. Anaheim, CA, 2010, 457–460.

35. Bai L and Choi J. Lattice reduction-based MIMO iterative receiver using randomized sampling. *IEEE Transactions on Wireless Communications*, 2013, 12(5): 2160–2170.

36. Zheng X, Xie Y, Li J, *et al*. MIMO transmit beamforming under uniform elemental power constraint. *IEEE Transactions on Signal Processing*, 2007, 55(11): 5395–5406.

37. Lee J, Nabar RU, Choi JP, *et al*. Generalized cophasing for multiple transmit and receive antennas. *IEEE Transactions on Wireless Communications*, 2009, 8(4): 1649–1654.

38. Xiao Z, Bai L and Choi J. Iterative joint beamforming training with constant-amplitude phased arrays in millimeter-wave communications. *IEEE Communications Letters*, 2014, 18(5): 829–832.

39. Maltsev A, Maslennikov R, Sevastyanov A, *et al*. Characteristics of indoor millimeter-wave channel at 60 GHz in application to perspective WLAN system. *Proceedings of the Fourth European Conference on Antennas and Propagation (EuCAP)*. Barcelona, 2010, 1–5.

40. Park M and Pan H. A spatial diversity technique for IEEE 802.11 ad WLAN in 60 GHz band. *IEEE Communications Letters*, 2012, 16(8): 1260–1262.

41. Tse D and Viswanath P. *Fundamentals of Wireless Communication*. Cambridge: Cambridge University Press, 2005.

Chapter 8

Space-Based Cooperative Transmission System

The first two chapters introduce the ground-based transmission system and the air-based transmission system. This chapter focuses on the space-based transmission system. The traditional space-based transmission system is a satellite-based forwarding system. Since satellites are usually located at high altitudes off the ground, space-based systems have incomparable advantages in terms of coverage. In fact, satellite communication systems have played a crucial role in the process of data transmission and global information exchange, especially in maritime, earth observation, and all-weather surveillance.

Due to the bandwidth-constrained bottleneck of traditional satellite communications, with the increasing demand for bandwidth, service providers and related agencies have to find ways to increase the number of satellites, bandwidth, and power. However, the lack of geosynchronous orbital satellite orbits and the lack of available spectrum resources, as well as the increased complexity and increased operating costs, make these satellite-oriented improvements difficult to achieve. On the contrary, without increasing the transmission power, by using the multi-satellite common-orbit cooperation and multi-antenna technology, reasonable planning of the ground station layout to obtain multi-antenna multiplexing gain has become one of the important means to improve the spectrum efficiency. This new technology is the space-based cooperative transmission system to be introduced in this chapter.

The space-based cooperative transmission system utilizes multi-satellite common-orbit cooperation and multiple-input multiple-output technology to increase the system capacity and system bandwidth by increasing multiplexing gain without increasing system transmission power. Due to the full utilization of the renewable payload by the MIMO system, one can transfer the main workload to the ground station. As long as the orthogonality of the uplink and downlink is satisfied, the complexity of the satellite payload design will be reduced. This is also the advantage of MIMO satellite communication systems.

This chapter begins with an overview of space-based transmission techniques, followed by a multi-beam transmission technique for constellation systems. The traditional single-satellite system can be treated as a special case for cooperation with in a constellation. Subsequently, the constellation cooperative MIMO system modeling and system channel capacity analysis and optimization are carried out. Finally, the capacity results of the constellation cooperative MIMO system are given.

8.1 The Overview of Space-Based Transmission Technology

With the development of aerospace technology, the types and functions of space platforms with satellites as backbone networks are becoming more and more perfect. And it is the origin of space-based transmission technology to organically connect different satellite systems in space for information acquisition, transmission, processing, and other functions to establish a satellite-based spatial information network. Because satellite networks have the advantages of flexible networking, wide coverage, fast network construction, and no geographical restrictions, they have significant advantages for long-distance wireless communications, and this technology has become an active research topic in various countries.

In Europe, France, Germany, Italy, and other countries have actively promoted research on spatial information network technology through distributed satellite development plans. The Centre National d'Etudes Spatiales (CNES) proposed the Interferometric Cartwheel;[1] Deutsches Zentrum für Luft-und Raumfahrt e.V. (DLR) proposed the TSX/TDX (TerraSAR-X/TanDEM-X) two-satellite formation plan;[2] and Italy proposed the BISSAT plan.[3]

In North America, spatial information network technology is also attractive. National Aeronautics and Space Administration (NASA) and the United States Air Force (USAF) use Advanced Extremely High

Frequency (AEHF) military communications satellites and Transformational Satellite Communications System (TSAT)[4] to develop spatial information network technology to achieve rapid information access worldwide; and Canada has also proposed the RadarSat-2/3 program.[5]

The AEHF project[6,7] uses beamforming network technology and phased-array antenna technology.[8] The beamforming network technology can suppress the generation of interference signals by generating a null depth while providing services for legitimate users. And the phased-array antenna technology can change the direction of the radio frequency beam by means of electronic means, so that the beam between the users can be fast and agile, thereby effectively improving the transmission efficiency and flexibility of the channel. The TerraSAR-X/TanDEM-X two-satellite system developed by the German Aerospace Center also uses active phased-array antenna technology to create flexible beam pointing and provide array gain.

Although active phased-array antennas can improve the signal power and transmission efficiency to a certain extent, they are not capable of greatly increasing the channel capacity of the satellite communication systems. Instead, their improvement in channel transmission performance is largely governed by the load and power of the satellite.[9] In order to meet the growing demand for data rates, current satellite communications projects tend to use higher power satellite platforms and larger bandwidth transponders. In this case, the production, operation, and maintenance of these powerful and complex satellite platforms and communication loads become very expensive.[10] Therefore, if the spectrum utilization can be improved without increasing the satellite transmission power, it would be significant for satellite communications, even at the expense of increasing the design cost of the ground station.

However, limited by the satellite payload and the power carrying capacity, it is difficult for satellite communication systems to improve the information transmission capabilities by increasing the power and antenna size as in conventional ground communication systems. So far, improving the types of satellite systems, increasing the satellite loads, and enhancing the communication capabilities of satellite systems remain the next set of development goals for the major space nations. In addition, due to the lack of synchronous satellite orbitals and shortage of spectrum resources, single-satellite communication power is severely limited. Therefore, the use of limited orbital resources and satellite payloads to maximize the spatial information transmission capability has become the top priority for the development of space-based transmission systems at this stage.

In addition, the TSAT program[11] uses the virtual radar array consisting of a satellite constellation that has been formed for cooperative communication to perform tasks such as passive radio radiation measurement, navigation, and communication to verify that the constellation thus formed can effectively accomplish multiple tasks through cooperative communication.[12] At the same time, the Johns Hopkins University Applied Physics Laboratory and the US National Security Space Office proposed the idea of manipulating satellites in a geosynchronous orbit to perform military missions in a separate module, namely the "Space-based Group".[13] The "Space-based Group" uses a main satellite to provide core services such as the space–ground link for the group, and the cooperative satellites and the main satellite form a cooperative constellation to jointly perform tasks such as communication and investigation. The Defense Advanced Research Projects Agency (DARPA) proposed the F6 program to establish a future-oriented, flexible, and efficient spacecraft architecture.[14] Its idea is to decompose the overall traditional spacecraft into multiple combinable separation modules, with different modules having different tasks and functions. These separate spacecraft modules can be mass produced and independently launched on the ground. When operating normally in satellite orbit, they work together in formation flight, wireless data transmission, and wireless energy transmission to combine the discrete modules into one complete virtual space system. This "Space-based Group" transmission technology based on the separation module's way of working together to complete the task provides a new idea for the development of satellite communication systems.

With the wireless communication technology that is currently available, on the one hand, the requirements for transmission bandwidth are becoming higher and higher, and on the other hand, the spectrum resources which can actually be used are becoming more and more tense. As an important channel resource other than time, frequency band, and coding, the use of spatial dimension creates a broad prospect for MIMO technology in the field of wireless communication. Especially in satellite communication, MIMO technology has a higher information transmission rate than the single-input single-output (SISO) system, which effectively improves the spectrum utilization without increasing the transmission power or allocating additional bandwidth, thus making up for the deficiency of the single-satellite platform load and power limitation. Therefore, in order to improve the data rate and bandwidth efficiency, applying MIMO technology to satellite communication systems is very significant.

The existing research results show that the rational use of an active antenna array can form orthogonal channels on a typical line of sight (LOS) channel, and the channel capacity increases linearly with the number of antennas without increasing the satellite transmission power to realize spatial multiplexing gain.[15] Therefore, an active antenna array platform capable of achieving efficient communication can be constructed through the cooperation among the satellites in the constellation and the cooperation between the array antenna technology and the ground station antenna array.

8.2 Constellation Cooperative Multi-Beam Transmission Technology

In order to better use the spectrum without increasing the satellite transmission power, we apply the MIMO technology to satellite communication systems. On the one hand, cooperation within the constellation can be realized by the multi-satellites common-orbit technology, and on the other hand, multi-beam transmission can be realized by using the active antenna array.

Multi-satellites common-orbit technology can keep multiple satellites with the same or similar functions in the same orbital position, synchronize and exchange data through inter-satellite links, and form a satellite constellation with cooperative transmission and forwarding capabilities, so as to use limited satellite orbit resources more effectively.

Through the configuration of the active antenna array, the satellite channel can not only realize the efficient transmission mechanism of the cooperative multi-beam but also obtain the capacity gain. At the same time, it can adaptively optimize the transmission mode and improve the energy efficiency according to the continuous change of its own structure.

The proposed multi-beam transmission technology with cooperation within the constellation has been theoretically proved by improving the channel capacity and realizing the spatial multiplexing gain of satellite communication.

In terms of satellite channels, a frequency-selective MIMO satellite communication channel can be described by its channel matrix $\mathbf{H}(f)$, which consists of an LOS signal component and a multiplicity of multipath signal components. Considering the conditions of long-distance transmission of signals in the satellite channel, the LOS signal becomes the main component of the satellite radio channel due to its low fading characteristics; thus, we denote the channel matrix as $\mathbf{H}_{LOS}(f)$. Furthermore, we can assume that the channel is frequency stable, ignoring the frequency dependence of the baseband signal. This means that the satellite communication process, we finally discussed, is carried out in a fading-free and shadow-free LOS channel.

In ground wireless communication systems, we have demonstrated that orthogonal channels can provide optimal multiplexing gain in the LOS channel with equal number of antennas.[16] It has special requirements for satellite antenna placement and ground antenna placement when adopting orthogonal channels, and this optimized geometric configuration provides significant capacity gain over randomly arranged antenna arrays.[17] Considering that in many environments the movement of the ground station relative to the satellite end remains low, the geometric arrangement of the array of receiving and transmitting antennas is almost constant for a short period of time. In other words, the satellite channel is an excellent environment for realizing this channel capacity optimization scheme. Using the multi-beam transmission technology with cooperation within the constellation, we can achieve theoretical antenna optimization configuration, thereby increasing the capacity gain of the satellite communication system.

8.3 Constellation Cooperative MIMO System Modeling

In this section, considering a typical satellite downlink, we will build an MIMO satellite communication system model based on an active antenna array in the satellite in the presence or absence of array antennas.

Satellite communication systems can use any type of polarization and use two polarization directions simultaneously. In the calculation of the channel capacity, we can detect any polarization direction. Due to channel losses, we do not take polarization reversal into account. Of course, polarization reversal reduces the channel capacity not only in SISO but also in MIMO transmission. However, this phenomenon does not have much effect on the expected optimal value because the optimization criteria are not changed accordingly.

If two orthogonal polarizations are used simultaneously, their respective independent channels will optimize their respective channel capacities simultaneously. Two orthogonal polarizations and two orthogonal spatial channels can be considered as one MIMO system providing four orthogonal modes, but this point is not the focus of this section.

Finally, to demonstrate the pre-processing of the MIMO signal to the downlink, we assume a regenerated payload for the satellite. Therefore, a communication link can be established between multiple satellites through a high-bandwidth optical link, thereby realizing cooperation within the constellation. It should be noted that the regenerated payload is not a general assumption for the geometrically optimal solution; the transparency payload can also accomplish the above design at the expense of increased complexity.[18]

8.3.1 *Single-antenna constellation*

As shown in Fig. 8.1, the satellite downlink is established between a ground receiver having M_E receiving antennas and a cooperative constellation consisting of M_S satellites, each of which has one transmitting antenna. Considering further practical limitation, for the compactness of the devices at the receiving end, we require that the distance between the receiving antennas on the ground be as small as possible.

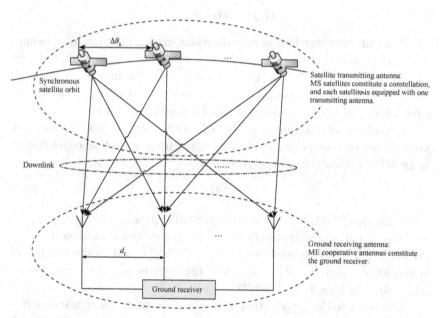

Fig. 8.1. The multi-satellite single-antenna MIMO communication system model (downlink).

A frequency-selective MIMO channel can be described by its channel transfer matrix, and it consists of one LOS signal component and another component consisting of multipath signals:

$$\mathbf{H}(f) = \mathbf{H}_{\mathrm{LOS}}(f) + \mathbf{H}_{\mathrm{NLOS}}(f) \tag{8.1}$$

In a satellite wireless communication channel, due to the low fading characteristics of the LOS channel, the main component of the signal is the LOS signal. In contrast to the moving ground environment, the multipath component is not the most important and the power of the LOS signal is much greater than the power of the reflected and scattered waves.[19] Therefore, we only consider the LOS signal component here:

$$\mathbf{H}(f) = \mathbf{H}_{\mathrm{LOS}}(f) \tag{8.2}$$

Furthermore, we assume that the satellite communication channel is a frequency-stationary channel, where the upper boundary f_u and the lower boundary f_l of the transmission band are within the range of the carrier f_c, namely $f_u, f_l \approx f_c$. In this condition, the frequency dependence of the channel is negligible:

$$\mathbf{H}(f) = \mathbf{H}_{\mathrm{LOS}}(f_c) \tag{8.3}$$

It means that satellite communications are carried out in a fading-free and shadow-free LOS channel. In fact, since signal fading occurs simultaneously in both the LOS channel and the multipath channel, the channel capacity optimization conclusion is also valid for the fading environment, although the total channel capacity is reduced.

Regardless of the noise generated during signal propagation, the propagation of a frequency-stationary signal from a satellite constellation in an MIMO channel can be expressed as

$$\mathbf{y} = \mathbf{H}\mathbf{x} \tag{8.4}$$

where the signal vector received at the ground is given as $\mathbf{y} = [y_1, \ldots, y_{m_{\mathrm{E}}}]^{\mathrm{T}}$ and the signal vector transmitted by the constellation is given as $\mathbf{x} = [x_1, \ldots, x_{m_{\mathrm{S}}}]^{\mathrm{T}}$. The channel matrix $\mathbf{H} \in \mathbb{C}^{M_{\mathrm{E}} \times M_{\mathrm{S}}}$, and as the number of transmitting antennas $M_{\mathrm{T}} = M_{\mathrm{S}}$ and the number of receiving antennas $M_{\mathrm{R}} = M_{\mathrm{E}}$, we have $\mathbf{H} \in \mathbb{C}^{M_{\mathrm{R}} \times M_{\mathrm{T}}}$.

According to the propagation principle of electromagnetic waves in free space, the equivalent baseband of the matrix element $[\mathbf{H}]_{m_{\mathrm{R}}, m_{\mathrm{T}}}$ of the m_{R}th row and the m_Tth column in the channel matrix is expressed as

$$H_{m_R,m_T} = a_{m_R,m_T} \exp\left\{-j\frac{2\pi f_c}{c_0} r_{m_R,m_T}\right\} \qquad (8.5)$$

where f_c is the carrier frequency and $c_0 = 3 \times 10^8 \text{m/s}$ is the propagation speed of light in vacuum. r_{m_R,m_T} is the distance between the m_Rth receiving antenna on the ground and the transmitting antenna on the m_Tth satellite, and its complex envelope

$$a_{m_R,m_T} = \frac{c_0}{4\pi f_c r_{m_R,m_T}} e^{j\theta_0} \qquad (8.6)$$

where θ_0 is the carrier phase angle at the time of observation. The matrix element represents the channel complex gain of the signal transmitted from the transmitting antenna on the $m_S = m_T$th satellite to the $m_E = m_R$th receiving antenna on the ground.

It is easy to verify that $|a_{m_R,m_T}| \approx |a|$, which is nearly constant.

8.3.2 *Array antenna constellation*

As shown in Fig. 8.2, the satellite downlink is established between a ground receiver with M_E receiving antennas and a coordinated constellation consisting of M_S satellites, each of which has M_L transmitting antennas.

Similar to the discussion in Section 8.3.1, the satellite communication system operates in a fading-free, shadow-free, and frequency-stationary LOS channel, so the system also satisfies Eqs. (8.3), (8.4), and (8.5).

The difference is that the channel matrix $\mathbf{H} \in \mathbb{C}^{M_R \times M_T}$. Since the number of transmitting antennas is $M_T = M_S \cdot M_L$ and the number of receiving antennas is $M_R = M_E$, we have $\mathbf{H} \in \mathbb{C}^{M_E \times (M_S \cdot M_L)}$. Correspondingly, the matrix element $[\mathbf{H}]_{m_R,m_T}$ of the m_Rth row and the m_Tth column in the channel matrix represents the channel complex gain of the signal transmitted from the m_Lth transmitting antenna on the m_Sth satellite to the $m_E = m_R$th receiving antenna on the ground, where $m_S \cdot m_L = m_T$.

For convenience, the channel complex gain of the signal transmitted from the transmitting antenna of the m_Sth satellite to the $m_E = m_R$th receiving antenna on the ground is defined as

$$H_{m_E,m_S\_m_L} = a_{m_E,m_S\_m_L} \exp\left\{-j\frac{2\pi f_c}{c_0} r_{m_E,m_S\_m_L}\right\} \qquad (8.7)$$

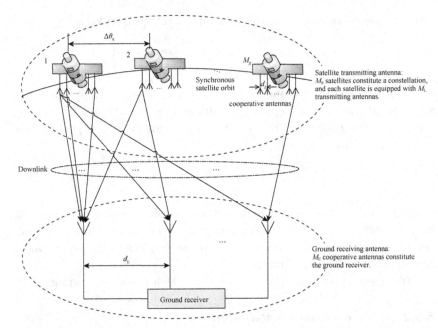

Fig. 8.2. **Multi-satellite multi-antenna MIMO communication system model (downlink).**

where r_{m_E, m_S-m_L} is the distance between the m_Eth receiving antenna on the ground and the m_Lth transmitting antenna on the m_Sth satellite and $a_{m_E, m_S-m_L} = \dfrac{c_0}{4\pi f_c r_{m_E, m_S-m_L}} e^{j\theta_0}$ is the complex envelope of the channel gain.

8.4 Constellation-Cooperative MIMO System Capacity

Based on the system model and channel model established in Section 8.3.2, we can deduce the relationship between the position of the satellite and the ground user, the antenna spacing, the array angle, and the degree of channel orthogonality and then obtain the relationship between them and the channel capacity by simulation.

8.4.1 *Capacity derivation*

For a time-invariant MIMO system, the highest spectral efficiency of the channel can be derived from the well-known formula of Telatar:[20]

$$C = \text{lb}[\det(\mathbf{I}_{M_R} + \rho \cdot \mathbf{HH}^H)] \tag{8.8}$$

where $(\cdot)^{\mathrm{H}}$ refers to the transposition operation of the matrix and ρ is the linear SNR of the channel. Define the logarithmic signal-to-noise ratio of the channel as $\mathrm{SNR} = 10\lg(\rho) = \mathrm{EIRP} + (\mathrm{G} - \mathrm{T}) - \kappa - \beta(\mathrm{dB})$ with EIRP, $(\mathrm{G} - \mathrm{T})$, κ, and β representing the effective isotropic radiated power, quality factor, Boltzmann constant, and logarithmic values of downlink bandwidth, respectively.[16]

Define

$$\mathbf{V} = \begin{cases} \mathbf{H}\mathbf{H}^{\mathrm{H}}, & M_{\mathrm{R}} < M_{\mathrm{T}} \\ \mathbf{H}^{\mathrm{H}}\mathbf{H}, & M_{\mathrm{R}} \geq M_{\mathrm{T}} \end{cases} \tag{8.9}$$

It is easy to prove that the MIMO channel can obtain the maximum multiplexing gain only if each non-zero eigenvalue γ_i that satisfies the matrix $\mathbf{V}$ (rank($\mathbf{V}$) = min($M_{\mathrm{R}}, M_{\mathrm{T}}$)) is equal, namely $\gamma_1 = \gamma_2 = \cdots = \gamma_{\min\{M_{\mathrm{R}}, M_{\mathrm{T}}\}} = |a|^2 \cdot \max\{M_{\mathrm{R}}, M_{\mathrm{T}}\}$. Its maximum channel capacity is $C_{\mathrm{opt}} = \min\{M_{\mathrm{R}}, M_{\mathrm{T}}\} \cdot \mathrm{lb}(1 + \rho|a|^2 \max\{M_{\mathrm{R}}, M_{\mathrm{T}}\})$.

Therefore, the transfer matrix $\mathbf{H}$ of the MIMO channel satisfying the maximum multiplexing gain is an orthogonal matrix. In other words, elements of any two rows of $\mathbf{H}$ are orthogonal for $M_{\mathrm{T}} > M_{\mathrm{R}}$ systems, and elements of any two columns of $\mathbf{H}$ are orthogonal for $M_{\mathrm{T}} \leq M_{\mathrm{R}}$ systems.

The parameters selected in this section for the simulation are shown in Table 8.1.

Table 8.1. Parameters of the MIMO system of the constellation cooperative array antennas.

Parameter symbol	Parameter value
Satellite constellation array center longitude, $\theta_{\mathrm{S,C}}$	11°E
Ground cooperative receiving antenna array center longitude, θ	11°E
Ground cooperative receiving antenna array center latitude, Φ	48°N
The angle between the ground cooperative receiving antenna array and the east–west direction, δ	0°
Carrier frequency f_0 in the MIMO channel	18 GHz
Signal to noise ratio ρ in the MIMO channel	$\mathrm{SNR} = 10\lg(\rho) = 224\,\mathrm{dB}$
Earth radius, R_{E}	6378.1 km
Synchronous satellite orbit radius, R_{S}	42164.1 km
The spacing between two adjacent transmitting antennas on the same satellite, d_L	2 m
The longitude difference between two adjacent satellites, $\Delta\theta_{\mathrm{S}}$	1°

8.4.2 *Single-antenna constellation capacity*

In the literature of Ref. 15, the necessary and sufficient conditions for establishing the orthogonal LOS channel matrix are derived by mathematical methods. The eigenvalues of matrix $\mathbf{V}$ can be solved by a $\min(M_R, M_T)$-order polynomial whose optimal solution is $\min(M_R, M_T)$ with identical roots.

8.4.2.1 *Establish LOS orthogonal channel*

Based on the system model established in Section 8.3.1, an orthogonal LOS channel matrix is established by taking the system with $M_T > M_R$ as an example.

In order to make the system satisfy orthogonality of the elements any two rows of $\mathbf{H}$, the transfer matrix of the MIMO system is given as

$$\mathbf{H} = \begin{bmatrix} H_{1,1} & H_{1,2} & \cdots & H_{1,M_T} \\ H_{2,1} & H_{2,2} & \cdots & H_{2,M_T} \\ \cdots & \cdots & \cdots & \cdots \\ H_{M_R,1} & H_{M_R,2} & \cdots & H_{M_R,M_T} \end{bmatrix} \tag{8.10}$$

It is given in the channel model such that

$$\begin{cases} H_{m_R,m_T} = a_{m_R,m_T} \exp\left\{ -\mathrm{j}\dfrac{2\pi f_0}{c_0} r_{m_R,m_T} \right\} \\ a_{m_R,m_T} = \dfrac{c_0}{4\pi f_0 r_{m_R,m_T}} e^{\mathrm{j}\theta_0} \approx |a| e^{\mathrm{j}\theta_0} \end{cases} \tag{8.11}$$

Therefore,

$$\begin{aligned} H_{m_R,m_T} &= \frac{c_0}{4\pi f_0 r_{m_R,m_T}} \exp\left\{ -\mathrm{j}\left(\frac{2\pi f_0}{c_0} r_{m_R,m_T} - \theta_0 \right) \right\} \\ &\approx |a| \exp\left\{ -\mathrm{j}\left(\frac{2\pi f_0}{c_0} r_{m_R,m_T} - \theta_0 \right) \right\} \end{aligned} \tag{8.12}$$

and $\because \forall k, l \in \{1, 2, \ldots, M_R\}$, the kth and the lth rows of $\mathbf{H}$ are orthogonal, so we can get

$$\begin{cases} \displaystyle\sum_{i=1}^{M_T} H_{k,i} \cdot H_{k,i}^* = \sum_{i=1}^{M_T} H_{l,i} \cdot H_{l,i}^* = |a|^2 \cdot M_T \\ \displaystyle\sum_{i=1}^{M_T} H_{k,i} \cdot H_{l,i}^* = 0 \end{cases} \tag{8.13}$$

Substituting $[H]_{m_R,m_T}$ into $\sum_{i=1}^{M_T} H_{k,i} \cdot H_{l,i}^* = 0$, we get

$$
\begin{aligned}
\sum_{i=1}^{M_T} H_{k,i} \cdot H_{l,i}^* &= \sum_{i=1}^{M_T} |a|^2 \exp\left\{ +j\left(\frac{2\pi f_0}{c_0} r_{k,i} - \theta_0\right) - j\left(\frac{2\pi f_0}{c_0} r_{l,i} - \theta_0\right) \right\} \\
&= |a|^2 \sum_{i=1}^{M_T} \exp\left\{ +j\left[\frac{2\pi f_0}{c_0}(r_{k,i} - r_{l,i})\right] \right\} \\
&= 0
\end{aligned}
\tag{8.14}
$$

Define $\phi_i = \frac{2\pi f_0}{c_0}(r_{k,i} - r_{l,i})$ and

$$
\sum_{i=1}^{M_T} e^{j\phi_i} = 0
\tag{8.15}
$$

Considering the system here, it is easy to prove that Eq. (8.15) can be satisfied by setting $\sum_{i=1}^{M_T} \phi_i = 2\pi v, v \in \mathbb{Z}, M_T \nmid v$.

Therefore, we propose a solution $\arg[\phi_i - \phi_j] = \frac{2\pi}{M_T}(i - j)$, as shown in Fig. 8.3. In this case, ϕ_i is equally spaced, and thus $(r_{k,i} - r_{l,i})$, which has a linear relationship with ϕ_i, also has a constant differential relationship.

Specifically, for the kth and lth receiving antennas on the ground and the ith and jth satellite transmitting antennas,

$$
(r_{k,i} - r_{l,i}) - (r_{k,j} - r_{l,j}) = \frac{c_0}{M_S f_0}(i - j) \cdot v, \quad v \in \mathbb{Z}, \quad M_S \nmid v
\tag{8.16}
$$

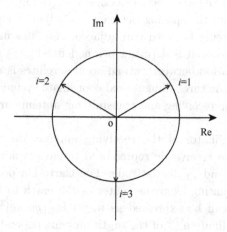

Fig. 8.3. Multi-satellite single-antenna system calculation Eq. (8.15).

Similarly, for the $M_T \leq M_R$ system, it should satisfy

$$(r_{k,i} - r_{k,j}) - (r_{l,i} - r_{l,j}) = \frac{c_0}{M_E f_0}(k - l) \cdot v, \quad v \in \mathbb{Z}, \quad M_E \nmid v \qquad (8.17)$$

Only systems which satisfy Eqs. (8.16) and (8.17), respectively, can guarantee that the channel capacity reaches its maximum. It is easy to identify a geometrical distribution form that satisfies this optimized solution. One possible implementation is that the receiving and transmitting antennas are all uniform linear arrays (ULAs), that are also the commonly used antenna arrangement in satellite communication systems.

8.4.2.2 *Optimize antenna layout in combination with geometric position*

In the following, the system is specifically analyzed using latitude and longitude coordinates.

(1) Establish a spatial coordinate system

The principle of Mercator projection is used to describe the position of the ground receiver and satellite constellation, which will be given by the longitude θ and the latitude Φ of the geographic location. The M_E receiving antennas on the ground receiver are placed in a uniform linear array, and the constellation consisting of M_S satellites is also uniformly distributed in a geosynchronous orbit wherein the angle between the ground antenna array and the east–west direction is δ (the ground antenna ULA direction angle) and the spacing between two adjacent receiving antennas is d_E(m). The spacing between two adjacent satellites in constellation in the geosynchronous orbit is d_S(m), which is defined as $d_S = \frac{\pi \Delta \theta_S}{180°} \cdot R_S$, and the angular separation between two adjacent satellites is $\Delta \theta_S(°)$.

Next, we use the three-dimensional coordinate system to represent the arrangement of the receiving and transmitting antenna arrays.

(1) Position coordinates of the receiving antenna on the ground. The position of the receiver is represented by geographic coordinates: θ_E for longitude and φ_E for latitude. The Cartesian position vector $\mathbf{R}_X$ is a vector pointing from the center of the earth to the center of the ULA, which can be expressed as $\mathbf{a}_E = [x_E, y_E, z_E]^T$. Therefore, the position coordinate $\mathbf{a}_{m_E}^{(E)}$ of the m_Eth antenna depends on the position

of $\mathbf{R}_X$ – ULA.

$$\mathbf{a}_{m_E}^{(E)} = \begin{pmatrix} x_E - p_{m_E}(\sin\theta_E \cdot \cos\delta + \sin\phi_E \cdot \cos\theta_E \cdot \sin\delta) \\ y_E - p_{m_E}(\cos\theta_E \cdot \cos\delta - \sin\phi_E \cdot \sin\theta_E \cdot \sin\delta) \\ z_E + p_{m_E}\cos\phi_E \cdot \sin\delta \end{pmatrix} \quad (8.18)$$

where $p_{m_E} = \left(m_E - 1 - \frac{M_E - 1}{2}\right)d_E$, $m_E \in \{1, 2, \ldots, M_E\}$ is the distance from the m_Eth receiving antenna on the ground to the center of the ground antenna ULA.

(2) Position coordinates of the satellite transmitting antenna. The position of the geosynchronous satellite is represented by the longitude $\theta_{S,i}$, $i \in \{1, 2, \ldots, M_S\}$, and the angular separation between adjacent satellites in the constellation is $\Delta\theta_S = |\theta_{S,1} - \theta_{S,2}|$ with $\theta_{S,C}$ representing the center point longitude of the constellation. Since the size of the satellite is much smaller than $\Delta\theta_S$, it is possible to use satellite coordinates to represent the position of the single antenna on satellite:

$$\mathbf{a}_{m_S}^{(s)} = \begin{bmatrix} R_S \cdot \cos\theta_{S,m_S} \\ R_S \cdot \sin\theta_{S,m_S} \\ 0 \end{bmatrix} \quad (8.19)$$

where $\theta_{S,m_S} = \left(m_S - 1 - \frac{M_S - 1}{2}\right)\Delta\theta_S + \theta_{S,C}$ and $m_S \in \{1, 2, \ldots, M_S\}$.

(2) Optimize the arrangement of the antenna

In order to apply Eqs. (8.16) and (8.17) to satellite scenes, the path lengths must be determined by mathematical derivation because they determine the phase angle of the complex channel matrix coefficients. An orthogonal channel matrix $\mathbf{H}$ requires a specific phase angle relationship, which requires adjustment of the distance r_{m_E,m_S}. And the path length r_{m_E,m_S} is defined as the distance between $\alpha_{m_E}^{(E)}$ and $\alpha_{m_S}^{(S)}$:

$$r_{m_E,m_S} = \|\alpha_{m_E}^{(E)} - \alpha_{m_S}^{(S)}\| \quad (8.20)$$

where $\|\cdot\|$ represents the Euclidean norm.

The detailed derivation of different paths depends on the position parameters of the satellite antenna. Taking into account the practical factors, for the system with $M_S = 2$, $M_E = 2$, the following equation can be obtained after mathematical derivation:

$$d_E\left(\frac{c_1}{2s_1} - \frac{c_2}{2s_2}\right) = v \cdot \frac{c_0}{M_E f_0}, \quad v \in \mathbb{Z}, \quad M_E \nmid v \qquad (8.21)$$

where

$$\begin{cases} s_{m_S}^2 = R_S^2 + R_E^2 - 2R_S R_E \cdot \cos\phi_E \cos(\theta_E - \theta_{S,m_S}) \\ c_{m_S} = 2R_S \cdot [\cos\delta_E \sin(\theta_E - \theta_{S,m_S}) + \sin\delta_E \cos(\theta_E - \theta_{S,m_S})\sin\phi_E] \end{cases}$$
$$(8.22)$$

Therefore, the ground antenna array spacing d_E at which the maximum channel capacity can be reached at this time is

$$d_{E\text{opt}} = v \frac{c_0}{M_E f_0} \cdot \frac{1}{\dfrac{c_1}{2s_1} - \dfrac{c_2}{2s_2}} \geq \frac{c_0}{M_E f_0} \cdot \frac{1}{\dfrac{c_1}{2s_1} - \dfrac{c_2}{2s_2}} \qquad (8.23)$$

Therefore, we can draw the following conclusions:

(1) If $d_E = \frac{c_0}{M_E f_0} \cdot \frac{1}{\frac{c_1}{2s_1} - \frac{c_2}{2s_2}} \cdot v$, $v \in \mathbb{Z}_+$, $M_S \nmid v$, the channel capacity can reach its maximum $C_{\text{opt}} = \min\{M_R, M_T\} \cdot \text{lb}(1 + \rho|a|^2 \max\{M_R, M_T\})$;
(2) The channel capacity curve fluctuates periodically with respect to d_E, and its period is $D_S = \frac{c_0 h}{f_0 \cos\delta \cdot d_S}$.

8.4.2.3 *Simulation comparison*

Taking the system with $M_S = 2$ and $M_E = 2$ as an example, the channel capacity of the multi-satellite single-antenna MIMO system varies with the adjacent antenna spacing d_E of the receiving antenna array on the ground under different satellite angular separations as shown in Fig. 8.4.

The simulation results show that the channel capacity is a periodic function related to d_E, and its period decreases as the satellite spacing increases. The spacing of the receiving antenna on the ground is important for achieving maximum channel capacity, which is given as $d_E = \frac{c_0}{M_E f_0} \cdot \frac{1}{\frac{c_1}{2s_1} - \frac{c_2}{2s_2}} \cdot v$, $v \in \mathbb{Z}_+$, $M_S \nmid v$.

8.4.3 *Array antenna constellation capacity*

Based on the system model established in Section 8.3.2, we discuss a multi-satellite multi-antenna constellation cooperative array antenna MIMO system.

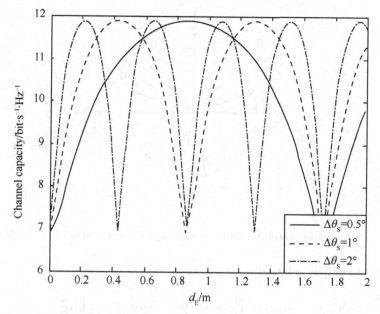

Fig. 8.4. Relationship between channel capacity and ground antenna spacing for multi-satellite single-antenna MIMO communication systems with different satellite angular separations.

8.4.3.1 *Establish LOS orthogonal channel*

Similar to Section 8.4.2.2, a system with $M_T > M_R$ is used as an example to establish an orthogonal LOS channel matrix. And in order to make $\mathbf{H}$ an orthogonal matrix, elements of any two rows of $\mathbf{H}$ must be orthogonal.

Then, after a similar mathematical derivation, Eq. (8.15) can also be obtained.

Considering the system here, the number of transmitting antennas is $M_T = M_S \cdot M_L$, the number of receiving antennas is $M_R = M_E$, and the distance between the m_Eth receiving antennas and the m_Lth transmitting antennas on the m_Sth satellite is defined as $r_{m_E, m_S\_m_L}$. Divide $e^{j\phi_i}$ into groups: make all the antennas on the same satellite a group, and define the nth transmitting antenna on the mth satellite corresponding to $e^{j\phi_i} = e^{j\phi_{m\_n}}$, where $i = (m-1)M_L + n$, then $\phi_i = \phi_{m\_n} = \frac{2\pi f_0}{c_0}(r_{k,m\_n} - r_{l,m\_n})$. Therefore, $e^{j\phi_i}$ is divided into a total of M_S groups.

It is easy to prove that as long as the argument difference $\Delta\theta$ between the two adjacent $e^{j\phi_{m\_n}}$ of the same group is kept consistent and $\sum_{m=1}^{M_S} \phi_{m\_n} = 2\pi v$, $v \in \mathbb{Z}$, $v \nmid M_S$ can satisfy Eq. (8.15).

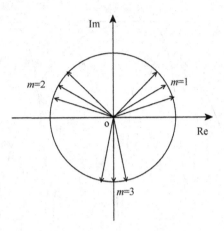

Fig. 8.5. Multi-satellite multi-antenna system calculation Eq. (8.15).

One possible solution is (as shown in Fig. 8.5):

$$\begin{cases} \arg[\phi_{m_1\_1} - \phi_{m_2\_1}] = \dfrac{2\pi}{M_\mathrm{S}}(m_1 - m_2) & \forall m_1,\ m_2 \in \{1, 2, \ldots, M_\mathrm{S}\}; \\ \arg[\phi_{m\_n_1} - \phi_{m\_n_1}] = \Delta\theta(n_1 - n_2) & \forall n_1,\ n_2 \in \{1, 2, \ldots, M_L\} \end{cases}$$

Similar to Section 8.4.3.1, $r_{k,m\_n} - r_{l,m\_n}$ with a linear relationship to ϕ_{m_n} has a constant differential relationship.

For the kth and lth receiving antenna on the ground, and the dth antenna on the cth satellite and the fth antenna on the eth satellite,

$$(r_{k,c\_d} - r_{l,c\_d}) - (r_{k,e\_f} - r_{l,e\_f}) = \frac{c_0}{f_0}\left[\frac{(c-e)}{M_\mathrm{S}} + \frac{\Delta\theta}{2\pi}(d-f)\right]\cdot v, \quad v \in \mathbb{Z}$$

$$(8.24)$$

Only when Eq. (8.24) is satisfied can the channel capacity be maximized. Therefore, both the receiving antenna and the transmitting antenna are uniformly arranged antenna arrays, and the arrays between constellations are also uniformly arranged.

8.4.3.2 *Optimize the antenna layout in combination with geometric position*

We discuss this problem in a scene of a constellation cooperative array antenna as shown in Figs. 8.6 and 8.7. The M_E receiving antennas on the ground receiver and the M_L receiving antennas on each satellite are all

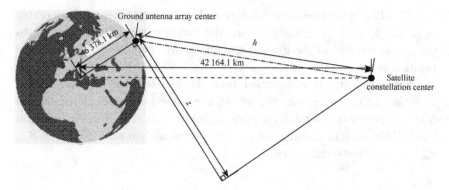

Fig. 8.6. The MIMO satellite communication system geometry model (a).

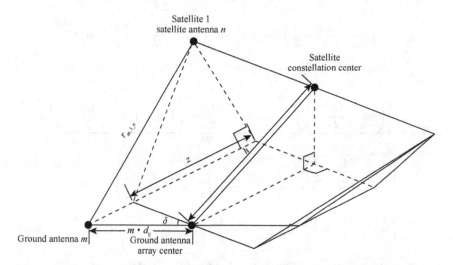

Fig. 8.7. The MIMO satellite communication system geometry model (b).

placed in a uniform linear array, and the constellation consisting of M_S satellites is also uniformly distributed in the geosynchronous orbit wherein the angle between the ground antenna array and the east–west direction is δ (the ground antenna ULA direction angle) and the spacing between two adjacent receiving antennas is d_E(m). The antenna array on the satellite is kept in the east–west direction, and the spacing between two adjacent transmitting antennas is given as d_L. The spacing between two adjacent satellites in the constellation array is d_S(m), denoted as $d_S = \frac{\pi \Delta \theta_S}{180°} \cdot R_S$, and $\Delta \theta_S$ (°) is the angular separation of two adjacent satellites.

The distance between the satellite and the ground antenna array center is about h, and the distance from the satellite constellation center to the connected line of the ground antenna array center and the geocentric position is z.

For simplicity, it is assumed that the constellation center and the receiving antenna array center are at the same longitude. Based on the MIMO satellite communication system geometry model (a) in Fig. 8.6, and the MIMO satellite communication system geometry model (b) in Fig. 8.7, $r_{m_E, m_S\_m_L}$ can be calculated.

$$r_{m_E, m_S\_m_L}$$

$$= \sqrt{\begin{array}{l} h^2 + \left[\left(m_S - \dfrac{M_S}{2} - \dfrac{1}{2}\right) d_S + \left(m_L - \dfrac{M_L}{2} - \dfrac{1}{2}\right) d_L \right. \\ \left. - \left(m_E - \dfrac{M_E}{2} - \dfrac{1}{2}\right) d_E \cos\delta\right]^2 + \left[\left(m_E - \dfrac{M_E}{2} - \dfrac{1}{2}\right) d_E \sin\delta\right]^2 \\ + 2z \cdot \left(m_E - \dfrac{M_E}{2} - \dfrac{1}{2}\right) d_E \sin\delta \end{array}}$$

$$\approx h + \frac{\left[\left(m_S - \dfrac{M_S}{2} - \dfrac{1}{2}\right) d_S + \left(m_L - \dfrac{M_L}{2} - \dfrac{1}{2}\right) d_L - \left(m_E - \dfrac{M_E}{2} - \dfrac{1}{2}\right) d_E\right]^2}{2h}$$

$$+ \frac{\left(m_E - \dfrac{M_E}{2} - \dfrac{1}{2}\right) d_E}{h} \left\{(1 - \cos\delta) \cdot \left[\left(m_S - \dfrac{M_S}{2} - \dfrac{1}{2}\right) d_S\right.\right.$$

$$\left.\left. + \left(m_L - \dfrac{M_L}{2} - \dfrac{1}{2}\right) d_L\right] + \sin\delta \cdot z\right\} \tag{8.25}$$

Substituting it into the left-hand side of Eq. (8.24), we obtain

$$(r_{k,c\_d} - r_{l,c\_d}) - (r_{k,e\_f} - r_{l,e\_f})$$

$$\approx \frac{\cos\delta}{h}(k - l) \cdot d_E[(e - c) \cdot d_S + (f - d) \cdot d_L] \tag{8.26}$$

Therefore, Eq. (8.24) can be rewritten as

$$\frac{\cos\delta}{h}(k - l) \cdot d_E \cdot d_S \left[(e - c) + (f - d) \cdot \frac{d_L}{d_S}\right]$$

$$= \frac{c_0}{f_0} \left[\frac{(c - e)}{M_S} + \frac{\Delta\theta}{2\pi}(d - f)\right] \cdot v, \quad v \in \mathbb{Z}, \quad M_S \nmid v \tag{8.27}$$

namely,

$$\frac{\cos\delta}{h}(k-l)d_{\mathrm{E}}\cdot d_L = \frac{c_0\Delta\theta}{2\pi f_0}(-v) \tag{8.28}$$

$$\frac{\cos\delta}{h}(k-l)d_{\mathrm{E}}\cdot d_{\mathrm{S}} = \frac{c_0}{f_0 M_{\mathrm{S}}}(-v) \tag{8.29}$$

$M_L = 1$ happens to be the case discussed in Section 8.4.1.

When M_{S}, $M_L \neq 1$, by Eqs. (8.28) and (8.29), the ground antenna array spacing d_{E} at which the maximum channel capacity can be reached is

$$d_{\mathrm{Eopt}} = \frac{c_0 h}{M_{\mathrm{S}} f_0 \cos\delta \cdot d_{\mathrm{S}}} \cdot \frac{-v}{k-l} \geq \frac{c_0 h}{M_{\mathrm{S}} f_0 \cos\delta \cdot d_{\mathrm{S}}} \tag{8.30}$$

and it also satisfies

$$\Delta\theta = \frac{2\pi}{M_{\mathrm{S}}}\cdot\frac{d_L}{d_{\mathrm{S}}} \tag{8.31}$$

Therefore, we can conclude that

(1) When $d_{\mathrm{E}} = \frac{c_0 h}{M_{\mathrm{S}} f_0 \cos\delta\cdot d_{\mathrm{S}}}\cdot u$, $u \in \mathbb{Z}_+$, $M_{\mathrm{S}} \nmid u$, channel capacity can reach the maximum $C_{\mathrm{opt}} = \min\{M_{\mathrm{R}}, M_{\mathrm{T}}\}\cdot \mathrm{lb}(1 + \rho|a|^2 \max\{M_{\mathrm{R}}, M_{\mathrm{T}}\})$;
(2) The channel capacity curve fluctuates periodically with respect to d_{E}, and its periodicity is reflected in two aspects. On the one hand, the peak-to-valley fluctuation is in a small order of magnitude (caused by multiple satellites) with its valley–valley period $D_{\mathrm{S}} = \frac{c_0 h}{f_0 \cos\delta\cdot d_{\mathrm{S}}}$. On the other hand, the period of the envelope function of the curve in a large order of magnitude (caused by multiple antennas on the satellite) is $D_L = \frac{c_0 h}{f_0 \cos\delta\cdot d_L}$.

8.4.3.3 *Simulation comparison*

A series of simulation comparisons are performed on the system using latitude and longitude coordinates. In the simulation, the number of satellites, the number of satellite antennas, and the adjacent satellite angular separation are changed, and the variation of the channel capacity of the constellation cooperative array antenna communication system with respect to the ground antenna array spacing d_{E} is observed.

In the multi-satellite multi-antenna MIMO communication system with $M_{\mathrm{E}} = 2$ and $M_L = 2$, the simulation results are shown in Fig. 8.8.

In the same system, consider the case where d_{E} is of a large order of magnitude. The simulation results are shown in Fig. 8.9.

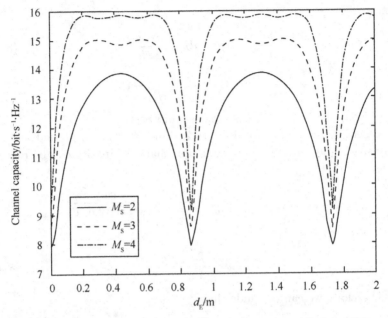

Fig. 8.8. **Relationship between ground antenna spacing and channel capacity of multi-satellite multi-antenna MIMO communication systems with different satellite numbers (small order of magnitude).**

In the multi-satellite multi-antenna MIMO communication system with $M_S = 2$, $M_E = 2$, the number of antennas on the satellite is changed, and the simulation result is shown in Fig. 8.10.

In the multi-satellite multi-antenna MIMO communication system with $M_S = 2$, $M_E = 2$, $M_L = 2$, the angular separation between two adjacent satellites is changed, and the simulation results are shown in Fig. 8.11.

The simulation results show that when d_E is of a small order of magnitude, the change in the channel capacity with d_E is similar to that discussed in Section 8.4.1, which means that both increasing the number of satellites and increasing the angular separation of adjacent satellites will initially result in a decrease in d_{Eopt} before reaching the maximum channel capacity.

When d_E is of a large order of magnitude, it can be seen that the channel capacity will fluctuate periodically with d_E with a period of $D_L = \frac{c_0 h}{f_0 \cos \delta \cdot d_L}$. In one period, due to the periodicity of $d_E = \frac{c_0 h}{M_S f_0 \cos \delta \cdot d_S} \cdot u$, $u \in \mathbb{Z}_+$, $M_S \nmid u$, the channel capacity will have a rapid jitter ripple on both sides. This situation will be improved around $\frac{c_0 h}{M_L f_0 \cdot d_L} \cdot p (p \in \{1, 2, \ldots, M_L - 1\})$,

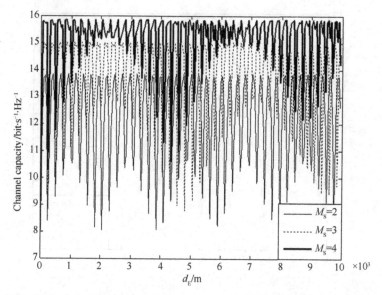

Fig. 8.9. Relationship between ground antenna spacing and channel capacity of multi-satellite multi-antenna MIMO communication systems with different satellite numbers (large order of magnitude).

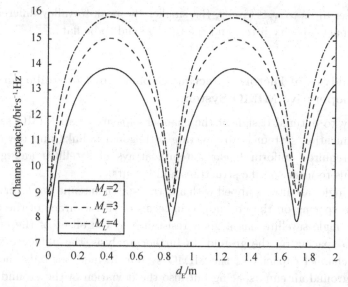

Fig. 8.10. Relationship between ground antenna spacing and channel capacity of multi-satellite multi-antenna MIMO communication systems with different satellite antenna numbers.

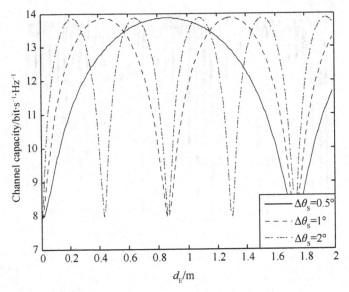

Fig. 8.11. Relationship between ground antenna spacing and channel capacity of multi-satellite multi-antenna MIMO communication systems with different angular separations.

the closer d_E is to $\frac{c_0 h}{M_L f_0 \cdot d_L} \cdot p$, the smaller the peak-to-valley difference of the channel capacity jitter, and the ripples tend to be flat.

8.5 Analysis of Factors Affecting Capacity of Constellation Cooperative MIMO System

The key to optimal design of the channel capacity of an MIMO satellite communication system is to generate orthogonal uplinks and downlinks, which requires uniform linear antenna arrays of satellites and ground terminals to meet specific structures and layouts.

A single satellite equipped with a narrow-pitch antenna has a very large antenna spacing on the ground, so in terms of the accuracy of the design size, a single satellite has a good resistance to the offset of the optimal antenna spacing on the ground. In further analysis, the influence factors of the channel capacity of the MIMO system include not only the error of the ground antenna spacing but also the deviation of the ground plane ULA azimuth δ, which is likely to be gradually superimposed to a large extent. Therefore, we need to find an optimal setting that can be actually manipulated.

For small-sized ground terminals, such as portable or mobile satellite communication terminals, the design of a small-sized ground-side antenna aperture is necessary. Under the condition of the multi-satellite MIMO system, it is theoretically achievable to have a large capacity gain and a design for satisfying a small-sized antenna aperture channel at the ground terminal.

Since MIMO utilizes the regenerative payload sufficiently, the main work in the design process is on the ground station. As long as the uplink and downlink remain orthogonal, the design complexity of the satellite payload will be reduced, which is the advantage of the MIMO satellite communication system. However, in practical applications, it is sometimes necessary to carry out a considerable amount of work for this not only to determine the appropriate antenna array arrangement but also to consider the limitations of practical factors, such as changes in the communication environment and the impact of the satellite's own mobility. These limitations make it difficult to maintain the orthogonality of the channel to a certain extent, which we have avoided in the design of satellite communication systems.

Therefore, it is necessary to make a compromise between channel design complexity and channel capacity optimization. In this section, we will analyze and quantify the channel capacity attenuation caused by practical factors in the MIMO satellite communication system and propose further reasonable improvement measures that can be taken in this case.

8.5.1 *Single-antenna constellation*

Considering the constellation cooperative system model established in Section 8.3.1, a preliminary discussion has been made on the relationship between the channel capacity of the system and the arrangement of the receiving and transmitting antennas.

According to the derivation in Section 8.4, we have obtained the relationship between the channel capacity of the satellite communication system and the ground array antenna spacing d_E:

$$d_{\text{Eopt}} = \frac{c_0 h}{M_S f_0 \cos \delta \cdot d_S} \cdot u \geq \frac{c_0 h}{M_S f_0 \cos \delta \cdot d_S}, \quad u \in \mathbb{Z}_+, \quad M_S \nmid u \quad (8.32)$$

For the multi-satellite single-antenna system, Eq. (8.32) is also true. It differs from the constellation cooperative array antenna system only in that the channel capacity peak-to-valley value of the single-antenna system is stable without the fluctuation of the channel capacity envelope. As a special case of the constellation cooperative array antenna system, the discussion of the influence of practical factors on the multi-satellite single-antenna communication system is relatively simple.

Because a typical base station antenna is unlikely to allow different satellites to simultaneously receive signals, the satellite antenna spacing is significantly larger in on-orbit multi-satellite systems equipped with different MIMO antenna elements than that in single-satellite application. Therefore, the antenna spacing of the ground terminal becomes smaller. When $u = 1$, the optimal value can be calculated. And when $u \in \mathbb{Z}_+$, $M_S \nmid u$ is selected, the optimal value $d_{\mathrm{Eopt}}(u > 1)$ can still be calculated, but its value is slightly larger. The optimal array antenna spacing of the ground terminal exhibits periodic changes with u. The channel capacity is a periodic function with respect to d_E, whose period is $D_S = \frac{c_0 h}{f_0 \cos \delta \cdot d_S}$ and peak is at $d_E = \frac{c_0 h}{M_S f_0 \cos \delta \cdot d_S} \cdot u$, $u \in \mathbb{Z}_+$, $M_S \nmid u$.

Based on the above factors, the following three phenomena can be observed regarding the optimal geometric arrangement of the antenna:

(1) The spacing of the satellites in orbit is inversely proportional to the spacing of the antennas at the ground terminals.
(2) As the ground antenna ULA direction angle δ increases, the optimal spacing of the ground terminal or satellite antennas increases.
(3) The optimal antenna spacing of the ground terminal changes periodically with the change of u value.

In the multi-satellite single-antenna MIMO communication system with $f_c = 18\,\mathrm{GHz}$, $M_S = M_E = 2$, and $u = 1$, the simulation results of the optimal geometric arrangement are shown in Fig. 8.12.

The fading of the channel capacity caused by actual factors mostly affects the orthogonality of the channel matrix from these aspects. In the following, we quantify the impact of the actual factors.

8.5.1.1 *Description and classification of factors affecting channel fading*

The fading of the channel capacity that is to be described in the actual MIMO system channel is caused by the antenna array deviating from the optimal geometric arrangement. For convenience, this case is expressed as "position error" hereinafter.

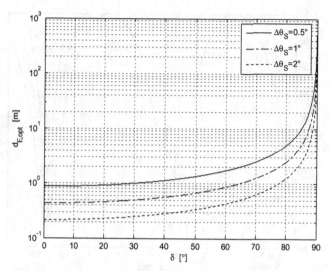

Fig. 8.12. The relationship between the optimal arrangement spacing d_{Eopt} of ground antennas and the ULA azimuth δ in a multi-satellite single-antenna MIMO communication system.

The actual causes of channel fading are summarized as follows:

(1) Deviation of the optimal antenna parameters at the ground end

    (a) geographical position θ_{E}, ϕ_{E};

    (b) internal antenna spacing d_{E};

    (c) uniform linear array (ULA) azimuth δ.

(2) Deviation of the optimal parameters of the constellation end

    (a) changes in the attitude of the satellite;

    (b) channel fading caused by the maneuvering of the satellite position.

8.5.1.2 *Possible factors affecting ground terminals*

(1) Deviation of the optimal geographical position

The actual result is that the influence of the geographic position (deviation of longitude θ_{E} and latitude ϕ_{E}) is negligible after correction of the ULA direction angle δ and the antenna spacing d_{E}. And it is this stable performance that makes the application of the MIMO system discussed in the previous sections to have a general meaning in different scenarios.

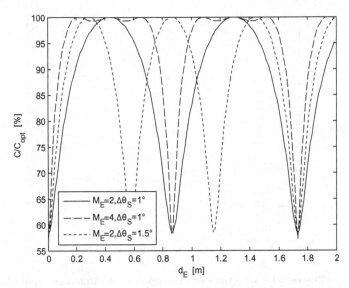

Fig. 8.13. **Relationship between channel capacity of the multi-satellite single-antenna MIMO communication system and ground antenna spacing d_E.**

(2) Deviation of optimal ground terminal antenna spacing

In Fig. 8.13, compared to the optimal value, the channel capacity is presented as an example of the "Miss-Positioning" Δd_E in the downlink system of the multi-satellite single-antenna in this section.

It can be seen that for the system with $M_S = 2$ and $M_E = 2$, in order to ensure at least 90% of C_{opt}, the position accuracy Δd_E ($\geq 90\% C_{opt}$) = ± 23 cm must be required first. Second, as the angular separation $\Delta \theta_S$ of the satellite increases, the allowable error d_E decreases and the required position accuracy increases. Finally, as the number of ground terminal antennas increases, the fading of channel capacity is also relatively reduced. Under the same conditions, if the number of ground terminal antennas is increased from 2 to 4, and the channel capacity is still required to reach $90\% C_{opt}$, the allowable error range is increased to ± 35.5 cm, and the required position accuracy is reduced.

Therefore, in order to reduce the positional accuracy requirement which is positively related to the practical workload, the following conclusions should be met as much as possible:

(1) The minimum spacing $d_{Eopt}|_{u=1}$ of ground array antennas should be as large as possible.

(2) The angular separation of orbiting satellites should not be too large.

(3) Ground terminals should use as many array antennas as possible.

Therefore, for a constellation cooperative communication system, the designer must perform a considerable amount of work in order to ensure the position accuracy of the ground antenna spacing d_E required by $90\%C_{opt}$. For single-satellite multi-antenna systems, the required position accuracy (± 20 km) is easy to maintain, but the deviation requirements for d_{Eopt} are extremely strict in the case of multiple satellites.

In the multi-satellite single-antenna MIMO communication system with $M_S = 2$, the simulation results are shown in Fig. 8.13.

(3) Deviation of the optimal ULA direction angle δ

It is easy to prove from the obtained conclusion that the channel capacity in Fig. 8.14 as a function of the ULA direction angle δ once again demonstrates the advantages of the ground terminal multi-antenna, since the increase in the number of antennas is advantageous for the stability of C_{opt}. As δ increases, the slope of the curve $d_E - \delta$ increases, $d_{Eopt}(u = 1)$ increases rapidly, and the requirement for the accuracy of δ is higher. For example, in the multi-satellite single-antenna system with $M_S = 2$ and $M_E = 2$ as shown in Fig. 8.14, if the channel capacity is required to reach $90\%C_{opt}$, the allowable error of δ must be maintained within the range $\pm 90°$. This is much better than the case of a single-satellite multi-antenna with approximately $\pm 10°$, indicating that the accuracy requirements for δ are reduced in the case of a multi-satellite single antenna. Finally, the d_E accuracy required by the communication system is directly related to the selected parameter u, which can be obtained from the simulation. And for higher values of u, relative to the minimum value $d_{Eopt}(u = 1)$, the ground antenna spacing $d_{Eopt}(u > 1)$, $u \in \mathbb{Z}_+$, $M_S \nmid u$ causes a more severe fading of C_{opt} in the case of deviations from δ_{opt}.

Based on the conclusions stated above, in order to further reduce the accuracy requirements for δ, the following conditions should be met:

(1) ULA azimuth δ should be as small as possible.

(2) The designed parameter $u(u \in \mathbb{Z}_+, M_S \nmid u)$ should choose a value as small as possible.

(3) Ground terminals should use as many array antennas as possible.

In the multi-satellite single-antenna MIMO communication system with $M_S = 2$, the simulation results are shown in Fig. 8.14.

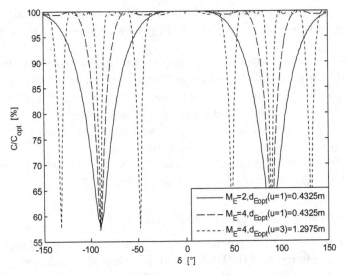

Fig. 8.14. Relationship between channel capacity and ULA azimuth δ for multi-satellite single-antenna MIMO communication systems.

8.5.1.3 *Channel fading caused by satellite maneuvering*

Literature in Ref. 21 explores the relevant knowledge on satellite motion affecting the communication systems.

Figure 8.15 shows the possible satellite movements. The altitude of the satellite can be described by a local coordinate system, whose vertical axis, the roll axis, and the yaw axis are extended from the origin of the centroid local coordinate system. The satellite will offset through tumbling, translation, and centrifugation/central motion along the three dimensions of longitude, latitude, and radial, respectively.

(1) Changes in satellite attitude

Fortunately, the effect of the offset of the satellite attitude on the orthogonality of the MIMO channel is negligible. Of course, a change in the attitude of the satellite within the range listed in Fig. 8.15 will result in drift of the coverage area and there may even be a reduction in the power received. It will reduce the overall data transmission rate but will not affect the orthogonality of the optimized MIMO satellite channel, so it is not the focus of the actual research.

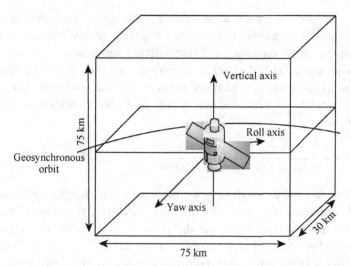

Fig. 8.15. **Possible satellite movements in the orbit of geosynchronous satellites.**

(2) The position of the satellite remains maneuverable

Finally, we discuss the effect of orbital offset due to independent motion on channel fading. The effect of this phenomenon in the case of a single satellite is negligible but imposes additional restrictions on the channel in the case of multiple satellites. The results again show that the fading of the channel capacity is closely related to the actual antenna spacing $d_E = u \cdot d_{Eopt}|_{u=1}$, so the stability of the channel capacity depends on the choice of u. Similar to the results of Fig. 8.13, the fading of the channel capacity is a function of the ground terminal antenna spacing. The specific derivation is shown in Section 8.5.2.

In order to obtain any desired C_{opt} values, the conclusions of this section are summarized as follows.

The optimal antenna spacing d_{Eopt} of the ground terminal is limited to a particular maximum according to the number of antennas used by the ground base station, but this is independent of the actual satellite spacing.

8.5.2 *Array antenna constellation*

We use the array antenna system model of the constellation, which we established in Section 8.3.2, to further discuss the theoretical results.

In the preceding sections, a preliminary discussion has been made on the relationship between the channel capacity of the system and the arrangement of the receiving and transmitting antennas.

According to the derivation in Section 8.4, we have obtained the relationship between the channel capacity of the multi-satellite multi-antenna satellite communication system and the ground-array antenna spacing d_E:

$$d_{\text{Eopt}} = \frac{c_0 h}{M_S f_0 \cos\delta \cdot d_S} \cdot u \geq \frac{c_0 h}{M_S f_0 \cos\delta \cdot d_S}, \quad u \in \mathbb{Z}_+, \quad M_S \nmid u \quad (8.33)$$

In Section 8.4.2, we draw a simple conclusion that for systems with multiple antennas equipped with multiple satellites, the channel capacity is a periodic function of d_E as d_E is of a small order of magnitude. However, when d_E is of a small order of magnitude, the channel capacity will exhibit a rapid jitter, and the peak-to-valley envelope will periodically fluctuate with the change of d_E. In one period, due to the periodicity of $d_{\text{Eopt}} = \frac{c_0 h}{M_S f_0 \cos\delta \cdot d_S} \cdot u$ with $u \in \mathbb{Z}_+$, $M_S \nmid u$, the channel capacity will have rapid jitter ripples on both sides. And this situation will be improved near $\frac{c_0 h}{M_L f_0 \cdot d_L} \cdot p \, (p \in \{1, 2, \ldots, M_L - 1\})$, and the closer d_E is to $\frac{c_0 h}{M_L f_0 \cdot d_L} \cdot p$, the smaller the peak-to-valley difference of channel capacity jitter.

When d_E is of a the small order of magnitude, the variation of channel capacity with d_E is similar to that of the multi-satellite single-antenna MIMO system. Therefore, the conclusions derived from mathematical expressions are similar and as follows:

(1) The spacing between the on-orbit satellites is inversely proportional to the antenna spacing of the ground terminals.
(2) As the ULA direction angle of the ground antenna increases, the optimal distance of the antenna of the ground terminals or satellites increases accordingly.
(3) The optimal distance of the antenna in the ground terminals changes periodically as the value of u changes.

When d_E is of a large order of magnitude, the channel capacity has a special relationship with the change of d_E such that on both sides of a period, the channel capacity curve will have a rapid jitter ripple. This situation will improve near $\frac{c_0 h}{M_L f_0 \cdot d_L} \cdot p \, (p \in \{1, 2, \ldots, M_L - 1\})$.

Figure 8.16 shows the relationship between the ground antenna spacing d_E and the ULA azimuth δ of receiving antenna of the ground when the

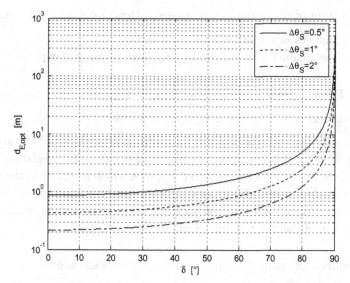

Fig. 8.16. The relationship between the optimal arrangement spacing d_{Eopt} of ground antennas in the multi-satellite single-antenna MIMO communication system and ULA azimuth δ.

channel capacity is optimized in a multi-satellite multi-antenna MIMO communication system with $f_c = 18\,\text{GHz}$, $M_S = M_E = M_L = 2$, $u = 1$.

In the following, we quantify the impact of practical factors on the fading of the channel capacity.

8.5.2.1 *Description and classification of factors affecting channel fading*

The fading of the channel capacity which appears in the channel of the actual array antenna MIMO system of the constellation is also caused by the "position error" of the antenna array deviating from the optimal geometric arrangement.

Similar to Section 8.5.1, the actual causes of channel fading are summarized as follows:

(1) Setting the deviation of the optimal antenna parameters at the ground terminal

    (a) Geographic position θ_E, ϕ_E.

    (b) Internal antenna spacing d_E.

    (c) Directional angle of uniform linear array (ULA) δ.

(2) Deviation of the optimal parameters of the constellation terminal

    (a) Changes in the attitude of the satellite.

    (b) The channel fading caused by satellite position maneuver.

8.5.2.2 *Possible factors from ground terminals*

(1) Deviation of the optimal geographical position

In fact, after the correction of the ULA direction angle δ and the antenna spacing d_E, the influence of the geographical position (the deviation of the longitude θ_E and the latitude ϕ_E) is negligible, which is similar to the multi-satellite single-antenna MIMO system. Therefore, the conclusions obtained for channel capacity and antenna arrangement proposed under typical ideal position conditions are also universal.

(2) Deviation of optimal ground terminal antenna spacing

In the multi-satellite multi-antenna downlink system, the simulation of the ratio of the channel capacity to the optimum value as a function of the "position error" Δd_E is shown in Fig. 8.17.

    An analysis similar to the one in 8.4.1 is given here.

    In order to ensure that the channel capacity reaches at least 90% of C_{opt}, first, the position accuracy must be $\Delta d_E(\geq 90\% C_{opt}) = \pm 25\,\text{cm}$.

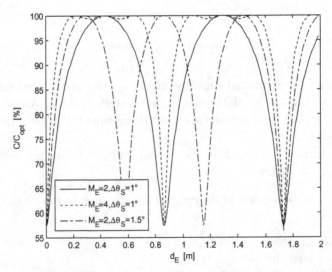

Fig. 8.17. Relationship between channel capacity and ground antenna spacing d_E in a multi-satellite multi-antenna MIMO communication system.

Second, as the satellite angular separation $\Delta\theta_S$ increases, the allowable d_E error decreases and the required position accuracy increases. Finally, as the number of ground terminal antennas increases, the fading of channel capacity is also relatively reduced. For example, under the same conditions, if the number of ground terminal antennas is increased to $M_E = 4$ and the channel capacity is still required to reach $90\%C_{opt}$, the allowable error range is increased to $\pm 35.5\,\text{cm}$, and the required position accuracy is reduced compared to the case of $M_E = 2$.

In order to reduce the position accuracy requirements which are positively related to the actual workload, our conclusions are similar and as follows:

(1) the minimum spacing of the ground array antenna $d_{\text{Eopt}}|_{u=1}$ should be as large as possible;
(2) the angular separation of orbiting satellites should not be too large;
(3) ground terminals use as many array antennas as possible.

In the case of a multi-satellite multi-antenna MIMO communication system, the channel capacity has very strict requirements for the deviation of d_{Eopt}.

In the multi-satellite multi-antenna MIMO communication system with $M_S = 2$ and $M_L = 2$, the simulation results of the channel capacity are shown in Fig. 8.17.

(3) Deviation of the optimal ULA direction angle δ

Similarly, the channel capacity in Fig. 8.18 as a function of the ULA direction angle δ indicates that the multi-antenna system helps to enhance the channel gain because the increase in the number of antennas is advantageous for the stability of C_{opt}. As δ increases, the slope of the $d_E - \delta$ curve increases, $d_{\text{Eopt}}(u = 1)$ increases rapidly, and the accuracy required for δ becomes higher. Similar to the multi-satellite single-antenna MIMO system, for larger values of u, C_{opt} is caused to degrade more rapidly in the case of deviation from δ_{opt}.

To further reduce the accuracy requirements for δ, the multi-satellite multi-antenna MIMO system should satisfy the following conditions:

(1) ULA azimuth δ should be as small as possible, although the allowable error is relaxed compared to multi-satellite single-antenna MIMO systems.

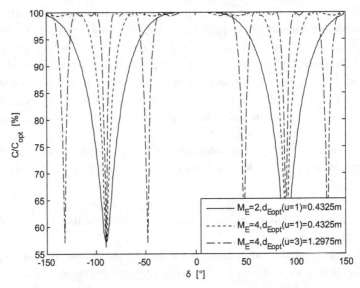

Fig. 8.18. Relationship between channel capacity and ULA azimuth δ for multi-satellite multi-antenna MIMO communication systems.

(2) $u(u \in \mathbb{Z}_+, M_S \nmid u)$ should be as small as possible.

(3) Ground terminals use as many array antennas as possible.

The simulation results of the channel capacity for in the multi-satellite multi-antenna MIMO communication system with $M_S = 2$ and $M_L = 2$, are shown in Fig. 8.18.

(4) Impact of channel capacity jitter when the ground antenna spacing is of a large order of magnitude

Due to the periodicity of the envelope function caused by u, in the case of a large order of magnitude, the channel capacity is a periodic function with respect to d_E, whose period is $D_L = \frac{c_0 h}{f_0 \cos \delta \cdot d_L}$ as shown in Fig. 8.19.

Different from the case discussed in Section 8.5.1, in one cycle, due to the periodicity of $d_{E\text{opt}} = \frac{c_0 h}{M_S f_0 \cos \delta \cdot d_S} \cdot u$, $u \in \mathbb{Z}_+$, $M_S \nmid u$, the channel capacity will have rapid jitter ripples on both sides of the cycle. This situation is seen to improve around $\frac{c_0 h}{M_L f_0 \cdot d_L} \cdot p(p \in \{1, 2, \ldots, M_L - 1\})$, and the closer d_E is to $\frac{c_0 h}{M_L f_0 \cdot d_L} \cdot p$, the smaller the peak-to-valley difference of the channel capacity jitter. We might call these points of improvement "flat jitter points".

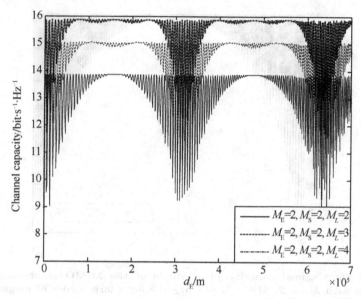

Fig. 8.19. Jitter corrugation generated by the channel capacity of a multi-satellite multi-antenna MIMO communication system with d_E of a large order of magnitude.

This suggests that increasing the value of u appropriately and approaching the flat jitter points will make the jitter of the channel capacity flat, and the capacity fluctuation caused by the error of d_E will become more tolerant.

Now, take the MIMO system with $M_S = 2$, $M_E = 2$, and $M_L = 2$ as an example to study its first cycle.

The channel capacity curve can be thought of as a ripple curve between the upper and lower bound envelopes wherein the upper bound is a straight line parallel to the x-axis, the y value satisfies the channel capacity equal to the maximum value C_{opt}. The lower bound is an axisymmetric upward convex curve with $\frac{c_0 h}{M_L f_0 \cdot d_L}$ as the symmetry axis.

As can be seen from Fig. 8.20, when $d_E \in [0.67, 2.54] \times 10^5 (\text{m})$, no matter how large the error of d_E is, the channel capacity will not be lower than 90% of the maximum value. At this time, it is no longer strictly required that d_E satisfies the optimal conditions, and it can also ensure that the system can achieve sufficient channel capacity even in the worst case caused by errors.

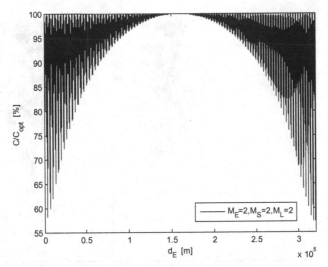

Fig. 8.20. **Channel capacity jitter ripple of the MIMO communication system with $M_S = 2$, $M_E = 2$, and $M_L = 2$ for a large order of magnitude of d_E.**

Therefore, we can conclude that increasing the value of u appropriately can effectively ensure the channel capacity of the multi-satellite multi-antenna MIMO system reaching the required minimum value even in the case of large errors.

8.5.2.3 *Channel fading caused by satellite maneuvering*

Refer to Section 8.5.1 for the geosynchronous satellite orbits listed in Fig. 8.15 for possible satellite motion: the satellite's center of mass is at the origin of the vertical, roll, and yaw axes; the satellite will move through tumbling, translation, centrifugal, and centered motion along three dimensions: longitude, latitude, and radial.

(1) Changes in satellite attitude

Similar to the multi-satellite single-antenna MIMO system, the influence of the satellite attitude offset on the orthogonality of the MIMO channel is negligible. Even the coverage area drifts by the change of satellite attitude or the received power reduction reduces, the orthogonality of the optimized MIMO satellite channel will not be affected when reducing the overall data transmission rate. Therefore, this is not the focus of research in this system.

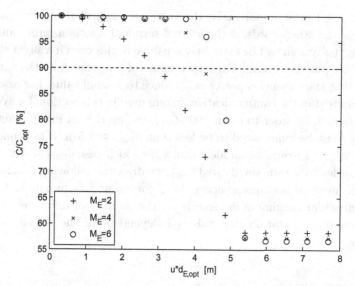

Fig. 8.21. For the multi-satellite multi-antenna MIMO communication system, the relationship between the channel capacity and ground antenna spacing considering the satellite orbital offset in the worst case of Monte Carlo simulation.

(2) The position of the satellite remains maneuverable

Finally, we discuss the effect of orbital offset due to independent motion on channel fading. The effect of this phenomenon in the case of a single satellite is negligible but imposes additional restrictions in the case of multiple satellites. The results again show that the fading of the channel capacity is closely related to the actual antenna spacing $d_E = u \cdot d_{Eopt}|_{u=1}$, so the stability of the channel capacity depends on the choice of u.

Similar to the result obtained from Fig. 8.17, the fading of channel capacity is a function of the ground terminal antenna spacing.

For the multi-satellite multi-antenna MIMO system with $M_S = 2$ and $M_L = 2$, Fig. 8.21 shows the relationship between the channel capacity and ground antenna spacing d_E considering the satellite orbital offset in the worst case of Monte Carlo simulation. The x-coordinate contains discrete values obtained by increasing $u \in \mathbb{Z}_+$, and each coordinate value $C(u \cdot d_{Eopt}|_{u=1})$ is a Monte Carlo simulation result representing the channel capacity in the worst case.

We find that if the number of receiving antennas is sufficient, the satellite orbital offset will not cause significant fading of the channel capacity, and most importantly, the value of u is still relatively small at this time. In other words, if the ground terminal selects a larger antenna spacing, the system will be extremely sensitive to this even if a slight change in satellite position occurs. For larger values of u as shown by the curve, it means that the channel capacity may reduce to a small value. For example, in the context of the communication system used in this section, for systems with $M_E = 2$, in order to ensure $90\%C_{opt}$, the maximum internal antenna spacing must be guaranteed to be less than $d_{Eopt} \approx 2.5\,\text{m}$. If the condition allows, $M_E = 4$ would be an ideal choice, in which case $d_{Eopt} \approx 4\,\text{m}$.

In order to obtain any desired C_{opt}, we draw the following conclusions.

The optimal antenna spacing d_{Eopt} for ground terminals is limited to a particular maximum depending on the number of antennas used by the ground base station, but this is independent of the actual satellite spacing.

8.6 Summary

Due to the application of the spatial dimension, MIMO technology is an effective method to improve the channel capacity of the satellite communication platform. The optimum multiplexing gain can be obtained by proper arrangement of the satellite and terrestrial terminal antennas to form orthogonal uplinks and downlinks.

The key to the maximum channel capacity of the satellite communication MIMO system is to generate orthogonal uplink and downlink channels, which requires the receiving and transmitting antenna array to meet certain arrangement rules. The constellation cooperative multi-beam transmission technology provides technical support for building a space-based transmission platform which satisfies the optimal conditions. For constellation array antennas, this arrangement needs to take into account the spacing of the ground antenna array and the ULA direction angle, the spacing of the constellation array, and the arrangement of the array antennas on the satellite. The simulation proves that the ground antenna arrangement scheme which satisfies the proportional relationship in the constellation MIMO system can achieve the maximum channel capacity, and it combines the advantages of the multi-antenna single-satellite and the single-antenna multi-satellite system.

Although these requirements impose many practical limitations on system's design, the amount of work which must be done in most cases is still acceptable. A single satellite equipped with a narrow-pitch antenna will have very large antenna spacing on the ground, so a single satellite has better resistance to the offset of the optimal antenna spacing on the ground. The multi-satellite multi-antenna MIMO technology can theoretically allow the ground terminal antenna to have a smaller and realistic spacing, while reducing the angular accuracy requirements of the ground antenna ULA. After taking certain measures, this technology can also ensure that the ground antenna spacing is minimized while having a high probability of achieving high channel capacity, and even in the worst case caused by errors, the channel capacity is also not that low. The optimized link limits the user's freedom of system design to a combination of parameters. The orbital offsets of satellites are not easily controlled, they are almost irrelevant in the case of single satellites, but they are a critical source of error in multi-satellite situations.

In addition, the optimized channel capacity and constellation MIMO systems are also affected by actual fading error sources. In terms of antenna pitch accuracy, with the currently available technology, antenna pointing accuracy and tracking performance can be simultaneously satisfied when satellites, ground base stations, and good performance channels are under a suitable workload.

References

1. Amiot T, Douchin F, Thouvenot E, *et al.* The interferometric cartwheel: A multi-purpose formation of passive radar microsatellites. *IEEE International Geoscience and Remote Sensing Symposium*, 2002, 1: 435–437.
2. Krieger G, Moreira A, Fiedler H, *et al.* TanDEM-X: A satellite formation for high-resolution SAR interferometry. *IEEE Transactions on Geoscience and Remote Sensing*, 2007, 45(11): 3317–3341.
3. D'Errico M and Moccia A. The BISSAT mission: A bistatic SAR operating information with COSMO/SkyMed X-band radar. *IEEE Aerospace Conference Proceedings*, 2002, 2: 809–818.
4. Burns R, Mclaughlin CA, Leitner J, *et al.* TechSat 21: Formation design, control, and simulation. *IEEE Aerospace Conference Proceedings*, 2000, 7: 19–25.
5. Girard R, Lee PF and James K. The RADARSAT-2&3 topographic mission: An overview. *IEEE International Geoscience and Remote Sensing Symposium*, 2002, 3: 1477–1479.
6. Yang HP, Hu XH and Li Y. Advanced Extreme High Frequency (AEHF) satellite. *Digital Communication World (DIGITCW)*, 2008, 6: 84–87.
7. Hang GR and Kang XL. Propulsion system of USA AEHF military communication satellite and its application on AEHF-1 satellite. *Journal of Rocket Propulsion*, 2011, 37(6): 1–8.

8. Wu XZ, Wu B and He RL. Foreign military's new-generation satellite communication system and key technologies. *Communications Technology*, 2012, 45(9): 7–12.

9. Arapoglou P-D, Liolis K, Bertinelli M, *et al.* MIMO over satellite: A review. *IEEE Communications Surveys & Tutorials*, 2011, 13(1): 27–51.

10. Alagoz F and Gur G. Energy efficiency and satellite networking: A holistic overview. *Proceedings of the IEEE*, 2011, 99(11): 1954–1979.

11. Steyskal H, Schindler JK, Franchi P, *et al.* Pattern synthesis for TechSat21-A distributed space-based radar system. *IEEE Antennas and Propagation Magazine*, 2003, 45(4): 19–25.

12. Feng SD, Zhang WF and Zhang JX. Design of the US Army's next generation transformational satellite operation control system. *Digital Communication World (DIGITCW)*, 2009, 9: 59–63.

13. Gou L, Wei YJ, Shen Z, *et al.* Research on fractionated spacecraft. *Journal of Spacecraft TT&C Technology*, 2012, 31(2): 7–12.

14. Liu H and Liang W. Development of DARPA's F6 program. *Spacecraft Engineering*, 2010, 19(2): 92–98.

15. Schwarz RT, Knopp A Ogermann D, *et al.* Optimum-capacity MIMO satellite link for fixed and mobile services. *2008 International ITG Workshop on Smart Antennas (WSA'08)*, Vienna, 2008, 209–216.

16. Telatar E. *et al.* Capacity of multi-antenna Gaussian channels. *AT&TBell Technical Memorandum*, 1995, 10(6): 585–595.

17. Knopp A, Schwarz RT, Hofmann CA, *et al.* Measurements on the impact of sparse multipath components on the LOS MIMO channel capacity. *4th International Symposium on Wireless Communication Systems*, Trondheim, 2007, 55–60.

18. Knopp A, Schwarz RT, Ogermann D, *et al.* Satellite system design examples for maximum MIMO spectral efficiency in LOS channels. *IEEE Global Telecommunications Conference*, New Orleans, LO, 2008, 1–6.

19. Maral G, *et al.* Satellite Communications Systems. Wiley&Sons, 2006.

20. Maral G, Bousquet M and Sun ZL. Satellite Communications Systems: Systems, Techniques and Technology. New Jersey, John Wiley & sons, 2002.

21. Schwarz RT, Knopp A and Ogermann D. On the prospects of MIMO SatCom systems: The tradeoff between capacity and practical effort. *6th International Multi-Conference on Systems, Signals and Devices*, Djerba, 2009, 1–6.

Conclusion

Spatial multidimensional cooperative transmission technology is a key component of the future-integrated mobile communication system. From the principle of multidimensional signal transmission in space and in multi-antenna systems, this book provides suggestions on how to maximize the use of spatial dimension resources to improve system performance and spectrum efficiency in a step-by-step manner and discusses the practical applications and the corresponding key technologies for ground-based, air-based, and space-based communication systems.

The book begins with an overview of the history of mobile communications and the characteristics of ground-based, air-based, and space-based cooperative communications systems and introduces the principles and basic theory of an array antenna pattern and an MIMO multi-antenna system for the spatial multidimensional signal and system modeling. And then, for adaptive antenna array technology, the methods of using space resources flexibly and efficiently by controlling the antenna beam in order to achieve anti-fading and anti-interference, improve spectrum utilization, and expand system capacity under the premise of ensuring communication quality are discussed in detail. For MIMO multi-antenna technology, methods to improve the channel capacity by the MIMO system; the MIMO space–time coding technology represented by space–time trellis code, space–time block code, and layered space–time code; the MIMO beamforming technology; and the design of the MIMO transceiver antennas are discussed.

In addition, in order to further achieve the theoretical channel capacity of the MIMO system, this book also introduces the basic principles of

iterative decoding of BICM systems and various iterative signal processing detection methods for the coding system in practical applications,
including optimal MAP, random sampling-based, and bit filtering-based
low-complexity, high-performance detection methods.

To introduce the theory of spatial multidimensional cooperative
transmission, the book further discusses the space–air–ground integrated
cooperative communication system. For the ground-based transmission
system, the following key technologies are introduced: multidimensional
joint resource scheduling, multi-user cooperative transmission, coordinated
multi-cell transmission, and anti-interference methods in the new generation
ground-based cooperative transmission system. Aiming at the air-based
cooperative transmission system, the high-altitude platform communication
system represented by the Google Project Loon is introduced, and based
on the two-dimensional filtering air-based beamforming technology, the
efficient transmission mechanism between the array air-based transmission system and the high-altitude platform is discussed. Finally, for the
space-based cooperative transmission system, the multi-beam transmission
technology of the constellation system is introduced. Furthermore, the
constellation cooperative MIMO system modeling and system channel
capacity are analyzed and optimized to obtain the optimal multiplexing
gain through the orthogonal links formed by the proper arrangement of the
transmitting and receiving antennas.

Looking forward to the development frontier of communication technology, countries around the world have focused on the research of
the 5G wireless mobile communication technology while promoting the
industrialization of the 4G mobile communication and strive to make a new
leap in the performance and industrial scale application of wireless mobile
communication systems. The space–air–ground integrated mobile Internet
technology with the new space-based and air-based platforms is developing
at an accelerated rate. With a gradual improvement in the high-altitude
platform technology, it will provide high-quality communication services
in all aspects and will become an important supplement to ground-based
communication systems. The application of large-scale array antennas will
ensure that high-altitude platforms achieve stable coverage of multiple cells
in the presence of random flutter. And multi-beam dynamic beamforming
and fast tracking based on antenna array, multi-cell dynamic program-
ming, and cooperative interference management between cells will be the
core technologies in high-altitude platforms, which require more in-depth
research. At the same time, the space-based cooperative transmission

system based on LOS-MIMO technology is considered to be an effective solution for improving the channel capacity of the satellite communication platform. However, considering the actual operational errors of satellite systems, such as measurement and control errors, coordination errors, satellite perturbations, the method to design a more practical space-based cooperative transmission system not only provides a rare opportunity for researchers but also brings with it a huge challenge. With the rapid development of the space–air–ground-integrated mobile Internet, these new technologies with broad prospects will surely ensure a promising future for people.

Index